A SHORT
HISTORY OF INDIA

A SHORT HISTORY OF INDIA

BY

W. H. MORELAND, C.S.I., C.I.E.

AND

ATUL CHANDRA CHATTERJEE
G.C.I.E., K.C.S.I.

FOURTH EDITION

WITH 11 MAPS

LONGMANS, GREEN AND CO
LONDON • NEW YORK • TORONTO

LONGMANS, GREEN AND CO LTD
6 & 7 CLIFFORD STREET LONDON W I
THIBAULT HOUSE THIBAULT SQUARE CAPE TOWN
605–611 LONSDALE STREET MELBOURNE C I

LONGMANS, GREEN AND CO INC
55 FIFTH AVENUE NEW YORK 3

LONGMANS, GREEN AND CO
20 CRANFIELD ROAD TORONTO 16

ORIENT LONGMANS PRIVATE LTD
CALCUTTA BOMBAY MADRAS
DELHI HYDERABAD DACCA

First Published 1936
Second Edition 1944
New Impression with Postscript **1945**
New Impression January 1947
Third Edition 1953
Fourth Edition 1957
New Impression August 1958

Permission has been given for this
book to be transcribed into Braille

PRINTED IN GREAT BRITAIN BY
SPOTTISWOODE, BALLANTYNE AND CO LTD
LONDON AND COLCHESTER

PREFACE TO THE FOURTH EDITION

AT the time of his death Sir Atul Chatterjee had in hand the preparation of the fourth edition of this book. The work of revision has been completed on the lines which he had planned.

Sincere esteem and enduring loyalty to the memory of Sir Atul have made the preparation and publication of this fourth edition possible: its aim is to add a more detailed account of those events for which an authoritative record was dependent on the publication of later documents and books and to include once again the valuable appendix on 'Indian Nomenclature and Chronology' for scholars wishing to pursue the study of Indian history in more elaborate works or in the original sources.

The invaluable assistance given to me so unstintingly cannot pass without recognition. My thanks are due to Sir John Walton for his continuous help; to Sir Mortimer Wheeler for generously supplying, from his great knowledge of the area, the latest information relating to the Indus civilisation; to Mr. Edwin Haward for advice on recent political developments, and for educational progress to Mr. Tapas Kumar Banerjee. I am also indebted to Miss Thorne, Librarian at India House, and to Mr. Matthews, of the India Office Library, for providing the necessary material and relevant authorities; and to Mrs. Williamson for her accurate work on the text.

Any errors of commission or omission must be laid at my door.

GLADYS M. CHATTERJEE

June 1956

PREFACE TO THE THIRD EDITION

The death in 1938 of my life-long friend W. H. Moreland deprived me of his collaboration in preparing the second and revised edition of this book, which was published in 1944. That edition contained an objective account of the developments in India between 1919 and 1943. Since then there has been a complete transformation of the situation there, and in August 1947 two sovereign and independent States—India and Pakistan—came into being. It is no longer possible to describe the history of these two countries in one connected narrative. It has therefore been deemed advisable to terminate the *Short History of India* at the date when these momentous changes took place.

In dealing with the complicated events of the period between 1943 and 1947, I have had the great advantage of the skilled and generous help of my friend Sir John Walton and I should like to take this opportunity of expressing my sincere thanks to him.

ATUL C. CHATTERJEE

September 1952

PREFACE TO THE FIRST EDITION

We have tried to tell the story of India as it appears in the light of the most recent research, but within a moderate compass, and in a manner which we hope will retain the interest of ordinary readers. It follows that our task has been selection rather than enumeration, for knowledge of the details of Indian history has increased so greatly in recent years that to tell all that is known is impossible: we have been forced to discard much that is of secondary importance in order to concentrate on the main theme, the evolution of Indian culture and its response to successive foreign contacts.

This formula, it must be understood, applies to the latest period as well as those which preceded it. We have not attempted to recount in detail the British achievement in India, a subject which has been adequately treated by various writers; our object has been rather to describe Indian reaction to the new influences, or in other words for this period we have tried to write the history, not of British rule in India, but of India under British rule.

Limitations of space have ruled out the provision of detailed references, which would have left little room for the story; and readers who wish to go further will find ample materials in the full bibliographies included in the volumes of the *Cambridge History of India*. The references we have given are confined to the sources of quotations in the text, and to a select number of authorities which are later in point of time, or have not been utilised by the Cambridge historians.

In the spelling of Indian names we have followed the practice of the *Imperial Gazetteer of India*, a description of which will be found in the Appendix. We have retained the established forms of a few foreign words, such as Mogul or suttee, which have found a place in the English language.

Our thanks are due to a number of scholars who have helped us on particular questions, linguistic, archaeological, or other. If we do not enumerate their names, the reason is that we are anxious lest readers should haply attribute to one or other of them mistakes for which the responsibility is ours.

April 1936

CONTENTS

CHAP.		PAGE
I.	THE LAND AND THE PEOPLE	1
	1. THE LAND	1
	2. THE PEOPLE	4
II.	THE BEGINNINGS OF INDIAN HISTORY	9
	1. THE CIVILISATION OF THE INDUS PLAIN	9
	2. THE COMING OF THE ARYANS	10
	3. THE EMERGENCE OF HINDUISM	15
III.	THE HINDU WAY OF LIFE	22
IV.	THE EARLY PERIOD OF HINDU SUPREMACY: A GENERAL VIEW	34
V.	THE RISE OF BUDDHISM AND JAINISM	40
VI.	THE EARLY HISTORY OF THE INDUS PLAIN	44
VII.	THE MAURYA EMPIRE: CHANDRAGUPTA	48
VIII.	THE MAURYA EMPIRE: ASOKA	53
IX.	THE SECOND CENTURY B.C.	59
X.	THE GREEKS IN THE PUNJAB	64
XI.	THE SAKAS AND PAHLAVAS	68
XII.	EARLY COMMUNICATIONS BY SEA	71
XIII.	THE KUSHĀN POWER	75
XIV.	THE GUPTA EMPIRE	86
XV.	THE WHITE HUNS	97

CONTENTS

CHAP.		PAGE
XVI.	Harsha of Kanauj	104
XVII.	From Harsha to Mahmūd	112
XVIII.	India in the Tenth Century	118
XIX.	Foreign Contacts	133
XX.	The Advent of the Turks	143
XXI.	The Turks in Delhi	152
XXII.	The Turkish Kings	160
XXIII.	Islam in Southern India	172
XXIV.	The Fifteenth Century	178
XXV.	The Results of Turkish Rule	185
XXVI.	The Coming of the Portuguese	197
XXVII.	The Mogul Conquest	204
XXVIII.	The Reign of Akbar	210
XXIX.	Akbar's Administration	221
	Note on Official Designations	229
XXX.	Jahāngīr	231
XXXI.	Shāh Jahān	240
XXXII.	Aurangzeb	249
XXXIII.	The Disintegration of the Mogul Empire	265
XXXIV.	The Work of Clive	273
XXXV.	India in the Eighteenth Century	280
XXXVI.	Warren Hastings as Administrator	294
XXXVII.	Warren Hastings as Diplomatist	305
XXXVIII.	From Cornwallis to Wellesley	313
XXXIX.	From Wellesley to Bentinck	326
XL.	Internal Changes, 1793–1835	332
XLI.	The North-West Frontier and the Punjab, 1836–1856	345
XLII.	Dalhousie's Administration	351

CONTENTS

CHAP.		PAGE
XLIII.	The Mutiny and its Consequences .	366
XLIV.	Economic Changes, 1860–1880 . .	376
XLV.	Cultural Developments, 1860–1880 .	391
XLVI.	The Frontiers, and Finance, 1860–1880	403
XLVII.	General History, 1880–1905 . .	413
XLVIII.	The Rise of Politics . . .	426
XLIX.	Unrest and Reforms, 1906–1914 .	442
L.	The Results of the First World War	453
LI.	India after the First War, 1919–1943 : External Relations . .	463
LII.	Constitutional Questions: First Phase, 1919–1935	473
LIII.	Constitutional Questions: Second Phase, 1935–1942	487
LIV.	Defence and Finance . . .	503
LV.	Economic Developments . . .	515
LVI.	Social Progress	528
LVII.	Constitutional Questions: Third Phase, 1942–1947	540
LVIII.	Partition and the Transfer of Power	560
	Appendix: Indian Nomenclature and Chronology . . .	571
	Index	580

MAPS

		PAGE
I.	INDIA : MAIN PHYSICAL FEATURES (*Coloured*) *facing*	xii
II.	INDIA : TO ILLUSTRATE CHAPTERS II–VIII .	8
III.	INDIA : TO ILLUSTRATE CHAPTERS IX–XVIII	58
IV.	INDIA'S FOREIGN CONTACTS	132
V.	INDIA IN THE TURKISH PERIOD : TO ILLUSTRATE CHAPTERS XX–XXV . . .	142
VI.	MOGUL INDIA : TO ILLUSTRATE CHAPTERS XXVI–XXXII	196
VII.	INDIA IN THE EIGHTEENTH CENTURY : TO ILLUSTRATE CHAPTERS XXXIII–XLI .	264
VIII.	MODERN INDIA : TO ILLUSTRATE CHAPTERS XLII–LVI	350
IX.	MODERN INDIA : PROVINCES AND STATES . . . . . *facing*	472
X.	MODERN INDIA : RAILWAYS AND INDUSTRIAL CENTRES . . *facing*	473
XI.	INDIA AND PAKISTAN, 1947 .	561

Alas, my Brother ! Mighty kings and lords,
  Proud princes, courtiers, loveliest maidens gay,
Bards, and their tales of ancient chivalry—
  Homage to Time !—all these have passed away.
                    From BHARTRI-HARI'S *Vairāgya Satakam*.

Think, in this batter'd Caravanserai
Whose Portals are alternate Night and Day,
  How Sultán after Sultán with his Pomp
Abode his destined Hour, and went his way.

They say the Lion and the Lizard keep
The Courts where Jamshýd gloried and drank deep :
  And Bahrám, that great Hunter—the Wild Ass
Stamps o'er his Head, but cannot break his Sleep.
          OMAR KHAYYÁM, in Edward FitzGerald's version.

         Cities and Thrones and Powers,
              Stand in Time's eye,
         Almost as long as flowers,
              Which daily die :
         But, as new buds put forth,
              To glad new men,
         Out of the spent and unconsidered Earth,
              The Cities rise again.
                         RUDYARD KIPLING.

MAP I.
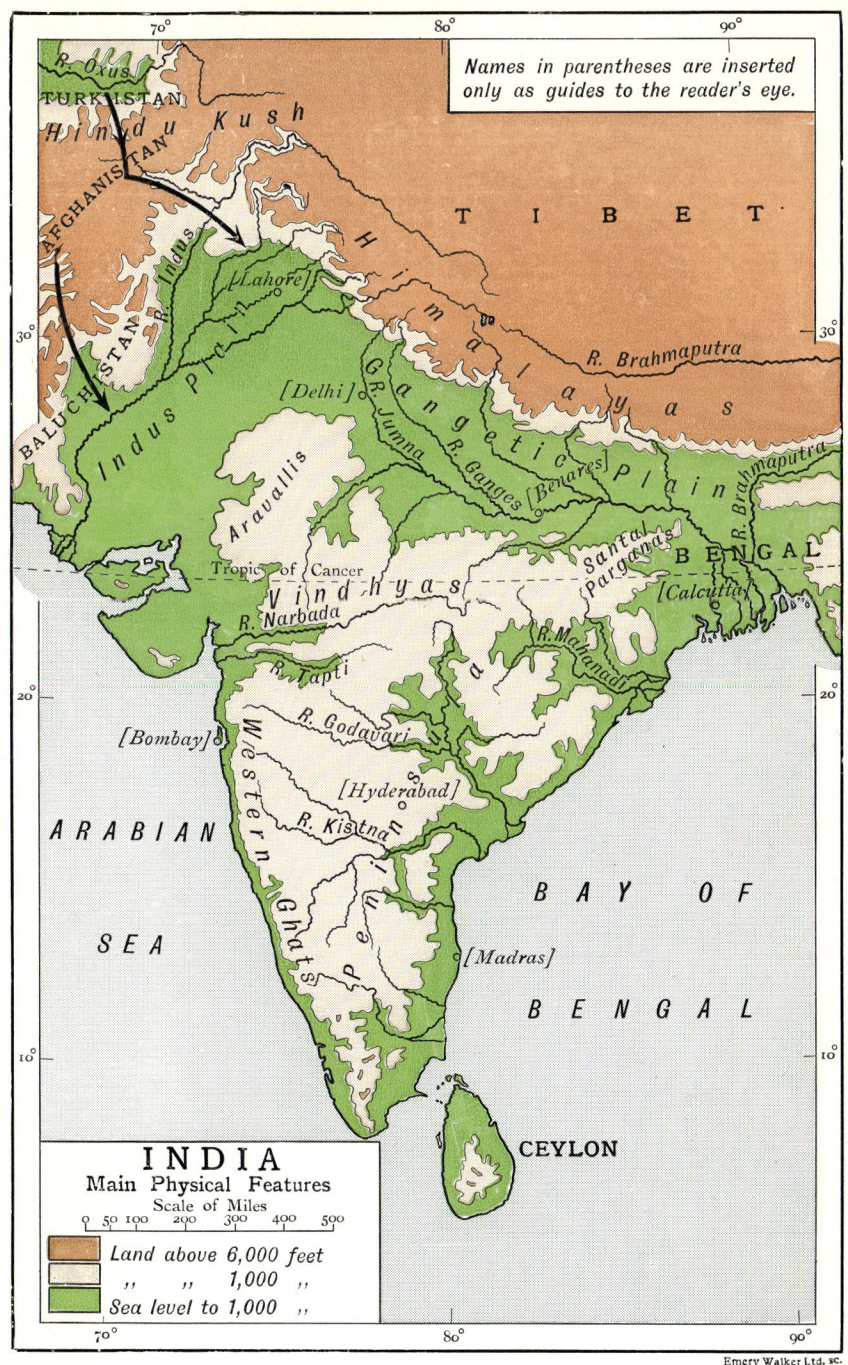

A SHORT HISTORY OF INDIA

CHAPTER I

THE LAND AND THE PEOPLE

1. *The Land*

WE must begin by defining our subject, for the name 'India' has in the past meant different things to different people, sometimes merely a narrow strip of coast, at others the greater portion of southern Asia. We mean by it the region lying between the Himalayas and the Indian Ocean; and we exclude Burma, which does not form part of India in this geographical sense, though in the course of the last century it was incorporated by degrees in the administrative unit known as the Indian Empire.

The main natural division of this great region of the world is into North and South. The dividing line is formed by what is popularly called the Vindhya range, a rugged tract of varying width and elevation, lying almost east and west along the Tropic of Cancer, and presenting a serious obstacle to communication, now partially overcome by roads and railways.

South India consists of a high triangular plateau. On the west, the scarp or wall of the plateau, known popularly as the Western Ghats, is steep and continuous from almost the extreme south northward to the river Taptī; the passes are few and difficult, and the narrow strip of coastal land which lies below them has in the past largely lived a life of its own. The chief rivers of the plateau flow eastward, and the eastern scarp, broken as it is by their valleys, is a much less important obstacle to communication, so that the South, as a whole, has in the past looked east rather than west. Through the eastern seaports intercourse has been maintained for an indefinite period with Java and Sumatra, with Burma, Siam and Indo-China, while on the west coast the harbours were important in former days mainly as accommodating the vessels engaged in the trade between the east of Asia and the Red Sea or the Persian Gulf. At the north-western corner of the plateau, however, two rivers, the Narbada and the Taptī, have broken through the western scarp, and the seaports at their mouths formed, until the development of Bombay, the main outlets of India towards the west.

North India extends from the Vindhyas to the Himalayas, with their western continuation, the Hindu Kush. The main chain of the Himalayas, running at an elevation of over 15,000 feet, presents perhaps the greatest natural obstacle to land communication in the world. It is not absolutely impenetrable, and thin streams of commerce flow through the passes to and from Tibet and Turkistan, but the movement across it of large bodies of men, or a large volume of bulky goods, is not a practical possibility. The eastern land-frontier, too, is mountainous, and almost equally difficult ; but there are two gaps, a narrow strip of lowland along the coast, which gives access to Arakan, and, further north, the valley of the Brahmaputra, by which it is possible, though not easy, to reach western China. On the west also the natural land-frontier is formed by mountainous country running from the Hindu Kush to the sea ; but a few passes, practicable for troops, lead through Afghanistan to Turkistan, and through Baluchistan to Persia, and it is by way of these passes that, at intervals throughout the historical period, India has been invaded—by Greeks, Scythians and Huns, by Afghans, Mongols and Persians.

Within these frontiers North India consists of the basins of two great river-systems, the Indus and the Ganges. The mountainous portions of these basins are extensive, but thinly populated, and the main life of the country has been lived on the wide alluvial plains. These are broken into three divisions by wedges projecting northward from the rugged central region. Towards the west, the tract known in modern times as Rājputāna separates the two basins, and at one point, close to Delhi, the modern capital, approaches the forests lying at the foot of the Himalayas, leaving a comparatively narrow gap of less than 200 miles, through which invaders from the north-west have had to pass in order to reach the Gangetic plain ; a series of decisive battles have been fought at this point, and there have been times when the Indus plain has had a history of its own. Further east, another wedge, now called the Santāl Parganas, projects northward, and serves to separate the main Gangetic plain from the region known as Bengal, where the waters of the Ganges unite with those of the Brahmaputra ; and in former times, when the country north of the river was not easily traversed, the separation was effective, so that Bengal, too, has had its own history.

An important difference in conditions between North and South lies in the fact that the former has snow-fed rivers, while the latter has not. The southern rivers are torrents in the wet season, with little water during the remainder of the year, and they have never been of much service as means of communication. The Indus and the Ganges, with their main tributaries, derive from the Himalayan snow-fields, and, with a more regular flow of water, navigation is possible at certain seasons from the Bay of Bengal to Agra, and from the Arabian Sea to Lahore. In old times both systems carried a large volume of traffic, but they have now been superseded by the railway ; in the deltaic parts of Bengal, however, boats are still, as they must always have been, an important means of transit.

As far back as we can see, India has lived mainly by agriculture, and her life has depended on the atmospheric phenomenon known popularly as ' the monsoon.' During the greater part of the year dry winds blow from the north-west, gradually curving southward as they traverse the country ; and while these bring a varying amount of rain, the fall is not by itself sufficient to make agriculture possible. About May a moist current from the south-west, ' the monsoon ' of ordinary speech, enters the Arabian Sea and the

Bay of Bengal. The former branch sweeps across the Indian coast, and usually gives adequate rain to the greater part of the country; the latter ordinarily curves, and flows westward up the plain of the Ganges, while later in the year it waters the south-east of the peninsula. The main currents vary in strength from year to year, while the distribution of their moisture over the land is irregular, affected by causes which are as yet imperfectly understood. Thus, year by year, the months from June to September are an anxious time. A 'good monsoon' has always meant, as it still means, at least sufficient food for the population, and an active demand for goods from every village in the country. A 'bad monsoon' has meant famine, in the literal sense, over larger or smaller areas, involving death from starvation, aimless migration, and sometimes actual depopulation. These effects have been minimised by administrative action in recent times, but they are written in bold characters across the story of the past.

2. *The People*

We do not know when, or from what sources, India was first populated. Working on linguistic and ethnographical data, scholars have analysed the population, excluding later accretions, into layers, attributed to successive waves of immigration from regions indicated with varying degrees of precision, but it cannot be said that any hypothetical reconstruction has yet won general assent in all its details, and we must confine ourselves to the broad facts which can be regarded as established. Three elements, or groups of elements, can be distinguished with confidence, which are described in popular language as the jungle tribes, the Dravidians, and the Aryans. In the hills and forests in the centre of the country are found certain tribes who still speak distinctive languages, and appear to be the oldest elements in the population. Their present location is most easily accounted for on the theory that at one time they occupied a much wider area and that they were gradually pressed back into the jungles by an immigrant race, or group of races, which eventually spread over almost the whole country. The name Dravidian, which properly denotes a group of languages, is loosely applied to this race, or group, and such indications as exist suggest that these Dravidians reached India from the west. The third element consists of the Aryans, whose arrival from the north-west may almost be described as a matter of history, and is discussed in the next chapter.

Later additions to the population include the Scythians and the Huns, whose incursions will be mentioned in due course, and, in more recent times, the Moslem conquerors and immigrants from Persia, Afghanistan, and beyond, who penetrated the north, and far into the centre of the country; but it is important to remember that in this case creed does not furnish a clue to race, for in the past wholesale conversions to Islam have occurred, principally in the Indus basin and in Bengal.

Such are the main elements which have gone towards building up the Indian people of to-day, but we have also to take account of minor accretions, which have contributed in some cases much more than their numbers would suggest— the Jews, the Arabs, and the Armenians, who settled in the country for trade, the Parsees who left Persia under the pressure of Islam, Africans and Asiatics imported as slaves, and, since A.D. 1500, the Portuguese and other European nations. Some of these minor elements have preserved their racial individuality, but the Arab traders on the West Coast intermingled with the inhabitants, and are now represented by the class known as Moplah, while to the advent of Europeans must be attributed the mixed race formerly called Eurasian, but now preferring to be known as Anglo-Indian.

This heterogeneous collection of races has necessarily resulted in a wide diversity of speech. The languages spoken by the jungle tribes, though they still survive, are now quite unimportant, and the country is divided into two main linguistic regions. The bulk of South India speaks Dravidian, but here several distinct languages have emerged; these are not mutually intelligible, and English is the nearest approach to a *lingua franca* which is known in this region.

In North India, and for some way down the west side of the peninsula, we find numerous languages fundamentally Aryan, but modified in varying degree by Dravidian and other contacts ; the most important group of these, known loosely as Hindi, is spoken in the Gangetic plain. These languages shade off into each other, and there is some mutual comprehension, while, in addition, a *lingua franca*, known to Englishmen as Hindustani, resulted from the intercourse of Persian-speaking invaders and immigrants with the Hindi speakers of the Gangetic plain. Knowledge of this expressive and adaptable medium will usually suffice to carry a man through the greater part of North India, but it will leave him almost helpless in the South ; while a Dravidian speaker has no resource but English to take him through the North. It is true that Sanskrit, the classical language of India, is read by some scholars throughout the country, but their number is comparatively small, and as a means of intercommunication its practical value is even less than that of Latin in modern Europe.

In attempting then to write the history of India, we have not to deal with a homogeneous whole. The country, it is true, forms a well-defined geographical unit, but its wide extent and its natural features combine to favour segregation into distinct entities, such as in other parts of the world have developed into separate nations, and in the past a tendency towards segregation has in fact operated. So far back, however, as we can see, there has also been an underlying tendency in the opposite direction, which has found scope for adequate expression only in the course of the last century. It is historically incorrect to think of ' Indians ' as we think of French or Portuguese : it is not less incorrect to think of them as we think of Europeans. The truth lies somewhere between these contrasted views.

MAP II

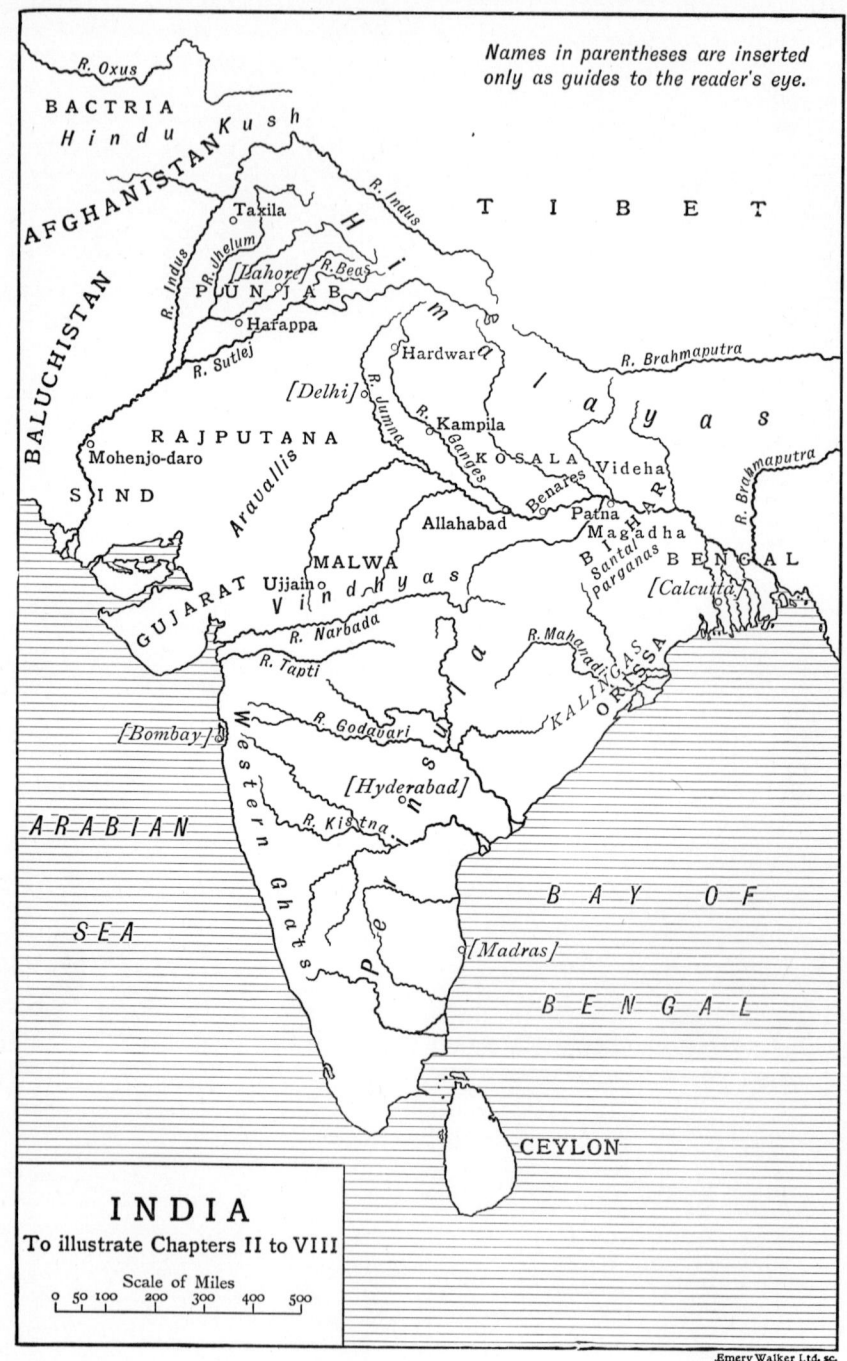

CHAPTER II

THE BEGINNINGS OF INDIAN HISTORY

1. *The Civilisation of the Indus Plain*

IN India, as elsewhere, relics of prehistoric stone ages have been discovered, seemingly linking India both with Africa and with south-east Asia. But our knowledge of these ancient peoples is too uncertain for incorporation in a general history. The first big fact known to us is that before 2500 B.C., an orderly and widespread civilisation existed in the Indus plain, a civilisation comparable with that of contemporary Mesopotamia and ranking, therefore, amongst the major achievements of man.[1] Since 1921, when this Indus civilisation was first identified, traces of it have been found over a vast area extending from the Himalayas to the Arabian Sea. Throughout this area the remains are sufficiently uniform to suggest a corresponding political unity on an imperial scale. The inference is supported by the metropolitan size of two of the Indus cities, Harappā in the Punjab and Mohenjo-daro, 400 miles away in Sind ; but whether this duality represents alternative capitals of a single state or adjacent and kindred principalities cannot now be determined. Both cities were more than three miles in circumference, and excavation has indicated that they were laid out on similar plans, each with a towering citadel defended by walls and towers, overshadowing a ' lower city ' with straight streets and elaborate courtyard-houses. A notable feature is the use of kiln-baked bricks rather than the sundried mud-bricks characteristic of Mesopotamia ; and this fact, combined with the skill wherewith jungle animals were represented by the Indus craftsmen, and the great fondness of the builders for elaborate brick drains and conduits, points to a wetter climate than today. The excavated structures include large granaries for the storage of the

[1] The most recent account is in Mortimer Wheeler's *The Indus Civilization* (Cambridge, 1953).

tributary grain which, as in Mesopotamia and Egypt, must have represented a great part of the state income. On the citadel of Mohenjo-daro, beside the granary, is a large tank of the ritual type familiar in more modern India, and smaller bathrooms are of frequent occurrence. Stone sculptures of an individual kind probably represent gods or priest-kings, and there is a great range of figurines and ornaments in clay, bronze, silver and gold. Above all, there is a now-famous series of steatite 'seals', generally bearing representations of animals, often with pictographic inscriptions which have not yet been interpreted. These are the earliest examples of writing yet found in India.

Who were the people who enjoyed these conveniences and luxuries? We can only say at present that the Indus civilisation was an essentially Indian product, developing in more or less remote contact with the older civilisation of Mesopotamia but having its own individual culture and language. If the so-called 'Aryans' come into the picture at all, it is probably as destroyers of the Indus Empire. On the latest level of Mohenjo-daro have been uncovered the contorted skeletons of some of the last inhabitants—men, women and children—lying where they fell in a final massacre. The tragedy seems to have occurred a little before 1500 B.C., and it is a guess (though not much more) that the ruthless invaders may have been some of those Aryans to whom we must now turn.

2. *The Coming of the Aryans*

Scientifically, the term 'Aryan,' like 'Dravidian,' is linguistic, not racial, but in popular use it has come to be applied to people who spoke an Aryan language. For the Aryans who came to India, we possess no such archaeological data as have just been described, and the nature of their life renders similar finds unlikely, for at first they did not dwell in towns, while their houses were built of wood and other perishable materials. Our knowledge of them is derived primarily from the Rigveda, the oldest Sanskrit text, and secondarily from the comparative study of the languages to which Sanskrit is allied. The facts to be obtained from these sources are meagre when compared with what we want to know, and they have fired the imaginations of many scholars in the West as well as in the East, so that the scanty knowledge we possess is associated with an extensive mass of conjecture, and it is not always easy to separate the two.

In essence, the Rigveda is a hymn-book, though a large one, approximating in bulk to the Iliad and the Odyssey taken together. It is a compilation of hymns written at different periods, and no precise dates can be assigned either to the compilation or to the component parts, but it is safe to say that the earlier hymns carry us back beyond 1000 B.C. The information to be gathered from such a source is naturally very unequal. It tells us much of religion, and comparatively little of other aspects of life, still less of history; and, in regard to religion, it is concerned mainly with the elaborate ritual of the sacrifices offered by kings and nobles, and throws little direct light on the actual beliefs of ordinary people. It is thus an unsatisfactory source, but it is all we have.

When Europeans came in direct contact with India, Sanskrit was at first regarded as an obscure language, not related to anything else within their knowledge. Soon, however, its obvious similarity to Greek and Latin was recognised, and towards the close of the eighteenth century Sir William Jones, a judge of the Supreme Court in Calcutta, and the founder of modern Indian scholarship, put forward the view that it is one of a large family, and that Greek and Latin, Gothic and Celtic, Sanskrit and Old Persian, must all have sprung from a common source. Working on this hypothesis, scholars have developed the idea of an Indo-European language, spoken by a group of tribes which from their original habitation gradually spread over large parts of Europe and Asia, and in the regions where they settled diverged in life and in speech under the influence of their new environment.

This main idea can be accepted with confidence, but as yet there is little certainty as to detail. We do not know where these tribes originally lived, or when or by what routes they scattered. Their home has been placed in various parts of Europe and Asia, as far west as Hungary, and as far north as the Arctic Circle, while the date of their migration has been assigned to several millennia; it is, however, reasonably certain that, wherever they came from, the Aryans entered India through Afghanistan, and there are no strong grounds for supposing that they began to arrive before 2000 B.C., several centuries later than the life which has been discovered in the Indus plain. They must be thought of as immigrant tribes, not invading armies, for they brought their families and live-stock; there are some indications that tribe may have followed tribe in successive waves, separated, perhaps, by considerable intervals of time; and it has been suggested that they may have belonged to more races than one.

Ethnographical and linguistic data suggest that the immigrants first settled in the Indus plain, dispossessing the inhabitants whom they found, and that their penetration eastward came later. The geographical allusions in the Rigveda point to a stage when the community for whom it was composed were living mainly on the watershed between the Indus and the Ganges systems, a short distance north-west of Delhi, and they were certainly more familiar with the region to the west than with the Gangetic plain. The Aryans were grouped in tribes, which had occasional wars among themselves, while they were normally at war with the 'black-skinned Dasyus,' who may reasonably be identified with the peoples speaking Dravidian languages, who were presumably darker in complexion than the invaders.

An Aryan tribe was composed of families, never polyandrous and usually monogamous, in which the father held a patriarchal position, and the mother an honourable though subordinate station. There is no hint of city life, and it has been conjectured that at this period each family lived apart, and that the village, which is still the Indian unit of population, arose in this region as the family multiplied, and occupied several houses side by side. The tribe was ruled by a king, whose position was usually if not always hereditary, and there was a council, apparently composed of the heads of families; but the relations between king and council are uncertain, and perhaps were in fact indefinite, the evolution from tribal leader to territorial sovereign being in progress. Apart from the tribesmen there were numerous slaves, consisting of prisoners taken in war; but there are indications that an insolvent tribesman might become the slave of his creditor.

The tribesmen lived mainly by the land, but were apparently more interested in stock than crops. Cattle were the most highly prized animals : wealth was reckoned largely in cows, which served as a unit of value, and were on the way to attain the peculiar sanctity they now enjoy; but the flesh of oxen seems to have formed part of the ordinary diet. Next to cattle came horses, which drew the chariots used by the great men in war; there were also sheep and goats, donkeys and dogs. The texts indicate that woollen cloth or tanned skins were worn, and cotton is not mentioned; weaving was women's work, and besides weavers we read of tanners, of wood-workers, and of smiths, though it is uncertain what metal the last-named worked. Fishing was apparently rare, but hunting was common; the most prominent recreation was the chariot-race, and gambling with dice was prevalent, leading on occasion to debt, and thence to slavery.

As regards the religion of the Aryans, the gods to whom the hymns in the Rigveda are addressed are usually the great phenomena of nature,[1] the sky, the sun, the thunderstorm, fire, and the like, conceived as living beings, and usually represented in anthropomorphic shapes; they were regarded on the whole as benevolent, and their favour could be won by sacrifices, the ritual of which was in process of elaboration. But there are traces of development in ideas as well as in ritual, and it would be a mistake to regard the religion of the Aryans as static. In the tenth book of the Rigveda, which as a whole is certainly later than the rest,

[1] Some of the Vedic gods, which cannot easily be brought under this description, look like heroes who had been deified by the people, and accepted by the priests, but not yet fitted into the general sacerdotal scheme.

philosophical speculations appear, the beginnings of the continuous effort to get beyond polytheism which is one of the most prominent characteristics of Indian thought : the idea emerges of the universe as a whole, and of its creation by a single supreme power, superseding the earlier conception of a number of deities, more or less co-ordinate.

What the Aryans thought about a future life is obscure, and perhaps at this period they had not thought the matter out. There is only the barest hint of anything resembling the doctrine of successive rebirths, which is so firmly established in the later literature, and there are some indications that a man's future fate was believed to depend on his conduct, but it is scarcely possible to say more than that the doctrine of individual survival was accepted.

It is natural to ask if the Aryans had anything corresponding to the system of caste, under which a man's social and economic status is determined by his birth. The growth of this system has been gradual, and in one of the later hymns of the Rigveda we meet the names of the four original castes familiar in the next period ; but the main body of the text does not disclose the institution in a precise form. Kingship and priesthood were commonly hereditary; but fighting was the business of all tribesmen, not of a separate class, and there is nothing to suggest that weavers or other craftsmen were segregated in any way. The one clear distinction drawn in the texts is that of colour. As has been rather crudely said, the Aryan of the Rigveda ' was a white man, and proud of it ' ; he loathed his dark-skinned enemies ; and his captured slaves were undoubtedly a class apart. To this extent, caste existed ; but it is doubtful whether the system had developed further, and whether priestly and kingly families were as yet definitely segregated.

The Rigveda thus enables us to form some idea, however indistinct, of Aryan life ; of the life of the hostile inhabitants it tells us scarcely anything. They possessed large herds of cattle, and they had some sort of refuges in which they sheltered themselves against the Aryan attacks ; the word applied to these refuges means in later literature ' towns,' but some scholars have questioned whether this meaning is applicable so early, and there is nothing to show the precise nature of these strongholds. It is clear that they were dangerous enemies in the field, though an impartial view of the fighting is not to be expected in the hymns of their opponents ; and that is practically all we know about them. The view has occasionally been put forward that they were mere savages, but it seems to rest only on a too literal acceptance of the hatred and scorn expressed in the Aryan texts ; and it will be negatived decisively if the Indus civilisation is proved to be Dravidian.

While, however, the relations between Aryans and Dravidians depicted in the texts were purely hostile, there must have been a certain amount of intercourse of a different type. The Aryans possessed many captured slaves, a fact which renders probable the beginnings of a population of mixed descent, while there are some hints of alliances with Dravidian forces in the wars between Aryan tribes. The language of the Rigveda contains numerous words, and some forms, which must be accepted as Dravidian ; and it is probable that these were more frequent in the everyday speech of the Aryans, which according to linguistic scholars was already diverging from the written language of the learned. It is reasonable to infer then that a beginning had already been made at this period towards the fusion of cultures which undoubtedly occurred.

3. *The Emergence of Hinduism*

For the period following that of the Rigveda, our only sources are still the religious literature, consisting of later collections of hymns and ritual, together with explanations and commentaries on them. The dates of the texts are uncertain, but the oldest of them overlap the latest parts of the Rigveda, while the rest of the group are certainly earlier than 550 B.C. ; and, when taken together, they enable us to form some idea of the developments which had occurred in the course of about four or five centuries.

The main fact disclosed by this literature is the emergence

of that distinctive way of life which is most conveniently called Hinduism : the Rigveda is an Aryan text, but the later documents are the result of the gradual fusion of cultures which was apparently in a very early stage at the time the Rigveda was compiled. Hinduism is sometimes described as a religion, but when that word is used it must be understood in its older and wider sense ; the present tendency is to confine 'religion' to that department of human activity which is concerned with creed and worship, but Hinduism, like Judaism, is a complete rule of life, arising from a distinctive outlook on the universe, and the term covers not merely creed and worship, but law, both public and private, and practically the whole of social and economic life.

Hinduism must be regarded as both Aryan and Dravidian, but it cannot yet be analysed into its elements. We know only a little about the Aryans, about the Dravidians we know practically nothing, and an apparently new element may be either a Dravidian contribution or an Aryan element which has escaped earlier record, or a novelty resulting from the interaction of the two cultures. Analysis must therefore wait until archaeologists have succeeded in reconstructing Dravidian civilisation as it existed before contact with the Aryans.

The locality to which the sources now refer shows a definite change. The Rigveda belongs to the watershed between the Indus and the Ganges, but now we are concerned with the upper Gangetic plain, the 'Middle Country' of the texts, and the Holy Land of Hinduism. Many Indian rivers are sacred, but none of them has in full measure the peculiar sacramental quality attributed to the Ganges ; and while places of great sanctity are found all over the land, to the Hindu none of them carries just the same significance as the three names, Kāshī, Prayāg and Hardwār. At the present day many pilgrims make the long and difficult journey to the sources of the Ganges, far up in the Himalayas, but their number is trifling compared with the crowds who go to bathe at Hardwār, where the river enters the plain ; at Prayāg, renamed Allahabad in later times, where it is

HINDU LIFE

joined by the Jumna; or at Kāshī, usually known as Benares, the most sacred city of all. Kāshī was not, however, the centre of the life of this period. That position was occupied by Kāmpīla, now merely a village, lying near the Ganges, about midway between Agra and Lucknow. The scope of our authorities extends thence eastward to the border of Bengal, and westward to the Indus plain; South India remains outside it, but some 'outcast,' that is to say, unassimilated, tribes are mentioned, whose names suggest that they lived in, or just beyond, the Vindhya country.

In this region the conditions of life were apparently more settled than in the period covered by the Rigveda. It becomes appropriate to speak of kingdoms rather than tribes; the territorial units were of larger size; city life had developed; and the power of the king over his subjects was increasing, while the lack of information regarding the councils suggests that their importance was on the wane. We meet, too, the beginnings of a local administration, an institution so conspicuous in later times, with a man at the head of each village receiving orders directly or indirectly from the king. In the family there are some signs that the position of the women was deteriorating, and the desire for sons rather than daughters becomes prominent.

It is clear that the bulk of the subjects were settled on the land, and that their chief business was raising crops; we hear of wheat and barley, rice and millets, pulses, sugarcane and oilseeds, the main staples of the country at the present day, but as yet there is no mention of cotton. Iron and silver come into the list of metals in use, and the long array of handicrafts shows that specialisation of work had made much progress since the days of the Rigveda. It is, by comparison, an orderly and settled life, though still broken by wars between the kingdoms, and with the unassimilated tribes on their borders.

Segregation of the people into castes had advanced, though not to the point reached in later times. A caste is a social group, the membership of which is determined by birth; a child is born into a particular caste and cannot change to another. In the fully-developed system a caste presents four main characteristics. In the first place, it is endogamous, that is to say, nobody can marry outside the circle of his or her caste ; and within the caste there are commonly groups known as sub-castes, which are also endogamous, so that people must marry inside their sub-caste. In the second place, a particular form of occupation is appropriate to each caste, so that a son usually follows his father's calling, as a weaver, a blacksmith, or whatever it may be ; but this has never been altogether obligatory, and agriculture in particular may be practised by anyone. In the third place, each caste has an elaborate code of rules regarding food, drink, smoking and the like, which operate to restrict social intercourse between different castes. In the fourth place, there is what may almost be called a masonic element : men of the same caste are ' brethren ' ; they help each other in work, and enjoy themselves in common ; they extend charity to brethren in distress ; while a man who has been ' put out of caste ' for some breach of rules or for conduct offensive to his brethren is practically deprived of all social amenities, has no friends, and must face the world as an isolated unit. The system is, however, by no means rigid. New castes arise from time to time ; the social rules are frequently changed by agreement ; the restrictions on occupation are increasingly elastic ; and it is the limitation on marriage which has been the most stable feature of the institution.

This description applies only to modern times. In the period of which we are writing there were four main groups, the Brāhman or priestly class, the Kshatriya or royal and warrior class, the Vaishya or commoner, and the Sūdra or servile class. Intermarriage among these groups was not yet absolutely barred, and the offspring of mixed marriages were tending to form distinct classes ; while apparently some of the Sūdras were rising in rank, and becoming assimilated to the poorer freemen, among whom the craftsmen were being segregated from the agriculturists as being of inferior status. The position was thus developing in the direction of increased numbers of groups : the motives underlying this development are obscure, and, while it is easy to put forward conjectural theories, all that can safely be said is that, starting from the ' colour-bar ' between Aryans and Dravidians, a tendency has in fact operated continuously in the direction of increased subdivision of classes, and increased rigidity of the distinctions between them.[1] The actual starting-point may indeed lie much further back, if, as some scholars hold, there were already caste-divisions among the Dravidians before the Aryans arrived ; but on this point definite evidence is wanting.

Religion remains, on the surface, polytheistic, and the deities of the Rigveda reappear, but with marked changes in emphasis. The most significant novelty is the growing primacy of Siva and Vishnu, the two deities between whom the bulk of popular worship is divided at the present day. In the Rigveda Vishnu appears as one form of the sun-god, but is accorded no special prominence : in the later Vedic literature he emerges as one of the main objects of popular adoration. His position is not, however, so prominent as that of Rudra, who is hailed as ' great god,' and is given the epithet Siva, which has since become the recognised name. There are some grounds for thinking that we have here traces of a non-Aryan cult, for, according to Sir John Marshall, a representation of the ' male god ' found at Mohenjo-daro is ' recognisable at once as a prototype of the historic Siva ' ;[2] it is possible then that this early deity of the Indus plain was in course of time identified with the Aryan Rudra, and the primacy accorded to him may be the outcome of his prominence in the older popular worship.

A second important change is the increased power of the priesthood arising from the elaboration of ritual, and the development of what may be called the magical side of sacrifice. The idea had gained ground that the priest could

[1] It is possible that a stage in this development is indicated by the *sreni*, an institution mentioned occasionally in the early Buddhist literature. The word is usually rendered gild (or guild), but enough is not known of the institution to justify the use of a term carrying such precise connotations. A *sreni* was a group of families following the same craft, and co-operating under the control of a president or headman ; it looks like an occupational caste in the making, but more than this cannot usefully be said about it.
[2] Marshall, *op. cit.*, p. 52.

influence, to the point of compulsion, the god to whom he offered a sacrifice, provided that he observed the accepted ritual in its minutest details; but only an expert priest could do this, and an error in ritual, whether accidental or intentional, would be fatal to success. The Brāhman had thus come to stand out as indispensable to the layman, to be reverenced, and propitiated, as controlling the favour of the gods.

This, however, is not the whole story. While the priests were developing their power over the people, they, or some of them, were carrying further the ideas already foreshadowed in the Rigveda, which, if logically interpreted, would render priests and ritual unimportant. The group of commentaries known by the name of Upanishads insist on the ultimate unity of the universe, and on an absolute reality which cannot be approached directly by human beings; the consequences of these conceptions are not fully developed, but they form the starting-point of the elaborate metaphysical discussions which characterise the literature of later times, and they mark the increasing divergence between the popular polytheistic religion and the best thought of the best minds.

Of more immediate significance was the formulation of the doctrine of successive rebirths, together with the allied doctrine of *karma*, a term which has no precise equivalent in English. Etymologically the word denotes 'action,' and the consequences of human action form the subject of the doctrine. On one side it approaches the principle of philosophic determinism, that the present is the sum of the past, and that the future depends inevitably on the present; but it departs from this principle in postulating the freedom of the individual will. What happens to a man in the present is the inevitable result of the sum total of his past actions, and as such must be accepted with resignation; but his action in the present is not predetermined by the past, for he is free to choose his course. At the moment of death, then, there is an accumulation of the consequences of past action, which determines the condition of the individual in the next birth, whether as a man or as a higher or lower animal. Rebirth may not, however, be immediate, and there may be an interval of retribution for past conduct, which in the popular speech is denoted by words usually rendered as 'heaven' and 'hell.' The succession of rebirths may be long, but it is not necessarily infinite : the ideal of life is to become one with the absolute reality which is termed Brahman, when the series of rebirths comes to an end. This union, or absorption, is described by some Indian writers as 'immortality' or 'eternal life,' but it is something essentially different from the meaning which those words carry in ordinary English speech : in one case the separate individuality is lost, in the other it persists to all eternity. This ideal, that the termination of a separate existence is the greatest good, leads naturally to the position that individual existence is in itself an evil ; the inference does not appear in our authorities for this period, but it must have been quickly drawn, for the pessimistic view of life lies at the root of the doctrines taught by the religious reformers of the sixth century B.C., whom we shall meet in Chapter V.

It may be said then that the main lines of Hinduism had emerged in the upper Gangetic plain by the end of the later Vedic period. There is no record of the process by which it spread over the rest of India. Some writers have pictured the activities of hosts of Brāhman missionaries, preaching the new gospel successfully throughout the country, but no facts have been brought forward to justify this view, and all that can safely be said is that Hinduism extended, it may be supposed gradually, until it became the accepted way of life alike in North and in South.

CHAPTER III

THE HINDU WAY OF LIFE

SUBJECT to local and temporary interruptions, Hinduism dominated India politically until the thirteenth century of the Christian era ; and when eventually political authority passed to Moslem conquerors, the Hindu rule of life remained substantially unchanged, governing, or claiming to govern, the conduct of the great majority of the population, as it does to-day. It will be well, therefore, to give at this stage a general account of the institution, not as it stood at any particular date, but as it appears throughout the period of Hindu political supremacy.

The rule of life is Dharma, a term which is really equivalent to ' the whole duty of man,' but is conveniently rendered as the Sacred Law. It is embodied in a literature which runs from portions of commentaries on the Vedas, written, perhaps, as early as 800 B.C., and extends for at least twenty centuries ; indeed it may be described as still incomplete, for even at the present day the rules which deal specifically with personal law may be the subject of interpretation by judges exercising jurisdiction in British India. The most important texts are known as Dharma-sāstras, but in some cases later commentaries on these texts have practically superseded the originals. The dates of the texts are uncertain, some of them bear marks of successive recensions, and even in the case of the Mānava-Dharma-sāstra, or ' Laws of Manu,' the most famous text of all, modern scholars are content to allow a wide margin, as from 200 B.C. to A.D. 200, for the period to which it belongs.

The Sacred Law is equally binding on kings and on

THE SACRED LAW

subjects. No machinery exists for its formal amendment, but in the course of time particular provisions have been substantially altered by the refinements and elaborations of successive commentators, and it must be regarded as to some extent a gradual growth, influenced by the views of individuals or schools of thought, and by their reaction to changing environment. The main outlines are, however, unchanged, and it is these which we proceed to summarise.

The Sacred Law contemplates the existence of many kingdoms, and of war between them as the normal state of things. Within his kingdom, the king is ' a great deity in human form,' and his paramount duty is to protect his subjects, punishing the criminals who molest them, and receiving in return the revenue which it is their duty to pay. He is expected to employ a learned priest as his chief minister, and to maintain a body of councillors whom he should consult daily. The bulk of his subjects live in the country, and a regular bureaucratic hierarchy must be maintained for their government, extending from the ' lord of ten ' to the ' lord of a thousand ' villages, though it is possible that these precise numbers represent a theoretical scheme rather than the actual practice of any particular period.

On the face of it the king stands out as a despot, but some recent writers have argued that he was bound by the decisions of his councillors to an extent which rendered his position practically the same as that of a constitutional monarch of the present day. The evidence on this point cannot be discussed here, but it may be remarked that if such a position was in fact contemplated by the early text-writers, the institution must have atrophied, for nothing resembling it was found in the Hindu kingdoms which in later periods came under the observations of foreign visitors; to them, the Hindu king was obviously a despot. At the same time, it must be borne in mind that his despotism was not unconditioned. He had been educated in the principles, and in the atmosphere, of the Sacred Law; he was exposed to the influence of councillors trained on the same lines; and it is a question of fact, and one which owing to want of evidence can scarcely ever be answered, how far the ideal of public service inculcated by the Law prevailed over the temptations to which a despot is exposed. We can safely infer that there were good kings as well as bad, but we cannot even guess which type predominated.

The idea of empire, that is to say, of a political institution superior to the kingdom, had existed in India at any rate since the period of the Vedas, when a special form of sacrifice was recognised as appropriate to the 'conqueror of the whole earth,' and during the historical period large empires emerged from time to time. As a rule these were superimposed on existing kingdoms as the result of conquest or submission, the constituent units ordinarily remained intact, subject to the payment of tribute, and, when the empire broke up, the old kingdoms, or most of them, resumed their independence as a matter of course. The Hindu king, therefore, should not be thought of as necessarily holding the position of an uncontrolled sovereign : the conception of a king under an emperor was recognised in the Hindu period, it recurs during the centuries of Moslem rule, when Hindu kingdoms submitted to foreign conquerors, and it is apparent in the position of the Indian States at the present day.

Within the kingdom the status of the individual subject was determined by his birth. The caste-system was not so elaborate or so rigid as it has since become, for intermarriage frequently took place, and social segregation was apparently less complete ; but already each caste had its appropriate occupation, which every man born into it was expected to follow in the ordinary course. The most important occupation was necessarily agriculture, which was organised in the units known in India as villages. To English readers this term is misleading : the Indian village must be thought of rather as a civil parish, that is to say, a recognised administrative unit of area, which need not have a resident population, though ordinarily the land of a village was cultivated by people living within its limits.

The Indian village of the remote past has been the subject of some rather imaginative literature, in which conjecture has occasionally run beyond the few facts furnished incidentally by the texts of the Sacred Law. Interpreting the texts in the light of facts recorded at later periods, it may be said that most villages, but probably not all, contained a resident community or brotherhood, held together by the tie of a common ancestry, and managing, as a body, the affairs of the village, subject to whatever orders the administration might give. Each member of the brotherhood had separate possession of the land which he cultivated; and his holding passed by inheritance, and could in some cases, if not in all, be sold or mortgaged. A share of the produce of the land was due to the king in return for the protection he offered, and it was largely for the realisation of this share that the local administration was organised. Outside the brotherhood there were serfs who worked as labourers on the land, and in some cases were probably allowed to cultivate portions of it, either in lieu of, or in addition to, the grain or other produce paid to them for their maintenance. There may also have been persons, not belonging to the brotherhood, allowed to cultivate land as its tenants, but the evidence on this point is too scanty for a definite statement, and it is quite uncertain when the free tenant emerged. Apart from these ordinary villages, there are some indications of areas held as the peculiar possession of the king, or of prominent men; and these may have been cultivated by serfs, or by tenants, or in both ways.

The scanty facts on record regarding the tenure in the ordinary villages have been interpreted in three ways. Some writers have contended that the king was owner of the soil, and the brotherhood were his tenants, paying a share of the produce by way of rent. Others have argued that the members of the brotherhood owned the land, paying a share of the produce to the king by way of tax. Others, again, hold that the juristic conception of ownership of land had not emerged when the texts of the Sacred Law were compiled, and that the relation between king and brotherhood was contemplated as political, not legal, in its nature: cultivation of land within a kingdom was a fact, which necessarily involved allegiance to the king and payment to him of a share of the produce, while failure to pay was a breach of the Sacred Law and a definite act of rebellion. These conflicting views cannot be discussed in a book like this, and we must be content with recording the divergence.

Of greater practical significance is the question what share of the produce had to be paid, and the passages bearing on this point are of interest as showing how the Sacred Law might in fact develop. The text-writers fixed the ordinary share at one-sixth, or less, though the Laws of Manu allowed one-fourth to be taken in emergencies. One of the later writers, however, used the phrase ' what is called one-sixth,' suggesting that by his time the fraction, like the word ' tithe ' in modern English, had come to bear a technical signification. A commentator on Manu inserted the words ' or one-third ' in the provision for emergencies, while another later writer explained, much in the fashion of a modern parliamentary draftsman, that the term one-sixth included one-fourth or one-third. It is probable that these writers reflect a change in practice, and that, as time went on, the higher charges, at first recognised as permissible in emergency, came to be levied in ordinary circumstances, so that the burden was in fact doubled ; and this view is borne out by a few records which have survived in South India, showing that the actual charge was much greater than the traditional fraction.

Payments of the king's share of produce did not always reach the royal treasury. It was a common practice to assign the amount due from a given area as the salary of an official, who made his own arrangements for collecting it, or as an endowment for a temple or charitable foundation, the assignments in the first case being merely temporary, while those with a charitable or religious object might be intended to be permanent. This practice of alienating future revenue prevailed right into the British period, and was one of the causes which contributed to the financial collapse of various kingdoms ; but its practical convenience in the circumstances cannot be denied. Notwithstanding these alienations, it is probable that the great bulk of a

ADMINISTRATION

Hindu king's revenue was drawn from his share of the produce of the soil; but all classes of his subjects were required to pay for the protection to which they were entitled, and the result was an elaborate system of taxation on trade and industry, much of it injurious when judged by modern canons. This system, too, was destined to continue, in spite of the occasional efforts of financial reformers, right through the Moslem period, and traces of it are still to be found in the India of to-day.

As has been said above, a regular bureaucratic hierarchy was required to execute the king's duties and collect his dues. Administration had of course to be conducted in accordance with the Sacred Law, but the subject was of sufficient importance to be recognised by Hindu thinkers as a separate department of activity, requiring a literature of its own. The outstanding text of this literature is known as the Arthasāstra [1] of Kautilya, and is traditionally attributed to a famous minister of Chandragupta Maurya, who was reigning at Patna in the year 300 B.C. Some modern scholars accept this attribution, but others date the treatise at least five centuries later, while others again regard it as a gradual growth, which cannot be dated at all. According to some authorities it may be confidently accepted as indicating the administrative practice prevailing at the time it was written, while according to others it should be taken as originally a theoretical work, which in course of time came to exercise an important influence on rulers and administrators. Regarded from the former standpoint, the picture it presents must be described as unpleasant in modern eyes, for the sole aim of the administrator was efficiency, and he had no scruples as to the means he employed. In view, however, of the existing uncertainties as to date and authority, it would be dangerous to assume that any Indian kingdom was in fact governed in accordance with the detailed rules given in this manual, or to use it as more than a warning that the environment in which it was drawn up was not a golden age of honesty and simple truth.

[1] An English version will be found in *Kautilya's Arthasāstra*, tr. R. Shamasastri, Mysore, 1923.

We must recognise that what would now be called gross administrative oppression was contemplated as possible, and even appropriate, by the writer, or writers, of the manual, but we cannot be confident that it reflects the actual practice of the Hindu period as a whole, though it may serve to illustrate the complexity of the administrative machinery, and the nature of the system of taxation to which reference has already been made.

Passing from public to private life, the Sacred Law contemplates a monogamous family as the unit ; but the religious requirement that death ceremonies should be performed by a male descendant was allowed to override the strict rule of monogamy, and a wider latitude in this matter was permitted to kings than to private persons. The same requirement accounts for the gradual rise to prominence of the practice of adoption, so that at the present day an adopted son becomes a member of the family precisely as if he had been born in it, and can thus perform the obligatory ceremonies. Probably the insistence of some of the text-writers on the practices of child-betrothal and early marriage is derived from the same source, the imperative need for male offspring, but the imaginative literature of the Hindu period shows incidentally that, while these practices existed, they were by no means so general as in later times.

In the matter of property also, there appears to have been a gradual development of rules restricting the freedom of the head of the family, until the position was reached in most parts of the country that males acquire at birth a right in the family property, the father is manager rather than owner, and on his death the sons take equal shares. Actual division of the property is, however, unnecessary, for the family may hold together for successive generations, the rights of individuals being maintained, and being recognised when eventually partition takes place. As a rule females have no share in the family property, though there is a complicated set of provisions regarding the

SUTTEE AND PURDAH

devolution of possessions which a woman has acquired in particular ways ; and the legal position of women is throughout inferior to that of men, the sex receiving respect from the text-writers only as potential or actual mothers of sons, and as essential partners of a householder in religious and ceremonial rituals.[1]

In this connection reference may be made to two exceptional institutions familiar under the names of ' suttee ' and ' purdah.' The former denotes the practice of a widow allowing herself to be burnt on her husband's funeral pyre. Such customs have been recorded in the early stages of many races, but it is only among Hindus that they persisted into modern times. The source of the Indian practice is unknown, but it was recognised in some texts of the Sacred Law, and it excited the interest of the Greek invaders in the fourth century B.C., so that it certainly belongs to the Hindu period. It persisted under Moslem rule, in spite of the efforts made by some administrations to suppress it, and its final prohibition by law dates only from the year 1830. The practice had two sides. When enforced by family or priestly opinion on an unwilling victim, it resulted in a long series of what were in effect cruel and callous murders : when followed voluntarily, as it so frequently was, it expressed the highest ideal of unselfish love, that a wife should accompany her husband in death as in life ; and many western observers must have shared the attitude of William Methwold,[2] an English merchant of the seventeenth century, whose experience left him ' yet unresolved whether their love to their dead husbands be more to be admired or pitied.'

The other practice, purdah, or the seclusion of ladies of position from the public eye, does not appear in the Sacred Law, nor is it clearly exemplified in the literature of the Hindu period ; and the usual view is that it originated under Moslem rule, when the subjects adopted the practice introduced by their conquerors. There are, however, some

---

[1] The question of the right to property of Hindu women is at present receiving much attention from the legislature in India and some changes are taking place.
[2] *Relations of Golconda* (Hakluyt Society, 1931), p. 28. Much information on this subject will be found in Altekar's *The Position of Women in Hindu Civilisation* (Benares, 1938).

signs that, even in Hindu times, the ladies in a royal palace lived in apartments specially reserved for them, and it is not entirely certain that the Indian institution was originated by Moslems, though their practice must undoubtedly have contributed to its prevalence in northern India in later times.

Slavery was recognised by the Sacred Law. Prisoners of war and their descendants were naturally slaves, and the same status might result as a punishment for crime, or on failure to discharge a debt; while there are definite provisions regarding the voluntary surrender of freedom under economic pressure, as in time of famine. From the general literature of the Hindu period it appears that slaves were quite common in domestic service, but there is nothing to show that their labour was employed in organised industry, as was the practice in some other countries. There are also some indications of a class of serfs living in the villages, and held at the disposal of the free community, though not treated as slaves in the strict sense, but the references in the literature are too scanty for any precise statement to be made regarding the legal position of this class.

Turning to the religious side of Hinduism, it may be said that the creed was not embodied in any precise formulas, and that in practice an individual enjoyed considerable latitude in regard to belief, so long as he paid due respect to Brāhmans, the sacred caste, venerated the cow, the sacred animal,[1] and did not hurt his neighbours' feelings. For popular worship, there was an extensive array of gods, from which the individual might choose the object of his special devotion; not all of these gods were regarded as benevolent, and sacrifice might be desirable not merely to obtain favour, but to propitiate some malignant power.

[1] This sentiment appears to have grown up by degrees. In the earliest days of Hinduism cows' flesh was still eaten, as it had been among the Aryans; in the second stage it was offered to honoured guests, who, it seems, were expected to refuse it; but the view that killing, or wilfully injuring, a cow is a heinous sin was well established by about the Christian era, and had extended its protection to oxen as well as cows.

The two great gods, Siva and Vishnu, stood out far above the rest; in the literature Brahmā, the creator of the universe, ranks along with these, but it does not appear that his worship was ever really popular, as that of Siva or Vishnu was. In the case of the latter of these, popular devotion tended to concentrate more and more on two incarnations, Krishna and Rāma, and to become practically monotheistic, as will be told in a later chapter.

In all formal religious ceremonies the intervention of the Brāhman was indispensable, because he alone was in position to conduct the ritual without which sacrifices and offerings would be ineffective; and the magical side of his powers seems always to have been emphasised in the popular view, that is to say, the belief prevailed that he could compel the gods to act in a particular way. But this idea of compulsion is most prominent in connection with the practice of asceticism. The Sacred Law prescribed a period of ascetic self-discipline for Brāhmans, and in practice this developed into the life of austerity, culminating in self-torture, led by some groups of religious mendicants. The development is no novelty, for it attracted the attention of the Greek invaders under Alexander the Great; and, while the underlying idea was self-discipline, the magical conception seems to have supervened that a man could become more powerful than the gods by subjecting his body to extremes of torture. Popular tales represent even the greatest of the gods as terrified by the threats of some particular saint, and as hastening to grant his prayer, or rather to obey his orders, in the fear that otherwise they themselves would be annihilated.

The allied doctrines of *karma* and rebirth, the emergence of which was mentioned in the preceding chapter, formed an integral part of the popular mentality, and they, too, tended to derogate from the position of the gods, of whom their operation is almost independent; and speaking generally, Hinduism as a religion must not be regarded as mere polytheism. It cannot be defined in terms of strict logic, which is irrelevant to popular belief, but it may be said that polytheism did not satisfy religious needs, and that there was continuous effort to get beyond it to a region where satisfaction might, perhaps, be found. The pantheon was not discarded, but its power was limited, and people were seeking, more or less consciously, for a road by which it might be superseded.

So far we have spoken of Hinduism as a popular religion. In the schools the search for a way of escape was more conscious and more systematic. An immense mass of philosophical literature was produced during the Hindu period, containing practically all the metaphysical conceptions which are now current in the West ; it is marked by extraordinary intellectual acuteness, it presents very different views of the ultimate reality, and it is unified only by the fact that all thinkers alike leave polytheism far behind. It would probably be a mistake to infer that this conscious intellectual effort exerted much direct influence on the popular views : the two movements should be regarded rather as different expressions of the same need. The scholar sought escape in the profoundest regions of speculative thought, while the ordinary man chose from among a wide variety of cults that which seemed to offer the best prospect of concrete satisfaction. This wide variety is in fact one of the most obvious characteristics of the popular religion. There have in the past been cults which centred in sanguinary sacrifices, or in orgies of lust ; alongside of them there have been, and still are, others of pure spiritual aspiration ; and midway between, there is the worship which so far as we know has always been that of the vast majority of Hindus, traditional rites scrupulously performed, with a varying degree of confidence in their efficacy.

Some scholars have attributed this variety, or part of it, to absorption into Hinduism of cults which had grown up among the earlier inhabitants of the country, and judging by the experience of later times, this explanation is not improbable. Even in the present century several millions of souls, constituting the jungle tribes, have been enumerated in the census as Animists, that is to say, worshippers of spirits believed to reside in particular natural objects such as stones or trees. The absorption of these tribes into Hinduism is a simple affair when once their isolation has given way as the result of the development of the country. It is sufficient for a Brāhman to point out that the spirit which the members of a tribe 'ignorantly worship' is in fact a manifestation of Siva or some other member of the Hindu pantheon ; the idea is accepted as reasonable, the Brāhman is appointed priest, the ritual is regularised, and the tribe is brought within the circle of Hinduism without more ado. There is no reason to doubt that this process has operated in the past, but evidence is wanting to prove that it accounts for the existence of all the cults which have been conjecturally attributed to it.

CHAPTER IV

THE EARLY PERIOD OF HINDU SUPREMACY :
A GENERAL VIEW

THROUGH the long period of Hindu political supremacy, we must think of India as usually parcelled out among a number of kingdoms of varying size and importance, occupying more or less completely the productive regions of the country, while the forests, hills and deserts were the home of tribes in a lower stage of organisation ; and we must regard the kingdoms as frequently at war among themselves, as well as with the tribes on their borders, except for the limited intervals when peace was imposed by the authority of a transient paramount power. The political history of this period cannot be recounted as a whole, because the facts are not on record. The literature produced during it was, indeed, varied and extensive ; in addition to the works on law, religion and philosophy, which have already been mentioned, there is extant a rich mass of poetry, epic, dramatic and lyric, a wealth of technical literature, dealing with a wide range of arts and sciences, from grammar and mathematics to erotics, and, belonging to the later centuries, a smaller number of tales and romances embodying some historical matter ; but there is practically nothing that can fairly be called history, or even chronicle.[1] Certain historical traditions, to which we shall come later, are embedded in the literature, but it is a remarkable fact that among all the learning, fancy, and speculation of the period, there is nothing to be compared with what we have received from

[1] The only known exception is a work of the twelfth century A.D., known as the *Rājataringinī*, which purports to be history ; but it is quite untrustworthy for the earlier period.

CHRONOLOGY

the Hebrews, the Greeks or the Romans—no Book of Kings, no Herodotus, no Livy. Such knowledge of political events and conditions as we possess is derived largely from foreign sources, in some cases Greek, in others Tibetan or Chinese, supplementing the extensive, but incomplete, series of coins and inscriptions discovered in recent times ; and the story has to be told in successive episodes rather than as a continuous narrative.

For the earliest centuries the chronology remains uncertain, but as time goes on dated inscriptions and coins come to our aid. Their interpretation has not been a simple matter, for the various eras used in them had already become obsolete when western scholars first approached the subject ; but a starting-point was obtained when Sir William Jones recognised that the Sandrokottos mentioned by the Greek historians about 300 B.C. must be the Maurya Emperor Chandragupta, and from about this date onwards Indian chronology becomes increasingly precise, though there is still room for difference of opinion regarding particular points.

Unfortunately this chronological precision does not extend to the dates at which the literature was produced. Very few works can be ' dated ' in the usual sense of the word, and for some of the most important of them it is impossible to assign even the century with certainty, so that the information they furnish regarding social and economic life cannot be placed in its correct historical setting. It is possible, for instance, to reconstruct in broad outline the life depicted in the epics, but we cannot be confident that all the data relate to one period, either that of the events described or that of the authors who described them, nor can we say what that period was. Such historical value therefore as the epics possess depends mainly on the traditions which they embody.

There is but little to be learned in this way from the *Rāmāyana* of Vālmīki, the second of the great Indian epics, which recounts the adventures of Rāma, King of Kosala, or Oudh, at an epoch which is quite uncertain. The story itself, how Rāma's wife, Sītā, was abducted by a demon king and carried away to Ceylon, whence Rāma eventually recovered her, is perhaps the most popular tale in India, and is presented every year in elaborate dramatic performances; it has been interpreted in various ways by western scholars, but the historian can say only that probably there is a nucleus of fact. The kingdom of Kosala was, as we shall see, certainly important in the early part of the Hindu period, and there are some faint indications that the story may belong to about the seventh century B.C., though the epic was not written till long after; but it seems impossible to disentangle any concrete facts from the fantastic tales of South India, or to say more than that Rāma was probably a real person whose exploits excited the popular imagination, until in course of time he was deified in tradition, and that later on the Brāhmans, recognising the strength of this tradition, regularised it by additions to the epic which present the hero as an incarnation of Vishnu.

The other great epic, the *Mahābhārata*, embodies elements of somewhat higher value to the historian. It is a gradual growth, containing a nucleus of royal traditions, which later priestly writers have enriched with huge masses of didactic matter. The nucleus consists of true epic stuff, and may be regarded as glorified history. Two parties, the Kurus and the Pāndus, living near Delhi, furnish the principal actors. In the course of a gambling match, marked by a certain amount of sharp practice, the king of the Pāndus lost everything he had—wife, family, and kingdom—and, as the result of the last throw of the dice, went into banishment for twelve years; after these had elapsed, he collected allies, with whose aid he eventually defeated and exterminated the Kurus. The name of the latter tribe is prominent in the Vedic literature, and the nucleus of the epic may record events which occurred as far back, perhaps, as the tenth century B.C.; but the story has been enriched in the course of the long time which elapsed before the poem assumed its present form, and tribes or nations which belong to later periods have been brought in as allies to one or other of the original protagonists. It is impossible, therefore, to accept with entire confidence the interpretations which have been put forward, representing the war as a clash of cultures or philosophies determining the fate of India : there may have been some great principle at stake, or there may have been merely a tribal quarrel, fought out to the end.

Of greater cultural significance is the appearance in the *Mahābhārata* of Krishna as the charioteer of the Pāndu leader, and his recognition as an incarnation of Vishnu. The most important of the didactic enrichments of the epic story, known as the *Bhagavadgītā*, or ' Song of the Adorable One,' is put into his mouth, and the action of the battle is suspended while he explains at length the relation of the practical life to the pursuit of ultimate salvation. It is probable that Krishna, like Rāma, was originally a popular hero, and that he reached the pantheon by the same road, so that the two most prominent figures in modern Hindu worship have a similar origin.

Related to this epic are the later texts known as Purānas, which, like it, contain a nucleus of royal tradition, embedded in a mass of didactic matter. The nucleus consists mainly of traditional genealogies of the royal families ruling in the Gangetic plain after the war described in the *Mahābhārata*, but these have been greatly corrupted in the course of time, and, taken by themselves, cannot be used with confidence as the basis of political history. They suffice, however, to furnish the outlines of political geography as it stood in the sixth century B.C., and may thus be employed to set the stage, as it were, for the events to be described in succeeding chapters. Using the administrative nomenclature of the present day, the various states may be located as follows, though of course their boundaries cannot be determined with precision.

One important kingdom was Magadha, situated in that portion of Bihār which lies south of the Ganges, and across the river was Videha, or North Bihār, while to the west of these lay Kāshī or Benares, and Kosala or Oudh. The region which comprises these four states was the scene of the most conspicuous events of which there is a record during the early part of the period ; it was here that two new religious movements, Jainism and Buddhism, arose ; and Magadha expanded in course of time into the first of the great Indian empires of which we have any definite knowledge.

Bengal and Orissa, the countries lying to the east of this region, barely appear in the early history; while for the upper Gangetic plain on the west, occupied by the Pūru [1] and Panchāla kingdoms, practically nothing has survived beyond the corrupt dynastic lists. Similar lists show merely that there were other Hindu kingdoms south and west of the Jumna, occupying East Rājputāna and Mālwa, as far almost as the Narbada. South India, the great region beyond this river, scarcely comes into the picture before the third century B.C., while the Indus plain lies outside the scope of these records, and, as we shall see, a portion of it belonged to the Persian Empire for a large part of the earlier period.

In this connection it may be noted that, while hereditary kingship was the standard institution, it had not yet become universal, for in the early period considerable areas were ruled by tribal oligarchies, either independent, or subject to the overlordship of a king. The Buddhist literature indicates that in the sixth century North Bihār contained a group of ten such oligarchies, among them Videha, which has been mentioned above; and, while this particular region was soon to pass under the sovereignty of Magadha, similar oligarchies persisted further west, along the Himalayas, in the Punjab, in Rājputāna, and in Sind. Their history is obscure in detail, but in a general way it may be said that, as time went on, oligarchy tended to give way to kingship as each strong ruler in turn subdued the tribes on his borders and incorporated them in his kingdom.

A question of great interest in connection with the sources of history for these early days is the date when the art of writing came into use. Apart from the script found at Mohenjo-daro, and not yet deciphered, two early forms of writing, kharoshthī and brāhmī, are known in India. The former was derived from the Aramaic alphabet which was used in the Persian Empire, and was introduced thence in the sixth century into the Indus region, but did not spread

---

[1] The Pūrus of these records include tribes known by different names in earlier texts, particularly the Kurus

THE ART OF WRITING

over the rest of the country. The brāhmī script has been recognised as the source of all the Indian alphabets now in use, except of course the Arabic, which arrived much later; but its history is as yet uncertain. Some scholars have supposed that it was brought to India by Mesopotamian traders, and was used at first only in commerce[1]; more recently the view has been put forward that it is a development of the script which has been found at Mohenjo-daro; but all we know is that its adaptation to express the sounds used in Sanskrit had been completed by or before the fourth century B.C. The older view was that India did not possess the art of writing, at any rate before 800 B.C., and that the large mass of Vedic literature was both composed and transmitted orally. The obvious difficulties presented by this view as regards composition have been reinforced by recognition of the fact that writing is a very old art, and that it was already practised in the Indus plain in the third millennium. We know now that it existed at that period not only in India but also in China, in Mesopotamia, and in the Mediterranean region; and when the art had once been acquired, it is very difficult to believe that it should ever be discarded, though from time to time one script might supersede another. We know, too, that the usual writing materials in India were birch-bark in the North and palm-leaves in the South, and their perishable nature would account sufficiently for the absence of any surviving manuscripts, while the practice of making inscriptions on stone or metal has not been traced back beyond the third century B.C. The history of writing in India cannot then be the subject of any dogmatic statements: we know that it was common in the Indus plain in the third millennium, but we do not yet know whether the practice continued, with a development of the script, into the historical period, or was abandoned and then reintroduced from outside.

---

[1] Buhler derives it from the most ancient form of the North Semitic alphabet. See his *On the Origin of the Brahma Alphabet*, 2nd ed. (Strassburg, 1898).

CHAPTER V

THE RISE OF BUDDHISM AND JAINISM

THE first events to which tolerably precise dates can be assigned in Indian history are two movements of religious and moral reform, or revolt, which occurred, or rather culminated, simultaneously towards the end of the sixth century B.C., and which resulted in the establishment of the religions of the Buddhists and Jains. The two movements had many points of similarity. Both were revolts not against Hinduism in the wider sense, but against the traditional polytheism and the spiritual claims of the Hindu priesthood. Both started from the allied doctrines of *karma* and rebirth. Both regarded existence as in itself an evil, and both offered a path leading ultimately to escape. In both cases the leaders belonged to the Kshatriya caste, and the original teaching of both was practical rather than philosophical; while it may be added that both religions have in course of time diverged somewhat widely from the ideas of their founders. The extant literature of both is voluminous, and it is an interesting fact that the earlier records were composed, not in classical Sanskrit, but in the simplified forms of everyday speech which are known as Prākrit, and are the parents of the modern languages of India.

The man who established Jainism as a faith was named Vardhamāna, but he is better known by the title Mahāvīra, or in current speech Mahābīr, and his life probably ran from 540 to 468 B.C. He belonged to a noble family living in Videha, or North Bihār, but at the age of thirty he became a wandering ascetic. After twelve years he attained enlightenment, that is to say, he felt that he had found what

THE BUDDHA 41

he was seeking ; and he then set out to teach the truth which he had learned, that escape from existence can be secured by right knowledge, to be attained only by a life of asceticism. Disciples gathered round him, and he was welcomed at the court of Magadha and elsewhere, but Jainism never became an important factor in political history. At first its adherents were found mainly in Bihār ; later on the religion spread to other parts of India ; and at the present day the Jains number about $1\frac{1}{2}$ millions, most of whom live in Bombay or Rājputāna. According to tradition, Mahābīr was not the originator of the Jain doctrine, but stands twenty-fourth in a line of prophets, all of them Kshatriyas, who appeared at intervals during a period which must be measured by billions of years. The traditional account is clearly fantastic, but some scholars hold that the twenty-third prophet of the series may have been an historical personage ; everything, however, before Mahābīr is wrapped in obscurity.

The founder of Buddhism was Siddhārtha Gautama, known also as Sākyamuni, and, after his enlightenment, as the Buddha. His life may be taken to have extended from about 560 to 480 B.C., the precise dates being matter of argument, and he belonged to the Sākiya tribe, an oligarchy occupying the lower slopes of the Himalayas on the eastern border of Kosala, or Oudh. A mass of legends gathered round him in the course of time, and the details of his life are hard to disentangle from the later myths, but it is clear that, starting as a Kshatriya of position, he became dissatisfied, and like Mahābīr, set out as a wandering ascetic to learn the truth. He too became enlightened, and spent the rest of his life in preaching the truth which had been given to him. His doctrine was practical rather than philosophical, and the early texts are not free from ambiguity on the speculative side ; but his main principle was the elimination of all desire as the condition necessary for escape from the evil of successive rebirths and attainment of the goal of nirvāna, or extinction of personality ; and his practical method was to master the mind rather than the body. Actual asceticism was of less value to him than to

Mahābīr; meditation and concentration on the essential truth was the essence of the discipline which he preached. But his outlook was wide, and he did not confine his efforts to the perfection of a limited band of disciples. For ordinary men and women his teaching was essentially moral, and he set before them the ideal of righteousness substantially in the form in which it has been presented by other great ethical teachers of humanity.

His teaching attracted followers, the discipline took root, and it was to become a factor in political history in later times; but in the early period the significance of Buddhism, as of Jainism, is religious rather than political. It would be a mistake to regard the two movements as new departures: Mahābīr claimed to carry on an ancient tradition, and the early Buddhist texts show that there were many seekers after truth, though they allow only one finder. The two men clearly took a road which was already familiar, when, dissatisfied with their environment, they became wandering ascetics; the doctrines which they evolved follow naturally from the basic idea that existence is in itself an evil, and do not differ greatly from teaching to be found in the priestly writings of the period. We must recognise then that in the sixth century, and perhaps earlier, the popular religion failed to satisfy men of action and not merely its priestly expositors; we do not know why other enquirers have left no mark on history, but we may reasonably conjecture that the success of Mahābīr and of the Buddha was due in the first instance to their personal qualities, and later to the qualities of their disciples.

The fact that the two successful leaders belonged to the Kshatriya caste may be of some significance. As has been said already, the power of the priesthood had increased since the age of the Rigveda, and there are some faint suggestions in the literature that the change was not welcomed by the kings, whose authority it necessarily affected. Nearly all our information comes, however, from priestly sources, which from this point of view cannot be accepted as either complete or impartial, and we do not know how far, or with what success, individual kings may

THE SIGNIFICATION OF BUDDHISM 43

have resisted the encroachments of the priests. It is not improbable that, as some writers have suggested, a long struggle between the two powers had marked the period before Mahābīr and the Buddha became ascetics, and that it may have been an important factor in their environment ; but we know only that both of them denied the authority of the Brāhmans, and thus separated themselves definitely from the priestly tradition.

CHAPTER VI

THE EARLY HISTORY OF THE INDUS PLAIN

From Bihār and Oudh we turn to the Indus plain, the region now divided between the Punjab, Sind, and the North-West Frontier Province. It will be recalled that there are some grounds for believing that the Aryans had extruded their predecessors from this region, so that there was less opportunity here for such a fusion of cultures as occurred further east; and it has been conjectured that the Aryans of the Punjab may have maintained relations with their kinsmen who had occupied Persia. There are some indications in the later Vedic literature that the Punjab was despised by the inhabitants of the Gangetic plain, and it is possible that in the early days it looked west rather than east; but our knowledge of facts begins only with the end of the sixth century B.C., when a portion of it belonged to the Persian Empire.

The history of Persia is an alternation of glory and eclipse, and one of its most glorious periods dates from the reign of Cyrus (558–530), familiar to western readers as the ruler who allowed the Jews to return from their captivity in Babylon. In the course of his efforts to extend his empire, Cyrus advanced eastwards from Persia, and conquered the country then known as Bactria, which corresponds roughly to the part of Afghanistan lying north of the Hindu Kush; but it is improbable that he actually penetrated as far as India. The attention of his immediate successors was turned rather to the west than the east, but Darius I (522–486) annexed a portion of the Indus plain, probably about the year 518, and Persian rule appears to have continued in this region for nearly two centuries. An Indian contingent, wearing cotton clothes, was included in the army which Xerxes, the successor of Darius, sent against the Greeks in 480, and Indian troops, together with a small force of elephants, appeared among the Persian forces defeated by Alexander the Great a century and a half later, while the tribute paid by the Indian provinces is recorded in an inscription of Darius I. We may infer that these ordinary features of political domination, tribute and military service, persisted during the intervening period, or most of it, but we know nothing else regarding the nature of the Persian administration, or how far it affected the life of the Indus plain. Nor is it possible to speak with confidence regarding its extent; it covered the course of the Indus down to the sea, but its eastern limit is uncertain, and we cannot say how much, if any, of the Punjab was included.

In 330 B.C. Alexander the Great crushed the declining power of Persia, and proceeded to complete the conquest of its eastern dependencies, and to penetrate beyond them. After subjugating the countries which now constitute Afghanistan, he entered India in 326, and, marching and fighting close under the Himalayan foot-hills, reached the Beas, the fourth of the five eastern tributaries of the Indus which give the modern name to the Punjab (Persian *panj-āb*, 'five rivers'). He contemplated the conquest of the Gangetic plain, but his army refused to go farther, and he marched down the Indus, which he was thus forced to accept as the boundary of his dominions, leaving India in the autumn of 325. His appearance in the country was merely an episode, and its importance for the history of India lies in the fact that for a time it established communication between Indian and Hellenic culture.

Alexander himself meant to do much more than this. He regarded his conquests as definitive, divided the Indus plain into satrapies, or provinces, and established at strategic points walled cities with a nucleus of Greek population drawn from his army, which were intended to develop into permanent colonies of the ruling race. These plans were, however, frustrated by the disputes among the Greek leaders which followed on his death in 323 ; the Greek satraps, or viceroys, whom he had appointed, left India to take part in the fighting further west, and were probably accompanied by the bulk of the colonists ; and eventually the eastern portions of Alexander's conquests fell into the hands of Seleucus I, who, when he was firmly established in Mesopotamia, decided to recover the Indian provinces. Meanwhile, however, the position in India had been entirely changed by the establishment of the Maurya empire under Chandragupta, as will be related in the next chapter. Seleucus advanced to the Indus, probably very soon after 305, but came to terms with Chandragupta and withdrew from the whole country, handing over to the latter the Indus plain and the greater portion of Afghanistan. In this region Bactria alone remained to the Seleucid empire, until in the middle of the next century it became an independent Hellenic kingdom, which, as we shall see further on, eventually furnished two Greek dynasties to rule in the Punjab.

Several of Alexander's officers wrote books describing their experiences in India, and, if these works had survived, they might have furnished materials for a tolerably precise description of the life of the time. The originals, however, are lost, and the information taken from them by later writers is fragmentary and inadequate for this purpose ; but it suffices to show that, whatever earlier cultural relations may have been, the life of the Indus plain in Alexander's time was Indian rather than Persian. The political conditions, the methods of warfare, the presence of Brāhmans and of ascetics, the practice of suttee, the worship of Siva, and various other details fit in precisely with what we know of the contemporary life of the Gangetic plain, and indicate that, though there is no record of the process, Hinduism had by this time extended to the north-western borders of India.

Alexander came into relations with various Indian kings, and a large number of tribes not organised as kingdoms : the kings were at enmity among themselves, and also with the tribes on their borders, whom they were striving to

ALEXANDER THE GREAT

bring into subjection. The two chief kings in the Punjab were called by the Greeks Taxiles and Porus : the former name was derived from Taxila, the capital of his kingdom, lying between the Indus and the Jhelum, while Porus denotes the king of the Pūrus, whose dominions lay east of the latter river. These two kings were at variance, and the son of the former, named Ambhi, had negotiated with Alexander when he was still north of the Hindu Kush, while a little later the king himself waited on the invader in the Kābul valley. After Alexander crossed the Indus, he was received in Taxila by Ambhi, who had succeeded to the throne, and who asked him for formal investiture, thus recognising him as suzerain. Porus, on the other hand, decided on resistance, but was completely defeated in the battle for the passage of the Jhelum, made an honourable submission, and was reinstated in his kingdom, with large additions, under the conqueror's suzerainty. A third king, whose territories lay in the hill country east of Taxila, and who had hitherto played a double game, now made his submission ; other kings, whose countries lay further east, either submitted or abandoned their kingdoms ; and the tribes in this region were disposed of with little difficulty. Throughout there was no trace of solidarity among the Indian rulers : at variance among themselves, each played for his own hand, as was to be the ordinary rule in India for many centuries to come.

As has been said above, Alexander appointed governors for his Indian provinces : some of them were Greeks, but Ambhi and ' Porus,' whose personal name is not known, were left in charge of much of the Punjab, their domains being separated by the Jhelum ; and, when the Greek power was eliminated from this region, they naturally resumed their former position as independent rulers, but in a few years' time their territories were included in the expanding Maurya empire.

CHAPTER VII

THE MAURYA EMPIRE : CHANDRAGUPTA

WE have seen in Chapter IV that, about the year 500 B.C., Magadha, or South Bihār, was already an important kingdom. During the half-century which followed, its limits extended, and it acquired supremacy over North Bihār, Benares, and Oudh ; and to this period belongs the establishment on the bank of the Ganges of its capital of Pātaliputra, the Palibothra of the Greek writers, and the modern Patna. The course of events for the next century or so is uncertain, but the importance of the kingdom was maintained, and under the dynasty known in the traditions as Nanda its dominion extended over the western Gangetic plain, and possibly further to the south-west, while its fame appears to have been one of the chief attractions which tempted Alexander to march eastward from the Punjab. A few years after his departure from India, the Nanda dynasty was displaced by Chandragupta Maurya, under whom the power of Magadha became sufficiently great to justify the use of the word ' empire.'

The story of Chandragupta's exploits is obscure, for there are no precise records, and the traditions vary ; even the origin of his second name is uncertain, for one account makes it a tribal appellative, while another derives it from his mother, Murā, said to have been a concubine of the Nanda ruler. Whatever his origin, it appears that he was employed in the service of the Nandas, rose to the rank of commander-in-chief, conspired unsuccessfully against his master, and fled to the north-west, accompanied by his fellow-conspirator Kautilya, whom tradition represents as his guiding genius, and also as the author of the *Arthasāstra*, the manual of public administration which has been mentioned in an earlier chapter. According to a Greek historian, Chandragupta visited Alexander's camp in the Punjab; and subsequently, having obtained support in this region, perhaps from 'Porus,' he attacked the Nanda king, who was defeated and killed, leaving the victor to ascend the throne of Magadha. The details of all this are obscure, but we know that, very soon after the year 305, Chandragupta, with a great army, confronted Seleucus on the Indus, and that terms were arranged under which his empire was extended to a large part of Afghanistan. His death occurred not long after, the most probable date being 297. The extent of his empire is uncertain. There is no doubt that his rule ran from Bengal right up to the Hindu Kush; and there are some grounds for thinking that it covered also Mālwa, and even Gujarāt, which certainly belonged to his successors, but how and when they were acquired is unknown.

Friendly relations were maintained by Chandragupta with Seleucus, whose envoy, Megasthenes, spent some time at Patna, and wrote a description of India, which furnished one of the main sources of the information collected by later Greek writers regarding the country. Had this description survived, we should know much, if not everything, about Chandragupta's empire, but we possess only such portions as the later writers thought worthy of preservation, and even these are usually paraphrases rather than quotations. Attempts have been made to provide an account of the empire by dovetailing these fragments into the Indian literature, but the process is very dangerous while the dates of the texts remain uncertain, and it is safer to take Megasthenes by himself, unsatisfying as the result may be. It must be remembered that we do not know what he actually wrote, or the precise sense in which he used various terms of art; the context of what we possess is quite uncertain; we can only guess at the sources of his information; and we must recognise that there may have been serious difficulties in interpreting the Prākṛit speech of Magadha into his provincial Greek.[1]

Of the personal characteristics of Chandragupta we are told very little,[2] but he is presented as living closely guarded in his palace, and as leaving it to spend the day on the seat of justice, or occasionally to offer sacrifices, or go hunting. Much stress is laid on the precautions taken for the Emperor's safety, and here Megasthenes doubtless wrote from personal observation, but we must remember that Chandragupta was a usurper, who would naturally be guarded with exceptional care. Regarding the administration, we can see in the fragments that it was elaborate and highly organised, and that a distinction existed between country and town; but such details as have survived are not easily to be reconciled with Indian literature.

A striking feature of the fragments is the distinction drawn between the empire generally and the 'autonomous cities,' to reproduce the Greek term; the rulers of these 'cities' are presented to us as receiving the revenues which elsewhere belonged to the Emperor, and as exercising various administrative functions independently of him. In the Seleucid empire this term had a technical signification, denoting certain privileged cities, which were relieved of most of the ordinary taxes, and allowed to manage their own affairs; nothing corresponding precisely to this institution is known in Indian literature, and it is probable that Megasthenes applied the technical term, necessarily familiar to him, to what was for him a novelty—the subordinate kingdoms included in Chandragupta's empire, which retained their internal autonomy subject to the payment of tribute.

The fragments dealing with land tenure have been the

---

[1] When Alexander the Great tried to learn the wisdom of the ascetics at Taxila, one of them objected, with good reason, that to try to convey their teaching through a series of three interpreters, ignorant of the subject, ' would be like trying to make water flow clear through mud.' (*Cambridge History of India*, i. 359. This book is cited below as *Camb. Hist.*)

[2] The remarks which follow are based largely on the latest edition of the principal fragments, B. C. J. Timmer, *Megasthenes en de Indische Maatschappij* (Amsterdam, 1930).

subject of much discussion, and have been interpreted in various ways. It is possible that here also Megasthenes used terms of art derived from his experience further west, but now obsolete, and the most that can be said is that he certainly knew of a practice by which the cultivators paid one-fourth of the produce to the treasury, and apparently he mentioned another practice by which the cultivators retained the same share. The former is the recognised Indian system, and it is noteworthy that the share paid was one-fourth, not the traditional one-sixth of the texts : the latter may possibly refer to the private domains of the Emperor and the prominent men, and would indicate that the serfs or labourers employed on them were paid a quarter of the crop as wages. As regards the course of agriculture, we are told that, with the aid of irrigation, two crops were usually raised in the year, and that famine was unknown. The former statement may safely be accepted as based on personal observation, but recurring liability to famine is established incidentally by the literature of the Hindu period, and the most probable explanation is that Megasthenes, not having personal experience of such a calamity, inferred its impossibility from the productiveness of the soil which he observed.

As regards social organisation, Megasthenes recognised that the population was divided into endogamous occupational groups, and this is important as showing that by his time the caste system was firmly established in this part of India ; but his enumeration of the seven constituent groups —philosophers (or sophists), peasants, herdsmen and hunters, artisans and merchants, soldiers, spies, and officials—cannot possibly be made to square with the system of caste as it is known from other sources, and we are driven to conclude that he simply made a list of the occupations which had come to his notice, ignorant, for instance, that some ' officials ' at least were certainly ' philosophers,' that is to say, Brāhmans, and that merchants were distinct from the various classes of artisans. Similarly his statement that there were no slaves in India is directly contrary to what we know from all other sources, and can be explained only by the absence of the organised industrial slavery which was familiar to the writer; he saw freemen doing the work which he regarded as appropriate to slaves, and he did not notice the mild domestic slavery which undoubtedly prevailed.

This summary review of some of the more important statements attributed to Megasthenes will show the need for caution in accepting them as they stand. The fragments which have survived do not suffice to furnish a full description of the empire, but what they show us is a population predominantly agricultural, ruled by a despot with the help of an organised bureaucracy, a large standing army, and an elaborate system of espionage. The people were frugal in their food, but lavish in clothes and ornaments; and they were honest according to the standards of Megasthenes. The caste system prevailed, though it was not so rigid or so highly developed as in later times. Brāhmans were held in great honour, and offered sacrifices for the other castes; the main distinction in worship was between the followers of Siva and Krishna, identified by the Greeks with Dionysus and Heracles respectively; and ascetics were conspicuous. We see, then, the outlines of an ordinary Hindu community, but we learn little which is not known to us from other sources, and the chief value of the fragments is that they enable us to say that various institutions had taken definite form at least as early as 300 B.C.

CHAPTER VIII

THE MAURYA EMPIRE : ASOKA

CHANDRAGUPTA was succeeded by his heir Bindusāra, who reigned for a quarter of a century, and of whom practically nothing is known ; but in Bindusāra's son and successor, Asoka, we meet the first Indian ruler whose personality stands out clearly in history. His fame bulks largely in Buddhist literature, but the story there given has been coloured or distorted in the process of hagiography, and for the facts of his life we are indebted primarily to the edicts which, following an old Persian practice, he caused to be inscribed on rocks and pillars throughout his dominions. Many of these are still in existence, and in their simple, earnest language, marked by endless repetitions, there is no difficulty in recognising the man. We may question the extent to which his ideals were realised in practice, but there can be no question that we are in the presence of a great apostle of righteousness.

Asoka succeeded to the throne of Magadha about 274 B.C., the precise year being uncertain, and reigned, most probably, for thirty-seven years. For the first quarter of this period there is nothing to distinguish him from the ordinary Hindu ruler: apparently he had to fight for the succession, though it is safe to refuse credit to the legend that he killed ninety-nine of his brothers in the process; and, following the usual course of kingship, he conquered Kalinga, a region lying on the east coast between the Mahānadi and the Godāvarī rivers, corresponding to the modern Orissa with the most northerly portion of Madras. This was the turning-point of his life. Distressed by the suffering and misery caused by war, he resolved to abandon the traditional course, and turned to the teaching of the Buddha. The remainder of his life was spent in philanthropical administration, in promoting moral reform, and in propagating the doctrines which he had embraced.

For the administration of the empire Asoka employed three viceroys, one at Taxila for the north-west, a second at Ujjain in Mālwa for the west and south-west, and a third for Kalinga on the south-east, apparently retaining direct control of the central region. It is impossible to distinguish the tracts in this area which were held by vassal kings, but probably most of it was administered in this way, so that the empire may be regarded as a confederation of states. Its southern limits are not clearly defined, but the presence of inscriptions in the north of what is now the Mysore State indicates that Asoka's influence, if not his actual rule, extended well to the south of the river Kistna. The principles governing the administration were drawn from the Sacred Law, and accepted by Hindus and Jains as well as Buddhists; but Asoka laid particular stress on those which bear the names of *ahimsā* and *maitri*, or 'non-violence' and 'friendliness,' applied to all living creatures. In accordance with these principles we find him insisting on the provision of shade and water along the roads, and of medical aid for animals as well as human beings; restricting the slaughter of animals; enjoining the just and humane treatment of prisoners; and appointing high officials, in addition to the existing administrative staff, charged specially with the organisation of charity, the redress of wrongs and the inculcation of moral principles.

The frontier policy of Asoka represented an entire breach with the Indian tradition of enlarging the borders of a kingdom by conquest. He desired [1] that ' the unsubdued borderers should not be afraid of me, that they should trust me, and should receive from me happiness, not sorrow '; and he hoped that they too would accept the moral principles which he preached to his own subjects. The extent to which

[1] The quotation is from the first Kalinga edict, as translated in *Camb. Hist.*, i. 515.

his hopes were realised is not on record, but there is no reason to doubt that during his reign the frontiers were ordinarily peaceful.

As a moral reformer Asoka was essentially practical. If he cared anything about metaphysical speculations, the fact does not appear in his edicts ; he laid stress on simple duties, which he considered had been too much neglected, obedience to parents, kind treatment of servants, slaves and animals, respect and generosity to priests and ascetics, toleration, friendliness, charity, simplicity of life—in a word, righteousness. In matters of religion he was no bigot : he discountenanced certain popular ceremonials, but he inculcated respect for Brāhmans among other classes, and he claimed as a merit that he had extended the knowledge of the gods of Hinduism among the jungle tribes. His activities in promoting Buddhism do not stand out as directed against the popular religion, and it is not possible to infer from the language of his edicts that he regarded himself as the champion of one creed against another ; he was the champion of a life rather than a faith.

One side of these activities was the establishment of Buddhist shrines : tradition attributes to him an enormous number of such buildings, and, while the number is an obvious exaggeration, there is no doubt of the essential fact. Another side was the attempt to secure unity among the followers of the Buddha ; a Council was held under his patronage at Patna, when the differences between various schools were composed, and the canon of authoritative scriptures was determined ; and one of his edicts imposed penalties on schism. A third side was the despatch of missionaries throughout the empire and beyond its limits. There is nothing to show that his envoys achieved any success in the distant countries they are said to have visited, in Syria, Egypt or Greece ; but nearer home, in north-west India, in Burma and elsewhere, the progress of Buddhism was marked. The most important results were secured in Ceylon, which may be described as the second home of the faith ; here the doctrine laid down in Asoka's Council was preserved and codified ; and when this school of Buddhism disappeared from India the authority of the Sinhalese canon was accepted in Burma and Siam.

No confident estimate can be made of the results of Asoka's efforts within the limits of his empire. So far as we know, his distinctive policy was not continued by his successors, under whom the empire fell to pieces; his edicts are more concerned with the future than the past; and there is no other source of information. We know only that a high ideal of righteousness was authoritatively set before the people; we can safely conclude that it was not realised in its entirety; we may be equally sure that it was not wholly without effect. The edicts stood for future generations to read; but the characters in which they were engraved became obsolete, and their decipherment belongs to the period of British rule. The survival of Asoka's fame in tradition shows at least that his figure struck the popular imagination; but his actual achievement cannot be determined.

On the material side Asoka's reign marks an epoch in the development of the arts of building and sculpture in the Gangetic plain. No work in cut stone or burnt brick [1] of an earlier date has yet been found in this region. Megasthenes recorded that in areas liable to flood the towns were built of wood, while those on high ground were of brick and mud, the bricks being probably sun-dried rather than burnt. In Asoka's buildings the burnt bricks which have been found are of an inferior class, indicating want of experience on the part of the makers; on the other hand, the workmanship and sculpture on his columns are of very high quality, and are recognised by experts as undoubtedly displaying a combination of Persian and Hellenic influences, so that it is safe to infer that some at least of his stone-workers were imported from the north-west, probably from Bactria, where the establishment of Greek rule would have facilitated such a combination. The inference as to the introduction of brick-burning is less certain, for the excavations at

[1] Burnt bricks of very large size were used in a building on the Nepal frontier, which some scholars have assigned to the fifth century, but the present view (*Camb. Hist.*, i. 623) is that it belongs to the Maurya period.

BUILDING AND SCULPTURE

Mohenjo-daro have shown that the art was well established in the early Indus civilisation, while so little digging has yet been done in the Ganges plain that the negative evidence is not conclusive ; but in the present state of our knowledge it is probable that burnt bricks were not in use, at least generally, before the Maurya epoch. From this time on their use was well established ; while sculpture quickly became the most important medium for expressing the artistic feelings of the people, the foreign influences being gradually eliminated.

MAP III

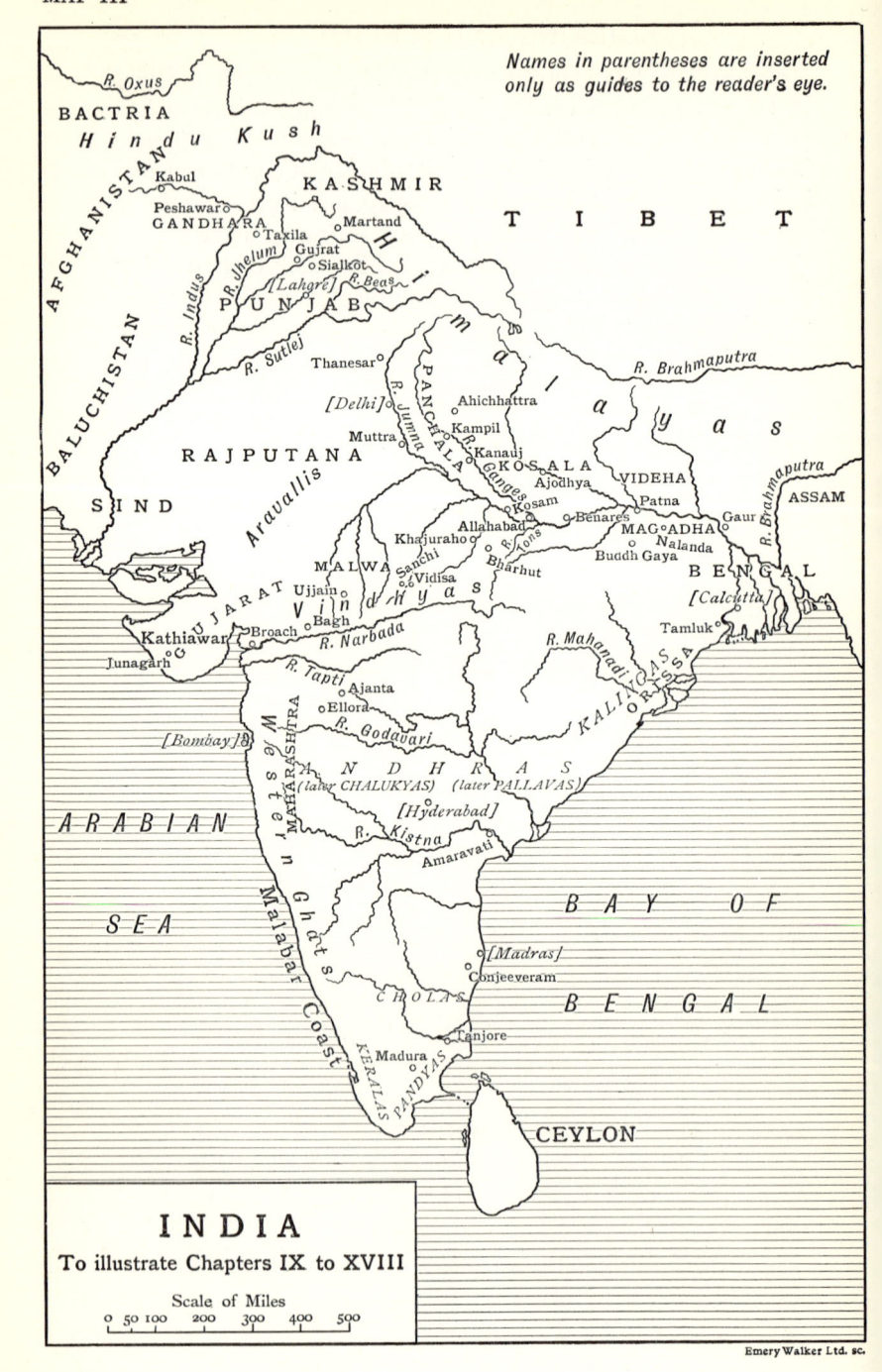

INDIA
To illustrate Chapters IX to XVIII

Scale of Miles
0 50 100 200 300 400 500

CHAPTER IX

THE SECOND CENTURY B.C.

AFTER the death of Asoka the Maurya empire broke up, and for some centuries there was no really paramount power in northern India, though from time to time one dynasty or another claimed the overlordship of a larger or smaller portion of the country. The history of these centuries is still obscure, but an outline of it has been laboriously drawn by interpreting the traditional dynastic lists with the aid of inscriptions and coins, so that we can see dimly the rise and fall of the various conflicting kingdoms. From this time on, coins become one of the main sources for political history, and it will be well to approach the period by a short account of what is known of the development of the use of money in India.

So far nothing has been found to suggest that money was current in any form in the early Indus civilisation,[1] nor can it be traced in the Rigveda, where the usual standard of value appears to have been the cow. The first rudiments of a monetary system occur in the literature of the later Vedic period, in which the berry of a certain plant, known to botanists as *Abrus precatorius*, appears as a unit of weight, a unit which still survives under the name *ratī*; pieces of gold weighing 100 of these berries, equal to about 180 grains, are mentioned in the texts and were doubtless used in commerce, but there is nothing to suggest that as yet they were stamped or marked as coins. Metallic currency was clearly common when the earliest Buddhist literature was written, but the dates to be assigned to these texts are

[1] Certain copper tablets, which were at first taken to be coins, are now regarded as amulets.

uncertain, and the most that can be inferred from them is that the use of money was well established in northern India before the time of Asoka—how long before we cannot say with confidence.

The earliest coins hitherto found in the North are rectangles cut from a sheet or strip of metal, trimmed at the corners, and punched on one side, or occasionally on both, with a variety of marks the significance of which is still matter for conjecture ; at present they are of little value to the historian, but they may eventually be deciphered. The practice, now so familiar, of striking coins by means of double dies must be attributed to foreign influence ; the first Indian coins which have been found of this type were pieces of silver, which were issued by a local ruler in the Punjab about the time of Alexander's invasion, and they are obviously direct imitations of the Greek coinage of the period. The adoption of the new method was, however, gradual, and there is as yet no evidence that it was ever followed by the earlier Maurya emperors. The suggestion has been made that the use of the old rectangular coins, which are known as *purānas*, was the result of early commercial dealings with Mesopotamia, where similar coins were current, but here again definite evidence is wanting : we know only that these coins were used in India for some centuries, and that, soon after Alexander's invasion, they began to give way to pieces struck from double dies, and bearing the name [1] of the ruler who issued them. It is these names, with the accompanying descriptions, which give their historical value to the coins of the second century B.C., for the practice of inscribing the date of issue was not adopted until much later; from about A.D. 175 onwards the named and dated coins are sources of the highest value for the historian, but even names without dates are of substantial service in interpreting the traditional dynastic lists and the occasional allusions in the literature.

Using such sources as exist, the probable course of events may be summarised as follows. Soon after the death of

[1] A few coins with names appear to belong to a period earlier than Asoka, but they cannot as yet be identified with particular dynasties.

POLITICAL GEOGRAPHY

Asoka two of the three vice-royalties broke away from the Maurya empire: on the north-west Taxila became independent, and its history will be traced in the next chapter; on the south-east Kalinga resumed the position it had recently lost, and increased in power. The remainder of the empire, comprising the bulk of the Gangetic plain and a large part of Central India, was held, though with diminishing authority, for about half a century by the Mauryas, and then passed to a new dynasty, the Sungas, which maintained itself, probably, from about 184 to 72 B.C., the seat of power passing during this interval from Bihār to Mālwa. It may be conjectured that the constituent states were now increasing in importance relatively to the central power, and it becomes necessary to take account of the separate units.

Beginning from the east end of the Gangetic plain, the position of Bengal is uncertain, but some recent discoveries suggest that the northern portion at least had been incorporated in the Maurya empire, and may have remained subject to the Sunga dynasty. West of Bengal, we know of four states on the south of the Ganges and three on the north, which together occupied the great bulk of the plain. On the south these were, in order, Magadha itself, Kāshī (or Benares), Karsāmbī, and Muttra. The position of the capital of Kausāmbī has been the subject of much discussion, but the evidence of surviving monuments and inscriptions appears to justify its identification with the village of Kosam on the Jumna, about 30 miles west of Allahabad. Muttra, also on the Jumna, north-west of Agra, has survived as a city of some importance, and is the centre of the popular worship of Krishna; the northern limit of this kingdom is quite uncertain. North and east of the Ganges lay Videha (or North Bihār), Kosala (or Oudh), and Panchāla. The two former have been mentioned in earlier chapters; the chief capital of Panchāla was Ahichhatra, now a ruin near Bareilly in Rohilkhand, but the kingdom extended across the Ganges, with a second capital at Kampil. These states, however, are not conspicuous in the story of the next few centuries.

In order to describe the Central Indian kingdoms, a few words are necessary regarding the physical aspect of the land. From about Agra to Allahabad the Jumna marks the base of the wide belt of rugged country, which rises towards the south to the range of hills overhanging the valley of the Narbada. Thus the latter river has no important tributaries on the north; the whole country drains to the Jumna by a succession of rivers, some of them rising within a very few miles of the course of the Narbada, and, while none of them is navigable, their valleys provide practicable routes from the Gangetic plain towards the south. In the past, therefore, this central belt was as a rule more closely connected with the northern powers than with the kingdoms of the peninsula.

The road from Patna to Ujjain left the Jumna at Kausāmbī, and struck southwards for about 80 miles along the valley of the Tons as far as Bhārhut, then the seat of an important kingdom, but now known only for the remains of buildings belonging to this period. At a distance of about 180 miles south-west of Bhārhut lay Vidisā, and 120 miles further was Ujjain, these two places being the capitals of East and West Mālwa respectively. In comparison with the broken country further north, Mālwa may be described as a level plateau, comprising large areas of productive soil; Ujjain is still an important city, and the commercial capital of the whole region, but Vidisā, now Besnagar, a few miles from Bhilsa, is, like Bhārhut, known only for its monuments. These three kingdoms, Bhārhut, Vidisā, and Ujjain, constituted the bulk of the dominions of the later Mauryas outside the Gangetic plain, though there may have been other units the memory of which has not survived.

The scanty evidence available suggests that the Sungas were originally kings of Vidisā subordinate to the Maurya empire. About 184 B.C., one of the race, named Pushyamitra, who was commander-in-chief of the Maurya forces, rebelled, killed his master, and seized the throne of Magadha. His dynasty lasted for a little more than a hundred years, in the course of which period the capital seems to have been transferred from Patna to Vidisā; Bihār now passes into obscurity for some centuries, and Mālwa takes its place as

THE CENTRAL AND SOUTHERN POWERS 63

one of the main centres of political interest. It is probable, though not certain, that Buddhist influences remained powerful among the Mauryas, but the Sungas reverted to the ordinary practice of employing Brāhmans as ministers, and it was a Brāhman minister who, probably in 72 B.C., brought the dynasty to an end by the murder of its last representative. There are some indications that the Sungas remained overlords of Kausāmbī, Muttra and Panchāla in the Gangetic plain, as well as of the kingdoms of Central India, but there is no evidence to show how far their power extended towards the east.

It was during the period of the Sungas that the Andhras of southern India first became an important factor in the politics of the North. This kingdom lay on the east coast, adjoining Kalinga on the south ; and soon after Asoka's death it underwent a remarkable expansion right across the Peninsula, as is shown by Andhra inscriptions surviving in the mountains above Bombay. During the reign of the first Sunga king, the Andhras appear to have struck northward, and captured Ujjain, thus dividing Mālwa with the Sungas at Vidisā, and it is probable that they retained their conquest for some time, until Ujjain became a bone of contention between conflicting powers. Kalinga also increased in importance during the second century B.C., and inscriptions show that it was occasionally engaged in hostilities with the Andhras, as well as in Bihār, but the extent of its actual achievements is uncertain.

About the beginning of the first century B.C., then, the political situation of India may be described as follows. The Sungas held the centre of the country, and probably the western side of the Gangetic plain ; the Andhras held the north of the peninsula, and had extended into Mālwa ; Kalinga was well established on the east coast ; the position in Bengal and Bihār is uncertain. To the south of the Andhras, the peninsula was occupied mainly by three extensive kingdoms, the Cholas on the east, the Keralas on the south-west, and the Pāndyas on the south-east, but these powers, called collectively the Tamil kingdoms, do not yet come into the picture. There remains the Indus plain, the story of which is told in the next chapter.

CHAPTER X

THE GREEKS IN THE PUNJAB

NOTHING is known of the circumstances in which the viceroyalty of Taxila became separated from the Maurya empire, or of the political conditions which supervened; but it may be inferred that no strong kingdom emerged in this region, for, half a century after Asoka's death, the Punjab was being conquered, or absorbed, piecemeal by the Greeks of Bactria. It will be recalled that, in the settlement made between Chandragupta and Seleucus I, Afghanistan south of the Hindu Kush passed to the former, while Bactria was retained by the latter. Half a century later, Bactria became an independent kingdom, expanded largely in area, and increased in power. Very soon after 200 B.C. the Bactrian Greeks were masters of nearly the whole of Afghanistan, and of a large part of the Punjab; but while Demetrius, the reigning king, was in India, Bactria itself was seized (175 B.C.) by a rebel named Eucratides, who in his turn came south, and the Punjab was divided into two Greek kingdoms, separated by the Jhelum. The country east of this river was ruled by the house of Demetrius with the capital at Sākala, the modern Sialkot; to the west, the house of Eucratides was established in the Kābul valley and in Gandhāra, the name then given to the region which stretches from the Jhelum westward into Afghanistan. These two kingdoms survived for about a century, when they fell into the hands of nomad invaders, and Hellenic power disappeared from India. Their limits towards the south are uncertain; according to a Greek historian, Sind, and even

NOMAD MIGRATIONS

Kathiāwar, were conquered, but it is doubtful whether these countries were held for any length of time, and Hellenic rule was probably confined mainly to the Punjab.

The southward move of the Greek power is closely connected with one of the outstanding events in the history of the world, the migration of the nomad hordes from High Asia, which was destined to change the history of Europe. The westward track followed by the hordes was well north of the Hindu Kush, and Bactria lay on its southern flank. It is probable, though not certain, that when the Greeks first moved in the direction of Kābul, the danger from the north and east was already realised ; but, in any case, there is no doubt that Eucratides was driven out of Bactria by the pressure of the Parthians on the west and the Sakas [1] on the north. Records which have been preserved in China show that about 165 B.C. the Huns were pressing from the east on another horde named the Yueh-chi ; the latter in turn pressed on the Sakas, and drove them in the direction of Bactria ; and the Greeks, unable to resist the Sakas, and confronted on the west with the Parthian power in Khorāsān, could find security only to the south of the Hindu Kush.

The details of the Greek dynasties in the Punjab have been reconstructed mainly from their coins, some of which are marvels of artistic work, particularly in the matter of portraiture ; but, with one exception, the individual rulers left no definite mark on the history of India. They seem to have played their part as Indian kings, so far as war and diplomacy are concerned ; their conquests, or raids, towards the seaboard have already been mentioned ; and according to tradition one of them marched victoriously down the Gangetic plain to the neighbourhoood of Patna, but was compelled to return by dangers nearer home. A more precise record of the period is a stone column at Besnagar, the inscription on which shows that it was erected in honour of Krishna by Heliodorus of Taxila, ambassador from Antialcidas, a king who was reigning about the year 100 B.C. The

---

[1] The Sakas are sometimes spoken of as Scythians, but the latter name is ambiguous, being applied indifferently to the nomads of Europe and of Asia ; it is therefore more convenient to adhere to the term **Saka**, which occurs in Indian literature.

Greeks had thus diplomatic relations with the Sunga dynasty at this time, while the fact that one of them described himself as a follower of Vishnu is suggestive of the processes of assimilation which must have been at work, though we have no precise knowledge of their operation.

The one Greek ruler who has left a name in India is Menander, King of Sialkot, who appears in Buddhist literature as Milinda. In a famous text, known as the ' Questions of Milinda,' he is presented as a vigorous controversialist, who first criticised, and then accepted, the doctrines of his Buddhist interlocutor. The description [1] given of him in this work is enthusiastic: ' as in wisdom, so in strength of body, swiftness, and valour there was found none equal to Milinda in all India. He was rich too, mighty in wealth and prosperity, and the number of his armed hosts knew no end.' Language such as this is obviously subject to a high rate of discount, but the fact that it was used may indicate that Menander was, if not actually a Buddhist, at least favourably inclined towards that discipline, and that, like the ambassador in Mālwa, he had come under the influence of Indian teaching.

Direct contact between India and the culture of independent Greek states extended over a period which practically coincides with that of the Maurya and Sunga dynasties, and it is natural to ask what India gained from it. The new methods of coinage, and the introduction of western styles in sculpture, have already been mentioned. The monuments which have survived from the second and first centuries B.C. show clear traces of the eastward spread of Perso-Hellenistic influence, which can be observed in the remains found at Bhārhut, Buddh Gaya (in Bihār), Sānchī (near the modern Bhopal) and elsewhere ; as time went on, the quality of the workmanship was maintained, but the foreign forms were transmuted, and the result was, not a mere borrowing from abroad, but a synthesis producing, in Sir John Marshall's words, ' essentially a national art, having its root in the heart and in the faith of the people, and giving eloquent expression

---

[1] *Milindapanha*, tr. T. W. Rhys Davids, in *Sacred Books of the East*, xxxv, pp. 6, 7.

GREEK AND INDIAN CULTURE

to their spiritual beliefs and to their deep and intuitive sympathy with nature.'[1]

Outside the domain of art, there are grounds for holding that India may have learned something in the region of science, as the term was then understood, but there is little or no sign of influence in literature,[2] politics or religion. The Indian texts which deal with medicine, astronomy, and astrology show clear evidence of Greek influence, and in particular the art of casting horoscopes, which was extensively practised right into the British period, and is not yet extinct, was characterised by Greek methods, and employed Greek technical terms. The uncertainties regarding the dates of these texts make it impossible to say precisely when the influences in question operated, and some of them at least must be attributed to later contacts with Alexandria, but it is possible that others date from this period of direct contact.

In philosophy there are some obvious similarities between principles developed by Greek and Indian thinkers, and it has sometimes been suggested that these denote actual borrowing by one side or the other, but there is no evidence of the process, and the facts can be explained sufficiently by the hypothesis of parallel development : Greeks and Indians alike were thinking over problems which must present themselves to anyone who tries to think at all, and it is no matter for surprise that both should on occasion reach similar results from consideration of similar data. We cannot entirely exclude the possibility that a wandering philosopher, whether from the East or from the West, may have dropped seeds which germinated in congenial soil, but it is unnecessary to assume that there was anything like systematic mutual study, which differences of language would have rendered very difficult. Apart from this uncertainty, there is nothing to suggest that the Greeks learned much from India beyond the knowledge of concrete facts, and the occasional legends, which have been preserved by their historians.

[1] *Camb. Hist.*, i. 644.
[2] Some scholars have attributed the origin of the Indian drama to Greek influences, but the relation is disputed ; the question is discussed in Dr. A. A. Macdonell's *India's Past*, pp. 98 ff.

CHAPTER XI

THE SAKAS AND PAHLAVAS

WE have seen in the last chapter that the Sakas replaced the Greeks in Bactria. They did not stay there long, for the pressure from the east was maintained, and very soon after 125 B.C. Bactria was in the hands of the Yueh-chi. There are some indications that the Sakas first tried to move westwards, but their progress in this direction was barred by the Parthian empire, and eventually they passed through Afghanistan and Baluchistan into India. The Parthian power was first established in Khorāsān, or north-east Persia, in the third century, when the strength of the Seleucids was waning in this region; and it was transformed into an empire by the conquests of Mithridates I (170–138), which extended over the greater part of Persia. There are no precise records of the southward movement of the Sakas, but the most probable account is that, after they were finally repulsed from Khorāsān by Mithridates II (123–88), they traversed western Afghanistan into Baluchistan, became closely associated with the Parthians in this region, and in union with them turned eastwards, and entered Sind through the passes in the neighbourhood of Quetta. In India they spread southward to the coast, and on into Gujarāt, while towards the north-west they conquered the Punjab.

It appears that about this time the Parthian empire was weakening on its eastern side, for in the first century B.C. the title 'King of Kings,' which denotes independent sovereignty, was used on coins by a dynasty in eastern Persia, and also by the closely allied dynasty in the Punjab; it is

SAKA-PAHLAVA KINGDOMS

not possible to distinguish these dynasties as either Saka or Parthian, and the only convenient course is to speak of the Indian rulers as Sakas and Pahlavas, the latter name, which is philologically equivalent to ' Parthians,' being adopted to distinguish these local elements from the main Parthian power familiar in the history of the West.

The conquest of the Punjab was made in two steps. About 75 B.C. Gandhāra, the western kingdom, fell to Maues, the first Saka-Pahlava ruler of whom a record has survived; and about twenty years later his successor, Azes I, conquered the eastern kingdom of Sialkot. The rule of the Sakas and Pahlavas lasted till about A.D. 50, when they were overcome by the Kushāns, as will be told in a later chapter; their dominions included the kingdom of Muttra, but there is no evidence of extension of their rule further into the Gangetic plain; and, as might be expected, it left practically no mark on Indian culture.[1]

The southward movement produced more durable results, for the Saka kingdom in Kathiāwar, the western portion of Gujarāt, was destined to persist in one form or another for some centuries. Gujarāt adjoins Mālwa, and we now return to that portion of the country, which we left in Chapter IX divided between the Sungas in the east and the Andhras in the west. About 72 B.C. the Sunga dynasty came to an end, and the Andhras appear to have come into possession of their territory, and, as rulers of the whole of Mālwa, to have become involved in a long-drawn struggle with the Sakas. There is precise evidence of this struggle only from about the year A.D. 100 onwards, but it seems impossible to reject entirely the legends which relate to the earlier period, and which introduce us to the name of Vikramāditya (' Sun of power '), one of the outstanding figures in Indian tradition. One of these legends is to the effect that an oppressed faction in Ujjain asked the Sakas of Gujarāt for help against the Andhra despot: the Sakas defeated the despot and occupied Ujjain on their own account; Vikramāditya, the despot's son, then gathered forces in the country to the south, and drove the Sakas out. The approximate date of these events is fixed by the attribution to him of the

---

[1] For a different view of the Pahlava influence on Indian culture, see Dr. Vogel's remarks at p. 145 of *Revealing India's Past* (London, 1939). See also below, p. 82, footnote.

Vikrama era, which is reckoned from 58 B.C., and which obtained a very extensive vogue in northern India. It must be recognised that the name Vikramāditya was borne by many rulers at various times, and one of them was the Gupta Emperor who, more than four centuries later, finally crushed the Saka power ; the acts of all the various Vikramādityas seem to have been fused into one cycle of legends, and it is possible that this story may be merely an echo of the Gupta achievement, but it is perhaps more probable that there is a nucleus of fact, and that the struggle between Andhras and Sakas actually began in the middle of the first century B.C.

CHAPTER XII

EARLY COMMUNICATIONS BY SEA

WITH the arrival of the Sakas in Gujarāt, we come into contact for the first time with that portion of the Indian seaboard which forms the natural doorway to the West, and it will be well to summarise at this point the scanty knowledge we possess of the beginnings of communications by sea. Discoveries at Mohenjo-daro prove that there was intercourse between the Indus plain and Mesopotamia in the third millennium and perhaps earlier; it is not yet certain whether communication took place by land or by sea, but the use of the latter route is considered by some authorities to be possible, or even probable.

The occurrence of the Sanskrit word for ' ocean ' in the hymns of the Rigveda has led some authorities to infer that the Aryans of that period had reached the coast, and even engaged in extensive navigation, but others hold, with perhaps greater probability, that in those days the word denoted only the Indus, and that the meaning ' ocean ' was acquired in later times. If the latter view is correct, it is possible that the earliest mention of sea-communication with India occurs in some familiar passages in the Old Testament [1] describing the commercial activities of Solomon in the tenth century. Nobody reading the English version of these passages would see the connection, and it is impossible to state in a few words the arguments which have induced various commentators to infer that at this period some Indian curiosities—peacocks and possibly monkeys—

[1] 1 Kings, ix, x; 2 Chronicles, viii, ix.

and, less probably, some raw materials—gold, ivory, and sandalwood—were brought up the Red Sea in Phoenician and Israelitish vessels. Accepting their conclusions, the question whether there were Indian ships at this time depends on the location of Ophir, the southward destination of the Phoenician fleet. This question has not yet received a final answer. If, as has often been argued, Ophir lay at the mouth of the Indus, then there would be no reason to infer the existence of Indian sea-going vessels; but if, as appears to be more probable, it was somewhere on the southeast coast of Arabia, then there is at least a suggestion that the coasting-trade between Arabia and India had already been established.

There is somewhat better evidence for sea-transport between India and the Persian Gulf in the seventh and sixth centuries B.C. It is known that Sennacherib of Assyria (c. 700 B.C.) placed on the Gulf a fleet built by Phoenician shipwrights brought from the Mediterranean, and that a little later there was intercourse by sea between the Euphrates and the coast of China; the inference is obvious that the ships must have called somewhere in India during these long voyages. Other facts belonging to the sixth century suggest that shipping had developed between the west coast of India and Babylon, then the great mart of the world; but so far the indications are that the ships belonged to the latter region rather than India.

The decay of Babylon dates from the rule of Darius I, and it appears to be probable that Indian trade then passed to the Red Sea route, but there is still no precise evidence that any of it was carried in Indian ships, for it is possible that then, as in some later times, the merchants of Mocha and Aden, the principal ports of transhipment, sent their vessels to India to fetch the commodities they required. In point of fact, the first vessels known to have left India were those which Darius I sent to explore the Indus about 510 B.C. This expedition started from somewhere near Peshāwar, and eventually reached Egypt, but no account of the voyage has survived, and we do not know whether the vessels were Indian-built in the ordinary sense, or whether they were constructed on the Indus by foreigners from Persia or further west. It is not possible, then, to say when sea-going ships began to be built on the western side of India. The early Buddhist literature shows incidentally that shipbuilding was practised, but it gives no clue as to dates; the texts are indeed later than 500 B.C., but they incorporate some older stories, and all that we really know is that Indians used the sea freely in the centuries between the foundation of Buddhism and the Christian era, and that they made coasting voyages to Ceylon and other neighbouring countries: there appears to be no clear evidence that in the earlier days they sailed the open sea. We know, however, that ship-building was well established on the Indus by the time of Alexander, because he was able to procure the large number of vessels on which a portion of his army embarked for the Euphrates.

From the third century B.C. onwards, the trade of the Red Sea was systematically developed from new seaports established in Egypt, and Indian goods reached the Mediterranean by this route, but there was no direct shipping; the goods were bought at Mocha or Aden, or at other places near the Straits of Babelmandeb, and we do not know definitely how they reached those ports, but probably by this time the voyage across the Arabian Sea was being regularly made by Indian ships. Our precise knowledge of this commerce dates only from a few years before the Christian era. Augustus, the first Roman Emperor, devoted much attention to the Red Sea trade, a taste for Indian luxuries developed in Rome, and Alexandria quickly became the centre of commercial intercourse between East and West. We know that at this time Indian vessels sailed regularly into the Persian Gulf and to the Straits of Babelmandeb, but they were excluded from the Red Sea by the local owners, who asserted a monopoly of those waters. This monopoly was broken in the time of Augustus by Egyptian ships, manned by Greek crews, which sailed down the Red Sea, and at first coasted to Indian ports; then, about the middle of the first century A.D., the new-comers learned the secret of the seasonal winds, and began to sail direct from the Straits to the mouth

74   EARLY COMMUNICATIONS BY SEA

of the Indus,[1] to Broach on the Narbada, to the pepper ports of Malabar, and even to the east coast.

The result was a remarkable expansion of Indian trade, carried almost entirely by foreign ships, an expansion comparable in some ways to that which was to occur in the seventeenth century. The chief exports were pearls and precious stones, pepper and other spices, drugs, materials such as ivory and ebony, fine muslin, and a long list of curiosities—almost entirely a luxury trade. Imports consisted mainly of base metals, coral, and some western luxuries, and the large balance was settled in gold and silver, constituting a drain of coin and bullion eastwards which alarmed Roman financiers. This direct trade lasted for about two centuries; then the Egyptian effort failed, and the declining commerce returned to the old channels, Indians bringing goods to the mouth of the Red Sea, and selling them to the Arabs for transport further north.[2]

Our knowledge of the development of shipping on the east coast is exceedingly scanty. It is clear from European sources that when the Egyptian ships first rounded Cape Comorin, there was already an active coasting-trade from Ceylon to the Ganges, and that Indian vessels of considerable size crossed the Bay of Bengal to Sumatra and the Malay Peninsula, but there are no records to show for how many centuries this had been going on, or what were the main staples of the trade. All that can be said with confidence is that Indian-built ships, with Indian crews and Indian merchants, had been busy in these waters for an indefinite period before the Christian era.

[1] Changes in the Indus mouths have given a long succession of ports in this region, one after another emerging and disappearing without leaving any precise record. Alexander found a city named Pattala. In Roman times the port was called Barbaricon. Moslems knew successively Daibal or Diūl, Lāharī-bandar, and Shāh-bandar; it was only in the eighteenth century that Karachi emerged, not actually in the delta, and so exempt from its vicissitudes.

[2] A detailed account of the Roman trade will be found in E. H. Warmington's *The Commerce between the Roman Empire and India* (Cambridge, 1928).

CHAPTER XIII

THE KUSHĀN POWER

For the first three centuries of the Christian era our present knowledge of what was happening in India relates mainly to the western side of the country, but the story of the kingdoms further east is being gradually put together as new material comes to light, and may eventually be reconstructed as a coherent whole. For the peninsula we possess a nucleus of fact owing to the practice which was growing up of recording inscriptions on sheets of metal, usually copper.[1] Many of these documents have survived, and the gradual process of their recovery and decipherment has made it possible to draw up tentative lists of the rulers of various dynasties, and to form a general idea of their mutual relations. The three Tamil kingdoms, Chola, Pāndya and Kerala, continued to exist, and fought frequently among themselves; the boundaries of each may have expanded or contracted, but their substantial identity was preserved. To the north of these kingdoms lay the Andhras, who, as we have seen in Chapter XI, were ruling from the east coast right across the country to Ujjain, and were in conflict with the Sakas of Gujarāt: the remainder of their story is involved with the rise of the Kushān power, which forms the main subject of this chapter.

It will be recalled that, shortly before 100 B.C., the Yueh-chi horde of nomads had driven the Sakas out of Bactria. According to the account usually accepted, this

---

[1] The first copperplate recorded in *The Historical Inscriptions of Southern India*, by R. Sewell, ed. S. Krishnaswami Aiyangar (Madras, 1932), is dated about A.D. 234.

horde comprised five tribes, one of which, the Kushān, eventually became supreme over the others, so that the name Yueh-chi disappeared, and Bactria became the centre of the Kushān kingdom. An alternative account states that the Kushāns were really Sakas, who successfully reasserted themselves against their Yueh-chi conquerors. Whoever they were, the Kushāns, like their predecessors, quickly came south; one of their kings was in the Kābul valley by about A.D. 50, and a few years later the dynasty was supreme in the Punjab, and was extending thence towards Sind and Gujarāt, and also in the Gangetic plain.

While the earliest rulers of this dynasty were powerful and successful conquerors, the one name that has survived in tradition is that of Kanishka, who is now generally accepted as the third of the line, and who ranks with Asoka in popular fame, not merely in India itself, but throughout Central Asia and as far as China. Our knowledge of him is, however, vague. As a patron of Buddhism he has a high place in the hagiography of that faith, but many of the stories told of him are obviously mere echoes of the life of Asoka, and very little of historical value can be extracted from the traditions; in particular, it is quite safe to disregard the statements that before his conversion, if he was converted, he was a monster of wickedness, for that is part of the hagiographer's stock-in-trade; and our knowledge is practically confined to what can be inferred from coins and inscriptions.

The chronology of the dynasty is still uncertain; the more usual view is that Kanishka ascended the throne in A.D. 78, but some scholars place that event about half a century later; and while it is agreed that his reign was glorious, its precise length has not yet been determined. His capital was the city of Peshāwar, where the main route from Afghanistan enters the Indus plain, and we are thus entitled to regard him as an Indian ruler; but the Kushāns had spread, not been driven, southward, and his empire comprised Bactria and country still further to the north and east. Its extent in India is hard to define with precision, but it certainly included the Punjab and Sind, Kashmīr, and the parts of Mālwa and Gujarāt which had been held by the Sakas and Pahlavas, as well as the kingdom of Muttra, on the west side of the Gangetic plain. According to tradition, it extended in this direction at least as far as Patna, and numerous finds of Kushān coins in different parts of Bihār, Bengal and Orissa lend some support to the theory that either Kanishka himself or his immediate successors ruled on this side of India, but to what point is uncertain. Scarcely anything is known of the way in which this great empire was administered; we get glimpses of high officers, who may be styled viceroys, at Muttra and Ujjain, but we can say nothing of the methods which they followed, or their relations with the people whom they ruled.

Of the Emperor himself, we know only that he was successful in war, and that he was a patron of Buddhism. His principal military achievements were in Central Asia, where he extended his dominions, and freed his empire from the tribute to China which had been paid by his predecessor; and we do not hear of extensive conquests in India beyond the area which had been subdued by his predecessors. His position in regard to Buddhism is not entirely clear. He undoubtedly patronised the faith, as is testified by his buildings and endowments; it is probable that he convened the Council, which was certainly held during his reign, to formulate an authoritative canon of the doctrine; and in the legendary accounts to be gathered in China and Tibet he appears as a Buddhist of great eminence. His extant coins, on the other hand, do not suggest exclusive devotion to a single faith, for, while the image of the Buddha occurs, the great majority present a variety of Indian, Greek and Persian deities: we can infer from these that he was no bigot, and while he may have adopted Buddhism as his personal creed, there is no reason to think that he imposed it on his empire.

A few words may be said regarding the Buddhist Council convoked in this reign, the fourth of the series, and the last of which there is any record. The traditional account, which is all that we possess, is that the initiative came from Kanishka himself, who in his study of the faith found so much conflict of doctrine that he decided to obtain an authoritative exposition. An assemblage, said to number 500 theologians, was accordingly convoked, and a series of elaborate commentaries is said to have been compiled ; but it is impossible to be certain as to either the doctrine established or the individuals who formulated it.

Whatever the Council may have done, the Buddhism which Kanishka patronised differed substantially in creed and worship from the discipline preached by the Buddha. The original idea of a path by which an individual could escape from the evil of successive rebirths and attain the goal of nirvāna still persisted, but alongside of it had emerged the larger conception that an individual might rise to the position of a saviour of the world, bringing nirvāna within the reach of the whole human race. This conception appears to have grown up by degrees, and was eventually systematised under the name of Mahāyāna, or ' the Great Vehicle,' as contrasted with Hīnayāna, or ' the Lesser Vehicle,' the term applied to the original doctrine ; its precise formulation is usually assigned to a somewhat later date, and possibly was assisted by the deliberations of Kanishka's Council ; but from about A.D. 200 onwards the two schools subsisted in India side by side.

The change which had taken place in worship is at first sight startling, for the Buddha, whose original teaching was essentially atheistic, had by this time been elevated to a position indistinguishable in the popular eye from that of a personal god—a god seated in heaven, surrounded by an obedient hierarchy, and worshipped in costly temples with an elaborate ritual, his words spoken on earth accepted as carrying divine authority, his relics preserved in magnificent shrines and exposed periodically to the veneration of the faithful. This developed form of popular Buddhism is now scarcely to be traced in India, but it remains the creed of those parts of Central Asia which have not accepted Islam ; and in the neighbourhood of Kanishka's capital it found expression in a distinctive school of sculpture.

The country round Peshāwar has yielded in very great numbers specimens of the work of this school, which has been described variously as Graeco-Buddhist, Indo-Hellenic, and otherwise, but the most convenient label is Gandhāran, since the specimens which have been found are practically confined to the region known in old days as Gandhāra, of which Peshāwar was the centre. These sculptures are characterised by Greek methods of composition and technique, but the subjects are purely Indian, and are drawn almost entirely from the newer form of Buddhism. The earlier Buddhist sculptures, which we know from the survivals at Bhārhut, Sānchī and elsewhere, depicted scenes from the traditions which had accumulated round the teacher, but, so far as is yet known, never showed the teacher himself : in the Gandhāran school the Buddha is the most conspicuous figure, and his worship is everywhere the inspiring motive. At first the artists depicted their subject in various ways according to their individual conceptions, but a conventional type gradually emerged, the type which now prevails throughout the Buddhist countries to the north and east. In this way the school made a permanent contribution to the religious conceptions of a large part of the world, but in India it was confined to a small locality, where it persisted for a time, with a gradual disappearance of the foreign elements, and in this region it left no successor. Its influence on the art of other parts of India is estimated differently by different critics, some of whom detect it right across the country, while others hold that it was limited in area and unimportant in its results.

The development of strictly Indian sculpture during this period must be studied, not in Gandhāra but mainly in the remnants which have been preserved of the great Buddhist shrine at Amarāvatī, a name familiar to all who have used the main staircase of the British Museum. Amarāvatī is situated on the river Kistna, about 80 miles from the east coast, and at this time lay in the Andhra dominions. Between A.D. 150 and 250 the shrine, already of old standing, was enriched with an elaborately carved railing and other embellishments, all of white marble ; but in the course of time much of the material was used by the neighbours for lime-burning, and we possess only the fragments which survived, and which have been placed in the museums in London and Madras. The style of the sculpture is readily recognisable as a development of that which characterises the monuments found at Bhārhut or Sānchī, and there is nothing extant to prove that the artists had any direct knowledge of the work which had been done in Gandhāra ; but the appearance of the figure of the Buddha in the seat of honour and worship shows that the ideas of the newer Buddhism had become established on the east coast as well as in the far north.

As has already been said, the length of Kanishka's reign has not yet been accurately determined. He was succeeded by Huvishka, who was probably his son, and who retained, and possibly extended, the empire ; but decay soon set in, and the Kushān power appears to have shrunk by the third century to portions of the Punjab, and to some of its territories in Afghanistan and beyond. The causes of the collapse are unknown, and all that can be said is that the later coins of the dynasty show marked signs of Persian influence, and thus lend some support to the Moslem tradition, recorded many centuries later, that early in the third century one of the first Sassanian rulers of Persia invaded the Punjab and received the homage of its rulers.

In western India also the political situation is not entirely clear. This region continued under Saka rule till nearly the end of the fourth century, the rulers being designated Satraps (in Sanskrit, *Kshatrapa*) or ' viceroys.' For a time they were subject to the Kushān power, and the designation was thus appropriate, but apparently they resumed their independence at some uncertain period during the decline of the suzerain power. We have seen in Chapter XI that contention had arisen between the Sakas and the Andhras of the South, possibly even before the Christian era. In the first century of that era a Saka satrap was ruling in Mahārāshtra, the country to the south of the Narbada, but about the year A.D. 120 this satrapy was destroyed by the Andhras. Very soon after, Rudradāman I, the Satrap of Ujjain, revenged this defeat, and re-established Saka rule for some distance beyond the river ; thenceforward Ujjain remained the Saka capital of Western India, from Sind to the borders of Mahārāshtra, until, just before A.D. 400, the territory was conquered by the Guptas.

An interesting memorial of this Satrap Rudradāman has survived in what is known as the Jūnāgarh inscription, discovered in the Kathiāwar peninsula in the course of the last century. The inscription was cut on a rock which already bore the edicts of Asoka, and it recorded the history of an artificial lake which had been constructed to provide for irrigation. The work was taken in hand under the Maurya Emperor Chandragupta, and was completed under Asoka ; in the year A.D. 150 the embankment gave way, and Rudradāman caused it to be rebuilt 'three times stronger' than before. Later records show that his work lasted for three centuries, but had to be reconstructed in the Gupta period ; and in the end the jungle swallowed up the lake and the cultivated area dependent on it. Inscriptions such as this are rare, but the facts which it records are typical of what has happened all over the hilly parts of India from time immemorial. Almost wherever a stream or drainage-line exists, embankments have been thrown across it, given way before exceptional floods, been reconstructed only to be wrecked again, and at last perhaps abandoned because there was nobody on the spot able or willing to undertake the needful work. There is no doubt that in the past collapse was often due to neglect of timely repairs, but it is only in quite recent times that the progress of engineering science has rendered possible the construction of dams which can justly be described as permanent in the conditions which exist in India. It is easy to be critical of the failures of the past, and expatiate on the enormous waste evidenced by the surviving ruins of such works : it is perhaps more profitable to recall that, long before the days of scientific engineering, such a dam might remain serviceable for as many as four centuries, a period sufficient at least to justify the original expenditure.

While the Sakas persisted, the Andhra power was declining. The details of the process are almost unknown, but by about the end of the second century A.C. it had withdrawn from western India, and shrunk to practically its original dimensions, the Telugu-speaking area near the east coast. Then the original dynasty was crushed by a rebel governor, who established his own family as kings in this region; thenceforward the name Andhra disappears, and we hear only of the Pallavas, the name borne by the new dynasty, which was to persist for six centuries, and play an important part in the history of the South.[1]

It cannot be affirmed that either Sakas or Kushāns left any important mark on the culture of the regions which they ruled. Speaking generally, the nomads of Central Asia appear to have been highly adaptable, and, when they settled down, they conformed to their new environment, assimilating, or rather being assimilated by, the culture prevailing in the locality. From the nature of the case, such a development could not leave many conspicuous records, and all that we possess are a few hints that the process was at work. The names of the foreign rulers became Indianised as time went on: among the Saka satraps we find such purely Hindu names as Rudradāman or Satyasinha; and while the earlier Kushāns bore foreign names, we come in due course to a Vāsudeva. Kanishka and Huvishka, again, patronised the Buddhism which they found in their dominions; but the coins of Vāsudeva, the next ruler, are characterised by the figure of the great Hindu god Siva, accompanied by the appropriate emblems, and it is hard to resist the inference that he was in substance a Hindu.

This fact may serve as a timely reminder that Hinduism continued on its way during the centuries for which we have so few records of its existence. Our precise knowledge of

---

[1] The origin of the name Pallava is uncertain. Some writers, e.g. P. T. Srinivas Iyangar (*History of the Tamils* (Madras, 1929), p. 329) and J. Allan (*Cambridge Shorter History of India* (Cambridge, 1934), pp. 195–6), make the new rulers Pahlavas, or adventurers from the north-west; others, such as V. A. Smith (*Early History of India* (Oxford, 1924), pp. 490 ff.), find their origin in the Tamil country or in Ceylon; while K. P. Jayaswal has recently connected them with a dynasty ruling in the Vindhyan region (*Journal* of the Bihar and Orissa Research Society, 1933). It is generally agreed that the name represents a dynasty, not a people.

THE SPREAD OF HINDUISM

Buddhism or Jainism at this period is derived mainly from architecture and sculpture : the fact that we have no similar evidence for Hinduism is best explained on the view that the practice of building in durable materials had not as yet spread to India as a whole, but was confined to the adherents of particular creeds. As usual, the uncertainty of all literary dates makes it impossible to say what Hindus in the mass were doing, and thinking, during this period ; but we must infer that in many centres learned men were pursuing the studies which bore fruit in the extant Sanskrit literature, and that the way was being prepared for the culmination of that literature which was to take place in the next period.

There are also grounds for inferring that Hinduism was increasing its hold on the peninsula, though its final supremacy was to be delayed for some centuries. The early religion of the Dravidians in this part of the country centred in spirits localised in trees, or other objects, and in some cases regarded as malevolent ; but both Jainism and Buddhism had gained a footing in the country by the third century B.C., while Hinduism was gradually absorbing the indigenous deities. We possess no knowledge of the details, but we may reasonably regard the period as one of religious ferment in the South, and of intimate contact between the preachers of competing doctrines.

To these doctrines it is almost certain that Christianity must be added.[1] The very old tradition that the Apostle Thomas preached the gospel in India has found new defenders in recent years, and cannot be summarily rejected on the lines followed by critics of the Victorian age ; but, whatever view may be taken of the evidence on this point, there is little doubt that before the end of the third century Christian congregations existed in the south-west of India, in communion with what was then the flourishing church of Mesopotamia ; and these congregations persisted with many vicissitudes until their ' heresies ' shocked the orthodox

[1] In addition to the authorities discussed in V. A. Smith's *Early History of India* (4th edition), pp. 260-2, reference may be made to the papers by Dr. J. F. Farquhar and Dr. A. Mingana in the *Bulletin of the John Rylands Library*, 1926, 1927.

Portuguese ecclesiastics who came to Goa in the sixteenth century.

It would, however, be a mistake to picture the preachers of these new doctrines as missionaries to savage peoples. The Tamil language, which is spoken in the south of the Peninsula, possesses a valuable body of literature, which is now generally regarded as dating from the period we are considering ; and this literature shows incidentally that, as may indeed be inferred from the facts of commerce summarised in the last chapter, the South had already developed a civilisation of its own. Its exportable products, mainly pepper, pearls, and precious stones, enabled it to indulge in foreign luxuries ; the royal courts were ornate, and patronised literature, music and the drama ; and there are traces of what some scholars have regarded as an approximation to constitutional government. The King was supreme, but his action was influenced to an important, though uncertain, extent by what are known as 'the five great assemblies,' bodies of which the composition and functions are still obscure ; while there are hints of local assemblies also, composed of representatives of the villages, which exercised considerable power in matters concerning their own affairs.

Some little caution is required in drawing facts from the old Tamil literature, which cannot be checked from other sources, and occasionally seems to strike a note of conventional idealism ; but it suggests that under these institutions the peasants of the Tamil country were on the whole reasonably well governed, and led a quiet and laborious life. Extreme poverty certainly existed, but in ordinary seasons there was enough to satisfy the simple wants of most of the people. Probably they were not as yet much influenced by the newer religious ideas, but adhered to the traditional worship of the country, and were concerned mainly with the routine of peasant life, ploughing and sowing, watering and reaping, the occupations described so vividly in some of the poems, along with hunting game in the hill country and fishing on the coast.

In the towns the position was more complex. The poems give us pictures of a pleasant family life, and also of

EARLY TAMIL CULTURE

the dangers to which it was exposed from the seductions of the numerous and attractive courtesans, the chief exponents of the arts of music and dancing. There were crowded streets and well-stocked shops, foreign merchants with their wares, the king's court and his troops; there were the representatives of the newer creeds; and there were the literary men to whom we owe our knowledge of these facts. Madura, then the Pāndya capital, and still one of the principal cities of the South, appears to have been the chief, though doubtless not the only, centre of Tamil literary activity; and according to tradition it was the seat of what has been described as a literary academy, to which poems were formally submitted for approval, but the validity of this tradition has been questioned.[1] This Tamil culture was not, however, isolated, for the presence of Sanskrit words in the poems indicates that intercourse with northern India must have proceeded for a long time before the later ones at least were composed.

Another centre of culture was Kānchipuram, a town which is situated a short distance south-west of Madras, and is now usually known as Conjeeveram; in the old days it lay near the northern limit of the Tamil country, and in the third century became the capital of the Pallava dynasty, which, as we have seen, then ruled over the Andhra country to the north. The culture of Kānchipuram appears to have been Sanskritic rather than Tamil, and there are some grounds for the view that it formed, so to speak, an outpost of Hinduism in its gradual advance towards the south.

Taking into consideration, then, the facts depicted in the literature, it is perhaps reasonable to infer that by this time the urban, though not the rural, population of the Tamil country had progressed to a point where the primitive indigenous religion no longer afforded satisfaction, and thus offered a favourable field for missionary effort to the representatives of the newer creeds.

---

[1] Mr. P. T. Srinivas Iyangar (*op. cit.*, ch. xvi) argues strongly against the validity of the traditional account. This work contains English renderings of many passages from the Tamil poetry of the period. Another account of this period will be found in the early pages of Professor Nilakanta Sastri's *The Colas*, Vol. I (Madras, 1935).

D

CHAPTER XIV

THE GUPTA EMPIRE

THE political history of northern India in the period following the Kushān power is at present in process of reconstruction,[1] and cannot yet be told as a series of ascertained facts. We come to firm ground only in the opening years of the fourth century, when a conquering dynasty emerged in Bihār, which was to establish a great empire over northern India, and make its power felt far into the south. The name Gupta empire, which is ordinarily used, is drawn from the practice of its rulers. The founder bore, or possibly assumed, the name of Chandragupta, which, it will be recalled, had been borne six centuries before by the founder of the Maurya empire, and the termination *-gupta* (meaning ' protected ') reappeared with each successive emperor, not as a surname in the modern sense, but as an integral part of the official title which he adopted.

Chandragupta I appears to have been originally a petty king, or chief, in Bihār. An advantageous marriage gave him possession of Magadha with its capital, Patna ; thence he extended his rule over the remainder of Bihār, the east of Oudh, and perhaps part of Bengal ; and by the year 320 he considered himself justified in assuming a title denoting paramountcy, and in establishing a new era, dating from that year. His successor, Samudragupta, enjoyed a long reign, probably from about 330 to 375, and spent much of it in successful wars, for the facts of which we have to rely on

[1] A notable work on this period, Mr. K. P. Jayaswal's *History of India, c.* A.D. 150–350, published in the *Journal* of the Bihar and Orissa Research Society, 1933, has not yet received the expert examination it deserves before a final verdict can be passed on its conclusions.

a panegyric which he caused to be inscribed on one of Asoka's pillars now standing in the fort at Allahabad. Before summarising his achievements it will be convenient to explain a distinction, recurring frequently in Indian military history, between two classes of operations, which may be labelled conquests and raids. The material object of a conquest was to secure a regular revenue from the conquered country; and this might be effected either by accepting tribute from its ruler, or by setting him aside and undertaking the administration of his territory. A conquest was thus intended to be lasting, but a raid had for its object merely the attainment of military glory, and, usually, possession of the wealth which had been accumulated by the enemy and could easily be carried away. Using these terms, it may be said that Samudragupta conquered most of northern India and successfully raided far into the south.

The empire, as organised by him, extended on the east almost as far as the Brahmaputra; it incorporated the greater part of Bengal, while kingdoms covering the rest of Bengal and Assam are enumerated among the tributary states. On the west his administration reached to the Jumna, and on the south-west to the line of the Narbada, but in this direction it stopped short of the dominions of the Western Satraps, and thus did not extend to the coast; beyond the Jumna, he received tribute from portions of the Punjab and Rājputāna, so that he may reasonably be styled Emperor of northern India.

The laudatory account of Samudragupta's raid into the south is astonishing, and some recent students hold that the inscription magnifies his actual achievement. It is however certain that marching south from his capital through the jungles and subduing the tribes on the way Samudragupta met and defeated a number of rulers belonging to Kalinga, where it will be remembered Asoka had waged his last war. It is uncertain whether Samudragupta was able to proceed further south than the banks of the Kistna where he had a contest with the Pallavas. He then turned back and marched north until he reached the frontier of his own dominions on the Narbada. He must have carried back considerable booty including the hoarded gold of the southern rulers which enabled him to introduce a gold coinage. He had marched over eight hundred miles from his capital, and we must recognise that such a march in those days called for exceptional powers of organisation and leadership. His exploit was rivalled only after nearly a thousand years in the reign of the Turkish ruler Alāuddin.

Samudragupta was succeeded by his son, Chandragupta II, who assumed the additional title of Vikramāditya, and reigned until 413. He rounded off his dominions by conquering the last of the Western Satraps, who now disappear from history, and the annexation of their dominions gave free access to the ports on the Arabian Sea. This appears to have been the last important extension of the empire, which was enjoyed by his successors, apparently in peace, until the invasion of the White Huns, recorded in the next chapter; then the empire seems to have shrunk to small dimensions, and from about the year 500 onwards the Gupta dynasty survived merely as a local power.[1]

Some glimpses of the working of this great empire are furnished by inscriptions which have been recovered in recent years, relating mainly to Bengal. The chief territorial unit was the *bhukti*, or province, in charge of a governor; and under him in succession were districts, subdivisions and villages, much as in modern times. The district administrator had some sort of council, containing representatives of financiers, merchants and craftsmen, but it is uncertain whether this body was merely advisory, or exercised any specific functions; and there was a staff of record-keepers concerned in particular with the registers of lands. The inscriptions give us some idea how these authorities worked. When, for instance, a man wanted to establish a religious endowment, he applied to the district administrator and his council to sell him the land he required: the record-keepers reported on the application; on their report the administrator fixed the terms of sale, directed

---

[1] Dr. Basak has recently advanced reasons for holding that the empire, as such, lasted well into the sixth century (*History of North Eastern India*, ch. iv).

GUPTA ADMINISTRATION

the local officials to measure and demarcate the land, and exhorted them to give the purchaser peaceful possession, free from all further payments. It is an orderly bureaucratic system, such as we meet all over India whenever we obtain a glimpse of the working of the administration.

Of the effect of the administration on the people such records naturally tell us nothing, but something can be gleaned from the narrative of a visit to India made by a Chinese pilgrim between 399 and 414, that is to say, during the reign of Chandragupta II. Fa-hien, or Fa-hsien, for the name is written in various ways, came overland to India to visit the Buddhist holy places and obtain authentic copies of the scriptures.[1] Entering India at Peshāwar, he made a detour through the mountains to the north and west, re-entered the Indus plain from the direction of Bannu, crossed the Punjab to Muttra, and passed on through Kanauj and Ajodhya to the holy places in Bihār, and so to Patna. Here at last he was able to obtain some of the scriptures for which he was searching, and he stayed for three years, learning the language and copying the sacred books. Thence he travelled to Tamluk, near the mouth of the Hooghly, where two years were spent in similar occupations; and then he sailed for Ceylon on his journey homewards. He thus had ample opportunities for observing the life of northern India, but, unfortunately for posterity, his concentration on the object of his search seems to have left him little inclination to record his observations on secular matters, and he is silent regarding much that we desire to know. What he tells us is, however, consistent with the view that under Chandragupta II the empire was prosperous and well administered.

Parts of the country indeed were desolate. The holy places in North Bihār were situated in a wilderness, peopled only by some priests and a few families living near the shrines; and the pilgrim heard of desert tracts towards the south, which he did not visit. The bulk of the Gangetic

---

[1] Several translations of his narrative have been published; we have used the latest of these—*The Travels of Fa-hsien*, re-translated by H. A. Giles, Cambridge, 1923.

plain, however, from Muttra through Kanauj and Benares to Patna, was well populated and thriving. The subjects of the empire were free from most of the bureaucratic restrictions with which the pilgrim was familiar in China : the land revenue of course had to be paid, but there was no 'registration or official restriction,' and 'those who want to go away may go.' Judged by Chinese standards, the criminal law was lenient ; fines were the usual penalties for misconduct, and 'even for a second attempt at rebellion the punishment is only the loss of the right hand.' The bulk of the population were abstemious and vegetarian : 'they do not keep pigs or fowls, there are no dealings in cattle, no butchers' shops or distilleries in their market-places' ; but the outcast tribes went hunting, and dealt in flesh. These outcasts were segregated ; 'and when they approach a city or market, they beat a piece of wood, in order to distinguish themselves. Then people know who they are, and avoid coming into contact with them.' These are glimpses only, but they enable us to form some sort of an idea of administrative and social conditions in the empire.

It is difficult to write with precision regarding the religious situation at this period. There is no doubt that during the great days of the dynasty the emperors themselves were definitely Hindu, not Buddhist ; but they were certainly not fanatical, there is no hint anywhere of official persecution, and some of them on occasion patronised the latter faith. From the scanty facts on record, some writers have inferred that the Gupta period was characterised by the decay of Buddhism as a popular creed, and by a vigorous Hindu renascence ; but the record is too imperfect to justify confident deductions, and the facts seem to be consistent with the view that the change was in the royal, rather than the popular, attitude. Imperial or royal patronage left durable memorials, some of which have survived : in its absence there is no record to which we can appeal.

Some idea of the extent to which Buddhism prevailed can be formed from the facts recorded by Fa-hien, if we remember that he travelled with a purpose, and presumably

PREVALENCE OF BUDDHISM

visited only those parts of the country where he had reason to hope that copies of the Buddhist scriptures could be obtained, neglecting the regions where the faith was not established. He found the faith ' very flourishing ' in the Punjab, and ' becoming very popular ' in the country round Muttra ; in Bengal, too, in the country near the mouth of the Hooghly, it was ' very flourishing ' ; but for the wide plains between these limits we have no similar appreciations, and can say only that the faith existed. There were twenty monasteries along the Jumna near Muttra, and a few were to be found in the wildernesses near the holy places ; but there were only two establishments of the kind at Kanauj, none at Ajodhya, one at Kausāmbī, two at Benares, and two at Patna ; if there were others between these points, the pilgrim failed to notice them, but his enumeration appears to be exhaustive, and his observation that the faith was spreading near Muttra shows, at least, that it was not predominant in that region. Of the relations between Hindus and Buddhists, the pilgrim recorded very little ; legends reproduced by him indicate that in the past there had been occasional bickerings with ' Brāhman heretics ' at Ajodhya and elsewhere, but there is no hint of persecution under Chandragupta II, and the statement that Brāhmans took part in the annual Buddhist festival at Patna points to the existence of amicable relations at the imperial capital. The most probable conclusion to be drawn from his observations, taken as a whole, is that Hinduism predominated in the great bulk of the Gangetic plain : Buddhism had more adherents in the east and in the west than in the centre of the country, but there are not sufficient grounds for describing it as predominant in either region.

When we supplement the pilgrim's observations by the few scraps of information available in other sources, the view appears to be justified that, while Hinduism, Buddhism and Jainism existed side by side, they were not ordinarily in actual conflict. It would be a mistake to think of the period as one of ' acute communal tension,' to use the phrase of the moment ; and perhaps a more enlightening analogy can be drawn from the position in England early in the last century.

In those days the Church was quiescent, the Dissenters were active : bigots might occasionally emerge on one side or the other ; but the ordinary Anglican watched the competing activities with a tolerant eye, disapproving some of the methods employed, but recognising that good was being done, and prepared to allow that there might be room for both. On the scanty evidence available it is permissible to hold that the Hindu attitude under the Guptas was not very different.

For the development of Hinduism itself the Gupta period is of particular importance in that it covers the production, substantially in their present form, of the group of texts known collectively as the Purānas. The historical traditions embedded in some of these texts have been mentioned in Chapter IV ; but about this time the traditional matter was elaborated and enriched so as to produce the moral and religious treatises now extant, the most striking feature of which is the exaltation of one particular deity, in some cases Siva, in others Vishnu, at the expense of all others. The Purānas thus take their place in the history of India's secular struggle to get beyond polytheism, while their practical influence has been very great, for, along with the epics, which have been similarly enriched, they constitute the scriptures of the masses of the people, and comprise much of the moral teaching which has gone to mould the Indian character in its present form.

Apart from the production of these, and other, texts, the Gupta period was a time of great activity in art and literature, so much so that it has been compared by European writers to the age of Pericles, or of Shakespeare. In literature it is dominated by the figure of Kālidāsa, who is regarded by western as well as eastern critics as the greatest poet of India, and one of the great poets of the world, known alike for his epic, lyric and dramatic work, but most familiar for his romantic play *Sakuntalā*, which is usually accepted as the finest flower of the Indian theatre. Kālidāsa, however, does not stand alone, for there is a large volume of good literature which can be attributed with some confidence to the same period and which is distinguished by its comparative freedom from the artificiality of later ages.

GUPTA LITERATURE

The language used in this literature was classical Sanskrit, which had now become the regular medium of expression for lay as well as ecclesiastical writers. Sanskrit developed from the original Aryan language used in the Rigveda, and its classical forms had been fixed as early as the fourth or fifth century B.C., but at first its use was confined to Brāhman scholars. The early Buddhist and Jain literature was produced in Prākrit, the simpler speech of everyday life ;[1] and the same medium was employed in the edicts of Asoka and other early inscriptions which have survived. As time went on, Sanskrit was adopted first by Buddhist, and later by Jain writers, and it begins to appear in secular inscriptions from about A.D. 150. In the Gupta period its literary use had become general, and this was to remain true for several centuries—in fact, until the emergence of vernacular literature in comparatively modern times ; but, by a convention which nowadays seems curious, the plays were bilingual, the speeches of kings and men of position being Sanskrit, while women and uneducated men express themselves in Prākrit.

A few words may be said here on the controversy regarding the debt of the Indian theatre to Greek inspiration. Some scholars have traced the beginnings of Indian dramatic representations back to the days of the Rigveda : others attribute their origin to Greek actors performing before Alexander the Great and his successors in India. The direct evidence in favour of either view is scanty, and cannot be discussed here, but it may be said in a general way that the theory of a Greek origin is not absolutely required to explain the few facts which are known, and that there is no real difficulty in the way of the alternative view that the Indian drama grew up independently, though some details may have been borrowed from the practice of the Greek theatre.[2]

There are good grounds for holding that architecture

[1] Pāli, the language in which the Buddhist canon was eventually formulated in Ceylon, is a form of Indian Prākrit, somewhat developed on the literary side.
[2] Reference may be made to the summary of the discussion in *India's Past*, pp. 98 ff., and to the literature cited on p. 114 of that volume.

also flourished under the Guptas, but survivals are so few that it is difficult to write with confidence on the subject. The imperfection of the record is sufficiently explained by a combination of causes. In the first place, the climate, with its torrential falls of rain and sudden changes of temperature and humidity, makes for rapid decay. In the second, the idea of preserving monuments of the past is quite modern in India, as in most other countries; and disused edifices have been commonly treated as convenient sources of building materials for the needs of the moment. In the third, some of the Moslem invaders were active iconoclasts: idols of any sort were repugnant to their religious feelings, while the wealth concealed, or supposed to be concealed, in the temples ensured the coincidence of interest with sentiment.[1] There is no doubt that, along the tracks followed by some of the invaders, religious buildings were destroyed wholesale, and it must be remembered that in the Hindu view a temple which has once been desecrated cannot be restored; the historian of the art is therefore dependent on a small number of examples, which owe their preservation mainly to their remoteness.

These examples, again, are confined to buildings of a single class. We have no private houses, no palaces or other secular buildings; and it appears to be certain that wood was still the ordinary material for all general purposes, stone or burnt bricks being employed solely for religious edifices. Judging from the survivals of these, it would appear that about this time the types of permanent buildings which had been originally evolved for Buddhist use began to be adapted to Hindu worship. These types were two: the shrine with its covering, and the monastery, consisting of cells built round a quadrangular enclosure. The shrine, at first a receptacle for relics, was at once available as the resting-place of the image of the deity; the developments, which probably began in the Gupta age and culminated

[1] *Cf.* the account of Constantinople quoted by Gibbon in chap. lxvii of the *Decline and Fall*: 'The works of ancient sculpture had been defaced by Christian zeal or barbaric violence; the fairest structures were demolished; and the marbles of Paros or Numidia were burnt for lime or applied to the meanest uses.'

later, consisted in the elaboration of the covering from a plain hemispherical mound into the 'towered structures high' which are so characteristic of the country, and the addition of subsidiary buildings such as porches and enclosures. The quadrangle of the monastery, too, was readily available as the type of residence for holy men of any faith; and in southern India it was transmuted later on into the ground plan of the enclosed temples which are found in that region.

The Buddhist shrine was not, however, always a building in the ordinary sense of the word, for in some places, most of them in western India, both shrines and monasteries were hewn and carved out of solid rock, giving the 'cave-' or, more accurately, rock-temples which are among the greatest glories of Indian art. The oldest of these go back beyond the Christian era, and the most famous of all, those at Ajanta, in the extreme north-west of the Hyderabad State, contain a series of work ranging from the first to the sixth century. Other remarkable examples are situated at Ellora, about fifty miles from Ajanta, and at Bāgh in the south of Gwalior. It is to these rock-temples, the older of which are Buddhist and the later Hindu, that we owe almost all our knowledge of early Indian painting, for in some cases the interiors were lavishly decorated with frescoes,[1] many of which can still be seen. They were also elaborately carved, and furnish most of the materials for study of the sculpture of the period—sculpture which has won the praise of connoisseurs throughout the world; but these materials have of late been supplemented by the recovery of many images, probably thrown down by iconoclasts, and buried in the debris of their work, so that they have been preserved for the modern excavator.

The study of such specimens as have survived suggests that for this period it would be wrong to draw a sharp distinction between Buddhist and Hindu art. What we have is a true indigenous art, employed in the service, first of Buddhism as well as Jainism, and then of Hinduism:

[1] Frescoes, in the popular sense of mural paintings. Technically the work is in *tempera*, not *fresco*.

the subjects change, but not the technique, nor, at first, the inspiration; and it was only by degrees that the influence of developed Hindu ideas reacted on the artists so as to produce the distinctive features recognisable in the later work known usually as Hindu. The Gupta period, then, seems to have been one of transition, in the limited sense that artists were turning from one set of subjects to another; but even this generalisation is subject to the caution that the record is very imperfect, and, while so many hopeful sites remain unexcavated, it is dangerous to write with confidence of the trend of art in India as a whole.

The literary and artistic activity of the Gupta period has seemed to some scholars to call for a precise explanation, which has been sought in foreign contacts—with China in the East, and Rome, or rather Alexandria, in the West. It may be agreed that such contacts existed, though the direct trade between Egypt and India had come to an end a century before the first Gupta ruler came to power; but clear evidence of foreign influence is hard to find, and it is doubtful whether the facts require such a theory. Some at least of the emperors were men of culture: Samudragupta, the greatest conqueror of the line, was also a poet, a musician, and a theologian; and possibly the facts may be adequately explained by the existence of a wealthy and cultured court, extending its patronage to the best talent that could be found, and thus stimulating and bringing into the light of day energies which in less favourable circumstances might have remained hidden, and possibly unfruitful.

We have described the fourth and fifth centuries as the Gupta period, but it must not be inferred that there were no other important powers in India, and, indeed, there is definite evidence of a considerable kingdom, or even empire, that of the Vākāṭaka dynasty, lying between the Guptas and the southern states, and for a time dominating the centre of the country. We know the names of its rulers, and the claims to conquests which some of them made; we have some grounds for thinking that their culture was allied to that of their northern neighbours; but as yet we possess no knowledge of the life of the people under their rule.

CHAPTER XV

THE WHITE HUNS

WE have seen in Chapter X that when, in the second century B.C., the Yueh-chi pressed the Sakas out of Bactria, the Huns were behind them. The westward movement of the hordes had continued since those days, and, while the Guptas were reigning in northern India, the Huns had reached Europe, and were earning there the reputation for wanton brutality which still adheres to the name. At the same period a tribe, or group of tribes, known as the White Huns were settled on the Oxus: the nature of their connection with the Huns proper is uncertain, but the fact that they are described in Sanskrit literature and inscriptions as Hūna suggests that, whatever their claim may have been, they must have brought the name of Hun with them to India. From the Oxus the White Huns came south by the regular route through Afghanistan, and just after the middle of the fifth century they were defeated by the Emperor Skandagupta, who recorded his achievement on a pillar of victory. The locality of the battle is uncertain, but the position of the pillar, some distance east of Benares, suggests that the invaders may have penetrated to about this point.

So far as is at present known, the White Huns did not become permanent masters of the Gangetic plain, but soon after the year 465 they were overrunning the north-west under a leader named Toramāna, who before the end of the century was reigning in the Punjab and as far south as Mālwa, and had assumed an Indian title. His son Mihiragula (or -kula) appears to have dominated these regions from his capital of Sialkot; the Guptas continued to rule in Bihār and northern Bengal, and possibly elsewhere, but their claim to the paramountcy of the north had passed away. Of Mihiragula's activities we possess no direct evidence, but concurrent traditions represent him as a ruthless and bloodthirsty oppressor, and, while they are doubtless exaggerated, they may be taken as having a substantial basis of fact. The story of his fall is still obscure, and the present position of the question may be summarised as an illustration of the state of our knowledge of this period, and a justification of the recurring cautions which we have to inflict on our readers against assuming that everything is known.

It may be premised that soon after the middle of the sixth century the main power of the White Huns in Central Asia was broken by the Turks, the next figures in the long procession westwards, and from that time, if not earlier, the Indian section was isolated and left to its own resources. The only literary account we possess of the fate of Mihiragula was given by a Chinese pilgrim, Yuan Chwang, whom we shall meet in the next chapter. According to him, Mihiragula decided on the extermination of Buddhism, and with this object invaded the territory of the Gupta ruler Bālāditya, who was a zealous Buddhist. His enterprise failed, and he himself was taken prisoner. Subsequently he was released, but finding that his throne had been usurped, he sought a refuge in Kashmīr, where, a little later, he seized the kingdom, renewed his persecution of the Buddhists, and died suddenly among portents of divine displeasure.

This account, written by an enthusiastic Buddhist more than a century after the event, presents many difficulties in regard to date and other details; and it has usually been rejected by scholars since the discovery in Mālwa of two inscriptions, recording that about the year 530 one Yasodharman crushed the White Huns, and made himself Emperor of northern India from sea to sea. Of the position previously occupied by this conqueror nothing definite is recorded, and he still remains a shadowy figure; but a phrase

DEFEAT OF THE WHITE HUNS

in one of the inscriptions suggests that he belonged, not to Mālwa, where they were inscribed, but to Thānesar, a town in the Punjab about 100 miles north of Delhi.

It is possible to bring the two stories into some sort of harmony if we assume that, while the White Huns were dominating the north-west, Yasodharman established himself on their flank, and extended his power to the east over the territories of the Guptas; then, with the aid of his new vassals, he drove the White Huns south and west, until he had cleared the eastern Punjab and the Mālwa plateau, and thus made himself paramount, broadly speaking, over northern India. A century later Yuan Chwang must have obtained from Buddhist sources a distorted version of the story, in which the whole credit for the achievement was given to the zealous Buddhist Bālāditya instead of to the Emperor whom he assisted: the statement that Mihiragula himself found a refuge in Kashmīr may well be true, but it has not yet been confirmed by contemporary evidence. This hypothetical account squares with the facts, so far as they are known, but it is not established, and may have to be revised at any time in the light of subsequent discoveries; all that can be said with confidence is that Yasodharman's claim to have crushed the White Huns and obtained the paramountcy of the north is justified in the present state of our knowledge.[1]

It seems to be certain that Yasodharman's empire did not last for long. In the middle of the century two dynasties named Maukhari became prominent in what is now the United Provinces, and claimed dominion as far as the Bay of Bengal; and a little later we meet a line of kings whose names end in -*vardhana*, ruling in Thānesar, and extending their power towards the north-west. The relation of this line to that of Yasodharman is at present unknown, and, speaking generally, the sixth century is still a dark period in history; but it is certain that the Vardhana dynasty of

[1] A recently published inscription (*Epigraphia Indica*, January 1929, pp. 37 ff.) has been read as proving that Bālāditya was in fact a vassal of Yasodharman, but the interpretation is still a matter of controversy. A somewhat different account of the events of this period will be found in Mr. K. P. Jayaswal's *Imperial History of India* (Lahore, 1934), pp. 35 ff.

Thānesar developed into the empire of Kanauj, which forms the subject of the next chapter.

The Turks did not at once follow the White Huns into India ; they began to arrive about five centuries later, and during this interval the country, so far as is known, was not invaded in force by nomads from the north-west. When at last the Turks came, they did not find Sakas, or Kushāns, or White Huns, recognisable as such ; they found only Hindus, and the question inevitably arises, What had happened to the descendants of the earlier conquerors ? At present this question can be answered only in general terms. Absorption is much more probable than extermination, and, having regard to the system of caste, it is more probable that the invaders, in the course of their assimilation to Hinduism, became new castes, or new sections of existing castes, than that they were absorbed piecemeal by irregular unions of individuals. It is distinctly probable then that the foreign tribes became Hindu castes : but many difficulties arise when we ask the further question, Which of the existing castes represent these foreign tribes ?

The most plausible case is that of the Gūjars. In Sanskrit literature and inscriptions we meet a tribe named Gurjara associated with the White Huns in such a way as to suggest that, if they were not themselves Huns, they were foreigners who entered India about the same time ; and later on we find various Gurjara kingdoms in the north and west of India. Now the everyday form of the name Gurjara is Gūjar, and country formerly held by some of these kingdoms still bears the name of Gujarāt, which is found in the Punjab as well as in Bombay ; while at the present day the Gūjar caste is represented in both regions. Gūjars are quite obviously Indians, and some of them are Hindus, while others have been converted to Islam, but they have some characteristics of their own, which distinguish them from the mass of Hindu peasants. It is thus tempting to infer that we have here a caste which originated about the fifth century as an invading tribe, enjoyed for a time the position

FATE OF THE NOMAD INVADERS

of a ruling race, lost its pre-eminence, and eventually settled down as one caste among many ; but the base of this inferential structure is still uncertain, because the foreign origin of the Gurjaras has not been definitely proved.

Other conjectural identifications are more uncertain, and, in particular, it may be mentioned that the theory of the existence of a strong Saka element among the Marāthas, which was suggested on anthropometrical data in the *Imperial Gazetteer of India*, has not won general acceptance, the facts being considered explicable on other lines. The most interesting problem of the kind is concerned with the great Rājput or Chhattrī caste. The former name etymologically denotes royalty, while the latter is the everyday form of Kshatriya, the royal and warrior class of the early days ; all Rājputs claim to derive directly from Kshatriya stock, and those of any position cherish detailed pedigrees which go back to one or other of the mythical ancestors of the race, whether sun, or moon, or fire. Outside the Rājput circle, however, it is now widely, though not universally, held that the modern caste is composite, and that some of its most important subdivisions represent certain tribes or families, some Indian and some foreign, which at one time or another attained the status of royalty, were thereupon accepted as Rājputs, and were furnished in due course with fictitious pedigrees by obsequious bards. From the nature of the case, no precise record of such a process is likely to have been made, and the inference that it operated has been drawn from the accumulation of a large number of details regarding one subdivision or another of the caste, evidence which cannot be examined adequately in a book like this, and the strength of which may be variously estimated by different students. One point, however, which has emerged in the course of this study may be mentioned here. For the period before the sixth century Rājput traditions are vague and scanty, while from the seventh century onwards they become more precise and detailed ; there are thus reasonable grounds for inferring that the invasion of the White Huns, of which we know so few details, left a definite mark on northern India, obliterating much of the older tradition, and forming the starting-point of the later cycle, which has been so well preserved.

We must now turn to southern India, and see what had been happening there during the three centuries which in the North are covered by the Guptas, the White Huns, and their successors. Our knowledge is still scanty and fragmentary, and all that can be done is to sketch the general situation. In the first place, it must be borne in mind that in the interior of the peninsula there were various independent tribes, one or another of which might for a time rise to political importance as an enemy, or an ally, of one of the larger kingdoms; these tribes have to be considered by the historian of the South, but in a general account of India they must be passed over. Neglecting the tribes, we have in the south of the peninsula the Tamil kingdoms, occasionally fighting among themselves, but retaining their identity and position during the three centuries under review. North of the Tamils, the eastern portion of the peninsula was held by the Pallava dynasty. The fact that its capital was Conjeeveram, which lies inside the traditional Tamil country, indicates that the Chola kingdom had been pressed back in this direction, and we get occasional glimpses of fighting between Cholas and Pallavas. Of the Kalinga country, to the north of the Pallavas, we hear practically nothing.

There remains the north-western portion of the peninsula, where, as we have seen, the Sakas had for some time secured a footing after the withdrawal of the Andhras. Here also our knowledge is fragmentary. We have glimpses of a tribe of Abhīras ('cowherds') ruling near Bombay in the fourth century, and of other tribes in other localities; the most important of these seem to have been the Rāshtrakūtas, who come into prominence in a later period, but in the fourth and fifth centuries they are still shadowy figures. It is only in the middle of the sixth century that we reach firm ground, in the emergence in this region of the Chalukya dynasty, which was destined to become a great power in the centre of India.

The traditions of this Rājput tribe derive their origin from Ajodhya, far away in the north, but we first meet them on the uplands of the peninsula approximately in the latitude of Goa, conquering the Rāshtrakūtas and various other tribes in all directions. Their greatest ruler was Pulakesin II, who came to the throne in 608, and whose dominions extended right across India, from the coastal strip known as the Konkan on the west to the mouth of the Godāvarī on the east, while his armies were known as far north as Mālwa and as far south as the Tamil country. As we shall see in the next chapter, it was the existence of this great power which prevented Harsha, the Emperor of Kanauj, from extending his dominions into southern India.

It is possible then to form a general view of the political situation in the South : of religious and social conditions we know scarcely anything, but we can infer from the records of the next period that during these centuries Hinduism was steadily advancing by absorption of the indigenous gods, while Buddhists and Jains maintained their position in some regions. We can infer also that Conjeeveram, under its Pallava rulers, continued to be a centre of Hinduism, and it is known from inscriptions that an institution for the study of Vedic and Sanskrit literature existed there in the fourth century. Some scholars attribute the extension of Hinduism among the Tamils largely to the fact that, somewhere about the year 400, this city was held for a time by the Cholas, so that its culture could more easily spread southward ; it is doubtful, however, whether political frontiers offered a serious obstacle to that process, and, in the absence of precise evidence, we must be content with the fact of the spread of Hinduism, without assigning definite dates to the stages by which it spread.

CHAPTER XVI

HARSHA OF KANAUJ

IN the present state of our knowledge, the story of the empire of Kanauj stands out as an episode, which lasted for less than half a century and ended in confusion. Our information regarding it is drawn mainly from two sources, one the work of an Indian poet, the other of a Chinese pilgrim. The *Harshacharita* of the poet Bāna purports to relate the life of Harsha, the Emperor. It has sometimes been described as an historical romance, and it undoubtedly contains a romantic element, while its laudatory tenor, together with its abrupt termination, forbids its acceptance as a complete biography; but there is a solid basis of fact, verifiable from other sources, which can be extracted from the extravagant eulogies and artificial rhetoric of the poet. Hard facts are more in evidence in the narrative of the pilgrim known as Yuan Chwang or Hiuen Tsang, who travelled in India from 630 to 644, visiting the Buddhist holy places, and collecting manuscripts; but, like his predecessor Fa-hien, his interests were confined almost entirely to his faith, and he left out many of the things we most wish to know, while the lack of precision in his topography renders it at times difficult to say exactly to what part of India his statements should be applied. When, however, these exceptional sources are employed along with the data furnished by coins and inscriptions, they make it possible to form a general idea of the life of northern India in the first half of the seventh century.

The empire arose out of the relations between three regions, Thānesar, Kanauj, and Mālava. As we have said

THE VARDHANA DYNASTY

in the last chapter, Thānesar was the centre of an expanding kingdom, which comprised, at any rate, a substantial portion of the eastern Punjab. The city of Kanauj, the remains of which lie near the right bank of the Ganges, about 50 miles north-west of Cawnpore, was apparently a capital of the Maukhari dynasties, whose sway seems to have extended through Oudh and North Bihār as far as the west of Bengal. There is an extensive, but still inconclusive, literature regarding the situation of Mālava, and all that can be said is that it is not the same as the modern Mālwa, with its capital of Ujjain, but probably lay farther to the west, partly in Gujarāt and partly in Rājputāna. The boundaries separating these regions cannot be defined even approximately, but from the course of events we must infer that they were contiguous.

In the year 605 Prabhākara-vardhana, the King of Thānesar, died, leaving two sons and one daughter who come into the story. The elder son, Rājya-vardhana, succeeded to the throne, and just then news came that the daughter, Rājyasrī, a child of twelve or thirteen, was in serious trouble ; young as she was, she had been married to the ruler of Kanauj, but her husband had been attacked and killed by the King of Mālava, who was subjecting her to confinement and ill-treatment. Rājya, already a soldier of some experience, marched at once on Kanauj, and defeated the Mālava king, but was treacherously murdered at a conference. He was succeeded by his brother Harsha-vardhana, a lad of about sixteen, who in his turn marched promptly to rescue his sister, and punish the murderer. On the way he met his brother's army, returning with the spoils of victory, and learned that his sister had escaped from her captors and fled to the jungles beyond the Jumna. Harsha turned his march in that direction, found his sister in despair, and on the point of performing the rite of suttee, dissuaded her, and brought her back, to be his constant companion during his reign.

This task having been accomplished, the young King decided on the conquest of India, an enterprise in which he achieved considerable, but not complete, success. The details of his campaigns are quite uncertain, and we can merely indicate the results by defining the limits of his empire. Its northern boundary was the Himalayas, and on the north-west it reached to the line of the Beas and Sutlej, which perhaps represented the limit of his hereditary kingdom of Thānesar. To the south-west it extended to Gujarāt, while on the south it was bounded by the Narbada. It was at this point that Harsha received his most serious check, for he attempted to invade southern India, but was defeated by Pulakesin II, the Chalukya ruler, and apparently he did not renew the attempt. On the north-east he ruled as far as the Brahmaputra, while his neighbour in that direction, the King of Kāmrūp (Assam), was, at the least, a submissive ally; and further south the empire touched the Bay of Bengal.[1]

The desire of conquest seems eventually to have declined or been satiated, and in his later years Harsha devoted himself to the administration of his great empire, to the promotion of religion and philanthropy, to the patronage of literature, and, there is good reason to believe, to writing the plays and poems traditionally attributed to him. He died about the year 647, and his empire died with him, as will be related further on.

In accordance with the usual Indian practice, the empire consisted largely of subordinate kingdoms, the rulers of which on occasion attended in person at the Emperor's court; and its ultimate basis was a strong standing army. In one way Kanauj may be thought of as the capital, but Harsha made long and frequent progresses through his dominions, accompanied by the civil administration as well as by the army, and thus the actual capital was the place where he happened to be at the moment. We know the designations of a large number of the civil officials, but their powers and duties are for the most part a matter of guesswork, and all that can safely be said is that the

[1] There is some doubt as to the position of the kingdom of Gaur in Bengal. At the beginning of the century it had been ruled by a King named Sasānka, who was in alliance with Mālava against Kanauj, and was probably responsible for the death of Rājya. Some years later, either in the lifetime of Sasānka or after his death, Bengal lost its independence, but it is uncertain whether the suzerainty over this region passed to Harsha or to the King of Assam.

ADMINISTRATION

administration was elaborate and highly organised, but that it left the individual in greater freedom than was the case in China. The empire was not exempt from violent crime, and Yuan Chwang had a few unpleasant experiences, including an attack by river-pirates; but, judging from his narrative, the most dangerous part of India lay outside the empire, on the western side of the peninsula, where the jungles were in places 'infested by troops of murderous highwaymen,' or 'harried by banded robbers'; and his general conclusion was to the effect that the criminal class was small. Trials were conducted by ordeal, while punishments, if more severe than under the Guptas, were still light when measured by Chinese standards. According to the same standards, taxation was not heavy, and forced labour was sparingly employed. The land-revenue was said to be one-sixth of the produce, but we cannot be certain whether this statement represents the facts of the time, or the traditional figure which the pilgrim had heard in the course of his enquiries; the only other taxes which he mentions are the transit dues paid on merchandise, and these also he considered to be light.

Regarding social conditions, Yuan Chwang depicts the higher castes as leading a simple and frugal life, with great ceremonial cleanliness, while their chief extravagance was in the matter of jewellery. The disreputable classes, 'butchers, fishermen, public performers, executioners and scavengers,' were segregated, living outside the city, and avoiding contact with respectable people. The walls of the cities were of brick, but houses were still built mainly of wood or wattle, and either tiled or thatched. Of the lighter sides of life the pilgrim naturally tells little or nothing, but the imaginative literature of the period indicates, perhaps with some exaggeration, that the Court at least was gay and festive, or even on occasion what would now be called dissipated, and that in the north, as in the south, of India courtesans played a conspicuous part in the revels. In ordinary times, however, we get the impression of a cultured Court, with the ladies trained in singing, dancing and painting, and interested also in more serious matters.

The religion of the Court was comprehensive. The royal family were traditionally worshippers of Siva, but Harsha himself, while not discontinuing the patronage of Brāhmans, showed much devotion to Buddhism. At first he adhered to the Hīnayāna, or 'Lesser Vehicle,' but under Yuan Chwang's influence he accepted the doctrine of the Mahāyāna, and at a great assembly for religious discussion, which he held in Kanauj in the year 643, the pilgrim was allowed to have matters very much his own way. That the Emperor's views remained comprehensive, however, is shown by the fact that from this assembly he went to Allahabad for a quinquennial gathering at which, in accordance with custom, he distributed his accumulated wealth among Buddhists, Brāhmans, Jains, and various other sects, as well as the poor in general. The ceremony is described by the pilgrim in picturesque terms; everything was given away, except the necessaries for the army, and at last the Emperor, having parted with his clothes, ' begged from his sister an ordinary second-hand garment, and having put it on, paid worship'; but the account adds that the treasury was again filled within ten days of its depletion.

The Court, then, patronised all religions, though with a definite preference, at this period, for the Mahāyāna form of Buddhism. As for the religion of the people, the pilgrim's notes of his experiences make it possible to say that Hinduism predominated throughout India as a whole; that Buddhism was most prominent in the Punjab, Kanauj, Bihār, Bengal, Mahārāshtra and Gujarāt; and that signs of its decline were most obvious in the Punjab, Rājputāna, Allahabad, and Mālwa in the North, and in the Pallava and Tamil country in the South, the general result being one of decreasing vigour. Relations between the competing religions or sects were ordinarily harmonious, but there were important exceptions. Controversy sometimes ran high between the two Buddhist schools, as well as among the various sects into which the 'lesser' school was divided; Brāhmans objected strongly to the favour shown by the Emperor to Buddhism; and the proceedings of the Kanauj assembly were marred by incidents of a more serious nature.

Some followers of the 'lesser' school conspired to murder Yuan Chwang, the champion of Mahāyāna; certain Brāhmans hired an assassin to murder the Emperor; and it is clear that religious animosities ran high on the occasion.

Of actual persecution there are two well-authenticated instances at about this period, both of them outside the limits of Harsha's empire. Sasānka, the King of Gaur, or Western Bengal, a zealous worshipper of Siva, attempted to extirpate Buddhism from his dominions, desecrated the holy places, broke up the monasteries, and drove the monks into exile. Later in the century the Jains in the far south were persecuted by a Pāndya king who had been converted from that faith to the worship of Siva, and who, according to the traditional account, which, however, is not universally accepted, impaled some thousands of martyrs on their refusal to apostatise. Other incidents of the kind may possibly have escaped record, but it is quite safe to infer from Yuan Chwang's narrative that persecution was not a general practice in his time; the instances which have survived must be taken merely as showing that extremes of bigotry were not unknown in the seventh century of our era.

The available authorities leave the impression that about this period there was a widening gap between popular and learned Buddhism. The popular worship was approximating to the lower forms of Hinduism and developing in the direction of a magical cult, relying largely on spells and charms; but some of the monasteries were centres of serious and profound studies, and must have exercised a definite influence on the general culture of the country. The most important centre was Nālandā, a group of monasteries situated some distance south of Patna. Here some thousands of monks studied and discussed doctrine and philosophy; and foreign students were welcomed, provided they could pass the severe preliminary test, which was apparently of the nature of an entrance examination. The institution was not limited to a single school or sect; and its studies comprised, in addition to the Buddhist texts, the old Vedic literature, and the sciences and arts represented in Sanskrit works on logic, grammar, medicine, and the like. Such institutions must have operated in the direction of unifying the higher learning of the country as a whole, and at the same time widening the gap between learned men and the cults followed by the masses of the people.

Before taking leave of Harsha's empire, a word of caution is perhaps desirable on one point. Stress has been laid on the culture which prevailed at his Court, as at the Court of the Guptas two centuries or so before; but this does not imply that the position was exceptional. We know but little of the facts, but all that we know indicates that patronage of art and literature was a normal feature of Hindu Courts, and was recognised as a duty comprised in the ideal of kingship. It follows necessarily from the nature of the records we possess of the Hindu period taken as a whole that conquest and dominion stand out as the most prominent elements in the kingly ideal, more prominent even than the primary duty of protecting the subjects enjoined by the Sacred Law; but they leave room for various other elements, such as the promotion of learning, art and letters, and we know at least that many kings, though probably not all, were in fact liberal patrons. The difference between them and a Harsha or a Chandragupta was one of magnitude rather than of kind; and perhaps we may describe the ideal king as a patient and laborious administrator, an expert and chivalrous soldier, sincere in his religion, but tolerant of other creeds, a sportsman, and a cultured gentleman according to the standards of the times.

In northern India the kings to whom this description applies were ordinarily Rājputs, but royalty was by no means confined to a single caste. From time to time we meet with Brāhman dynasties, founded in some instances by usurping ministers of state; Harsha himself belonged to the Vaishya caste, the third of the traditional groups; and kings of the fourth group, Sūdra, were not unknown. Rājputs frequently, though not invariably, ruled in the more northerly parts of the peninsula, but the Tamil kings belonged to the principal land-tilling caste of that part of India; and, speaking generally, kingship was not a monopoly of Rājputs, while the kingly ideal was recognised by rulers of all castes alike.

Of the end of Harsha's reign we know few details. The Emperor died in 646 or 647, leaving no heir. One of his ministers usurped the throne, and—for whatever reason—attacked a Chinese diplomatic mission which had just arrived. The leader of the mission escaped to Tibet, at the time a powerful kingdom, obtained troops there, invaded Bihār, defeated the usurper, and carried him away to China as a prisoner. In these conditions the empire inevitably dissolved, and it is a curious fact that for a short period the northern portion of Bihār remained subject to the king of Tibet.

CHAPTER XVII

FROM HARSHA TO MAHMŪD

IN a book of this scope it is impossible to tell all that is known of the political history of India during the three centuries and a half which elapsed between the death of Harsha and the first recorded inroads of the Turks, for the mass of detail is very great, and there is no single thread on which all the facts can be strung. In northern India the story is one of several dynasties striving for paramountcy but failing to attain it; the situation is not materially different in the South; and all that we can attempt is to give a brief account of the protagonists in the struggles, and of the more important incidents which have come to light.

First, however, a few words must be said regarding the Indus plain. In the course of his travels Yuan Chwang found an extensive kingdom under a Sūdra ruler in Sind and Baluchistan, but he did not record, and probably did not know, that it was already threatened by the Arabs. The extraordinary outburst of energy which followed on the preaching of Muhammad (569-632) is part of the history of the world; and it was only a trifling fraction of his victorious nation which about 650 established itself in Baluchistan, and sixty years later conquered the remainder of the kingdom from a Brāhman dynasty which had meanwhile replaced the Sūdra rulers. From 712 onwards, Sind, along with the adjoining portions of the Punjab, continued under Moslem rule, at first as a province under the Caliph (more accurately, *Khalīfa*) of Baghdad, and later as two principalities, acknowledging the Caliph's supremacy but in fact independent. The impetus towards further expansion in this direction

THE STRUGGLE FOR EMPIRE

seems, however, to have died away, and, while the Arabs played a minor part in the struggle for the North, the influence of Islam did not extend materially from this nucleus ; its effective introduction in India was to be the work of the Turks, not the Arabs.

Leaving Sind out of account, the struggle for northern India was conducted by four protagonists—Kashmīr, the Pāla dynasty of Bengal, the Gūjars of Rājputāna, and the Rāshtrakūtas from the South ; and it may be said that the earlier part of the eighth century belonged mainly to the first of these. As has been mentioned in an earlier chapter, Kashmīr is the one part of India for which we possess a chronicle going back beyond the Moslem conquests, and its contents are generally accepted as more or less historical from about the time of Harsha onwards. Strictly speaking, the name denotes the upper valley of the Jhelum river, a tract secluded among lofty mountains, but in the seventh century the King of Kashmīr had acquired a substantial portion of the Punjab plains, and in the eighth a definite bid was made for the paramountcy of northern India. It is worthy of note that at this time Kashmīr had more intimate political relations with China than with India. The struggles which were taking place in Central Asia lie outside the scope of this book, and we must content ourselves with saying that about this time the power of the Chinese Empire extended over the countries to the north of India, as far as, and sometimes beyond, the Oxus, and it is recorded that in 720, and again in 733, successive kings of Kashmīr acknowledged the overlordship of China by accepting investiture from the Emperor. This situation, however, did not last for long ; the limits of the Chinese Empire contracted, and Kashmīr again became politically part of India. About the year 740 we find Kashmīr obtaining a decisive victory over Kanauj, which had just successfully invaded Bengal, and somewhat later there is a more dubious story of its penetration further eastwards ; but after this we hear nothing of its achievements in the plains, and the interest of the story passes to Bengal.

There is general agreement among historians that in the

first half of the eighth century the internal condition of Bengal and Bihār was anarchic, and that the country suffered from repeated invasions until the emergence of the great Pāla dynasty, named from -*pāla* (protector), which formed the latter portion of the titles of successive rulers. The date and origin of the dynasty are still uncertain, but there are good grounds for holding that Gopāla, the first of the line, was reigning in, or just after, the middle of the eighth century. It is on record that he was chosen to be king : we do not know for certain who chose him, but the probable view is that the choice was made by the Chiefs of the small principalities into which the country was divided. His ancestry too is uncertain, but there are grounds for inferring that he was neither Brāhman nor Kshatriya, though his descendants intermarried with families of the latter caste. The dynasty which he founded was destined to rule for four centuries, constituting the traditional golden age of Bengal; and its rulers were usually men of culture, patrons of art and literature, and, above all, zealous Buddhists. Their part in the struggle for northern India was, however, played only for a short time at the beginning of the ninth century.

Dharmapāla, the second of the line, having consolidated his position in the east, turned his eyes westward, conquered Kanauj and placed his nominee on the throne. His further progress was then stayed by the Gūjars of Rājputāna and the Rāshtrakūtas, or in everyday speech, the Rāthors, from the South ; the details of the events which followed are uncertain, but after a few years Kanauj came definitely into the possession of the Gūjars. There are some indications that the struggle was continued for a time by Devapāla, the successor of Dharmapāla, but from about 830 onwards Kanauj under its Gūjar rulers became the most prominent power in the North, and the rule of the Pālas was confined to the eastern side of India.

We first meet the Gūjars ruling in the south of Rājputāna, and we do not know the circumstances in which they entered the Gangetic plain, but it appears that after capturing Kanauj they made it their capital, and two successive kings, Mihira Bhoja and Mahendrapāla I, who between them ruled

THE PĀLAS AND THE GŪJARS

from about 840 to 910, were paramount in northern India, excluding Sind on the west, and the territory retained by the Pālas on the east. Of the history of their reigns we know only that fighting on the frontiers was common; nothing has yet been found to throw light on their personal characteristics, or on the nature of their administration. In the tenth century the power of the Gūjars waned. In 916 Kanauj was captured by the Rāthors, who, however, were prevented from retaining it by dynastic troubles, and the Gūjars maintained themselves for some time longer, though with decreased prestige and diminished authority over their vassal kings. By about 950 their paramountcy had finally passed away, and when the Turks appeared in India towards the end of the century they found the North divided among a number of independent kingdoms. Such in barest outline is the story of three of the protagonists in the struggle; the fourth, the Rāthors, belong rather to the South, to which we now turn.

We have seen in Chapter XV that at the beginning of the seventh century the leading powers in the peninsula were the Chalukyas in the north, the Pallavas on the east, and the three Tamil kingdoms in the south. After a few years the Chalukyas split into two branches. The eastern branch, located near the mouth of the Godāvarī river, persisted into the eleventh century, but did not play a prominent part in the struggles which ensued : the western spent a century and a half mainly in fighting with the Pallavas, who during this period were on the whole the strongest of the southern powers; but about 750 the Chalukya dynasty was overthrown by a chief of the Rāthor clan.

The Rāthors were not new-comers, for they had been powerful in this region before the rise of the Chalukyas. They maintained themselves for more than two centuries, during which they, like their precedessors, were frequently at war with the Pallavas, but their ambition seems to have been directed mainly to the North. A branch of the dynasty established itself in Gujarāt, Mālwa was occupied, the Pālas of Bengal and the Gūjars of Rājputāna were confronted, and on one occasion Kanauj itself was taken, as has been recorded above. The Rāthors seem to have regarded the Gūjars as their special enemies, and in accordance with the usual diplomatic practice they sought the friendship of the Arabs in Sind, who also were at enmity with the Gūjars; Arab merchants were consequently welcomed in the Rāthor country, and in this way it happens that, when Chinese pilgrims had ceased to visit India, we begin to obtain a few glimpses of the country in the literature of Arabia. Not unnaturally, the merchants and travellers whose narratives we possess were enthusiastic admirers of the friendly Rāthor kings, whom they describe under the dynastic name of Balharā; and the merchant Sulaiman, who wrote in the middle of the ninth century, regarded 'the Balharā' as the fourth power in the world, inferior only to Baghdad, China and Constantinople. In the tenth century decline set in, and in 973 the north-west of the peninsula passed to a new Chalukya dynasty.

As has just been said, the Pallavas were in the seventh century the most prominent power in the South, but their strength then declined, perhaps as the result of frequent fighting with the Chalukyas and Rāthors on one side, and with the Tamils on the other, and about the year 900 their kingdom fell finally to the Cholas.

Of the three Tamil kingdoms, the Keralas on the south-west maintained their independence until nearly the end of the tenth century, when they too were conquered by the Cholas. The Pāndyas in the far south were strong from the seventh to the ninth century, when the Cholas were in eclipse; but our knowledge of them is practically confined to their recurring wars with the Pallavas and the Keralas, as well as with Ceylon. The outstanding feature of the period in this region is the recovery of the Cholas from the middle of the ninth century onwards. For a long time they had been almost negligible, pressed between the Pallavas and the Pāndyas; then we find them defeating both powers, and, after an interval of dynastic troubles, a great conqueror, Rājarāja, emerged, who subdued in succession the Keralas, the Pāndyas, the Eastern Chalukyas, the tribes in the interior of the peninsula, Kalinga on the east coast, and finally Ceylon. The eleventh century thus opened with one great power paramount over almost the entire peninsula, a situation which, so far as we know at present, had never previously existed.

It will be obvious from this summary account that, when the tenth century was drawing to its close, India was not in a favourable position to resist invasion from the north-west. The Cholas in the South, the one great power in the country, were far removed from the point of danger, and there are at present no signs that they were interested in the politics of the North. Thirteen centuries before, Chandragupta Maurya, from his capital in Bihār, had successfully confronted the attempted invasion of Seleucus I : now there was no emperor of northern India, but a number of independent kingdoms, at variance among themselves, and unfamiliar with the difficult art of uniting their forces against a common enemy. The gates of India lay open.

It would be unjust to close this chapter without a word of tribute to the scholars whose labours have made its compilation possible. Not many years ago, the period following the reign of Harsha was almost entirely dark ; the reconstruction of its political history has been effected mainly by the decipherment and interpretation of inscriptions, the accumulation of which has gradually furnished lists of the various dynasties with dates, either actual or approximate, and information regarding some at least of the decisive factors in the struggles between them. The work is by no means simple, for inscriptions do not always bear their meaning on their face, and the tentative interpretations offered by the first decipherers have in many cases had to be revised ; Indian scholars are now devoting themselves particularly to this task of critical revision in the light of later discoveries, and while finality has not yet been attained, the claim can fairly be made that the main course of events in each important portion of the country has been established on firm foundations. The scope of this book necessarily excludes most of the new facts which have thus been brought to light ; and it is all the more incumbent on us to recognise the value of the work which has been done.

E

CHAPTER XVIII

INDIA IN THE TENTH CENTURY

In the last chapter we have reviewed the political situation in India up to the end of the tenth century : the more difficult task remains of presenting a general view of the life of the country as a whole, and estimating its progress up to the point of its first effective contact with the religion and culture of Islam. The impression left by the extant literature which can be attributed to the period beginning with the decline of the Gupta empire is that during the intervening centuries the genius of India had been regulative rather than creative. We do not meet with many new ideas : what we find is increasing precision of statement, classification, subdivision, and refinement of the ideas already current, along with detailed rules for action in almost every conceivable situation. There is no room for doubt as to the general tendency ; but the question remains how far the numerous codes and manuals of practice reflect actual life, and how far they consist of theories elaborated in the study by men who were not necessarily in close contact with affairs. The literary material has thus to be checked, wherever possible, by such other sources of information as may be available.

The sphere of politics was dominated by the figure of the king : the kingless tribes in the hills and forests did not play an important part in the life of the country. Kingship was certainly hereditary, and ordinarily the eldest son succeeded, but it would be going too far to say that primogeniture was a universally accepted rule. We hear of kings nominating their successors, and incidents in the literature suggest that an heir apparent who was a minor, or was

THE HINDU CONSTITUTION

unsuitable for other reasons, might be set aside in the interests of the kingdom, or possibly to make way for a stronger competitor; and the most probable view is that an invariable rule of succession had not emerged.

The ideal of an empire embracing many kingdoms, and covering, perhaps, the whole of India, was well established, and, while it had never been completely realised, it probably lay at the root of most of the political history of the period. Apart from this conception, no machinery for securing peace had been evolved, and it would be hard to produce any evidence that peace between kingdoms was an ideal of the time. According to the texts, a king was normally at enmity with his immediate neighbours, and it was his duty to find allies on their further frontiers. There was thus ample scope for the art of diplomacy, which, again according to the texts, was practised without any regard to ordinary rules of morality; but in this case we have scarcely any materials by which theory can be checked.

As regards the art of war, we are fortunately in possession of accounts of battles with the Arabs in the eighth, and with the Turks in the eleventh, century, which tell us how Indians in the North actually fought. The traditional array of battle consisted of an open line of elephants covering the infantry, mostly bowmen, in the centre, with cavalry, covered by war chariots, on both flanks. It was just such a line as this which confronted the Arabs and the Turks, except that we do not read of chariots being employed, and this arm, a heritage from the Aryan invaders, had apparently become obsolete. The elephants were the distinctive feature of Indian warfare; they must be thought of as movable strong-points, giving stability to the line so long as they stood fast, and furnishing vantage-ground for the discharge of arrows and other missiles. Their stability, however, had a limit, and when some of them turned and bolted, the breach in the line, and the confusion caused to the infantry behind, gave the opposing cavalry their chance; to stampede the enemy's elephants was consequently one of the main objects of a commander right up to the time when the development of artillery rendered their employment impossible. In battle there was an element of single combat, in the sense that when the king, who usually commanded in person, fell, or became invisible, his army ordinarily fled. Thus the fight for Sind in 712 was decided by the fall of Dāhir, the king of the country; while an important victory gained by Mahmūd in 1008 was due to the flight of the elephant on which his opponent was mounted. To kill, or put to flight, the opposing king was thus the primary object in each battle.

Hindu kings usually, though not, it seems, invariably, maintained standing armies, trained and paid in time of peace; in war these forces were supplemented by contingents recruited from the wilder tribes, and possibly also by levies from the subjects of the kingdom. It is probable that in the Rājput kingdoms the standing troops consisted largely of men of the royal tribe, bound to their king by permanent ties of loyalty; but in some states mercenary troops were employed, and the fact that almost from the outset the Turkish invaders had Indians in their armies suggests that among certain classes fighting was a regular trade, as it continued to be throughout the Moslem period.

Turning to the civil side of the kingdom, there was no legislation in the modern sense of the term; the 'codes of law' which we possess were elaborated by text-writers, not by Kings, Ministers, or Assemblies, and differ essentially in their nature from the codes of modern times. The writers clearly had a twofold object, to codify existing practices, and at the same time fit them into the framework of royal and priestly authority; their views were obviously conditioned by their environment, so that on occasion they differed among themselves; the extent to which the 'codes' were accepted varied from place to place, particularly in regard to private rights and duties; and, while it is reasonable to infer that their influence increased as time went on, it is not possible to fix a period at which they became formally authoritative, or to say how far their provisions might prevail against the will of an autocrat.

In India, both North and South, there was elaborate machinery for securing the execution of the King's com-

ADMINISTRATION

mands, with Ministers at the capital in touch with the villages through the officers in charge of districts and subdivisions. For the Tamil country in the South, there is ample evidence to prove the existence of village assemblies consisting of the male residents, which conducted the business of the village through committees, managing the agricultural land, the sources of irrigation, the local roadways and such matters, and also directing police-work and disposing of criminal cases, though the severer punishments were apparently inflicted by order of the King. The inscriptions suggest that there was ordinarily harmonious and effective co-operation between the royal officers and these village-assemblies, and their perusal leaves the impression that the villagers could transact their own business without much interference from above.[1]

We have no clear evidence that similar institutions existed in northern India. We know only that there the royal officers dealt with the villages through representatives, who are conveniently described as headmen; we do not know how these headmen were appointed in early times; and we can only guess that then, as in later periods, they were chosen by the brotherhood of resident peasants, with a tendency for the position to become hereditary in practice. Nor have we any precise knowledge of the powers exercised by the headmen in the transaction of local business or in dealing with crime; the most probable view is that the brotherhood and the headmen, between them, had a free hand, so long as their actions did not conflict with the royal policy, but as yet there is not sufficient evidence to establish this view as a fact.

In regard to religion, it is safe to say that, while India contained Animists, Christians and Moslems, Jews and Parsees, Jains and Buddhists, by the end of the tenth century the country, both North and South, was predominantly devoted to Hinduism in one or other of its forms. The wilder tribes were doubtless Animists, as some of them still are, but, as we have said already, they counted for little in the life of the country. The Christian community was small, and localised near the south-west coast. The Moslem

[1] See Note on p. 131.

power was confined to Sind, while the small numbers of Moslem merchants in the seaports were as yet unimportant from the cultural aspect. The Parsees, whose arrival will be recounted in the next chapter, were localised on the west coast, and were a people apart ; and the same description may be applied to the Jews, who for some centuries had been established in Malabar. The Jains persisted in some localities, mainly in the centre of the country; the Buddhists were by this time almost confined to the Pāla territories in Bengal and Bihār.

The view which will be found in some older books that Buddhism was extirpated from India by ruthless persecution is not borne out by evidence. Our knowledge is still very imperfect, but all that is known points to the conclusion that, while the idea of persecution in one region or another cannot be entirely ruled out, the main forces at work were assimilation and absorption. To explain the operation of these, we must look back. In the beginning, Buddhism had offered a path to salvation independent of gods and priests alike ; in the course of the centuries it became transformed, and offered a personal god, with an extensive celestial hierarchy, and with worship conducted by priests or monks. Meanwhile Hinduism had, as we have seen, developed in the direction of one supreme god (not always the same) ; and it may fairly be said that the ordinary man, in search of salvation, was now offered a choice between the cults of Buddha, Siva and Vishnu, differing mainly in matters of ritual. Assimilation had, however, gone still further. The Buddha was commonly represented in sculpture as accompanied or attended by some of the gods of Hinduism, so that in the eyes of ordinary laymen the hierarchy and the pantheon must have become very much alike ; while Hindus recognised the Buddha as an incarnation of Vishnu, that is to say, as on the same footing as Rāma or Krishna.

In this position, with three cults similar in essence, and each of them offering a measure of satisfaction to the religious needs of the individual, it may reasonably be inferred that the expansion of one or the other depended largely on secondary causes such as fashion or patronage. In earlier

THE DECLINE OF BUDDHISM 123

times Buddhism had enjoyed the patronage of many powerful rulers both in the North and in the South ; and we know that under Harsha Buddhist monks in great numbers had flocked to Kanauj. After Harsha, we hear of no powerful patrons except the Pāla dynasty ; and the probabilities are that the monks, the preachers of Buddhism, gradually concentrated in Bengal and Bihār, where they were assured of favour and support, leaving the rest of the country to the competing cults, which could rely on the patronage of the Rājput kings.

Account must be taken also of the tendency, which is apparent in the literature of the period, to strengthen the institution of kingship by invoking divine authority in its support. Kings were presented as great gods in human form ; their pedigrees were carried back to the pantheon ; and their Brāhman ministers, too, were exhibited as divine in their origin and in their powers. Such theories fit much more easily into Hinduism than into Buddhism, and it was natural for rulers and ministers, intent on the aggrandisement of their authority, to accord their patronage to the former rather than to the latter.

Another cause of the decline of Buddhism which is suggested in the literature of the period is the moral deterioration of the monastic system. From the earliest times there had been Buddhist nuns as well as monks ; it was easy for a woman to cast off her family obligations and enter on a freer life ; and the resulting threat to the integrity of the social system must have told strongly against the creed by which it was rendered possible.

The prevalent conditions then were such as to promote Hinduism at the expense of Buddhism among ordinary people. At the two ends of the scale the position was somewhat different. The lower forms of popular religion were mainly matters of spells and charms, in which the differences between one cult and another could count for little ; success would depend rather on the astuteness of the priesthood. The highest intellects, on the other hand, were busy in regions where differences of cult were almost immaterial, in arguing out with extraordinary subtlety the world-problems of the fundamental nature of matter and of personality. Some of them, however, were alive to the daily needs of the people whose nature they discussed ; and in particular the great philosopher Sankara, known as Āchārya, or 'the Master,' who in the ninth century was the protagonist of the strict theory of monism, expounded also the practical side of life on the definite lines of Hinduism, and became the founder of a Hindu sect. It is perhaps fair to say that the influence of intellect was on the side of Hinduism, even when it was employed in the most abstruse metaphysical speculation.

We may conclude then that by the end of the tenth century Hinduism held the field, except in Bengal and Bihār, and that it had attained to the conception of a single personal God, in direct relation with individual men. The nature of this relation, as it was understood by some of the best thinkers of the time, is embodied in the doctrine of *bhakti*, which can be interpreted precisely in the terms Grace and Love, as used in the theology of the West. The first recorded apostle of this doctrine was Rāmānuja, who belongs to the twelfth century ; he lived in the Tamil country, and some scholars, who have regarded him as the originator of the doctrine, have inferred that he learned it from the Christian community in the south-west. The central idea is, however, much older, for it occurs in the portion of the *Mahābhārata* known as the *Bhagavadgītā*, which, whatever its actual date may be, was certainly in existence in the Gupta period ; and its rudiments have been traced back in Indian literature which is earlier than the Christian era, by some scholars even in the Rigveda. There is no evidence that Rāmānuja was ever in personal contact with Christians ; it is quite possible that he may have been, and that intercourse with them may have influenced the development of his thought, but the root-idea must be accepted as having an independent origin in India. The spread of the developed doctrine will occupy our attention in later chapters ; here we must be content to quote a summary of it as it was preached by Rāmānuja himself. ' There is first the belief in a Primal Being who is indeed infinite, but infinite in qualities of goodness : secondly, the doctrine that in his love

THE DOCTRINE OF BHAKTI

for his creatures the Supreme becomes incarnate in divers blessed forms to save men from sin and sorrow, and lead them to union with him ; and, thirdly, the teaching that the Supreme may be reached by any suppliant, whatever his birth or rank, who worships him in perfect self-forgetting love.'[1] That is in essence a gospel of Love and Grace : God's love for man, manifested in His grace, and man's love for God, manifested in his devotion.

Rāmānuja found his Primal Being in Vishnu, but substantially the same ideas had by this time gathered round Siva, whose worshippers regarded the individual soul as bound by the triple fetters of ignorance, *māyā*, or illusion, and its accumulated *karma*. 'But God in His grace wills that it shall be redeemed and shall dwell in blessedness for ever with Him in a union not of unity but of perfect association ; and therefore the soul must be born in man, in order that through human experience salvation may come. Then, when merits have balanced demerits, the defilements of *māyā* and *karma*, which have attached themselves to it in its human incarnation, are taken away by the divine Grace, and the soul is gathered into the bosom of the infinite Love.' It was along lines such as these that Hindu religious thought had been travelling in the period which we are reviewing.

It must not, however, be inferred that this doctrine of *bhakti*, or salvation through Grace and Love, was held universally and consciously by Hindus in the tenth century. It had been attained, but, so far as we know, had not yet been preached widely or effectively ; and probably the older idea of the efficacy of sacrifice still predominated among the masses, degenerating at the lowest end of the scale into reliance solely on the magical power of the priest, but with an increasing demand for something better—a demand which was to be met by the preachers of *bhakti* in the centuries that lay ahead.

In the region of culture, the tendency we have mentioned towards regulation rather than creation is obvious in the

[1] The quotations are from Dr. L. D. Barnett's *The Heart of India* (London, 1913), pp. 42, 80.

literature of the period. Good literature continued to be produced in Sanskrit after the age of the Guptas, but the bulk of what has survived is characterised increasingly by artificiality and convention, by strict adherence to form, and by extraordinary verbal ingenuity. In addition, a popular literature was coming into existence, expressed in the developing vernacular languages, but too little of it is extant to justify a pronouncement on its quality. As regards painting also, the paucity of surviving specimens prevents any precise statement, but it is reasonable to infer that its development was parallel to that of sculpture, where a definite change can be observed. The difference may be stated in phrases borrowed from Sir John Marshall.[1] The purpose of the earlier art, ' free alike from artificiality and idealism, was to glorify religion by telling the story of Buddhism and Jainism in the simplest and most expressive language which the chisel of the sculptor could command ' : after the age of the Guptas, the artists, now employed in the service of Hinduism, sought rather ' to embody spiritual ideas in terms of form.' The aesthetic value of this change is a matter of controversy, for while some critics regard it as an advance to a higher plane of art, others see only a sacrifice of truth, and a submission to convention of an ever-increasing rigidity: to decide between these conflicting views is no part of our purpose.

In regard to architecture, there is happily no similar controversy. Surviving examples are still limited to religious edifices, but, whatever may have been the case in other departments of activity, there is no doubt that it was a great age of temple-building. Some western critics indeed object to the quantity and elaboration of ornament, which tends to obscure the fundamental qualities of the edifice, but all of them recognise that the union of strength and grace displayed in the best examples is unsurpassed. These examples are spread over a wide area, beyond the range of Moslem iconoclasm. In the far north, the temple of Martand

[1] *Camb. Hist.*, i. 644. The difference can be readily observed in the British Museum by comparing the Amarāvatī figures (second and third centuries) exhibited on the main staircase, with those in the two rooms devoted respectively to Indian Religion and to Buddhism.

ART AND ARCHITECTURE

stands as a memorial to the rulers of Kashmīr in the eighth century; while the Chandel dynasty, which ruled in Bundelkhand in the tenth and eleventh centuries, is commemorated by the group of temples at Khajurāho. In the peninsula, the Kailas temple at Ellora is a monument of Rāthor rule; the Pallavas are recalled by the temple at Conjeeveram, and the great days of the Cholas by that at Tanjore. When allowance is made for the destruction wrought by time and by man, it must be recognised that during these centuries Hinduism commanded the best that India could give, not only in money, but in taste and skill.

Our knowledge of the social life of the period is necessarily imperfect. We can, however, safely accept the current view that it was characterised by increasing rigidity of the framework furnished by the system of caste, a necessary result of the decline of Buddhism, which ignored caste differences, and the extension of Hinduism, to which they belonged. But the process was not yet complete. The best available picture of the life of the time is to be found in a collection of tales [1] known as *The Ocean of Story*, which was compiled in Kashmīr in the eleventh century, and the glimpses afforded by incidents in these tales suggest that, while the rules of caste may have been hardening, they were not so rigid as in later centuries. There is no hint of the endogamous subdivisions of caste which are now familiar; men could on occasion take a wife from a lower caste; among Brāhmans at least, a wide latitude was allowed in the choice of occupation; and merchants made sea-voyages in a way that would have been unthinkable a hundred years ago.

As regards the position of women, nothing like the rigid seclusion of later times can be traced in these stories, but ladies of the upper classes led a sheltered life, and the idea of actual seclusion must have been known, because a character in one of the stories condemned it as a useless custom. Polygamy was recognised, but instances of it appear usually among royal families, and the difficulty of supporting many wives is suggested as a reason why ordinary men were content

[1] The Sanskrit name is *Kathāsaritsāgara*. A translation by C. H. Tawney, edited by N. M. Penzer, was printed in London, 1924-28.

with one. Child-marriages were known, and were occasionally advocated, but judging from the stories, were not the usual practice of the time. The rite of suttee was practised, but it was not obligatory, and the remarriage of widows is implicitly recognised as permissible. Music and dancing were popular recreations among ladies, there were picture-galleries in the royal palaces, and the general impression is of a diversified and cultured life. It may be added that courtesans play a prominent part in *The Ocean of Story* as in so much of the literature of the country.

In the matter of diet, the stories suggest that, while northern India was mainly vegetarian, more meat, though of course not beef, was eaten then than now. A more striking difference is in the matter of intoxicating drink; drunkenness was by no means uncommon, and we read of drinking-bouts being enjoyed by princesses. The familiar practice of chewing the betel leaf by way of stimulant was well established, but, on the other hand, there is no hint of indulgence in opium or hemp-drugs, and the question when these forms of intoxicants obtained their vogue is one of the numerous unsolved problems of the social history of India. Nor is there any mention of the practice of smoking, and in the present state of our knowledge we must infer that the great social importance of the habit has grown up since the introduction of the tobacco plant in the sixteenth century.

Of the economic basis of this social life as yet we know very little. It is clear that the great bulk of the income of the country was provided by peasants working on the land and raising most of the crops which are now familiar, rice, wheat and barley, millets and pulses, oilseeds and sugar-cane, for food, and fibres and dyes for use in industry; but the extant literature does not enable us to say whether the peasants were worse or better off than at the present day. We know that drought was their great enemy, for famine, in the literal sense, was a stock topic for story-tellers, while in the North as in the South the provision of means for irrigating the land was regarded as a meritorious act. We can say in general terms that the position of the peasants must have depended largely on the share of their produce which was taken as revenue by the king, but we do not know how much was usually taken. The traditional claim was, as we have seen, one-sixth, but the texts allow of a higher proportion in emergencies ; and there is good evidence to show that the practice of levying cesses in addition to the share was already well established. Inscriptions recovered in South India show that on occasion the share actually taken was much above the traditional figure, but as yet there are not sufficient data for confident generalisation, while for the North there is even less evidence. The most probable inference from the recorded experience of the first Moslem conquerors is that in the North the king's claim was usually either one-third or one-half the produce ; but all that can safely be said is that it would be dangerous to assume that the traditional figure represents the facts of the period.

Another question which must be asked, but cannot yet be completely answered, is the extent to which peasants were dependent on the markets : did they deliver the king's share in kind, or had they to sell produce in order to pay the treasury in cash ? We know that coined money had been current in India for many centuries, but we do not know how far its use had spread from the towns to the villages. Inscriptions show that in the South payments of revenue were frequently made partly in kind and partly in cash, so much rice and so much gold, so that the cash-nexus between the town and country had already come into existence in that region, though it was not yet universal. In the North also there are clear indications in the inscriptions that some payments, though certainly not all, were made in money, but many of the technical terms used in these sources are hard to interpret, and the data are not yet sufficient for any general statement. The most probable view is that at this period cash-transactions were increasing slowly throughout India as a whole, and that their prevalence varied widely in different parts of the country, but that in the more highly developed regions the peasants had to sell a substantial portion of their produce in order to pay the revenue due from them, so that conditions were already operating to produce that great bane of peasant countries, the ' harvest glut.'

when everybody has to sell at the same time, and harvest prices are consequently depressed.

Of the condition of rural labour we know nothing: the literature of the period shows the existence of slavery, but it was purely domestic, an incident of urban rather than rural life, and there are no grounds for inferring that the village labourers were technically slaves. Inscriptions establish the fact that the authorities could on occasion exact compulsory labour from the villages. The extent of this burden is quite uncertain, but there are some indications in the literature that it was most severe in the Himalayan region, where goods have often to be carried by men instead of pack animals. Of industry, too, we know scarcely anything: the production of cotton goods and other articles was widespread and diversified, but the literature throws no light on the economic position of the craftsmen who produced them. Merchants travelled freely over the country, but the volume of their transactions and their methods of business are matters for conjecture; we know only that there was an elaborate system of transit dues and other taxes on commerce. The subject of foreign trade will be noticed in the next chapter.

Lastly, a few words must be said on the practice of making pilgrimages to the holy places, a practice which, though primarily religious, has had important influences also on social and economic life. We do not hear of pilgrimage in the earliest period of Hinduism, and apparently the practice was originated by Buddhists and Jains, who gathered at the places sacred to the memory of the founders of their faiths; but, whatever its origin, there is no doubt that by this period it was well established among Hindus. There are allusions to places of pilgrimage in the works of Kālidāsa, the great poet of the Gupta age, while in *The Ocean of Story* the practice is quite familiar, and we read of gatherings at some of the centres which pilgrims still throng to-day. In estimating the life of the tenth century, therefore, we must take account of the fact that Hindus from distant places were meeting at such centres, each at its appropriate season, and, whether at their destination or along the roads leading to it, were forming acquaintances, exchanging news and views, listening to preachers, bards or story-tellers, and thus acquiring a wider outlook than if they had stayed at home. For the Indian pilgrim is seldom wholly absorbed in the ceremonies which are his primary object : the event is a holiday in his life, and while the ceremonies are scrupulously performed, there is usually plenty of time for conversation, shopping, sightseeing, and all the various interests which combine to make travel an important element in education. We must, in fact, regard pilgrimage as one of the great factors making for the unification of Hinduism.

NOTE
Village Government in South India

The account of government by assemblies and committees on p. 121 gives the view which used to be generally accepted. Dr. A. Appadorai has recently argued (*Economic Conditions in Southern India* (Madras, 1936), pp. 135 ff.) that this elaborate system of government was not general, but was confined to a relatively small number of villages held in a special form of tenure, and that the great bulk of the southern villages were governed less elaborately on the lines which prevailed in the North. A larger number of relevant inscriptions must be found and studied before the question can be fully determined.

MAP IV

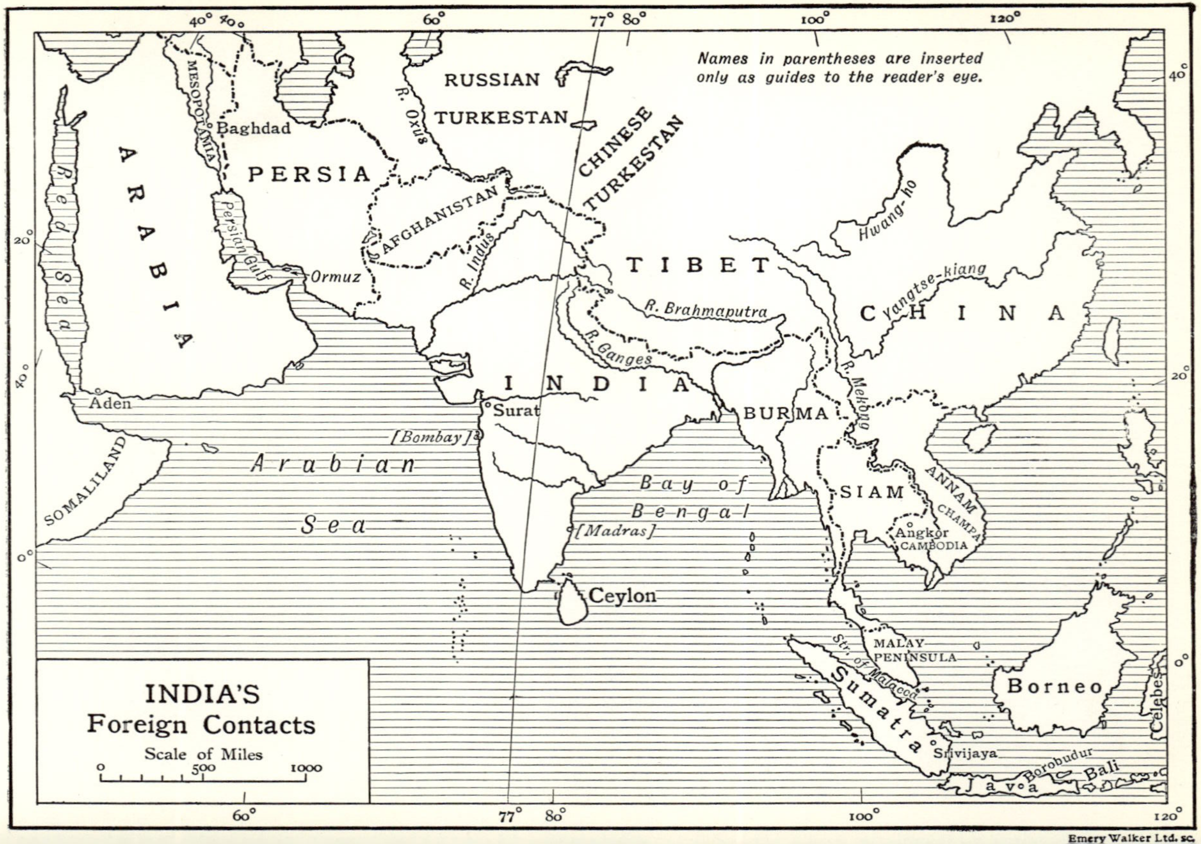
INDIA'S
Foreign Contacts
Scale of Miles
0 500 1000
Names in parentheses are inserted only as guides to the reader's eye.
RUSSIAN TURKESTAN
CHINESE TURKESTAN
PERSIA
AFGHANISTAN
ARABIA
MESOPOTAMIA
Baghdad
Persian Gulf
Ormuz
Red Sea
Aden
SOMALILAND
Arabian Sea
R. Oxus
R. Indus
TIBET
R. Brahmaputra
R. Ganges
INDIA
Surat
[Bombay]
[Madras]
Ceylon
Bay of Bengal
BURMA
CHINA
Hwang-ho
Yangtse-kiang
R. Mekong
SIAM
ANNAM
CHAMPA
Angkor
CAMBODIA
MALAY PENINSULA
Str. of Malacca
Sumatra
Srivijaya
Borneo
Celebes
Java
Borobudur
Bali
40° 40° 60° 77° 80° 100° 120°
20° 40° 0°
Emery Walker Ltd. sc.

CHAPTER XIX

FOREIGN CONTACTS

WE have now to sketch the position of India in relation to other countries towards the end of the tenth century; but the area to be covered is wide, the usual uncertainty as to dates prevents precise chronological treatment, and in order to give an intelligible account we shall have to look back, and occasionally forward, for considerable periods. As a first approach to the subject, we may divide Asia by a line drawn north and south through Delhi, or, say, the 77th meridian. To the west of this line commerce on the whole counted for more than culture; to the east we are concerned mainly with the spread of Indian religion over almost the whole of eastern Asia, and of Indian civilisation, including religion, over the region, insular as well as continental, lying to the south of China.

On the northern land frontier such a line marks very roughly the meeting-place of Chinese and Islamic culture at this period. We have seen in an earlier chapter that at one time the Chinese power had extended into the basin of the Oxus, but since then Islam had gained ground, for Persia had been conquered by the Arabs in the seventh century, and their faith had now extended north and east into the countries which we call Afghanistan and Russian Turkistan. We possess no knowledge of the relations of India with the latter country in the period preceding the first incursions of the Turks into the Punjab; but in regard to the former we must distinguish, for the eastern portion was ruled by a Hindu dynasty until nearly the close of the tenth century, and it may reasonably be inferred that Indian influences predominated in this region as far as the frontiers held by Arabs on the west and by Turks on the north.

At present we have no evidence to show to what extent Indian influences crossed these frontiers, but further south there had been active intercourse with Baghdad during the period when Sind was subordinate to the Caliphs. Under Mansūr (753–774) and Hārūn (786–808), Indian works in astronomy, medicine and philosophy had been translated into Arabic with the aid of Sanskrit scholars, some of them summoned for the purpose, and formed an important contribution to the new body of learning which was growing up in Baghdad; but after a short time the Arabs turned their eyes definitely to the West, and the earlier Indian current gave way to that which flowed from Greek sources.

The sea routes from India to the Persian Gulf and the Red Sea remained open; we have no precise knowledge of the trade carried by them at this period, but we know that it was by them that Parsee and Arab settlers reached the west coast of India. The former were Persians who adhered to the old national religion of Zoroastrianism, or 'fire-worship' in the popular phrase, and in the course of the eighth century left their homes, and sought a refuge from Islam in India; they were allowed to settle on the coast between Bombay and Surat, and there they established themselves, following their own religion, and leading a peaceful and industrious life. Their prominence in commerce, finance and industry dates only from the rise of the city and seaport of Bombay in modern times.

In order to account for the Arab settlements on the west coast, we must glance at the chief trade-route of the Asiatic seas, that which connects the ports of China with the Red Sea and the Persian Gulf. This route falls naturally into three sections, from China to the narrow waters between Sumatra and the Malay Peninsula, from Sumatra to the south-west coast of India, and from India to the western termini. The complete voyage is very long and dangerous for sailing vessels, dependent, as they are, on the seasonal winds; if owing to any accidental delay a ship 'loses her season,' as the phrase goes, she can only wait till the next season comes round, and may perhaps have become unseaworthy by the time it arrives. There were thus sound commercial reasons for the change in practice which is known to have occurred on this route; the through voyages were gradually discontinued, and goods changed hands at entrepôts in the Straits, or on the Indian coast, or both. Through voyages were certainly made between the fifth and the seventh centuries, when Chinese junks were familiar objects in the Persian Gulf, and also, it seems, at Aden, while about the year 650 the Arabs had commercial agencies on the coast of China; but later on we find the junks terminating their voyage on the Indian coast, where their goods were sold to Arabs for transport farther west. From somewhere about 900 then, and perhaps earlier, Arab merchants were settling on the Indian coast in order to pursue this trade, buying and selling with the junks, and also dealing in pepper and other local products. Their objects were purely commercial; there was no idea of conquest, and apparently there was little or no religious propaganda; but the settlers, who adhered to their own faith, took wives in the country, and they are represented at the present day by the race known as Moplahs, who still live in the region where their ancestors once traded.

The scope of the Arab traders in Africa is uncertain. In earlier days, we do not meet them farther south than Somaliland; but somewhere about this time they were extending their settlements towards Zanzibar and Mozambique, and it is possible that the direct trade between India and East Africa, which later on became of great importance, may already have begun. Traces of Indian culture have been found on the island of Madagascar, but their date is uncertain; by some students they are believed to be due to contact with Java rather than the mainland, but precise knowledge is wanting. South Africa was, so far as we know, entirely outside the Indian circle until the arrival of the Portuguese five centuries later.

Crossing the Indian Ocean, and passing by Ceylon, which was for the time incorporated in the Chola empire, we come to the islands which are now known as the Dutch East Indies. Here we find Indian culture established over a wide region, but the history of its extension cannot yet be written. Indian literature furnishes barely a hint that the process was at work; only a little more has been gleaned from Chinese sources; and the story is being slowly reconstructed mainly by the labours of Dutch scholars who in recent times have been active in archaeological research. We know that both Buddhism and Hinduism were well established, and that Indian cultural influences were prominent up to the fifteenth century, when Islam reached the islands; but we do not yet know when the extension began, or where it originated. Definite evidence of its existence has been found on the north-eastern side of Sumatra, in Java and some smaller islands further east, on the coast of Borneo, and quite recently in Celebes; but the possibility of a still wider extension cannot be ruled out, and it is perhaps significant that the earliest survivals which can be approximately dated occur on the eastern side of the region just described. Sanskrit inscriptions show that somewhere about the year 400 Hindu, or Hinduised, kings were ruling on the east coast of Borneo, and that sacrifices were offered there by Brāhman priests; but we have as yet no knowledge how the kingdom was founded, from what part of India the Brāhmans had come, or by what route they had travelled, while the later history of this kingdom is unknown. Similarly, we know that, about the same period or a little later, Hindu ideas were familiar in western Java, and that in the seventh century Srīvijaya, near the modern Palembang at the eastern end of Sumatra, was a great centre of Indian Buddhism, where the Chinese pilgrim I-tsing was able to learn Sanskrit; but the origins of these influences are still matters for speculation.

Towards the end of the eighth century a maritime power known as the Sailendra empire emerged in these regions and, with occasional vicissitudes, dominated the narrow waters till about 1250. The history of this power is in process of reconstruction. Until quite recently it was believed to be an expansion of Srīvijaya in Sumatra, but the more probable view [1] is that it arose on the coast of the Malay Peninsula, and thence extended its sway over the islands to the south. The origin of the dynasty is still unknown, but its inspiration was certainly Indian, and it patronised the Mahāyānist form of Buddhism. That it maintained relations with the motherland appears from inscriptions which have been discovered in India, showing that an early Sailendra ruler founded a monastery at Nālandā in Bihār, and that a later one did the same thing in the Chola country in the South. It is to this dynasty that the world owes the greatest surviving monument of Indian Buddhism, the shrine at Borobudur in central Java; but Buddhism was not the only religion in that part of the island, for remains of Hindu temples have been found in the vicinity.

In the eleventh century we meet with new kingdoms in eastern Java, and find evidence of a further cultural development. The survivals in central Java and Sumatra are still definitely Indian in character, though they comprise indigenous elements, but in eastern Java the two streams coalesce, and the result is no longer Indian, but a distinctive culture in which much that is Indian has been assimilated. The religion of Islam spread over the archipelago in the course of the fifteenth century, but not in its most aggressive form, and survivals of the earlier Indian culture can be traced in Java and Sumatra; while in the smaller island of Bali, lying east of Java, where Islam did not establish itself, the national religion is still definitely Indian in its character.

Passing from the islands to the mainland, we find a position similar in essence to that which has just been described. There is no doubt that for ten centuries or more Indian religion and culture were prominent features in the life of the countries which are now known as Burma, Siam, Cambodia, Annam, and the Malay Peninsula; but the story of the extension is being gradually put together by the

[1] See the articles by Dr. R. C. Majumdar, Dr. G. Cœdès, and other writers in the *Journal of the Greater India Society* for 1934 and 1935.

labours of archaeologists, and cannot yet be recounted as a whole. The earliest survival so far recovered in this region is a Sanskrit inscription, assigned to the third, or possibly the second, century, which establishes the existence of a Hinduised kingdom on the coast of southern Annam, in the region formerly known as Champa. Later inscriptions show that Champa continued as a powerful kingdom for many centuries, but its history is still in process of reconstruction by French archaeologists; the Chams of to-day are mostly Moslems, and have lost nearly all the old Indian tradition, but a few of them are still worshippers of Siva.

Chinese annals tell us that about the same period there was an extensive Hinduised kingdom lying south and west of Champa and covering part of what is now Cambodia; and they attribute its origin to the first century, when a Brāhman conquered the country and married the reigning Queen. Later there are hints of fresh emigration from India to this region, and a great mass of inscriptions, some of them in Sanskrit, combine with other records to furnish the history during several centuries of the Khmer empire, a powerful state essentially Indian in constitution and in culture, whose principal monuments are the famous temples at Angkor in the heart of Cambodia.

In Siam archaeological research has been pursued actively in recent years, but much ground remains unexplored. The present kingdom is known to have been built up out of several states, each with its own Hindu culture, but the origins of these are unknown, and their history is not yet written. Substantially the same may be said of Burma, where research has made less progress: we know that Indian culture prevailed, and we know little more. In the Malay Peninsula there are traces of Hindu influences as far back as the second century of our era, and later on we come to the Sailendra empire which has already been mentioned, so that it is possible to say that about the tenth century Indian ideas prevailed over the whole of south-eastern Asia.

Later on they were to be overlaid by cultures of different

types. Islam spread up the Malay Peninsula, and also in Champa, while the southward migrations of various races brought Burma, Siam, Annam and Cambodia definitely within the Chinese sphere. Taking a wide view, then, we may say that in the tenth century Indian culture was in contact with Islam on the west and north-west, and with China on the north-east, while to the east and south-east it had no definite limits. The changes which occurred during the next five centuries resulted in its enclosure between Islam and China, which met first in Turkistan, and again at the head of the Malay Peninsula ; but just when the ring seemed to be complete, the arrival of the Portuguese round the Cape of Good Hope opened a way for new contacts of a very different nature—contacts which were ultimately to determine the position of India as it stands to-day.

We know of intercourse between India and China by two routes, both of them long, difficult and dangerous. The sea route has already been described : the land route ran from the western provinces of China through Turkistan to the basin of the Oxus, and thence southward over the Hindu Kush to the Kābul valley and Peshāwar. On the map this is a very roundabout journey. Its explanation lies in the fact that from about the Christian era onwards successive Chinese dynasties attached very great importance to the east-and-west route by which silk goods could be carried to the markets of the Roman Empire ; for long periods the road was policed right up to the Oxus basin, and thus offered a comparatively safe journey to the point where a traveller to India had to turn south over the passes of the Hindu Kush. Modern explorations along this route [1] have shown that Chinese Turkistan was the meeting-place of Indian and Chinese culture, and there is no doubt that regular communication went on as late as the ninth century, after which the importance of this road declined.

At present there is no evidence that any substantial

---

[1] A fascinating description of this portion of the route will be found in Sir Aurel Stein's *On Ancient Central-Asian Tracks* (London, 1933).

volume of trade passed between India and China by this route. Its importance for our present purpose lies rather in the fact that somewhere about the Christian era it carried the first news of Buddhism to China; and later on, when that faith had become established in the Far East, it was followed by many of the Chinese pilgrims who came to India, some by land and others by sea, to visit the holy places and obtain authentic versions of the scriptures. From China Buddhism spread to Korea, and thence to Japan, so that the seed first carried from India across the deserts of Central Asia nearly twenty centuries ago has borne a marvellous crop. In Tibet also the establishment of Buddhism was the result of Indian influences, but it was independent of the main movement across Central Asia, and cannot safely be dated earlier than the seventh century. Later on, intercourse became active with northern India, particularly with the Pāla kingdom, and the extant Tibetan versions of lost Sanskrit texts testify to the intimate cultural relations which were established between the two countries.

If we have so far said very little of the commercial relations of India with the countries farther east, the reason is that for the period we are considering there are no facts on record. One inference, however, is so nearly certain that it may be mentioned here. We first get precise knowledge of the commerce of this region early in the sixteenth century, and we find that at that time the whole commercial situation was dominated by the trade in cotton clothing made in India. In Indo-China and in the islands practically everybody who wore clothes at all obtained them from India; the trade was highly organised, and along the east coast of India, as well as in Gujarāt, large numbers of weavers, dyers and cloth-printers were kept busily employed in producing the goods required by the varying tastes of the consuming markets. In regions like the Moluccas, where as yet money was scarcely current, Indian clothes of definite types formed the usual medium of exchange; and merchants who desired to buy cloves or nutmegs, gums, resins, and other produce, began their operations by obtaining a stock of clothing from India. Obviously such a system was of long and gradual growth, and we may reasonably infer that its origins go back to the distant period when Indian merchants first carried their civilisation across the seas, and that it was already established, if not fully developed, by the tenth century.

MAP V

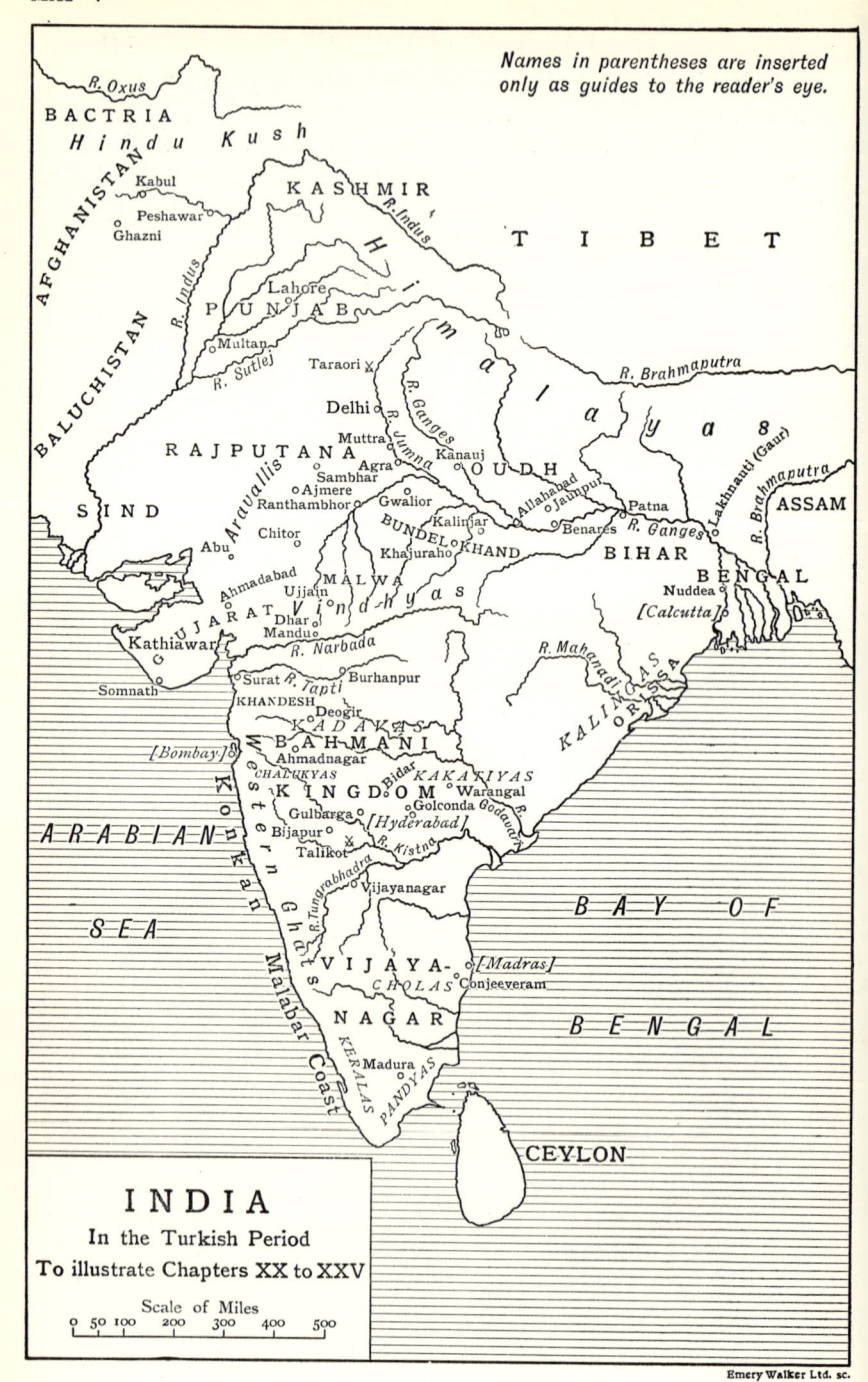

INDIA
In the Turkish Period
To illustrate Chapters XX to XXV

Scale of Miles
0 50 100   200   300   400   500

Names in parentheses are inserted only as guides to the reader's eye.

Emery Walker Ltd. sc.

CHAPTER XX

THE ADVENT OF THE TURKS

WE are now approaching the period of Moslem political predominance, and may begin with a very short summary of the events which lie before us. During the eleventh and twelfth centuries the north-west of India was governed for the most part by Turks from their capital in Afghanistan. In the thirteenth a Turkish kingdom established in Delhi became paramount over the best part of northern India, and in the fourteenth its power extended also over a large portion of the South. The fifteenth century was a period of conflict, out of which a new kingdom of Delhi emerged under an Afghan dynasty. In the sixteenth the North fell to Mogul invaders, and in the seventeenth the Mogul empire extended over almost the whole of India. Its collapse was followed by another century of conflict, which ended in the political supremacy of the East India Company.

We have seen in an earlier chapter that the Turks had followed the Huns in the westward movement of the nomads; they established themselves as a great power in the region of the Oxus, and eventually broke up into various independent states. The branch which brought Islam effectively to India was originally a small principality founded in 933 at Ghaznī, a fortress lying about eighty miles south of Kābul. Its territory adjoined that of the Hindu Sāhi dynasty, which then ruled part of Afghanistan as well as a large portion of the Punjab, and the first recorded clash between the neighbours occurred in 973, when Jaipāl, the Sāhi king, unsuccessfully invaded Ghaznī. Four years later, a great conqueror, Sabuktigīn, succeeded to Ghaznī, and by a series of victories towards the north and west enlarged his principality until it became a formidable power. Incidentally he carried on hostilities with Jaipāl, and established his frontier on the Indus, but he did not attempt the conquest of any part of India. On his death in 997 he was succeeded by his son Mahmūd, with whom the story of Islam in India really begins.

The Turks who came to India as conquerors must not be thought of as savages, though they could behave savagely on occasion. Along with the creed, they had accepted the culture of Islam, as it came to them by way of Persia. The royal courts were elaborate and well ordered; there was an organised administration, conducted in the Persian language; the rulers were often discriminating patrons of literature, great builders, and cultivated men. One feature of the new culture calls for special mention: the Turks, who were already familiar with the use of paper, brought to India the practice of writing chronicles, based on the Islamic calendar, and henceforward the chronology of India becomes precise, so far as the facts recorded in the chronicles are concerned.

Islam, like Hinduism, is a complete rule of life, and, again like Hinduism, it has its Sacred Law, which in theory is binding on rulers as well as subjects. The primary source of Islamic law is the Koran, which records the revelations given to Muhammad, but these are supplemented by his traditional sayings, and the somewhat fragmentary materials have been worked up by a succession of jurists into a consistent whole. The creed is pure monotheism: any subdivision of the omnipotent power is the worst form of heresy; and any visible representation of the deity is a heinous sin. Moslem theologians did not shrink from the logical implications of omnipotence: according to them, each individual has his allotted destiny, at which it is impious to repine; and in India as elsewhere this doctrine has operated to give fortitude in adversity, but not to restrict the initiative of a conqueror.

In its origin, the Islamic polity was based on equality. All Moslems were brothers, banded together under the rule

THE ISLAMIC POLITY

of the Caliph against the rest of the world; and, while they were subject to certain restrictions, notably the prohibition of intoxicating liquor, their social life was in general free. They were, however, bound to follow the Caliph when he summoned them to a religious war, and, after victory, each soldier was entitled to an equal share of the spoil. For the vanquished the choice lay between Islam and either death or slavery. Acceptance of the former alternative involved merely the repetition of a short formula, followed by the rite of circumcision: if it was refused, the adult males were put to death, and the women and children treated as booty.

By the time of Mahmūd this original polity had undergone important modifications. The temporal power of the Caliph had waned, and numerous sovereign states had emerged: jurists regarded Moslem kings as deputies of the Caliph, and it was usual for a king to solicit his formal recognition, but for practical purposes the kings had become independent. In these circumstances it was inevitable that individual rulers should think more of the safety of the kingdom than of meticulous compliance with the Islamic constitution, and the practice arose of distinguishing between public and private law; in the latter sphere the rules laid down by Moslem jurists were duly enforced, but in matters of state some kings claimed, and exercised, entire freedom of action. In face of this position, the jurists hesitated. They maintained the validity of the Islamic constitution, but they did not proclaim the deposition of a king who violated it; they relegated his punishment to the next world, and, as we shall see in later chapters, some of the greatest of Moslem kings in India were prepared to take that risk.

Another modification of great importance for India was in the treatment of the vanquished. Originally the only exception to the stern rule of Islam or death was in the case of 'the people of the Book'—that is to say, Jews and Christians, who acknowledged the authority of the Old Testament: these classes could enjoy freedom and protection under Moslem rule if they accepted the position and paid a special tax, known as the *jizya*. This exception was extended in the course of the first conquest of Sind, when the victor granted to Hindus the position legally confined to Jews and Christians; and by the end of the eighth century the jurists had agreed that a conqueror might allow the conquered population to remain undisturbed subject to the payment of *jizya*, and of revenue (*kharāj*) representing a share of the annual produce of the cultivated land.

In this way the conquest of India was enormously facilitated. In the original polity, conquest would have involved the extirpation of Hinduism from the conquered territory, and the distribution of the land among the conquerors. In actual fact, a conquest involved no very great disturbance to the general population: the peasant sowed and reaped as before, but paid his revenue to a Moslem instead of to a Hindu ruler. An even simpler arrangement was often adopted, for when a Hindu ruler submitted, and agreed to pay tribute representing the revenue due from his dominions, he was allowed to retain his position and authority, so that to some extent the earlier Moslem kingdoms took substantially the form of a Hindu empire—a number of vassal states acknowledging the supremacy of an overlord.

From the administrative standpoint then the adjustments following on a conquest were comparatively easy; but in social and religious matters the initial clash must have been terrible. To a sincere Moslem of those days, every Hindu temple, every wayside shrine, was an utter abomination, to be desecrated as effectively as time might permit; and Hindus, when unable to resist, could only watch the desecration. Again, the invading armies consisted almost entirely of cavalry, and, at the pace at which they moved, they must have lived on the resources of the country. Food and forage were indispensable, and, seeing that the Turks were great eaters of meat, we must infer that to the loss and distress occasioned by forced requisitions or indiscriminate looting was added the horror of wholesale slaughter of cattle for food. We possess no formal record of these happenings, but we must recognise that they were inevitable in the circumstances, and that they must have left a legacy of bitterness to tax the statesmanship of the future.

From these general observations we return to Mahmūd, the conqueror. A precise estimate of his character is scarcely possible, for he quickly became the subject of conflicting traditions, and, in the absence of impartial records, he may be regarded as a great militant apostle, as a monster of cruelty and avarice, or, more probably, as something between the two. Throughout his reign he was concerned primarily with the maintenance and extension of his empire in Persia and Turkistan, but between 1000 and 1026 he invaded India as often as the military situation elsewhere permitted, and in the result he conquered and annexed the Punjab, while his raids extended beyond Kanauj to the east, and as far south as the coast of Kathiāwar.

Mahmūd's Indian province extended from the Indus nearly to the Jumna, but not as far as Delhi, and from the Himalayas down to beyond the point where the five rivers of the Punjab finally unite. It comprised, firstly, the territories of the Hindu Sāhis, which were finally annexed in 1021, and, secondly, the Moslem state of Multān, extending some way into Sind. Lower Sind was conquered, but not annexed, and local dynasties continued to rule in that region for some centuries, while the province was ordinarily administered by a viceroy with his capital at Lahore.

A little must be said of Mahmūd's two principal raids into India. In 1018 he started from Ghaznī with an army of more than 100,000 horse, crossed the Punjab, and, avoiding Delhi, marched down the Jumna, seized Muttra, where the temples were plundered and desecrated, and then turned east to Kanauj, which submitted. Beyond this point his course is uncertain. According to some authorities he advanced as far east as Jaunpur, but the more probable view is that the territories of Kanauj marked the limit of the raid, and that he now returned, still conquering as he marched, until he reached Ghaznī with enormous booty, including so many prisoners that Indian slaves became common throughout Persia and Turkistan. During this raid we hear of the rite of *jauhar* : the garrison of one fortress, finding further resistance hopeless and scorning to surrender, killed their wives and children, and then rushed out of the fortress to fight to the death. We read of the same thing frequently in later chronicles ; the origin of the rite is unknown, but its traditional object was to preserve the honour of the women, and doubtless it had already been practised in the days of the Huns and other invaders from the north. The sources on which we are dependent for the history of India treat warfare as such a commonplace matter that it requires incidents like this to bring home to modern readers the grim tragedies which then as always it brought in its train.

Six years later occurred the raid to Somnāth, where, on the coast of the Kathiāwar peninsula, there was one of the richest temples in India. Mahmūd marched southwards into Gujarāt, defeating all who opposed him, sacked Somnāth, desecrated the temple, and broke the great image into fragments. The effect of this raid is shown in the various legends which grew up round it, and we may be confident that in far distant parts of India the name of Islam was associated primarily with this spectacular act of iconoclasm.

Mahmūd died in 1030, and his successors quickly lost most of his great empire, but for more than a century the dynasty retained Ghaznī and the Indian province ; in 1158, however, Ghaznī was lost, and the latest rulers of the line possessed nothing outside India. We know but little regarding the relations between Hindus and Moslems during this period. Towards the south the Ghaznavid boundary was extended into Rājputāna, but on the east it remained practically fixed, with occasional losses and gains of frontier fortresses. In 1033 the holy city of Benares was raided ; we hear of another raid in that region about 1100, and it is possible that similar expeditions may have been made from time to time ; but all that can be said is that the rest of India must have been acutely conscious of the political and religious danger in the north-west. Meanwhile, predominance in Afghanistan had passed to another Turkish dynasty, that of Ghor, or Ghūr ; and in the last quarter of the twelfth century the Ghūrīs entered India, conquered the last of the Ghaznavids, and initiated a new phase of the expansion of Islam over northern India. Before relating their achievements, we must glance at the situation in the rest of the country.

In Chapter XVII we left the Cholas paramount throughout the greater part of the peninsula. They maintained their position more or less during the next two centuries, and for a time they extended their interests beyond the sea, for about the year 1025 they were fighting in Sumatra and the Malay Peninsula.[1] Their achievements in these regions were, however, not destined to be durable, while their hold over Ceylon was lost, and the story of southern India for these two centuries centres in their struggle with the later Chalukya dynasty, which had succeeded to the Rāthor dominions in the north-west of the peninsula. In the course of this struggle the Chalukyas on the whole gained ground, but its interest lies mainly in the rise of new powers within their territory. On the south the Hoysalas, originally a family of petty chiefs, became prominent as governors of the frontier, and gradually worked their way towards independent possession of the country which is now known as Mysore : on the north the Yādavas, and on the east the Kākatīyas, similarly rose to power, and when the Chalukya dynasty collapsed, the bulk of its territories was divided between these three houses. The Yādavas and Kākatīyas did not last for long, succumbing to the early Moslem conquerors, but a family of Hoysala nobles became the founders of the kingdom of Vijayanagar, which from the fourteenth to the sixteenth century was to stand out as the single great Hindu power remaining in the country.

In Bengal and Bihār the Pāla dynasty survived with

[1] Most scholars are now agreed that the story of a Chola conquest of Lower Burma has no historical foundation.

F

fluctuating fortunes during the eleventh century, but by the middle of the twelfth it had become unimportant, and the bulk of Bengal had passed to the Senas, who retained it until they were dispossessed by the Turks. About the same time most of Bihār had apparently fallen to the Gaharwārs of Benares, and thus the last stronghold of Buddhism in India came under the rule of orthodox Hindus. The Senas are known to have regularised the system of caste in their dominions, and, while there is nothing to suggest that they actively persecuted the Buddhists, we must attribute to this period the effective advance of Hinduism in this region.

To the west of Bihār, political instability continued to prevail in northern India. The country was divided among numerous Rājput dynasties, quickly waxing and waning, and the details of their vicissitudes have no important bearing on the main course of history; but a little must be said of four regions, Kanauj, Bundelkhand, Mālwa and Sambhar, by way of introduction to the Turkish conquest. We have seen that the power of the Gūjars in Kanauj had declined during the tenth century, and that in 1019 Kanauj itself submitted to Mahmūd. The later Gūjar rulers were unimportant, but about 1090 their territory seems to have come into the hands of the Gaharwārs, a Rājput dynasty which from its capital of Benares governed most of what is now the United Provinces, and, as we have just seen, extended its authority into Bihār. The kingdom was thus extensive, but few visible memorials of the period have survived, and the bulk of it fell to the Turks in 1193.

To the south-west of the Gaharwārs, the country beyond the Jumna, now known as Bundelkhand, was ruled by a dynasty of the Chandel tribe, which was powerful from the tenth till nearly the end of the twelfth century. The Chandels were great builders, and, apart from their temples at Khajurāho and elsewhere, they are commemorated by many of the artificial lakes and reservoirs which still play an important part in the agriculture of this region. The Chandels were heavily defeated by the Chauhāns in 1182, and the dynasty was finally broken in 1203, when the Turks entered their principal fortress of Kālinjar, plundered its wealth, enslaved its inhabitants, and converted the temples into mosques.

Further to the south-west we meet the Pawār dynasty, which flourished in Mālwa in the tenth and eleventh centuries, ruling not at the old capital, Ujjain, but at Dhār, about fifty miles farther south. The Pawārs, like the Chandels, are commemorated by artificial lakes : some of the kings were famed as authors as well as patrons ; and one of them, Rāja Bhoj (1018–1060), stands out in Hindu tradition as the model king. His long reign ended, however, in defeat at the hands of a confederation of enemies, and the dynasty shrank into insignificance.

Lastly we come to the Chauhān dynasty, which had ruled for a long time at Sambhar in Rājputāna, but is noteworthy only for one great name, that of Prithvīrāj, who stands out in Hindu tradition as the embodiment of chivalry, as Rāja Bhoj is the embodiment of kingship. Among ordinary people at the present day he is known mainly as a gallant and daring lover ; in prosaic history he appears rather as an able general in the field. He crushed the Chandels, as has just been said, and in 1191 he inflicted a severe defeat on the invading Turks ; but a year later he was outmanœuvred, defeated, and put to death after what must be reckoned as one of the decisive battles in the history of India.

These brief illustrations must suffice to give a general idea of life in northern India during the eleventh and twelfth centuries. We see dynasties emerging from obscurity, rising to prominence, and then decaying or collapsing under the pressure of their neighbours. What we do not see is any sustained and deliberate effort to present a united Hindu front against the danger impending from the northwest.

CHAPTER XXI

THE TURKS IN DELHI

The spectacular rise to empire of the Turkish house of Ghūr, which was originally subject to the Ghaznavids, can be appreciated from the following summary of their advance across India. In 1173 they obtained possession of Ghaznī; in 1175 they had Multān; and in 1186 Lahore fell to them, and the rule of the Ghaznavids was at an end. In 1191 the Ghūrīs sustained a defeat at Taraorī,[1] near the watershed between the plains of the Indus and the Ganges, but in the next year they won a decisive battle at the same place over their former opponents, Prithvīrāj and his allies, and in 1193 their headquarters were in Delhi. Meanwhile they were established beyond the Ganges as far as Oudh, and had raided into Bihār; in 1194 the Gaharwārs were crushed, and Benares was plundered; in 1202 the Senas of Bengal were driven into the extreme east of their country; and thus in less than thirty years the power of the Ghūrīs had extended eastward from Ghaznī practically to the Bay of Bengal. In other directions Sambhar in Rājputāna had been annexed, Gujarāt had been plundered, the fort of Gwalior had submitted, and the Chandels had lost Kālinjar, so that the greater part of northern India had come under Moslem domination.

The interests of Ghūr were not, however, confined to India, and a defeat sustained elsewhere by Muhammad,[2] the ruling king, resulted in rebellion in the Punjab.

[1] The name appears variously as Taraorī, Tiraurī, Talāwarī, and Tarain.
[2] His full name was Muizzuddīn Muhammad *bin* [i.e., son of] Sam: some writers call him Muhammad *bin* Sam, others prefer Muhammad Ghorī (or Ghūrī), and others again write of Muizzuddīn.

Muhammad marched to India in person, and crushed the rebels; but he was assassinated in March, 1206, on the banks of the Indus, and the power of Ghūr died with him. Effective rule passed to his viceroys, one of whom, Kutbuddīn Aibak, assumed the title of Sultan of Delhi; he was accepted as sovereign by the various Moslem governors from Bengal to Multān, and thus the kingdom of Delhi came into existence. Before recounting its history, we will attempt a sketch of its general organisation.

The king was an autocrat, except in so far as he chose to be guided by the public law of Islam. The business of the kingdom was organised in departments, dealing respectively with finance, the army, and so on; a minister was in charge of each department, that of revenue and finance being held by the Vazīr or Prime Minister. The power of the kingdom rested firstly on the royal army, and secondly on the provincial governors, each of whom had an army of his own. The royal army at first consisted almost entirely of cavalry, but elephants were soon added; no reliance was placed on infantry. During the thirteenth century the troopers were ordinarily paid on the assignment system, that is to say, they collected and retained the revenue due from the villages assigned to them for their support, and many of them lived in those villages, presenting themselves at the capital only when summoned; the delays in mobilisation resulting from this system proved to be a danger to the kingdom, and in the next century a large standing army was kept at the capital and paid in cash.

It is convenient to speak of the subdivisions of the kingdom as provinces, but the word must be understood with reference to the circumstances of the time, and we must think of a province, not as an area of uniform administration, but as a region with authority located at the centre and extending just as far as the conditions allowed. The governor lived in a fortress, from which the province usually took its name; his duties were to prevent rebellion and collect the revenue; and to enable him to perform them he was permitted to maintain an army of a specified size. His success depended primarily on his personal qualities:

rebellion was always to be expected in one direction or another, and its prompt suppression required a competent commander of a well-trained force, while the frequency of its occurrence depended on the relations which the governor was able to maintain with the prominent or influential inhabitants of his province. From the revenue which he collected the governor was allowed to retain specified sums for the payment of his troops or other expenses, and the surplus was remitted periodically to the capital. In practice, the amount of the surplus was frequently an agreed sum, so that in effect the governor was a farmer of the revenue.

It will be obvious that the stability of the kingdom depended on an adequate supply of strong and loyal governors, at a time when loyalty could not be assumed as a matter of course. A weak governor meant a rebellious province, as well as a loss of revenue: a strong and disloyal governor was a potential candidate for the throne. There were times when a king appointed to these posts merely the highest bidders, and administration became speculative farming pure and simple; but this did not continue for long, and as a rule the king chose his governors for their qualities rather than their offers. At the outset there was nothing that can be described as a free nobility from whom to choose, and in fact most of the early governors were, or had been, slaves of the king who appointed them.

In trying to understand the Turkish kingdom, care must be taken not to introduce the idea of degradation which the term 'slavery' now connotes. Slavery was a status, not a stigma. In the practice of the time, as opposed to the strict provisions of Islamic law, Moslems as well as unbelievers were held as slaves; a king's son, if captured in war, might be enslaved, though it might be safer to kill him; and a slave might easily become a king. Sabuktigīn of Ghaznī had been a slave; Kutbuddīn, the first king of Delhi, had been a slave; and for almost a century his successors were of servile origin.[1] Each king in his turn

[1] According to tradition, the founder of the Tughluk dynasty, which reigned from 1320 for almost a century, was the son of a slave: if the tradition is true, practically the whole series of Turkish kings may be reckoned as of servile origin.

THE PALACE

held numbers of slaves, and it was mainly from these slaves that governors were chosen, until in the course of time a free nobility emerged—largely from among their descendants.

In one of its aspects, the palace of those days must be thought of as a school of administration, and also of ambition. It contained a large number of lads, some of them Indians, others brought from distant places like Samarcand or Baghdad, employed directly under the king's eye, serving at first as pages or in even humbler positions, promoted in time to the charge of a household department such as the wardrobe or the stables, and then selected, whether before or after manumission, for more responsible duties as governors of provinces or commanders in the field. Discipline was strict, and the cane was freely used for trifling faults, but each boy admitted to the palace knew that he had his foot on the ladder which he might be able to climb, by merit or by favour, or by both, to the highest positions in the kingdom. From such material, a king who was a good judge of character, and whose judgment was not warped by passion, could hope to select officers who would be loyal as well as competent, and, in the circumstances of the time, it would not be easy to point to any alternative offering an equal prospect of success.

Another aspect of the palace brings us to an unpleasant topic, on which a few words must be said. The Turks who came to India, while they professed to be sincere Moslems, did not conform to all the moral precepts of their faith. For one thing, they drank heavily and convivially; for another, some of them, particularly in high places, were addicted to homosexual practices, a fact which must have been as great a scandal to Hindus of the period as it would be to all Indians at the present day. There is no doubt that some at least of the boys bought for the palace had been chosen for their personal attractions; and some of the most disastrous incidents of the period were due directly to the promotion of favourites to positions for which they were not qualified. At the same time, repugnance to their origin must not blind us to the abilities of some of these favourites. The man who carried the flag of Islam from the Narbada to beyond Madras had been bought, at a fancy price, as a eunuch-catamite, and less conspicuous instances of military or administrative success are scattered through the chronicles of the time. A favourite might be worth promoting, or he might not : everything depended on the judgment of the king.

A more serious weakness of the system lay in the fact that the loyalty of the promoted slaves was strictly personal to the master who had promoted them. Succession to the throne did not proceed automatically. The king usually nominated a successor from his family, but the ministers and courtiers occasionally made another choice, and a weak king could rarely hold his position for long. Many of the serious internal troubles of the kingdom arose from the factions formed by the old slaves of preceding rulers, who held together as a body, sometimes advanced their own candidate for the throne, and were always a potential danger to the ruling king.

Such was the general organisation of the kingdom. Regarding its attitude to its Hindu subjects, we must distinguish between town and country. In the garrison towns the Turks undoubtedly behaved as a ruling race, but there is no evidence that they oppressed the citizens as a regular thing, and it is a significant fact that the Brāhmans of Delhi, the capital city, were for a long time able to escape payment of the *jizya* tax, which was collected from other Hindus. Iconoclasm was an incident of conquest, but not, so far as we know, a function of the settled administration ; the value of the Hindu mercantile community was well appreciated ; and, while isolated acts of oppression undoubtedly occurred, the towns were probably able to live quietly enough, except when the succession to the throne was disputed, and fighting became the order of the day.

The country districts were administered in part directly by the governors, and in part indirectly through Hindu men of position. In the first case, it was the governor's duty to assess and collect the revenue to be paid by the peasants, and to secure them in the peaceful pursuit of their occupation. The attitude of the Turks to the Hindu cultivators

POSITION OF HINDUS

was expressed in the aphorism that soldiers and peasants 'are the two arms of the kingdom.' The peasant paid the revenue by which the kingdom lived, and he was to be so treated as to make that revenue as large as possible; in particular, he was to be encouraged to extend his holding by bringing new land into cultivation, and to increase the revenue by growing the more valuable crops. We read in the chronicles of occasional acts of what would now be called gross oppression, but, speaking generally, a reasonable *modus vivendi* between the conquerors and the peasants had been established, and one very different from what was contemplated by the strict Islamic system.

In much of the kingdom, however, the governors did not deal directly with the peasants, but received agreed sums by way of tribute from Hindu men of position, some of them entitled to rank as kings, others merely petty chieftains, claiming authority over a few villages. The Turks treated all these as one class, which soon came to be known by the name of *zamīndār*, or 'landholder'; but this name acquired various meanings in later times, and is now ambiguous, so that it is safer to describe the class as Chiefs. The Hindu Chiefs were regarded as a danger to the kingdom, because it was assumed, with good reason, that they would rebel whenever a suitable opportunity offered, and there were two currents of opinion regarding the way in which they should be treated. One course was to break their power once for all: the other was to make the best of them, allowing them to retain full authority over their territories so long as they remained loyal, and proved their loyalty by paying the stipulated revenue. The detailed history of the period is largely concerned with the interaction of these contrasted policies, but all that need be said here is that, except for one brief interval, the Chiefs as a body retained their position and authority, and probably the larger portion of the kingdom was ordinarily in their hands.

Submission to the Turks was not, however, universal, and bands of Rājputs, in particular, set out to found new kingdoms for themselves in the less accessible and more defensible parts of the country; some, though not all, of the

States which now exist in Rājputāna and in the Himalayas derive their origin from such movements, as do some of the large landed estates still held by Rājputs in Oudh and in Bihār. The position of these new foundations varied from time to time : they might be practically independent states, or they might be merely privileged units subject to a Moslem ruler, but their individuality has survived to the present day.

The foreign policy of the Turks in India was substantially that of an ordinary Hindu king—extension of the kingdom by conquest—but their activities in this direction were restrained by a danger on their north-western frontier. The rise from insignificance to empire of the Mongols under Chingīz Khān (*c.* 1155-1227) is part of the world's history : Chingīz himself did not invade India, but from about 1220 onwards Mongols were massed in the region of the Indus, at times occupying portions of the Punjab, on occasion threatening Delhi itself, and always separating the Turks in India from their fellows in the countries beyond Afghanistan. To the Moslems of Delhi this Mongol danger was the governing consideration, and the thirteenth century witnessed consolidation rather than extension of the kingdom. In the early years of the next century a new era of expansion supervened. The defence of the frontier was effectively organised ; Mālwa and Gujarāt were incorporated in the kingdom ; and a series of successful campaigns carried the flag of Islam right down the peninsula to Madura in the far south. To some extent these conquests were transient, but Moslem power was definitely established in southern India as far as the line of the river Kistna.

Something must be said here of the routes leading from Delhi towards the south, because the military history of the period requires a knowledge of the topography in this direction. Rājputāna is divided into two portions by the Aravalli range, the northern spurs of which extend to Delhi itself. West of this range the country is arid and generally unsuitable for military operations ; to the east there are three routes to Gujarāt, which are now traversed by the railways leading respectively to Ajmere, Rutlām, and Jhānsī, and which in the old days were commanded by the forts of Ajmere, Ranthambhor (near Siwai Madhopur junction), and Gwalior. When these forts were held by the Turks, the roads to Mālwa and Gujarāt lay open ; but none of these roads could safely be used so long as the fort commanding it was in the hands of an enemy, and the first step towards an extension of the kingdom southward was either to defeat or to come to terms with the Hindu Chiefs in possession. The forts changed hands at short intervals : a strong Turkish king would seize one or all of them, in a period of weakness the Chiefs would regain them, and their names recur constantly in the chronicles of the period.

Lastly, a few words may be said regarding Delhi, the capital of the Turkish kings. The action of the *Mahābhārata* takes place mainly in this region, and one of the principal cities mentioned in the epic must have been situated close to Delhi ; but the absence of any records renders it probable that the place was of no importance during the historical period, until a fortress was built there in the middle of the eleventh century by the local Rājput ruler. The Turks made it their capital from the outset of their rule, building one new city after another according to the taste of successive kings ; and, with brief intervals, it remained the centre of Moslem power until the opening years of the sixteenth century, when Sikandar Lodī moved to Agra. A new Delhi was built as his capital by the Mogul Emperor Shāh Jahān, and the shadow of an emperor still resided there in 1857 : fifty-four years later it was chosen to be once more the imperial capital of India, and another new Delhi has now come into existence

CHAPTER XXII

THE TURKISH KINGS

ONLY a few of the twenty-six Turks who sat on the throne of Delhi deserve to be remembered ; the majority are now merely names, either weaklings who could not maintain their position, or puppets who were elevated and degraded by the factions at the capital. Kutbuddīn, the first king of Delhi, died in 1210, as the result of an accident at polo, and after an interval of a year the throne fell to Iltutmish,[1] his slave and son-in-law. The new king's first task was to reconstitute the kingdom, for Bengal on the east, Multān on the west, and part of Rājputāna on the south had broken away, and twenty years elapsed before his authority was restored in these regions ; he then proceeded to extend his dominions, but died in 1236 before much could be achieved. The ten years that followed saw five reigns, among them that of Raziya, the only queen in the history of Moslems in India ; they were marked by intrigue at the capital, rebellion in the provinces, and occasional incursions of Mongol raiders ; and the stability which was recovered under Nāsiruddīn Mahmūd (1246-1266) was due not to the personality of the king, who was pious, amiable, scholarly and ineffective, but to the energy of a slave named Balban, who had been purchased by Iltutmish, and had risen rapidly to eminence. Except for a period of two years, during which his opponents gained the upper hand, Balban was practically king of Delhi during Mahmūd's reign, and eventually succeeded him on the throne, so that his power lasted almost without interruption from 1246 to his death in 1287.

[1] In older books this name usually appears incorrectly as Altamsh.

Balban was a man of great ability and iron will, who devoted all his powers first to consolidating the kingdom, and then to establishing his house upon the throne. After his formal accession, he conformed strictly to the ordinances of his creed so far as they affected his personal conduct, but in matters of state the interest of the kingdom was his only law, and his stern justice was enforced by punishments not authorised by the regular Islamic system. The earlier portion of his rule was spent in mastering his opponents among the Turks, and punishing the rebellions of his subjects; when his authority was at last firmly established in the North, the recrudescence of activity among the Mongols prevented him from undertaking further conquests; and then, in his old age, he learned that the Governor of Bengal had gone into open rebellion. Two expeditions sent against him were defeated; Balban, rendered furious by these reverses, marched in person on Bengal, the rebel was killed, his army captured almost *en masse,* and his family and principal adherents impaled in the chief streets of Lakhnautī, the rebel capital.[1] Balban now determined to create a subordinate kingdom in this region, and placed his younger son, Bughrā Khān, on the throne, after which he returned to Delhi.

Meanwhile, the main burden of the defence of the frontier had fallen on his elder son, Muhammad, who held the province of Multān, and who stands out in the chronicles as representative of the highest ideals of the Turks of those days, as soldier and administrator, scholar and patron, a courteous, loyal and clean-living gentleman. In 1285 Muhammad was killed in a skirmish with Mongols, and Balban's heart was broken; he died two years later, and the ministers at court placed on the throne his grandson Kaikubād (1287-1290), the son of the vassal king of Bengal. The new king, who was about eighteen years of age, had been brought up under very strict discipline, but he promptly threw off all restraints, and his reign was one continuous

[1] Ruins extending over an area of more than 20 square miles on the left bank of the Ganges are now the only memorial of this great city. The earlier name, Gaur, had been changed under the Sena dynasty to Lakhnautī.

debauch ; paralysis soon supervened, and he lay helpless in his palace when the emissary of a successful rebel put an end to his sufferings. The dynasty which Balban had laboured so hard to found thus came to an inglorious end, but his line survived for about half a century in the subordinate kingdom of Bengal.

The usurper, who took the title of Jalāluddīn (1290–1296), belonged to the Khaljī tribe, which had long been settled in Afghanistan, and was unpopular with the rest of the Turks, but in the new circumstances it naturally furnished most of the high officers of the kingdom. Jalāluddīn was an old man, who soon passed into senility, and his reign is noteworthy only for the fact that it introduces us to his nephew and son-in-law, Alāuddīn Khaljī, the strongest of the Turkish kings, and the man who brought most of southern India under Moslem supremacy. Intensely ambitious and entirely unscrupulous, cruel, treacherous, and an evil liver, Alāuddīn stands out as one of the most repulsive characters in Indian history, but of his strength there can be no question : his reign of twenty years (1296–1316) was a reign of terror, but, so long as his health lasted, it was also a reign of triumph for himself. Like Balban, he knew no law but the interest of the kingdom, and the ferocity of his punishments could be defended on no other grounds.

At the opening of the new régime Alāuddīn found himself in high favour, and established as Governor, first of one province, and then of two ; but his restless ambition, aggravated by an unhappy domestic life, sent him far afield. A successful raid into Mālwa whetted his appetite, and in 1294 he struck due south with a force of about 8,000 horse, raided the Yādava capital of Deogīr, about 500 miles distant from his headquarters, bluffed and fought his way back, and returned with enormous booty in gold and silver, silks, pearls and precious stones. He delayed in fulfilling his obligation to hand the spoils over to the treasury ; negotiations followed ; a meeting was arranged with the king on the banks of the Ganges ; and the old man, who had disregarded the warnings of his entourage, was treacherously murdered—a crime so brutal that it shocked even the Turks of those not over-sensitive days. Alāuddīn then marched on Delhi, employing his booty lavishly to win momentary support, and, after a short period of uncertainty, ascended the throne in October, 1296.

At the outset his position was precarious. He had practically no personal following beyond a few able officers who had been concerned with him in the murder of his uncle, and whom he could not trust without reserve; the Turks were recalcitrant; the Chiefs were rebellious; and the Mongols were active in the Punjab. The measures by which he overcame these dangers, and reached a position where his lust for conquest could be gratified, must be recounted in some little detail, for they throw a vivid light on the life of northern India. The most imminent danger came from the Turks, who, as a ruling race, naturally expected to live on the resources of the kingdom; many were employed in lucrative posts, and those who were not on the salary list enjoyed stipends paid from the public treasury, or grants of the revenue due from specified areas. Alāuddīn abolished summarily all these grants and stipends, and, since no alternative means of livelihood existed in the kingdom, the Turks who had lost their income had either to go elsewhere or to depend solely on his continued favour. To this economic motive for loyalty he added social pressure. Convinced that the convivial drinking parties characteristic of the time were hotbeds of seditious conspiracy, he brought them to an abrupt end, prohibiting the use of wine under ferocious penalties, and organising so effective a system of espionage that nobody dared to whisper a seditious word. The jovial atmosphere of the capital turned to suspicious gloom, but conspiracy was, for the time being, at an end.

In the case of the Hindu Chiefs, the weapon used was economic pressure. The details of their tenures are not on record, but we know in a general way that up to this time they had been allowed to enjoy a regular income, which some of them had supplemented by clandestine means. The tribute which they paid was less than would have been assessed directly on their peasants, the balance being spoken of as their 'right' or 'perquisites'; while some of them took from their peasants more than would have been assessed directly, so that, in the chronicler's phrase, the burden of the strong fell upon the weak. Alāuddīn and his advisers were convinced that the Chiefs used their income to maintain and equip troops to be employed in rebellion at the right moment, and we may safely accept the substantial justice of this view; but in any case he decided that the true preventive of rebellion was impoverishment. The revenue was fixed at half the gross produce of the land; the Chiefs were not allowed to handle it, but assessment and collection were entrusted to a large staff of officials; and practically nothing was left to a Chief beyond the land he cultivated personally, and so much as he could extract from his peasants after the very heavy revenue had been taken for the royal treasury. We are not in a position to estimate the burden in precise terms; but it is possible to say that a revenue of half the produce must have come very near to the entire surplus income of the country, after the necessary expenses of the inhabitants had been met, so that practically nothing would be left for rebellion or other luxuries. The chronicler gloats over the impoverishment which in fact resulted, and we must infer that the provinces shared the gloomy atmosphere of the capital; but the policy succeeded, for we hear of no serious rebellions throughout the greater part of the reign.[1]

There remained the danger from the Mongols on the frontier. Very early in his reign Alāuddīn devoted his attention to opening the roads leading to the south, but he learned quickly by experience that he could not neglect the north-west. Successive Mongol invasions culminated in the arrival of an army stated to be 120,000 strong in the immediate neighbourhood of Delhi; the king himself was besieged in a fortress, the country was ravaged, and the

[1] The language of the chronicler suggests on a first reading that these measures were directed against the Hindu population as a whole; but detailed scrutiny of the relevant passages shows that he used the word 'Hindus' in a restricted sense, practically equivalent to Chiefs. The insistence of the regulations on equality of sacrifice as between the strong and the weak points in the same direction, implying protection of the weaker Hindus against the stronger

REGULATION OF PRICES

kingdom was almost lost; but at the last moment the Mongols withdrew, for reasons which can only be surmised.

Alāuddīn now reorganised the frontier defences, and placed them in charge of a strong commander named Tughluk, who for nearly a quarter of a century held the Mongols effectively in check; but more than this was required for complete security, and the decision was taken to maintain a large standing army in the immediate neighbourhood of Delhi, ready for war at any moment, and necessarily paid regularly in cash. The difficulties experienced in giving effect to this decision bring out clearly some of the essential features of the economic life of the period.

In the kingdom of Delhi there was an insistent demand for the precious metals, to be used for currency, for display, for the presents required by etiquette, and, perhaps most of all, for hoarding. There was no local production, and the supply depended mainly on what could be obtained, by trade or by tribute, from the distant seaports, where, as has been said already, gold and silver were received on balance as a normal feature of commerce. In the thirteenth century supplies from the coast were not large, and coins were scarce in the North, which is another way of saying that prices were low, and the citizens or soldiers of Delhi could live cheaply. The lavish distribution of the spoils brought by Alāuddīn from the South had, however, changed the situation; for the time being, money was locally cheap, that is to say, prices were high, and the cost of maintaining the standing army was more than the treasury could bear. To meet this situation, Alāuddīn resolved to lower prices, and keep them low; and here, as in his other activities, he achieved entire success.

In essence his methods were sound. He relied on complete control of supplies and transport, with rationing of demand where this measure was necessitated by the state of supplies. In the area which provided the capital with food, he caused some or all of the revenue to be paid in grain, which was stored at the capital; and peasants could sell their surplus, when they had any, only to the controlled merchants, who had bound themselves to deal only at the fixed prices, and to deliver all produce to the royal storehouse. From these stores supplies were issued to the retailers, who, in turn, were bound to sell only at the prices fixed by royal authority. It is in the details of the scheme that we get vivid glimpses of life in Delhi. Control of the merchants was a simple matter; they were made to deposit their wives and children as security for their conduct, and these pledges were settled close to Delhi in charge of a superintendent. Control of the peasants' supplies was also simple, for the existing administrative machinery sufficed. Control over the shopkeepers and speculators of the city was more difficult, and involved the further development of the system of espionage which Alāuddīn had already organised. Several distinct bodies of spies were employed, each spying on the others, and all spying on the citizens, while the king himself would occasionally send trusted servants to spy independently; and when the shopkeepers persisted in giving short weight, the drastic order to cut the equivalent of the deficiency from their flesh eventually brought them into line. And so the system worked. There were difficulties at times, but the king's iron will surmounted them, and the security of the kingdom was ensured.

While these measures were being elaborated, the expansion of the kingdom had been taken in hand. The roads to the South were opened, Mālwa and Gujarāt were annexed, and then, between 1306 and 1311, southern India was overrun in three spectacular campaigns. Their story will be told in a later chapter; for the present it must suffice to say that Alāuddīn did not take part personally in them, but remained at Delhi, entrusting the operations to a eunuch named Kāfūr, who had been brought as booty from Gujarāt, became the king's favourite, and developed into one of the greatest military commanders that India has known.

The last few years of Alāuddīn's life make a sorry tale. Excesses had ruined his health, his judgment failed, and his will weakened. Palace intrigues supervened, rebellion began to occur, and it is probable that at last Kāfūr put an end to his master in order to gain the throne for himself.

ALĀUDDĪN'S SUCCESSORS

A month later he himself was murdered, and a son of Alāuddīn became king, with the style of Kutbuddīn Mubārak Shāh. Four years of utter debauchery ended in his murder by a singularly vile favourite, who usurped the kingdom, only to be crushed by Tughluk, the old warden of the frontier, who, in the absence of anyone with greater claims, succeeded to the throne.

Tughluk (1320-1325) stands out as the pleasantest figure in the line of Turkish kings, equally successful as soldier and as ruler, a man who thought of his troops first, and of his peasants next. His immediate task was to reorganise the kingdom, for Alāuddīn's elaborate regulations had lapsed, and the government of the provinces had fallen into the hands of mere speculators. Upright governors were now appointed, the burden of the revenue was mitigated, extortion by subordinate officials was checked, and the Chiefs were restored substantially to their former position, reforms which were effective in practice, and must have made a vast difference to the subjects of the kingdom. At the same time disorders which had arisen in distant parts of the kingdom were suitably dealt with. At the outset of his reign Tughluk had sent his son, Muhammad, to deal with the situation in the south, and a few years later he went in person to restore order in Bengal; but in returning thence to his capital he was killed, along with his favourite son, by the fall of a temporary building where he had halted to rest. It seems impossible to reject the evidence which shows that this was no accident, but a deliberate murder, skilfully planned and carried out by Muhammad in order to secure his succession to the throne.

It is not easy to characterise in a few words the reign which followed (1326-1351), for Muhammad Tughluk was a complex personality. In modern times he has been praised as a genius, and diagnosed as a madman; his contemporaries gave him up as incomprehensible, and it is tempting to say no more; but the facts which are on record point to a restless and versatile man, obsessed with grandiose projects—some of them merely fantastic, others indicating flashes of political insight—but unable to bring them to fruition owing to instability of purpose, ferocity of temper, and lack of ordinary judgment. Such a man necessarily dreamed of a wide extension of the kingdom; we read of a great army assembled for the conquest of Persia, which melted away for want of pay; another sent against a hill state perished in the foothills of the Himalayas; but the reign saw only the definite loss of Bengal and of practically all the territory south of the river Narbada, while rebellion was almost endemic throughout the North. In internal affairs, too, we read only of instability. Experiments in administration ended in a relapse to speculative farming in its worst form; an attempt to introduce a token coinage caused ruinous loss to the treasury; and a change of capital resulted in an extraordinary fiasco. Instead of describing all these matters in detail, we will merely sketch the course of the last of them, which gives a vivid idea of what life must have been like in those days.

One of Muhammad's earliest projects was to transfer his capital to Deogīr, the administrative centre of his southern possessions, which he renamed Daulatābād. The idea itself was probably sound, for the new capital was central, and might be considered safe from the Mongols, who still threatened the old. At first, the measures taken to effect the transfer were reasonable, but the citizens of Delhi grumbled, the king's temper blazed up, and he ordered the whole city to migrate *en masse* to Deogīr. The order was enforced rigorously and Delhi was left empty. Many of the citizens died on the long march of nearly 700 miles, the survivors could not accommodate themselves to the new climate, and after some years the project was abandoned, and a return march was decreed. When the citizens got home, however, there was nothing for them to eat, and they had to march again to a temporary city erected near Kanauj, where supplies could be obtained from across the Ganges; and here they remained until Delhi could be provisioned, and could at last resume its place as the capital of the kingdom.

There were two causes why Delhi could not be fed. For one thing, the monsoons had been bad, and in some parts of the country famine was rife; but the region on which the capital mainly depended for supplies was already desolate when the rains failed, having been deliberately ruined by the king. The chief source of supplies was the tract of fertile land between the Jumna and the Ganges, which is now known as the Upper Doab (Persian *dū-āb*, 'two rivers'); the peasants in this tract depended solely on Delhi to buy their surplus produce, and Delhi depended mainly on them for its daily food. Muhammad had made a ruinously heavy enhancement in the revenue due from these peasants, and almost simultaneously he had deprived them of their only market; they naturally responded by growing less produce, or abandoning their holdings altogether, and taking to highway robbery as an alternative; and they burnt their surplus stocks of grain, presumably in the hope of mitigating the inevitable fall in prices. Reduced cultivation meant less revenue, which was assessed season by season on the area actually sown; Muhammad therefore regarded the peasants as rebels, led his army against them, slaughtered them like sheep, and desolated the whole region, which naturally remained unproductive. Later in the reign, when Delhi was restored as the capital, efforts were made to accelerate the recovery of the desolate region, and eventually the king embarked on a grandiose scheme of agrarian reconstruction; but the horde of incompetent officials appointed for the purpose embezzled most of the money with which they were entrusted, no substantial improvement was effected, and it was only in the next reign that prosperity returned.

This brief outline must suffice as a sample of Muhammad's methods, and of the results which they secured. For the rest, the reign may be pictured as one of constant rebellions and ferocious repression. The world-traveller Ibn Batūtah, who spent some years at the Court, was revolted by the cruelty of the king, which he witnessed day by day; ferocity bred rebellion, and rebellion bred ferocity; Muhammad's growing sense of his own failure only increased his severity, and things went steadily from bad to worse. The survival of the kingdom must be attributed mainly to relaxation of the Mongol pressure on the frontier ; we hear of no invasions in force after 1330, and later on Muhammad spent large sums in inducing Mongols to settle peaceably in India, so that a measure of security was established in this direction.

In 1345 Muhammad travelled South to deal in person with the increasing disorder in that region. Two years later he abandoned what was left of southern India in order to crush rebellion in Gujarāt, and, when this had been accomplished, he marched to Lower Sind to punish the ruler for having harboured some rebels ; there he fell sick, and early in 1351 the chronicler tells us that ' the king was freed from his people, and they from their king.' The leaderless army placed on the throne a cousin of Muhammad's named Fīrūz, who succeeded in bringing it back to Delhi, and was there accepted as king.

Fīrūz (1351–1388) was a man of middle age, reasonably intelligent, benevolent, indolent, and essentially weak ; his mother was a Hindu lady of position, but, unlike most of his predecessors, he respected the public law of Islam, and usually, though not invariably, he lived as a good Moslem should. The successes of the first half of his reign were due almost entirely to an able and loyal Minister named Makbūl, a Brāhman who had accepted Islam, and who practically governed the kingdom for more than twenty years. Fīrūz himself engaged in some rather futile military enterprises in Sind and in Bengal, but after ten years he forswore aggressive warfare ; and, since the Mongols on the frontier still showed little energy, the kingdom enjoyed a short interval of peace, and quickly recovered prosperity under Makbūl's just and sagacious administration. In essence his policy was that of Tughluk—exclusion of speculators from the provinces, and the appointment of honest governors, charged with the duty of protecting the peasants and levying from them only a reasonable revenue ; under this policy the disorders of the previous reign quickly disappeared, the desolate country was brought under cultivation, the capital and the troops enjoyed ample supplies at low prices, and the king was in a position to gratify his taste for large and costly public works—new cities and towns, mosques and palaces, tombs, bridges and monumental pillars, as well as a number of canals for irrigation. The tradition of this short golden age still lingers vaguely in the villages of northern India.

After twenty years the scene changed. Makbūl died in 1372, and two years later Fīrūz, now an old man, broke down under the death of his favourite son. His judgment failed; we read of ferocious reprisals on rebels, of speculation in provinces, of factions in the capital, of disloyalty among ministers; and when at last the old king died, no one emerged to restore the kingdom. Six reigns are reckoned in the decade which followed; the provinces began to break away; and then, in 1398, a new enemy arrived in earnest before Delhi, where there was no power to offer effective resistance.

The empire founded by Chingīz Khān had not lasted for long, and in the fourteenth century the Mongols, who had now accepted Islam as their creed, were distributed in several independent states, while among the neighbouring Turkish kingdoms there emerged the great figure of Tīmūr, the Tamerlane of English literature, who in 1369 was crowned in the Oxus country, and aspired thence to conquer the world. Khorāsān and Persia, Chinese Turkistan and much of Russia, fell to him, and then it was India's turn. Marching through Afghanistan, he was before Delhi in December, 1398, and after one battle entered the city, which was sacked effectively for several days, many of the citizens being slaughtered, and others carried away as slaves. Tīmūr continued his march from Delhi as far as the Ganges, slaughtering and plundering as he went, and then returned by a more northerly route, leaving India after a visit of six months, with the remnant of the Turkish kingdom in ruins, though its final disappearance was delayed for fifteen years. It is not certain that he ever meant formally to annex any part of India, but in any case he did not do so; he left the country because his presence was needed in western Asia, and six years later he died on the long road to China. In India he had broken the Turkish kingdom, and left nothing in its place.

CHAPTER XXIII

ISLAM IN SOUTHERN INDIA

DURING the thirteenth century only one important change occurred in the political situation in southern India; the power of the Cholas decayed, and practically the whole Tamil country came under the Pāndyas of Madura, who had for so long been their recalcitrant vassals. For the rest, the period was one of conflict, and at its close the four leading powers—Yādavas, Kākatīyas, Hoysalas and Pāndyas—were at variance among themselves, and were not in a position to present a common front to invasion from the North.

Alāuddīn's raid on Deogīr, which has been mentioned in the last chapter, marked the first direct contact with the Turks. On that occasion he stipulated for the annual payment to him of the revenue of one province by way of tribute; and default in this payment was the pretext for the first expedition which, in 1306, he sent under Kāfūr against Deogīr. The expedition was entirely successful, for the Yādava ruler submitted, visited Delhi, and was restored to his country as a tributary of the Turks. In 1308 Kāfūr was sent on a second expedition to Warangal, the capital of the Kākatīyas, south-east of Deogīr. The city was besieged, and eventually the ruler surrendered, paid a heavy indemnity, and engaged for an annual tribute for the future.

Delhi was now in touch with southern India, and news of the great hoards of wealth held by the rulers, and by the temples, induced Alāuddīn to despatch a third expedition. In 1310 Kāfūr started from Deogīr, plundered the Hoysala capital, advanced thence to Madura, which had been

THE CONQUEST OF THE SOUTH

evacuated, and was also plundered, and finally reached the coast opposite Ceylon. The booty collected during this expedition was enormous, far exceeding the spoils of Deogīr in the weight of gold and jewels carried to the North; but it must not be inferred that the South was thereby crippled in its economic life. The wealth taken away was almost entirely unproductive; the temples merely hoarded the bulk of the valuables which they received as offerings, while we have good evidence to show that the treasure accumulated by the kings was not meant to be expended. The tradition was that a king should never touch the treasure left by his predecessors, but should gather a fresh treasure for himself, which in its turn would ordinarily remain intact in the hands of his successors. The loss of these royal accumulations would have very little economic significance so far as the South was concerned; the impoverishment of the temples may have reacted injuriously on the neighbouring villages, which looked to them for help in times of stress, but their endowments in land remained intact and available for such purposes; and the final result of Kāfūr's expeditions was to leave the people under their former rulers, but subject, in at least two out of the four states, to recurring liability for tribute.

This arrangement, however, did not last for long, because the stipulated tribute soon fell into arrears. In 1315 the Yādavas were forcibly displaced from Deogīr, in 1323 the same fate befell the Kākatīyas at Warangal, and at some uncertain date a Moslem governor was appointed to Madura, so that of the four Hindu powers only the Hoysalas remained in possession of their territories, while the Pāndyas still held part of the country beyond Madura. Then the tide turned against Delhi. In 1334 the Moslem governor of Madura rebelled, and founded a line of independent sultans, which survived for nearly fifty years, and in 1347 Deogīr also became independent under a Moslem dynasty, while Warangal was recovered temporarily by a branch of the Kākatīyas. Thus in the middle of the century there were two independent Moslem kingdoms in the South.

The events which followed resulted in the division of

southern India between a single Moslem power and the Hindu kingdom of Vijayanagar. The line of division between them was formed by the river Kistna with its tributary the Tunga-bhadra. North of the Kistna Moslems were supreme; south of the Tunga-bhadra Hindus were unchallenged; while the land between the two rivers was claimed by both sides, and changed hands from time to time. The Moslem kingdom is known by the name of Bahmanī,[1] derived from the leader of the rebels against the rule of Delhi, who, on his acceptance as king in 1347, took the title of Alāuddīn Bahman Shāh. During his reign (1347–1358) he established his authority as far as the sea on the west, and over Warangal on the east; he organised his kingdom in provinces, and transferred his capital from Deogīr to Gulbarga, some way further south; and at his death the new power was a definite political fact. Its independence was admitted by Fīrūz, the King of Delhi, and was formally recognised by the Caliph in Egypt.

The city of Vijayanagar ('Victory City'), lying on the right bank of the Tunga-bhadra, was established as the Hoysala capital by about the year 1336. Not long after, the line of the Hoysalas became extinct, but their territories remained intact under the officers of the kingdom, and from among these a new dynasty emerged, which is known by the name of the recently founded capital. Just at first Vijayanagar lay between two Moslem powers, but about 1378 it destroyed the sultanate of Madura, and thenceforward the whole country south of the Tunga-bhadra was united under one rule. We hear little more of the three Tamil kingdoms, which had persisted in this region for so many centuries. The Cholas had come to an end. The Pāndyas survived into the seventeenth century as subordinate rulers under Vijayanagar and its successors. The Keralas, too, survived as subordinates, and, though their

[1] It is also known as the Kingdom of the Deccan, but this name is liable to mislead. It is an Indian word meaning 'south,' and was applied by the Turkish rulers of Delhi to the country adjoining their kingdom on the south. In this way it came to mean not the south of India, but the north and centre of the Peninsula, excluding the true South which constituted the kingdom of Vijayanagar; and this usage has survived, so that at the present day Poona and Hyderabad are in the Deccan, but Mysore and Madras are not.

VIJAYANAGAR

history is at times obscure, it may fairly be said that they are still represented as a political entity by the States of Travancore and Cochin.

The first clash between the two dominant powers occurred in 1365, and two years later Vijayanagar sustained a severe defeat. War was renewed in 1377, and again in 1398; on both occasions the Bahmanī forces drove their opponents into the fortifications of Vijayanagar, but were unable to capture the city and so reach a decision; and further fighting occurred at intervals until the middle of the sixteenth century, as will be related further on. It is natural at the present day to regard this long struggle as essentially a religious war, but there is not much positive evidence on the point. Apart from the instinct of self-preservation, which certainly counted for much, desire for conquest was inherent in the Hindu mentality of the period, and was the dominant incentive of the Turkish invasion of India; the extent to which these motives were reinforced by religious zeal remains a matter for conjecture. It is certain, however, that in the course of time the struggle became political rather than religious. At the beginning of the fifteenth century Vijayanagar was engaged in friendly negotiations with the Moslems of Gujarāt and Mālwa; by the middle of the century it was employing large forces of Moslem mercenaries against the Bahmanīs; and the complicated diplomacy of the years which follow shows that the Moslems had been fitted effectively into the well-known theory that neighbours were natural enemies, and that allies should be sought on their further frontiers.

The methods of warfare in southern India differed in one important feature from those which prevailed in the North. The Turks, as we have seen, relied almost entirely on well-mounted and highly trained cavalry, their best horses being obtained from Afghanistan and beyond. Horses fit for cavalry were not bred in the South, and the wastage of imported animals was very heavy, owing partly to the climate and partly to unskilful treatment. There was a regular trade in horses brought by sea from Arabia and Persia, but, while it was very large for the period—one writer speaks of 10,000 animals being imported yearly—it could not suffice to maintain great masses of cavalry such as were employed by the Turks. Accordingly, we find that the Vijayanagar army usually consisted of a huge levy of infantry, supported by elephants and a relatively small mounted force : in 1365, for instance, the numbers given in the chronicles are 30,000 horse and 900,000 foot ; and the concurrent testimony of various observers suffices to establish the fact that something like a million men might be brought into the field. Naturally they could not be kept there for long, and an ordinary campaign consisted of some preliminary manœuvres and a single battle, followed by a rapid dispersal. The Bahmanīs, on the other hand, maintained the Turkish tradition of relying mainly on cavalry, which was certainly more efficient than that of their opponents ; their tactics were also better on the whole ; and, when once the Vijayanagar line was broken, the slaughter of the infantry must have been appalling.

Non-combatants, too, suffered terribly at times. The story of this feature of the struggle, which was entirely contrary to Indian traditions, is recorded as follows by the Moslem chroniclers. In the first clash, a Moslem citadel was captured by the Vijayanagar forces, and the entire garrison with their families were put to the sword. Thereupon Muhammad, the second Bahmanī king (1358-1375), vowed that he would slaughter a hundred thousand Hindus in revenge for this outrage, and after the battle of 1367 there was an indiscriminate massacre of the Hindu population, the number of victims being stated at 400,000. After this, an agreement was made to spare non-combatants ; but it was not always carried out, and a breach of it by the Hindus was punished by another appalling massacre in the year 1423, accompanied by the destruction of temples, the slaughter of cows, and everything that could wound the feelings of the vanquished side. The population of Vijayanagar must therefore have been prepared for such a sequel to each Bahmanī success, while, even when the agreement was respected, it did not operate to prevent the enslavement of any non-combatants that might be worth carrying away. The South had travelled a long way from the old Indian tradition that war was a matter which concerned only the armies actually engaged.

A few words may be said here of the new capital cities which emerged at this time in southern India. Gulbarga, the first capital of the Bahmanīs, was already a place of some importance under the Kākatīyas, but its surviving monuments, a mosque and the tombs of some of the Bahmanī kings, belong to the period 1350–1430, during which it was the centre of the Moslem kingdom. After the transfer of the capital to Bīdar, it fell into decay, but has of late taken its place as a thriving commercial town and an important administrative centre of the State of Hyderabad. Bīdar, about 60 miles north-east of Gulbarga, has also a tradition of importance in Hindu times, but its history centres in the Bahmanī dynasty, whose memorials—palaces, mosques, a college, and numerous tombs—may still be seen. It is now a small commercial and administrative centre.

Unlike these towns, Vijayanagar is a mere ruin, practically uninhabited, but in the fifteenth century it must have far surpassed them in magnificence. As with the other great Hindu cities of the past, we possess no contemporary Indian descriptions, but are dependent on the observations of foreign visitors—in this case an Italian merchant adventurer, an envoy from Persia, and a Russian monk, supplemented by various Portuguese narratives of the early sixteenth century. The massive walls, which can still be traced, enclosed an area of more than sixty square miles, much of which was occupied by fields and gardens watered by canals from the river. The population cannot be estimated with precision, but it was certainly very large when judged by the standards of the fifteenth century. The great majority of the houses were naturally small and undistinguished, but among them were scattered palaces, temples, public buildings, wide streets of shops shaded by trees, busy markets, and all the equipment of a great and wealthy city. The principal buildings were constructed in the regular Hindu style, covered with ornamental carving, and the fragments which have survived suffice to give point to the enthusiastic admiration of the men who saw the city in the days of its magnificence. It was destroyed in 1565 after the decisive battle of Tālikot, and so far as is known was never repopulated.

CHAPTER XXIV

THE FIFTEENTH CENTURY

ALMOST throughout India the fifteenth century was a period of conflict, the details of which we can pass over, because they throw little light on the main story of the country. In the South the chief struggle lay between Vijayanagar and the Bahmanī kingdom, with complications in the directions of Orissa, Gujarāt, and Mālwa. In northern India the collapse of Delhi generated a large number of independent, or quasi-independent, political entities, each struggling to maintain itself and expand at the cost of its neighbours. The Hindu Chiefs had recovered control of the roads leading to the South, and Mālwa and Gujarāt, cut off from Delhi, became independent Moslem kingdoms at the end of the fourteenth century, while about the same time the 'eastern province,' as it was called, developed into the Moslem kingdom of Jaunpur. Between Delhi and Jaunpur there was no fixed frontier, and on both sides of the Ganges various Hindu Chiefs asserted themselves in the debatable area, while on the other side of Delhi the Punjab also tended to break away, leaving only a small tract of country dependent on what had been the capital of India.

In this contracted area the line of the Tughluks survived till 1414, when it was displaced by Khizr Khān, who became the founder of what is known as the Sayyid dynasty.[1] Khizr Khān had been patronised by Tīmūr, and considered, or affected to consider, himself merely a viceroy, but the

[1] The term Sayyid properly denotes a descendant of the prophet Muhammad, but it has been assumed in many cases without adequate historical justification, and Khizr Khān's claim to it is dubious.

THE AFGHAN DYNASTY 179

power of Tīmūr's successors was waning, and this attitude was abandoned by the later Sayyids, who called themselves kings—of the little that was left to them. Their rule was marked by incompetence and increasing impotence, and in 1448 the last of them retired into private life.

After a short interval the throne of Delhi fell to Bahlol, an Afghan of the Lodī tribe, who had for some years governed part of the Punjab nominally on behalf of the Sayyids, but practically as an independent ruler. His reign (1451–1489) was marked mainly by a long struggle with Jaunpur, which lasted, with brief interruptions, for more than thirty years before the eastern kingdom was definitely subdued; but he was a competent administrator, and with the aid of his tribesmen, whom he attracted to India by the offer of generous terms, he maintained a firm hold on his territories. His son, Sikandar Shāh (1489–1517), ruled effectively over the plains from the Indus to the western border of Bengal, and also made some progress in reducing the power of the Chiefs to the south and west of the Jumna; and it was mainly for the convenience of these latter operations that he transferred the capital of the kingdom to Agra, then a place of little importance, but destined to become in the next period the greatest city in India. Ibrāhīm, the third Lodī king, was less successful, for he distrusted the powerful Afghans who constituted the official nobility of the kingdom, and by capricious acts of tyranny drove them to disloyalty. The result was seen first in a serious rebellion in Bihār, and a little later in the relations which the Governor of Lahore opened with Bābur, the Mogul ruler of Kābul, relations which eventuated in 1526 in the transfer of northern India to a new conquering dynasty.

Incidents scattered through the chronicles of the period make it possible to form a general idea of what this century must have meant to the peasants in the North. Under the Sayyids the ordinary administrative machinery ceased to function. When money was needed, the king led, or sent, his troops to collect the revenue; and the process commonly resolved itself into extracting from the peasants whatever they could be made to pay, after they had already satisfied the demands of other claimants, whether Hindu Chiefs or Moslem Governors, on the spot. There was no pretence of policing the country, and armed bands of robbers also took their share; in fact, robbery was the only profession that offered reasonable prospects to a man of enterprise. Out of this confusion Bahlol Lodī established a rough but effective administration. Something like one-sixth of the kingdom was held by loyal Chiefs: in the remainder the great bulk of the revenue was assigned to the Afghan nobles, each of whom took charge of his territory, governed it with the aid of troops raised and paid by himself, and exercised in it practically royal power. These nobles were not fools, and they recognised that it was necessary to protect the peasants from whom they drew their income, while one of them at least adopted a deliberate policy of restoring the half-ruined agricultural industry; but they were strong men, and would stand no nonsense. A recalcitrant village would be raided by the assignee's forces; a rebellious Chief might be put to death, and his family sold as slaves; judged by modern standards, the administration was summary, and at times brutal, but it was a vast improvement on the anarchy which had preceded it.

Turning now to the remainder of northern India, it may almost be said that Bengal forms an exception to the general statement that the century was one of conflict. The country was independent from the middle of the fourteenth century to the first transitory Mogul conquest in 1538; for a time it was subject to invasion from Jaunpur on the west, but otherwise its frontiers were more or less stable throughout this period, and most of the fighting which occurred was incidental to dynastic intrigues. One episode which deserves mention is the rise to power of a Hindu Chief known as Rāja Ganesh, who about the beginning of the fifteenth century became the actual ruler of Bengal, and was succeeded by his son, a convert to Islam; but the story of this episode is very obscure, and the details must be passed over. Taking the period as a whole, about one-third of the kings died violent deaths or were deposed, and it is noteworthy that here, as had been the case in Delhi, the royal slaves were responsible for much of the trouble which occurred. The most serious disturbances were due to the Africans. Soon after the middle of the century the ruling king set the fashion of employing large numbers of African slaves, some of them in important positions, and for a time they formed a powerful party at the Court. In 1486 their chosen leader had the king murdered, and usurped the throne, which for the next seven years was held by Africans, and it seemed likely that they would establish themselves as a ruling caste ; but the tyranny of the last of their number led to a successful rebellion, and a new dynasty was founded by the leader, himself a foreigner, who finally expelled the Africans from Bengal. This new dynasty lasted until 1538, when, after some vicissitudes, the country came temporarily under Mogul rule.

To the west of Delhi, the bulk of the Punjab was never formally detached, though for a time it was practically independent, but a distinct Moslem dynasty held Multān and Upper Sind from 1438 to 1528. Lower Sind was ruled by a line of Rājputs who had accepted Islam, and who likewise became independent after the collapse of Delhi ; their rule lasted almost to the end of the fifteenth century, when the country passed into the possession of a Mongol tribe. To the north, the mountain kingdom of Kashmīr, which had not been subject to Delhi, came in 1346 into the hands of a Moslem adventurer, whose line continued, with vicissitudes, for more than two centuries. To the south, Hindu Chiefs dominated the broken country, and beyond them lay Mālwa and Gujarāt.

Here we come into a region of persistent conflict. The Moslem governors of these two provinces had established independent kingdoms by the beginning of the fifteenth century; to the south of Mālwa lay another small Moslem kingdom, Khāndesh, which had broken away, not from Delhi but from the Bahmanī kingdom ; beyond Khāndesh were the Bahmanīs, and beyond the Bahmanīs was Vijayanagar. The story of the fifteenth century in this region is intricate and confused ; we will not attempt to tell it in detail, but will confine ourselves to a sketch of the fortunes of the two protagonists.

G

The main fact in the political history of the Bahmanīs is the deterioration of the original stock, and the resultant need for employing foreign mercenaries or adventurers. The foreigners came largely from Persia and the neighbouring countries; in war they proved themselves definitely superior to the resident Moslems; at times they secured practical control of the administration; and a persistent feud was established between the two classes. Later on large numbers of Africans were also employed: these formed a third party, usually in alliance with the residents against the haughty foreigners, who despised them; and with these feuds added to the intrigues to be expected in every Turkish capital, it can easily be understood that the course of the dynasty was not smooth. Of the twelve kings who ruled until 1487, three were murdered, two others were deposed and blinded, scarcely one can be said to have enjoyed a tranquil reign. For the rest, most of them were drunkards, several devoted themselves mainly to their harems, and one of them, Humāyūn the Oppressor, became proverbial as a monster of tyranny.

Notwithstanding these drawbacks, the Bahmanīs had the best of the struggle with Vijayanagar for most of the century. Our knowledge of the period is derived mainly from Moslem sources, which cannot be regarded as impartial, and may possibly exaggerate the Bahmanī achievements; but they represent Vijayanagar as paying tribute from 1400 onwards, and assign the periodical defaults in payment as the cause of most of the fighting which occurred, and which ended on each occasion in payment of the arrears, accompanied by various humiliating conditions. After the middle of the century there was an interval of repose on this frontier, during which Vijayanagar was embroiled with an aggressive Chief in Orissa, while the Bahmanīs were engaged with Mālwa and Gujarāt; and then the situation was abruptly altered by revolutions in both kingdoms.

In Vijayanagar a noble named Narasimha [1] had come

---

[1] The popular form of the name is Narsingha; and the Portuguese, who reached India during Narasimha's reign, frequently wrote of Vijayanagar as ' Narsinga.'

THE STRUGGLE IN THE SOUTH

into prominence in the course of the struggle with Orissa, and had gradually consolidated his position in the country near Madras. The reigning king was inefficient and oppressive; and in 1487 Narasimha deposed him and usurped the throne. Twenty years later a second usurpation occurred, and in 1509 the throne fell to Krishnadeva, who may be regarded as perhaps the greatest of the Vijayanagar kings. Meanwhile the Bahmanī kingdom had broken up. It consisted of four large provinces, each of them held by a strong governor; and the hopeless inefficiency of the king led three out of the four to assume independence in 1490, while the fourth followed their example shortly afterwards. The Bahmanī dynasty retained Bīdar for a short time, but almost ceased to count; the four new kingdoms were Ahmadnagar and Berār on the north, Bījāpur and Golconda on the south, and, as a glance at the map will show, it was Bījāpur which succeeded to the long-disputed frontier in the direction of Vijayanagar.

The period following these changes was one of intricate diplomacy, shifting alliances, and almost incessant war. The Moslem kingdoms fought among themselves, and one or other of them sought the support of Vijayanagar, now the strongest single entity, which was sometimes fighting Bījāpur, and at others helping Bījāpur against its enemies further north. Holding the dominant position, the rulers and the troops of Vijayanagar became arrogant, their marches through the Moslem country were marked by desecration of mosques, insults to the honour of women, and other outrages to be expected in the circumstances; and the imminent danger to their continued existence at last drove the principal Moslem powers to combine. In 1564 their united armies faced the full strength of Vijayanagar, and in the first days of 1565 destroyed it in a decisive battle, which has received the name of Tālikot. The city of Vijayanagar was occupied and devastated, the surrounding country was ravaged, the dynasty withdrew to the southeast, and, though it was destined to survive for some time, it no longer threatened the supremacy of the Moslem kingdoms in this region.

In an earlier paragraph we have attempted to show what the period of conflict meant to the peasants of northern India. For the South the materials for a similar estimate are scanty; but, as we have seen already, the sufferings of non-combatants were at times terrible, the huge size of the armies must have involved the periodical disorganisation of agriculture, and the burden of military expenditure must have fallen very heavily on those who had to pay—a burden aggravated by the luxurious extravagance of the Courts and nobles. A few scattered observations of foreign visitors suggest a sharp contrast between the unbounded luxury of the cities and the extreme poverty of the villages, a result which would follow naturally from the conditions we have stated; but materials for a more exact description are not available.

The face of the country still bears testimony to the lavish expenditure in which the rulers indulged. We have mentioned in the last chapter the surviving monuments of Vijayanagar, Gulbarga and Bīdar; to these we may add the great buildings of Bījāpur, of Golconda, and of Burhānpur, the capital of Khāndesh, as well as, farther to the north, of Māndū, the fortress-capital of Mālwa, and of Ahmadābād, the chief city of Gujarāt, all of them familiar names to students of Indo-Moslem architecture. We can infer also that it was a prosperous period for the artistic handicrafts carried on in these and other capitals, crafts which have in the past depended largely on Court patronage; and, in more general terms, that the cities flourished, if the villages suffered.

CHAPTER XXV

THE RESULTS OF TURKISH RULE

THE sixteenth century was marked by new and important contacts of India with the outer world, with the Moguls in the north-west, and with the Portuguese on the coast: before we describe these, we must pause to trace the effects of the three centuries of Turkish rule, the political aspects of which have been outlined in the foregoing chapters. The earlier nomad conquerors, bringing with them no definite cultural system of their own, had been gradually absorbed, but the faith and the culture of Islam were too precise and too virile to experience that fate, and from the thirteenth century onwards the life of India must be thought of as two distinct currents flowing side by side, mingling to a varying extent along the line of contact, but not uniting to form a single stream.

There were several obstacles to the development of friendly intercourse between Turks and Hindus. In the first place, there was the embitterment which necessarily resulted from the methods and the incidents of conquest. In the second, the Turks kept their women in strict seclusion, so that the opportunities for what we think of as social intercourse were reduced by half. In the third, the convivial propensities of the Turks were incompatible with the restrictions imposed by the system of caste, which prevented anything in the way of common meals, while their taste for beef was an offence to all Hindus. Against these obstacles must be set the important factor of intermarriage. There is nothing to suggest that any Hindu ever married a Turkish woman, but the chronicles furnish instances of Turkish nobles obtaining wives from Hindu families of position, while the conditions of the conquest—masses of cavalry over-running a distant country and settling down wherever circumstances permitted—make it practically certain that many of the rank and file also must have married Hindu wives, and that, from the second generation onwards, there was a definitely Indian strain in the race which continued to be known as Turks.

This strain was found even in the highest places. We have said in an earlier chapter that Fīrūz, the King of Delhi, had an Indian mother, and according to tradition the same is true of an earlier king, Tughluk. Further south, the second king of Bījāpur was the son of a Hindu mother, and his three sisters were married respectively to the rulers of Bīdar, Ahmadnagar and Berār. The first 'Turkish' King of Gujarāt was in fact the son of a Rājput who had been converted to Islam, while the founder of the kingdom of Berār was himself a Brāhman convert. On the basis of recorded conduct, however, it is not possible to draw any clear distinction between the rulers who were purely foreigners and those who were wholly or partly of Indian blood.

The old Islamic theory of social equality had by this time given way. In practice all the Moslems in India were not 'brothers,' for various social distinctions had come into existence ; but facts recorded in the chronicles indicate, at least, that there was no effective prejudice against Indian converts on the ground of their origin, and that they might rise to the highest positions in a Turkish kingdom. The extent to which unconverted Hindus were employed in the large public offices at the capitals is uncertain ; but there is no doubt that the Turks made free use of the existing machinery of local administration, the headmen and accountants of villages or aggregates of villages, who were in all cases Hindus, and in this sphere of activity relations must have been intimate. In northern India, however, the position of the Turks as a ruling class is perfectly clear ; and the same is true of the South until the practical super-session of the Turks by other foreign immigrants.

SOCIAL RELATIONS

As regards the medium of intercourse, the emergence of the *lingua franca* known to Englishmen as Hindustani must be attributed to this period. Hindustani is in essence the form of Hindi spoken in the neighbourhood of Delhi, but with the addition of many Persian words and a lesser number of Persian turns of speech. So far as we know, it was not employed during this period as a means of literary expression, but grew up as a spoken language, used for, and adapted to, the needs of the moment ; and it was carried with them by the Turks in the course of the expansion of their rule to the south and west.

In some respects Bengal forms an exception to the statements which have just been made. There the numbers of immigrant Turks can never have been large, and, more than elsewhere, the foreign rulers were dependent on local support. Large numbers of the inhabitants accepted Islam, as we shall see further on, while there are some indications that Hindus were employed more freely in the administration than was the case in the other Turkish kingdoms. The Persian and Hindustani languages did not obtain the same vogue as in the north-west, and some of the rulers are known to have patronised the production of literary works in Bengali. Speaking generally, we may say that the peculiar conditions of the region operated to bring rulers and ruled together, and that in Bengal, alone of all the Turkish kingdoms, some progress was made towards an effective synthesis.

Turning now to the current of Hindu life, we can say in a general way that the study of law, philosophy and allied subjects continued on the established lines of subtle elaboration, and apparently without material changes in method ; but the texts are not yet dated, nor for the most part are they localised, so that no precise account of them can be given. We may conjecture that the main centres of Sanskrit studies in the Turkish period were those which survived into the early days of British rule, places like Nuddea on the Hooghly or Benares on the Ganges, where in the shelter of temples and monasteries learned Brāhmans went on their way, undisturbed except for some occasional outburst of iconoclasm, refining and distinguishing as their predecessors had done, but not introducing many new ideas. Further than this we can scarcely go.

Imaginative Sanskrit literature was dying or dead. We have seen that poetry and the drama had depended largely on the patronage of wealthy and cultured Hindu Courts, and it was probably inevitable that the political change in northern India should result in their decay: we might indeed expect to find a survival at Vijayanagar, but as a matter of fact no important productions are known to have originated there, or in the smaller Hindu Courts of Bundelkhand, Rājputāna and Orissa. Against the disappearance of this highly conventionalised literature must be set the marked development of the vernacular languages as a medium of literary expression, a development which was independent of patronage except in Bengal. Nearly everything of value in this new development is primarily of religious significance and it will be described in later paragraphs; but mention must be made here of the versified chronicles, recording, sometimes in most effective style, the fortunes of the various Hindu dynasties which, after the arrival of the Turks, established themselves in Rājputāna and elsewhere. These chronicles, composed by the Court bards, and recited periodically at festivals, have preserved into modern times the traditions of Rājput chivalry, and furnished to each succeeding generation an incentive to emulate the glories of the past.

As regards the recreative arts, music, singing and dancing, we know that they flourished at Vijayanagar as they had flourished at earlier Hindu Courts; and that the skill of the artists was appreciated by the Turks also can be inferred from the fact that on one occasion the terms imposed by the Bahmanīs included the surrender of 2,000 musicians and dancers from the Hindu capital. Of painting we know that the art survived in various Hindu Courts, to experience a remarkable development in the next period. The remains of Vijayanagar, and the temples built or restored about this time in Orissa, at Mount Abu and elsewhere, show that architecture and sculpture proceeded on the established

HINDU AND MOSLEM CULTURE

lines; and, speaking generally, it is not possible to point to any important literary or artistic development in Hindu culture which can be attributed directly to contact with the Turks.

The learning patronised by the conquerors consisted essentially of the science and theology which had been elaborated in Baghdad; as we have already seen, it embodied some elements derived originally from India, but on its secular side it was predominantly Greek. The Turks themselves did not play a very prominent part in these studies, but they welcomed learned men from Persia and elsewhere, who were held in honour at Court, and provided with liberal stipends from the treasury. In letters, the standard was set entirely by Persia, then enjoying its golden age of literature, and some of the Persian poets whose names are now familiar throughout the world appear in the Indian chronicles. Shaikh Sadi, for instance, reluctantly declined an invitation to visit Balban's son at Multān, while Hafiz actually started for the Bahmanī Court, but, deterred by the dangers of the voyage, turned back, and sent a well-known ode by way of apology. Amīr Khusrū (1253–1325) and the other writers of Persian poetry in India followed these models closely; the chroniclers enriched their prose with appropriate quotations from the Persian classics; and down to quite recent times Persian continued to be the language most favoured by cultured Indian Moslems.

Islam offers no scope for statues or images, and the surviving specimens of Turkish carving are purely decorative, an integral part of the architecture which has furnished the visible memorials of the period. The Turks brought with them to India a taste for building, and they required in particular two types of edifice—mosques and tombs—which were new to the country. They brought also an expert knowledge of the use of cement and mortar, which had hitherto been little used in India; and this enabled them to elaborate the dome and the true arch, the forms which, along with the minaret, are characteristic of Moslem buildings in general. They did not, however, introduce a merely exotic style, for, from the opening of the period onwards, many of the characteristics of Indian architecture are obvious in their work, particularly that union of strength and grace which Hindu builders had already achieved. The result was the evolution of the distinctive style usually known as Indo-Saracenic, though Indo-Islamic is a more appropriate description, specimens of which, adapted variously to local conditions and influences, can be seen wherever Moslems ruled in India, and not merely in their capital cities, but in the smaller centres of administration. Many of these buildings have suffered grievously from neglect, and some of them from injudicious restoration, but there has been no active iconoclasm such as befell those of the earlier period ; in the towns and cities of the greater part of India they still dominate the prospect ; and the ordinary traveller from the West brings back fewer memories of the towering temples than of the mosques and tombs, the arches, minarets and domes, which the Turks introduced.

In describing the religious developments of the period, we may begin with the subject of conversion. There is nothing to suggest that any appreciable numbers of Turks were converted to Hinduism as individuals, or that groups or tribes of them were absorbed as new castes, but it is certain that large numbers of Hindus accepted the creed which the conquerors introduced. Forcible conversion was not entirely unknown, but it was relatively unimportant. In Kashmīr, at a time when Islam had already gained many adherents, the king who is known as Sikandar the Iconoclast (1390–1414) insisted on the conversion of the remainder of the population, with death as the alternative ; about the same time there seems to have been a brief outburst of persecution in Bengal, in the course of which some scholars have inferred, on somewhat slight grounds, that large numbers of Hindus were converted by force ; while, nearly a century later, another Sikandar, the Lodī king of Delhi, is also credited with forcible propagation of the faith ; but with these exceptions the chronicles are silent on a subject which their writers would not have overlooked, and we are driven to the conclusion that most of the conversions which occurred were independent of official pressure.

A general idea of the regions where Islam found new adherents can be formed from the position at the present day. In the north-west—that is to say, Kashmīr, the western Punjab, the Frontier Province and Sind, taken together—Islam is professed by the great bulk of the people, more than three-quarters of the whole ; in the north-east, more than half the population of Bengal are Moslems, the proportion being highest in the northern and eastern districts ; in the rest of India Moslems constitute a small minority, ordinarily less than one in ten, and most of them living in the cities and towns. The large numbers found in the north-west can be explained as due partly to the immigration of Moslems from beyond the frontier, and partly to the vigour of the new faith—a vigour which rapidly weakened in Indian surroundings ; but these explanations cannot be used to account for the success of Islam in Bengal. Its causes are not on record, and the subject is too intricate to be discussed fully in these pages, but the most probable view is that the main factor was a reaction of the lower classes against the strict Hinduism enforced by the Senas. It will be recalled that the indigenous Pāla dynasty, which ruled from the eighth to the twelfth century, had been devoted to Buddhism, a faith under which the lower classes enjoyed practical freedom. In the twelfth century the Senas, entering Bengal from the south, brought with them the severe rules of Hinduism, under which the lower classes were subjected to many onerous restrictions ; and, at the end of the same century, before these restrictions had become customary, Islam arrived, preaching freedom and equality for all, even if the equality was not always apparent in practice. In these circumstances a mass movement towards the new creed is so inherently probable that it is unnecessary to seek further afield for other hypothetical causes.

Outside these two regions, conversions were merely sporadic. Many of them were doubtless due to sincere conviction, though social and economic motives may also have played their part. It is known, for instance, that some families which drew their livelihood from the public offices in the neighbourhood of Delhi quickly accepted Islam, and it is probable that the Turks depended largely on them for the rank and file of their administrative staff; and doubtless similar motives operated elsewhere, though the facts are not on record.

It is clear that conversion usually proceeded by families, or groups of families of the same caste, rather than by individuals, a fact which is entirely in accord with the social framework of Hinduism; and the result was a transfer of customs and even of ideas. The descendants of many converts retained usages in regard to marriage and other family events which they had practised as Hindus, and also in some cases the rules of their caste; and in this way the idea of caste itself was carried over into Islam, overriding the fundamental principle of equality, and the imported faith received a distinctive bias. Among uneducated Indian Moslems caste remains, even to-day, an essential fact; and Islam from being a single brotherhood has become in India an association of brotherhoods, held together by creed, but separate in some important departments of their social life.

Another feature which distinguishes Islam in India is the development of the practice of adoring saints, a practice which, though it exists in some other Moslem countries, does not rest on any precept of the founder of the faith. It is impossible now to extract the true stories of these saints, who are known as *pīrs*, from the mass of legends which have grown up round them, but we know in a general way that, even before the establishment of the kingdom of Delhi, pioneers of Islam had penetrated into the Gangetic plain, some as missionaries, others as soldiers of fortune, that something in their lives, or their deaths, caught the popular imagination, and that their tombs became shrines, where their anniversaries were, and still are, celebrated by the lower classes. The same is true of many Moslem missionaries of later times, whose shrines are found in

ISLAM IN INDIA

various localities, particularly in Bengal. The most remarkable thing about this development is that Hindus as well as Moslems take part in the ceremonies, which are Indian rather than Islamic in their details; adherents of both faiths make their offerings side by side; and, while theologians, in India as elsewhere, draw a nice distinction between the worship of God and the adoration of saints, the masses of the people do not feel the difference.

During our period, then, Islam contributed what to the popular eye are in effect new members of the Hindu pantheon. In order to consider the question whether it influenced Hinduism on a higher level, we must return to the development of the latter. The outstanding fact of the period is the spread over northern India of the doctrine of *bhakti*, or salvation by Grace and Love, which, as we have seen in an earlier chapter, had existed for an indefinite number of centuries, but had first been preached effectively by Rāmānuja. The story of this development is not known in detail, but the fifteenth century was marked by an extraordinary outburst of devotional poetry inspired by these doctrines, and thus stands out as one of the great formative periods in the history of northern India, a period in which on the one hand the modern languages were firmly established as vehicles of literary expression, and on the other the faith of the people was permeated by new ideas. We cannot even enumerate all the contributors to this outburst, but a few words must be said of five names which are household words to-day: Rāmānand and Mīrā Bāī, Nānak, Chaitanya and Kabīr.

Rāmānand belonged to the religious order which had been founded by Rāmānuja, but broke away from it, came to the North, settled in Benares, and preached the doctrine of *bhakti* with such success as to found a new order, the members of which produced a large volume of Hindi poetry embodying their faith. Mīrā Bāī was a Rājput princess, who, meeting with adversity, fled from her home in Chitor, became the disciple of a follower of Rāmānand, and embodied the new doctrines in Hindi and Gujarati verse of high poetic quality. Nānak preached in the Punjab, and he too relied largely on hymns composed by himself, partly in Hindi and partly in Punjabi. Chaitanya preached in Bengal, and inspired an extensive literature in Bengali. Kabīr is the centre of so many legends that it is impossible to ascertain the facts of his origin, but we know that he was a weaver in Benares, associated closely with Moslems if not actually a Moslem by birth, that he was influenced by the preaching of Rāmānand, that he attempted a synthesis comprehending Hinduism and Islam on the lines of the new doctrine, and that he composed or inspired a very large volume of poetry in Hindi. To complete the story, we may look a little ahead, and add the name of Tulsī Dās, the greatest poet of all, who in the sixteenth century retold the story of Rāma in the light of the new doctrines.

On the literary side then, this epoch furnished all over northern India the great bulk of the poetry which, read or recited in the villages, has ever since formed the basis of the imaginative life of the people. On the religious side it furnished new ideas which permeated, rather than superseded, the sacrificial cults of the temples; and, when we take both sides into account, the effect of the literature produced during the fifteenth and sixteenth centuries may justly be compared to that of the Bible in the life of England —for the common people the one great accessible source of inspiration as of consolation. The peasant may still follow scrupulously the ancient ritual appropriate to the worship of this deity or that; but in his mind, or rather in his heart, there is the idea of something larger and more universal, and when his feelings find expression, it is in an appeal to Parmeshar, the one Supreme Being, whom he has been led by this literature to know and love.

We have seen in an earlier chapter that the doctrine of *bhakti* might centre on either Siva or Vishnu. The former was the more usual in the South, where the doctrine spread widely though unobtrusively, but in northern India the Sivaite cults did not become equally prominent, and we meet much more often the names of Krishna and Rāma, the two principal incarnations of Vishnu. The distinction between these two cults is that the former is the more sensuous. The poems present the sexual life of the traditional Krishna, transfigured as allegory ; and, as has happened in other religions, the line between the sensuous and the erotic is sometimes crossed, while the moral dangers inherent in such teaching have been made manifest in India as elsewhere. The teaching which centres on Rāma has been spiritual rather than sensuous, and its literature is characterised by high ideals of personal conduct as well as by the self-surrender in devotion which is common to both. The movement in northern India was not, however, confined to worship of these two incarnations. To Kabīr the idea of incarnation was as unacceptable as the idea of sacrifice, and his teaching tended towards a pure theism, centring on a single Supreme Being who comprehended Allah and Rāma in Himself; and the same spirit is apparent in the teaching of Nānak in the Punjab, teaching which was largely inspired by Kabīr.

The question whether this great spiritual movement, which in spite of all distinctions is undoubtedly a single phenomenon, owed anything to the influence of Islam cannot be answered in set terms, except in the case of Kabīr and his followers, where the relationship is obvious. It is probable, however, that the imported creed was not without effect. Islam in India was no hole-and-corner religion. In every town where Moslems gathered, the mosque asserted itself, often on the site of a former temple, and built in part of its materials. From its minarets the daily call to prayer sounded in the ears of Moslems and Hindus alike, proclaiming the universal truth of the unity of God. Hindus might resent but they could not ignore this assertion, which at any rate familiarised them with an outlook different in essentials from the orthodox teaching of the Brāhmans. It is probable that this change in atmosphere may have facilitated the work of the preachers of *bhakti*, but more than this cannot be affirmed ; and *bhakti* in its origin is older than Islam.

MAP VI

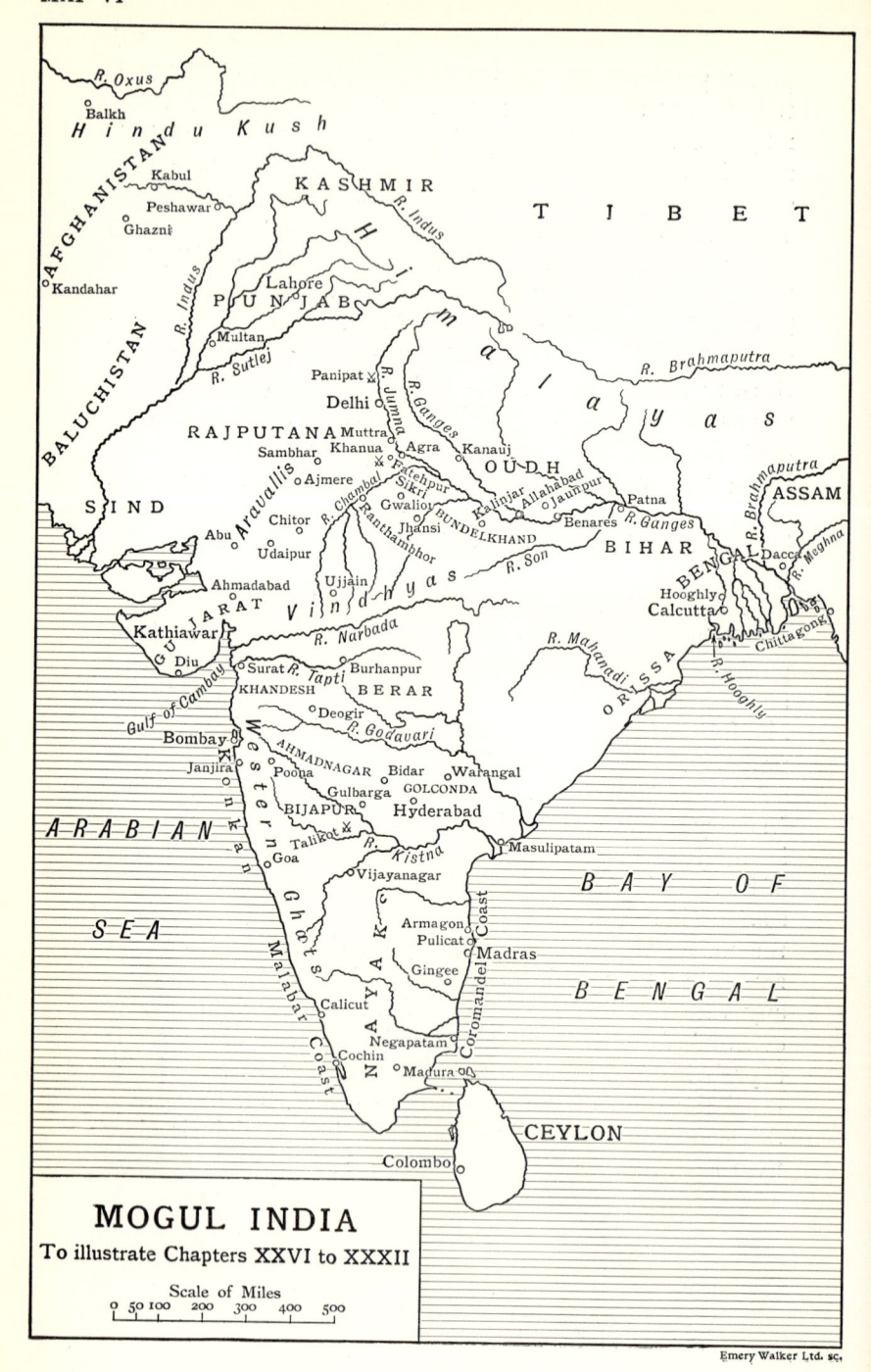

MOGUL INDIA
To illustrate Chapters XXVI to XXXII

Scale of Miles
0 50 100   200   300   400   500

CHAPTER XXVI

THE COMING OF THE PORTUGUESE

WE have seen in Chapter XIX how, towards the end of the fifteenth century, India had become enclosed in a ring-fence by the cultures of China and Islam, and in later chapters how the latter had spread over a large portion of the country. The causes which led the Portuguese to break the ring require a few words of explanation. Portugal was a small but enterprising nation, with little scope for expansion on land, but placed in a favourable position for development on the sea. During the fifteenth century her seamen had gradually worked their way down the west coast of Africa through waters then unknown to Europeans, trading as they went, but some of them inspired by the dream of finding a road to the Indies, and diverting to it the large and lucrative trade which then reached Europe through Egypt, Syria and Turkey. Desire for profit existed, but it was not the only motive at work. The Portuguese had a bitter hatred of Islam, as they knew it in north-west Africa, and they shared the apprehensions which then prevailed in Europe of the imminent danger to Christendom from the great Moslem powers established on the east of the Mediterranean; these powers drew a very large revenue from the goods which passed through their territories, and diversion of their trade would strike a heavy blow at their prosperity. Again, the Portuguese were ardent Christians, inspired by missionary zeal; and access to the Indies offered a prospect of preaching the Gospel to nations doomed by their ignorance to eternal damnation. These three motives, commercial, political and religious, appealing variously to individuals, combined to inspire what may almost be regarded as a national endeavour.

The exploration of African waters took a long time, but at last the Cape of Good Hope was discovered, and in 1498 a royal fleet commanded by Vasco da Gama anchored off the Malabar Coast, the name usually given to the southern portion of the western seaboard of India. In order to explain the results which followed, we must return to the great trade-route of southern Asia. We have seen in an earlier chapter that through voyages on this route gave way to arrangements by which goods changed hands, first in the Straits, and then on the coast of India. Early in the fifteenth century Malacca became the great entrepôt in the Straits. Indian ships came there, laden mainly with cotton goods, and returned to India with silk, spices, drugs, and other merchandise. Some of these goods were carried to the east coast, and distributed throughout India; some reached Gujarāt, partly for India, partly for transhipment to the Red Sea and Persian Gulf; a large portion reached the Malabar seaports, almost entirely for transhipment. The Malabar ships did not sail westward: the goods for the Red Sea were carried in Arab and Egyptian vessels, the agents for which lived in the ports, not as subjects of the rulers, but under special concessions which secured them rights of self-government; and since the various seaports, each under its own petty King or Chief, competed eagerly for the lucrative transhipment trade, these foreigners were assured of favourable treatment, and could exert much influence at the Courts, while acting, as they did, in concert, they could sometimes dictate terms to the Indian importers.

The vogue of the Malabar ports depended partly on their favourable position, and partly on the fact that, in addition to imported goods, they offered ample supplies of pepper, which for various reasons was an important article of consumption throughout northern Europe, and which in bulk, if not in value, was the largest single item in the cargoes for the Red Sea. Pepper was grown, as it still is, on the slopes of the Western Ghats, close to the seaports in this region; the narrow strip of country below the Ghats lived largely by its production; and a state might almost be ruined if the Arab and Egyptian merchants deserted it. The various small states were subordinate to Vijayanagar, but were not as a rule subject to much control, and in their commercial politics they acted as independent units, negotiating, and occasionally fighting, among themselves without interference from above.

The appearance of the Portuguese in this environment led necessarily to a conflict of interests. It was not, as it has occasionally been represented, a struggle between Christians and Moslems, but one between importers and exporters. The Indian importers, many of whom were Moslems, welcomed the Portuguese as new customers; the Arab and Egyptian exporters objected to them as new competitors, who might break the existing monopoly; and the upshot of a complicated series of intrigues was that, while the new-comers quarrelled with the ruler of Calicut, the principal seaport on the Malabar Coast, they established friendly relations at other centres, especially at Cochin, which offered the largest supply of pepper, and for a few years their annual fleets carried on a profitable trade, though one which was subject to occasional vicissitudes.

A share in the trade did not, however, satisfy the Portuguese; they aimed at controlling it, and their early experiences showed them how this could be done. No large territorial acquisitions were required; what was wanted was a navy strong enough to command the seas, with fortresses to guard the narrow waters, and, somewhere on the west coast of India, a central establishment from which operations could be directed and on which the navy could be based. The naval strength needed was not great, because there was little opposition; the only real fleet the Portuguese had to face was one which was equipped in Egypt, and this was destroyed in a battle fought early in 1509, after which date they were masters of the eastern seas.

The foundations of this maritime empire, as it may justly be called, were laid by Afonso de Albuquerque, Governor in the East from 1509 to his death in 1515, and one of the outstanding European names in the history of India; to quote a recent writer, 'his lofty vision was accompanied by a commanding character and by a tenacity of purpose which few leaders have possessed; he had a genius for civil administration as well as for war, while in diplomacy he could meet Orientals with their own weapons.'[1] In 1509 Albuquerque obtained possession of Ormuz, the island fortress which commanded the entrance to the Persian Gulf; in 1510 he seized Goa, a seaport in the territory of Bījāpur, which soon became the Portuguese capital in the East; and in 1511 he captured Malacca after desperate fighting, and thus secured the domination of the Straits. The possession of Aden, at the mouth of the Red Sea, which would have made the scheme formally complete, was sought for, but never secured; and later acquisitions on the Indian coast, especially the fortress of Dīū at the entrance to the Gulf of Cambay, rendered it unnecessary, for the Portuguese were in a position to dominate all the seaports whence ships could start for the Red Sea, and in point of fact most of the Arab shipping agents soon left India.

The methods adopted to control the trade were briefly as follows. Some routes, and some commodities on all routes, were monopolised for the benefit of the kingdom of Portugal. Subject to these restrictions, Indian or other ships could obtain licences to ply between specified ports on payment of substantial fees. Any unlicensed vessel was good prize, and the gunboats employed by the Portuguese to patrol the routes were more than a match for the cumbrous merchantmen even when armed. By these methods the Portuguese dominated the main trade-routes throughout the sixteenth century, and the fact that some goods continued to reach Europe overland was due mainly to the increasing corruption of their officials, who came to look on their posts as sources of private gain, and could be bribed to pass contraband goods.

The possessions of the Portuguese on the west coast of India were integral parts of the kingdom of Portugal, obtained either by conquest or by cession; but on the

[1] *Afonso de Albuquerque*, by E. Prestage (Watford, 1929), p. 83.

THE PORTUGUESE MARITIME EMPIRE

east coast settlements of a less regular type grew up as the century went on. At various places in Bengal and on the Coromandel Coast, Portuguese merchants settled with the consent of the local rulers, and then, relying on the prestige of their nation, fortified their settlements, assumed rights of self-government, and eventually in some cases repudiated the authority of the Viceroy at Goa. These petty republics, as they may almost be called, became centres of lawlessness, and in some cases nests of pirates, to the serious injury of commerce in the Bay of Bengal; but this result was due, not to Portuguese policy, but to the collapse of the national power.

The immediate effects produced by the Portuguese in India were not great. In the field of politics, their capture of Goa necessarily involved them in enmity with Bījāpur, while on the whole they maintained friendly relations with Vijayanagar; they quickly realised the importance of the horse-trade, but they did not render the Hindu power any material help in the struggle for the South; and, from the Indian standpoint, their appearance merely added one more element in the confused politics of the time. In war, they undoubtedly introduced higher standards of efficiency in both artillery [1] and musketry; and these, combined with the magnificent courage they displayed, produced a legend of invincibility, which in its turn contributed to their success.

In commerce, it cannot be said that the diversion of trade was accompanied by any great expansion in the exports of Indian goods; it is probable that more pepper reached western Europe than before, but the only new development which can be asserted with confidence was the opening of new markets for Indian cotton goods in West Africa and Brazil. Nor were the Portuguese successful in developing the import trade; the great bulk of their purchases were paid for in silver, and they could sell little except luxuries and curiosities from Europe. The chief commercial service

---

[1] The date of the introduction of artillery in southern India is a very obscure topic, but guns were certainly in use there before the Portuguese arrived.

which they rendered to India was the effective policing of the coastal trade. There were nests of pirates along the Malabar Coast, who lived mainly by depredations on the small vessels which plied in great numbers between Gujarāt on the one side and Ceylon, Madras and Bengal on the other; the Portuguese provided gunboats to convoy the fleets of these vessels, and thereby established a reasonable degree of security on the main line of Indian trade. Against this service must be set the toll, whether in licence-fees or in bribes, which they levied on Indian commerce, both coasting and foreign, the loss to Indian shippers on the trade transferred to Portuguese vessels, and the vexatious restraints which their system involved on the possible extension of Indian maritime enterprise.

The Portuguese were devoted to their religion, and Christianity was firmly established wherever they settled, much of their territory being given as endowments for churches and monasteries. The various religious orders despatched saintly and heroic missionaries through India, and as far as China and Japan; in Goa itself the Holy Inquisition was established for the protection of the faith; and the Archbishop held a position second only to the Viceroy. The attitude of the ecclesiastics towards Indians in general presents a mentality which is difficult to realise at the present day. To them Moslems were reprobates, who had known and rejected the eternal truth; Hindus were heathen, waiting for their souls to be saved; but even more deplorable was the heretical condition of the Nestorian Christians whom they found in Malabar, and who were eventually brought into nominal subjection to Rome.

The Portuguese who came to India were characterised by great individual courage, enthusiasm for conquest, personal and national pride, but many of them were cruel, factious, and domineering; and their early successes encouraged their inborn arrogance, so that they came to regard Asiatics in general as their natural subjects. The arrivals from Europe included very few women; and from the time of Albuquerque onwards the men were encouraged to marry Indian wives, and make their homes in the various settlements, which, it was hoped, would in this way become self-supporting in soldiers and sailors. The mixed race which thus came into existence during the sixteenth century was inferior to the original stock, less brave, but not less arrogant, and increasingly avaricious and corrupt. Records of gallant exploits became fewer, instances of treachery and rapacity increased, and by the end of the century the Portuguese in India, though still feared, were generally detested. Their prestige collapsed promptly when they were confronted by the Dutch and the English, and fifty years later their influence in India had become insignificant. This period of decadence has given the Portuguese an evil name in modern India, but it should not be allowed to obliterate the memory of their initial achievement, with its magnificent record of courage and endurance, a record which is preserved for all time in two worthy monuments, the *Asia* of the historian João de Barros, and the *Lusiad* of the poet Camoens.

CHAPTER XXVII

THE MOGUL CONQUEST

WHILE the Portuguese were still new-comers on the coast, the north of India was conquered by the Moguls.[1] Bābur, the conqueror, was of mixed blood, part Turk and part Mongol; he was a direct descendant of Tīmūr, while on his mother's side he derived also from Chingīz Khān, and he was justly proud of his ancestry. As a child he succeeded to a petty kingdom in Turkistan, and his boyhood was adventurous, sometimes seated on a throne, sometimes wandering in a desert; but at the age of twenty-one, having been driven out of Turkistan, he settled down as King of Kābul, then the chief fortress in eastern Afghanistan. We know the sort of man he was mainly from his *Memoirs*, a book which takes a high place in the autobiographical literature of the world; its dominant note is the joy of life in all its aspects—scenery, gardens, and buildings, hard drinking and harder fighting, friendships and enmities, intricate diplomacy and practical jokes, and, behind all these, a steadfast purpose and unconquerable will.

Kābul did not offer scope for such a man, and he decided to conquer the Punjab, which, as he recalled, had once belonged to his great ancestor, Tīmūr. His resources were, however, inadequate, his position in Kābul was not too secure, he matured his plans slowly, and gained experience by a series of raids across the Indian frontier. The opportunity for which he was waiting seemed to have come when

[1] Etymologically the words Mongol and Mogul are identical, but the distinction which has grown up in English use corresponds to facts, 'Mongol' denoting the whole following of Chingīz Khān, while 'Mogul' is confined to Bābur's family and adherents in India. The original word is reproduced by some writers as Mughal and by others as Mughul.

the Governor of Lahore, convinced that he had been marked out for destruction by his sovereign, Ibrāhīm Lodī, renounced his allegiance, and asked for help from Kābul. The parties were, however, at cross purposes, for each of them wanted the Punjab for himself; and the upshot of a period of intricate diplomacy was that Bābur invaded India, and, crossing the Punjab without much difficulty, reached the edge of the Gangetic plain, where in the first battle of Pānīpat, fought in April, 1526, he destroyed the power of the Lodī dynasty and became master of its dominions.

The battle was in many ways noteworthy. Ibrāhīm's forces probably numbered about 50,000 men, with 1,000 elephants; Bābur had not more than 8,000 effectives, but he had obtained from Turkey serviceable artillery and musketry, which the Lodī army lacked, and his dispositions were directed to give these arms full play. As the result of his masterly tactics, the enemy's forces found themselves crowded together in a mass, with the Mogul cavalry on each side and the guns in front; the slaughter was terrific; the king himself was killed; and at last the remnant of the Lodī army fled in disorder. Bābur took possession unopposed first of Delhi and then of Agra, and settled down to the task of organising his conquest.

The obstacles in his way fell into two classes, the Afghan nobles and the Rājput Chiefs. We have seen that under the Lodīs each Afghan noble was practically supreme in the territory assigned to him. After the battle of Pānīpat some of these agreed on a claimant to the throne, while others assumed independence, and it was necessary to crush the latter one by one. Bābur's energy was equal to the task. The army supporting the claimant dispersed without fighting, and many nobles rallied to the new conqueror, while the others were driven out of their strongholds, and most of them retired to Bengal, where they were welcomed by the king and provided with assignments. Before, however, the plains had been cleared of enemies, Bābur had to face the Rājputs from the South.

It will be recalled that in the course of the Turkish conquest bands of Rājputs had left the Gangetic plain and carved out kingdoms for themselves in the country which now bears their name. These kingdoms had on the whole maintained their independence, and occasionally fought among themselves, but in the reign of Ibrāhīm Lodī a confederacy had emerged among them under the leadership of Sangrāma, the Rāna of Mewār,[1] the object of which was to drive the Lodīs out. True to the Indian tradition, Sangrāma had entered into negotiations with Bābur as a possible ally, and had promised co-operation with him, a promise which was not fulfilled; but when Bābur had succeeded in his enterprise, the confederacy turned against him, and its forces marched north and threatened Agra. Bābur took the field in person, and in March, 1527, the Rājputs, in spite of their great superiority in numbers—probably seven or eight to one—were completely defeated at Khānua, about forty miles west of Agra, the guns again serving to decide the issue. Many of the Rājput Chiefs were killed, Sangrāma their leader was severely wounded, the confederacy dissolved, and Bābur was in no further danger from this quarter.

The short remainder of Bābur's life was spent in consolidating his kingdom, and disposing of such opposition as remained; but his health was failing, and in 1530 he died, at the age of forty-seven. The story of his death is characteristic of the man. Humāyūn, his eldest son, lay dying. Bābur decided to follow an old custom, and sacrifice his most precious possession in exchange for his son; and so, with due ritual, he offered his own life, the thing he valued most. The son recovered, and not long afterwards the father died. Humāyūn, who succeeded to the throne, was a man of ability and culture, but indolent by nature, and addicted to opium. His first few years were spent in organising and extending his kingdom, and in 1535 he was fighting successfully in Mālwa and Gujarāt; but in the following year he had to return hastily to the North to deal with a dangerous situation which had arisen in Bihār, and which introduces us to Sher Khān, one of the most remarkable men who ever ruled in India.

[1] Mewār is sometimes called Chitor, and sometimes Udaipur, after its successive capitals.

SHER SHĀH

Sher Khān was an Afghan, and one of the nobles of Ibrāhīm Lodī. After the battle of Pānīpat he attached himself to the conqueror, but, falling under suspicion, retired hastily to his assignment in Bihār, in country which had not yet been pacified. After much skilful intrigue, with occasional hard fighting, he emerged as a quasi-independent ruler in the broken country between the Ganges and its southern tributary the Son, and proceeded to extend his territory in the direction of Bengal, where he laid siege to the capital Lakhnautī. Humāyūn, after some procrastination, marched in that direction. Sher Khān was not yet in a position to resist him in the field, and, having secured a great treasure by the capture of Lakhnautī, withdrew with his booty through Chota Nāgpur to his strongholds in Bihār while Humāyūn occupied Lakhnautī, and spent three precious months in relaxation. Here his army was weakened by disease and desertion; news came of a rebellion in Delhi; and Sher Khān's forces threatened his line of retreat. He turned his face westward, but Sher Khān by a combination of tactics and treachery practically destroyed his army in two battles, and in 1540 fairly chased him out of the Gangetic plain. He sought help in Rājputāna and Sind, and eventually with a following of only forty men found a refuge in Persia, leaving his conqueror, henceforward styled Sher Shāh, in undisputed possession of northern India from Bengal to the Punjab.

Sher Shāh's equipment for kingship was exceptionally complete. An expert soldier, he was also a great military administrator, and kept his troops on a very high level of efficiency; in diplomacy he was astute, and absolutely unscrupulous; in the art of government he was experienced, diligent and sagacious; above all, he was a master of men, before whom opposition was apt to melt away. Extension of his kingdom was naturally an object of his policy. He quickly secured the key position of Gwalior, and thence overran Mālwa; designs on the country farther south were considered, but postponed till the roads were cleared; and he made himself master of two other key positions, Ranthambhor and Ajmere. There remained the great fortress of

Kālinjar, about 120 miles east of Jhānsī, which was in the hands of a hostile Hindu Chief; early in 1545 Sher Shāh laid siege to it, was fatally wounded in an explosion of ammunition, and died after a reign of less than five years.

His conquests were transient, and his importance in history is based rather on his administrative work. The early Moguls had made no advance on the rough system of the Lodīs, merely sending their own followers to replace the Afghan nobles: Sher Shāh established a regular bureaucratic hierarchy, taking orders direct from his Court. Officials were appointed to administer each of the traditional groups of villages, which were known to Hindus as parganas; and these parganas were grouped in what may be called districts, with superior officers in charge. One most important duty of these officials was the assessment and collection of the revenue, that is to say, the king's share of the produce of the country; Sher Shāh fixed the proportion to be paid in all ordinary cases as one-third of the produce, and introduced methods by which the sum due from each peasant could be determined with substantial accuracy without the labour of weighing and dividing the crops. We do not know how far these methods were successful at the moment; their interest lies in the fact that they formed the starting-point of the agrarian system elaborated during the reign of Akbar.

For the security of the country forts were suitably garrisoned at the dangerous points, and placed in charge of officers selected for their capacity. The village headmen were held personally responsible for highway robbery and other violent crime, on the theory that they must be acquainted with the criminals; while the main roads were equipped with walled rest-houses where merchants and travellers could halt in safety. Nor were the amenities of life neglected. Shade-giving trees were planted along the roads, supplies of drinking water were provided, and, speaking generally, the reign of Sher Shāh was marked by a great bureaucratic development, in which the central authority concerned itself actively with the lives of its individual subjects, which under the Lodī régime had been matters for

THE END OF AFGHAN RULE

the nobles on the spot. Such a system is exposed to the obvious criticism that it must have involved great oppression on the part of minor officials, and the only possible reply is that under personal rule the personality of the ruler is the determining factor. Sher Shāh, a tireless worker, listened to all complaints, and is credited by the chroniclers with a strong sense of justice as well as a taste for drastic punishments ; it is reasonable therefore to infer that oppression was kept in check by fear of his wrath, and that his rule was on the whole beneficial to his subjects, though under weaker successors his system might have disastrous results.

Little need be said here of those successors. The kingdom held together for barely ten years, and then the western portion was reconquered by Humāyūn, while Bengal broke away and became independent under an Afghan dynasty. We have said that Humāyūn had found a refuge in Persia. The Shah furnished him with a force of cavalry, with the aid of which he established himself in Kābul, and there he sat waiting, as his father had waited, for a favourable moment to invade India. A disputed succession offered a suitable opportunity, and in 1555 he traversed the Punjab, defeated the claimant who for the moment had the upper hand, and resumed the throne which he had lost fifteen years before. His reign was not, however, destined to be long, for only a few months later he died from the effects of a fall, and was succeeded in India by his son Akbar, then a boy of thirteen, while Kābul fell to a younger son, **Muhammad Hakīm.**

CHAPTER XXVIII

THE REIGN OF AKBAR

WE may preface the account of Akbar's achievements with a few words about the dynasty to which he belonged. The great days of the Mogul empire are comprised in four reigns, and English readers may find it helpful to remember that these reigns coincided, to a couple of years or so, with dynastic events nearer home. Akbar (1556–1605) was contemporary with Elizabeth, Jahāngīr (1605–1627) with James I, Shāh Jahān (1627–1658) with Charles I and Cromwell, while Aurangzeb (1658–1707) ruled from the Restoration to the middle of the reign of Queen Anne. The despotism of the first three Emperors was untrammelled, but Aurangzeb considered himself bound by the public law of Islam, which he applied with results disastrous to the dynasty.

The Emperor nominated his successor, and this practice was the cause of a long series of dynastic troubles, which we shall not narrate in detail. There were endless intrigues to secure the coveted nomination, or discredit the favourite of the moment, intrigues in which the ladies of the palace played active parts; we can only imagine what an Emperor's private life must have been like, but in the field of public affairs we know that these intrigues resulted from time to time in rebellions, and in cruel and treacherous murders. Jahāngīr rebelled against Akbar, Shāh Jahān rebelled against Jahāngīr, Aurangzeb deposed and imprisoned Shāh Jahān, Prince Akbar rebelled against his father Aurangzeb. Jahāngīr, again, arranged the murder of Abul Fazl, Akbar's most trusted officer, who was believed to be hostile to his claims, and he was widely suspected of poisoning Akbar himself; it is practically certain that Shāh Jahān ordered the murder of his brother, Prince Khusrū, who had been entrusted to his care, and on his accession he exterminated all possible competitors for the throne; Aurangzeb, after his successful *coup d'état*, had two of his brothers murdered, and the same fate would certainly have befallen the last of them, if he had not escaped to Burma, only to die there miserably.

Such incidents as these were normal. That there were not more of them is explained in part by the death of several Princes from drink, to which the Moguls in general were much addicted. They did not, like the Turks, content themselves with the light wines of Persia, but either drank strong spirits, or fortified their wine with intoxicating drugs; and the chronicles relate melancholy stories of able and cultured Princes degenerating into hopeless drunkards, and being eliminated by death from the contests for the throne.

The ladies of the Court were kept in strict seclusion, but it must not be inferred that they were nonentities. We get occasional glimpses of strong-minded and strong-willed ladies playing active parts in public affairs, and we know that the general level of culture in the palace was high. Nor was seclusion incompatible with outdoor enjoyments; Jahāngīr tells us of his wife's prowess in shooting tigers, and some of the early English merchants were advised that ladies' riding hats and gloves of the latest European fashions would be acceptable presents at Court. The contemporary chronicles, however, are marked by reticence as to what actually happened behind the veil, and it is often impossible to make a precise estimate of the influences operating thence on the Emperor or the Princes; we know that the ladies counted for much, but for how much we can rarely say.

There was no hereditary nobility in the strict sense of the term. Everybody of position lived on grants or assignments of revenue, which were resumable at pleasure, while the Emperor was heir to the entire personal property left by each noble. In theory then each generation had to make a fresh start, but in practice many noble families persisted; portions of the estate of a deceased noble were commonly restored to the family as a matter of grace, while the sons, if they had secured the Emperor's favour, were sure of substantial assignments, and of a good start in life. In this matter, however, as in everything else, the favour of the Emperor was the decisive factor: without it, there was no career for a gentleman within the empire, and the man who failed to gain it could only transfer his allegiance to some other ruler. An exception to these statements must be made in the case of those Hindu Chiefs who were recognised as nobles of the empire; in their case hereditary succession was the rule, subject to the approval of the Emperor, which was usually accorded.

From these general remarks we turn to the reign of Akbar. He succeeded as a boy to a precarious hold on part of the Punjab: when he died half a century later, he was undisputed master of northern India, and had made substantial progress towards the conquest of the South. Practically the whole of this achievement was his own, for after six years of regency he assumed personal control, and thenceforward he was ruler in fact as well as name, deciding on the policy to be pursued, choosing the men to carry it out, and attending to the administration in all its details. The sources of our knowledge of his character and achievements are, for the period, unusually varied. The *Akbarnāma*, the official record of his reign, was compiled by Abul Fazl, an ardent admirer, and is characterised by hero-worship, or even what some western readers would describe as flattery. There are also several unofficial chronicles, one of which, the work of a zealous Moslem and disappointed place-hunter, is definitely hostile to the Emperor; while in addition we have various sidelights on the reign from European sources, the most important of them the reports of Jesuit missionaries from Goa, who spent long periods at Court, and had exceptional opportunities of studying the Emperor's character.

Physically, Akbar was well equipped for his position, being endowed with a strong constitution and remarkable powers of endurance. Like others of his family, he occasionally drank to excess, but he did not, like so many of them, become a slave to intemperance or other vices, and he preserved his health by dint of an active life, with plenty of riding, walking and shooting, for he had a passion for every form of sport. In action he was prompt and courageous, or even rash; but in policy he was deliberate, and knew how to choose his time.

As a boy he had preferred sport to lessons, and as a man he never read or wrote; nor was there any reason why he should. For study or relaxation he could command the services of expert readers; while all business was brought before him by word of mouth, and his orders taken down by the secretary in attendance, a method of procedure which gave full scope to his natural gifts, a clear head, a very retentive memory, and the power of going straight to the heart of a complicated question, and promptly reaching a decision.

We know less of his motives than of his acts, for the working of his mind was by no means simple, and even when reasons for a particular decision are assigned in our sources, they cannot always be accepted as the whole truth; his Jesuit guests, though experts in the study of character, were frequently left wondering what he really meant. It is safe, however, to say that his dominant motives were ambition and curiosity. The former is obvious in the records of his conquests, while all our authorities agree in stressing the wideness of his interests, and his eagerness for concrete facts; nothing came amiss to him in art or sport, in mechanics or theology, in metallurgy or natural history; and when the facts were in doubt, he was quick to devise experiments for their ascertainment.

Something must be said of Akbar's personal position in regard to religion, because it was one of the dominant factors in his life. He was always drawn to mysticism, seeking for direct intercourse with God, and occasionally experiencing religious ecstasy. In early life he appears to have found satisfaction within the pale of Islam, the religion in which he had been brought up, but this phase soon passed, and when he was about thirty-three he organised a series of formal discussions intended to discover the truth. At first these discussions were confined to various schools of Islamic thought, but presently Hindus, Jains and Parsees were included; then Akbar sent to Goa for Christian priests, and a Jesuit mission reached his Court in the year 1580, and took an active part in the debates. The Emperor's eagerness to learn raised high hopes among the members of the mission, but disillusionment came as they realised that his interest in their doctrine was primarily intellectual, and that he would accept no dogma which did not commend itself to his reason; he had by this time definitely broken away from Islam, but he could not be led to accept Christianity, and eventually the missionaries asked leave to depart.

As the outcome of these discussions, Akbar, in 1582, promulgated a new religion, the Divine Faith (*Dīn Ilāhī*). In essence it was a rather vague theism, of which he was the sole authoritative exponent; and his attitude was such as to give some excuse for the assertion of strict Moslems that he claimed divine honours for himself. The motives which prompted this action are somewhat obscure: it is certain that he was still seeking spiritual satisfaction for himself, but at the same time there was probably a hope of providing a common faith which might help to unify the subjects of the empire. If so, the hope was disappointed, for the new creed gained practically no adherents except at Court, and did not long survive its founder. Whether it continued to satisfy Akbar himself is uncertain. Additional Jesuit missions were invited to Court, and were in constant relations with him for the last ten years of his reign, but they could never be certain of his real attitude. The evidence regarding his death-bed is conflicting, and all that need be said here is that it is important to remember that throughout the second half of his reign Moslem orthodoxy was definitely out of favour.

Turning now to the political history of the reign, we may begin by a sketch of the process by which the petty and precarious kingdom of 1556 extended into a great

THE BEGINNINGS OF EMPIRE

empire. At the time of Akbar's accession, the principal Afghan claimant to the throne was represented by a Hindu named Hemū, a merchant by caste, who had become his Prime Minister, and was in command of his army. Encouraged by the news of Humāyūn's death, Hemū attacked the Moguls, and drove them out of Delhi, where, disregarding his absent master, he assumed the throne for himself. The Moguls rallied, and battle was again joined at Pānīpat in November, 1556; Hemū, with much the stronger forces, had secured an apparently winning position, when he was incapacitated by a wound, his leaderless army broke, and he himself was captured and executed. Within a year the other Afghan claimants were accounted for, and the danger from this side was at an end. Expansion could then begin, and before the end of the regency the kingdom had been extended to Jaunpur on the east, and included the fortress of Gwalior on the south.

As regards Akbar's personal achievements in this field a few general remarks may be made. In the first place, it is unnecessary to seek for *casus belli*; conquest was his accepted policy, and excuses for an attack could always be found. In the second place, Akbar treated Moslem rulers differently from Hindus: on conquest, a Moslem was usually displaced and his territories taken under direct administration, but a Hindu who accepted the situation was assured of an honourable position within the empire, and ordinarily retained practically complete authority within his domains. In the third place, the formal annexation of a kingdom was sometimes only the beginning of a long story; in various directions, particularly Bengal and Gujarāt, the defeated dynasty was able to reassert itself from time to time, and the suppression of these rebellions, as they were regarded by the Moguls, was no easy task. Subject to the campaigns undertaken for this purpose, Akbar's conquests fall into four groups, to the south, to the east, to the north-west and west, and finally to the south again.

Holding the fortress of Gwalior, it was easy to overrun Mālwa, which was annexed in 1561. Rājputāna next received attention for ten years, and some Chiefs were conquered while others were won over. Ranthambhor fell in 1569, and by 1571 Rājputāna as a whole was within the empire, though a few portions were still recalcitrant. Next came the turn of Gujarāt, which was annexed in 1572, and Akbar was able for the first time to look upon the sea. Subsequent operations in this direction were confined to the suppression of rebellions, and attention was turned towards the east. In 1574 Akbar in person conquered Bihār; the campaign against Bengal was then entrusted to others and was for a time mishandled, but in 1576 the Afghan king was defeated and put to death. Most of Bengal was then brought within the empire, but some years elapsed before the Afghan resistance was finally crushed, while part of the country east of the Meghna, which not long before had been overrun by Arakan, remained foreign territory until the middle of the next century.

Akbar had now to turn his face towards the north-west. We have said in the last chapter that, on the death of Humāyūn, Kābul was allotted to Akbar's half-brother, Muhammad Hakīm, who ruled there in practical independence. Quite early in life he seems to have coveted a share in the wealth of India, and in 1566 he had invaded the Punjab, but soon retreated. In 1580 many of Akbar's officers in Bengal and Bihār, alienated by the Emperor's apostasy from Islam, turned to the younger brother as the orthodox head of Indian Moslems; a party at Akbar's Court took the same view; and early in the next year Muhammad Hakīm, encouraged by the situation, again invaded the Punjab in the hope of finding local support. For a time the position was serious, but the invader was not the stuff of which conquerors are made, being cowardly, irresolute, and a drunkard, and he retreated hurriedly without attempting to face the large army which Akbar put into the field. Akbar occupied Kābul without serious fighting, but he was reluctant to press matters to extremes, and he tacitly allowed Muhammad Hakīm to return to the fortress. The younger man died in 1585 of chronic alcoholism, and Kābul then became part of the empire in fact as well as in name. Kashmīr was annexed in the following year,

CONQUESTS IN NORTH AND SOUTH

Lower Sind in 1591, eastern Baluchistan in 1595, and in the same year the Persian Governor of Kandahār, the great fortress of southern Afghanistan, handed over his charge without fighting.

Northern India as a whole was now within the empire, for the Viceroy of Bengal had in 1593 extended his authority over Orissa, and Akbar prepared for the conquest of the South. Berār fell in 1596, Khāndesh in 1600, and the capital of Ahmadnagar in the same year, but only a portion of the latter kingdom was brought under Mogul rule. Akbar was not yet satisfied. He still hoped to conquer Bījāpur, Golconda, and the country beyond, to expel the Portuguese from India, and to extend his power indefinitely over Central Asia; but these projects were not destined to be accomplished, and the few remaining years of his life were occupied, and embittered, by the rebellion of his son, Jahāngīr.

We now turn to the methods by which Akbar consolidated and ruled the great empire he had acquired : for the present, we confine ourselves to the principles on which he acted, leaving the mechanism of his administration for the next chapter. From the outset of his effective reign he recognised that an Indian empire, such as he aspired to found, could not rest merely on the small numbers of adherents of the dynasty, or on the Turks and Afghans who might rally to success, and would certainly desert in the event of failure. He aimed, therefore, at securing the acquiescence of his Hindu subjects as a whole, and the active support of the leading Rājput Chiefs ; and these aims he was able to realise.

As regards the Chiefs, it will be recalled that Bābur had been confronted by a powerful Rājput confederacy, and the possibility of its revival must have been present to Akbar's mind, while the forces of horsemen whom the Chiefs could put into the field were certainly the best fighting material in India ; to have these forces on his side instead of against him was the motive of his policy. Adhesion of the Chiefs to the paramount power was made easy, and fighting was where possible avoided, though a battle might on occasion be a necessary preliminary. Once a Chief had submitted and placed his forces at the Emperor's disposal, he was given an honourable position at Court, and welcomed socially. So far as we know, he was not required to pay tribute, beyond the conventional presents due to every Oriental monarch, nor had he to fear administrative interference within his own territories. Akbar himself married daughters of some of the leading Chiefs, while his son Jahāngīr, whose mother was a Rājput lady, received another as his first wife, the wedding being celebrated with many Hindu rites.

As the result of this policy the great bulk of Rājputāna became definitely loyal to the Emperor, who could thus command the services of something like 50,000 of the best horsemen in India. Its one conspicuous failure was in the case of the Rāna of Mewār. In 1567 Akbar attacked and captured his capital, Chitor, after the ladies had sacrificed themselves in the traditional rite of *jauhar*, but the survivors of the tribe withdrew to the hills. A second attack made in 1576 was unsuccessful, and Rāna Partāb Singh, now the leader, and the hero, of his tribe, maintained a defiant attitude until his death in 1597, preoccupations in other directions preventing Akbar from undertaking a decisive campaign.

Justice and toleration were the keynotes of the policy adopted towards Hindus in general. One of Akbar's first measures after he assumed personal control was to forbid the levy of a special tax which had been collected on Hindus visiting places of pilgrimage, and a year later he prohibited collection of the *jizya*, the differential tax claimed from non-Moslems in a Moslem state. Like other foreign rulers, he was opposed to the practice of suttee, and on one occasion he intervened, personally and alone, to prevent it, but his formal orders permitted the practice so long as it was voluntarily performed. He deferred also to Hindu veneration of the cow, the slaughter of which he made a capital offence; and, in the second half of the reign, after the failure of the orthodox movement to supplant him by Muhammad Hakīm, his regulations were certainly less favourable to

Islam than to the other faiths professed by his subjects. That his policy was successful may be inferred from the tranquillity of the empire which resulted. The occasional rebellions, of which we read in the chronicles, were not popular movements; they were undertaken by Moslems, whether representative of conquered dynasties, or officers who had grievances of their own, but there was nothing in the nature of a mass revolt; and the tradition of a golden age, which survived into the British period, is good evidence of the honour in which Akbar's name was held in the villages of northern India.

The width of Akbar's interests is obvious in the accounts we possess of his Court, which was stately and magnificent, but not extravagant by the standards recognised in Asia. The literary culture was, of course, predominantly Persian, and writers from many countries gathered to benefit from the imperial patronage; but the great library of manuscripts which Akbar collected comprised also many translations of Sanskrit works, such as the *Mahābhārata*, which had been made under his orders, and which he enjoyed hearing. There is nothing to show that his patronage extended to writers of any of the modern Indian languages, but he gathered large numbers of the best Hindu musicians and artists from the smaller Indian Courts. The artists were, it seems, set to work on pictures in the established Persian manner, but they brought to the task their own gifts and traditions; the foreign influences were for the most part either extruded or assimilated; and the outcome was the distinctive Mogul style, which culminated in the seventeenth century, and the work of which is now appreciated so highly by western connoisseurs.

Akbar was a great builder, but most of his work was meant for use, and his personal activities in this department dealt largely with the practical question of getting good value for the money which he spent. The massive stone forts at Agra and Allahabad show the scale on which he could work, but his principal monument is his ruined capital, Fatehpur Sīkrī, about twenty miles west of Agra. The Lodīs, who had made the latter place their capital, had not done much in the way of building; Akbar considered the city unlucky, and in 1569 he decided to build a new capital at a village called Sīkrī, the residence of a Moslem saint to whose intercession he attributed the birth of two of his sons. Work went on rapidly for the next decade under the Emperor's personal supervision. The material used was mainly the red sandstone of the ridge on which the city stands, and the buildings display in varying proportions such a combination of Hindu and Moslem features that the place may be described as having a style of its own, and a style of rare charm and beauty.

Under Akbar, however, as under some earlier Emperors, the effective capital was the place where he happened to be, for the large public offices ordinarily accompanied him on the march. He left Fatehpur Sīkrī in 1585, and spent the next twelve years in the north-west; when he returned, he resided chiefly at Agra, and the city he had built quickly fell into decay. The reasons why it was abandoned are not on record; possibly it was merely an autocrat's whim, but it may be that prosaic considerations of a sanitary nature were the determining factor in this, as in some other cases, where a change of capital took place.[1]

Apart from official activities, the reign was marked by a revival of temple-building, rendered possible by Akbar's tolerant attitude. The most remarkable specimens are found in the neighbourhood of the city of Muttra, a centre of the cult of Krishna, and they display the same combination of diverse features as characterises Fatehpur Sīkrī, the dome and true arch taking their place harmoniously in structures of a definitely Hindu type.

[1] A generation later an English merchant was told that the abandonment of the city was due to the badness of the water supply (*Early Travels in India*, ed. W. Foster (London, 1921), p. 150).

CHAPTER XXIX

AKBAR'S ADMINISTRATION

We have now to attempt a sketch of the administrative machinery by means of which Akbar achieved the results recorded in the last chapter. As an administrator he was not less distinguished than Sher Shāh, but the two men had very different tasks. Sher Shāh had to improvise a system out of nothing : Akbar built on Sher Shāh's foundations, not improvising, but modifying and developing to meet each difficulty as it arose, and guided always by the hard facts of each particular case. The story of his successive adaptations is long and interesting, but cannot be recounted here : the most that can be done is to describe the system reached in the later years of his reign, a system which in its main lines persisted into the British period. Our knowledge of it is derived mainly from the *Aīn-i-Akbarī*, a supplement to the official chronicle of the reign, which consists in essence of a selection of documents illustrating the Emperor's activities in each department of the administration.

Staff is the first concern of the administrator. Akbar developed what can only be called a State Service, in which everybody was graded, from the Princes and the loyal Chiefs down to what would now be called sergeants and corporals, the rank of each individual being stated in terms of a cavalry command, of 5,000 horse, or 1,000, or 500, down to 10. The idea underlying this method of grading goes back far beyond Chingīz Khān, whose conquering army was organised in thousands, hundreds and tens, with a commander over each group ; but by Akbar's time the system had become conventionalised, and while each officer was, as a rule, required to maintain a body of horse, the number which he had to maintain was not the number indicated by his conventional rank, but was ordinarily very much less.

Except for a short period, during which salaries were paid in cash, each officer after presenting his troops for inspection was granted an assignment of revenue; the calculation of salary was an elaborate affair with various distinctions of detail, but all that need be said here is that the remuneration of the higher grades was extremely liberal when account is taken of the value of money—somewhere between five and ten times what it is in India to-day. The Service was in no way specialised. Each unemployed officer was required to remain in attendance at Court, and to take up whatever task the Emperor assigned to him; and Akbar's success must be attributed largely to his judgment of character, and his ability to ' pick the right man for the job.' He was not infallible, and occasional mistakes had disastrous results, but, as a rule, he was able ' to get things done,' the primary business of the administrator.

The administration was organised under three main heads, the Court, the Army, and the Empire, but these terms must not be interpreted too strictly; the Court, for instance, included the mint, the artillery and household troops, and the office of works, in addition to the departments which would now be classed under that term. Akbar administered the Court departments himself, and his regulations are characterised by minute detail, designed mainly to ensure effective financial control; he was no cheese-paring economist, but his constant aim was to get full value for the money spent.

The Emperor was necessarily Commander-in-Chief of the army, and chose the officers to command when he did not take the field in person. Military administration, as distinct from command, was in charge of a high officer, the Paymaster-General, whose most laborious duty was to ensure that officers actually maintained the contingents required of them. In this matter fraud was traditional. The practice was to save money by keeping less than the prescribed number of horsemen, and to improvise by borrowing horses

THE COURT AND THE ARMY 223

or otherwise when an inspection was imminent: Akbar fought against this practice by a long series of regulations, and while fraud was never entirely eliminated, it is probable that the proportion of effective to nominal strength was higher in his reign than at any other period. Cavalry was still the main arm, the great bulk of the troops classed as infantry being of little fighting value, but the beginnings of a change are apparent in a corps of 12,000 musketeers. It is impossible to calculate with any approach to precision the force which Akbar could have put in the field: reckoning together the household troops and the contingents furnished by Chiefs and officers, he may have had at his disposal somewhere about a quarter of a million of horsemen, varying greatly in efficiency; but a substantial proportion of these would always be required for watching the frontiers and maintaining internal tranquillity, so that the army mobilised for attack would have been smaller.

Turning to the third head, the administration of the empire, a preliminary caution is needed regarding nomenclature. In India as in other countries, the significance of official designations has tended to change, and much confusion has resulted from interpreting one century in terms of another. In the account which follows, English designations are used throughout, but readers who wish to pursue the subject further will find the Indian equivalents in a note at the end of the chapter.

Akbar eventually made an almost complete separation between the general administration of the country and the business of the land revenue, a distinction of which survivals may be traced even at the present day. General business was brought before the Emperor by the Prime Minister: revenue business was dealt with in a separate office in charge of the Revenue Minister, who had direct access to the Emperor. For general purposes, the empire was divided into provinces, each in charge of a Viceroy, who was appointed by the Emperor, received orders directly from him, and represented him in everything except the revenue administration. In addition, officers who may be styled Commandants were appointed by the Emperor to particular centres, charged with the duties of suppressing, or rather forestalling, rebellion, keeping the roads open, and putting down violent crime. Each of the larger cities had a City-Governor, who, subject to orders from above, was a local autocrat, combining the functions of magistrate, police commissioner, and mayor and corporation. In each smaller centre there was a Governor,[1] who belonged, as will be explained below, primarily to the revenue administration, but also exercised powers of a general nature, and who stands out in our European sources as the official with whom members of the public usually had to deal, though he might on occasion refer their business to the Viceroy of the province.

There were Judges at the principal centres of population, but they must not be thought of as constituting an independent judiciary. Akbar himself was the fountain of justice, which flowed indifferently through his judges and his governors, always with a final appeal to himself. The main concern of the judges was with Islamic law, and it may be assumed that in personal questions affecting Moslems their opinions were decisive, or at the least carried great weight; but in both civil and criminal proceedings the judge sat beside the Viceroy, or Governor, or City-Governor, as the case might be, and the decision was that of the bench rather than of an individual.

The revenue administration was concerned primarily with the assessment and collection of the land-revenue, the traditional share of the gross produce of the soil, but in some provinces, if not in all, it dealt also with customs, the salt tax, and a few other items. The bulk of the revenue was assigned to officers of the State Service, but certain areas were reserved for the imperial treasury, and the work of the Ministry thus fell into two main divisions, the management of the reserved areas, and the allocation of assignments. For the former purpose the Minister had a Commissioner in each province, taking orders directly from him, and independent of the Viceroy; and the Commissioner had a staff

---

[1] 'Governor' conveys, perhaps, too high an idea of the position of these officers, but the term is consecrated by tradition, appearing regularly in the Portuguese, Dutch and English literature of the period.

THE REVENUE ADMINISTRATION 225

of Collectors, whose main duties were to assess and collect the revenue of their circles, but who also acted as Governors for the purpose of the general administration. Allocation of assignments was done at the headquarters of the Revenue Ministry, not by a local staff. Each officer was, it may be said, in the position of a Collector within the area assigned to him, but as a rule he appointed a representative to live on the spot, and this representative acted as Governor for the area in his charge.

Such was the bureaucratic machinery. In addition there were certain local functionaries, a headman and an accountant in each village and in each pargana, survivals of the Hindu period, who were not exactly government officials, but whose position was recognised by the administration, and who may be regarded as standing between it and the peasants, required by the former to help it, but inclined on the whole to take the latter's side.

As regards the assessment of the revenue, it will be readily understood that to weigh and divide the produce of the land, field by field, and season by season, was not a practical proposition, and far back in the Hindu period we get glimpses of various simplifications of procedure. From the time of the Turks onward, there were two schools of opinion, one of which favoured assessment by simplified methods of the sum payable by each peasant, while the other preferred to assess a lump sum on the village as a whole, leaving the peasants to calculate the share due from each. The latter course was obviously the simpler, but it was open to the objection that the stronger peasants might be tempted to oppress the weaker. In Akbar's eyes this objection was conclusive, and he decided on the alternative of individual assessment. To begin with, he worked the system introduced by Sher Shāh, who apparently had taken the same view ; after a short time that system broke down badly, and a period of experiment followed, resulting in the evolution of an alternative which, so far as we know, was workable and substantially just, though the charge on the peasants was very high when judged by modern standards. Akbar, however, was not obsessed by the principle of administrative uniformity, and was ready to allow for local conditions : in the hill country and in Lower Sind, in Bengal and in the provinces beyond the Narbada, he permitted the continuance of the practices already in force, even though they conflicted with the conclusions he had reached ; and his distinctive system was confined to the plains of northern India, outside Bengal.

The essence of his system, which applied to assignments as well as to the reserved areas, was that each unit of area sown was charged with a sum of money (varying with the crop), calculated to represent the average value of one-third of the produce ; each peasant thus knew, when he planned his season's cropping, what liability he was incurring. When the crops came up, measuring parties went to work under the Collector's supervision, and ascertained the area of each crop sown by each peasant ; the Collector's clerks then calculated the sum due from each peasant at the rates in force, and this sum was collected at harvest, with an allowance for any area on which the crop had failed to mature.

The weak point in this system was that, while the peasant could tell beforehand what he would have to pay, he could not forecast the price his produce would yield, and, owing to imperfect means of communication, prices fluctuated within very wide limits both from market to market and from time to time. The peasant was reasonably well protected against bad harvests, for if his crops failed, he had nothing to pay ; but if the local market was glutted, his produce might for the time be almost unsaleable. This actually occurred between 1585 and 1590, when very large sums of revenue had to be written off because a series of exceptionally good harvests had left the country from Delhi to Allahabad overstocked with produce, and the peasants could not turn their crops into money.

It may be mentioned here that Akbar's method of assessment did not survive its founder for long. There is no record of a formal change, but we know that within half a century of his death the general practice was to assess the revenue annually as a lump sum payable by the village as a unit and to hold the headmen responsible for its payment.

Besides assessing and realising the revenue, Collectors were required to follow a policy of agricultural development designed to increase its amount, and they, or the Commissioners, had wide discretionary powers to vary the system when necessary, so as to bring waste land under the plough, and increase the area of the more valuable crops ; for these purposes they could reduce the rates ordinarily charged, and they could also advance the capital required. Assuming then an honest and efficient staff, the system made for the economic improvement of the empire ; how far this object was attained is uncertain, but the absence of agrarian troubles suggests that the peasants as a whole were contented, and in the circumstances of the time content would ordinarily imply development.

No single man can be named as the author of this agrarian system, which, as we have said, was developed by degrees. For portions of it Akbar himself was certainly responsible ; apart from him, the main credit is due to Rāja Todar Mal, a Hindu belonging to one of the mercantile castes, who, beginning life as a clerk, rose to be Revenue, and for a time Prime, Minister. It is characteristic of Akbar's methods that on several occasions he sent Todar Mal, his chief agrarian expert, to command troops in the field, and his consistent success in these operations would almost justify us in describing him as the most efficient General of the reign ; but, as soon as each war was over, he came back to the Revenue Ministry, where his main work was done. His fame, with legendary accretions, lived on in the villages, and even in the British period he served as a standard by which revenue officers could be judged ; but he was by no means a perfect Minister, being obstinate, bad-tempered, and vindictive, and Akbar's treatment of him may fairly be described as a display of administrative genius. His gifts were indispensable ; his faults could be avoided, or corrected ; and from time to time we find him, not sole Minister, but associated with colleagues who could be trusted to keep him in check. Always a strict Hindu, in his old age he retired to die beside the Ganges, but Akbar called him back to duty, and he worked until the end.

The prosperity of a peasant empire depends mainly on the peasants. As regards the artisans, we must distinguish between the great majority, who made coarse clothes and other goods for the peasants, and the smaller numbers who produced articles of luxury for the Court and the nobles. We know nothing of the condition of the former class under Akbar, but can safely assume that they shared in the fortune of the peasants, whatever it was. The latter class certainly profited by the patronage of the Emperor, and of the nobles who naturally followed his lead. The best craftsmen were taken into the imperial workshops, where the supply of materials was organised, processes were studied and improved, and new designs provided, all under the stimulus of Akbar's personal interest ; and it is safe to conclude that these branches of industry benefited from the artistic as well as the technical standard.

In regard to commerce Akbar followed and extended Sher Shāh's policy of making the roads safe, and he also abolished practically the whole mass of petty and vexatious imposts on trade, which, as we have seen in earlier chapters, prevailed in the old Hindu times, and had survived under the earlier Moslem rulers. He also provided a serviceable, though not a perfect, currency. It will be recalled that under Alāuddīn the treasure brought from the South had led to a period of high prices in northern India. The plethora was absorbed before the end of the fourteenth century, and for a time gold and silver commanded a scarcity value, only copper remaining in general circulation. Sher Shāh was able to re-establish a silver currency, and the coin which he introduced, and which came to be known as the rupee, has survived till now with some change in its silver content. Under Akbar, while the rupee continued to be the standard coin, an extensive subsidiary coinage, in both silver and copper, was also issued ; gold, too, was coined, but did not become generally current, being quickly absorbed in hoards. The coins were artistically meritorious, but the technique of production was still imperfect, and it was easy to diminish their weight. The exchange ratios between the different metals, and between different issues, also fluctuated ; and for these reasons merchants had still to employ the old-established professional money-changers in practically all their transactions.

The success of Akbar's administrative machinery can be estimated only in general terms. It was not unqualified, for from time to time serious scandals required his personal intervention, and we are thrown back on the principle that under personal rule it is the personality of the ruler which counts. Like the rest of his race, Akbar was subject to fits of terrible anger, and in matters of state he was at times unscrupulous ; but in all ordinary cases he was inflexibly just. An untiring worker, accessible to all complaints, and with an elaborate system of intelligence, the probabilities are that he was able to maintain a reasonable standard of conduct among his officers taken as a body ; and if his success was not complete, it is at any rate certain that he approached success more nearly than any of the emperors who followed. It may be added that from the financial standpoint his administration was brilliant when judged by the standards of the time, for he was able to secure a recurring surplus, which, added to the spoils of victory, left an overflowing treasury, so that he died, as was commonly said, the richest ruler in the world.

Note to Chapter XXIX
Official Designations

This note gives the Indian equivalents of the designations used in the text in the order in which they occur ; but the warning must be repeated that their significance varied from time to time, and the interpretations here given should not be applied to either the fourteenth or the eighteenth century without examination of the facts of the period.

State Service : There is no term for this as a whole : the higher grades were designated Umarā (nobles), the lower, Mansabdārs (office-holders).

Salaries : Usually Tan.

230 AKBAR'S ADMINISTRATION

ASSIGNMENTS: Usually Jāgīr; synonyms, Iktā, Tuyūl.

PAYMASTER-GENERAL: Bakhshī; but this term was applied also to officers of his staff, and a complimentary adjective, 'high,' or 'chief,' was often used to distinguish him.

GENERAL AND REVENUE ADMINISTRATION: Mulkī (of the kingdom) and Mālī (of the revenue).

PRIME MINISTER: Vakīl.

REVENUE MINISTER: Vazīr. (This, the traditional Islamic term for Sole, or Prime, Minister, had now fallen to the second place.) Synonym, Dīwān, usually with a complimentary adjective.

PROVINCE: Sūba.

VICEROY: Sipāhsālār (official); Sūbadār (usual).

COMMANDANT: Usually Faujdār; in some areas Kilādār (fort-commandant).

CITY-GOVERNOR: Kotwāl.

GOVERNOR: Usually Hākim, occasionally Zābit.

JUDGE: Kāzī. (The word is written Kādī in Arabic, the *d* representing one of a series of peculiar dental sounds which Persian speakers transformed into sibilants.)

RESERVED AREAS: Khālisa.

COMMISSIONER: Dīwān.

COLLECTOR: Amalguzār (official); Āmil (usual); also Karorī.

HEADMAN, etc.: In parganas, Chaudhrī (headman) and Kānūngo (accountant); in villages, Mukaddam (headman) and Patwārī (accountant).

THE ASSESSMENT SYSTEM: **Zabt**: synonym, Paimāish.

CHAPTER XXX

JAHĀNGĪR

WHEN Jahāngīr succeeded Akbar, he was already a man of experience, being thirty-six years of age. We have said in an earlier chapter that he was widely suspected of having poisoned his father, but the evidence is very inconclusive, and the significant point is that among the entourage of the Court parricide was considered to be probable in the circumstances. We possess ample knowledge of Jahāngīr's personality, for the self-revealing Memoirs which he wrote, for the most part with his own hand, are supplemented by descriptions from European sources, from the Jesuits who were at Court for the greater part of the reign, and from various Dutch and English visitors.

In many ways Jahāngīr was his father's son, though on a smaller scale. Ambitious and curious, subject to outbursts of ferocity, but ordinarily just and considerate, a sane and competent administrator, an enthusiastic sportsman and naturalist, the main lines of the picture are similar ; but he was lazy, self-indulgent, and wanting in steadfast purpose. His ambition thus remained a sentiment, without furnishing a policy, while his curiosity became mere dilettantism, seeking always for something new. At one time he nearly drank himself to death, but when he realised his danger, he limited his consumption of spirits to a quantity which, taken regularly in the evening, sent him to bed more or less fuddled. He soon tired of the drudgery of administration, and handed it over to his Persian wife, Nūr Jahān, a competent and ambitious woman, who, with her father and her brother, the Prime Minister, thenceforward practically ruled the empire. His attitude towards religion was in keeping with his character. He considered himself at least equal to the great prophet of Islam; he could enjoy long conversations with Hindu ascetics or with Jesuit missionaries; but there is nothing to show that he really cared much about the matter, and the hopes which the missionaries entertained of his conversion were probably the resultant of his politeness and their enthusiasm.

Under such a ruler the empire naturally did not expand. Much of the ground which Akbar had gained in Ahmadnagar was soon lost, and a desultory war on this front went on throughout the reign with no tangible results. On the west, Kandahār reverted to Persia; Jahāngīr meditated a great effort to save the fortress from capture, but his attention was diverted by the rebellion of his son Shāh Jahān, and the matter was eventually dropped. The one vigorous campaign undertaken during the reign was directed against the Rāna of Mewār, who at last made his formal submission and was honourably received into the empire.

In his internal policy Jahāngīr followed the same lines as Akbar, securing the loyalty of the Rājput Chiefs and aiming at the contentment of his Hindu subjects; but the quality of the administration deteriorated when actual power passed to the Empress. She and the members of her family were inevitably more intent on consolidating their personal position, and amassing the wealth which it brought within their reach, than on ensuring the stability of an empire which might not be in their hands for long. The State Service suffered from divided allegiance, rapid promotion and sudden dismissal became the order of the day, and practically everybody in authority tried to make hay while the sun shone. Violent crime increased, the roads became unsafe, and the commandants and governors were widely suspected of favouring criminals in return for a share of the booty. The taste for luxury and display increased greatly during the reign, so that there was all the more incentive to rapacity on the part of those in authority; and the practice by which the assignments granted to officers were changed suddenly and at short intervals had most injurious results, for the ordinary assignee could think only of squeezing his peasants dry, and then making interest or giving bribes to get a fresh assignment where the same process could be repeated. The financial administration also deteriorated. Peculation became rife, income fell off while expenditure rose, and a large part of Akbar's accumulated treasure was dissipated in meeting the recurring annual deficits. It is uncertain whether or not Jahāngīr realised what was going on; but, if he did, he took no effective action to put things straight. He had his daily rides and his evening receptions; in his later years he usually spent the summer in Kashmīr; he seems to have retained his capacity for enjoyment almost to the end; but affairs of State had ceased to trouble him.

The most important event that happened in India during the reign was one which attracted very little notice at the moment, the settlement of Dutch and English merchants on the coast. To explain the forces which operated to bring the merchants into Asia would require a summary of much of the history of Western Europe during the latter portion of the sixteenth century: here we must be content to say that from 1596 onwards various groups of Dutch merchants had been trading successfully in Java and Sumatra, and that in 1602 they were united in the powerful Dutch East India Company, while at the end of 1600 an English Company had been chartered by Queen Elizabeth to carry on the same trade. From the outset the Dutch Company, which was in effect a national institution with large financial resources and very wide powers, deliberately confronted the maritime force of the Portuguese in Asia, which collapsed as soon as it was seriously challenged, and aimed at succeeding to the monopoly of eastern sea-borne commerce; on the other hand, the English Company, which was a purely commercial body, sought only a share of the trade which the Dutch desired to monopolise; and the contest between the rivals was decided during Jahāngīr's reign, with the result that the Dutch became commercially supreme in the seas eastward of Batavia, the fortress in Java where they established their capital, while the trade to the west of this point was carried on by both Companies, for the most part in active competition.

The development of the Companies' businesses in Asia can be summed up in the formula, Voyage, Factory, Fort. At the outset, ships sailed straight to eastern seaports, sold what they could, bought spices, silks and drugs, and returned home as soon as possible. Time was the essence of such a voyage, for delay in the ports meant not merely loss of interest, but deterioration of the ships, and danger to the health of the crews; and the merchants of Bantam in Java or Achin in Sumatra, seeing the strangers to be in a hurry, naturally made the most of the position in order to buy cheap and sell dear. It was thus essential for profitable business to establish agencies, or factories as they were then called, which could buy and sell at leisure, and have cargoes ready against the arrival of the next ships. At this time the procedure for establishing a factory was substantially the same in Europe and in Asia; in both continents it was necessary to negotiate with the local government, and obtain definite terms on which the strangers could settle in a foreign seaport and carry on their business without molestation; and accordingly we find the Dutch, and then the English, securing capitulations, to use the time-honoured term, at Bantam and elsewhere.

A factory consisted merely of residences, offices and storehouses, occupied under the protection of the local government. Where the government was both efficient and friendly, nothing more was needed; but cases occurred where the government, though willing, was not able to provide protection, and allowed the merchants to fortify their factory and arrange for their own defence. The advantages of such a fort as a safeguard against disturbances, or against the rapacity of local officials, were quickly proved by experience, and the fashion caught on, so that in the course of time forts held by Europeans were to become a feature of the Indian coast, and were to pave the way for the territorial changes of the eighteenth century; but at the end of Jahāngīr's reign the fashion had not yet been introduced in the Mogul empire, though the Dutch already had

THE EUROPEAN COMPANIES

a fort in the Hindu territory in the far south and the English were erecting one in the vicinity. Another fort in the same region was in possession of the Danes, who also had entered the Eastern trade, but the part which they played in India was insignificant.

The causes which brought the Dutch to the mainland of India were purely commercial. The islands where they began to trade required very little in the way of European goods, and were not usually anxious for silver, which in some of the remoter markets was practically valueless. On the other hand, every market demanded Indian cotton goods, and the obvious way to get these was to buy them where they were made, and where silver was always in demand. We hear of Dutch buyers from Achin reaching Gujarāt in 1601, and the Coromandel Coast shortly afterwards, probably in 1603. The first Gujarāt venture was a failure, and several years elapsed before a regular factory was established in Surat; but, under the able management of Pieter van den Broeke, who was in charge of the factory from 1620 to 1629, the Dutch secured a leading position in the trade of western India. On the Coromandel Coast there was no set-back, and in 1606 a factory was opened at Masulipatam, the principal seaport of Golconda, while in 1610 another, of greater importance, was started at Pulicat, a town lying about twenty miles north of Madras, where the artisans had specialised in the types of clothes worn in the Spice Islands.

A few years later the Pulicat factory was fortified under circumstances which may be briefly related. When the Dutch first applied for capitulations, the King of Vijayanagar, in whose territories Pulicat lay, suggested that they might like to have a fort; but this would have been expensive and the Dutch envoy replied that he would rather live under the King's protection. Soon after the factory had been established on these terms it was raided and burnt by the Portuguese of St. Thomé, one of those quasi-independent communities which we have already mentioned.[1] The King was thus placed in a difficulty, for while he owed

[1] St. Thomé is now a suburb of the city of Madras.

the Dutch protection, he was not in a position to control the Portuguese; and an agreement was made under which he was to construct a fort to be garrisoned jointly by Indians and Dutch. The fort was promptly begun, but after a short time the work was interrupted; the Portuguese threatened another attack; and the President of the Dutch factories took matters into his own hands and finished the work which the King had started. The joint garrison was tried, but naturally it led to friction; the King withdrew his troops, and the Dutch found themselves in undisputed possession of a fort which was destined to set a new fashion in India. Thus by the end of Jahāngīr's reign the Dutch had a footing at three points on the coast, the fort at Pulicat, and the factories at Masulipatam and Surat. In addition to these, they had several branch factories, opened and closed as business required, but the only one which calls for mention here was at Agra, where they were brought into touch with the heart of the Mogul empire.

The motives which brought the English to India were also essentially commercial, but somewhat different from those which had influenced the Dutch. Very early in the century it was found that the spice trade was being overdone, and the English Company decided to broaden the basis of operations by establishing itself in new markets. In furtherance of this policy, the *Hector* arrived off Surat in 1608, and William Hawkins, the captain, travelled to Agra, where at first he won the favour of Jahāngīr. As a diplomat, however, he was no match for the Jesuits, who at the time were also in high favour and who exerted themselves against him in the interests of the Portuguese; and his mission eventually proved fruitless. Meanwhile other English ships had come to Surat, and a quarrel having broken out between the Moguls and the Portuguese, the new-comers were welcomed, capitulations were obtained, and a factory was established at the end of 1612; but the terms proved to be unsatisfactory, and James I was persuaded to send an ambassador to Jahāngīr to negotiate a regular treaty. Sir Thomas Roe, who was chosen for this duty, was in India from 1615 to 1619; he failed to obtain a formal

ARRIVAL OF THE ENGLISH

treaty, but secured substantially improved terms, under which the factory at Surat was maintained, and various branches opened. The Company had also sent ships to the Coromandel Coast, and in 1616 was able to establish a factory at Masulipatam. Ten years later the merchants opened another factory at Armagon, some distance north of Pulicat, and received permission to fortify it.

There is no need to look far for reasons explaining why the Dutch and English were welcomed in India. They offered just the sort of trade which India liked, buying her goods for hard cash, and offering commodities which suited her taste ; and that was enough for everybody concerned. In Gujarāt, however, there was an additional reason : there the new-comers were welcomed as a counterpoise to the Portuguese, and the Mogul officials quickly realised that, so long as they could play off the Dutch against the English, their position would be much better than when a single foreign power was master of the sea.

Both sides had thus reason to be satisfied, but still causes of friction were not wanting. Europeans regarded capitulations, once settled, as stable institutions, and considered a breach of them to be a hostile act. The view in India was different. There a king did not regard himself as bound by his predecessor's acts, though he might be persuaded to confirm them ; while an order addressed to a particular officer did not necessarily bind his successors, who expected to make something in return for any favour they might show. Occasionally, then, the merchants found that conditions which they regarded as established were not observed, and they undertook what they called reprisals, that is to say, they seized Indian ships, or blockaded a port, until the authorities could be brought to terms. That they were sometimes able to do this with success was due to the entire absence of naval power in the seaports ; neither in Gujarāt nor in the kingdom of Golconda was there anything of the sort, not even a single gunboat to police a harbour ; and a display of force, however small, might be effective when there were no means of opposing it.

Such incidents were, however, exceptional, and by

degrees the parties came to understand each other better. The officials recognised that the merchants were dangerous if provoked too far, while the merchants realised that the local officials could make or mar the success of their ventures. An occasional mission to Court might be indispensable, particularly on the accession of a new ruler, but it was a costly business, requiring many presents or bribes, and taking time which could ill be spared, and the best course was to keep on good terms with the local officials, who were ordinarily reasonable enough, and expected merely a courteous attitude and an occasional present of substantial value. In this way the Dutch and English found their place in the commercial life of India.

The effect on Indian trade was substantial. On the import side, anything that India wanted from Europe was promptly obtained, but the main feature was the steady inflow of silver, the thing which India demanded most. Among exports, indigo at first was the most important; then new and large markets for calico were opened up in Europe and North America; then yarn, saltpetre, sugar and other commodities came into the list. The importance of particular articles of export fluctuated from time to time; the permanent feature was the establishment in India of a new commercial organisation, much more effective than that of the Portuguese, or of the overland traders who preceded them. The Dutch, while they continued to make large purchases for their business in eastern Asia, quickly followed the English lead in developing trade with Europe; in Amsterdam, as in London, some of the ablest merchants of the day were constantly engaged in studying the Indian markets, while their agents on the spot were working in close touch with the leading Indian firms; and all alike were concerned in finding out what people wanted, and in satisfying their needs on profitable terms.

One particular want of the Indian market was for novelties and curiosities. Jahāngīr was not alone in his taste for these; the same appetite existed in the South, among Hindus as well as Moslems; and from the outset of their activities the European merchants found it indispensable to provide articles which would be acceptable as presents, not for their intrinsic value, but for their rarity in India. The various Courts thus became familiar with a wide range of European luxury goods, from mirrors to coaches, from chandeliers to greyhounds and mastiffs. The trade in such articles was not extensive, but to the merchants it was necessary in order to secure official favour, while their success in meeting the demand probably contributed to the growth of extravagance which characterised the period.

The increase of the export trade brought direct benefit to India, but it was not of such magnitude as to affect the economic life of the country as a whole. Most of the benefit accrued to merchants or middlemen at the few centres which produced goods for export; a portion of it went in taxation; and it is uncertain whether any substantial share reached the actual producers, the weavers or indigo-growers, who themselves constituted only a small fraction of the total population.

While the new intercourse between Europe and India was primarily commercial, it necessarily produced reactions in a wider field. Indians came to know a type of European differing from the Portuguese, not actively concerned in politics, not ardent missionaries, but men of cooler blood, hard-headed merchants, steadfast or even stubborn, some of them men of culture, but all of them putting business first. The West, too, learned something of the facts of Indian life, of its splendour and its frugality, of its abounding wealth and its deep poverty; in the pages of *Purchas his Pilgrimes*, published in 1625, the home-keeping scholar could read the observations of many who had visited the country; and a comparison of Shakespeare's allusions to the Indies with Milton's gorgeous similes affords some measure of the new knowledge which the West was gaining.

CHAPTER XXXI
SHĀH JAHĀN

THE death of Jahāngīr was followed by a short period of intrigue regarding the succession, but eventually his son Shāh Jahān attained the throne without serious difficulty. Our knowledge of the new Emperor's personality is defective, for the official record of his reign does not go below the surface, the other chronicles are not very enlightening, and, as it happened, he was not intimately known to European visitors during his active life; but we can safely affirm that his ruling passion was magnificence. In early life he showed himself a capable administrator, usually prompt and decisive, and he put the finances of the empire on a sound footing; but, for whatever reason, his character weakened in the course of his reign, the close of which makes melancholy reading.

Like his father, Shāh Jahān was the son of a Rājput mother, so that by blood he was more than half a Hindu; but he is the first of the dynasty who can be described as an orthodox Moslem. It would be going too far to call him a systematic persecutor, but the administration was invigorated on the religious side, and the interests of Islam were put first; Hindus were prevented from building new temples, the Jesuit missionaries at Agra were for a short time actively persecuted, and in the chronicles Moslems stand out quite clearly as the ruling class.

Shāh Jahān's first serious task was to bring to a close the long-drawn war on the southern frontier. As will be related further on, Ahmadnagar was finally conquered, and

FOREIGN AFFAIRS

the bulk of it annexed, while shortly afterwards Bījāpur and Golconda were brought formally within the empire, though the rulers retained their position as kings. In 1638 the empire received a windfall in the fortress of Kandahār. The Persian Governor, fearing that he had been doomed to death by his master, transferred his allegiance, and his charge, to Shāh Jahān, who welcomed him with extraordinary honours; but the change was not permanent, for the fort was recaptured by Persia eleven years later, and Shāh Jahān's prolonged efforts to recover it were fruitless. In 1645 the Emperor undertook the task of extending his dominions to the north-west, and began by the conquest of Balkh, the country north of the Hindu Kush, which in older days was known as Bactria. It proved easier, however, to conquer Balkh than to hold it, and after some vacillation the country was restored to its former ruler, the designs of further extension in this direction being abandoned. Shāh Jahān thus failed in the north-west, though he was successful in the south.

Our knowledge of the internal condition of the empire during the reign is incomplete. In the earlier years the administration was vigorous, and the lawless sections of the people, who had made head under Jahāngīr, were to a certain extent curbed, but there seem always to have been disturbed areas, and it is not possible to infer from the fragmentary records of the period whether things got better or worse as time went on. Nor can the economic position be described with confidence, for we possess no formal records, though a few facts stand out clearly. We know that the revenue drawn from the reserved areas was more than doubled in the course of the reign, and that the salary-list of the State Service grew by leaps and bounds; we may be confident, therefore, that in both assigned and reserved areas much more money was taken from the peasants of the empire than in the days of Akbar. We do not know where this money came from, but it is quite certain that very shortly after the end of the reign peasants were deserting the land for other occupations to an extent which caused serious embarrassment to the revenue administration. We know further that the officials were required to strain every nerve to extend cultivation, and that they were empowered to flog peasants who did not sow sufficient land. These facts, taken together, suggest that Shāh Jahān, in pursuing his ideal of magnificence, took from the peasants more than could safely be taken, with the result that agriculture became an unpopular occupation, and that the economic foundations of the empire were undermined.

Whatever the economic results, there is no question about the magnificence. The splendour of the Court was famed throughout the world. Shāh Jahān was a munificent and discerning patron of the arts. Extensive workshops were maintained, not only at the capital but in the chief industrial centres of the empire, where carpets, shawls, muslins and other luxury goods were produced of a quality previously unknown, and at a cost which nowadays sounds fantastic. As a single example of the scale of expenditure, we may mention the Peacock Throne, the costliest of the eleven—all of them jewelled—which were in use; its construction took seven years, and the cost of the materials was returned officially at more than one million sterling.[1]

Such productions were ephemeral, destined to serve as a conqueror's booty, and Shāh Jahān's buildings form his true memorial. He reconstructed much of the palace at Agra, and built the great mosque in that city. Later, he decided to remove the capital to Delhi, where he laid out the city known as Shāhjahānābād, and where much of his palace can be seen in the fort beside the Jumna. Other buildings in various parts of the empire are also his work, but they fade into insignificance beside the Taj Mahal, the tomb which he built for his wife's body, and which stands, serene above criticism, on the river bank near Agra.

Readers will have noticed that, in recording the achievements of Indian architecture, we have said nothing of the architects. The reason is that anonymity was the practice of the country, and it is thus impossible to trace the inter-

[1] The French jeweller, Tavernier, was assured that the total cost exceeded twelve millions sterling (*Travels in India*, translated by V. Ball, i. 385); but the official figure, recorded in the *Bādshāhnāma* (I. ii. 79 of the *Bibliotheca Indica* text), is sufficiently striking.

SOUTHERN INDIA

action between genius and environment which is such a prominent topic in the history of European art. Even in the case of the Taj Mahal, the official record, while it preserves the names of the officers who superintended the construction, tells us nothing of the architect, beyond the fact that the ' officers at the capital ' were ordered to design a suitable memorial, and his identity is a matter of controversy, into which we cannot enter.

We must now turn to the history of southern India. After the power of Vijayanagar had been broken at the battle of Tālikot, the Moslem kingdoms in this region were left free to bicker among themselves, and the squalid story of decadent dynasties, factions at Court, and shifting alliances can be passed over. When, however, the intention of Akbar to conquer the South had become manifest, the surviving kingdoms, Ahmadnagar, Bījāpur and Golconda, were drawn together, and the two latter gave some assistance to the former, which from its position necessarily had to bear the brunt of the attack. That Ahmadnagar survived throughout Jahāngīr's reign was due primarily to the genius of one man, an African named Malik Ambar, originally a slave, who rose to be Prime Minister, and in his old age displayed a capacity for guerilla warfare which kept the Mogul forces at bay. Shortly before the end of Jahāngīr's reign Malik Ambar died at the age of eighty, and no competent successor emerged, so that Shāh Jahān, who took the field in person, was able to conquer the kingdom without serious difficulty; the bulk of it was annexed and most of the remainder transferred to Bījāpur. The Mogul advance was then checked for a time, but a few years later the Emperor returned to the South and laid siege to the fortress of Bījāpur; and, though he failed to capture it, he was able to secure a recognition of his supremacy from both Bījāpur and Golconda, which then turned their attention to what had been the territory of Vijayanagar, farther to the south.

Vijayanagar continued as a political entity for half a

century after the defeat at Tālikot. In 1614, however, on the death of the reigning king, civil war broke out among the principal nobles, who were known by the designation of Nāyak, and in the result the country was split up among a number of Chiefs, at variance among themselves, and acknowledging, when it suited them, some sort of allegiance to the shadow of the old dynasty which still survived. The conditions were thus favourable for an advance towards the south on the part of the Moslem kingdoms, who made substantial conquests in this direction ; but in 1656 they had to face northwards again, for the Moguls, under Prince Aurangzeb, had now undertaken their definite subjection. At this juncture, however, Shāh Jahān fell seriously ill, and Aurangzeb's attention was diverted to the struggle for the succession, so that Golconda and Bījāpur secured a temporary respite.

We have said in an earlier chapter that little is definitely known regarding the conditions of life in the southern kingdoms during the fifteenth and sixteenth centuries. The observations of Dutch and English residents, recorded soon after 1600, show us in actual operation in Golconda a system of administration, apparently of old standing, which must be regarded as the most oppressive in the whole history of India. Each source of revenue was sold to the highest bidder, and the successful farmer-governor exercised very wide administrative powers during his short term of office, commonly a single year. The one thing needful was that he should make the stipulated payments punctually, and any deficiency was extracted from him by means of the bastinado or some other form of torture. Under this system, administration necessarily meant extortion from anyone who appeared able to pay ; new taxes, compulsory presents, or forced loans might at any moment be demanded ; and there was little hope of redress from the higher authorities, whose interest in the administration was primarily financial. There are some indications that substantially the same system prevailed at this period in Bījāpur, and in the territories of some of the Nāyaks farther south ; we do not know when it originated or how it developed ; but there is no doubt of its injurious effects on the people, whether peasants, artisans or merchants.

The reign of Shāh Jahān was marked by some important changes in the position of Europeans in the empire. We have spoken in a previous chapter of the deterioration of the mixed race, which still claimed the name of Portuguese, but came to be known in Bengal as Feringees, that is to say, Franks. As time went on there was a gradual drift of the worst characters away from Goa and other centres, where a civilised government existed, to the quasi-independent communities in the Bay of Bengal, where there was little or no restraint on the conduct of individuals. The greatest desperadoes gathered on the coast of eastern Bengal, then partially under the King of Arakan, who was known to protect pirates in return for a share of their spoil. The Feringees entered this trade with alacrity, and equalled or surpassed the Arakanese in depredations along the coast and in the waterways of the delta. Passengers and crews were good prize to these pirates, and a considerable export of Indian slaves developed at the port of Chittagong.

In the Mogul empire, the only important Portuguese community was at Hooghly, the chief port on the river which now bears that name. Here the residents were in touch with the pirates farther east, and marketed some of their captives; scandals arose regarding the sale of Mogul subjects, and other matters; and, in 1632, Shāh Jahān decided to exterminate the settlement. The inhabitants made a gallant resistance behind improvised fortifications, but at last the place fell, and most of the survivors were carried away to Agra as slaves.

The fall of Hooghly had important commercial results. Both Dutch and English were eager for a share of the trade of Bengal, but the venture was not worth while so long as the principal port was in the hands of the Portuguese, and their friends, the pirates, were active on the coast. Soon after Hooghly fell factories were established at the mouth of the river; then both Companies moved to Hooghly itself; and an active trade with Europe arose in the saltpetre of Bihār, the silk of Bengal, and, a little later, the fine muslins of Dacca.

Farther south, the English, finding that their modest fortress at Armagon was badly placed, obtained leave from the local Nāyak to establish themselves in the little fishing village which has since grown into the city of Madras, and here Fort St. George was built in 1640. In the disturbed conditions of the country, merchants and craftsmen flocked to the vicinity of Madras and of the Dutch fort at Pulicat, where they could hope for some sort of security; towns grew up rapidly at both places; and the merchants of both nations found that they had to turn their attention to problems of municipal administration.

Meanwhile the Portuguese were gradually losing their strongholds in the Asiatic seas. Ormuz had fallen in 1622 to the Persians, in alliance with the English Company; the Dutch took Malacca in 1641, Colombo in 1656, Negapatam in 1658, and Cochin, with some minor forts, in 1663; all their efforts against Goa were, however, unsuccessful, and the Portuguese retained their capital in India, but very little else. Friendship between the English and the Portuguese was established in 1635 and has since continued unbroken; the real question now was whether the Dutch, having destroyed the power of the latter, could exclude the former from the eastern trade, and this was settled by the result of the war between England and Holland, which broke out in 1652, and which left the English Company free to pursue its business.

To complete the story of European development about this period, we may record that the island of Bombay was ceded by Portugal to England as part of the dowry which Catherine of Braganza brought to Charles II in 1661; and six years later the island was leased to the Company. Up to this time Bombay had played no part in the history of India, and the question is often asked why the one great natural harbour on the coast had not been developed. The answer is to be found in its situation. It lay too far north for the transhipment trade by which the Malabar ports lived, while the rugged mountains to landward cut it off effectively from the productive regions to the north and

THE GREAT FAMINE

east ; potentially it was a great naval station, but it offered no prospects of profitable commerce, and at the time of cession its Indian population consisted largely of fishermen, while what land there was was tilled by peasants under Portuguese landholders.

One event of Shāh Jahān's reign remains to be recorded, the appalling famine of 1630-1631. We have said in earlier chapters that in India a failure of the seasonal rains had always meant famine, in the precise sense of a deficiency of food throughout the area affected. From time to time the Moslem chroniclers record the horrors of famine in one region or another, but their descriptions are rhetorical rather than precise, and now for the first time we are in a position to check their rhetoric by the observations of Europeans on the spot. The monsoon of 1630 failed almost completely over a tract comprising Gujarāt and Ahmadnagar, with portions of Bījāpur and Golconda, and before the end of the year the local stock of food was exhausted. Supplies were available elsewhere, but it would have been impossible to bring them to the heart of the affected region, because transport animals need food and water along their routes, while the country was bare of grass, and the streams and ponds were dry. The choice before the population thus lay, as the chronicles show it always lay, between flight and starvation. The former alternative was chosen by the more energetic, and the country was largely depopulated ; many of those who remained died of starvation, sometimes evaded by suicide, or postponed by robbery and by cannibalism. The official record of the reign tells us that ' men began to devour each other, and the flesh of a son was preferred to his love ' ; a Dutch merchant, who lived through the calamity, noted that ' men lying in the street, not yet dead, were cut up by others, and men fed on living men, so that even in the streets, and still more on road journeys, men ran great danger of being murdered and eaten.' [1]

[1] *Bādshāhnāma* (*Bibliotheca Indica* text), I. i. 362 ; and Ch. iii of J. van Twist's *Generale Beschrijvinge van Indien* (Amsterdam, 1648).

Indian and European accounts are thus in substantial agreement regarding the horrors of the time.

The historian, however, is more concerned with the lasting results than with the momentary horrors of such a calamity. We know that much of the land of Ahmadnagar lay uninhabited and unproductive for a quarter of a century, when a vigorous and successful effort was made to attract peasants from other regions. We know, too, that in Gujarāt the scarcity of peasants remained serious for almost as long, while the great weaving industry was completely disorganised for the time. The latter fact had important consequences. In 1630 Surat handled the great bulk of the trade with Europe, exporting mainly calico and indigo. After the famine, there was no calico to be had, for in the contemporary phrase the weavers were 'dead or fled'; the merchants turned their attention to other markets; and the discovery was made that the European demand could be met more effectively on the Coromandel Coast. By the middle of the century the main calico trade had shifted from Gujarāt to Madras; about the same time Indian indigo was driven out of Europe by the competition of the West Indies; and the result was that the western port lost most of the trade, and that Madras and Bengal, rather than Gujarāt, became the chief centres of European commercial activity, a fact which is reflected in the political developments of the eighteenth century.

The famine of 1631 does not stand by itself. The sources of our information are very incomplete, but we know that famine conditions prevailed with varying intensity in one part of India or another in 1636, in 1643, in 1645, in 1646, in 1648, in 1650, in 1659, and, over an exceptionally wide area, in 1661. The extent and intensity of the calamity of 1631 stand out; but the record we have given forbids us to think of famine as something outside the ordinary experience of the time. We must regard it rather as a spectre in the background, always visible to peasants, labourers and artisans, and coming forward from time to time to wreck the social and economic life of one region or another.

CHAPTER XXXII

AURANGZEB

We have seen in the last chapter that, on hearing of Shāh Jahān's illness, Aurangzeb turned his face northwards in order to assert his claim to the succession. Three other Princes were candidates for the throne : Aurangzeb quickly disposed of them, imprisoned his father in the fort at Agra, and was crowned Emperor in the summer of 1658, being then nearly forty years of age, with a wide experience of war and peace. When he died, half a century later, the empire was visibly falling to pieces, with the treasury depleted, the fighting spirit of the army destroyed, and the civil administration demoralised. This result was due primarily to fundamental errors of policy, and secondly to unsuitable methods of administration.

Aurangzeb had many good qualities, great personal courage, a cool and clear head, untiring industry, a deep sense of religion, and complete control over the ordinary passions of human nature ; but these could not avail against his lack of statesmanship. Himself a rigid Moslem, his guiding principle was to organise the empire in strict accordance with the public law of Islam, and he pursued this course without any recognition of the facts which it is a statesman's business to take into account. His reign was thus a tragedy, for his religion, as he understood it, compelled him to wreck his empire by reversing the policy adopted by Akbar, which had made its existence possible.

The most important measures adopted in pursuit of this principle may be summarised as follows. In finance, customs duties were differentiated in favour of Moslems, and the *jizya* tax was reimposed on all 'infidels.' A deliberate policy of temple-destruction was adopted, and was carried out in such holy places as Benares and Muttra. The practice of suttee was formally forbidden. The prohibition of killing cows had apparently lapsed during the previous reign; that the idea of prohibition found no favour with Aurangzeb can be inferred from the fact that, on at least one occasion, he desecrated a temple by having a cow slaughtered inside it. At one time he closed the revenue department to Hindus, but this order had to be modified because the administration could not be carried on without them; and in the second half of the reign no high office was held by a Hindu. Old-established grants of land to Hindu institutions were withdrawn: converts to Islam were honoured, rewarded, and provided with appointments; but insulting sumptuary laws were enacted against the Hindus, their religious fairs were prohibited, and the celebration of their festivals curtailed.

The cumulative effect of these and other measures, introduced not all at once but in the course of the reign, was to bring home to the subjects the idea that the empire existed for the benefit of Moslems, and Moslems alone. The idea excited widespread resentment. In the northern plains there were occasional revolts, not of the masses but of particular communities, which made considerable head before being crushed; in the broken country farther south, rebellious Hindu Chiefs found it easy to rally the people to their support; while the operations undertaken in Rājputāna, which will be described further on, made it impossible to rely on the loyalty of that region. Aurangzeb thus destroyed the foundations on which Akbar had built the empire—the acquiescence of the masses and the active support of the Rājputs.

The second great error of Aurangzeb's policy, the expansion of the empire to a point where it became unmanageable, will be sufficiently obvious from the account of his proceedings in the South. In administration, his great fault lay in the treatment of his officers. Tortuous in his methods, he distrusted almost everybody, and won universal

ERRORS OF POLICY

distrust in return. Competent officers disappeared, and their places were filled by sycophants. As time went on, he drew matters more and more into his own hands, and attempted to do everything personally, while his subordinates at a distance were concerned mainly to hoodwink their master and make money for themselves. His Generals, uncertain of receiving support, were frequently in collusion with the enemy; and, in the last phase of the reign, the old man of over eighty found himself obliged to conduct all military operations in person because there was nobody on whom he could rely.

From the economic standpoint the reign was ruinous. The supply of men, and of money, was exhausted in ineffective wars; large areas were devastated; increasing exaction drove more and more peasants off the land, and turned them into robbers, preying on commerce, and thereby disorganising the staple industries; production fell off, while consumption and waste increased. The artistic handicrafts decayed, for the puritanical simplicity of the Court offered no patronage. Culture almost disappeared; music was banished from the Court; portraits were obliterated from the palace walls; literature found no scope, and even the writing of chronicles was discountenanced. That we know so much of the reign is due in great measure to the survival of large numbers of letters written by the Emperor himself and some of his principal officers—letters which have been utilised effectively by Sir Jadunath Sarkar, the learned historian of the period.

The political history of the reign falls into two parts. For the first half of it, Aurangzeb remained in the North, while affairs in the South were managed, or mismanaged, by his officers. Late in 1681 he crossed the Narbada and assumed personal charge of the South, while the administration of the North gradually deteriorated in his absence. In the first period the centres of interest are successively Bengal, Afghanistan, and Rājputāna.

One of Aurangzeb's earliest measures was to direct the Viceroy of Bengal to conquer Assam, which was then in the possession of the Ahoms, a dynasty of Mongoloid origin.

The Viceroy, a very remarkable man, is usually known as Mīr Jumla, which is in fact a designation rather than a name. A Persian, and originally a merchant, he had become Prime Minister of Golconda, where his growing wealth and power alarmed the king. To save his life, he transferred his allegiance to Shāh Jahān, who welcomed him, and appointed him Minister of the empire. Aurangzeb sent him to Bengal, where he organised the Assam campaign with the energy which had characterised all his actions; a gallant advance was followed by a forced retreat; and in 1663 he died of fever, a result which, according to popular rumour, was not displeasing to his suspicious and distrustful master. The war in this direction was renewed at intervals for nearly twenty years, but Assam retained its independence.

Further south, Mīr Jumla's successor had an easier task in the recovery of the country about Chittagong, for he was able to win over the Feringee pirates, who were dissatisfied with their treatment by the King of Arakan, and in 1666 he captured Chittagong with their assistance, and so restored the old frontier of India in this direction. The Feringees were settled in the neighbourhood of Dacca, where some of their descendants still live, and in this part of India piracy ceased to be a serious menace to trade.

The trouble in Afghanistan was a matter of greater importance, for strategically Kābul was one of the key positions of the empire, the gateway by which so many conquerors had entered India, and the starting-point for any enterprise beyond the Hindu Kush. The hills between Kābul and the Indus were occupied by various tribes, living in practical independence. Their country was too poor to support them, and its yield had to be supplemented in one way or another—by subsidies, robbery, or blackmail. The Mogul cavalry could not operate effectively in the defiles by which alone communication was possible, and from time to time the passes were closed by the tribesmen until they were either driven or bought off; the real strength of the Moguls lay in the fact that the tribes were ordinarily at variance among themselves, and the position became serious only when a leader emerged strong enough to effect a temporary consolidation. Such a leader appeared in 1672; war blazed up, and the Moguls suffered a series of heavy reverses. After two years of failure, Aurangzeb took charge of the situation in person, and by a judicious combination of force and diplomacy broke up the confederacy; but for about three years the needs of the north-west made it impossible to reinforce the army in the south, and this fact contributed materially to the developments in that region.

From Afghanistan Aurangzeb turned his attention to Rājputāna. In pursuance of his fundamental policy, he determined to break up this essentially Hindu region by annexing Mārwār, the Rāthor state lying west of the Mogul territory of Ajmere; and he put this determination into effect in 1678, when the Mahārāja died on duty in Afghanistan, leaving no direct heir. For the moment the Rāthors were helpless, but the birth of a posthumous heir changed the situation; the tribe rallied to their infant Chief, guerilla war broke out, the accessible towns in the state were seized and pillaged by the Moguls, the temples were desecrated, and the Rāthors were driven into the hills of the desert. The adjoining state of Mewār prepared to help the Rāthors; it, too, was overrun by the Moguls, and the attack was pressed so that the enemy was confined to the Aravalli hills with the Mogul forces on both sides.

At this point a complication ensued. One of Aurangzeb's sons, Prince Akbar, who was in command of one section of the operations, and had fallen into disfavour owing to the inefficiency he displayed, determined to rebel; and in 1681 he joined the Rājputs, proclaimed his father's deposition, and crowned himself as Emperor. For the moment Aurangzeb's position was critical, for he had very few troops with him at his base in Ajmere, and it is quite possible that, if Akbar had advanced promptly, he might have secured the throne; but he was not the right sort of man for such an enterprise, and he delayed his attack until his father was in a position to take the offensive. When the armies were in touch, Aurangzeb resorted to diplomacy, and by the astute use of forged letters and other devices he succeeded in splitting the enemy ; the Rājputs withdrew, the Moslem troops joined the Moguls, and Akbar fled with only a handful of followers. He found a refuge with the Rājputs, who by this time had learned how they had been duped, and they conducted him into the South, where for some time he remained with the Marāthas, but eventually he left India for Persia, and did not return.

Soon after this episode, Mewār made peace with Aurangzeb, but in Mārwār the guerilla war continued, and ended only in the next reign, when the Chief who had been born thirty years before was formally acknowledged by the Emperor. The outstanding result of these operations was that Rājputāna as a whole ceased to be a recruiting ground for the Mogul army. Some of the Chiefs continued to render loyal service to the Emperor, but others were openly hostile, and others again were, at the most, lukewarm ; there were thus fewer Rājput troopers to be had for the war in the South.

A few months after the peace with Mewār, Aurangzeb started for the South, where the situation had become complicated. The kingdoms of Bījāpur and Golconda still remained to be conquered ; but a new hostile power, that of the Marāthas, had grown up, and at the moment the rebel Prince Akbar was in their camp. The fate of the two old kingdoms need not detain us. The fortress of Bījāpur surrendered in 1686 ; Golconda fell by treachery a year later ; the territories of both were annexed ; and the Mogul empire was thus extended to the east coast, well to the south of Madras. The rise of the Marātha power calls for fuller notice, for it was the beginning of a movement which was destined to dominate the history of India.

The Marāthas [1] lived mainly on the uplands of the Western Ghats, east and south-east of Bombay. Their

[1] The term Marātha is sometimes used vaguely. Strictly speaking, it denotes one agricultural caste, living in this region ; but sometimes it covers a group of such castes, and sometimes the whole population of the region, which is now frequently described as Mahārāshtra, the Sanskrit form of the name.

THE MARĀTHAS

country was agriculturally poor, and, accustomed as they were to a hard and frugal life, they were excellent military material. As such, their services were in demand in the southern kingdoms, where bands of them were employed as mercenaries under their own leaders. One of these leaders, Shāhjī Bhonsle, had an adventurous career in the first half of the seventeenth century, in the course of which he served successively Ahmadnagar, the Moguls, and Bījāpur; and to him was born in the year 1627 a son named Sivājī, who founded the Marātha independent power.

The historian must approach this topic with caution, for in the process of time it has been overlaid with sentiment and prejudice. In the villages of the North, the brutal excesses of the Marātha armies, committed half a century or more after Sivājī's death, left an enduring memory, and for a long time the very name of the Marāthas excited hatred as well as fear. In western India, on the other hand, Sivājī has become a popular hero, and his exploits have been celebrated in an extensive literature, some of the texts of which are certainly spurious, while the authority of others is dubious. Some modern writers have seen him as the expression, almost as much as the leader, of a great popular movement, which they regard as a renaissance of the Hindu power; others have regarded him merely as a successful freebooter; others, again, as a military and political genius, whose mental horizon widened as he went forward—originally a freebooter who was also a dreamer, but later a soldier, statesman and administrator of unquestioned eminence. Such differences cannot be discussed adequately in a book like this, and we shall confine ourselves to his achievements, leaving his personality to be studied in the voluminous literature of which he is the subject.

A few words must, however, be said regarding the idea that the Marāthas were already in a condition of emotional ferment when Sivājī emerged to guide the new force into definite activities. There is not very much positive evidence in support of this view, but it is certain that new religious ideas had recently spread among the Hindus in this region; and in the first half of the seventeenth century they had been further popularised by the songs of Tukārām, the most highly esteemed of all the poets who have written in the Marāthi language. Ideas of a Hindu revival were thus in the air, and Sivājī himself had a deep personal sense of religion; but it is not easy to correlate his varied political activities with Tukārām's pure gospel of love.

Sivājī was brought up by his mother, mainly at Poona, on the assignment held by his father, who was employed on military duty elsewhere. At the age of twenty he was managing this assignment, and had already gathered a small band of adherents, with whose help he set out to enlarge the assignment into an independent kingdom. For the first few years his progress was slow and cautious, but after 1655 his enterprises became more important, and brought him into collision sometimes with Bījāpur and sometimes with the Moguls. Some years of inconclusive fighting followed, but in 1664 Aurangzeb sent Rāja Jai Singh, the most efficient of his Generals, to bring matters to a decision, and the Rāja succeeded so well that next year Sivājī submitted, and became a vassal of the Emperor.

The settlement, however, did not last for long. Sivājī was prevailed on to present himself at Aurangzeb's Court at Agra, was disappointed at his reception, and showed his feelings in such a manner that the Emperor, who already distrusted him, placed him under arrest; he made a spectacular escape, and returned to his own country, where he renewed negotiations with the Moguls. Hostilities recommenced in 1670. On the one side was Sivājī, now in unquestioned command of a strong and united power; on the other the Moguls, deprived of necessary reinforcements by the claims of the Afghan campaign, and crippled by recurring dissensions among the commanders, who, even when united, were not disposed to bring the campaign to a conclusion, preferring, in the words of an English report, to 'maintain a politic war for their own profit.' The result of three years' fighting was a large extension of Sivājī's territory, and even more of his prestige.

In 1674 Sivājī decided to regularise his position by a formal coronation. An objection raised by the Brāhmans

THE CAREER OF SIVĀJĪ

of his territory that only a member of the Kshatriya caste could lawfully be crowned as king was met by the production of a pedigree [1] tracing his descent from the Rājputs of Mewār; the pedigree was accepted by an eminent scholar of Benares; and the traditional ceremonies were duly performed, at a cost which left the treasury empty. The years which followed were marked by continuous fighting. The most important event was Sivājī's incursion in 1677 into the Madras country, which he overran and plundered, or 'peeled to the bone,' in the words of an English record. Three years later he died, and was succeeded by his son Sambhujī.

It is not easy to define the Marātha territory in precise terms, for the boundaries fluctuated, but it may be said in a general way that about 1670 Sivājī's kingdom consisted of a long and comparatively narrow belt of country above the Ghats, from about the latitude of Surat to that of Goa, together with the coastal lowlands, known here as the Konkan, from the neighbourhood of Goa to Bombay. In addition, the Marāthas held various forts to the south-east of this region, and were thus in military occupation of large parts of Mysore and Madras.

When, therefore, Aurangzeb had annexed Golconda and Bījāpur, he found himself confronted to the west and the south by this Marātha power, hostile and aggressive, and ready at any moment to raid his dominions. Frequent raids were in fact a necessary feature in the policy of the Marāthas. Their country, though its condition had improved under Sivājī's able administration, was still poor, and could not support the forces required for its protection, while the Moguls, enjoying a large revenue from the northern provinces, could afford to fight in the South for a long time, though not indefinitely. Many of Sivājī's military operations had been in essence financial; he had twice plundered Surat, the chief Mogul seaport, his incursion into Madras had been rendered necessary by the state of his treasury, and, speaking generally, the spoils of war formed an indispensable part of the state revenue. A distinctive feature

[1] Modern scholars are at variance as to the authenticity of this pedigree.

of his system was the levy of what became known as *chauth* from those portions of Mogul territory which he was in a position to raid periodically. The name means 'one-fourth,' and it came into use because the practice was to spare from spoliation those areas which agreed to pay a quarter of the annual revenue by way of blackmail; its importance can be judged from the fact that, at the time of Sivājī's death, the *chauth* was reckoned to be nearly as great as the regular revenue of the kingdom.

With such neighbours Aurangzeb could not avoid action, even if he had wished to do so, and at first his cause was favoured by the fact that Sambhujī was a very different man from his father—personally dissipated, and a thoroughly inefficient administrator. Factions arose among the Marāthas, many of their commanders deserted to the Moguls, the kingdom suffered from the rapacity of officials and the depredations of minor Chiefs, and in 1689 the king himself was captured as the result of a daring raid on a pleasure-resort where he was engaged in debauch. The prisoner was publicly degraded in the Mogul camp, tortured, and at last executed with barbarous cruelty; his son, Shāhu, who had also been captured, was kept as a prisoner of the Moguls.

For the moment it seemed that the Marāthas were crushed, but this proved to be a mistake. Operations were not pressed to a conclusion, the various Marātha commanders fought as independent units, and a guerilla war ensued, affecting not only the Marātha country proper, but also the territories they occupied farther to the south-east, where the new king, Rājārām, a younger brother of Sambhujī, had established himself in the fortress of Gingee, about eighty miles south-west of Madras city.

Some years of indecisive fighting followed. In 1698 Gingee at last fell, after a desultory siege of seven years, but Rājārām reached his own country in safety; and Aurangzeb, having thus cleared the eastern theatre of war, settled down to the systematic reduction of the forts with which the Marātha territory was thickly studded. From 1699 to 1705 he pursued this object, conducting all operations in person.

DECAY OF THE EMPIRE

The story of his efforts is pitiful. After a long siege a fort would be captured, often by bribing the commander; then the Emperor would move to the next fort; his last capture would be recovered by the Marāthas, and things would go on as before. Eight principal forts, and several smaller ones, were besieged in this period, during which the spirit of the Mogul army was finally broken by the fruitless hardships of the campaign, the treasury was depleted, and Aurangzeb alone remained steadfast to his purpose. At last, in 1705, his health failed, and the old man of eighty-eight retired to Ahmadnagar, where he died.

Meanwhile Rājārām, the Marātha king, had died in 1700, and had been succeeded by a minor son under the regency of his mother, Tārā Bāī. The final failure of Aurangzeb was due largely to the energy and administrative genius of this lady, who succeeded in restoring some degree of unity among the Marāthas, and directed the conduct of both civil and military affairs. Aurangzeb's death reduced the pressure on the Marāthas, for his sons engaged in a war of succession, which was fought out mainly in the North; while the infant king was displaced in favour of Shāhu, the legitimate heir of Sambhujī, who returned to the South after nearly twenty years' captivity in the Mogul camp.

We have said that the administration of the North had become demoralised during Aurangzeb's absence of a quarter of a century. The collapse cannot be described in detail, but the main facts are that, while the Mogul officers, left largely to themselves, were engaged in strengthening their personal position, Hindu Chiefs were asserting themselves in all directions. In Rājputāna the war with Mārwār was dragging on, and other Rājput Chiefs were raiding into Mālwa, where the Marāthas also had made their appearance. In the Punjab, in Agra, and in Oudh, in Bengal, in Bihār, and in Bundelkhand, we hear of local Chiefs becoming active, with varying success; the central authority was weak; the decay of agriculture affected the power of the officers, who could not maintain adequate contingents out of the decreasing income of their assignments; loyalty to the empire brought no reward, and energetic men were already 'staking out claims' in view of the future. The evil was probably not yet beyond a remedy; another Great Mogul might have succeeded in restoring the empire in the North, but, as we shall see in the next chapter, the Moguls who followed Aurangzeb were in no way great, and disintegration proceeded steadily.

We must now turn to the maritime history of the reign, which was marked by the establishment of Indian naval forces on the west coast. The story of this development begins in the fifteenth century, when some Africans, known by the general name of Sīdīs, settled in the small island of Janjīra, nearly fifty miles south of Bombay, and secured some territory adjoining it on the mainland. In 1636 this part of the country came under the rule of Bījāpur, and the Sīdī Chief was recognised as an officer of that kingdom, on condition of protecting the maritime trade, a task which he performed by means of an efficient flotilla of armed coasting vessels. The Sīdīs, fine seamen and hard fighters, constituted a formidable obstacle to Sivājī's enterprises in the Konkan, and in 1659 he began to organise a similar flotilla of his own, manned largely by the piratical classes of the Malabar Coast. Ten years of fighting followed, in the course of which merchant vessels were freely captured or plundered by both sides; but the Marāthas were winning, and in 1670 the Sīdī Chief, despairing of support from Bījāpur, transferred his allegiance to Aurangzeb, by whom he was appointed Admiral of the empire.

From this time on, the war between Aurangzeb and the Marāthas was carried on in the coastal waters as well as on land, and led incidentally to various complications with the Europeans on the coast, but neither flotilla could cope effectively with armed sea-going ships. This weakness was important, for European pirates were now infesting the Indian Ocean. The trouble was not entirely new, for, from the beginning of the century, pirates from Europe had occasionally visited these waters, but in Aurangzeb's reign such piracy became endemic, and the Moguls, unable to deal

MARITIME DEVELOPMENTS

with the evil themselves, endeavoured to make the European merchants responsible for the safety of the seas, an endeavour which eventually proved unsuccessful. Indian commerce thus suffered severely at the hands of pirates as well as belligerents.

The European merchants on the coast were less affected by such matters than by wars nearer home, the details of which we must pass over. The Portuguese were at times involved with the Marāthas, but they were now outside the main current of Indian history, nor need the activities of the Dutch detain us. The French East India Company, founded in 1664, had appeared on both sides of India, but as yet it counted for little. For the English on the west coast the chief development was the growth of their new settlement at Bombay, to which their headquarters were transferred from Surat. The insecurity of the neighbouring Indian ports led to a large influx of merchants and artisans, anxious to carry on their business under English protection, and, though the place was very unhealthy, the population had risen to more than 50,000 before the century closed.

Developments in Bengal were more important. Here there had been for many years a dispute of the kind which has already been outlined, the English insisting on the permanence of a concession regarding taxes which the Moguls considered to be temporary; while the unauthorised exactions made by the local officials at last drove the former to the conclusion that they must have a fort for their security in Bengal, as in Madras and Bombay. In 1686 the authorities in England directed that an attempt should be made to seize Chittagong by force; but in October of that year hostilities were precipitated by an attack made on the factory at Hooghly by the Mogul Governor, and a state of war continued until 1690. Chittagong proved to be invulnerable, and the terms of peace granted by the Moguls, who could not afford the continued loss of trade, allowed the English to settle at a little village on the Hooghly, at the spot where Calcutta now stands. About this time the Mogul administration in Bengal was in the hands of an amiable but incompetent Viceroy; various neighbouring

Chiefs were in rebellion; and in 1696 the English, Dutch and French were permitted to fortify their factories on the Hooghly, which the Viceroy was not in a position to protect. Two years later, the English were allowed to rent three villages, comprising the site and environs of their new possession, the first Fort William, and one of these villages, known as Kalikātā, gave its name to the settlement, which increased rapidly in population.

This renting of villages was an incident of the fourth stage in the gradual approach of the Companies towards territorial possessions in India. We have seen in Chapter XXX how the trading voyage led to the factory, and the factory to the fort. In the disturbed condition of India during Aurangzeb's reign, forts became more and more indispensable, but the cost of the garrisons formed a heavy overhead charge on the commerce which they safeguarded, and the idea emerged of self-supporting settlements, each fortress being provided with a sufficient area of land to pay for its maintenance out of rents and taxes. The first step in this direction had been taken by the Dutch at Pulicat by the middle of the century. Of the English forts, Bombay had sufficient land for the purpose; Madras obtained three villages in 1693, and five more a little later; and Calcutta, as we have seen, began with three. The merchants on the spot thus gained some experience of rural as well as urban administration, finding tenants, and assessing and collecting their rents; while the security afforded by the fortresses attracted settlers of all classes. It may be added that a first step in the direction of local self-government was taken at Madras in 1688, when a municipal corporation was established with Indian as well as European aldermen.

The possession of villages under grant or lease from Indian authorities was not, of course, tantamount to sovereignty; but the latter idea had already emerged in England, where Sir Josia Child, Governor of the Company from 1681 to 1699, had maintained that Bombay and Madras should be developed on the lines followed by the Dutch at Batavia, and should form 'the foundation of a large, well-grounded, sure English dominion in [*not* over] India for all time to come.'[1] His conclusion was based directly on the growing insecurity of conditions in India, which made it impossible for merchants to rely on the authorities for protection ; but the measures taken to give effect to it were not immediately important, probably because of the uncertainty of the Company's own position. From 1689 onwards it was in conflict with Parliament, in 1698 a new competing company was established, and ten years elapsed before the conflicting interests were finally reconciled in the United Company, which thenceforward held the field. Bombay, which was already English territory, was developed to some extent in the direction indicated by Child, but Madras was still under the sovereignty of Aurangzeb, as successor to the rights of the kingdom of Golconda.

[1] Quoted in *Camb. Hist.*, v. 102.

MAP VII

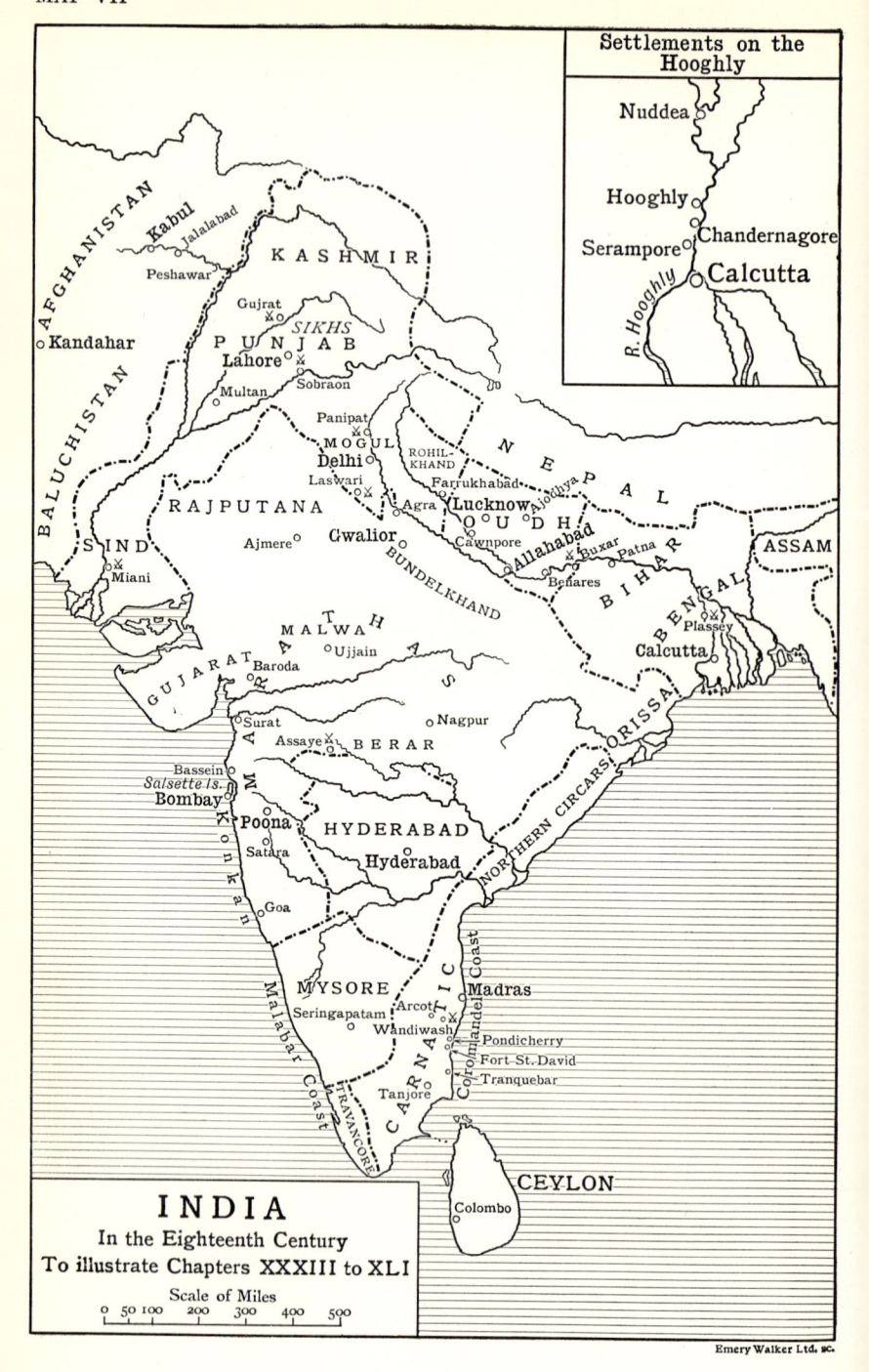

INDIA
In the Eighteenth Century
To illustrate Chapters XXXIII to XLI

Scale of Miles
0 50 100 200 300 400 500

Settlements on the Hooghly

CHAPTER XXXIII

THE DISINTEGRATION OF THE MOGUL EMPIRE

In the course of the half-century following Aurangzeb's death, the Mogul empire disintegrated, and the political map of India was redrawn. The disintegration cannot fairly be described as violent. It was helped by invasion from outside India, and in some cases by the incursions of the Marāthas, while some of the succession states fought among themselves; but, speaking generally, the provinces simply dropped away, and became independent of Delhi, which could not control them effectively. Towards the middle of the century there were independent Moslem states in southern India, separated from the Moslems in the North by the Marāthas, who occupied the centre of the country from Gujarāt to Orissa, and extended their influence to the neighbourhood of Delhi and Agra.

The chief Moslem ruler in the South was the Nizām of Hyderabad; the first Nizām had been Mogul Viceroy of a province formed by Aurangzeb from the conquered kingdom of Golconda, and this province became his territory. More or less subordinate to him was the Nawāb [1] of Arcot, who ruled over the eastern side of the peninsula, a region known at this time as the Carnatic, almost as far south as Tanjore. To the west of the Carnatic, Mysore was held by a Hindu dynasty, but just at the close of the period this region was coming under the sway of Haidar Alī, a military adventurer

[1] The designation of 'Nawāb,' the English 'nabob,' did not originally denote sovereignty. The word means 'deputy,' and its use at this period reflects the gradual transformation of Moslem viceroys or governors into sovereigns.

who in the third quarter of the century was to dominate the politics of the South.

In the North, Bengal and Bihār formed a practically independent state under a Nawāb, and on its western frontier lay Oudh, then much more extensive than the region which now bears that name, and also ruled by a Nawāb. Beyond Oudh, a dominion in Rohilkhand, north of the Ganges, had been carved out by a Moslem military adventurer, while between the Ganges and the Jumna another soldier of fortune, also a Moslem, ruled at Farrukhābād. West of these two states lay what remained to Delhi—still a fairly extensive kingdom until 1739, when, as we shall see, the Punjab, Sind and Kābul were annexed by Persia, and then very little was left to the Moguls. To the south-west of Delhi, Rājputāna remained under its Chiefs, independent in a way, but most of them dominated by the Marāthas, who had extended far beyond their original territories.

Shrunken and almost powerless as it was, the Mogul empire was still a political fact, for to the Moslems of India, who saw their faith and culture threatened with submersion, Delhi was still the centre and the great hope of Islam. A *de facto* king of Oudh might on occasion be also Prime Minister of the empire, a candidate for the throne of Hyderabad might look to Delhi for moral support, and the Emperor could grant, or sell, designations and appointments to successful adventurers who might wish to regularise their gains, though he could not guarantee continued possession.

A change had meanwhile occurred in the constitution of the Marātha power. Sivājī had governed through a council of Ministers, in which authority was distributed between the military leaders and the Brāhmans and other literate classes responsible for the civil administration. As time went on, the Brāhman Prime Minister, who was known as the Peshwā, drew all power into his own hands; by 1720 his position had become hereditary, and though Shāhu, the grandson of Sivājī, was still recognised as the titular king, the Peshwā was the actual ruler of most of the original Marātha territory with its capital at Poona, while the military leaders, Marāthas in the strict sense, carved out new dominions for themselves, acknowledging the Peshwā's general supremacy, but each acting largely on his own initiative. In this way the single power developed into a confederacy. The Gaekwar family established itself in Gujarāt, the Bhonsles in what is now known as the Central Provinces, and the Holkars and Sindhias in Mālwa. The two latter extended their authority towards the Jumna, while the Bhonsles spread eastward, raided into Bengal, and eventually obtained the cession of Orissa.

Such were the main lines of the territorial rearrangement which took place during this period, but the struggle for power went on also on a smaller scale. Chiefs, officials, and adventurers alike, all were busily engaged in extending their spheres of influence, and consolidating their authority over larger or smaller portions of territory, which might, or might not, develop into independent states. Ideas of prescriptive right were of no practical significance, though they might still be invoked to justify facts already established by force; the time was one in which energy and unscrupulous ambition held the field. The details of this struggle cannot be recounted here, but its existence must be borne in mind; some of the Indian States of to-day, and many of the large landed properties in northern India, trace their origin to these conflicts of the eighteenth century, and it was sometimes a matter of luck whether, in the course of the eventual reorganisation, a particular individual emerged as a ruling Prince, or as an influential landholder in a British province.

We must now sketch the history of the Moguls in Delhi. The twelve years following the death of Aurangzeb in 1707 were marked by five reigns, with three wars of succession. Muhammad Shāh reigned from 1719 to 1748, and watched, rather than contested, the progress of disintegration, while his Court was the scene of intrigue between various factions; but in 1739 came the Persian invasion. It cannot be described as a bolt from the blue, for in the previous century Persia had more than once shown a disposition to conquer part of India, or at least to secure the Indus as her frontier; and the importance which she attached to the retention of Kandahār is explained by the fact that it commanded the road. The idea, however, only came to fruition under Nādir Shāh, who won the throne of Persia in 1736. Five years later he marched from Kandahār, conquered in succession Kābul and Lahore, and defeated the Mogul forces at Karnāl a little north of Pānīpat. Terms were then made, and the conqueror entered Delhi peacefully in company with Muhammad Shāh; but a tumult arose in the city, many Persians were killed, and Nādir Shāh replied with an indiscriminate massacre of the inhabitants. After this had taken place, the treasures of the empire were seized, a heavy ransom was collected from the city, the Punjab, Sind and Kābul were ceded by treaty, and Nādir Shāh returned to Persia with his spoils.

Eight years later, on the assassination of Nādir Shāh, an event occurred which was to have an important influence on the history of India. An Afghan officer, who came to be known as Ahmad Shāh Durānī, succeeded in uniting the Afghan tribes into an independent kingdom, possessing both Kandahār and Kābul, and it now becomes possible, for the first time, to speak of Afghanistan as a political unit, lying outside India, but holding India's gates. The new ruler naturally regarded himself as entitled to the Punjab in succession to Nādir Shāh, and promptly entered it, but was driven back for the time in 1748.

The decade which followed the death of Muhammad Shāh in that year is covered by the reigns of some ineffective emperors. Faction continued to dominate the situation; presently the Marāthas were called in to help one side; and they did this so successfully as to become all-powerful, and overran what was left of the Mogul territory. The leading Moslems of Delhi, along with the rulers of Oudh and Rohilkhand, eventually sought assistance from Afghanistan; in 1761 yet another battle was fought at Pānīpat, in which the Marāthas were completely defeated by the joint forces of Afghans and Moguls; and for the next few years an officer of Afghan origin ruled in Delhi, while the titular Emperor, Shāh Alam (1759–1806), after endeavouring unsuccessfully to establish himself in Bihār, settled down

EVENTS AT DELHI

for a time under British protection at Allahabad. In order to explain how this was possible, we must return to the story of the European Companies on the coasts.

So far as the west coast is concerned, the period was uneventful. Friendship with the Marāthas was the accepted policy of the authorities at Bombay, and, while there were occasional disputes with neighbours, and recurring trouble with pirates on the coast, the settlement grew in population, wealth and commerce. In Bengal disputes with the local authorities were frequent, but Calcutta continued to prosper, and its population increased largely after 1742, when the Marāthas from the Central Provinces began to raid into Bengal. These raids, which were repeated at intervals for some years, make a terrible story. We have said in the last chapter that in the seventeenth century the spoils of war were indispensable to the continued existence of the Marātha power: this justification no longer held good when the various members of the confederacy were established in productive country, and were not threatened by a powerful enemy, but the practice was maintained, and plunder was now the chief aim of the raiders. Again, the discipline maintained by Sivājī had been strict, and even in his most violent raids women had been protected: in Bengal, we read of murder and mutilation, of arson and rape, practised indiscriminately and without restraint. A contemporary description speaks of the Marāthas as 'slayers of pregnant women and infants, of Brāhmans and the poor, fierce of spirit, expert in robbing the property of everyone and in committing every sinful act. . . . They slay the unarmed, the poor, women and children. They rob all property and abduct chaste wives.' Other accounts tell of cutting off ears, noses and hands, of women ravished by the members of a gang one after another, of houses and temples wantonly burnt; Bengal was terror-stricken, and safety could be found only in flight, or within the lines by which the settlement at Calcutta had been hastily protected.[1]

[1] The phrases quoted are taken from pp. 36–39 of Sir Jadunath Sarkar's *Bihar and Orissa during the Fall of the Mughal Empire* (Patna, 1932).

The Coromandel Coast was the scene of the really significant events of this period. There the English at Madras, and the French in their fortress of Pondichery, carried on business prosperously and peaceably till the outbreak of the War of the Austrian Succession. Fighting went on in India from 1746 to 1748; Madras was captured by the French, and, until its restoration under the treaty of peace, the English headquarters were established at Fort St. David, further down the coast; but it was essentially a European war, and its main effect in India was to establish the reputation of the French forces as superior to any opposition which the country could offer. When Madras was besieged, the English invoked the help of the Nawāb of Arcot, who did what he could, and sent troops for its relief. His forces, which consisted of cavalry according to the established Indian practice, met trained musketeers supported by effective field artillery, and the result was a conclusive demonstration that the Indian practice had become obsolete; horses were useless against guns and muskets, and European superiority on land became as obvious as European predominance at sea.

The French forces were not, however, entirely European, for they included some companies of sepoys, a name which came into use to denote Indians trained as infantry by European officers. The first sepoys of whom we hear were employed from about 1720 onwards at a French settlement on the Malabar Coast; and two companies of these were brought to Pondichery, where they served in this war. In its final year, the French example was followed by the English, the sepoys quickly proved their value, and from this time on they became an integral part of European armies employed in India.

The news of peace between England and France produced a difficult situation in the South, for both sides had troops which they did not need, but could not send home till the sailing season came round; and the Governors of Madras and Pondichery independently hit on the expedient of saving the heavy cost of their maintenance by lending them to some Indian power. The first English experiment in this direction was insignificant, but the action taken by Joseph Dupleix, the French Governor, must be regarded as a turning-point in the history of India. Dupleix, who, after previous experience in Bengal, had come to Pondichery as Governor in 1742, was a man of wide knowledge and great ideas. By the time the war ended, he had realised the instability of the southern states, and their helplessness against guns and muskets; and, starting from these facts, he conceived a new political development, which should transform the commercial position of the Company he served.

Commerce between Europe and India still continued on the established lines: India wanted little from Europe except silver, and the annual remittances of treasure which were needed to keep trade moving constituted a heavy drain on French resources. Dupleix conceived the idea that his Company should acquire territory in India yielding sufficient revenue to make such remittances unnecessary; or, in other words, that the surplus revenue of its Indian possessions should be exported in the form of commodities. He did not, however, obtain the Company's sanction to this scheme, but worked towards it on his own initiative, hoping presumably that he would be able to present his masters with an accomplished fact, and one of such value that it could not be refused.

To begin with, he aimed at predominance rather than formal sovereignty, and his first step was to support two claimants who were active in 1749, one to Hyderabad and the other to the Carnatic. In the former region he achieved definite success, and from 1750 to 1755 his able representative, Charles de Bussy, was the practical ruler of Hyderabad, the coastal districts of which, known as the Northern Circars,[1] were assigned in the regular way to provide the cost of the French troops. In the Carnatic things went differently. There the initial advantage gained by the French convinced the English Governor that, in order to save his Company's trade, he must support the Nawāb whom Dupleix aimed at displacing; and from 1751 to 1754 the two Companies were at war in this region, though there

[1] Properly *Sarkār*, a word used by the Moguls to denote an administrative unit of area corresponding to the modern 'district.'

was peace in Europe. The incidents of the war need not detain us; fortune varied, but on the whole the English gained predominance in the Carnatic, and established in Indian eyes a military prestige equal to that which the French had already won. The latter result was due in large measure to the successes achieved by Robert Clive, who earned in this war the reputation which brought him to the front in the next period. The end of the war came in 1754, when the French Company, determined on peace, recalled Dupleix, and abandoned for the time the struggle for the Carnatic.

The year 1756 saw events which led to the beginning of a new period in the history of India. It witnessed the outbreak of the Seven Years War, the result of which was fatal to French aspirations in the South; and it witnessed also the capture of Calcutta by the ruler of Bengal, an act which ultimately led to the establishment of British sovereignty over that region. These events form the subject of the next chapter.

CHAPTER XXXIV

THE WORK OF CLIVE

IN June, 1756, the English settlement of Calcutta was attacked without warning by Sirāj-ud-daula, a young man who two months earlier had succeeded his grandfather as Nawāb of Bengal. His motives are not on record, and his character was such that almost any discreditable hypothesis would be permissible ; but the most probable view is that he was influenced by news of what had been happening in the South, and feared that, if he did not take the initiative, the Europeans would fight over Bengal as they had fought over the Carnatic. Calcutta was not in a position to resist, for the fort had become indefensible owing to long-continued neglect, the garrison was below strength, the officers were inefficient, and there was nobody to lead. The Governor and some of his Council fled to the ships, the troops got out of hand, and the fort surrendered after a short defence. Those who surrendered were crowded for the night into a single room known as the ' black hole,' which had been used as the military prison of the fort, and the great majority of them died of suffocation.[1] When information of this disaster reached Madras, a relief expedition was despatched under the command of Clive, who, in January, 1757, recovered Calcutta, and, after a little fighting, negotiated a treaty with Sirāj-ud-daula. Just then came the news of the outbreak of the Seven Years War. The Nawāb, angry at the loss of Calcutta, was inclined to favour the French ; but he vacillated, and, after some intricate diplomacy, the English

[1] The view advanced in the present century that the story of the ' black hole ' is an invention is discussed in *Camb. Hist.*, v. 156.

forces, claiming his authority, captured the French settlement at Chandernagore, and thus eliminated the possibility of attack from that quarter.

Meanwhile Sirāj-ud-daula had alienated the wealthy and influential Hindus who had been favoured by his predecessor; they expected a campaign of active extortion, and some of the leading bankers had been threatened with forcible conversion. The officers of the army were also dissatisfied, Sirāj-ud-daula was unpopular with all classes, a revolutionary movement was initiated by the Hindus, and Mīr Jafar, an officer who had been in administrative charge of the Nawāb's troops, and had been dismissed and insulted by him, came forward as a candidate for the throne. The English authorities, convinced that the revolution would be successful, decided to be on the winning side; Mīr Jafar promised very favourable terms; and Clive marched against the Nawāb with a force of 3,000 men, mainly trained sepoys who had come with him from Madras. On 23rd June, 1757, this force met the Nawāb's army [1] at the battle of Plassey; Sirāj-ud-daula fled when the English attacked; and a few days later Clive placed Mīr Jafar on the throne of Bengal. The new Nawāb was weak, irresolute, and, like his predecessor, inclined to extort money from the wealthy Hindus who had secured his accession. Clive felt himself bound to protect them, and in the diplomatic struggle which ensued proved himself to be by far the stronger man, so that he acquired a predominant position in Bengal. In the following year he was appointed Governor of the English settlement; and in 1759 he found himself confronted by the Dutch. Hitherto the Dutch merchants had not played a very active part in Indian politics, but they were now alarmed for the future of their lucrative trade in Bengal; there, as in the Carnatic, political predominance was likely to result in commercial monopoly; and they sent a small expedition from Batavia in order to back their claims. The Nawāb at Clive's instance forbad the expedition to enter the

[1] Sirāj-ud-daula's force was estimated at about 50,000 men, but a substantial proportion, who were under the command of Mīr Jafar and other revolutionaries, took no part in the fighting.

DEVELOPMENTS IN BENGAL

Hooghly. The Dutch tried to force an entry; but their ships were captured, their troops were defeated, and they had to accept a humiliating treaty.

When therefore Clive sailed for England in 1760, he left Calcutta reasonably safe from European enemies, but its position as regards the Nawāb was uncertain. The English troops, though few in number, were a powerful factor in the situation, but the predominance which had been gained in Bengal belonged to Clive personally, and not to the men whom he left behind him; it was the result of his exceptional insight, his promptitude in action, and his power of imposing his will on others. Before continuing the story, we must say a few words regarding certain ethical questions which arise out of his conduct during these three years.

Clive himself wrote that the history of the period would contain 'fighting, chicanery, intrigues, politics, and the Lord knows what,'[1] and his view may be confidently accepted; but controversy has settled on two incidents in particular, the large sums paid to individual officers by Mīr Jafar on his accession, and the use by Clive of a fictitious document in the course of some intricate negotiations. The payments to Clive and other officers, aggregating something like half a million sterling, were fiercely denounced in England, and some part of the hostility was doubtless sincere, though in reading the passionate invectives of the eighteenth century it is always necessary to be on the watch for personal and political spite masquerading in the garments of righteous indignation. There is no evidence to show that the payments were considered unusual in India, where officers were accustomed at this period to make personal profit out of public business in the form of either bribes or presents.

As regards the second count, the position was that during the progress of the revolutionary movement, one of the leaders of the bankers, whose name usually appears as Omichund, was found to be playing a double game, negotiating in his own interests with the Nawāb whom he had conspired to replace; and, in order to keep him quiet, he was shown what purported to be the treaty made with Mīr

[1] Letter to the historian Orme, quoted in *Camb. Hist.*, v. 151.

Jafar, but was in fact a fictitious document containing a provision in his favour which did not appear in the authentic treaty. Clive's conduct in this matter was justly condemned in England, but it is doubtful if Indian diplomatists of the day would have seen any reason for objecting to it. We have said in an earlier chapter that the leading administrative treatise of the Hindu period presents administration in general, and diplomacy in particular, as an art entirely untrammelled by ethical considerations; and the known practice of the Moslem period was precisely in accordance with this doctrine. To give two illustrations only, Aurangzeb, as we have seen, made use of forged letters to break up the coalition which had been formed in favour of Prince Akbar; while the oldest Hindu biographers of Sivājī state as a matter of plain fact that he ordered assassination in the guise of diplomacy.[1] There was no reason to suppose that Indian views on this subject had changed in the interval which separates Aurangzeb and Sivājī from Clive, indeed it might be argued that the conditions prevailing during that interval were likely to operate in favour of a relaxation of moral principles; and on this count also it must be said that Clive followed the Indian practice of the day. Whether he was justified in doing so is a question which must be left to casuists.

As soon as Clive left Calcutta, a difficult situation arose between the English authorities and Mīr Jafar, who was not content to be a mere figurehead, and who was known to have intrigued with the Dutch at the time of their expedition to the Hooghly. The idea was mooted of obtaining for the Company an appointment as perpetual Viceroy of Bengal under the Mogul Emperor, but eventually it was decided to replace the Nawāb, and, in response to a show of force, Mīr Jafar withdrew, and was succeeded by Mīr Kāsim, a

---

[1] The evidence regarding the assassination of Hanumant Rao Moré is discussed on pp. 42–45 of Sarkar's *Shivaji and his Times* (Calcutta, 1929). On the general question, Mr. A. L. Srivastava writes: 'Political morality was at its lowest. Mean intrigue and treacherous conspiracy were the very breath of the life of the nobles and officers, and violation of plighted word, perfidy and assassination were common occurrences with our rulers of the first half of the eighteenth century' (*The First Two Nawabs of Oudh* (Lucknow, 1933), pp. 268–9).

FRESH COMPLICATIONS

much stronger man, under an agreement which left several dangerous questions unsettled. Mīr Kāsim quickly showed that he intended to be a real ruler, and the inevitable clash came when he interfered with the trade carried on in Bengal by the Company and its servants—a subject which requires a few words of explanation.

For a long time the Company had been exempt under the orders of the Mogul Emperor from paying the ordinary transit dues levied on commodities passing through Bengal; and the Company's servants had claimed that this exemption extended to the trade which they carried on for their personal benefit, a claim which had been rejected both by the Company and by the Nawāb. After the battle of Plassey, however, Mīr Jafar issued orders exempting from these duties all goods covered by a pass (known by the Indian name 'dustuck') issued by the head of any English factory; such passes were in fact used for the private goods of the Company's servants; and the practice grew up of selling them to Indian merchants, who were only too glad to secure the exemption they conferred. Mīr Kāsim objected entirely to such practices; negotiations proved fruitless; and in 1763 matters came to a head at Patna, where the Nawāb threatened the English factory. The merchant in charge of the factory then seized the city, but the Nawāb's troops recovered it by force, and a state of war resulted. The English forces advanced from Calcutta, and defeated the troops of Mīr Kāsim, who sought help from the Nawāb of Oudh. The result was the battle of Buxar, fought in October, 1764, when the Oudh forces were crushed, the Nawāb fled, and Shāh Alam the titular Mogul Emperor, who had accompanied him in the campaign, submitted to the victorious English commander.

Before this had happened, the English in Calcutta had restored the former Nawāb, Mīr Jafar; and on his death in 1765, they recognised his son as his successor, but on terms which made him practically a figure-head, for his principal Minister was to be an English nominee, and was not to be removed without English sanction. At this juncture Clive returned to Calcutta for his second term of office (1765-1767) as Governor, and it fell to him to settle the affairs of Bengal, Oudh and the Emperor—affairs which the battle of Buxar had thrown into the melting-pot. Nobody in India could have objected if he had established the sovereignty of the Company on the basis of conquest and effective possession, but this course would probably have involved trouble with Parliament, and also diplomatic difficulties in Europe with the French, the Dutch, and possibly other Powers; and the settlement actually made avoided such risks. The titular Emperor received as his territory a portion of Oudh lying south of the Ganges, including the city of Allahabad, which became his residence; the fugitive Nawāb of Oudh was restored to the remainder of his kingdom as the Company's ally; and the Company was appointed by the Emperor as Dīwān, or revenue administrator, of Bengal and Bihār. It will be recalled that Akbar had separated the revenue from the general administration throughout his empire, and this arrangement still held good in theory, though it was not always respected in practice. The effect of this appointment was to make the Company supreme in Bengal; it already controlled the general administration under its arrangement with the Nawāb, and it now received entire control over the revenue, subject only to fixed annual payments to the Emperor and the Nawāb.

Clive left India for the last time in 1767, with the political situation in the North settled on these lines—Bengal definitely though not formally English, and bounded on the west by two friendly Powers, the Emperor, and the Nawāb of Oudh, beyond whom were the other Powers which have already been enumerated; it was an arrangement which served for the time, but was not destined to endure for long. We must now turn to affairs in the South.

The Seven Years War brought great changes in Madras. At the outset there was little fighting, because there were few troops on the spot; the French forces were mainly in Hyderabad, while most of the English had accompanied Clive to Bengal. Reinforcements reached both sides from Europe, and from 1758 the war was actively prosecuted.

THE COMPANY SUPREME IN BENGAL 279

The English obtained command of the sea, the French were defeated decisively at the battle of Wandiwash (January, 1760), Pondichery fell in the following year, and the final result was to leave the English predominant in the Carnatic, while the French had lost their hold on Hyderabad. The arrangement which Clive made with the Emperor took account of the position in the South as well as in the North. The Carnatic was made formally independent of Hyderabad, thus recognising the facts of the situation, and the Northern Circars, the coastal districts which for a time had been held by the French, were granted to the English Company. The latter grant must be regarded as a matter of form, because these districts were actually part of Hyderabad; but it became a reality under an agreement made in 1766, by which the English at Madras and the Nizām of Hyderabad undertook to help each other in case of need, an agreement which was aimed primarily at the growing danger from Mysore.

Haidar Alī, an adventurer of exceptional ability, had now made himself master of Mysore, and, in accordance with Indian tradition, was eager to extend his territory. On the north his neighbours, and consequently his potential enemies, were the Marāthas and the Nizām; to the east lay the Carnatic, ruled by a Nawāb who was practically dependent on the English; and the political situation was thus one of four powers, any number of which might combine against the remainder—a situation which involved the complicated diplomacy and ever-shifting alliances characteristic of the Indian politics of the period. As early as 1767 the Company was assisting the Nizām against Mysore, and was then left to carry on the war alone; two years later it made peace, and entered into alliance with Mysore; and the game was destined to go on for a long time before stability was reached.

CHAPTER XXXV

INDIA IN THE EIGHTEENTH CENTURY

WHEN Clive left India in 1767, the Company, already dominant in Bengal, and committed to a share in the struggle for the South, had taken the road which was to lead it to the sovereignty of India : before continuing the story of its progress on this road, we may attempt a short description of the India to which it was to succeed. Enough has already been said regarding the political situation : everywhere might counted for much more than right, and in the conduct of public affairs there was no room for ethical considerations. In regard to war, the fact had been established that, under a competent commander, troops armed and trained in European style could defeat many times their number of troops organised on the lines traditional in India ; the lesson was being learned, and the latter portion of the century is characterised by the spread of the new methods in various Indian armies. Among Indians fighting was regarded not as a patriotic duty, but as a respectable, and sometimes lucrative, occupation. Many Marāthas had fought in Aurangzeb's armies ; European artillerymen were regularly employed by the Marāthas and the Moguls ; and no discredit attached to the Indians who served the English Company as sepoys. They were merely following their trade.

Administration was, as always in India, essentially bureaucratic, the ruler or minister transmitting his orders through a chain of subordinate officials, who looked to him, and not to the people, for guidance and control. Bureaucracy, however, did not present in India that aspect of impersonal uniformity which the term suggests in Europe, for, so long as he retained his superiors' favour, the individual officer had in practice very wide discretionary powers. The regular emoluments of office were as a rule less important than the total of perquisites, presents, and bribes which a competent man could hope to secure. The tenure of a post was of quite uncertain duration, and an official who found himself well off might have to spend much time and money in counteracting the intrigues of competitors who desired to oust him, while at the same time he might be engaged in similar intrigues to secure his own promotion : personal interests were thus apt to count for more than the welfare of the people. As regards regular emoluments, the practice of assigning the revenue of a stated area in payment of salary, which prevailed throughout the seventeenth century, had become unpopular by the close of Aurangzeb's reign, mainly, it seems, because there was no longer any certainty of peaceful possession, and in the Moslem succession states payment in cash appears to have been more usual ; but assignments continued to be made in Marātha territory.

The spirit of the administration was aptly expressed in an aphorism [1] which may be paraphrased as ' Hit before you hear ' ; action was prompt, summary and drastic, except when an opportunity offered of making money by delay, in which case a trifling matter might drag on for an indefinite period. The whip was the symbol, and the instrument, of executive power, used not only as a punishment, but also in order to obtain evidence of guilt, or, perhaps, merely to assert the authority of the wielder ; and there is nothing to suggest any regulations restricting its employment. Each local official was thus very much of an autocrat within the area of his jurisdiction.

The economic life of the country was dominated by the prevailing insecurity, for war might break out almost anywhere, while bands of robbers made the roads unsafe, and harried the villages at their pleasure. There are some indications that life and property were somewhat more secure in the Marātha territory than elsewhere, but outside its limits the Marāthas were the greatest danger of all ;

[1] In Hindi, *pahle lāt pīchhe bāt,* ' first the blow, then the talk.'

their activities in Bengal, which have been described in a previous chapter, might be repeated in any other region which they were in a position to raid. An Indian account [1] of what is now the western portion of the United Provinces, written about the year 1788, tells of the inhuman measures taken to extract money from the peasants in a period of famine by the officers of Mahādjī Sindhia, who then dominated that region. One of his tax-collectors, we read, ' tied rags to the bodies of the rich and poor alike, and, pouring oil on them, set them on fire. . . . Crowded rows of men are seen streaming from one place to another in search of food. Famine and robbery have enhanced their agony, and a third evil, viz., Mahādjī's tax-collectors, has now been added to the other two.' In Rājputāna, again, the Marāthas were a terror to Chiefs and peasants alike, and the enmity between these fighting races was destined to be an important factor in the extension of the Company's territories.

Looking at the records of the time, it is impossible to resist the conclusion that the conditions of life in the villages were far worse than they had been in the reign of Akbar, worse perhaps than they had ever been before. Under Akbar, peasants could ordinarily pursue their business in peace, and, while the revenue demanded from them was high, it was assessed and collected on generally equitable lines. In the eighteenth century the standard rate of assessment was higher than under Akbar, being nearer one-half than one-third of the produce, but in practice the amount claimed was decided by no standard other than ability to pay under the severest pressure ; and when one collector had done his worst, the officers of some rival claimant might come to glean whatever had been overlooked. To possess visible or tangible wealth was merely to invite stronger men to take it by force ; and, to men of energy, agriculture offered no attractions comparable with a career of active spoliation.

While, however, their numbers had been depleted by the superior attractions of fighting and robbery, the peasants

[1] Quoted from Mr. G. S. Sardesai's *Main Currents of Maratha History* (Bombay, 1933), pp. 178-80.

VILLAGE LIFE

still constituted the principal element in the economic life of India. If we have said nothing about the development of agriculture during the period of Moslem rule, the reason is that there is practically nothing to say. A few new crops —among them maize, potatoes and tobacco—had been introduced from America by the Portuguese, and were spreading over the country, but, speaking generally, the products, and the methods, of agriculture continued on the traditional lines. Important changes had, however, occurred in the relations of the peasants with the revenue administration. We have seen that, under Akbar, individual peasants were, as far as possible, assessed to revenue by officials in accordance with definite orders. This practice had changed by the middle of the seventeenth century, when village-assessment had become the general rule. At the beginning of each agricultural year the official assessor came to terms with the headmen of each village for a lump sum to be paid for that year by the village as a whole; and the headmen then allocated this sum among the individual peasants by methods which differed from village to village, but were in essence substantially just.

By the end of the seventeenth century a further development had occurred. The revenue of a village, or aggregate of villages, was commonly farmed for a period of years, and it was now a farmer, not an official, who came to terms annually with the village headmen. This change had an important bearing on the struggle for territorial spheres of influence,[1] which, as we have already said, characterised the eighteenth century. The headmen still held the traditional view that they were entitled to protection in return for the revenue they paid; and, when the administration had lost the power to protect them, they were prepared to pay revenue to anyone who could give them peace. The path of ambition was thus clearly marked. A man could begin with the possession of a fort, and a small body of retainers;

[1] For the benefit of readers who wish to study this subject in the contemporary authorities, it may be explained that the ordinary word for a sphere of interest was *taluk* (more accurately, *ta'alluka*), while the holder was *talukdār*. The connotation of these words has changed, and they now mean different things in different provinces.

he could then obtain farms for the villages round, which would pay him so long as he could protect them ; and out of the profits of his farms he could by degrees increase his forces and extend his sphere of influence, looking to the time when he might be strong enough to withhold the payments stipulated in his farms, and thereby become an independent Chief.

Obviously the persons in the best position to follow this path were those who were already established as Chiefs of a larger or smaller area ; and many Chiefs in fact extended their spheres by taking farms of neighbouring villages, with which they had had no previous connection. Meanwhile the ordinary farms were tending to become hereditary, as the line of least resistance, and, as time went on, the distinction between farmers and Chiefs tended to disappear. The obvious fact was a man exercising authority for the time being over the peasants of a larger or smaller area ; the question how his authority originated was of no practical importance. The agrarian position towards the close of the eighteenth century was thus essentially unstable. Scattered over the country there were these spheres of interest, differing widely in their origin, but alike in the fact that their holders exercised within them some or all of the powers of sovereignty, sometimes acknowledging, and at other times denying, the superior authority of the formal sovereign, whoever he might be. Such spheres might extend, or contract, or disintegrate, as fortune might decide ; and stability was reached only when sovereignty passed to the Company. The new sovereign recognised some of the spheres as constituting states subject to its paramountcy, while it accepted others as constituting landed estates within the territory it administered, and the distinction was drawn less on logical principles than on the conditions prevailing at the moment, so that, as we have said in an earlier chapter, it was sometimes a matter of luck whether an individual emerged as a Prince, entitled to assess and collect the revenue due from his peasants, or as a landholder, liable to pay the revenue assessed on his property, and entitled to collect rent from the peasants who cultivated it.

The foregoing account applies primarily to the Mogul

THE STRUGGLE FOR POWER

succession states. In the Marātha territory and in parts of the South, while farming of the revenue was extensively practised, direct relations between the revenue administration and the peasants did not entirely disappear, and the theory at least survived. There is thus some historical justification for the division of India into *zamīndārī* and *ryotwārī*, which grew up under British rule. Broadly speaking, northern India is *zamīndārī*, that is to say, there are landholders (*zamīn-dār*) intermediary between the State and the peasants, while in the South the State deals directly with the peasants or ryots, assessing and collecting the revenue due from each.

Turning to other aspects of the economic life of the eighteenth century, the production of minerals was at a low ebb. Old workings show that gold, and perhaps silver, had been procured at some period, but this must have been earlier than the Turkish conquests; the diamond-fields of Golconda, which had been profitably exploited in the seventeenth century, were now unproductive; and the yield of gems was small, though the pearl fishery continued in the far south. The copper mines in Rājputāna and Central India, which had supplied most of the North, decreased in productivity in the course of the seventeenth century, and the bulk of India was now dependent on imports of that metal. Iron and steel of excellent quality were produced in many places, but the existence of the coal-fields was still unknown, and the iron industry was limited, as was the case in other countries, by the supply of charcoal for smelting; vigorous exploitation led quickly to exhaustion of the forests within reach of the mines, and then the locality would have to be abandoned till the forests grew again. In most parts of India iron, though procurable, was relatively dear, and this fact may reasonably be correlated with the economy of the metal which is observable in the indigenous processes of agriculture and industry.

The only other minerals requiring notice are salt and saltpetre. The former was mined in the Punjab, and elsewhere was extracted by evaporation from inland sources or from sea water; it was everywhere heavily taxed, and in some places monopolised by the rulers; but its distribution over the country constituted one of the most important branches of internal trade. Saltpetre, then an indispensable ingredient of gunpowder, was produced in many regions by lixiviating the soil; but the great export trade to Europe was at this time concentrated in Patna, the capital of Bihār, where the different Companies maintained factories primarily for its supply.

In Bengal most of the trade was carried on boats through the inland waterways; elsewhere it passed by roads, not metalled or surfaced, but merely open strips of land, sometimes defined by avenues of trees, and provided at intervals with wells and walled halting-places. The Mogul system of policing the roads had definitely broken down; where police posts survived, they were usually in effect blackmailing agencies, and a merchant who could not provide an adequate escort had to compound as best he might for his protection on the road, as well as for the transit dues levied by anyone who was in a position to exert his authority. In some cases carts drawn by teams of oxen were in use, but pack-animals were more generally employed. The inland trade in grain was in the hands of the 'brinjarrees' (more accurately, *banjāra*), who were itinerant merchants, possessed of substantial capital and owning the large numbers of pack-oxen which they employed; in the eighteenth century their business consisted mainly of providing for the needs of troops on the march, and their huge convoys are familiar features in the records of the British army in India, which in the early days depended mainly on them for its supplies.

We know practically nothing of the condition of the ordinary handicrafts, but it is reasonable to conjecture that they had suffered from the decline of agriculture and the dangers of transit. The artisans who worked for export tended more and more to congregate at the European settlements, where they found their markets, and where they were comparatively safe; the export trade therefore suffered less than inland commerce from the prevailing insecurity. The most important exports were still cotton goods, but there had been some remarkable fluctuations in the European demand for these. In the middle of the seventeenth century

INDUSTRY AND TRADE

the exports consisted mainly of plain calico to be used as household linen in Europe, and as clothes in America and West Africa; but some printed goods also were taken by Europe for decorative purposes. Later on fine muslins and prints became the rage in England, and large quantities of these were exported. The art of cotton-printing was, however, developing in England, and in 1700 the use of Indian printed and dyed calicoes was prohibited, a measure of protection to a growing industry which appears more natural to-day than it did to the classical economists. Importation for re-export was still permitted, and the trade in cotton goods, taken as a whole, was not very seriously affected by these and other protective measures; but its days were numbered, for the invention of power-driven machinery eventually placed the English cotton industry beyond the reach of competition by Indian handworkers, and the tide of trade was soon to be reversed. Apart from cotton goods and saltpetre, the most important item of trade was the silk of Bengal. In this case also the English industry was protected, but the raw material was largely imported from India.

The trade with Europe was carried on mainly by the Companies' ships, but Indian vessels continued to be active in Asiatic waters. It is impossible to form any precise idea of the extent of Indian ownership, for the records of the period are apt to lump together under the term 'country ships' the vessels owned by Europeans in India with those owned by Hindus, Moslems and Armenians; we know only the fact that activity continued. In regard to navigation the most important event of the century was the reopening of direct trade between India and China. We have seen in earlier chapters how the old direct trade had given way. In the sixteenth century Portuguese vessels sailed between India and Macao, at the mouth of the Canton river, but this trade was not formally open to Indians. After the decay of Portuguese shipping, trade again became indirect, mainly through various Dutch seaports in Java and elsewhere; but at the end of the seventeenth century the port of Canton became available, and as time went on it was frequented not only by the Companies' ships, but by country vessels, the latter carrying in particular Indian opium, which, despite its formal prohibition by the Emperor of China, found a lucrative market on his coasts.

This branch of trade was largely in the hands of Armenian merchants who had settled in Calcutta. We first meet Armenians engaged in the overland trade between northern India and the countries farther west, and some of them were already living on the east coast when the Dutch arrived there, while others had settled in Gujarāt. The Armenians found their chance in the rising settlement of Calcutta, where they were accorded the status of Europeans, and quickly became an important element in the commercial population. Similarly, the settlement of Bombay was taken advantage of by the Parsees living on the coast of Gujarāt, who obtained a large share in its commerce, and, as time went on, in the great industrial development which centred there; and in the same way the Jews, who had been settled on the coast for many centuries, found in the new conditions scope for a wide extension of their commercial activities.

The commercial life of India depended less, however, on the men of these races than on the merchants and financiers, whether Hindu or Moslem, whose firms ramified over the country, and undertook whatever business offered a chance of profit, not merely buying and selling, but also remitting funds by means of bills, insuring goods in transit, and lending money in large sums. The European records of the seventeenth century show that the leading merchants in places like Pulicat or Surat were comparable in point of resources as well as of ability with those of London or Amsterdam, and one of them, Vīrjī Vora of Surat, was commonly spoken of as the richest merchant in the whole world. The conditions prevailing in the eighteenth century were necessarily unfavourable to such firms, and the tendency was for the ablest financiers to establish themselves in the European settlements, where their capital was comparatively safe; but we get occasional hints indicating that in the interior of the country business continued to be carried on in spite of all obstacles.

In this connection it may be mentioned that public

THE PUBLIC DEBT 289

debts first come into prominence during the eighteenth century. The older Indian practice was to hold large accumulated balances in the treasury, and to draw on these for wars or other emergencies. In the Mogul period we occasionally hear of loans being taken from bankers, sometimes under pressure, by a claimant to a throne, but not by an actual ruler. Treasuries were now generally depleted, for the decline of agriculture had reduced the revenue, and rulers were borrowing from their subjects as a regular practice. Towards the end of the century the Nawāb of Oudh was heavily in debt, and Sindhia was being pressed for payment by his creditors; while, somewhat earlier, the Nawāb of Arcot was living largely on credit. The European Companies had long been accustomed to borrow from Indian bankers for commercial purposes, and the English Company had bonds outstanding in Bengal in 1772; but these were paid off by Warren Hastings, who avoided fresh borrowing by some very undesirable expedients. Thus the public debt of India had not yet come into existence, but the practice of governmental borrowing was well established.

From what has already been said, it will be obvious that the conditions of the eighteenth century were unfavourable to cultural development. With few exceptions, neither the Marātha rulers nor the Nawābs stand out as patrons of art or literature; the capitals of the former are now distinguished chiefly by the temples which they built, while of the latter only Lucknow requires a short notice. The first Nawābs of Oudh lived in or near the old Hindu city of Ajodhya on the bank of the Gogra; but after the middle of the century Lucknow was chosen as the capital, and its worthiest public buildings date from this period, as do most of the art industries which have survived. Its architectural horrors came later.

The artistic crafts were at this period beginning to suffer from the growing demand for competing European products. In the Mogul empire wealthy connoisseurs had sought, in particular, rarities and curiosities, wherever they came from, and had looked indifferently to Europe and to China. This taste persisted, but as time went on purchasers came to look mainly to the West; pictures and ornaments were chosen more for their origin than for their artistic worth; and a foundation was thus being laid for what must be described as the degradation of Indian taste which characterised most of the nineteenth century, when almost anything European found a ready market, but local craftsmen could not sell their best work.

The art of painting, which had already suffered from the puritanical attitude of Aurangzeb, declined still more all over India, and the tradition of the earlier schools survived only in Rajputana and some small hill states. Of literature there is little to be said. Sanskrit studies persisted, but their products were unimportant. In the modern languages, both in North and South, the place of honour was still held by the poetry of the *bhakti* faiths, but the quality was not maintained, and there are not many outstanding names to be placed beside those of the earlier period. Two points regarding this literature require notice. In the first place, it was still almost entirely poetical; modern Indian prose belonged to the nineteenth century. In the second place, it was not yet printed, but was for the most part communicated by word of mouth. Printing presses had been used by missionaries in India as early as the sixteenth century, but their use had not spread, and the effective introduction of the art was to be the work of the early British administration.

The only noteworthy development of the period was the spread of Hindustani as a literary language. We have described in a previous chapter the origin of this *lingua franca* in the days of the Turkish conquests. About the year 1600 some writers in Hyderabad began to use Hindustani as a medium of literary expression, and in the course of a century it achieved a definite standard of form, along with a greater bias towards Persian than was present in the spoken language. During the eighteenth century Urdū, as the written language is called, became popular in the North, particularly in Delhi and in Lucknow, and much poetry,

CULTURE AND RELIGION

some of it of high quality, was produced in these centres; in this case also, prose was to come later.

In matters concerning religion there are no striking developments to record. Among the Moslem community two conflicting tendencies were at work. On the one hand, the collapse of the Mogul empire made for unity in face of the danger that their faith and culture might be submerged; on the other hand, the struggle for power tended to emphasise the racial and sectarian cleavages which had existed for so long, and faction still dominated most of the centres of Moslem rule. The great days of Islam in India were gone; the *jizya* tax, the symbol of its supremacy, was no longer claimed; the future was dark; and the devout Moslem, aloof from the factions of the Courts, could find a refuge from the present only in that resignation to the will of God which his faith enjoins.

The restoration of Hinduism to political power had no counterpart on the religious side, and the only feature of the period which deserves mention is the increasing popularity in parts of northern and eastern India of what is known as tāntrism. We have seen that popular religion in the North had come to centre on one or other of the incarnations of Vishnu. Along with the idea of incarnation came another conception, the ' energic power ' (*sakti*) of the god, represented in the consort of the god incarnate; and the name tāntrism covers the forms of worship devoted specially to this energic power. The motherhood aspect of divinity which it emphasises is a not unfamiliar concept, but otherwise it is an unattractive cult, full of spells and magic, dominated in its extremer forms by sexual ideas, and sometimes expressing power in terms of violence or even cruelty; its popularity in the eighteenth century, when some of its most important manuals were compiled, may fairly be taken as evidence of the moral degradation to be expected in such a period.

Finally, a few words may be said regarding the social life of Europeans in India. In the days when their interests were confined to trade, the merchants on the whole lived in European style, while borrowing such Indian practices as they found convenient; their tables were served in European fashion, though Indian dishes figured on them, and they usually appeared in public dressed as Europeans, though they might wear Indian clothes for comfort in their houses. European women were, however, still rare in India, and some of the merchants contracted more or less durable alliances with Indians, sometimes slaves bought for the purpose; such alliances naturally tended to promote the adoption of Indian habits, while the offspring already began to present the problems familiar in the case of mixed races.

Europeans were in close commercial relations with the great Indian wholesale houses, but in so far as these belonged to Hindus, social intercourse was limited by caste-restrictions which prevented anything in the way of meals in common. With Moslems, whether merchants or officials, similar obstacles did not exist; they could meet Europeans at table, or join with them in sport, and intimate friendships between individuals were not unknown; but Moslem officers expected, and generally received, the deference which was due to their position.

The establishment of European garrisons in the various settlements had unfortunate social results. The merchants had usually been gentlemen, or at least men of some education: the soldiers were drawn mainly from the lowest classes, they were not always well disciplined, and, when they were not on active service, they had plenty of time on their hands. Their intercourse with Indians took place mainly in taverns and brothels, and it may fairly be said that in this environment India and Europe saw each other at the worst.

About the middle of the century a change in the social position was impending, in that the English merchants were about to step into the position of authority hitherto held mainly by Moslems; and from this time on English influences reached India in two distinct currents. There were, first, the higher ranks of the Company's servants, merchants in process of transformation into administrative officers, and acknowledging progressively that in their conduct in India *noblesse oblige* : there were, second, soldiers and others of lower rank, claiming more or less consciously the same position of authority, but not as a rule acknowledging the corresponding obligation. The two classes were not entirely distinct, for some members of the first fell below, and some of the second rose above, the prevalent standard, but the distinction was nevertheless real, and its effects became manifest in the social position which characterised the nineteenth century.

CHAPTER XXXVI

WARREN HASTINGS AS ADMINISTRATOR

WARREN HASTINGS, who had previously served the Company for fifteen years in Bengal, and was now a member of the Council at Madras, was appointed Governor of Bengal in 1772, five years after Clive's departure; two years later, under the Regulating Act passed by Parliament in 1773, he became Governor-General in Council, with authority in some matters over Madras and Bombay, a position which he retained until 1785. As Governor, he had no serious opposition to meet : as Governor-General, he was at first opposed by a hostile majority of his Council, led by his bitter enemy, Philip Francis, and for two years he was almost powerless; but from 1776 onwards he was generally able to attain his objects, either by the support of a majority, or by the use of his casting vote in a divided Council.

The Regulating Act requires a few words of introduction. During the seventeenth century the Company derived its legal existence, and its monopoly of eastern trade, from letters patent issued by the Crown; but, after the Revolution of 1688, Parliament took the place of the Crown, and the Company's monopoly was acknowledged and extended by successive statutes. For some time, however, the affairs of the Company lay outside the region of political controversy, and the period of active intervention in its business dates from the achievements of Clive, when English statesmen and politicians came to recognise that the developments in India concerned the nation as well as the Company. Intervention was in fact necessary, but the Act was tentative,

THE REGULATING ACT

and left some important questions undecided; in particular, while it authorised the establishment of a Supreme Court of Justice in Calcutta, entirely independent of the Company, it failed to define the court's jurisdiction in precise terms, a failure which resulted in serious practical difficulties. The court was given jurisdiction over British subjects in India, but the term 'British subject' was not explained, and the question whether it covered Indians was left open; in other words, the Act avoided a pronouncement on the question of sovereignty. To dispose of this topic once for all, we may say that this evasion characterised also the later statutes passed during the eighteenth century; and it was only in the year 1813 that Parliament formally recorded the undoubted sovereignty of the Crown of the United Kingdom over the Company's territorial acquisitions in India, a position which was accepted by France and by Holland in treaties made in the following year. British sovereignty in India has thus been a legal and diplomatic fact since that time; it had long existed over the island of Bombay, but the question when it became a fact in other parts of India is still open to academic argument.

The main task of Hastings, the organisation of an administrative system in Bengal, was, however, imposed on him by the Company, not by Parliament: he had to transform a great commercial machine into a government, and he was given a free hand to do so, but he had to make use of the existing staff, which, owing to historical causes, was ill suited for the purpose. In its early days the Company had engaged merchants and factors for short periods, and the Directors had selected individuals for their qualifications for particular duties. Re-engagements soon became usual, so that a service of experienced merchants came gradually into existence, and this service was organised on the basis of early recruitment and promotion by seniority from grade to grade. In course of time the service became so popular that it was decided to confine it to the nominees of individual Directors; and appointments thus went by favour, the only technical qualification required being a knowledge of book-keeping.

The popularity of the service was not due to the emoluments, for there were no pensions, and the salaries were very small; nor was it due to the amenities of life in India, where conditions were often most unpleasant, and the rate of mortality was sometimes terribly high; the real attraction was the hope of quickly making a fortune by private trade, carried on with capital obtained from friends in England or borrowed from Indians. At first the Company had endeavoured to prevent this practice, but it failed to do so, and eventually it allowed its servants to trade for their own benefit, subject only to certain restrictions which were not infrequently evaded. The ordinary servant of the Company thus led a double life: he was carrying on the Company's business, and he was in business for himself in conditions where his personal interests would often clash with those of his employers.

There were, too, other ways of making money. We have mentioned already the sales to Indians of the 'dustucks' or passes which secured them exemption from transit dues; and, in the practice of the country, money, whether called a bribe or a present, was freely offered in return for any favour which an individual had it in his power to grant. The whole environment was in fact thoroughly demoralising; and it appears to be the case that demoralisation was progressive, and that it had reached its height about the middle of the eighteenth century, when Clive himself and his principal officers could accept presents on the scale already indicated. It might well seem a hopeless task to construct an administration from staff trained on these lines; but the most striking feature of the records of the period is the way in which men rose above the past, and juniors who, only a few years before, had come out to make money for themselves, emerged as zealous administrators, pressing the needs and claims of the people on their superior officers.

The evolution of what came to be known as the Covenanted Civil Service was, however, a matter of time. Clive, in his second term of office, had enforced the Company's orders against the acceptance of presents, and had attempted unsuccessfully to raise the scale of salaries. Hastings abolished the abuse of 'dustucks,' and laid the foundations of an administrative service separated from the commercial organisation; and his successor, Lord Cornwallis, built on those foundations the structure which gradually became the civil government of India, a body of men still owing their start in life to patronage, but coming to India for an administrative career, enjoying adequate emoluments which they were forbidden to supplement, and developing that tradition of public service of which the germ had already appeared in the time of Hastings.

The main administrative work of Hastings consisted of the liberation of internal trade, the reorganisation of the revenue system, and the establishment of courts of justice. Regarding the first of these, it will be recalled that the old Hindu fiscal system recognised a very large number of duties on commerce and industry, and that Akbar had abolished these *en masse*. His orders clearly had no durable effect, for Aurangzeb abolished the same duties again; and the old system quickly recovered in the disorganisation of the eighteenth century. Not merely the established governments, but local Chiefs and landholders, set up custom-houses on the roads within their authority, and levied onerous duties on everything that passed; and it was in fact this multiplicity of taxing-posts that made the sale of 'dustucks' such a remunerative business. Acting under the Directors' orders, Hastings suppressed all the smaller posts, reduced to a trifling figure the duties levied at the five centres where regular custom-houses were maintained, and thus enabled goods to pass freely throughout Bengal and Bihār.

This beneficent reform was comparatively easy to effect, but the revenue system presented a much more complex problem, and one which baffled Hastings as well as his successors. Holding the position of Dīwān, the Company was responsible for the assessment and collection of the land-revenue, that share of the peasants' produce which was due to the State; but the Company's officials knew nothing whatever about the matter, and nobody in Bengal was anxious to enlighten them as to either the records of the past or the practice of the time. Clive had merely retained the organisation which he took over; an Indian expert staff, working under ignorant English supervisors, was clearly an unsatisfactory arrangement; and it was universally believed, though it could not be formally proved, that the experts were defrauding the Company, and oppressing the peasants, in their haste to get rich. By orders which were published in India in 1772, the Company announced its determination 'to stand forth ... in the character of Dīwān,' or, in other words, to create its own machinery for assessment and collection of the revenue.

The actual position in Bengal at this time may be described as follows. First, there were the peasants, who cultivated the soil, and made payments in cash representing the share of produce due to the State; English officers had no means of knowing how these payments were calculated. Second, there were landholders (*zamīndār*), who received these payments, and handed a portion of them over to the treasury as land-revenue; English officers had no means of knowing how much a landholder received, how much he was really bound to pay, or what was the actual relationship between landholder and peasant. Naturally most of them tended to think of the position in terms of the landlord-and-tenant system with which they were familiar in England, and in fact the analogy was sufficiently close to be seriously misleading.

The agrarian history of Bengal is still in some matters obscure, but the following outline gives the main facts with substantial accuracy. At the time of Akbar's conquest much of the country was in the possession of Chiefs, that is to say, men of local influence who paid an agreed sum as revenue, and had a free hand in dealing with their peasants. Early in the seventeenth century most of these Chiefs were set aside, and the revenue due from the peasants was either assigned as salary or gathered in by official collectors, who accounted for it to the Revenue Minister of the empire. At some uncertain period these collectors were transformed into farmers, by undertaking to pay a round annual sum instead of accounting for their receipts; and as the central administration became progressively less efficient the farmers tightened their hold on the peasants, secured a hereditary position, and came to be known by the general name of landholders.

So far the process was similar in its essence to what we have already described in northern India, but in Bengal there was the peculiar feature that the farmers' payments became formally, though not actually, stabilised. The amount of 'revenue' due from them was never altered, but their total payments were from time to time increased arbitrarily by what were called 'cesses' added to the 'revenue,' so that the State in fact continued to assert its claim to share in the varying produce of the country, though in point of form it had accepted the position of receiving merely a fixed rent-charge. This constituted the true differentia between the Bengal landholder and the English landlord of the period; in Bengal it was open to the State to demand from the landholders whatever it might choose on account of its claim to a share of the produce of the soil; while the known practice of the Moslem period establishes the freedom of the State to alter from time to time the methods of realising the share due ultimately from the peasants. From the Indian standpoint, then, it was open to the administration to set the landholders aside in favour of some alternative method of assessing and collecting the State's share of produce; but Englishmen, with a greater respect for prescription than prevailed in India, might hesitate to go so far.

In point of fact, Hastings began by setting the landholders aside, and, in order to ascertain the true value of the State's right to revenue, farmed the revenue for five years to the highest bidders, who, in accordance with Indian practice, paid certain allowances to the dispossessed landholders. The result was disastrous, for much of the country fell into the hands of mere speculators, who oppressed the peasants cruelly in order to snatch the maximum of profit, or sometimes to cover their miscalculations of what the country could yield. Some such evil was an inevitable consequence of the method of farming by auction, but its magnitude was determined largely by the abnormal economic situation.

A failure of the rains of 1769 had resulted in acute famine throughout the greater part of Bengal; and, as has been said in an earlier chapter, famine in those days meant disorganised agriculture for something like a generation. The loss of population was estimated to have amounted to one-third of the whole, and it may be assumed that the loss of plough-oxen had been proportionately greater; for want of men and cattle the usual area of land could not be cultivated; it was certain that the former revenue could not be paid; and nobody, whether official or speculator, could do more than guess vaguely what the country could yield. For five years then the administration was trying vainly to collect an impossible revenue from speculative farmers who were trying to extort it from the surviving peasants. At the conclusion of this period the practice of farming by auction was discarded, and various experiments were tried; but the opinion steadily gained ground that it was a mistake to set the landholders aside, and as a rule the revenue was whatever sum a landholder could be prevailed on to offer.

So far, the English administrators merely attempted to work an existing system about which they knew very little; but in the course of the discussions an idea emerged which was entirely new in India, the idea that the sums payable by landholders should be fixed once for all, and that they should thus be given in effect the status of English landlords, subject only to the payment of an unvarying quit-rent. This idea was eventually accepted, and received effect in 1793, but during Hastings' term of office it was only a matter for discussion, and when he left India the revenue administration was still the field of experiment.

The third branch of his administrative activities was the establishment of local courts of justice. In this matter a distinction must be drawn between Calcutta, Madras and Bombay, the three 'presidency towns' as they came to be known, and the rest of the country. The former had been gradually equipped with institutions on the English model, appropriate to settlements in a foreign country, while in the case of the latter an attempt was now made to provide for Indian needs. We have seen in a previous chapter that in

COURTS OF JUSTICE

the Mogul empire litigation was disposed of by executive officials, sometimes sitting with the kāzī, or judge. No clear-cut line of division was drawn between civil and criminal cases, but in practice officials seem to have dealt with the matters which concerned their particular business, so that cases affecting the public peace fell to officers of the general administration, while the revenue officers dealt with questions concerning landholders and peasants. Under Hastings this distinction was made precise, and was modified so as to separate civil from criminal jurisdiction as the terms were understood by Englishmen. Two sets of local courts were established, the one consisting of magistrates and judges who dealt with offences, the other, known as Dīwānī Adālat (literally, revenue courts), having jurisdiction not merely in questions affecting the revenue, but in all civil disputes between individuals. From these local courts appeals lay to the chief courts; the final authority in civil litigation was the Sadr Dīwānī Adālat, which at first consisted of the Governor-General in Council, while in criminal matters the ultimate decision still lay with the titular Nawāb, who was under the Council's supervision.

This system was far from perfect, but it was much better than what preceded it, and the new courts quickly became popular with the people. Their early working was, however, disturbed by a clash of jurisdiction with the Supreme Court established in 1774 under the Regulating Act. Sir Elijah Impey, the first Chief Justice of this court, was not a paragon, but he was certainly not the monster of iniquity painted by Macaulay in his essay on Warren Hastings; he was a competent lawyer, somewhat meticulous and pedantic, determined to uphold the authority of the bench, and to exercise its jurisdiction to the full. But, as we have said already, the jurisdiction of the Supreme Court was not clearly defined; Impey held that it extended over all the inhabitants of Bengal, the Council held that it did not, and by the year 1780 matters came to a deadlock. Hastings, who had previously proposed the amalgamation of the Supreme Court with the Sadr Dīwānī Adālat, now met the difficulty by appointing Impey to be President of the latter body, while remaining Chief Justice of the former. This practical unification of the judicial system removed the immediate deadlock, and a year later the jurisdiction of the Supreme Court was defined by Parliament in such a manner as to obviate further disputes.

The establishment of courts of justice led incidentally to the remarkable development of the legal profession which characterised the nineteenth century. In the Indian system of justice there were no practising lawyers; litigants presented their own cases, and, if they got help from outside, it was from persons of influence whom they could persuade, or bribe, to interfere. We read of Portuguese lawyers practising in Goa in the sixteenth century, and the first Indians who are known to have entered the profession were clerks taken into partnership by their Portuguese employers, but these firms were purely local. The English courts established in the Presidency towns were from the outset assisted by attorneys or solicitors; the charter of the Supreme Court empowered the judges to enrol advocates and attorneys; and a number of these came out to Calcutta to practise before it. In this way Indians became familiar with the idea that skilled legal assistance could be had on payment, as an alternative to the reliance on bribes and influence which had hitherto been their only resource, and they were quick to avail themselves of the new facilities. At first the practitioners were necessarily Englishmen; the entrance of Indians into the profession came later, but its effective establishment in India belongs to this period.

Another development which was closely connected with Hastings' administrative measures was the study of Indian languages by Europeans. In the case of Sanskrit the need was primarily legal; the courts had to administer Hindu law, but at the outset none of the judges was in a position to consult the texts in which that law is contained, and when Hastings commissioned some Indian scholars to prepare a code, nobody could be found able to translate it directly from Sanskrit into English, so that it was necessary first to turn it into Persian. A few Englishmen, led by Sir William Jones, whose philological achievements have been mentioned

STUDY OF INDIAN LANGUAGES 303

in Chapter II, then took up the study of Sanskrit, and in 1784 founded the Asiatic Society of Bengal, the first institution of its kind; then translations of the Sanskrit classics began to be printed, some in Calcutta and others in Europe; texts, dictionaries and grammars followed in due course, and the new study became firmly established.

The impetus given about the same time to the study of Persian arose from diplomatic rather than legal needs. When the Company was merely a trading body, its servants had for the most part been content with a colloquial knowledge of whatever language they had to use, and for reading and writing employed interpreters, usually Indians with an imperfect knowledge of English. Such methods were obviously unsuitable for the conduct of intricate diplomatic negotiations, and Hastings, as well as some of his contemporaries, recognised that they required a first-hand knowledge of Persian, the accepted language of diplomacy throughout the greater part of India. The study of the written language advanced rapidly, and texts and translations began to appear before Hastings left India, some of them due directly to his inspiration.[1] He had at one time thought of a Persian school in England, where recruits for the Company's service could learn the language, but this scheme did not mature, and the systematic training of the service began with the establishment, in 1800, of a college in Calcutta, followed in 1806 by the opening of the East India College at Haileybury.

These linguistic studies necessarily involved the use of the printing press. The Arabic alphabet, which serves for both Persian and Hindustani, had long been familiar to compositors in Europe, and there was no difficulty about type; but Sanskrit characters were not printed until the later years of the eighteenth century, while the first fount of the Bengali alphabet was cut in 1778 by a Calcutta

---

[1] Gladwin's translation of the *Ain-i Akbari* (Calcutta, 1783) was dedicated to Hastings, who had interested himself in its preparation. Major W. Davy, the translator of the *Institutes . . . of Timour* (Oxford, 1783), was Persian Secretary to Hastings, and his letter, printed at the end of the volume, stated the official case for the study of Persian in precise terms.

304 WARREN HASTINGS AS ADMINISTRATOR

blacksmith under English direction. The production of official text-books in Bengali and Hindustani, which now began, paved the way for one of the outstanding cultural features of the nineteenth century, the development of Indian prose. So long as knowledge was contained in rare manuscripts, and for the most part communicated by word of mouth, poetic forms continued to hold sway, presumably for facility in memorising; but when it became possible to produce as many copies of a book as could be sold, the need for memorising ceased to exist, and Indian writers soon discarded the trammels of metre for the freedom of prose.

These developments were, however, for the most part undesigned consequences of Hastings' administrative work: his actual achievements may be summarised as follows. He laid the foundations of a civil service, distinct from the commercial officials who purchased the goods required for export on account of the Company; he organised a system of law courts open to all subjects in the Company's territory; and he freed internal trade from a mass of vexatious imposts; but he failed to devise a workable administration of the land-revenue. The other main branch of his activities, the conduct of the Company's external relations, forms the subject of the next chapter.

CHAPTER XXXVII

WARREN HASTINGS AS DIPLOMATIST

IN estimating Hastings' conduct of the Company's external relations, it is necessary to bear in mind the financial difficulties which beset him throughout his term of office. The Company had now discontinued the annual remittances of treasure which for so long had been the foundations of its trade in Bengal, as of the trade of all foreigners who did business in India ; the revenues of Bengal had to provide the cost of administering the country, and also the annual 'investment,' as it was called, that is to say, the commodities exported for the Company's account ; and, as we have seen, receipts fell far below expectation, owing primarily to the after-effects of famine, and partly also to the mismanagement of an inexperienced administration. In the past, Indian governments had usually held large sums in their treasuries available for wars and other emergencies, but the Company had no reserves of the kind, the idea of raising loans in India was not favoured, and a plea of necessity may reasonably be entered in partial explanation of some transactions of the period which cannot otherwise be defended. At the same time, it must be recognised that Hastings was a very incompetent financier, and another man could probably have done better.

When Hastings assumed charge of Bengal, he was concerned directly with two powers only, the titular Emperor and the Nawāb of Oudh ; but on his appointment as Governor-General under the Regulating Act, he was required to superintend the governments of Madras and Bombay in making war or peace, and he was thus brought into touch with the complicated politics of the south and west. It must not, however, be supposed that he was really supreme over the English in India. The subordinate presidencies continued to receive orders direct from London; their means of communication with Calcutta were liable to interruption; their governments, inclined to be jealous of interference, did not always keep Calcutta informed of what was happening; and the decisions of Hastings and his Council might amount merely to the acceptance of unpalatable but accomplished facts. The seat of authority was not Calcutta, but London; and, owing to the time occupied by the double voyage, London was even less able than Calcutta to exercise its authority with effect, while its decisions were apt to be swayed by personal and party intrigues. Sudden changes in India might render orders obsolete before they arrived; neither Hastings nor anybody else really knew where he stood; and to the various Indian powers the action of the Company's officers must sometimes have seemed hopelessly incomprehensible.

An important change had occurred in northern India between the departure of Clive and the arrival of Hastings. The Marāthas, recovering from their defeat at Pānīpat, had re-established their hold over Delhi, and had invited the Emperor to return, an invitation which he accepted against English advice; and for the rest of his life he was practically a prisoner in his capital. Hastings treated this action of the Emperor as annulling the settlement made by Clive, discontinued the annual payments which the Emperor had received from the revenues of Bengal, resumed the territory of Allahabad, which he had been forced to promise to the Marāthas, and transferred it to Oudh in return for a substantial payment in cash. The result was to establish the friendly power of Oudh as a barrier between the English and the Marāthas, whose hostility was already obvious; and the maintenance of this barrier was a primary object of Hastings' policy.

The Rohilla War of 1774 must be reckoned as a result of this policy. We have seen in an earlier chapter that an Afghan soldier of fortune had established himself in

AFFAIRS IN THE NORTH

Rohilkhand, the country lying to the north-west of Oudh. At this time Rohilkhand was held by a confederacy of Afghan chiefs under a leader who had usurped the rights of the previous ruler. The country was coveted by the Nawāb of Oudh, and also by the Marāthas; and it was undoubtedly in the Company's interest that it should belong to the former rather than to the latter, since it could scarcely be expected to stand alone. After much preliminary manœuvring, Hastings agreed to join forces with the Nawāb, the Rohillas were decisively defeated, and the great bulk of their country was incorporated in Oudh.

About the same time, the state of Farrukhābād, lying to the south of Rohilkhand, became tributary to Oudh, and thus the Company, together with its ally, dominated the larger portion of the Gangetic plain, with the hostile Marāthas to the south and west. In western India the small settlement of Bombay was in direct contact with the Marāthas, who were also one of the powers concerned, as we have seen, in the intricate politics of the South; and the stage was thus set for the first conflict between the Marāthas, still intent on aggression, and the Company, not at this time aggressive, but determined to maintain what it held.

We have seen how the Marātha power had become a confederacy under the lead of the Peshwā at Poona. A succession of able Peshwās held the confederacy together until 1772; then followed a period of disputed successions and minority rule, during which faction and intrigue held sway; and henceforward the leading Marātha houses must be thought of as in practice independent powers, not yet openly breaking away from Poona, but each working primarily for its own aggrandisement. The story of the conflict is thus complicated by the fact that the Marāthas were disintegrating, while the English had not yet attained unity of action.

The clash came in western India, and arose out of a question of merely local importance. The road northward from Bombay to Gujarāt lay through the adjoining island of Salsette, possession of which was a commercial as well as a strategical necessity for the settlement. According to the

English view, Salsette was included in the cession of Bombay made in 1661, but the Portuguese denied this, and retained its possession until 1739, when they were ousted by the Marāthas. The Bombay Council then attempted to obtain it by negotiation, but without success, and in 1773 they gladly seized the opportunity presented by a request for help from Raghunāth Rao,[1] one of the protagonists in the struggle for power at Poona, who had recently lost the position of Peshwā, having been replaced by an infant under the guardianship of a Council of Ministers. After some preliminary negotiations an agreement, known as the treaty of Surat, was made in 1775, under which Raghunāth offered to cede the territory desired, along with other concessions, in return for a promise of armed assistance. The Bombay troops then successfully attacked the Marātha army, while the navy destroyed the Marātha fleet; but at this juncture Calcutta intervened on the ground that the action taken by Bombay was directly contrary to the Regulating Act, ordered a suspension of operations, and negotiated the treaty of Purandhar (March, 1776) with Nānā Phadnavīs, the effective head of the Marātha Ministers then in power in Poona. By this treaty the arrangement made with Raghunāth Rao was formally annulled and he was to be pensioned off; but Salsette and certain other concessions which he had promised to Bombay were retained.

Fresh complications now ensued. A despatch from London approved the treaty of Surat, which Calcutta had condemned, and encouraged Bombay to renew its support of Raghunāth Rao; while a subsequent despatch agreed, with regret, to the treaty of Purandhar, with the proviso that if Poona attempted to evade its provisions Bombay should be at liberty to form a fresh alliance with Raghunāth Rao. As a matter of fact, Poona, distracted by intrigues, and, we may reasonably assume, at a loss to know what the English really meant, had made no attempt to carry out the treaty, and consequently the new alliance between Raghunāth Rao

---

[1] His name sometimes appears as Raghoba, while he is also described by the soubriquet Dādā Sāhib.

THE FIRST MARĀTHA WAR

and Bombay was duly made; and in 1778 the Bombay Council decided to install its candidate as regent for the minor Peshwā at Poona.

The weak Bombay forces marched for Poona in November of that year, but the operations were mismanaged throughout, and eventually the commander submitted to terms which both Calcutta and Bombay repudiated. Hastings had meanwhile sent a force to march from the Jumna in support of Bombay, and this column reached Surat in time for its leader, Colonel Goddard, to take charge of the military situation. Most of the year 1779 was spent in negotiations, but towards its close Goddard learned that the Marāthas had come to terms with Hyderabad and Mysore for a series of simultaneous attacks on the English possessions throughout India. In order to explain this confederacy we must turn to the story of events in the South.

The Council at Madras had not yet become an administrative body like that in Bengal; officially, it was concerned mainly with trade, while the individual Englishmen were for the most part intent on acquiring fortunes for themselves. The Nawāb of Arcot, under British protection, administered the Carnatic on lines which were disgraceful to his protectors; but he was heavily in debt to many of them as individuals, and his creditors necessarily formed a party in his favour, because his displacement would have involved the loss of their money. Not unnaturally, he made the most of his advantage, evaded all attempts at reform, and obtained English help in enlarging his dominions while intriguing on his own account with the neighbouring powers.

Meanwhile both Mysore and Hyderabad had become hostile to the Company as the result of the inept diplomacy of the Madras Council, aggravated by the effect of the injudicious orders which occasionally arrived from London, and by 1778 the English were practically without friends in the South. The situation was further complicated by the war which broke out at this juncture between England on the one side, and France, the United States, and, later, Holland on the other. The fighting which took place in

India was merely incidental, but French diplomatists and adventurers were naturally active at the various Indian Courts; and thus the prospects of the confederacy formed in 1779 were undoubtedly good. Its members were not, however, really united, and each ruler who was a party to it placed his own interests first. In the result, Hyderabad did nothing of importance, some of the Marāthas turned to the English side, and only Mysore acted with the vigour which the occasion demanded.

The four Marātha houses may be accounted for as follows. The Bhonsle ruler at Nāgpur was not enthusiastic, and was easily bought off by Hastings. In Gujarāt there was a dispute among the Gaekwar family over the succession; early in 1780 Goddard took the side of one claimant who had already received English support and forcibly established him in possession, despite the opposition offered by the two remaining houses, Holkar and Sindhia. Of these two, Mahādjī Sindhia was much the more important, equally expert as soldier and as diplomatist, still paying formal homage to the Peshwā's supremacy but working steadily for his own aggrandisement; he was firmly established in Mālwa, where he held the historic capital of Ujjain, but his most valued possession was the great fortress of Gwalior, which commanded the road to Agra and Delhi on the north. In view of the weakness of the English forces in Bombay, Hastings had decided to effect a diversion in this direction, and in August, 1780, the fortress, hitherto deemed in India to be impregnable, was carried by a night attack. On hearing this news Sindhia hurried north; in the following February he was defeated by the English, and he then came to the conclusion that his interests required peace. In October, 1781, he signed a treaty on his own account, and a little later he negotiated the treaty of Sālbai (May, 1782), which established peace between the English and the Marāthas as a whole.

The diversion effected by Hastings was thus decisive in its effects; and peace was welcome to the English, for in the west Goddard had experienced a reverse and had only just been able to hold his own against the remainder of the

THE FIRST MYSORE WAR

Marātha forces, consisting of the Poona army supported by Holkar, while in the south Madras was hard pressed by Mysore. At the moment the affairs of Madras were in incompetent hands, warnings were neglected, and in 1780 Haidar Alī was able to overrun the Carnatic without opposition. The campaign which followed was mismanaged on the English side, and Madras appealed to Calcutta for support; Hastings responded promptly, and the war continued through the next two years without reaching a decision. Haidar Alī died at the close of 1782; his son and successor, Tipu, had now the support of a large French force which had arrived by sea; the English command was still ineffective, and the army was saved only by news which arrived in June, 1783, that peace between France and England had been settled. Tipu was still at war with the English, who were weakened by dissensions between Hastings at Calcutta and the Governor of Madras. The latter, however, made a reasonable peace with Tipu in March, 1784, and though its terms were condemned by the former, it was not disallowed. The anti-English confederacy of 1779 had thus definitely failed when in 1785 Hastings resigned his appointment and sailed for England.

In order to complete the account of his activities in India, it is necessary to mention his efforts to extract contributions from various sources, particularly from the Nawāb of Oudh, and the Chief of Benares. The details of these transactions are important for an estimate of Hastings' character, but not for the history of India, and it must suffice to say that the methods he adopted were at once harsh and tortuous, so much so that on occasion they failed to secure their object, which was purely financial. His conduct in these matters, along with practically the whole of his administration, was examined in detail in the course of his impeachment before the House of Lords. The proceedings, which were spread over the years from 1786 to 1795, ended in his acquittal on all the charges which were pressed to a decision; their significance for India lies in the fact that, underneath all the spite and rancour by which they were marked, and marred, there was manifested the determination, common to the best men of all parties, that the Company's rule in India should be conducted in accordance with those English ideals of which Parliament is the guardian—the ideals of justice and fair play.

We may close this chapter with a few words on the modernisation of Indian armies which took place about this period under the direction of European officers. The first step in this development seems to have been taken in Travancore, the State in the far south which represents the Keralas of olden times; here, towards the middle of the century, the army had been trained by a Flemish officer, and it may be noted that later on the State was able to maintain itself successfully against the attacks of Haidar Alī. It was, however, in the last quarter of the century that the practice spread. The armies of Sindhia, Holkar and Hyderabad were all organised and trained to a greater or less extent on European lines, mainly by Frenchmen, and the fighting which now took place was of a very different character from that of the days of Clive; it was no longer a case of the old model being pitted against the new, but a contest between essentially similar forces, frequently led by European commanders.

CHAPTER XXXVIII

FROM CORNWALLIS TO WELLESLEY

DURING the later years of Hastings' administration Indian affairs had been the subject of acute conflict between English parties, and eventually the Regulating Act was modified by Pitt's India Act of 1784, which was supplemented by some other measures passed in 1786. The constitution thus provided, which survived in essentials until 1858, subordinated the Company to a Board of Control, the President of which was a member of the English ministry of the day. As time went on, the powers of the Board became concentrated in the President, and thus the ministry was supreme in the last resort; but in practice all important questions were discussed informally between the President and the Directors of the Company, and the action to be taken was ordinarily decided by a compromise. Henceforward, with rare exceptions, the Governor-General was chosen from outside the Company's service; he had power to overrule his Council in emergencies; his control over Madras and Bombay was effective; and on occasion he could assume the duties of commander-in-chief. The position was thus much more of a reality than in Hastings' time, and, so long as he retained the confidence of the ministry, a Governor-General could act with effect throughout the Company's territories in India.

The first man to hold the post on these terms was the Marquess Cornwallis (1786–1793), a soldier-statesman of high position and character. His task in India was mainly administrative organisation, but he was unable to keep entirely aloof from diplomacy and war. In Europe, while England and France were for the time being at peace,

French statesmen continued to cherish hopes of establishing their power in India, relying on their influence over Holland, on the French-trained forces of Sindhia and Hyderabad, and on Tipu's hostility to the English. In India the political situation was essentially unstable, and while the Company was for the moment in friendly, or at least correct, relations with the leading powers, Cornwallis had to keep a vigilant watch on affairs in both continents.

We may begin with an account of his administrative activities in Bengal. Hastings had not succeeded in establishing a really workable system, but during his term of office the government and its servants had been learning their business, and in 1786 the experience they had gained had been embodied in a new scheme which was published before Cornwallis arrived in India. Working on the basis of this scheme, and on the instructions which he had received from the Company, Cornwallis developed the system which in essence prevailed throughout the nineteenth century and was extended by degrees over the greater part of India. His personal contribution was insistence on strict discipline and on the maintenance in India of the ethical standards which had now won acceptance in England. Himself absolutely loyal to his superiors, he sought to imbue every servant of the Company with the same quality, and he embodied the duties of each in a code of Regulations, completed in 1793, which applied to all alike and were designed to eliminate individual idiosyncrasies; and these Regulations, which form the first chapter in the voluminous statute-book of British India, were built on the current English standards of integrity and justice, not on a compromise with the lower standards which had come to prevail in Calcutta and Madras.

We have seen that the Company's commerce had already been separated from its administration. When Cornwallis arrived in Calcutta, he found that the Board of Trade, which managed the former branch, made a practice of contracting with its own servants, styled Residents,[1] for the supply of

[1] The designation 'Resident' now denotes an officer representing the Government of India in a State or group of States.

the commodities required for export; the result was that some of the Residents, concerned mainly to make personal profit out of the annual contracts, cheated the Company and oppressed the Indians from whom they purchased goods. Cornwallis succeeded in abolishing this practice and in purging the staff of its most dishonest members; the Residents ceased to be contractors, and worked as subordinates of the Board. In this department his reforms were quickly effective, and also durable; but the Company's commerce became progressively of less importance as time went on, and we may take leave of the topic by recording that by the Charter Act of 1813 it was deprived of its monopoly of the trade with India, though not of that with China, while under the Act of 1833 it finally ceased to be a trading body.

Administration presented more complex problems than commerce, and Cornwallis worked towards a solution by degrees, and occasionally retraced his steps. In its final form as embodied in his Regulations of 1793, his scheme may be described as follows. At the top was the Governor-General in Council with the necessary secretariat. Next came two boards, the Board of Trade (which has just been mentioned) and the Board of Revenue, each presided over by a member of the Council. The local unit of administration was the District, to which officers were posted to perform three main functions: to keep the peace, collect the revenue and administer justice. We have seen that in the Mogul system, perpetuated under the Nawābs of Bengal, the two former functions had been separate; and according to administrative theory there should now have been three district officers in all, Magistrate, Collector, and Judge. The instructions issued to Cornwallis required, however, not merely justice, but also energy, simplicity and economy, and for a time all three functions were assigned to a single officer; but in his final arrangements the Judge was distinct from the Magistrate-Collector. This scheme was not universally approved, and a little later we find for a time a Judge-Magistrate distinct from the Collector; but the grouping made by Cornwallis eventually won the day, and the typical arrangement in British India is still the Magistrate-Collector in charge of each district, with a separate Judge or Judges, appointed either to a single district or to a group of districts.

Cornwallis also laid the foundations of the modern police force. It cannot be said that any regular system of police existed in Moslem India. Each village maintained its watchman, usually hereditary, and frequently associated with the criminal classes: for the suppression of violent crime Viceroys and Commandants employed the troops which they had to maintain as a condition of their service; and each local Governor employed a miscellaneous body of retainers to give effect to his orders. In Bengal this function of the local Governors had passed to the landholders; they were now relieved of responsibility for keeping the peace, their retainers were disbanded, and a network of police circles was established in each district, subject to the Magistrate's control.

One feature of the new régime was a substantial increase in the number of Englishmen employed in the administration. Hastings had left some important duties, notably the exercise of criminal justice, in the hands of Indians, but under Cornwallis every responsible post was filled by an English officer, and Indians were employed only in subordinate capacities. The change followed necessarily from the determination to establish purer standards of conduct, for those classes of Indians who were otherwise qualified for administrative work were not then expected to conform to standards of which they had no experience, and, as we have seen, the standards prevailing in the country were at this period definitely lower than those which Cornwallis aimed at establishing; the rule was thus needed at the time, and Cornwallis is not to be blamed if most of his successors were too tardy in relaxing it when conditions in India had changed.

Taken as a whole, the Cornwallis code marked the beginning of that 'Rule of Law' which has been one of the chief contributions of England to the life of India, but it was concerned mainly with procedure, and did little in the way of laying down the law which was to rule. The local courts continued to apply the existing law, whether Hindu or Islamic; and, since the sources of these laws were not yet available to them, they had to obtain their knowledge from experts appointed for the purpose. This unsatisfactory arrangement was superseded by degrees, as translations of the texts became available. Sir William Jones published his translation of the *Lawbook of Manu* in 1794; and thenceforward English methods of legal interpretation were gradually applied, and Hindu law, in particular, assumed a more precise form, and received a greater degree of authority, than it had previously possessed.

The change was not an unmixed blessing, for it crystallised, so to speak, customs which had previously been susceptible of modification in response to social development. Hindu scholars, when confronted with new facts, could regularise them by some ingenious reinterpretation of old texts: English judges, holding themselves bound by the wording of the texts and the interpretations adopted by their predecessors, had no such resource, while English legislators naturally hesitated to trespass on a domain guarded by the sanctions of religion; and the resulting rigidity of family law has in fact been felt as a serious inconvenience by Hindus desirous of effecting social reforms.

The chief contribution made under Cornwallis to the substantive law of India was in the field of land-revenue. At the time of his appointment, the Company had already accepted the view, which had come to the front in Hastings' time, that the revenue should be fixed once for all, and, as a step in this direction, his instructions required him to make a 'settlement' (the term for assessment used by Englishmen in India) with the landholders for the revenue to be paid, in the first instance, for a term of ten years. This work was completed in 1790, and Cornwallis, differing from his expert advisers, held that the information which had been gathered was sufficient to justify the Company in forthwith making this settlement permanent; his view was accepted by the authorities in England, and in 1793 the Permanent Settlement of Bengal came formally into existence.

The motives for this decision, which is now widely regretted in India, fall into two groups. In the first place there were the ideals of simplicity and certainty in government, which, under the influence of Adam Smith and other writers, were then so much in favour in England, and had been definitely accepted by the Company and by the Board of Control: periodical reassessment is a laborious task as well as a disturbing factor in economic life, and Cornwallis, taking the short view of a practical man, was anxious to set his staff free for other work. In the second place there was the characteristically English hope that the landholders of Bengal, when relieved from the risk of enhanced payments, would emulate the 'spirited proprietors' who in times then recent had done so much to transform the agriculture of England. This hope was not destined to be realised, and the chief effect of the Permanent Settlement was to alienate in advance the main source from which an increase in the income of the State could be expected. No steps were taken to give security to the peasants, and thus the seed was sown of the trouble which was to arise when the growth of population led to acute competition for arable land; the landholder knew what he had to pay, and he was left free to make the peasant pay as much as he could.

Another unfortunate effect of the new system was the displacement of many of the old-established landholders. The administration insisted on punctual payment of the revenue, and the rights of a defaulter were put up to auction without more ado, sometimes in circumstances where corrupt motives had free scope. In this way large areas passed into the permanent possession of mere speculators, bound to the peasants by no ties of personal or local sentiment, and concerned only to make the most they could out of their bargain.

From the administration of Bengal we turn to political events in India during Cornwallis' term of office. The only war in which the Company was involved during this period was that with Mysore. Tipu, intent on aggrandisement, and dissatisfied with the peace of 1784, planned first to crush

THE SECOND MYSORE WAR

the Marāthas and Hyderabad, and then to destroy the English power in the South. In 1786 he was at war with the two former, but failed to crush them; a little later he sent envoys to France to secure help against the English, and received encouragement but no formal promises; and in 1789 he attacked Travancore, a small State in the far south which was in alliance with the English. Cornwallis found it necessary to intervene, entered into an alliance with the Marāthas and Hyderabad, and initiated hostilities. The campaign of 1790 having been disappointing, Cornwallis assumed command in person, and early in 1792 he was able to besiege Tipu in his capital, Seringapatam. Tipu then made peace and surrendered about half his territory, most of which was distributed among the allies; but it was not a final settlement, and another war was to follow in a few years' time.

In Oudh and the Carnatic, the two Indian States under the Company's influence, internal conditions remained thoroughly unsatisfactory, but no important change occurred under Cornwallis. In the rest of India interest centred on the efforts of Mahādjī Sindhia to consolidate and extend his authority. For a time he was unsuccessful. The cost of his French-trained army involved him in financial difficulties; he suffered a reverse at the hands of the Rājputs; and in 1788 an Afghan officer seized Delhi, plundered the palace, and blinded the titular Emperor.[1] Next year the tide turned. Sindhia recovered Delhi, restored the Emperor to his nominal position, and regained control over the imperial territory. He then defeated the Rājputs, and in 1792 destroyed the army of Holkar, who all this time had been in open or secret opposition to his schemes, acting in concert with the Ministers at Poona, who were anxious to preserve a reasonable balance of power. Sindhia was now definitely predominant in the North, and he visited Poona in order to establish his position there also.

[1] This barbarous act derives from a very old Asiatic tradition that blindness is a disqualification for a throne. In the Turkish period in India, there are numerous instances of a dethroned ruler, or a candidate for the throne, being blinded, instead of executed, and the practice was not unknown in later times.

Such was the political situation when Cornwallis retired in 1793. He was succeeded by Sir John Shore (1793–1798), who had served the Company for nearly a quarter of a century, and had risen to be President of the Board of Revenue. Essentially a loyal servant, Shore carried to completion the administrative work which Cornwallis had initiated, though he had been the main opponent of the Permanent Settlement; while outside the Company's territories he maintained an attitude of non-intervention in circumstances where a more active policy would probably have been in the interests of India as well as England. The situation developed rapidly in two continents. In Europe the war broke out between England and France, which was to continue with brief interludes till 1815; while in India, where personalities counted for so much, a series of deaths brought important changes in the political conditions. Among the Marāthas, Mahādjī Sindhia died suddenly in 1794, and was succeeded by his young nephew, Daulat Rao. A year later died Ahalya Bāī, a lady who during her rule had made the Holkar domains in Mālwa an oasis of peace and happiness; and, shortly after, the death of her successor threw that State into confusion. Poona itself was the seat of a complicated struggle for power following on the suicide of the titular Peshwā in 1795; while, in other parts of the country, the Nawāb of Arcot died in the same year, and the Nawāb of Oudh in 1797. India, taken as a whole, was thus in a condition of instability when Lord Mornington, soon to become Marquess Wellesley, arrived in India to succeed Shore.

By this time Napoleon's ambitions in Asia had become well known; French troops had indeed already landed in Egypt; to Wellesley (1798–1805) the war in Europe was the thing that mattered most; and all the resources of England in India, as elsewhere, were to be employed against the enemy. From this standpoint, immediate action was required in the South, for while the French-trained army of Hyderabad was a potential danger, Tipu had solicited an alliance with France, and had actually secured the despatch of a small French force from Mauritius. Wellesley succeeded in effecting an arrangement with the former power, under

THE LAST MYSORE WAR

which hostile influences were eliminated from Hyderabad, and he then called on Tipu to repudiate his alliance with the French. The negotiations which followed showed that Tipu was not prepared to accept the stern conditions which Wellesley thought it necessary to impose, and in February, 1799, the latter ordered the Madras army to open hostilities. The attack was entirely successful. By April Tipu was besieged in Seringapatam, and early in May the fortress was taken by storm : Tipu himself was killed in action, his son surrendered, and Mysore fell into the hands of the English.

The death of Tipu was no matter for regret to the Hindu population, for his rule had been that of a persecutor. His kingdom was now dismembered; the western, southern, and south-eastern portions were included in the presidency of Madras, while the centre was made over to a representative of the old Hindu dynasty on terms which secured to the Company a position of predominance. The new State of Mysore was made a reality by Colonel Arthur Wellesley, to be known later on as the Duke of Wellington, who cleared it of the bands of freebooters by which it was infested, and established peace within its borders.

These events were followed promptly by a final settlement of the Carnatic. Among the papers found at the capture of Seringapatam were letters proving that successive Nawābs of Arcot had been in secret correspondence with Tipu, and had thus broken the conditions under which they held the Carnatic ; and Wellesley decided to take the opportunity of effecting the change which had so long been desired. At this juncture the Nawāb died. Wellesley invited his son and successor to surrender the country in return for an assured position of dignity, and an income sufficient to maintain it ; the youth refused the offer, and was set aside in favour of another claimant who accepted it.

A similar arrangement had shortly before been made with the ruler of the State of Tanjore, which lay to the south of the Carnatic, while Hyderabad now ceded in return for the protection of an English force the districts which had been transferred to it from Mysore, and thus by the year

1800 the Madras presidency had assumed substantially its present form. The entire southern triangle of the peninsula came under the Company's rule, excluding only the friendly and protected States, Mysore, Travancore and a few others of smaller extent ; to the north-west were the Marāthas, to the north, Hyderabad, while a narrow strip of British territory, the Northern Circars, extended along the coast as far as Orissa. In all this region there was now no danger from the French, or from their dependent allies the Dutch, for the Indian settlements of both nations had already been taken by the English : the Dutch [1] eventually disappeared from the mainland, but, under the treaties made after Waterloo, Pondichery and some smaller stations were restored to the French, who still retain them. To complete the story, it may be added that when Denmark came under French domination, the fort at Tranquebar was taken ; it was restored to Denmark after the war, but, along with the other Danish possessions in India, was eventually purchased by the Company in 1845.

Turning to the affairs of northern India, Wellesley had to deal with a difficult situation in Oudh. The question of French influence did not arise here, for under the existing agreements the country was defended mainly by British troops, for whom the Nawāb made a yearly payment in cash. Under their protection maladministration and corruption flourished and the annual payments fell into arrear, while English adventurers infested the capital and ministered to the debauchery of the Court ; and the position was further complicated by the threat of an invasion from Afghanistan, against which the Nawāb was clamorous for aid.[2] After long negotiations a treaty was made in 1801, by which the Nawāb ceded to the Company the eastern, southern and western portions of his territory, the revenue from which was to cover the cost of the troops maintained

---

[1] The Dutch Company gradually declined during the eighteenth century, and in 1795 the administration of its possessions in Asia was finally taken over by the Republic of Holland, which had been established under French influence, and was thus the enemy of England.

[2] Afghanistan was still nominally sovereign over the Punjab, and was thus within striking distance of the north-western border of Oudh.

for his protection ; the portion which he retained, now known as Oudh, was thus cut off from the rest of India by districts under British rule, and within it he undertook to establish a proper system of administration. In this way the Bengal presidency underwent a large extension towards the north-west, and was brought into direct contact with the Marāthas on nearly the whole of its southern boundary : Oudh as a buffer state ceased to exist.

The perennial disputes among the Marāthas came to a head in the year 1800, on the death of Nānā Phadnavīs, the Minister who for nearly half a century had ruled at Poona in the name of the titular Peshwā. Bājī Rao, who then held this position, determined to assert himself ; Sindhia supported him, but Holkar took the other side, and defeated the allies. Bājī Rao then sought British protection, and by the Treaty of Bassein (1803) accepted the paramountcy of the Company, and was installed in Poona by English troops. This action offended the Marāthas as a whole ; the armies of two houses, Sindhia and Bhonsle, moved southward threatening Poona, and on their refusing to withdraw, Wellesley declared war. From the English point of view the campaign which followed was brilliantly successful. In the South, Arthur Wellesley, now holding the rank of General, completely defeated the Marātha allies at the battle of Assaye, fought in September, 1803, and in the following December the Bhonsle ruler accepted the paramountcy of the Company, and ceded his territory in Orissa ; in the North, Lord Lake occupied Sindhia's possessions north and east of the Jumna, defeated what was left of his army at the battle of Laswārī, and forced him also to accept the Company as overlord.

The other two Marātha houses took no part in this war. The Gaekwar family was already under British protection, but Holkar, who was still independent, refused to come to terms, and early in 1804 Wellesley declared war against him. The campaign was marked by a serious reverse to a column which had advanced under Colonel Monson, and, on the destruction of this force, Holkar obtained support from quarters which had previously been on the English side ; but towards the close of the year he sustained two defeats, which would probably have been decisive had not the situation been altered by orders from England, where the authorities, thinking that Wellesley was going too far, decided to recall him. Lord Cornwallis was sent out to replace him, but died soon after arriving in India, and for two years the post of Governor-General was held by Sir George Barlow, a civil servant who carried out his masters' orders. The peace which he made with the Marāthas restored much of the territory which they had lost, but did not effect a final settlement. Its most unfortunate feature was that it left the Rājput Chiefs, who looked to England for help, at the mercy of Holkar and Sindhia, and during the next few years the eastern side of Rājputāna was almost ruined by their depredations and exactions.

Under this peace the Marāthas were excluded from the country north and east of the Jumna. The districts which they had held between that river and the Ganges, together with Delhi and a small territory to its west, came under British rule, and for administrative purposes were organised, along with Benares and the districts recently ceded by Oudh, as ' the Ceded and Conquered Provinces,' stretching up the Gangetic plain from Bihār to Delhi. This administrative area, enlarged by later accretions, formed the ' North-Western Provinces ' constituted in 1835, and, with the exclusion of Delhi and other minor readjustments, is now a part of the United Provinces. Thus during Wellesley's term of office the Madras presidency came into existence substantially in its present form, while the Bengal presidency was extended to the border of the Punjab, but the Bombay presidency was not yet a territorial entity of any considerable size.

Outside the presidencies, the relations between the Company and the various Indian powers (other than Sind and the Punjab) were expressed in treaties negotiated by Wellesley. The terms of these varied in detail, but they were alike in their recognition of the Company as the paramount power, and they thus form the basis of the constitutional system under which about two-fifths of the area of India is now ruled by Indian Princes subject to the paramountcy of the British Crown. Speaking in general terms, it may be said that under these treaties the Princes retained the powers of sovereignty within their dominions, though in some cases they bound themselves to maintain a certain standard of internal administration ; but in their external relations, in matters of diplomacy and war, they virtually submitted to the authority of the Company, exercised through the Governor-General in Council. Under Wellesley then the Company attained a position which, so far as we know, did not differ in essentials from that occupied by the Maurya or Gupta emperors of the old days, ruling directly over a large portion of the country, and holding a position of superiority over the sovereigns who ruled the rest.

CHAPTER XXXIX

FROM WELLESLEY TO BENTINCK

THE term of office of Lord Minto (1807-1813), like that of his predecessor, was dominated by the war in Europe. The measures already taken by Wellesley sufficed to exclude French influence from the interior of India, but Napoleon's Asiatic projects were still in being, and it was necessary to close the roads by which India could be reached. England now had command of the sea, and held the most important points on the maritime route, for the Dutch possessions at the Cape of Good Hope had been occupied in 1805, while Ceylon had been seized by the Company in 1796. The danger at sea came mainly from the French privateers which were busy in Asiatic waters, and caused great loss to Indian trade; but their activities were practically brought to an end by the capture of their bases, Mauritius and Bourbon in 1810, and Batavia in the following year, and thenceforward the Eastern seas were reasonably safe for commerce.

In order to close the route by land, Minto had to enter into relations with the rulers of north-western India. It will be recalled that Nādir Shāh had annexed Sind, the Punjab and Kashmīr to Persia, and that a little later these regions had come under Afghan rule. The Afghans continued to hold Peshawar but the Sikh clans obtained virtual possession of the Punjab. Sind became an independent kingdom in 1789, and a little later the great Sikh, Ranjīt Singh, established himself as ruler of the Punjab, and eventually also of Kashmir.

The story of the Sikh power goes back to the religious movement which occurred in the fifteenth century. We have seen that Nānak, one of the leaders in that movement, preached in the Punjab; he secured many adherents, mainly among the peasant and commercial castes, and his teaching was continued under a line of spiritual guides who were styled Gurūs, while their followers became known as Sikhs, a word which means 'disciples.' These disciples, it may be noted, did not form a closed caste, and they are still recruited from individuals belonging to other communities. The Gurūs appointed deputies in each place where the teaching of Nānak was followed, and received from them large sums by way of offerings, so that the organisation gradually became wealthy, and in the seventeenth century began to interest itself in political affairs. Bitter persecution carried out under the orders of Aurangzeb almost destroyed the organisation, but at the same time taught the Sikhs to fight, and in 1708 we meet them pillaging the country between Delhi and Lahore. In the first part of the century they appear occasionally as a militant organisation, but their political power was established in its closing years, when the Afghan ruler of the time recognised Ranjīt Singh as Governor of Lahore; the new Governor soon shook off his allegiance, and under him the Punjab became an independent state.

The Company came into contact with this state as the result of the annexation of the Delhi territory, which brought it astride of the Jumna, while Ranjīt Singh was preparing to extend his dominions southward from the Sutlej. The country between these rivers was occupied by several Chiefs, practically independent, and at variance among themselves: by a treaty of friendship negotiated in 1809, Ranjīt Singh abandoned his aspirations in this direction, and the cis-Sutlej Chiefs came under British protection, while the Sikhs were left free to extend in other directions, and gradually consolidated their hold over the Punjab as far as Multān and Peshāwar. Attempts made at the same time to establish relations with Afghanistan proved fruitless, but a treaty made between England (not the Company) and Persia barred the road from Europe to India, and, with a friendly power in the Punjab, the Company was free from anxiety in this direction for some years.

Elsewhere in India Lord Minto followed the policy of non-intervention laid down by the Company; but under his successor, Lord Moira (1813-1823), new developments occurred which brought the Marāthas and the Rājputs definitely inside what may now fairly be described as the Company's India. The settlement made with the Marāthas in 1805 did not result in stability, and sooner or later a clash was inevitable between the old Indian tradition of aggrandisement secured by diplomacy or war, and the Company's ideal of stable peace and orderly administration. During the years of non-intervention the condition of almost the whole centre of India went from bad to worse. The administration was oppressive, revenue was collected at the point of the sword, and the country was harried by the lawless bands known as Pindārīs. The name does not denote a definite caste or race, but covers adventurers of all sorts who, beginning as irregulars in the Marātha armies, organised themselves for independent and systematic pillage, and by degrees extended the area of their operations. So long as they confined themselves to country not under the Company's administration, the rule of non-intervention held good, but by 1812 they were raiding into Bihār, in 1816 they carried fire and sword into the Northern Circars, and at last the authorities in England ordered their extirpation.

With this object Lord Moira endeavoured to arrange for Marātha co-operation, and certain engagements were actually made; but they proved of little value, because the Marāthas were in fact on the side of the Pindārīs, who could on occasion be valuable auxiliaries. The power of these lawless bands can be judged from the fact that the English armies which were sent against them in the autumn of 1817 numbered over 100,000 men. The campaign was quickly successful, and the Pindārīs were annihilated once for all; but at an early state of the operations the Marāthas, perhaps apprehensive of Moira's ultimate intentions, took the initiative, and precipitated the final struggle. The English representatives in Poona and Nāgpur were attacked almost simultaneously, Holkar and Sindhia were clearly on the

THE LAST MARĀTHA WAR

same side, and the Gaekwar alone observed the engagements into which he had entered.

This last Marātha war was soon over. The Peshwā, after several defeats, surrendered in the following June, when his office was formally abolished, and he was allowed to settle down near Cawnpore as a pensioner of the Company. The representative of the Bhonsle house was defeated, and died as a fugitive; the forces of Holkar also were defeated in the field, and Sindhia submitted without fighting. The territorial arrangements which followed can be stated in a few words. In Mālwa, Holkar, Sindhia and some minor Marātha houses were allowed to retain the regions which they held; the greater portion of the Bhonsle territories was handed over to a minor representative of the family; in Gujarāt the territory held by the Gaekwar was defined; a moderate area was assigned to the Rāja of Sātāra, who represented the line of Sivājī; the Company took the rest, and the bulk of its acquisitions was included in the presidency of Bombay, which thus became a territorial entity. The Marātha houses accepted this settlement as final, and now came definitely within the circle of the Company's India. At the same time treaties were made with the Chiefs of Rājputāna, who as a body had never fought against the English, and who welcomed the relief from the long-drawn terror of the Marāthas; in this region the only territory acquired by the Company was the district of Ajmere, which had been an integral part of the Mogul empire, and which was now ceded by Sindhia.

The centre of India was thus pacified. In the North, Lord Moira had already been engaged in a war with Nepal, where in the course of the eighteenth century the Gurkhas had established an extensive kingdom, covering the southern face of the Himalayas from Kashmīr almost to Assam. Here, as in some other countries, the plains presented an irresistible temptation to the hillmen; raids across the border were frequent; negotiations were ineffective; and in 1814 Lord Moira declared war. Desperate fighting followed, and for some time the Gurkhas more than held their own; but eventually superior generalship on the

English side forced them to sue for peace. The western portion of the kingdom was ceded to the English, its limits on the east were curtailed and defined, and Nepal thus took the shape it now presents on the map, a long and narrow strip of mountainous country, with British territory on three sides. This settlement proved stable. For some time Nepal was treated as being included in the Company's India, though not exactly as an Indian State; but it has now been recognised as an independent kingdom, and maintains its own legation in London.

When Lord Moira, who had been created Marquess of Hastings, vacated office in 1823, the Company was predominant throughout India, except for the Punjab, Sind and Kashmīr in the north-west, and Assam in the north-eastern corner. The former regions were destined to remain independent for some time; Assam was included under the next Governor-General, Lord Amherst (1823–1828). We have seen that Assam had maintained its independence against Aurangzeb, and it continued a separate entity until 1816, when it was conquered by Burma. For eight years it experienced a cruel tyranny, during which its population is said to have been diminished by one-half, and the appeals for help made to Calcutta were rejected. The King of Burma was not, however, content with Assam. In 1818 he demanded the cession of those districts of Bengal which had once been held by Arakan, and in 1823 Burmese forces invaded Bengal with orders to take Calcutta, an action which now seems incomprehensible, but which was entirely in accordance with the self-sufficient ignorance characteristic of the Burma of those days. The first Burmese War, which followed inevitably, was concluded in 1826 by a treaty under which Assam, along with portions of Burma, was ceded to the Company; parts of the former region were then organised as a group of States on the model which had become established, and the remainder was incorporated in Bengal.

Lord Amherst was succeeded by Lord William Bentinck (1828–1835), whom the conditions allowed to adhere strictly to the policy of non-intervention in affairs outside the

THE FIRST BURMESE WAR

Company's territory. Bentinck, an experienced and sympathetic ruler, utilised this peaceful interval in inaugurating various social and administrative reforms which will be described in our next chapter. Both he and Sir Charles Metcalfe, who acted as Governor-General for a year until the arrival of Lord Auckland in 1836, endeared themselves to the now growing class of educated Indians by their liberal policy. Their rule was followed by two decades of renewed political and military activity, ending with the final elimination of the Company from the Indian constitution. Before describing this period, we must pause to review the changes which had occurred in internal conditions in the interval which separates Cornwallis from Bentinck.

CHAPTER XL

INTERNAL CHANGES, 1793–1835

WE have seen in previous chapters how the administration of the Company's territories had come under the supervision of Parliament, and how for a time it had been the subject of acute conflict between English parties. After the impeachment of Warren Hastings, the influence of party feeling became much less pronounced, and for the next half-century the action taken in Parliament in regard to India may be described with justice as an expression of the national will. The Company's charter came up for renewal at intervals of twenty years ; the successive Charter Acts were preceded by long and careful enquiries into the administration ; and the Acts themselves contained specific provisions, based largely on those enquiries, for reform and for new developments. Other Acts were passed from time to time dealing with particular administrative matters ; and it may fairly be said that during this period Parliament furnished in some measure that impetus from outside which is now generally recognised to be essential for the proper working of a bureaucratic government.

The Company's administration in India was also influenced materially by the training given to its recruits in the college at Haileybury. The actual teaching was perhaps less important than the inspiration derived from the traditions which came quickly into existence in that institution—a high standard of personal conduct, a sense of the magnitude of the tasks ahead, an ideal of loyal service to India as well as England. There were, of course, individual failures to realise this ideal, but the college was

THE COMPANY'S ADMINISTRATION

a factor of the utmost importance in setting up in India a standard of public life much higher than had prevailed there, whether among Indians or Englishmen, during the eighteenth century.

In approaching the administrative machine as it existed at this period, allowance must be made for the change in ideals which has taken place in the interval. Administration was not at that time directed towards a policy of active amelioration, or 'nation-building,' to use the phrase now current. In India there were no specialised departments charged with the maintenance of a general system of education or sanitation or economic development. The Company provided doctors, and also chaplains, for its servants, but not for the general population; public works were practically limited to the provision of administrative buildings, to occasional road-making and to some tentative irrigation schemes carried out by engineers drawn from the army; civil administration meant little more than keeping the peace, doing justice and collecting the revenue, the work of the magistrate, the judge and the collector.

The presidencies of Madras and Bombay still possessed a large measure of autonomy, and while their territories were organised on the general lines laid down by Cornwallis for Bengal, there were many differences in detail, rendered necessary by local conditions; in all cases, however, the unit was the district, ruled eventually by a Magistrate-Collector distinct from the Judge. It is important also to remember that as yet the Company had no Indian army; each presidency had its own military organisation, and the co-ordination between the three armies was far from perfect.

In civil matters the greatest divergence between the presidencies was in the revenue system. In the North the idea of a permanent settlement with the landholders for a time held the field; Bengal, Bihār and Benares had already been settled on these lines; and the officers sent to organise the Ceded and Conquered Provinces had instructions to do the same. The condition of this region was, however, such as to make a permanent settlement impossible, for agriculture had been ruined in the years of anarchy, and over large areas neither peasants nor landholders could be found. Contemporary accounts of the conditions prevailing in the 'conquered' districts, the country east and south-east of Delhi, make almost incredible reading at the present day. Regions which had been fully cultivated in the time of Akbar, as they are now, were then lying practically waste; the few remaining peasants tilled only the fields close to the village sites; and, when they ventured out to do so, they carried their weapons as they ploughed. In these circumstances the idea of making a permanent settlement forthwith was seen to be hopeless, and attention was concentrated on getting in whatever revenue could be paid at the moment, and on finding out who should be asked to pay it. The search for the landholders took a long time, and many mistakes were made by officers who attempted to apply the experience gained in Bengal to country where the practice had been different; conflicting claims had to be decided on imperfect evidence, and, at first, without any clear statement of the principles to be followed; but out of the initial confusion there emerged a new conception, the Record of Rights, which came to be one of the most important factors in the modern Rule of Law.

The Record of Rights is a statement, drawn up for each village, of all rights existing over its lands—what fields are held by each peasant and on what terms, what he pays for them, who receives the money, and many other details; and when it had been prepared, it became possible to decide with whom 'the settlement should be made,' that is to say, who should be recognised as the landholder of that particular village. The result of this elaborate investigation was to establish a very heterogeneous body of landholders. Some of them, representing the Chiefs, farmers, and grantees of the past, lived mainly on rent, and were thus comparable to English landlords, so long as they paid the revenue assessed; others were the peasant-brotherhoods, who lived mainly by tillage, and who now, in their collective capacity, undertook to pay the revenue due from the village as a whole.

REVENUE SYSTEMS

In Madras matters took a different course. Wellesley in 1798 ordered the introduction of the Bengal system, and some progress in this direction was made; but in the greater part of the presidency landholders, in the Bengal sense, did not exist, and attempts to create them proved unsuccessful, while officers with local experience pressed for a ryotwārī settlement, that is to say, one made with the individual peasants. Their view was accepted by the Select Committee which reported to Parliament in 1812, and thereafter ryotwārī became the rule, though a few landholders survived. The same rule was applied in the presidency of Bombay when its administration was organised a few years later; and thus the State entered into direct relations with individual peasants throughout southern India, while in the North it dealt either with landholders, or with the peasants of a village as an organised group.

As regards the amount of the revenue, the point which mattered most to those who had to pay, the Company's officers began by claiming the share which they understood to have been claimed by their predecessors; when dealing directly with the peasants, they demanded sums representing usually the value of half the gross produce, while landholders were asked to pay nine-tenths of what they expected to receive from the peasants. Experience soon showed that the collection of revenue assessed on these lines would be fatal to the recovery of the country, and the claim was progressively reduced, until, in the second half of the century, it became the general practice to demand one half of the net rent (not of the gross produce) from all revenue-payers, whether landholders or peasants; to reckon up this net rent periodically, usually at intervals of twenty or thirty years; and to leave the payers to enjoy any increment accruing between one settlement and the next. The ideal of a permanent settlement persisted for many years, but as experience accumulated it receded gradually from the region of practical politics, and it was at last formally abandoned in the year 1883.

During the period covered by this chapter little was done towards establishing a code of substantive law, though numerous Regulations were passed by the Councils in all three presidencies. The Charter Act of 1833 initiated a new system; Madras and Bombay then lost the power of legislating, which was confined to the Council of the Governor-General, strengthened for the purpose by a lawyer appointed in England, and thenceforward Acts took the place of Regulations. Under the first Legal Member of the Council, Thomas Babington Macaulay, a vigorous start was made on the much-needed formulation of the substantive law of India, but the pace slackened after he left the country, and the fruits of his work were not gathered for nearly a quarter of a century.

The absence of a code of laws did not, however, prevent the gradual establishment of internal peace and order; the lawless elements of the population were gradually brought under control, the people generally acquired the habit of bringing their disputes before the courts instead of fighting them out at home, and the idea steadily spread that obedience was now required, not to the orders of the individual who happened to wield executive power at the moment, but to a set of stable and permanent commands issued by the supreme authority: the Rule of Law had come into existence.

The establishment of internal peace was a tedious and inconspicuous business, involving the suppression, one by one, of the organised gangs of robbers, known in India as dacoits, who preyed on the people at large. We get glimpses of such gangs in the earlier history of the country, and they are not yet absolutely extinct; they had flourished in the anarchy of the eighteenth century, and indeed the Pindārīs were merely dacoits working on a larger scale; they had now to be hunted down, and their numbers gradually diminished as the executive gained in experience and efficiency. More spectacular was the attack on the organised bodies of criminals known as thugs, who practised murder for robbery as a fine art, in which young men were carefully trained by their elders, and who regarded each victim as a sacrifice to the goddess they worshipped. In 1836 an Act was passed, under which every member of such a gang was declared liable to imprisonment for life, and the special measures adopted for the enforcement of this drastic but necessary law eventually broke the chain of tradition, so that this form of crime became extinct.

We have said that little progress had yet been made towards producing a code of substantive law, but one momentous act of this period was the prohibition of the practice of suttee, the first occasion on which the Company's government deliberately interfered with an established custom of the country. Protests against this practice had been made by many English officers, by influential missionaries in India, and by humanitarian groups in England; a more significant opposition arose among Hindus under the leadership of Ram Mohan Roy, an outstanding figure to whose activities we shall return; in 1828 the Company instructed Bentinck to face the question, and less than two years later the practice was prohibited by regulation in all three presidencies. An influential body of opponents appealed against this decision to the Privy Council, but their appeal was rejected, and the prohibition remains a part of the law of India. Similar protests were being made against other Indian customs or institutions, notably the existence of slavery, and the practice of female infanticide by some sections of the people; action on these protests came somewhat later, but we may look forward a little and record the abolition of slavery.[1]

This institution is sanctioned by both Hindu and Islamic law; domestic slavery was quite common in India, and in a few places slaves were employed in cultivation, but not in organised industry. As a rule they were well treated, and it is arguable that they were better off than freemen, to the extent that in time of famine there was somebody interested in keeping them alive; but the humanitarian sentiment which was so influential in England was bitterly hostile to the institution as a whole, and under its inspiration the Charter Act of 1833 directed the Company to take action for abolition as soon as it should be safe and practicable. Exhaustive enquiries followed, and the result was the passing of Act V of 1843, which prohibited the courts from enforcing

[1] See Note on p. 344.

or recognising any claim to a slave. The institution was thus placed outside the law; there was no spectacular emancipation, but when deprived of legal support it gradually died out. It was only in 1860 that slaveholding became a punishable offence.

It will be apparent from the example of suttee that the Company was now envisaging its dominions in India as a whole. The same standpoint is seen in the action taken in a very different matter, the unification of the coinage. Up to 1834, rupees, varying slightly in value, were struck at several mints, and still recognised on their face the authority of the titular Mogul Emperor; in 1835 a single rupee (of 180 grains) was introduced for use in all three presidencies, and the new coins carried the portrait of the King of England, a tacit reminder that the sovereignty of India had changed hands.

Such were the main administrative developments of the period under review: we have now to relate the reaction of the population to the new influences which affected them. In economic life, the restoration of internal peace was what counted for most; agriculture and trade recovered rapidly, and the waste lands were brought gradually under the plough; but the desolation had been so extensive that some time had still to pass before increasing competition for land brought agrarian questions to the front. In industry, the outstanding feature of the period was the decline in cotton-weaving. We have seen in earlier chapters that India had for an indefinite number of centuries supplied clothes to most of southern Asia, that the efforts of European merchants had given her new and valuable markets in West Africa, Europe and America, and that early in the eighteenth century much of the English market was closed in order to protect home industry, but the other outlets survived. Indian artisans could not, however, compete with the new factory industry which emerged in England towards the close of the century, as the result of mechanical inventions and the use of steam-power; their export markets were gradually lost, their home market was invaded, and, after much suffering and distress, many of them turned to agriculture as the only available source of livelihood.

The administration took no action such as would now probably be taken in face of such an emergency; but in the circumstances of the time it could not have done more than facilitate the change of occupation. So far as the export trade was concerned, the only effective reply to the new competition would have been to imitate its methods, and for that purpose cheap coal was indispensable. A beginning had already been made in mining coal in Bengal, but the cost of transit rendered its use on a large scale impracticable, and though a few cotton factories were erected near Calcutta, the modern weaving industry could not become important until after the middle of the century, when the railway had reached the coal-fields.

The progress of invention, which ruined the old Indian weaving industry, was at the same time laying the foundations of the recent prosperity of a large portion of Bengal. The jute plant had been grown there for an indefinite period, and sackcloth had been woven from its fibre, but the industry was of purely local importance; the adaptation of machinery to its peculiar properties was a difficult matter, but in 1832 experiments made in Dundee proved successful, and the export of the fibre developed rapidly. In this case also the establishment of factories in India had to wait until coal could be brought by rail. The other great development in north-eastern India, the cultivation of tea, was just beginning to be contemplated seriously when Bentinck left India.

Passing to the social and cultural sides of life, it may be said that at this period the attitude of those Indians who came into direct contact with Englishmen was receptive, and to some extent imitative, rather than critical or hostile. In Bombay, the Parsees, who held the most prominent position in the city, were definitely Anglophile, and cordiality between the two races was well established. In Madras, where the leading Indians were Hindus bound strictly by the rules of caste, a similar social development was impossible, and there the most striking feature of the period was the rapid adoption of the English language as a *lingua franca*. In the north, the Moslems as a whole were inclined to hold themselves aloof, and some of the individuals who 'anglicised' took what was worst rather than what was best—the opportunities for extravagance and dissipation offered by the new régime. It was in Calcutta and the neighbourhood that the most significant developments occurred, and in order to explain them we must bring together three topics which are not necessarily connected—education, missions and journalism.

Our knowledge of education in India during the periods of Hindu and Moslem supremacy is very imperfect, but it is sufficient to show that literacy was not regarded as a necessary training for life in general: it was either an accomplishment for the few, or a path to certain definite vocations, especially the priesthood, commerce and administrative employment. Sanskrit texts prescribe an exceedingly elaborate course of training for priests; the other classes who required a knowledge of reading or writing obtained it either in the family or in the somewhat rudimentary schools which existed in greater or less numbers independent of the state. Higher education was given in institutions of a definitely religious character. We do not hear of anything comparable to the great centres of learning which had flourished under Buddhism, but groups of learned Brāhmans were to be found in various places of sanctity such as Benares or Nuddea, who taught particular branches of Sanskrit knowledge, and were sometimes in receipt of stipends provided by royal or wealthy patrons; while schools of Islamic studies, endowed in similar fashion, were attached to some of the principal mosques. Speaking generally, it may be said that the most characteristic feature of the old Indian education was the intimate relation between the teacher and the individual scholar, not the influence of a master over a class.

As a commercial organisation, the Company was not concerned with education, though in Madras it had maintained schools for the children of its Christian employees. The position was not materially changed when it emerged as an administrator, for according to English ideas education was no concern of governments.[1] There was, however, an active demand for English teaching on the part of those classes whose regular livelihood was drawn from the public offices; centuries before they had learned Persian when the need arose, and now they felt that in order to follow their traditional vocation they must learn the language of the new rulers. The task of meeting this demand fell at first on private enterprise, in which an important share was taken by missionaries.

The Company, as a trading body, had looked askance on missionaries as likely to be disturbing factors in its affairs. Some of the older Roman missions survived in its territories, and in Madras a few Protestants had been tolerated; but the atmosphere in Calcutta was hostile, and when a party of Baptists arrived there towards the end of the eighteenth century, they found it expedient to establish themselves, not in Calcutta itself, but in the neighbouring Danish settlement of Serampore. Here they opened schools, set up a printing press, and engaged actively in evangelisation. Meanwhile other institutions were growing up in Calcutta itself, where the hostility to missionary effort gradually disappeared; by the year 1820 there were two colleges there, and schools or colleges were soon to be found also in Madras, Bombay and Agra, giving not merely vocational training, but a general education on English lines.

The effective establishment of Indian journalism was due to the missionaries of Serampore. The first newspapers published in India had been designed merely for the English population in Calcutta, and were of the type natural in the circumstances, mainly personal, sometimes scurrilous, and usually short-lived. Wellesley, who was apt to be impatient of criticism, practically extinguished such ventures by the imposition of a drastic censorship, and, so long as it remained

[1] The first rudiments of the present Board of Education in England appeared in 1833, when a committee was appointed to administer a grant made by Parliament to supplement private subscriptions for the erection of schools for the poorer classes.

in force, the development of Indian journalism was impossible; but when it was abolished by Moira, a new type of enterprise emerged. A journal is said to have been brought out by an Indian in 1816, but it must have had a very short life; two years later the missionaries began to publish a weekly newspaper in Bengali, and a monthly magazine with the articles in both Bengali and English; and, following their example, Indians took up the profession in earnest. Its development was checked for the time by a Regulation issued in 1823, which required such publications to be licensed, but the press was set free again in 1835. Its early history in other parts of India is obscure, but at least one vernacular journal was published in Bombay from 1822 onwards.

During this period then India in general, and Bengal in particular, experienced a new intellectual atmosphere, provided by English education, newspapers, and the active preaching of evangelical Christianity. The nature of the response can best be shown by a sketch of the career of Ram Mohan Roy, whose name has been mentioned already. A Brāhman of Bengal, brought up in the doctrines of Grace and Love which had been preached by Chaitanya three centuries before, he had studied Islam, Christianity, and perhaps Buddhism, and, after serving the Company for about ten years, he settled in Calcutta in 1814, and devoted himself to extending his knowledge and to spreading the conclusions which he had reached. He found in the texts of Hinduism a pure theism which had become contaminated by idolatry; he found in the Gospels the same pure theism overlaid by much irrelevant matter; and his object was to propagate this doctrine within the circle of Hinduism, and to combat the social and religious practices which, in his view, were inconsistent with it. He met with vigorous opposition, from his friends the Serampore missionaries, who considered that he misrepresented the Gospels, as well as from the strict Hindus of Calcutta, but he held on his course; and in 1828 he founded a society, the Brahmo Samāj, ' for the worship and adoration of the Eternal Unsearchable and Immutable Being who is the Author and Preserver of the Universe,' without images, pictures or sacrifices.[1] On the social side, his objects comprised the spread of English education, the reform of the Hindu family, the abolition of polygamy and of suttee ; and he disliked the institution of caste, though he was not prepared to abandon it.

Ram Mohan looked to English influence for help in propagating his teaching, and in 1830 he made the voyage to England—a great adventure in those days ; his visit did much to bring home to Englishmen some idea of the new factors which were at work in his country, but it was cut short by his death in 1833. His influence in India for a time declined, but after a brief interval the Brahmo Samāj regained its vigour under new leaders, and it has remained an important factor in Indian life, not in point of the number of its actual adherents, but as the exponent of the view that Hinduism is a living faith with an inherent capacity of growth and development.

We have said above that at first the Company was not concerned with education, but it recognised the duty of an Indian ruler to patronise the old-established learning of the country ; Warren Hastings had assisted in the establishment in Calcutta of a school (known as the ' Madrasa ') of Islamic studies ; a Sanskrit college was endowed at Benares, and the customary stipends to learned men were continued at such centres as Nuddea and Poona. In 1811 Minto in India was pressing for further activity in this direction, while in England the powerful evangelical group led by Wilberforce was urging the need for the diffusion of useful knowledge ; and these different objectives were combined in a clause of the Charter Act of 1813, which authorised expenditure on ' the encouragement of the learned natives of India,' and also ' the promotion of a knowledge of the sciences.' For a time little was done. In 1823 a Committee of Public Instruction was formed to disburse the annual grant which had been sanctioned, and at first its efforts were directed towards the classical languages of India ; but the popular demand for

[1] The quotation is from the trust deed of the society's building, as reproduced in Dr. J. N. Farquhar's *Modern Religious Movements in India* (New York, 1918), p. 35.

English was insistent, the committee presently split into two parties, one for teaching in English, the other for employing the classical languages of the country, and a deadlock resulted, which lasted until 1834, when Macaulay, the new Legal Member of the Council, was appointed to be president of the committee. Early in 1835 he presented his famous minute, insisting that higher education should be imparted to Indians in the English language. His views were accepted by the Council, and the period which we have been reviewing closes with this momentous decision.

NOTE
FEMALE INFANTICIDE
(See p. 337.)

No religious sanction was ever claimed for the practice of female infanticide which was to be found among certain sections of the people in North India, particularly among some Rajput tribes, and had originated in the convention that a girl must be married into a family of a higher social status. Local British officials such as Duncan in Benares in 1789 and Metcalfe in Delhi about 1810 had been able to prohibit it. As a result of preventive measures the practice has since disappeared.

CHAPTER XLI

THE NORTH-WEST FRONTIER AND THE PUNJAB, 1836–1856

THE terms of office of Lord Auckland (1836–1842) and Lord Ellenborough (1842–1844) were dominated by the Russian menace on the north-west. We have seen that during the later years of the European war Persia had stood in the way of a French advance towards India through Turkey. The position was now different, for in 1828 Persia had been heavily defeated by Russia, whose forces were pushing southward to the east of the Caspian Sea ; and at the time when Auckland assumed charge of the post of Governor-General, Russia and Persia, working in harmony, were threatening Afghanistan. The situation there was complicated. The effective ruler at Kābul was Dost Muhammad, but his control over the country was by no means complete ; Persia was endeavouring to secure a footing at Herat, the western key to the country ; and Shāh Shuja, who had formerly ruled in Kābul, was seeking help in India to enable him to recover the throne. Ranjīt Singh in the Punjab also had ambitions in the direction of Afghanistan, and thus Dost Muhammad had some grounds for adopting a suspicious attitude towards overtures from the east.

Acting under instructions from England, Auckland entered into negotiations with Kābul, where a Russian agent was also active. The English diplomacy was ineffective, and in the spring of 1838 the envoy withdrew, leaving nobody on the spot to counteract the efforts of the Russian agent, and thus increasing the difficulties of Dost Muhammad, who was committed to neither side. In these conditions Auckland decided on action, and in June he made what is known as the 'Tripartite Treaty' with Ranjīt Singh and Shāh Shuja, under which the latter was to be restored as ruler of Afghanistan.

The resulting military operations were successful; Dost Muhammad withdrew, and in August, 1839, Shāh Shuja entered Kābul. As a ruler, however, he proved a failure, for he could not win over the Afghans to his side, and his position was maintained only by the aid of English garrisons. The situation was complicated by the death of Ranjīt Singh in June of that year. He had left the English to do nearly all the work of implementing the Tripartite Treaty, but, so long as he lived, his support was of some value; when he died, the Sikhs became involved in disputes regarding the succession, and no assistance from them could be expected. Notwithstanding this defection, the position in Afghanistan was maintained during 1840, towards the end of which year Dost Muhammad surrendered; but in 1841 things began to look black, for Afghan opposition to the new régime was increasing rather than diminishing, and in November of that year a serious revolt occurred in Kābul itself. The English authorities on the spot failed to take prompt action, and the revolt quickly made headway. In December negotiations were initiated, and the English undertook to evacuate Afghanistan and allow Dost Muhammad to return. The withdrawal of the Kābul garrison ended in disaster; the country was snow-bound; Afghan horsemen first harried the rear, and then attacked from both sides; and out of a total of about 16,000 men (reckoning troops and followers) a single survivor reached Jalālābād, midway between Kābul and Peshāwar, where an English force was stationed.

In February Ellenborough arrived in India to succeed Auckland. He saw clearly that the course of events had united the whole of Afghanistan in a war against the Company's forces, that the project to establish Shāh Shuja in Kābul had definitely failed, that it would be useless to attempt to recover possession of the country, and that the situation required a decisive success followed by voluntary withdrawal. Realisation of this policy was facilitated by

THE FIRST AFGHAN WAR

the fact that in April Shāh Shuja was murdered in Kābul, where he had remained as nominal king. The English forces moved from Jalālābād in June, and occupied Kābul in September: a column from Kandahār arrived there at the same time; and in October they finally withdrew, after placing a son of Shāh Shuja on the throne. He was, however, no more able to keep it than his father had been; early next year Dost Muhammad resumed his position as king, and the adventure initiated by Auckland was thus brought to an end.

The annexation of Sind was an incidental consequence of the Afghan war. In theory, Sind was still subject to Afghanistan, but in practice it was independent under the rule of a family belonging to Baluchistan, the head of which had established himself there in 1783. The leaders of this family were known collectively as the Amīrs, and at this period they had divided the country among themselves. The route to Kandahār lay through their territories, and in 1838 they were practically compelled to enter into treaties permitting the passage of the Company's troops, and giving possession of certain strategic points. Frequent difficulties arose in regard to the execution of these treaties, particularly when the situation in Afghanistan had become acute. Late in 1842 Ellenborough called on the Amīrs to execute a new treaty; they procrastinated and collected troops—a challenge which the Company's General was quite ready to accept. The result was the battle of Miānī (February, 1843), when the Amīrs were completely defeated, and their country was included in the presidency of Bombay.

Next year Ellenborough was recalled by the Directors of the Company, who objected to his general attitude, and it fell to his successor Sir Henry Hardinge (1844-1848) to deal with the situation which had arisen in the Punjab. The period of disputed successions, which began on the death of Ranjīt Singh, lasted till 1845. The Sikh army was now the only effective power in the State; it was anxious for active service, it suspected the English of contemplating annexation, and its hostile sentiments were fostered by some of the prominent Chiefs, who resented its domination, and desired its defeat. In December, 1845, the army crossed the Sutlej and invaded the Company's territory; Hardinge then formally declared war, and a hard-fought campaign was closed by the battle of Sobraon (February, 1846), in which the Sikhs were decisively defeated. Under the terms of peace dictated by Hardinge, Kashmīr was separated from the Punjab and constituted as a State under British protection; a small area on the east was annexed by the Company; and the rest of the Punjab was left in the hands of a minor, who was formally recognised as Mahārāja, supported by a British force.

The regency, however, was unable to stand alone, and the Ministers asked for a revision of the terms, under which the administration was practically handed over to the British Resident. This arrangement was disliked by the Sikhs as a body, and in 1848 a series of revolts made it clear that they were determined on a renewal of the war. Lord Dalhousie (1848–1856), who had just succeeded Hardinge as Governor-General, took the initiative, and a second hard-fought campaign ended in the decisive battle of Gujrāt (February, 1849), and the formal annexation of the Punjab. The pacification of the country which followed must be recognised as one of the greatest triumphs of administrative genius which India has seen. For four years the province was governed by a board, of which the leading members were the brothers Henry and John Lawrence, assisted by a staff of exceptional ability; in 1853 the board was dissolved, and John Lawrence, as Chief Commissioner, carried on the work. The people were disarmed and settled down to agriculture and commerce; the Rule of Law was established under regulations simpler than those of Bengal, and more closely adapted to local needs; the frontier was made reasonably safe, the interior was opened up by roads, a Record of Rights was prepared, and the settlement of the revenue was made for the most part with the peasant communities found in occupation of the land, at rates much lower than had been claimed by the Sikh government. In order to understand the rapidity and completeness of the pacification it is necessary to bear in mind that the

END OF THE SIKH POWER

establishment of the Sikh kingdom was still quite recent, that the Sikhs formed only a minority of the population, which consisted mainly of Moslems and Hindus, and that even this minority was not united, for some of the Sikh leaders preferred the Company as a ruler to the army of their own faith. When therefore the power of that army was finally broken, the Company was left without serious opposition.

Meanwhile the Russian menace had for the time disappeared as the result of an understanding reached in Europe in 1844, which remained effective until the outbreak of the Crimean war. Persia, however, was still seeking to extend into Afghan territory, and her repeated attacks on Herat induced Dost Muhammad to enter into friendly relations with the Company in 1855; there was thus a lull on the north-west frontier of India until his death in 1863. On the other side of India Dalhousie's term of office was marked only by the second Burmese War, fought in 1852, which ended in the annexation of what remained of the coastline, so that the Company's rule stretched without interruption from Assam through Arakan and Pegu to Tenasserim, while Upper Burma, which remained independent, was cut off from the sea. His activities in India itself form the subject of the next chapter.

MAP VIII

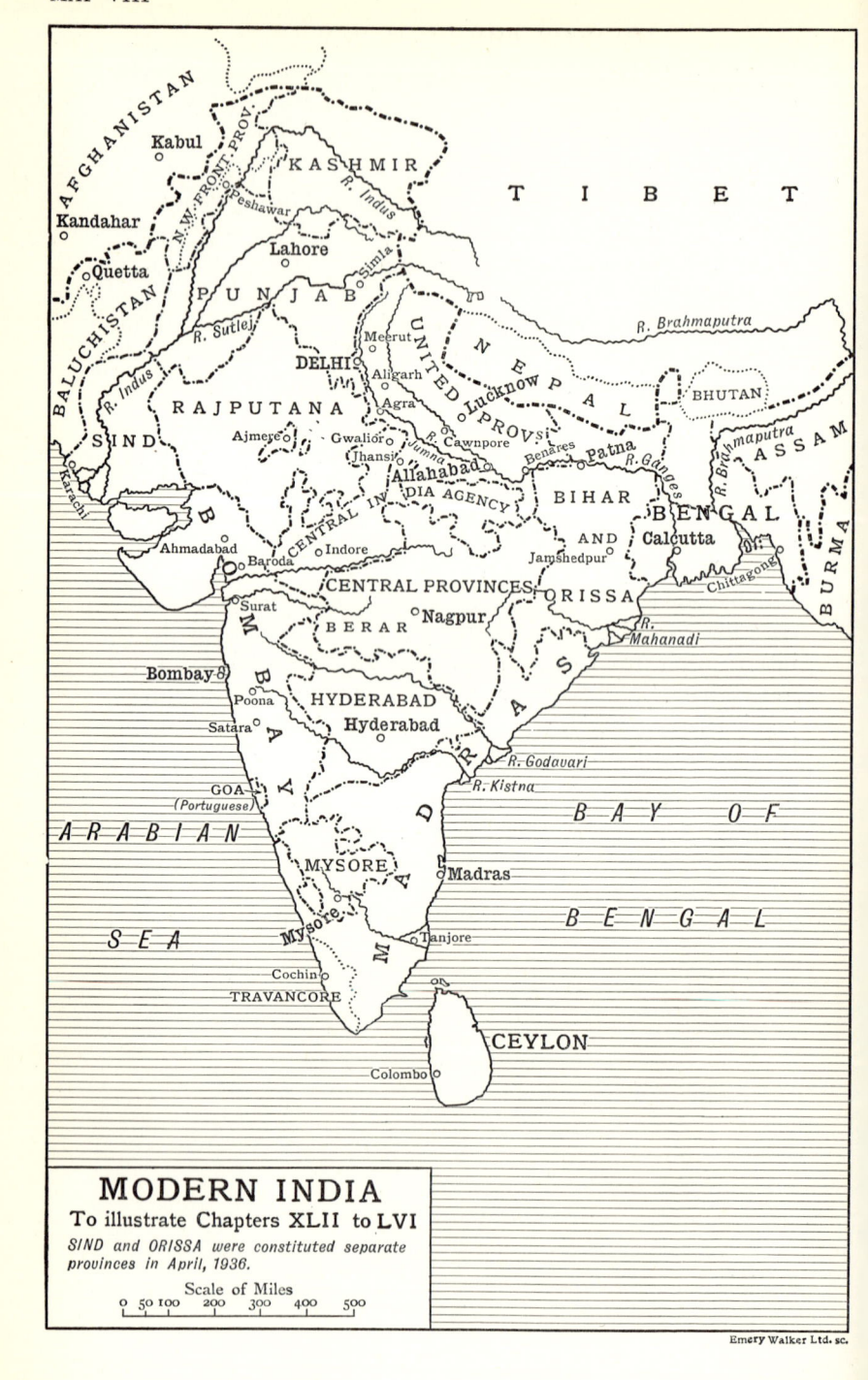

MODERN INDIA
To illustrate Chapters XLII to LVI
SIND and ORISSA were constituted separate provinces in April, 1936.

Scale of Miles
0 50 100   200   300   400   500

CHAPTER XLII

DALHOUSIE'S ADMINISTRATION

APART from the annexation of the Punjab, Dalhousie's administration is now remembered mainly for his treatment of various States, but it is memorable also as marking an epoch in the economic development of India. Under the former head we are concerned with two distinct principles, known respectively as Lapse and Paramountcy, the first a matter of merely historical interest, the second still practically important at the present day; but in order to understand Dalhousie's application of these principles it is necessary to bear in mind that his primary object was the welfare of the masses of the people, and that he thought much more of the peasants than of their rulers. He was firmly convinced that the people were better off under the Company than under Princes or Chiefs, and consequently he approached all questions concerning the States with a definite bias in favour of the Company's rule.

The principle of Lapse asserted that, on failure of the direct line of a subordinate ruler, the State lapsed to the superior Power, and that the line could not be continued by adoption unless the consent of the superior Power had first been obtained. There is good evidence that this principle existed in India, though not crystallised into a formal rule, and that the superior Power usually intervened in such cases, not to abolish the State, but to impose more or less onerous terms on the successor whom it decided to recognise; but in Dalhousie's hands the principle became an instrument of annexation whenever a suitable opportunity presented itself, and its application resulted in three Marātha States,

Sātāra, Nāgpur and Jhānsī, together with some smaller ones, being brought under the Company's administration. Similar annexations became impossible a few years later, when the power to continue their lines by adoption was formally granted to the rulers of all the more important States.

The other principle, that of Paramountcy, has a different history. To quote a recent authoritative description, 'it is based upon treaties, engagements and sanads, supplemented by usage and sufferance and by decisions of the Government of India and the Secretary of State embodied in political practice';[1] and its effect, stated in popular language, is that the Paramount Power will intervene in the internal affairs of a State when misgovernment reaches a stage requiring intervention, the Paramount Power being the sole judge of the necessity. The Company had already applied this principle on various occasions. In 1831 the large State of Mysore was taken over, after the people had been driven into rebellion by gross misgovernment, and it was not restored until 1881; while less important States had been annexed for various reasons in Assam and in Madras, and several others had received warnings from time to time. The most important of these was Oudh, where misgovernment had become chronic. In 1847 Hardinge had personally warned the king of the danger of annexation if the administration were not reformed within two years, but detailed local investigations made after that period had elapsed showed that things were going from bad to worse, and in 1856 the country was formally annexed under the orders of the authorities in England.

As the result of these changes, the administrative map of India assumed substantially the form which is familiar at the present day. By the Charter Act of 1853 the Governor-General had been relieved of the direct administration of Bengal, and the Presidency was now organised as five Provinces, the lieutenant-governorships of Bengal and

[1] *Report of the Indian States Committee* (Cmd. 3302), para. 19. The word 'sanad' means in this context a grant made in writing by the Paramount Power; the word 'political' is here used in the technical sense which is explained below.

THE PRINCIPLE OF PARAMOUNTCY 353

the North-Western Provinces, and the chief-commissioner-ships of the Punjab,[1] Oudh, and the Central Provinces, the last representing the territories of the Bhonsle rulers at Nāgpur; subsequently the size of Bengal was reduced further by the creation of chief-commissionerships in Burma (1862) and Assam (1874), but it still included Bihār, Orissa and Chota Nāgpur. The other presidencies were not broken up; Madras remained as a unit, while Bombay retained Sind, not as a separate Province, but under a Commissioner exercising certain exceptional powers. The boundaries of the various provinces were fixed mainly on historical or administrative considerations and they did not in all cases define homogeneous racial or economic units, a defect which was to become increasingly obvious as time went on.

One other territorial change made by Dalhousie deserves mention. The State of Hyderabad was bound by treaty to pay the cost of a force maintained for its defence by the Company; payments having fallen into arrears, Dalhousie effected an arrangement under which the northern districts of the State, now known collectively as Berār, were assigned to the Company in lieu of the cash payments, and these were administered as a separate unit for the next half-century.

The broad effect of the organisation completed under Dalhousie may be summarised as follows. On the north, the plains of the Ganges and the Indus were in the main administered by the Company, but comprised also some States of secondary importance; the rugged centre of the country consisted mainly of States, broken by some administered areas; and the south, apart from Hyderabad and Mysore, was mainly under the Company's rule. For administrative purposes, the bulk of the centre was grouped in two Agencies. The western, known as Rājputāna, consisted mainly of Rājput States, the Company's relations with which were in charge of an Agent of the Governor-General, who was stationed at Ajmere, and whose post dates from 1832. The eastern, known as Central India,

---

[1] The Punjab was shortly afterwards placed under a Lieutenant-Governor, when the Delhi country lying west of the Jumna was transferred to it from the North-Western Provinces.

was formed by Dalhousie in 1854, with the Agent stationed at Indore, and consisted mainly of the Marātha States of Mālwa and the Rājput States of Bundelkhand. The duties of these Agents, and of the Residents stationed in other States, are known as 'political,' a word which has acquired in India a meaning very different from that which it carries in England. In one aspect these duties are diplomatic, but they are also concerned with the principle of paramountcy, and the 'Political Officer' is more than a diplomat, because he may on occasion have to convey the orders of the Paramount Power to a subordinate ruler.

It would not be easy to point to any expressions of common feeling in the India thus parcelled out among Provinces and States: the importance of Dalhousie's economic policy lies largely in the fact that the measures taken by him to improve the means of communication rendered possible the steady approach towards unification which characterised the second half of the century; but before recording the developments in India itself we may glance at the changes which had taken place in its connection with Europe. The overland route had been opened in 1838, and had brought Bombay within about six weeks of London; in Dalhousie's time there was a regular monthly mail by this route—from 1857 onwards it was weekly—but the cost of the land journey across Egypt prohibited its employment for the transit of ordinary goods, and the trade-route by way of the Cape had still to be reckoned in months rather than weeks. As yet there was no telegraphic communication; the first line connecting India with Europe was not opened until 1865.

In considering internal communications, it is necessary to guard against misapprehensions resulting from changes in the connotation of certain familiar terms. Thus in the Mogul empire there was an efficient system for the transit of letters by relays of runners at a speed of perhaps 200 miles a day, but this cannot rightly be called a postal system, because its use was confined to official messages; private

COMMUNICATIONS

persons sent their letters by messengers, who in favourable circumstances covered about thirty miles a day. Under the Company's rule also, the mail lines were at first purely official, though the privilege of using them on payment was soon granted to private persons. A rudimentary public post was established in 1837, and, after experience of its working had been gained, the Indian Post Office was brought into existence by an Act passed in 1854, and letters then began to be carried throughout India at low, uniform rates prepaid by stamps. The effect of the change can be inferred from the fact that a letter from Calcutta to Bombay, which in 1837 would have cost two shillings, was now carried for less than a penny, while it became financially possible to distribute newspapers by post. Meanwhile, experiments with the telegraph having proved successful, Dalhousie obtained sanction to introduce the system, and in 1855 it became possible to telegraph messages, directly or indirectly, between Calcutta, Madras, Bombay, Agra and Peshāwar.

In regard to main roads also there is some risk of misapprehension, for in the Mogul period they were not metalled, while the Company aimed at providing a surface suitable for wheeled traffic. Its early efforts in this direction were governed mainly by the need for army transport, and road-making was entrusted to bodies known as military boards, which for various reasons were not very successful. When the Punjab was annexed in 1849, a new system was inaugurated there, in the creation of a department of public works, and by 1854 this system had been introduced in all provinces, which thus became responsible for the roads within their limits. The chief monument of the military boards is the Grand Trunk Road leading from Calcutta to Delhi, but, in spite of their limitations, they did valuable work in other regions also, and in particular it may be noted that the landward isolation of Bombay was broken in 1830 by the construction of a road up the Western Ghats to Poona.

It is, however, with the introduction of railways that Dalhousie's name is most closely associated. Proposals were first put forward in 1843 by financial interests in

London, and the discussion which followed makes curious reading at the present day. To the opponents of the project it was obvious that in Indian conditions the maintenance of a permanent way was wholly impracticable; but, even assuming the impossible, they were confident that railways could never pay, because the usages of caste would prevent their use by Hindus, the great majority of the population. These arguments were quickly disproved by experience: the first engineers made some mistakes, but they soon learned how railways in India should be made, while Hindus unostentatiously modified their usages to meet the new situation; and the main effect of the opposition was to delay a decision. The issues were clarified by Dalhousie in two elaborate minutes, in which he insisted on ideas which are now familiar but in those days were somewhat novel—that the State should retain an adequate measure of control, and that the railway system of the country should be planned as a whole, instead of being allowed to grow up at haphazard, as had been the case in England. As the result of his intervention terms were settled with various English companies, and construction was in active progress when he left India.

To pass from railways to canals comes naturally to English readers, but it must be remembered that all the principal Indian canals were constructed primarily for irrigation, and, while some of them also carry goods, the two objects are often incompatible. Irrigation in India has a long history. In an earlier chapter we have described the reservoirs [1] constructed for this purpose in great numbers under Hindu rule, but the methods used in them could not be applied to the great rivers of the northern plains, and the water of these could be employed only by means of what are called inundation canals, that is to say, channels cut through the river banks, so that a portion of the water can be drawn off when the river is in high flood. More advanced methods had been developed in the South, where on some

---

[1] Known in India as 'tanks.' The word is an etymological puzzle, but, in this sense, it probably came from the Portuguese *tanque*, cognate with the French *étang* (a pond or lake).

IRRIGATION WORKS

rivers Hindu rulers had constructed masonry dams across the main stream, forming reservoirs which would feed perennial canals, that is to say, channels which flow for most of the year and not only during floods. Some approach to such perennial canals had been made in the North during the period of Moslem rule, particularly on the Jumna, but, owing to want of proper maintenance, they had almost ceased to exist when the country came under the rule of the Company, and nearly the same statement can be made of most of the old works in the South.

Recurring seasons of famine drew the attention of the Company's administration to the potential value of these canals, and by 1830 those which drew supplies from the Jumna had been effectively restored, while the engineers employed in northern India had gained experience of work of a type then unknown in England. This experience was successfully utilised in the design of the Ganges Canal, a far larger undertaking, which was begun in 1842, and, after delays due to changes of policy, was opened in 1854, carrying water, by branches and channels progressively subdivided, through most of the country lying between the Ganges and the Jumna.

In the South development followed substantially the same lines. The works in the Cauvery delta, near Tanjore, which date from the days of Chola rule, were restored and improved in the years from 1836 onwards, and new works of the same type were constructed in the deltas of the Godāvarī (1849) and the Kistna (1854). The canals made at this period may be taken as the prototype of the modern irrigation system, not merely of India, but of the world at large, for every other irrigated country has drawn freely on the experience gained in India by the pioneers and their successors.

Regarded merely as investments, many of the large canals have proved highly remunerative to the State, but the motive which led to their construction was, as we have said, the desire to mitigate the horrors of famine. In this matter the early experience of the Company was similar to what we have described at the end of Chapter XXXI; up to 1838 there was usually famine, of greater or less severity, in one part of India or another; but for the next fifteen years seasons were generally favourable, and there was a respite for the country as a whole. Various methods of relief were adopted from time to time, but as yet no regular relief policy had been formulated, and in fact the conditions essential for such a policy did not exist. So long as large areas might suffer from actual want of food, palliative measures alone were possible; it was only when the spread of the railway system enabled ample supplies of food to be carried wherever they were needed that the basis of an effective policy could be found; and it was owing primarily to the railways that in the course of less than half a century the word 'famine' acquired a new meaning in Indian administration. In Dalhousie's time it meant, as it had always meant, starvation and depopulation: it now means widespread temporary unemployment, for food can be got by anyone who has money to buy it, and at the present day the essence of what is still called famine-relief is the provision of work wherever employment has temporarily failed.[1]

Passing to other aspects of Indian life, Dalhousie's term of office must be remembered for the formulation of a comprehensive policy of public instruction. The decision of 1835 to concentrate on English education had been followed by a period of experiment, during which each Province worked on its own lines, and in some cases efforts had been made to extend elementary teaching in the language spoken in the country; but the effective demand was still for English, mainly as a qualification for the public service, and by 1850 the supply of English-knowing candidates had in places already outstripped the Company's needs. Dalhousie drew up proposals for a general policy, and, after a Parliamentary enquiry, these were elaborated in England into the comprehensive scheme enjoined by the despatch of 1854, which is known by the name of Sir Charles Wood, the President of the Board of Control. This despatch provided for the establishment of a Department of Public Instruction in each Province, to promote elementary education in the

[1] See Note on p. 365.

vernacular, and higher education in English, by means of a co-ordinated scheme of schools and colleges, maintained or aided out of public funds, with, at the summit, external examining bodies on the model of the University of London as then constituted; and it laid stress on the education of girls as well as boys, a matter which the Company had hitherto avoided out of respect for Indian customs. Provision was also made for the extension of vocational training, which at the time was represented in India only by the medical colleges in Calcutta, Madras and Bombay, and by two institutions for training engineers. The scheme thus inaugurated was to govern the policy of the next half-century, and determine the direction of intellectual development throughout India.[1]

We have said already that it would be difficult to point to any expressions of common feeling in India at this period, and it would certainly be impossible to produce convincing evidence of any general disloyalty to the Company's rule; but the position was not stable, and there were various local or sectional elements of discontent which were important in the aggregate. The annexation of the Marātha States was not openly resented by the population in general, but it led necessarily to the hostility of the classes which were primarily affected, from the families and ministers of the displaced rulers down to their disbanded armies and the parasites of the Courts, whose prospects were injured by the change. The same thing occurred in Oudh, but there the early proceedings of the Company's administrators were such as to antagonise also a considerable portion of the general population. Oudh was a country of large landholders, whose tenures were of varied origin. Some of them were mere adventurers, who within living memory had succeeded in imposing their authority on the peasants, but others had behind them the traditions of five centuries or more, since their Rājput ancestors, retreating before the first Moslem conquerors, had carved out principalities for themselves. On annexation, a settlement of the revenue had necessarily to be made in a summary manner, and in the process most of the large landholders were set aside in favour of the

[1] See Note on p. 365.

peasants ; and this measure was resented not only by the landholders themselves but by the numerous Rājput tribesmen, who still regarded their landholder as their Chief, and were perfectly ready to follow him into the field, and also by some of the lower castes, whose loyalty to their old-established rulers was still an active sentiment. In 1856, therefore, Oudh was probably the darkest danger-spot in the Company's territory. Elsewhere, too, there were many persons of position who had lost the chance of high executive employment, or in other ways had suffered, or believed they had suffered, by the Company's rule, who regarded it merely as a temporary phenomenon, just as all recent governments in India had been temporary, and who were ready or anxious for a change.

As regards the general population, it may be said that among the Moslems of the North the Company's rule found little favour. The idea of a severance between Church and State is repugnant to the old Islamic polity, in which Church and State are one. The days were not yet distant when the greater part of India had constituted a Moslem State, but the annexation of Oudh deprived Islam of its last considerable possessions in the North, while Hyderabad, the one great Moslem power remaining in the country, was very far away. It was impossible for orthodox men to welcome the political predominance of a faith based on a revelation which, they considered, had been superseded by that given to Muhammad ; and in Dalhousie's time the leaders of the Wahābī sect, who claimed to be the exponents of the original teaching of the Prophet, were preaching the religious obligation of open war against the 'infidel' government of the Company. To men of more moderate views the activities of the missionaries were sometimes a cause of offence, for there were occasions when controversial zeal overstepped the limits imposed by Christian charity ; and, on a different plane, the official disuse of the Persian language was a grievance, practical as well as sentimental. In the law courts Persian had been displaced in favour of the vernacular, but in the public offices English was rapidly becoming universal. Moslems as a body held aloof from the new education which was now being offered, and saw the classical language of their community deprived of the predominance it had so long enjoyed. Except for the blessings of tranquillity, there was nothing in the new régime to win their active loyalty, and there was much in it to repel; even tranquillity had its drawbacks, when contrasted with the opportunities offered to strong men in time of anarchy.

So far as the literate classes were concerned, the position of the Hindus was more favourable. They had been quick to avail themselves of the new education, and many of them had secured positions in the public offices; but some of them had failed to do so, and, especially in Bengal, an independent educated class was emerging, disposed to be critical of the Company's rule. The tone of the Indian press showed a corresponding change; the sober type of informative journalism introduced by the missionaries was giving way to more vigorous, and sometimes hostile, comment, expressed in somewhat exuberant language, and paying less regard to facts than to personal views; the rudiments of an Opposition were coming into existence.

The adherents of the traditional forms of Hinduism had grounds for anxiety, for they were attacked from various directions, by the reformers within their own community, and by the missionaries from outside; the prohibition of suttee was a warning that their most cherished institutions might not be safe from official interference; new and disturbing projects, such as the railways, might excite alarm before their nature was clearly understood; and in some quarters there were even vague apprehensions, quite unwarranted by facts, that the Company contemplated a campaign of conversion. The operation of these varied forces did not, however, become manifest at once; the visible revival of the spirit of Hinduism developed later in the century; but already some of its exponents were becoming active in defending its institutions against attack, and in criticising the principles on which their opponents relied. It is hard to sum up in a phrase the characteristics of a time of gradual change, but perhaps it is not far from the truth to say that the most significant feature was the development of a critical spirit, along with a new boldness in its expression.

The masses of the people living in the villages were learning, or had learned, to accept the Rule of Law as a fact, but its stability or permanence might still be questioned, particularly in regions which had recently come under the Company's authority. Indian villages have long memories, and the lesson of the past was not stability but fluctuation. Men could look back to the period of anarchy, to the harsh rule of the later Moguls, to the golden age of Akbar, and still farther down the centuries; what they saw was a series of rulers or dynasties imposed on them from without, and rising or falling from causes lying outside their experience; the Company's Rule of Law was, in their eyes, merely the last of the long series. The burden of the land-revenue had been reduced, but in many places it still pressed heavily on the peasants; the new law courts were welcomed by many, but they could not be universally popular, for the gain of one party was the loss of another; and, speaking generally, the existing régime was accepted with acquiescence but without enthusiasm.

When Dalhousie left India, he could justly claim that the country was at peace without and within, but he was conscious of disturbing forces lying below the surface, and he would not venture to predict that peace would last for long. It must be allowed that the Company's administration was not in a position to make a precise estimate of the strength or direction of these disturbing forces, for by this time the process of social segregation was practically complete, and Englishmen in India stood out as a separate ruling class—so much so that a superficial observer might have described them as forming one caste out of many. This segregation was destined to produce unfortunate results, but it was the natural, perhaps the inevitable, outcome of the conditions of the time.

At the beginning of the nineteenth century there was no Indian 'society' in the sense which the word bears in

English, that is to say, there was not to be found a numerous body of persons, of both sexes, ordinarily cultured and well-to-do, and meeting openly on the common ground of similarity of outlook on life, in religion and politics, in art and recreation. There was a Moslem society in this sense, though it was marked by deep cleavages, for the Persian despised the Afghan almost as much as the Afghan despised his ' brethren ' of Bengal. Among Hindus the established usages of caste offered serious obstacles to social unity, particularly in the way of preventing the practice of eating and drinking together, which elsewhere has been almost of the essence of social intercourse. In early days some of the few Europeans in India were, as we have said, admitted to Moslem society, but the extent of common ground was too small to allow of assimilation ; and while they could be on friendly terms with men, they could not possibly meet a Moslem lady, so that social intercourse was at best imperfect.

While, however, there was no Indian society in the sense in which we are using the word, there was much friendly intercourse between Hindus of different castes, and also between Hindus and Moslems, men with men, and women with women ; they could not eat or drink together, but they could meet on occasions of ceremony, or in less formal contacts discuss topics of common interest. It would be a mistake to think of Indians of position as segregated socially into a number of compartments entirely distinct ; the obstacles to complete freedom of intercourse were serious, the compartments were there, but they did not absolutely prevent communication.

A marked characteristic of the Moslem society which we have described was that, in the regions where Islam was politically supreme, its members constituted a ruling class, and insisted on due deference from Hindus ; they might be on friendly terms with Rājputs of position, and with some of the wealthier merchants or individuals of other castes ; their authority might be shared with Hindus holding high executive positions ; but, broadly speaking, as rulers they stood above the subjects. When political power passed to the Company, its English servants stepped naturally into this position; they received the deference due to rulers, and accepted it as a matter of course; but the outward expression of this deference, which was reasonable among Indians, looked to Englishmen like cringing servility, and seemed to set them on a pinnacle of assured superiority, a position not in itself unpleasant. The problem of social relations was further complicated by the fact that Englishmen who held no official position claimed from Indians the same deference, or show of servility, so that the English as a whole, and not merely the English officers, took on the appearance of a ruling class.

When therefore the gradual increase in numbers made it possible for the Englishmen in India to be socially self-sufficient, it was natural that they should lead their own life, rather than seek admission to the society of men with whom they had so few interests in common; and it was no less natural that Indians should remain aloof from this exotic society, whose pursuits and amusements were very different from their own. This social self-sufficiency was, of course, dependent on the presence in India of Englishwomen, whose numbers increased rapidly in the first half of the century; and the same fact emphasised the disparity, so obvious in northern India, between the class whose women went about openly, and the classes whose women were never seen in public. The domestic architecture of the period is eloquent of this disparity: the English lived in bungalows, with every room opening on the outer world; the front of the Indian house was open, but the ladies' apartments were closed to the world, looking on to an inner courtyard, to which access was severely restricted. Incidentally, it may be noted that as the numbers of Englishwomen increased, the practice of concubinage tended to disappear; the change is no matter for regret, but it reduced the number of Englishmen with personal knowledge of the Indian attitude towards life, and thus contributed something to the process of social segregation.

It must also be recognised that a prejudiced view of India had grown up in England, so that young men came out ignorant, and sometimes contemptuous, of the civilisation of the country. To some extent this prejudice must be attributed to the zeal of missionaries and philanthropists, who in their eagerness for reform overstressed the darker shadows of Indian life. Suttee had prevailed until 1830; slavery was still legal in 1842; there had been cases of human sacrifices in a few localities until the practice was suppressed by the Company; some tribes were accustomed to kill their female children; there were thugs, and there were dacoits; these and other ugly facts were grave blots on Indian civilisation, but over-insistence on them produced a distorted picture, and the ' poor Indian ' of some popular preachers was presented as a being to be reformed or converted, to be pitied or despised, rather than to be understood and appreciated as he actually was.

There is room for difference of opinion regarding the relative importance of these various tendencies, but their operation is beyond dispute, and the result was that during the period when modern India was coming into existence the relations between the rulers on the spot and Indians of position were essentially formal and official, and it was a rare exception to have a free and open interchange of news or comments, such as would have been natural in a homogeneous society.

NOTES
(1) FAMINES
(See p. 358.)

The famine that prevailed in Bengal and some other parts of India in 1943 was caused by special circumstances which will be described in a later chapter. The general statement in the text does not require modifications.

(2) EDUCATION MEASURES
(See p. 359.)

As will appear in later chapters little progress was achieved for a long time in primary or vocational education and in the education of girls, defects from which the Indian social system is only now beginning to recover.

CHAPTER XLIII

THE MUTINY AND ITS CONSEQUENCES

LORD DALHOUSIE was succeeded by Lord Canning, whose term of office (1856-1862) was marked by the Mutiny and the subsequent reconstruction of the Indian constitution, as well as by much important legislation which will be noticed in later chapters. The Mutiny was practically confined to the Indian troops of the Bengal army; there was no trouble in Madras, and very little in Bombay. The initial successes of the mutineers won for them the support of some prominent individuals with real or imaginary grievances, but none of the important Princes took their side, and there was no movement which could be described as national; if some of the mutineers restored the Mogul Emperor, others proclaimed a new Peshwā of the Marāthas; and, so far as it is possible to draw any general inference from their conduct, their object was to return to the conditions of the eighteenth century by eliminating the Company's rule. Outside India the movement received no support; Afghanistan remained friendly, while Nepal sent a strong and efficient force to support the Company in Oudh.

In telling the story of the Mutiny, it is well to distinguish the conditions which rendered it possible from the causes which brought it about. Indian mercenary troops had won a high reputation for loyalty to the employers of their choice, but mutiny was not entirely unknown among them; they were at their best in the field, and in the monotonous garrison life of the period they were apt, like other mercenaries, to cherish grievances, formulate demands, and develop exaggerated ideas of their own importance. The

CAUSES OF THE MUTINY

maintenance of discipline was thus a task as difficult as essential. Now the Bengal troops, who were recruited not from Bengal itself but from the country farther west, had had no serious work since the conquest of the Punjab ; even at that period the standard of discipline had for various reasons fallen very low, and it was now still lower. The Indian officers, usually uneducated, and exercising very limited powers, were promoted from the ranks, whose fears and prejudices they shared, and had no prospects of rising to a position of real responsibility. The English officers as a body trusted their men blindly, and were resolutely opposed to any interference from outside ; even Dalhousie, who described the discipline of the army, officers and men alike, as scandalous from top to bottom, had felt unable to effect a reform ; and it was this want of discipline that made the Mutiny possible.

As to the actual causes of the Mutiny, it may be said that, while many of the men had grievances of the ordinary type regarding pay and conditions of service, these were reinforced by a general, if unfounded, apprehension of an attack on their religion and caste. Most of the sepoys were Brāhmans and Rājputs, while large numbers of them came from Oudh, and shared in the discontent which, as we have seen, was provoked by the measures taken after that Province was annexed. The need of a garrison in Burma had induced Dalhousie to order that future enlistments should be for general service, instead of for service within India ; and this order had been misrepresented by agitators as meaning that the men already in service were to be sent across the sea, which according to the ideas then prevalent would have put them ' out of caste.' In the same way, a missionary manifesto had been misrepresented as an official invitation to become Christians ; Canning, it was alleged, had brought out orders to convert the sepoys ; and, speaking generally, it may be said that at the end of the year 1856 they were genuinely alarmed, and were watching for the first overt act in the expected campaign against their faith and institutions.

At this juncture the authorities made a disastrous

blunder. The practice of the time was to bite the ends of cartridges when loading; and some cartridges served out to the sepoys had been greased with animal fat. Here was the overt act for which the sepoys were watching: they were to put into their mouths tallow made from the sacred cow, or lard made from the impure pig, and in this way forced to commit what was to them utter sacrilege, and to undergo unspeakable pollution: such a dastardly trick was more than enough to destroy any sentiment of loyalty among the mass of the sepoys; and of the minority who recognised that it was a blunder, not a trick, very few had the strength to withstand the general sentiment. In this way vague fears were transmuted into blind hate.

It is unnecessary for us to relate in detail the incidents of the struggle which followed. For a time Oudh as a whole, and some smaller areas elsewhere, became to the Company's government enemy's country, while the rest of the Gangetic plain westwards from Patna relapsed largely into anarchy, with a few centres of order here and there; the events which decided the issue took place at three centres, Delhi, Cawnpore and Lucknow, and our description may be confined to these; but some general remarks are required by way of preface. In the first place, such evidence as is available is opposed to the theory that the Mutiny was the result of a wide and well-organised conspiracy; its extension was gradual, and was in great measure the result of the success of the first outbreaks. In the second place, the first outbreaks were as a rule mishandled by the Company's authorities. In the Punjab, John Lawrence, the Chief Commissioner, and his picked staff of officers, acted with effect; the mutinous regiments were disarmed, the administration stood firm, and it was found possible to raise new troops, sufficient to decide the issue at Delhi; but elsewhere indecision or hesitation usually allowed the mutineers to get clear away with their arms. In the third place, there was much savagery on both sides. The mutineers sacked the treasuries, opened the jails, and slaughtered Englishmen at sight; in some instances they slaughtered women and children also. Some of the relieving columns of the Company's

THE PUNJAB AND DELHI

troops were equally savage in their reprisals on the country through which they marched; for a time there was blind hate on both sides, though there were many instances of mutual trust and goodwill among individuals of both races. Lastly, the mutineers found no effective leaders, while on the Company's side able commanders came quickly to the front.

The story of events at Delhi begins in May, 1857, with the mutiny of the sepoys at Meerut, a large military station lying forty miles to the north-east. The mutineers marched to Delhi, where they made common cause with the dependants of the titular Mogul Emperor, who still lived as a pensioner of the Company in the palace of his ancestors; the Moslem population of the city joined in; and thus there came into existence the appearance of an alternative government, still strong in tradition, to which everybody dissatisfied with the Company's rule could rally. John Lawrence immediately recognised the implications of this fact, and, owing mainly to his exertions, English troops from the north-west were before Delhi within a month of the outbreak at Meerut. The walls of the city were, however, too strong to be rushed, there were not enough men for a siege, and the English force took up a position on the Ridge, a line of low hills which commanded the city. Here, amid constant fighting, they were joined by successive reinforcements from the Punjab, while mutineers from various quarters continued to enter the city. In September heavy guns arrived, Delhi fell, and the Emperor was captured. Next year he was formally convicted of rebellion and sent to Burma in confinement; his position was finally abolished and the city and palace of Delhi ceased to have any special significance.

Cawnpore was of importance as one of the chain of military stations stretching up the Gangetic plain, and more particularly as commanding the road across the Ganges to Lucknow; close to it was one of the chief centres of disaffection to the Company's rule. It will be recalled that after the last Marātha war, the ex-Peshwā had been allowed to settle here; and he lived quietly until 1853 on the pension he received from the Company. On his death his adopted son, who is best known by the soubriquet 'the Nana Sahib,' was allowed to retain the estate, but was not favoured with a renewal of the pension, which had lapsed; he resented the refusal and became a bitter enemy of the Company. When some of the sepoys mutinied in June, the Company's commandant placed the few English troops, and the women and children, in an improvised entrenchment, which was besieged by the mutineers under the leadership of the Nana Sahib, recognised by them as Peshwā. After a short time, the commandant accepted the Nana's offer of a safe passage to Allahabad, and his party took their places in thatched barges for the journey by river. The barges were promptly set on fire, grape-shot and bullets were directed on them from the banks, and eventually nearly all the men were slaughtered, while a party of women and children were held for a time as prisoners, but were massacred a fortnight later.

The presence of this hostile force at Cawnpore had an important bearing on events at Lucknow. The elder Lawrence, Sir Henry, had arrived there as Chief Commissioner of Oudh in March, and had done what was possible to rectify his predecessor's mistakes; but he realised clearly that there had not been time to allay the hostility which they had created, and he prepared a refuge in what was known as the Residency, a group of buildings on rising ground which, before annexation, had been occupied by the Company's Resident appointed to the King's Court. Early in June most of the sepoys stationed in Oudh mutinied, the Company's administration disappeared, and in many places the landholders resumed control of what they still regarded as their estates. The ruling power was represented only by the Residency, where less than a thousand British soldiers and about seven hundred loyal sepoys, along with the European non-combatants, were besieged by a much greater force, consisting of the mutineers, strengthened as time went on by parties of the landholders' armed retainers. Lawrence died of wounds early in July, but the defence was maintained under his successor; a relieving column led by Sir Henry Havelock and Sir James Outram arrived near the end of September, after prolonged delays at Cawnpore, but could serve only to strengthen the garrison; and in November a second force under Sir Colin Campbell, the Commander-in-Chief, was able to withdraw the wounded and non-combatants.

The Commander-in-Chief had now to restore authority in the country at large. When once he had destroyed the forces of the Nana Sahib, the districts between the Ganges and Jumna were securely in his possession, but for a time he was in danger of an attack from the south. Early in 1858 columns from Bombay and Madras cleared Central India and Bundelkhand, and the Commander-in-Chief, having driven the enemy finally from Lucknow, was thus free to hunt down the bodies of mutineers who had spread over Oudh. It was a tedious task, for the enemy gradually disintegrated into scattered bands of marauders, but by the end of 1858 the great bulk of them had been accounted for, and a year later none were left. Meanwhile the civil administration was restored in Oudh, the decision to assess the revenue directly on the peasants was reversed, and most of the landholders received the estates which they claimed.

The news of the Mutiny produced both excitement and anxiety in England, and there was much bitter controversy over details; but the country as a whole decided, almost instinctively, that the rule of the Company had become an anachronism, and by the Act for the Better Government of India, passed in August, 1858, the authority of the Directors and of the Board of Control was transferred to a Secretary of State, responsible, as a member of the Cabinet, to Parliament. In the following November, Canning, now styled Viceroy as well as Governor-General, formally announced the change by publishing a royal proclamation, embodying a declaration of policy which was accepted in India as the fundamental document of the new constitution.

The changes in the machinery of government in India which resulted from this Act and others passed in the next few years affected mainly the army, the law courts, the legislature, and the central executive. Each of the Company's three armies had contained British as well as Indian troops; henceforward no British troops were recruited for the Indian armies, but the 'army in India,' to use the phrase now current, consisted partly of Indian cavalry and infantry under British officers serving permanently in the country, and partly of artillery, cavalry and infantry of the British army, the units of which came to India for a term of years. Local sentiment served to maintain the cumbrous organisation of the forces in three separate armies until almost the end of the century.

The dual system of law courts, which had survived from the time of Warren Hastings, came to an end in 1861, when a single High Court was established by charter in each of the three presidency towns, independent of the executive government, and exercising both civil and criminal powers throughout the area of its jurisdiction. Five years later, a similar court was established for the North-Western Provinces, but elsewhere the evolution was gradual; as a rule, a Judicial Commissioner was appointed for each new province, but when work increased in quantity and importance, he gave way to a Chief Court, not very different in practice from a High Court, and aspiring to become one eventually. In all cases, however, the principal court, whatever its designation might be, stood out as the guardian of the Rule of Law, watching over its working in the lower courts, and enforcing its observance on the executive authorities as well as on the people at large.

Up to 1853 legislation had been passed by the Governor-General and his Executive Council. The Charter Act of that year had constituted a Legislative Council of twelve officials; and in 1861, for the first time, provision was made for the nomination of unofficial legislators. The legislature now consisted of the members of the Executive Council together with additional members, at least half of whom were to be unofficial; but its functions were limited to discussing bills, and for many years to come questions could not be asked or resolutions moved. The power of legislation was restored to Madras and Bombay, with their Executive Councils

CHANGES IN ADMINISTRATION

similarly reinforced for the purpose ; a Legislative Council was established for the province of Bengal ; and power was given to establish others in the North-Western Provinces and the Punjab, but these came later, the former in 1886 and the latter in 1898.

The working of the Executive Council had been remodelled by Canning, who introduced what may be called the portfolio system of business. Each member was then placed in charge of a department or group of departments, in which he issued orders in the name of the Government of India, while the Council as a whole handled large questions of policy, and decided cases where the departments clashed. This portfolio system was legalised under an Act of 1861, which also increased the strength of the Council and authorised the appointment of an expert, financial or other, from outside the regular services. The Council thus came to consist of the Governor-General himself, who always held the 'political' portfolio, the Legal Member, who was a barrister appointed from England, the Military Member chosen from the army, and either three civil servants or two civil servants and one expert, among whom the remaining portfolios were distributed. The Commander-in-Chief sat on the Council as an extraordinary member, representing the army, but not holding a portfolio. The power of the Governor-General to overrule a majority of the Council in certain emergencies was retained, but its employment was rare.

All these changes in India may justly be described as necessary improvements in the machinery of government. The change in England was also necessary, but it had one undesirable result which its authors did not foresee : it operated to deprive the bureaucratic machine of that impetus from outside, which, as we have said in an earlier chapter, had been provided in some measure by Parliament. The India Office was now merely one of several ministries ; the Opposition, and its Press, was concerned with it mainly as furnishing potential 'party capital,' while the supporters of the party in power were disposed to let it alone. There were usually a few members of Parliament interested in

India for itself, but they carried little weight; the annual debate, when the Indian budget was presented in the Commons, came to be a byword for a few hours of futile boredom; and if an Indian topic became prominent, it was either as a matter of English party politics, or else as affecting the general diplomatic situation.

In this atmosphere, the Secretary of State, charged with the superintendence and control of the Government of India, was not likely to initiate reforms which might cause trouble in Parliament; and his initiative was further restricted by the Council appointed to provide him with expert knowledge. Most of the members of this Council had Indian experience, but it tended to become out of date during their prolonged tenure of office, at first 'during pleasure,' and from 1869 onwards ten years, which could be extended to fifteen. The Council was given large powers of controlling expenditure, and was active in the performance of its functions, but, from its constitution, it was more likely to criticise or delay, than to initiate or press forward, large schemes of reform.

In England then there was nothing to take the place of the independent parliamentary enquiries which during the first half of the century had scrutinised the administration from the outside. In India, public opinion was practically voiceless until late in the 'eighties, and the Indian press, though its influence was extending, had not yet developed in the direction of constructive criticism, while its exuberant and sometimes scurrilous tone repelled most English readers. The only possibility of effective independent scrutiny lay in the personality of the Viceroy; the instance of Lord Dufferin shows, as we shall see, that a Viceroy might intervene with effect; but, as a rule, the successive holders of the office, immersed in ceremonial or departmental routine, were content to be the head of the administration rather than look at it from the outside. Their environment, too, was unfavourable. From 1864 onwards the Government of India spent about half of each year at the summer capital of Simla, where contacts were purely official; in its winter capital, Calcutta, its contacts were less with Indians than with the influential and vocal European population of merchants,

ISOLATION OF THE GOVERNMENT

industrialists and professional men, supported by an able and enterprising press; and it was only in his periodical tours that the Viceroy, in the intervals of ceremonies, could hope to learn at first hand something of the currents of Indian life and thought.

These facts are important, for they form the background of the story of the half-century which we are approaching. In essence the story is one of an exceptionally able and high-minded bureaucracy, striving with remarkable success to do more and more for the people of India, and for the most part slow to recognise that, under the new forces and influences which had been set in motion, Indians were beginning to want to do these things for themselves.

CHAPTER XLIV

ECONOMIC CHANGES, 1860–1880

Viceroys: Lord Canning, 1856–1862;
Lord Elgin (eighth earl), 1862, died 1863;
Sir John Lawrence, 1864–1869;
Lord Mayo, 1869, assassinated, 1872;
Lord Northbrook, 1872–1876;
Lord Lytton, 1876–1880.

The two decades which followed the suppression of the Mutiny must be regarded as constituting one of the formative periods in the history of India, a period marked by changes in economic and cultural life which were to produce their full results in later years. These changes originated in the British Provinces, and extended slowly to the States, from which at this time there were few signs of leadership in any branch of activity; for the rest of the century the States must be thought of as following the Provinces at some distance. In this chapter we shall confine our attention to the economic sphere, and we may begin with the unification of Indian markets and their effective linking with the markets of the rest of the world.

The opening of the Suez Canal in 1869 reduced the voyage for cargo boats between London and Bombay from more than three months to about twenty-five days, and, for the first time in history, rendered possible a large-scale trade with Europe in Indian agricultural products. The Indian seaboard was thus linked to the markets of England, France, Italy and Germany; while the extension of railways, posts and telegraphs tended steadily to make the whole country one market instead of many. In Dalhousie's time it was still true that surplus food might be rotting in one part of

India while people were dying of starvation in another ; forty years later, the supply of food was being distributed throughout the country in accordance with needs in the ordinary course of commerce, and, except in a few tracts which were still inaccessible, the possibility of acute famine, in ordinary circumstances, had passed away ; for if there was not enough food in India itself, supplies could be drawn from Burma and more distant countries.

A less obvious result of the new conditions was that the economic balance between town and country was gradually restored. The extraordinary cheapness of food, which was noticed by so many of the early European visitors to India, can safely be attributed to the working of the revenue system. Under the Moguls, most of the peasants had to sell from one-third to one-half of their total produce within a few weeks of the harvest, merely to pay the revenue due from their land ; and the recurring harvest glut, which is a commonplace of rural economics, was thus always to be seen in India in an aggravated form. When, however, export to Europe became feasible, a limit was set to the possible fall of price at harvest, for exporters were busy in the markets, and Indian towns could no longer count on getting food below the cost dictated by world-conditions ; the gradual rise in the level of Indian prices which resulted from this and other causes was bitterly resented by townsmen, whose incomes were in most cases fixed in money, but it did more than anything else to tide the country at large over the period of agrarian difficulties which, as we shall see, was impending. The new export of grain operated also to secure a reserve of food against seasons of drought. More food was now grown in ordinary years than India could eat because there was a market for the surplus abroad ; in a bad season the rise in Indian prices put a stop to export for the time, and the entire produce of the country was available for its needs.

Indian merchants and bankers were quick to avail themselves of the new facilities for communication, and their business expanded, but its nature did not change materially. Meanwhile a European commercial and financial organisation had grown up, almost independent of that which already existed. In the early days the European firms established in the presidency towns were often bankers as well as merchants, and the recurring crises, resulting from injudicious speculation, caused heavy losses to many English officers, but had little effect on the country at large. Segregation of banking from trading followed in due course, and in 1860 the three presidency banks were already well-established concerns. The capital of these banks had been provided mainly by Europeans, except in Bombay, where a substantial proportion was subscribed at the outset by Parsees; their management and methods were definitely English; their operations were, at first, almost confined to the presidency towns; and such connection as they had with the indigenous system of finance came chiefly from their willingness to discount bills drawn by the more important Indian merchants. A new era seemed to be dawning in 1860, when the principle of limited liability in banking was for the first time recognised by law, but disaster quickly followed. During the civil war in the United States, Indian merchants in Bombay made very large profits by the sale of cotton to Lancashire; a wild outbreak of speculation followed; banks and financial companies were floated in large numbers; nearly all of them collapsed in the crisis of 1865; and thereafter, while a few additional banks were founded by European effort, Indians for a time left this branch of business alone.

The operations of the European commercial firms expanded largely after the opening of the Suez Canal, and it was due mainly to their efforts that, to borrow a picturesque phrase, the canal was extended to the foot of the Himalayas. In India, as in other countries, unorganised peasants usually got the worst of the market; the local buyers thought less of the market price than of the need of the individual seller; they kept most of a rise in price, but passed on a fall in its entirety; and they maintained or extended a variety of market customs, all of which operated in their own favour. A change came in each important country market when the railway reached it. The buyers of European firms appeared, offering a fixed price justified by the world-conditions, paying silver on the spot for what they bought, using accurate weights, making no deductions except for defects of quality, and in fact giving a demonstration of methods of trading of which Indian peasants had no previous experience. The peasant who was free to sell benefited immediately; his neighbour, who was in debt to a merchant and bound by his contract to sell only to his creditor, was less fortunate; but the general level of harvest prices was gradually raised, and the effect of the seasonal glut was mitigated for the country as a whole.

In industry, the weavers and other artisans who worked independently continued to suffer, but factories began to multiply. The low revenue-tariff on imports, ranging from five to ten per cent., afforded no material protection to these artisans, who could not compete with the factory-made goods of Europe, and such protection as it gave was lost on its abolition at the close of our period; and the artistic handicrafts in particular were depressed, for Indian taste was now at its lowest, and foreign ornamental goods were preferred merely as such. Some of the most characteristic crafts were preserved from extinction only by the efforts of individual English officers.

The railway had already reached the Bengal coal-field when the Mutiny broke out, and after its suppression mines and factories increased hand in hand. The first jute mill in the neighbourhood of Calcutta was opened in 1854, and the number increased rapidly. In Bombay, the number of cotton mills rose from ten in 1861 to over fifty in 1880, and the industry spread to other centres, such as Ahmadābād (1861), Cawnpore (1869), Madras (1874), and Nāgpur (1877). On a smaller scale other industries also appeared in these and other centres, producing leather, paper, woollen goods, and an increasing variety of manufactures from raw materials available in the country. In nearly all cases the pioneer factories were established, financed, and managed by Europeans, whose success brought in Indian competitors later on; and as a rule European management continued for a long time, though to some extent the ownership passed gradually to Indians, as they acquired the habit of investing in shares. The cotton industry in Bombay, however, was for some time owned and managed mainly by Parsees, while that of Ahmadābād, the second centre of spinning and weaving, was created by Hindu capital and enterprise. By the end of our period the need for factory legislation had arisen, and the Factory Act of 1881 prohibited the labour of children under seven and prescribed the fencing of machinery.

The employment provided by railways, mines and factories came at a time when it was wanted, for the pressure of population on the land, the outstanding new feature of the nineteenth century, was now becoming manifest by its results. The population question cannot be placed on a firm statistical basis, for the first complete census of India was not taken until 1881 ; but enough is known about the past to justify the statements that the birth-rate was normally high, and the tendency to increase rapid, subject to the operation of the familiar ' positive checks,' war, pestilence and famine. Sufficient has been said about war and famine in preceding chapters : as regards pestilence, there is no doubt that malaria, cholera, and smallpox have been endemic in India for an indefinite number of centuries, while bubonic plague, the fourth great scourge, has been imported at intervals, and has died out after a period of very heavy mortality. The knowledge of the aetiology of these diseases which has been acquired during the last half-century indicates that devastating epidemics imply a dense population, so that, while war was due to men, and famine to the weather, pestilence might almost be called a self-acting check on the natural increase.

In 1860 internal warfare was a thing of the past, mortality from epidemics had not recently been conspicuous, and, as we have said, there had been a respite from famine for nearly a quarter of a century, so that the natural growth of population must have been rapid. During our period it was supplemented in the North by small numbers of immigrants from neighbouring countries, attracted by the peaceful

THE POPULATION PROBLEM

conditions of life, while in the South it was counteracted by a certain amount of emigration. Ceylon had long attracted settlers from the mainland, and the annexation of Lower Burma in 1852 led to a new and progressive demand for Indian labourers in that country; but, with these exceptions, emigration, from the sixteenth century at least, had meant the slave trade. Slaves were brought down to the coast by Indian merchants, to be transported thence by shippers of various nations; and we know from Dutch records that the supply was ordinarily ample, but that it almost ceased for some years after each recurring famine. In 1789 Cornwallis prohibited the export of slaves from the Company's India, but it continued for some time longer from the French ports, and it was eventually replaced by the system known as indentured emigration.

Early in the nineteenth century the progressive abolition of slavery was followed by a demand for free labourers in various regions of the world, which looked to India for a supply, and found Indians, the successors of the slave-dealers, ready to act as recruiters. In return for his passage, an intending emigrant bound himself to work for a term of years, at the end of which he was entitled to benefits, such as repatriation, which varied in different cases; and it was labourers so recruited who furnished the bulk of the large Indian population to be found in Mauritius and Natal, in British Guiana, in Trinidad, and in various other islands. At its worst, the new system was very like the slave trade which it replaced; the recruiter, paid by results, cajoled ignorant men and women by lavish promises, bound them to him by loans of cash, and hustled them down to the seaboard, where the foreign exporting agencies, equally intent on making a profit, got them on board as quickly as they could. At its best, it was a valuable outlet for the surplus population, and many of the emigrants prospered abroad in a way they could never have done at home. The Indian administration endeavoured to prevent abuses, and the system continued to operate throughout the nineteenth century, undoubtedly a great improvement on the slave trade, but never with entirely satisfactory results.

In any case, neither immigration nor emigration proceeded on a scale large enough to affect the population problem as a whole. Under the Rule of Law the land had to provide subsistence for most of the natural increase, and also for the weavers and the other displaced artisans, for the soldiers no longer needed, and for many of those who had been living by lawless means: the result was the emergence of competition for productive land, a thing which scarcely anyone in India understood. Would-be peasants offered rents which they could not hope to pay; landholders accepted the highest offer, and evicted tenants in possession to make room for higher bidders; there was a scramble for land, and a scramble for rent, which threatened to destroy the stability essential to any system of peasant agriculture. This new danger appeared first in Bengal, and spread gradually over the landholders' country in northern India. The earliest attempt to cope with it by law was an Act passed in 1859, which aimed at protecting the bulk of the peasant-tenants from arbitrary eviction, and limiting the landholders' power to enhance rent unreasonably, or, in phrases which were to become familiar in England, its main objects were 'fixity of tenure' and 'fair rent.'

The period which we are considering was thus marked by the beginning of the struggle, which is not yet over, to induce the rural population to take long views instead of short. We cannot even outline the course of this struggle, for, while the first Act was general, the subsequent legislation was passed for each province separately, and was marked by progressive divergence in accordance with local conditions; but, speaking generally, the periodical attempts to stop evasions of the law produced an extremely complicated mass of rules the working of which taxed the administration severely. The broad result was that during the rest of the century the rise in rents lagged behind the rise in prices which, as we have seen, was in progress, and peasant-tenants, taken in the mass, remained in enjoyment of a portion of the economic rent, which in the absence of interference would have been taken by the landholders. The use which they made of this margin cannot be stated in quantitative terms,

Some of them improved their holdings, some of them secured a modest rise in the standard of living, some of them hoarded it, some of them spent it unproductively on marriages or funerals, and some of them used it to purchase leisure for themselves; the broad fact is that, owing to the progressive rise in prices, they had a margin at their disposal, and this eased the whole agrarian position at a time of unprecedented strain.

Something must be added regarding what we have called the purchase of leisure. The peasant in many cases sub-let his holding, or part of it, at the full economic rent, or more, and strove to live on the difference between the limited rent which he paid and the exorbitant rent which he could extract from his under-tenants. This meant the old evils in new forms, and legislators who had started to protect tenants against landholders found themselves compelled either to prohibit sub-letting, or to protect the under-tenant against the tenant, thus adding further complications to a body of rules which in the interests of the people ought to be as simple as possible.

So far we have written of the peasants who paid rent to landholders. In southern India, where most of the peasants paid revenue to the State, the margin left to them was relatively more substantial, because the standard of assessment was, as we have said, being generally lowered, while the progressive rise in prices during the long period for which the assessment remained unaltered meant a gradual increase in their resources. There was consequently greater scope for sub-letting in the South than in the North, and, as time went on, many peasants transformed themselves into petty landholders, living a hard, if leisured, life on what they could extract from their tenants.

It was in the South, too, that problems of agricultural indebtedness became pressing during this period. Peasants everywhere need finance, and in India the work of financing them fell almost entirely on the local money-lender, usually a produce-merchant as well as a banker. We know very little of the money-lender's business in Mogul times, but the high revenue then charged certainly made agricultural land an undesirable investment, even if investment had been possible, while it is probable that the summary justice of the revenue officers favoured the peasant rather than his creditor. The changes which we have described gave land a capital value as an investment, while the new law courts showed no favour, but insisted on the letter of the bond. The right to sell or mortgage their holdings was enjoyed by comparatively few tenants, but it was general among those peasants who paid revenue, whether individually in the South, or as members of the village community in the North. The money-lender, whose main business was in loans on personal security, involving very high interest and occasional heavy loss of capital, was glad to give credit on the security of land; but the bonds prepared by him, and accepted blindly by illiterate peasants, were very often unconscionable, and their rigorous enforcement by the courts gave rise to popular resentment, which in some localities became a menace to the public peace. During the period we are discussing, the trouble came to a head in parts of Bombay, and was met in 1879 by local legislation of a palliative character, but the general problem of peasant indebtedness was left over to be handled in the twentieth century.

The larger landholders, as well as the peasants, were prone to get into debt, not for improving their estates but to meet their personal expenditure. It was not easy for tribal chiefs or soldiers of fortune, brought up in the doctrine that might was right, to settle down as landholders under the Rule of Law, quietly managing their estates, cherishing their tenants, and accumulating reserves against bad seasons to come. Improvidence and extravagance were common, and many estates passed finally into the hands of money-lenders, who, as a rule, made bad landholders, concerned mainly to secure a monopoly of credit in the estates they purchased. The administration found itself compelled to check this process, and arrangements were made to bring improvident landholders under the management of the Court of Wards, an institution designed primarily for the protection of minors and secluded ladies; the court was able in many cases to restore an estate to a condition of

THE POSITION OF AGRICULTURE

solvency, and not a few of the great families of India owe their present position to its intervention.

Apart from debt, the worst feature of the peasants' life about this period was the progressive subdivision of holdings. Customs akin to primogeniture are exceedingly rare in India, and under the ordinary law, whether Hindu or Moslem, the death of a peasant is followed by the division of his holding among his heirs. In Mogul times, there was room for a family to expand, but, when the productive land was already fully occupied, expansion was no longer possible, and the original holding had to fill a gradually increasing number of mouths. The result was necessarily a progressive increase in the number of uneconomic holdings, that is to say, holdings which could not yield a livelihood to the persons who worked them; then followed debt till credit was exhausted, and eventually a descent to the ranks of labourers or criminals.

Increase of debt and subdivision of holdings were thus the dark side of the rural transformation which was progressing during this period. The most obvious remedy, the provision of alternative means of livelihood sufficient to reduce the pressure on the soil, was scarcely beginning to emerge; the most valuable palliative, the increase of production by the application of science, was already being talked about, but action in this direction came later; and, during the rest of the nineteenth century, the sole great force working in favour of the peasant was the rise in prices, which meant that he had to sell a progressively smaller proportion of his produce in order to pay his rent or revenue and provide the cash he needed for other purposes.

From the peasant we turn to the planter—the person or firm or company that raises crops on a large scale by hired labour. The area ' planted ' in India has never been a large proportion of the total, but the system has had results of considerable economic and social importance. During the period we are describing it was being applied in particular to the production of tea and coffee. The earliest 'gardens,' as the tea-plantations are called, were established in Assam soon after 1850, and in other places a little later ; in 1860 there were already over sixty gardens, and by 1880 the product had become one of the main exports of India, a position which it continues to hold. Practically all the gardens were established with European capital, mostly on land which had been lying waste ; the management also was in European hands ; and the additional demand for labour, in some cases brought from distant regions, made a substantial addition to the economic resources of the country.

In southern India coffee had been grown in a small way for a long time ; it began to be 'planted' about 1860, and for some years promised to become almost as important as tea, but severe competition from other countries has prevented this result. Indigo, the third great planting crop of the century, has a different history. We have seen that the European market for this dye was captured by the West Indies from about the year 1660 onwards ; a century later the West Indies had turned to other crops, and the Company then re-established the export from India. A planting industry quickly grew up, first in Bengal, but later farther west, and in the earlier period almost entirely in European hands ; but it differed from planting in the strict sense, because the indigo planters obtained most of the crop, not by growing it themselves, but by purchase from peasants to whom they had made advances in cash.

This practice was already known in India when the Company began its operations in the seventeenth century. The usual arrangement was that a peasant, on taking an advance, bound himself to grow a certain area of the crop, and to sell the produce to his creditor, ordinarily at a price below the market rate ; the result was often a pernicious form of debt-slavery, for at the end of the season a peasant might find himself still in debt, and then he was practically bound to do whatever his creditor wanted, to grow whatever area was ordered and take whatever price was offered. Sometimes, at least, this result was deliberately sought, the creditor's aim being to secure control over a submissive body

THE PLANTING SYSTEM

of peasants, so that he could be sure of getting as much produce as he wanted at his own price; this attitude was adopted by most of the European planters in Bengal, and in 1860 the endeavours which they made to force peasants to grow indigo rather than other and more profitable crops led to widespread riots, and to one of the earliest outbreaks of racial feeling in the press. In later years there were similar though less serious difficulties in Bihār and Benares, where the planters were mainly Europeans, and in the country near Delhi, where they were mainly Indian landholders; and the danger of trouble continued to exist until the production of indigo dye from coal rendered the crop commercially unimportant.

We now turn to the wage-earners. In Mogul times, the labourers in the towns and seaports were as a rule paid in cash at customary rates, but rates so near the subsistence-level that they had to be increased temporarily when the price of food was unusually high. The railways, mines and factories initiated a change, for their demand for labour was quickly felt in the market; competition tended to take the place of custom, and urban wages began to rise. The effect in the villages is more difficult to describe, for there the labourers did not regard themselves as free; the individual expected, and was expected, to work for some particular employer, and his remuneration was usually made up of a ration of grain with various periodical benefits and allowances which, taken together, just about kept him and his family alive. The call of factory industry was not at first heard in this environment; but from the outset railways and mines drew many of their hands from the neighbouring villages, and, as time went on, labour from one group of villages after another began to find its way to distant factories, or mines, or tea-gardens, attracted by the relatively high wages they offered, and conditions in the villages changed by slow degrees. Landholders and peasants bitterly resented the idea that their labourers should go elsewhere, and adhered as long as they could to the old rates; but a rise in wages set in sporadically, here an extra halfpenny a day, there a more liberal allowance of food, or a small ration of tobacco or some other luxury ; and the movement was thus initiated which was to produce general results later on.

To complete this economic survey, we may notice the rise of upper and middle classes not directly dependent for subsistence on the government of the moment, a change which belongs to the whole century rather than the portion of it with which this chapter is primarily concerned. In Mogul times the upper class lived almost entirely by grants or assignments of revenue, resumable by a stroke of the pen ; most of the few professional men looked to Court patronage for prosperity, if not for subsistence ; and, apart from priests, merchants and bankers, there was scarcely a middle class at all. Under the Company's rule, the great landholders emerged as an upper class, while the middle class was reinforced by the smaller landholders, the extension of trade, the introduction of large-scale industry, and the growth of professions.

The case of the landholders in general is obvious, but something must be said here of a special cause which operated in Bengal to produce the large middle class characteristic of that Province. We have seen that the land-revenue of Bengal had been fixed once for all, leaving to the landholders the entire prospective increment. Many of them proceeded to alienate this increment in advance, by giving permanent leases of portions of their estates, usually in return for substantial premiums, and these leases were eagerly taken by local merchants, who abandoned trade and set up as gentlemen of leisure. For a time they prospered, but as families grew in size, and the cost of living rose, the leasehold estates became insufficient to yield a gentleman's income ; the young men had to look for other means of livelihood ; and the result was the emergence of the problem of middle-class unemployment, which is now more acute in Bengal than elsewhere.

With two exceptions, the professions were slow to develop. Those Indians who qualified as doctors or engineers or architects usually entered the public service,

RISE OF NEW PROFESSIONS

and private practitioners were as yet scarcely to be found outside a few of the largest cities; but the extension of education was leading to an increased demand for teachers in private institutions, while lawyers multiplied with great rapidity, and were to be found wherever a law court existed. As we have said in Chapter XXXVI, the legal profession was no part of the older life of India, and the first practitioners were Europeans. The Indian profession grew up mainly in the Company's courts established by Warren Hastings. A class of men, calling themselves agents,[1] appeared in these, who, having picked up a smattering of procedure, conducted cases, or any other business which they could get, for persons who were willing to pay; the results were so unsatisfactory that Regulations passed in 1793 for Bengal and Madras, and somewhat later for Bombay, directed the courts to enrol suitable Indians as pleaders, and thus established the nucleus of the profession, which by subsequent legislation gradually acquired a definite character and status, and in the period which we are describing was already attracting most of the best brains in the country, apart from those employed in the public service or in commerce.

Three main causes operated to produce this result. In the first place, there was a real demand for lawyers. The eagerness of so many Indians for a fight, in court if not in the field, sufficed to ensure ample incomes for the leaders of the profession, if not for the rank and file; while the large increase in the number of courts, the rapid growth of the statute-book in complexity as well as volume, the extension of commerce and industry, and the general development of the country all combined to furnish opportunities for more and more litigation. In the second place, the type of intellect which had produced the refinements of Indian philosophy would naturally prefer words to things, minute legal distinctions to the facts of science or the details of trade or industry. In the third place, other openings for

[1] The common Indian name for a practising lawyer is *vakīl*. Etymologically the word means an agent of any kind, and its specialisation to denote a pleader occurred in the course of the nineteenth century.

the literate classes were few. Teachers and journalists were poorly paid, doctors in private practice could scarcely make a living, there was as yet little demand for Indian engineers or architects, the new industries were staffed almost entirely by Europeans, commerce was in the hands of particular classes, there was no career in the army or at sea ; for a young man who had no special connections or influence, who could not gain admission to the public service, and who had not the exceptional gifts required to strike out a new line for himself, the choice lay between a low-paid clerkship and the law. The result was, however, more important than the causes which produced it ; all over the British provinces, there was now a large body of able men, united by common interests, masters of the spoken and the written word, and imbued with the independent spirit of the English Bar, which for many years set the standard of the profession in every High Court. It was mainly these men who, in the next period, were to bring politics into the life of India.

CHAPTER XLV

CULTURAL DEVELOPMENTS, 1860–1880

In the cultural sphere the most important development of this period was the advance towards national unification. We have said that in Dalhousie's time it was nearly impossible to trace any common feeling in India, but by 1880 a common feeling had come into existence among the literate classes, and was already beginning to seek for means of expression. To a large extent this development was a by-product of the activities of the administration. The extension of railways, posts and telegraphs furnished a necessary condition precedent; the administration had to think of India as a whole, and the general legislation which characterised the period, together with the operation of the doctrine of administrative uniformity, produced a very definite response among the literate classes, who were now brought face to face with the idea of unity; more important than all was the spread of English education, on the lines laid down by the Despatch of 1854. At this point, however, we must recall what we have said in Chapter I, that the history of the country discloses not merely the obvious tendencies towards segregation, but also an underlying tendency towards unity. Had the administrative pressure which operated at this time in India been applied to Europe as a whole, the result would certainly not have been to evoke a common European feeling: it would rather have intensified the regional and separatist sentiments of the various nations. But India differed from Europe in the tendency towards unity which already existed, and the pressure from above operated to reinforce this tendency, and to bring it more definitely into the region of consciousness;

the ties which united Indians began to be talked about and thought about ; the forces which made for segregation became relatively less important, though they did not entirely disappear.

The period which we are considering was the golden age of the Indian statute-book. The pioneer work of Macaulay and his colleagues at last produced results—in codes of civil and criminal procedure, in the formulation of the rules of evidence, and in a large number of Acts declaring substantive law, headed by the Indian Penal Code, which quickly took its place as one of the outstanding laws of the world. Judges, magistrates and lawyers were now concerned in the course of their daily work with a uniform system of law ; in whatever province they might be, they had to study the rulings of the High Courts in Calcutta and Bombay, in Madras and Allahabad ; they saw varying interpretations harmonised by the final court of appeal, the Judicial Committee of the Privy Council ; and they realised that the Rule of Law now meant the rule of one law for all India.

Administrative activities produced similar results. The able and energetic men who formed the central government were determined that whatever was done should be done in the best possible way ; they compared methods followed in different provinces, and urged all to adopt those which appeared to be most suitable ; and in this way the idea of administrative uniformity throughout India steadily came to the front, until it became a doctrine, and the advantage of uniformity could be urged as by itself a reason for change. The over-centralisation which adherence to this doctrine did so much to produce was to become a serious evil later on ; but the immediate effect of its operation was to popularise the idea of the unity of India among the officials and clerks who handled the growing mass of administrative codes, resolutions prescribing policy, and other documents issued from the centre ; like the judges and lawyers, they were forced to think of India as a whole. Many of these official documents were used by journalists as raw material, so that the ideas which they contained reached everybody who read a newspaper ; and it may fairly be said that the unity of

India was pressed on all sections of the literate classes, with the exception of the more conservative elements in the world of commerce, which as yet had scarcely begun to concern themselves with the press.

The educational policy which had been laid down in 1854 was vigorously pursued, and schools and colleges multiplied. Their courses of English studies were determined mainly by the syllabus of the university which examined their students, and here too the idea of uniformity was prominent; Calcutta set the standard for the whole of northern India, and it was not materially different from the standards set for the South by Madras and Bombay. The courses were literary rather than scientific, a fact which will not excite surprise when it is recalled that in the 'sixties science was still fighting its way into the public schools in England; even where science was prescribed, the expense of the necessary equipment prevented most colleges from giving adequate training in it; while at this time there was no demand for Indian science-graduates in the sphere of industry. Now English history, from Elizabeth to Victoria, and English literature, from Shakespeare and Milton to Wordsworth and Tennyson, form no mean school of national unity, while the Englishmen who at first set the tone of the teaching were in general inspired by the robust patriotism and love of freedom which characterised the mid-Victorian age; it was in this atmosphere that the new generation of Indian students grew up.

The universities, unendowed as they were, and dependent for their income mainly on examination fees, were forced to aim at quantity rather than quality in their output. A degree was a qualification for employment, but the market did not as yet distinguish one degree from another; the 'pass,' or ordinary degree, was in greater demand than 'honours,' and the 'bachelor' seldom aspired to become 'master' or 'doctor' in the subjects of his study. A generation had still to elapse before Indian universities began to be centres of advanced study, but the ordinary graduate was nevertheless a national asset, with faculties sufficiently developed to be of real value to the country.

At the same time a few Indian students were coming to England, either to secure professional training or to enter for the examination which, as we shall see, now offered admission to the Indian Civil Service. The obstacles in their way were serious, for the expense was heavy, while at this period the social rule was absolute that a Hindu was automatically put out of caste by a lengthy voyage across the sea, and his readmission required ceremonies which cost much money, and were in some respects repulsive. The origin of this social rule is unknown. The early spread of Indian culture over Indo-China, Java and other regions shows that it is not a survival of a primitive taboo, while the imaginative literature of the eleventh century treats sea voyages as quite ordinary incidents in the life of Hindus of the higher castes. In the seventeenth century, however, foreign visitors noticed that such voyages were very rare, and by about 1800 they had been entirely abandoned. The rule continued to be respected up to the end of the nineteenth century, but it is now obsolete; during the period we are considering it operated effectively to ensure that the students who came to England were few in number, and men of exceptional energy and force of character. As a rule they were welcomed, but the earliest arrivals were debarred from Oxford, Cambridge and the Inns of Court by the old law which required subscription to the Church of England, and they studied either in London or in the Scottish universities, where 'tests' were not in force. The law on this subject was, however, changed in the 'fifties, and at this time Indian students were subject to no such restrictions in England. As we have said, the number of those who came was small, but most of them were successful, and later on they contributed very largely to the development of Indian public life.

The Despatch of 1854 had provided for primary education in the vernacular as well as for higher education in English, and, in spite of the hindrance caused by the want of adequate funds, a substantial measure of success was attained in urban areas by the schools established under it. In the villages, where money was still scarcer, less progress was made, for as a rule the peasants were not enthusiastic, and many of them were definitely hostile; the generation of peasants which grew up during this period remained substantially illiterate. Possibly this was not an unmixed evil, for as yet very little had been done to devise a curriculum of primary teaching suited to a peasant population, and the effect of the instruction given on urban lines was often, as in other countries, to tempt the best of the village boys into the towns, where they were not wanted, and to turn good peasants into indifferent clerks.

Along with the extension of literacy in the towns came a progressive increase in the output of vernacular prose, and also a closer adaptation to the needs of the public. Earlier in the century the pioneers of prose had enriched their medium by borrowing extensively from the classical languages—from Arabic and Persian in the case of Urdu, in other cases from Sanskrit—and the result had often been to produce matter which ordinary readers, unversed in the classics, could hardly understand; but as time went on, the excess of pedantry tended to disappear, common names were preferred for common things, and the language became at once more flexible and more intelligible. The great majority of the writers had received an English education, and it can scarcely be doubted that the change was due in large measure to their familiarity with a living language so well suited to express the ideas of the time; while the forms in which much of their output appeared, particularly in the case of works of fiction, bear testimony to the influence of English models. It is no paradox therefore to say that the decision to concentrate on teaching in English, which was taken under Macaulay's influence, has contributed largely to the development of the vernaculars into languages in which modern education can be effectively conducted.

The literary output of the period naturally varied in quality; much of it was worthless, and masterpieces were rare; but there was a substantial volume of good workmanship, worth reading for itself, and at once recording and stimulating the new impetus which the century had brought. The same cannot be said of other branches of art. Indian painting was scarcely heard of, though a few artists continued to work on traditional lines, mostly in places remote from the centres of intellectual life. Indian sculpture, too, continued to exist, but statues and monuments were ordered from England as a matter of course. Most of the public buildings belonging to the days of the Company, as well as to the period now under consideration, were purely utilitarian, the work of engineers rather than architects; but for a few of the more important edifices the Company and its successors adopted European styles, some of them stately and well-suited to the climate, others reflecting the eccentricities of contemporary English taste, but all alike unrelated to Indian tradition, and their example had been followed by some Indian rulers. English architects were, however, now beginning to seek for inspiration from Indian, or at least oriental, sources with results visible in many of the buildings constructed in recent times.

It was in this period, too, that the preservation of monuments of the past was seriously taken in hand. The tradition of vandalism was strong in India, both Hindu and Moslem, where it was generally held that religious merit was acquired by new foundations rather than the maintenance of those already in existence; men built grandly, but they seldom repaired the work of others; and great buildings were left to decay or used as quarries by the neighbours. There was much vandalism also in the Company's time, when, as we have said, utilitarian considerations were predominant, and a coat of whitewash might suffice to turn a frescoed mausoleum into a convenient rest-house for travellers. Some fitful attempts at conservation had been made from the time of Lord Minto down, but the first effective measure was the appointment of an archaeological surveyor in 1861; ten years later the Archaeological Survey was formally established; and thenceforward the work of saving the records, and the relics, of the past proceeded steadily.

The influences which were leading the way towards national unification did not, as we have said, entirely eliminate separatist tendencies. They operated also on a smaller scale to foster what may be called regional patriotism, and thus to produce the situation which later on was to be so puzzling to foreigners ; in the loose language of some sections of the popular press, there was not only the Indian ' nation,' but other ' nations ' forming part of it, the Sikh, or the Bengali, or the Marātha, as the case might be, and at times there was an apparent clash between the wider patriotism and the narrower ; but the expression of these developments belongs to the end of the century. The period we are discussing was characterised rather by movements which affected separately the adherents of the two great religions of the country.

In Islam a leader emerged in Sayyid Ahmad Khān, who, after holding office for some years as a judge, devoted the rest of his life to the service of his co-religionists, urging on them the need for social reform within the framework of their creed, and at the same time the importance of accepting western education, in order to enable them to play their part in the new India which had come into existence. He met with bitter hostility, but he fought steadfastly on, and when he died—as Sir Sayyid—his work was done, and Islam in India had acquired a new outlook. His visible monument is the college which he founded at Aligarh in 1875, and which later on became the nucleus of the Moslem University. It differed from the State colleges of the period in that moral training founded on religion was of its essence ; and before the end of the 'eighties its graduates were beginning to make their mark in the public service, less by their intellectual attainments than by their high character and practical efficiency.

Among Hindus, the Brahmo Samāj found a new and vigorous leader in Keshab Chandra Sen, who, between 1860 and his death in 1884, extended its connections over India, and led the way in social reform, as well as in the development of personal religion on lines which showed the influences of the teaching of Chaitanya, but still more of Christianity. The movement continued to be characterised by the quality rather than the number of its adherents, and its influence on Indian life was mainly indirect, while the forces lying behind it were manifested also in a negative way ; men discontinued the observances of traditional Hinduism, but adopted nothing in their place, and positivists or agnostics were to be found in intellectual circles, particularly in Calcutta.

On the other hand, the forces which lay behind traditional Hinduism were now beginning to find expression in various organisations, some of which defended the ancient faith as a whole, while others were in their nature eclectic, and discarded such portions of it as seemed to them to be irrelevant or untrue. In the first group the most prominent leader was Rāmakrishna, who in the 'seventies was preaching that, while all religions were true, or at least good, men should follow their own, and Hinduism was the best for Hindus. The distinctions which characterised the members of this group must be passed over ; the main result of their teaching was, so to speak, to restore the self-respect of Hinduism. Persecuted as it had been by Aurangzeb, lethargic during the anarchy of the eighteenth century, and attacked strongly by missionaries in the nineteenth, its adherents now began to show a defiant front, and advanced its claim to be one of the great living religions of the world, teaching an ultimate monotheism, but not disdaining the traditional ceremonies, images or sacrifices as aids to the worship of the ordinary man.

The most important movement in the second group is known as the Ārya Samāj, the founder of which, Dayānand, after many years spent as an ascetic, began preaching in 1868. His doctrine was that the true religion of India is contained solely in the Vedas, the oldest texts of all ; but he interpreted these texts on lines which are condemned by orthodox Hindus as severely as by western scholars, and the result was an eclectic system, comprising those elements of traditional Hinduism of which he personally approved, such as monotheism and the doctrine of *karma*, but excluding other elements, such as the authority of the Brāhman and caste in its modern form, which he considered to be objectionable. At the same time he urged the need for social and moral reform, for more and better education, and for recognition of the true position of women in the family.

His teaching, which in its essence was rationalist rather than mystical, was inspired by an ardent nationalism, and he attacked impartially all who differed from him, whether Hindus, Sikhs or Jains, whether Moslems or Christians, with a bitterness which provoked active reprisals, so that his system was definitely militant. The Ārya Samāj was founded at Bombay in 1875, but its initial success was greatest in the Punjab, and Lahore soon became the headquarters; the movement survived the death of Dayānand, and its dual inspiration, nationalist and militant, has counted for much in northern India.

Such were the main tendencies operating in India during this period—on the one hand, the growth of a sentiment of unity among the literate classes; on the other, a new self-assertiveness among different communities, tending to bring them into conflict with one another mainly in the sphere of religion. We now turn to a different topic, the organisation of the public service, but the transition is not so violent as it seems, for it was in relation to 'service questions' that the common feeling of the literate classes first found expression, while towards the end of the century the conflict between communities became apparent in the claims made by each for a due proportion of appointments. In Mogul times the public service provided a livelihood for a large proportion of the literate classes, while its higher ranks furnished the only career open to a gentleman, a career with enormous prizes, and one in which civil and military functions were not distinguished. Under the Company's rule the rank and file of the literary class continued to find employment in subordinate positions, but from the time of Cornwallis onwards the higher positions were filled only by Englishmen; and after the Mutiny the main 'service question' consisted of the claim made by Indians to a share of these higher positions.

At this time the claim did not extend to military service, which under the Company had been gradually divorced from civil. Literate opinion accepted the professional army as something apart ; the aspiration towards a national army is a new feature of the present century. On the civil side, the claim was concerned at first with the great administrative organisation known as the Indian Civil Service, which had enjoyed since 1793 a statutory monopoly of all the higher posts. Under the Company this service was, as we have seen, recruited from the Directors' nominees. An attempt to introduce an element of competition was made by the Charter Act of 1833, but was defeated owing to the opposition of the Directors ; and while that Act provided that no Indian subject should be disabled from holding office under the Company, it did not offer Indians the entry into the Civil Service which was a necessary preliminary to such appointments. The first step in enlarging the sphere of their employment came simply as a measure of economy ; the growth of work in the law courts outstripped the capacity of the English judges and magistrates, and Indians obtained a rapidly increasing share of judicial work, but their appointments remained definitely subordinate.

The Charter Act of 1853 provided for the introduction of a system of competitive examination for the Civil Service ; the examinations were conducted in London by the Civil Service Commissioners ; the training college at Haileybury was closed ; and a period of probation, to be spent at an English university, was prescribed. The examination was open to Indians, in accordance with a paragraph in the royal proclamation of 1858, which directed that ' our subjects, of whatever race and creed, be freely and impartially admitted to offices in our service, the duties of which they may be qualified, by their education, ability, and integrity, to perform ' ; but the syllabus was based on the existing English courses, and Indians found it necessary to study for it in England. A small number of exceptional men did so with success ; but admission was rendered more difficult for them in 1878, when the maximum age was reduced from 22 to 19, or, in other words, candidates were drawn from the schools instead of the universities, a practice which remained in force until 1892. The door was still open to Indians, but it was hard for them to reach the threshold.

THE PUBLIC SERVICES

Meanwhile the Secretary of State proposed to open a second door, and the necessary legislation was passed in 1870. Long discussions followed, but eventually rules were issued for the appointment, without examination, of a limited number of ' young men of good family and social position, possessed of fair abilities and education.' The ' statutory civilians ' appointed under these rules were not a success ; in many cases they could not hold their own in the work of administration with the abler and more energetic men recruited by examination ; and very few of them reached a high position in the service.

In the technical services, the conditions of entry varied greatly. The higher ranks of the medical department were recruited by examination in England, and a certain number of Indians secured admission in this way ; for the public works department, a proportion of the officers was drawn from the Indian engineering colleges ; while in the police, education, and forest departments recruits for the higher posts were almost entirely English. At this period, however, Indian opinion was not greatly concerned with such appointments ; a share in the general administration was the immediate objective. It would be a mistake to suppose that the motives behind this claim were purely economic. Indians were, in fact, attracted by the dignity and the emoluments which the administrative service carried ; but they were now beginning to think also of service in the other sense, that is to say, a new sentiment of patriotism was at work, and men wanted opportunities of rendering service to their country. This aspect of the question was not fully recognised either by the authorities in India or by public opinion in England. The official attitude was that the pledges which had been given must be honoured, and long years could be spent in discussing how this could best be done with due regard to the efficiency of the administration : Indians, eager to get to work, were naturally impatient of such delays, and, as the years passed, some of them became inclined to impugn the good faith of the administration, which failed to realise that time was of the essence of the question.

Opportunities of unpaid service were at this time rare, except in the presidency towns, where the municipal corporations and the benches of magistrates gave reasonable scope for the activities of public-spirited individuals. Elsewhere local self-government was still in a rudimentary state in urban, and still more in rural, areas ; the powers of the various committees were too small, and their financial resources too limited, to attract men of energy and capacity ; and, speaking generally, Indians who wished to serve their country had much difficulty in finding ways of doing so with effect.

One other development belonging to this period must be mentioned—the growth of a feeling of personal loyalty to Queen Victoria. Loyalty to the ruler is an Indian characteristic, and when once the impersonal Company had been eliminated, the sentiment did not take long to emerge. It was both displayed and increased during the visit of the Prince of Wales (King Edward VII) in 1875, and again on the proclamation in 1877 of the Queen as Empress of India, a step taken with the authority of Parliament. Queen Victoria never saw her new empire, but her published letters contain ample evidence of her insight into, as well as her deep interest in, its life, and as a knowledge of the numerous instances of her kindly tact and sympathy spread gradually over the country, the sentiment was confirmed and strengthened until even in her lifetime she became almost a legendary figure in the villages, the embodiment of the justice and the goodness which Indians expect from a ruler. The sentiment grew up in the palaces as well as in the villages. During this period the doctrine of paramountcy continued to develop, and the government in India became progressively more inclined to intervene in the affairs of the States when their administration fell much below the standard at which it aimed ; but, whatever irritation might be caused by its actions, the loyalty of the Princes to the Empress went on growing until it became one of the dominant factors in the life of India.

CHAPTER XLVI

THE FRONTIERS, AND FINANCE, 1860–1880

IN this chapter we deal with India's external relations and with the course of public finance, which was materially affected by them. The introduction of telegraphic communication with England wrought a fundamental change in the position of the Indian government in all its branches, but particularly in regard to frontier policy. In the old days, the Governor-General with his Council had to act in emergencies without orders from England, and the Directors of the Company were sometimes presented with accomplished facts, palatable or unpalatable as the case might be. In the new conditions, orders could be sought and obtained by telegraph; the action to be taken was decided in London; and the decision was often determined by the international situation, so that the Indian frontiers, it may almost be said, had been brought on to the diplomatic map of Europe.

To the east of India, friendly relations were maintained, though not altogether easily, with Upper Burma until the accession of King Thībaw, whose hostile attitude led to the withdrawal of the Resident from his Court in 1879. To complete the story, it may be added that the final breach came six years later, when Thībaw, having oppressed a company trading between India and his dominions, treated the consequent ultimatum with contempt; a British force then entered his capital, and received his unconditional surrender; the kingdom was annexed, and Burma as a whole became a province of the Indian Empire.

On the west, the area known as Baluchistan came formally within the Empire. The bulk of this country is occupied by States or tribal communities, with some of which relations had been maintained since 1854 ; the recurring trouble among these entities was brought to an end in 1875 by an agreement negotiated by Major (later Sir Robert) Sandeman. The Indian government then accepted the responsibility for keeping the peace ; Sandeman was appointed Agent to the Governor-General in 1877, a post which he retained till his death fifteen years later ; and his exceptional gifts of sagacity, tact and insight were employed with success to bring tranquillity and prosperity to the people.

The strategical importance of Baluchistan lies in the fact that one of the two main gates of India, the road through Kandahār and Quetta, passes across its north-eastern portion. During most of the period the country north and east of Quetta was in the possession of Afghanistan, but under the Treaty of Gandamak, which is mentioned below, this region was handed over to India, and at the close of the Afghan war it was brought directly under the administration of the Governor-General's Agent. The railway which was constructed between 1879 and 1892 to the border of Afghanistan enabled India to dominate this route effectively, for the first time since Kandahār passed out of the possession of the Moguls.

The story of Afghanistan remains to be told. We have seen that Dost Muhammad, the Amīr of that country, was, in his later years, a friendly neighbour to India. His death in 1863 was followed by a period of war between his numerous descendants, and for some time the Indian government held aloof from the contestants ; but at last it intervened by subsidising Sher Alī, who had been designated by Dost Muhammad as his successor, and who with this help was now able to dispose of his opponents. The reason for this change of policy was the Russian menace. Russia had recently been active in extending her authority over the independent states lying to the east of the Caspian Sea, and in 1867 she established a military government in this region, which became known as Russian Turkistan, and stretched right up to the northern frontier of Afghanistan. At the

AFGHANISTAN

time, this step was represented as the inevitable and beneficent advance of civilisation, but the primary motive was to secure such a position that the threat of intervention in India could be used with effect in European diplomacy.

In these circumstances it was more than ever the interest of India that Afghanistan should be held by a strong and friendly ruler. Sher Alī might perhaps have been so described, but his position was necessarily difficult, and in 1873 he asked for a definite promise of support against Russia. Lord Northbrook, the Viceroy, was prepared to give the necessary assurances, but was overruled by the authorities in London, and Sher Alī concluded that he must make the best terms he could with his northern neighbour. Then Disraeli succeeded Gladstone in London, and initiated a new foreign policy. Impressed by the menace to India, the British Government tried to persuade Russia to discontinue the friendly relations which she had established with Sher Alī; and on the failure of this attempt, it was decided to strengthen the military position on the frontier, and to induce the Amīr to accept British resident agents in his territory. As the result of this latter decision, Lord Northbrook resigned, and his successor, Lord Lytton, came to India with instructions to give it effect, but was unable to overcome Sher Alī's opposition.

The failure of his negotiations, in the spring of 1877, came at a time when conditions in Europe seemed to render war between England and Russia almost inevitable, but the danger was averted in the following year by the Treaty of Berlin. While that treaty was being negotiated, a Russian agent arrived in Kābul. Lytton insisted that a British agent also should be received, but the Amīr refused to do so; the British representative was stopped on the way; and the Cabinet authorised the despatch of an ultimatum. No answer being received within the fixed period, Afghanistan was invaded; Sher Alī withdrew to Russian territory, where he died; and his son, Yakūb Khān, agreed to the Treaty of Gandamak (May, 1879), by which he bound himself to receive a permanent British representative at Kābul, and to conduct his foreign relations in accordance with the Viceroy's advice.

Yakūb, however, was unable to establish his authority over the country. In September the British representative was murdered; a month later Sir Frederick (later Lord) Roberts occupied Kābul; and he maintained himself there while the authorities considered what should be done next. Yakūb was pensioned off, and plans were being worked out for the future of the country, when a new candidate for the throne appeared in the person of Abdurrahmān, a nephew of Sher Alī, who had been living under Russian protection for some years. Lytton decided to enter into negotiations with him, and eventually he agreed, in return for an annual subsidy, to place the management of his foreign relations under the government of India. While these negotiations were still in progress, another son of Sher Alī, named Ayūb Khān, who had established himself in western Afghanistan, attacked the British force stationed at Kandahār, and defeated it severely at the battle of Maiwand. Helped by the orders issued by the new Amīr, Roberts promptly led a column from Kābul to Kandahār, and defeated Ayūb Khān, leaving the country clear for Abdurrahmān. The new Amīr was a man of the type of Dost Mohammad, strong of will, and ruthless in action; he had deliberately bound himself to England rather than Russia; and there were good grounds for hoping that under his rule the primary need of India, a strong and friendly neighbour, would be secured.

The north-west frontier is one of the dominant factors in Indian finance, because the cost of the army, which is maintained primarily for its defence, forms the largest single item in the annual expenditure. The Company had not worked out a satisfactory financial system; it had taken over the sources of revenue enjoyed by its predecessors, and had altered or adjusted its arrangements in accordance with the needs of the moment, while its accounts continued to be kept in a form more appropriate to a commercial firm than to a territorial government. We have seen in an earlier chapter that Warren Hastings avoided borrowing, but this policy was not continued by his successors. War was paid for largely with money borrowed, sometimes in India and sometimes in London, and after the Mutiny the total debt taken over by the new government amounted to nearly one hundred millions sterling. In 1859 it was decided to appoint a financial expert as a member of the Viceroy's Council, and under his administration an effective system of budget and control was introduced ; by 1864 the budget was balanced ; and thereafter the country paid its way in ordinary years, loans being raised only to meet the cost of war or famine relief, and for the construction of railways or canals which in time would pay for themselves.

At first the central government retained control over all branches of finance, and doled out the revenue to the various provinces. In the 'seventies certain items of revenue were assigned to the provinces, which thus acquired a direct interest in developing them, and thenceforward each province had a budget of its own, distinct from the Indian budget proper. Towards the end of our period the total annual income, available for both central and provincial needs, was a little under 50 crores of rupees,[1] made up mainly of taxes (17 crores), non-tax income (10), and land-revenue (22), which last is treated by some writers as a tax, and by others as income from the public domain.

Among taxes, the most important was that on salt, a legacy from earlier rulers of India, who had all agreed in taxing the commodity, though rates and methods varied widely. This diversity persisted under the Company, and in the 'seventies a barrier made of thorns, stretching almost across India, was still maintained to prevent smuggling from the low-taxed to the high-taxed area ; but at the end of our period this vexatious institution was abolished, and a low, uniform rate of taxation introduced throughout the country. The salt tax was the only impost paid compulsorily by every inhabitant ; the others, such as excise, customs and stamps,

[1] The practice of stating Indian revenues in sterling became dangerous about this time, when, as we shall see, the sterling value of the rupee was falling. The most convenient unit is the crore, which denotes ten millions ; when the rupee was worth about 2s., the crore was equivalent to a million sterling ; at present, with the rupee at 1s. 6d., it is three-quarters of a million.

fell on special classes of the people. The first of these aimed at reducing the consumption of alcohol and intoxicating drugs rather than at raising the maximum revenue, but was not as yet effectively organised for either purpose. The general customs tariff of ten per cent. was reduced by half in 1875, and was abolished altogether in 1882, in deference to the then accepted doctrine of free trade, which regarded even five per cent. as a protective duty. Judged by modern standards, then, taxation was low, if the land-revenue is excluded from consideration. As yet there was no permanent income tax, though duties of the kind had been imposed more than once for temporary purposes.

As to the non-tax revenue, the process of developing the national estate was only in its infancy. Railways as yet scarcely brought in the interest which had to be paid on their capital cost; the irrigation canals were more than paying their way, but the net revenue was not yet large; while the forests were only beginning to show the effects of the systematic conservation which had been introduced in the 'sixties. The outstanding item under this head was the profit derived from the monopoly of the production of opium, a monopoly which the Company had taken over from its predecessors. The cultivation of the poppy was carried on by peasants who had obtained licences for the purpose; the raw product was delivered by them to the government factories, where it was worked up; and the sale of the drug to China and other Eastern countries brought an income nearly half as large as the total land-revenue, while the net profit equalled or exceeded the yield of the salt tax.

Lastly, there was the land-revenue. We have seen in earlier chapters that it was found impossible to maintain the standards of demand which had prevailed under the predecessors of the Company; they had claimed from one-third to one-half of the gross produce of the soil, but now the claim had fallen to about one-half of the net rental, and experience had shown that in ordinary seasons this share could be realised with remarkable regularity and punctuality. The inherent weakness of the financial system is expressed in the words 'ordinary seasons'; when the rains failed, and crops were bad, large amounts of land-revenue had to be forgone, the yield from taxes fell off, and exceptional expenditure had to be incurred on the relief of famine. A budget which was quite satisfactory in March might be obsolete in October, and, as one Finance Minister put it, his business was in essence a ' gamble in rain.'

On the expenditure side, the largest single item was the cost of the army, from 16 to 18 crores; the service of the public debt took 5 to 6 crores; the balance went on the civil administration, and in ordinary seasons substantial sums were available for roads and other public works which brought no direct financial return. The most striking feature of the civil expenditure is the comparatively small amount provided for what are now called ' nation-building ' activities; education, medical relief, and sanitation were only minor items in the budget, while the departments of agriculture and industries were not yet in existence; the great bulk of the money available was spent on the law courts, the police, and the establishments for collecting the revenue.

During this period, the balance of the budget was not upset by war until the closing years, when events in Afghanistan involved heavy expenditure, but there was much disturbance from famine, for the course of the seasons resumed its wonted irregularity. In 1860 there was severe drought in the North-Western Provinces, but the railway brought the necessary food, and this may be regarded as the first of the series of famines in the modern sense, a famine ' of work rather than of food,' as it was described at the time. In 1866 drought in Orissa and along the east coast caused a famine of the old type, for here there were no railways, and the heavy expenditure which was ultimately incurred came too late to save the people. In 1868 the scene of famine was Rājputāna, and here too the lack of transport involved heavy mortality in many of the States. In 1873 it was the turn of Bihār, and relief was organised on a scale which some critics considered was in excess of needs. In 1878 nearly the whole of southern India and considerable portions of the North were affected, and heavy mortality again occurred; but the series of droughts was then broken, and nearly twenty years elapsed before famine again became prominent. The experience of this period was reviewed by a Famine Commission, whose reports, issued in 1880, form a landmark in the economic history of India. Schemes of relief were formulated for use when famine came, but the more important recommendations related to anticipation and prevention by steady effort carried on from year to year, and to developing the economic life of the people to a point where a failure of the rains could be borne.

Meanwhile the unproductive debt had been increased by nearly one-half, partly owing to the Afghan war, and partly to meet the cost of famine-relief. A productive debt had also come into existence, consisting of capital borrowed for the construction of railways and canals which were expected to pay their way. Practically all the canals were constructed by the State, but the railway policy varied from time to time. The earliest lines were built by companies formed in London with a State guarantee of five per cent. on their capital, a reservation to the State of a share of the surplus profits, and a right to buy out the companies after a term of years. This system proved to be extravagant, for the companies had no great inducement to keep down the cost of construction and equipment on which they were sure of five per cent. in any case; and in 1869 it was decided to undertake future construction by State agency, and to borrow for the purpose in the open market. State construction prevailed until the close of our period, and proved to be too slow for the needs of the country; in 1880, when less than 9,000 miles of line were open, the Famine Commission found that at least 5,000 miles more were imperatively required in order to be sure of feeding the people, and it was decided to have some of them constructed by companies, but on terms less onerous to the State than had originally been given.

The main reason why construction had fallen behind needs lay in the difficulty of borrowing sufficient money. The habit of investing in securities was gradually being formed in India, and a small loan could be raised almost every year, most of it from inhabitants of the presidency towns; but the supply of capital from this source was

THE EXCHANGE QUESTION

strictly limited, and additional funds could be borrowed only in the London market and in terms of the pound sterling. The objection to borrowing in sterling lay in the depreciation of the rupee, which had begun about 1875, and which was destined to continue till near the close of the century. The government had to make large payments in sterling—allowances to officers on leave in England and pensions to them after they had retired, the cost of munitions and railway material bought in Europe, and interest on the sterling debt; while the guarantees of the older railway companies involved a further liability, for they were given in sterling and the loss by exchange thus fell on the government. So long as exchange remained stable, there was no objection to borrowing in London, but when the rate began to fall, and nobody could say how far the fall would go, it was obviously most dangerous to increase the recurring sterling liability, which might require an incalculable number of rupees for its discharge.

The fall in exchange may be explained briefly as follows. At this time England had an effective gold standard: the mint was open, and anyone who brought gold to it could obtain a stated number of sovereigns in return. In the same way, the Indian mint was open to silver; and consequently the number of rupees required to buy a pound sterling depended on the number of ounces of silver required to buy an ounce of gold, a figure which was determined in the long run by the conditions of demand and supply of the two metals. In the Company's time this figure had remained reasonably steady, and a pound cost about ten rupees, with only small fluctuations. In the 'sixties, however, conditions were changing in the world at large, and the tendency was for gold to become dearer in terms of silver. For a short time this tendency failed to operate, because the mints of several European countries were, like the Indian mint, open to silver; but these countries soon found that they were getting much more silver than they needed, and in 1873 and 1874 all the important European mints were closed, so far as that metal was concerned, thus making a large reduction in the demand for it. The depreciation of silver then became manifest, and, since the Indian mint remained open, it was reflected in the falling value of the rupee. In 1878, when the fall was not yet serious, the Indian government proposed to alter its system by establishing a gold standard, but this proposal was rejected by the home authorities, and the next decade was spent in fruitless attempts to deal with the problem by international agreement. The period of which we are writing thus closed in uncertainty; the rupee was still worth 1s. 9d. or so, instead of 2s., but the fall was continuing, and nobody could say what it would be worth in a year's time. The effect of this uncertainty was a most unfortunate delay in the economic development of the country, for construction of railways and canals was retarded, while capital in private hands tended to leave India rather than enter it; the century had almost ended before the country at last secured a stable currency.

We may close this chapter with the caution that it relates almost entirely to the portion of India under British administration. In the States, financial reform had scarcely begun, and most of them were still characterised by the practices of older days—rigorous collection of the largest possible revenue, lax control over expenditure, a lack of any settled economic policy, and, wherever possible, a large hoard of idle treasure, which could be drawn on to meet the ruler's whims.

CHAPTER XLVII

GENERAL HISTORY, 1880–1905

Viceroys : Lord Ripon, 1880–1884 ;
Lord Dufferin, 1884–1888 ;
Lord Lansdowne, 1888–1894 ;
Lord Elgin (ninth earl), 1894–1899 ;
Lord Curzon, 1899–1905.

The period with which we have now to deal was characterised mainly by development of the tendencies which have been recorded in the last three chapters, and in particular by the active expression of the common feelings—national, regional and communal—which had come into existence. Before describing these movements we will attempt to summarise the general history.

On the frontier the activities of Russia continued to be a disturbing element. In 1885, while negotiations were in progress for delimiting the boundary between Afghanistan and the country south of Merv, which had now fallen into Russian hands, an advance by the latter's forces brought about a crisis in European diplomacy, but war was averted, and the frontier was fixed in the following year. From 1891 Russia was again active for some time, on this occasion in the north-eastern corner of Afghanistan, but here too the boundary was settled by an agreement made in 1895. Seven years later the Indian government thought that Russia was aiming at the absorption of Tibet, which is contiguous with India on both sides of Nepal. The facts could not be ascertained, because at this time Tibet kept its frontier absolutely closed, and eventually it was decided to despatch a mission, which, after some fighting on the way, reached the capital in August, 1904, and came to terms with the Tibetan authorities. Meanwhile, however, the situation in Europe was bringing England and Russia together as friends, and the importance of the Tibetan question disappeared; the new relations were fixed by a convention signed in 1907, and for the time the Russian menace ceased to exist.

Afghanistan itself continued under the rule of Abdurrahmān until his death in 1901, when he was succeeded by his son Habībullah. Father and son alike chafed under the provisions of the treaty which fettered their relations with foreign countries, and sought without success to establish direct contact with the government in London; but a more serious cause of discord arose out of the conditions prevailing in the tribal country between Afghanistan and India. In Chapter XXXII we have described the activities of the border tribes in the time of Aurangzeb; their habits had not changed in the interval, raids into British territory were frequent, and communications were interrupted from time to time. These raids were followed by punitive expeditions into the tribal country, and occasionally by the fortification of advanced posts of strategical importance; and this 'forward policy,' as it was called, produced apprehensions that the Indian government intended to deprive the tribes of their cherished independence. During the 'nineties the whole frontier was in a state of unrest, aggravated by the Amīr's intrigues, for he, like the tribesmen, was alarmed by the forward policy. In 1893 an agreement negotiated with Abdurrahmān defined the Afghan and British spheres of interest among the tribes, but its immediate effect was not very great, and tribes within the British sphere still hoped for support from Kābul. The trouble came to a head in 1897, when the spirit of independence was reinforced by a wave of fanaticism among the tribes, and outbreaks occurred all along the frontier, necessitating extensive military operations and the occupation of still more outposts beyond the border.

A change of policy was effected under Lord Curzon. The more advanced posts were withdrawn, the communications of the remainder were improved so that they became part of the general military organisation, and the maintenance of peace beyond the border was entrusted to militia forces raised among the tribes, and assured of support from India when it might be required. By 1904 this system was in operation along the northern portion of the frontier, where the tribal trouble was reduced to small dimensions; but its effective introduction in the central portion, known as Waziristan, was delayed for twenty years, during which that region remained a centre of anxiety. In order to facilitate these reforms, Curzon in 1901 constituted the North-West Frontier Province, comprising five districts west of the Indus which had hitherto been included in the Punjab, together with the sphere of interest defined by the agreement of 1893. The new Province was placed under a Chief Commissioner, responsible to the central government for the control of the frontier as a whole, administering the settled districts on the ordinary lines, and maintaining relations with the tribes in the sphere of interest through their own political institutions.

Frontier policy has been the cause of such long and bitter controversy that it may be well at this point to summarise the conclusions which have at last emerged. As we have said in an earlier chapter, the root of the evil is economic, for the tribal country is poor, and does not offer an adequate livelihood to its inhabitants. No permanent remedy for this evil could be found either in a 'forward policy' of subjugation, or in the alternative of a 'closed border,' which would deprive the tribesmen of the hope of income from outside, and confine them to their poverty-stricken homes; the solution must be sought rather in a development of the system initiated by Sandeman in Baluchistan, which in fact operated to provide new means of livelihood. The construction and maintenance of roads, the promotion of such forms of agriculture, notably fruit-growing, as the conditions permit, the offer of employment in the local militia or in India or at sea—such measures as these have in recent years made a substantial addition to the income of the tribal country, and the future appears to depend rather on economic development than on political change.

From the frontier we pass again to the subject of finance. During the 'eighties the sterling value of the rupee continued to fall, and by 1890 it was only 1s. 4d. The attempts to secure international agreement had definitely failed, and in 1892 the Indian mint was at last closed, thus divorcing the rupee from silver. For a few years the value continued to fall, but then the tide turned, and in 1899, when it had risen again to 1s. 4d., it was stabilised at that figure; the rupee, which originally had been a stated weight of silver, now became a token representing one-fifteenth of a pound sterling, and it was maintained successfully at this level until the currency chaos after the first Great War.

The period from 1880 to 1900 was thus a time of financial stress, marked by rigorous economy in expenditure, delay in developing the national estate, and recurring increases in taxation. The salt tax was raised, income tax was imposed permanently in 1886, and in 1894 the revenue tariff on imports was restored. Political pressure in England caused the latter measure to be supplemented by an excise duty on those grades of cotton cloth produced in Indian mills which competed with the produce of Lancashire, a step which aroused bitter resentment in India; other Indian industries were allowed to enjoy the protection, such as it was, of a five per cent. duty on imported goods, but the influence of Lancashire interests was sufficient to secure this exceptional favour, which was forced by the British Cabinet on an unwilling government. This 'countervailing excise' continued to rankle until its final disappearance, and the suspicion of British motives which it engendered in India survived its abolition, to throw a dark shadow over all discussions of fiscal relations between the two countries.

Another set of countervailing duties, those on imported sugar, have a different history. Various European countries, aiming at national self-sufficiency, were producing more sugar than they needed, and were giving large bounties on exports in order to dispose of their surplus. This 'bounty-fed' sugar was being sold in India at prices which threatened to ruin the old-fashioned indigenous industry, and consequently to curtail the cultivation of sugar-cane, which in northern India was one of the staple crops of the most laborious peasants. In 1899 countervailing duties were imposed on bounty-fed sugar, which practically excluded it from the country, and the indigenous industry was thus kept in being, to be remodelled later on as the result of years of scientific research followed by high protective duties.

The stabilisation of exchange introduced the halcyon period of Indian finance, which was to continue up to 1914. Increased trade and industry raised the yield from taxes, though their incidence was in some cases lowered, the national estate was now giving a handsome and growing surplus, and, while borrowing continued for productive works, the unproductive debt was progressively reduced until it almost disappeared. The position was so favourable that even the loss of the bulk of the opium revenue could be faced with equanimity; and just after the close of our period an agreement was made with China, by which the exports to that country were to be gradually discontinued, and opium cease to be one of the principal sources of revenue.

The financial difficulties of the 'nineties were increased by the reappearance of famine, which was widespread and acute in the North in 1897, and in the South and centre in 1900. The methods of relief recommended by the Commission of 1880 were put to a severe test, and were developed in the light of the new experience; and the results were reviewed by expert Commissions which reported in 1898 and 1901. The position which had been reached in the new century may be summarised as follows. Firstly, the affected population could be relieved without the widespread migration which formerly occurred, and death from starvation could be practically eliminated. Secondly, it was more difficult to prevent increased mortality, especially among old people and children, which followed a famine, owing to the spread of diseases attributable to the pollution of the diminished water-supply and the reduced power of resistance of the people. Thirdly, the loss of production, which in older days continued for a generation, could be practically limited to the famine year, and, as soon as rain fell, the people could be enabled to return to their ordinary course of life. Fourthly, while the provision of temporary employment on public works must remain an essential part of the system, the need for it could be minimised by liberal advances of cash, made at the first onset of the calamity, to enable peasants and artisans to carry on their ordinary business till better times should come ; and by early announcement of such reductions in the land-revenue, with corresponding abatements in the rent paid by tenants, as would suffice to put heart into the people and encourage them to fight the calamity for themselves. Lastly, the extent to which effective relief and rapid recovery could be secured depended entirely on the quality of the administration—on careful planning, an accurate intelligence system, prompt action and continuous supervision. These conclusions were verified in the severe famine which occurred in the United Provinces in 1908, until recently the last in the long series of these calamities.

The larger question of the protection of the people by action in ordinary times figured prominently in the reports of all three Commissions, and the improved financial situation after 1900 enabled Lord Curzon's administration to translate their recommendations into a definite forward policy in irrigation, agriculture and co-operation. The Irrigation Commission, which reported in 1903, formulated a large programme of new works, the gradual construction of which has resulted in a steady increase in the area where crops can be saved in a year of drought, but its recommendations for the most part followed lines which were already familiar : the other heads of the programme were in some respects novel.

The scope for improvement in agriculture had indeed long been obvious. The nucleus of an administrative department for the purpose had been constituted by Lord Mayo ; and, after it had been suppressed as a measure of economy, it was restored at the instance of the first Famine

ECONOMIC DEVELOPMENT

Commission. At the start, its main function was to collect accurate information, and this was accomplished successfully in nearly all provinces; but want of funds, technical officers, and equipment, prevented much being done either in the way of research, or to bring ascertained results to the notice of the peasants. In 1905 provision was made for the employment of a staff of technical officers, for the building of colleges and research laboratories, and for a systematic attack on the problems presented by Indian agriculture.

Not the least of these problems is that of peasant finance—to enable the peasant to borrow cheaply for productive purposes, and at the same time control his propensities towards lavish unproductive expenditure of borrowed funds. In the second half of the nineteenth century a few pioneers, working mainly among German and Italian peasants, had discovered that this problem could be attacked by way of mutual credit; a society formed of peasants who knew and trusted each other could borrow on the joint security of the members much more cheaply than its members could borrow as individuals, while its joint responsibility for the loan operated to check the tendency to extravagance and ensure that borrowed money was wisely spent. This system of co-operative credit began to attract attention in India early in the 'nineties, and, after some experiments had been made, and the subject had been examined by a Commission, an Act was passed in 1904 to legalise co-operative societies and regulate the main lines of their development.

Meanwhile the continued and large expansion of organised industries was bringing to the front problems such as the control of factories and the position of labour, with which the administration had not hitherto been seriously concerned, though a certain amount of labour legislation had been undertaken from time to time. In 1905 the Viceroy's Council was enlarged and the distribution of portfolios was altered so as to place all questions relating to commerce and industry in the hands of a single Member; henceforward the development of industries, which had been almost entirely a matter of private enterprise, became one of the objects of administrative activity in the central government, and also in some of the provinces, but the efforts of the administration were soon afterwards crippled by restrictions imposed by Lord Morley, the Cobdenite Secretary of State.

The new policy of assistance to agriculture and industry was timely, for the pressure on the land had continued to increase. Mines, factories and transport were offering more and more employment, but the population was growing faster; the famine of 1877 had checked the rate, but there were nearly ten per cent. more people to be fed in 1891 than in 1881, and while the rate was again checked by famine, and also by plague, in the 'nineties, it recovered quickly in the more prosperous years which followed. India had been free from bubonic plague for more than half a century, but the disease appeared in Bombay in 1896, and spread rapidly to most parts of the country, causing over two million deaths within the period under review. Its appearance gave additional emphasis to the forward health policy initiated by Lord Curzon, directed to utilising the new scientific knowledge which had recently been gained in regard to the aetiology of epidemic diseases.

Until nearly the end of the nineteenth century sanitarians in India, as elsewhere, were fighting these diseases in the dark. In the case of smallpox, it is true, they had the resource of vaccination, and in India the average mortality from this disease fell during the period with which we are dealing by more than one-half. The cholera microbe was first recognised in 1883, but several years elapsed before the discovery won general acceptance; the plague bacillus was identified in 1894, and the part played by fleas in disseminating it was established in the course of the next ten years; and in 1897 the anopheles mosquito was proved to convey the infection of malaria. In the new century it thus became possible to attack these diseases on scientific lines, but the wide gulf between the expert knowledge of

MILITARY DEVELOPMENTS

the sanitarian and the ignorance of the people at large had still to be bridged before such epidemics could be effectively controlled.

The administrative changes which we have enumerated, together with others of less importance, combined to produce a huge and complicated bureaucratic machine, highly centralised, and steadily pursuing the ideal of efficiency. The story of the army during this period is not very different. The final disappearance of the old presidency system of organisation was marked by the formal adoption in 1903 of the title ' The Indian Army,' denoting a single force under the Commander-in-Chief; and, just at the end of our period, the troops serving in India were reorganised by Lord Kitchener, who then occupied that post, in commands and divisions so arranged that mobilisation for the defence of the frontier could proceed with mechanical efficiency. Kitchener's tireless pursuit of this ideal brought him into conflict with the Viceroy on one point. As we have said in an earlier chapter, military affairs were in charge of a member of the Viceroy's Council, distinct from the Commander-in-Chief. Kitchener held that this arrangement made for delay and hesitation in action, and proposed that the Commander-in-Chief should also be ' Military Member,' to use the phrase then current; Curzon, and the rest of the Council, held that the proposal menaced the final authority of the civil power; the home government accepted in substance the former view; Curzon resigned the office of Viceroy; and the ' Military Member ' disappeared from the Council.

In the ranks of the Indian army the pursuit of efficiency led to important changes in recruiting; fewer men were taken from Madras and the United Provinces,[1] more from the Punjab and the country outside India—Nepal, and the border area in the north-west. There was still no idea of a national army, and the defence of India came to depend more and more on what were called the ' martial races.'

[1] The North-Western Provinces had been united for administrative purposes with Oudh in 1877; on the constitution of the North-West Frontier Province, the name of this region was changed to ' The United Provinces of Agra and Oudh,' shortened in practice to ' United Provinces.'

The economic and social effects of these changes were greater, perhaps, than their authors realised. The soldiers, who were drawn almost entirely from the peasantry, were accustomed to send home a substantial proportion of their pay, and their periodical remittances often made all the difference between penury and modest comfort to their families; the stream of remittances was now diverted from some densely populated regions, where the need for it was greatest, while large tracts in the Punjab became, by comparison, affluent. At the same time the education of the soldier had been taken in hand, and the wider outlook which he acquired during his term of service tended to make him a better peasant than if he had remained in his village, so that, by the end of our period, the rural population of the Punjab was developing a spirit of independent enterprise more quickly than that of any other part of India.

A significant step taken during this period was the establishment of the Imperial Service Troops. The Princes continued to maintain armies of their own when the need for them had ceased to exist, and they served mainly for purposes of display. In the crisis of 1885 many of the Princes offered their forces for the defence of India against Russia; and four years later it was arranged that they should maintain fixed contingents, subject to their own control, but trained under the guidance of British officers, and to be placed for 'imperial service' under the Commander-in-Chief when the need for them arose. The significance of this change will be obvious when it is recalled that in earlier days the peace-time location of the Indian army was determined largely by the need for watching the forces of the States; now these forces had become firm allies instead of potential enemies, and the Indian army could be organised with its face to the north-west, where alone serious danger might then be apprehended.

We now pass to the measures taken during this period to enable Indians to render service, paid or unpaid, to their country. The report of the Public Service Commission of 1886 forms a landmark in the history of the 'service question.' In accordance with its recommendations the various superior services were divided into two sections, 'Imperial,' or 'Indian,' recruited in England on the existing lines, and 'Provincial,' recruited by each province for its own needs, and ordinarily from among its own inhabitants, while a varying proportion of the posts hitherto filled from England was allocated to the latter section. Under this arrangement the quality of the provincial staff improved progressively, but in some cases, and particularly in the main administrative service, the number of higher posts offered to them remained too small either to satisfy Indian aspirations or to maintain a regular flow of promotion, while the term 'Provincial' came in time to carry a suggestion of inferiority of social status. Indian opinion sought admission on equal terms to the Imperial services, rather than an improvement in the prospects of Provincial officers; and this opinion was expressed in the demand that examinations for admission should be held in India as well as England. A resolution in favour of such 'simultaneous examinations' was, in fact, passed in the House of Commons in 1893, but the Liberal government then in office declined to act on it, and the idea did not become a reality until after the first world war.

As regards opportunities for unpaid service, Lord Ripon, who recognised the growth of new aspirations, thought at one time of introducing an elective element in the legislative councils, but eventually decided to begin with local self-government, and the necessary legislation was passed with little opposition from the official element, and with the cordial approval of educated Indians. Elected municipal boards were a novelty in India outside the presidency towns, which had long been governed by their 'corporations.' The city-governor of Mogul times had been an autocrat with very wide powers, and the position of the English magistrate-collector was at first not materially different, though he soon obtained the informal co-operation of prominent citizens, and the practice of election began to appear here and there. In the new boards from half to three-quarters of the members were elected, and in many cases they were empowered to choose their own chairman. No general statement can be made as to the administrative value of these municipal boards. Some towns were better governed than before, and others worse ; on occasion a board might be superseded for corruption or gross inefficiency ; and the best results were obtained in those places where officials and elected members worked cordially together. Their educative value is less doubtful, for they formed a school of training for public life, and offered scope for the manifestation of public spirit ; in some places citizens began to display a new pride in their town and to be jealous of its reputation ; and it was possible for a man to spend himself on behalf of his neighbours. The rural boards which were established at the same time proved to be of less value, for their organisation was in some respects defective, while their powers and resources were too narrowly limited to give much scope for the spirit of service ; it was often hard to get electors to vote, or candidates to stand, and sometimes equally hard to get a quorum of members to attend a meeting where no exciting business was to be transacted.

The enlargement of the legislative councils, which Lord Ripon had postponed, was taken up by his successor, Lord Dufferin, who was impressed by the growing demand, and also by the increasing number of Indians qualified to make competent legislators. In 1888 he sent home a definite plan for enlarging the provincial councils, and for the introduction of the elective principle, while he also recommended that members should be allowed to ask questions and discuss the provincial budget. The idea of election proved to be repugnant to the authorities in England ; and the Act which was passed in 1892, after a delay caused by parliamentary exigencies, left the methods of selecting unofficial members to be decided by the Indian government.

The arrangement adopted was to invite certain bodies possessing a more or less representative character to recommend persons, whom the government could then nominate as members; and, since the recommendations were ordinarily accepted, the principle of electing legislators was thus recognised in fact, though not in form. The bodies invited to make recommendations were of two kinds: municipal and rural boards chose persons who may be regarded as representing the general population; universities, chambers of commerce, and associations of landholders chose persons to represent their special interests; while the government nominated members to represent other special classes which had no organisation of their own. In this way the legislatures acquired the hybrid character which they still retain, some of the members coming from local constituencies of the kind familiar in England, but others chosen by, or for, particular classes or interests, like the university members who form an exceptional element in the House of Commons. The legislatures so constituted continued to function until 1909. They still contained an official majority, and, while the numbers of unofficial members had been increased, and individuals were able to acquire a certain amount of influence, they soon proved to be inadequate either to meet the needs or to satisfy the aspirations of the country.

CHAPTER XLVIII

THE RISE OF POLITICS

THE year 1885 may be taken as the first significant date in the history of Indian politics. In Mogul times, and earlier, there had been no scope for politics, in the sense of free and open discussion of public policy and voluntary organisation of parties or groups for the expression of common views. In those days policy was decided by the ruler after secret consultation with his ministers or other advisers; and, the decision once taken, open opposition would have been tantamount to rebellion. Ordinary people were interested in men rather than measures, and questions of the succession to power, as ruler or minister or viceroy, often concerned them in their daily lives; but it was dangerous to take a side openly on such questions, for the partisans of a losing candidate had to expect the displeasure of the winner. Thus the nearest approach to politics in those days was to be found in covert personal intrigue.

The opportunity for political discussion, and also the example, came with British rule. Except for two short periods, the press had been free since 1836: Canning's restrictions, imposed during the Mutiny, lasted only for a year, while the Act for controlling the vernacular press which Lytton passed in 1878 was repealed four years later; and, apart from these intervals, journalists had been subject to no restraint other than the ordinary law of sedition and libel. The papers published for Englishmen in India had from the outset conformed to the English practice of vigorous independent criticism of the actions of the Government, and their example had been followed by Indian journalists, so that free and open political discussion had come into the life of India. Organisation for the expression of common views began to appear in the 'seventies, mainly in Calcutta, under the leadership of Surendra Nath Banerji and some other Indians who had been educated in England; and the new movement crystallised out in the first meeting of the Indian National Congress, which took place in 1885. This body was national in its aim, for it thought and spoke of India as a whole, but it was not national in its composition, for it represented directly only one fraction of Indian life, and failed to win the support of many important elements.

It would be a mistake to think of Indian politics in terms of the traditional British two-party system, as typified in the rectangular House of Commons; a closer analogy can be drawn from the continental semicircular Chamber, with the members arranged in groups from right to left. The original Congress may be described on this analogy as representing the intelligentsia of the Left; its outlook was urban rather than rural; it had no organic connection with peasants, labourers, or country traders; the landholders and the other interests which would naturally gather on the Right for the most part held aloof. Those who attended the annual meetings were mainly Hindus, with some Parsees and Moslems; but in the North the bulk of the latter community followed the lead of Sir Sayyid Ahmad, who considered the movement to be dangerous, and urged entire abstention. In the early stages there was no effective local organisation to choose delegates to attend the Congress, and in practice many of the representatives might almost be described as self-chosen. The great majority of those who attended the Congress were lawyers, teachers or journalists, that is to say, they belonged to the three new professions which had grown up under British rule; a few Englishmen or Scotsmen gave substantial help in the early stages; the procedure was modelled on English practice; and the movement may justly be described as an attempt to influence the Government within the existing constitution.

The chief concrete demands of the Congress were at first twofold: representation in the legislative councils, and simultaneous examinations for the Civil Service; but, as time passed, new items were added to its programme. In the early years its attention was directed towards social as well as political reform, but such topics provoked acute differences of opinion in a body which aimed at presenting a united front, and the Congress ultimately confined itself to politics, while a Social Conference, meeting at the same time and consisting for the most part of the same people, but with the addition of government officials who could not take part in the political gatherings, discussed the moral and social problems of the country. Somewhat later economic questions were transferred in the same way to the Industrial Conference, a body of similar nature, and Congress became purely political in the narrow sense of the term; but the presence in the same place of politicians, social reformers and economists necessarily resulted in informal contacts, which influenced the proceedings of all three bodies.

The desire for a united front was a powerful motive. In the early days there was, in fact, little difference of opinion on political topics, but in the later 'nineties a split began to appear between the Left Centre, which remained constitutional, and the Extreme Left, which was revolutionary, aiming at the termination of British rule. For some years the tension within the Congress was acute, but it was as far as possible concealed from the public behind the screen of what was known as the 'subjects committee,' a body which drafted the resolutions to be moved in the full Congress, and was usually able to find a formula which would secure a unanimous vote. Its most famous formula was the word *swarāj* (literally, ' self-rule '), which was declared in 1906 to be the objective of the Congress, and which was interpreted by one group as independence of England, by the other as responsible government within the British Empire. The fissure was, however, too deep for such expedients, and in the following year the Congress at Surat broke up in disorder, leaving the Left Centre, or 'Moderate Party' as it was called at the time, in possession of the organisation. This event marked the close of the first stage in the evolution of Indian politics.

During the two decades occupied by this stage, the

numbers of the literate classes increased progressively with the continued extension of English education, and there was a corresponding growth of the influence of the Indian press. Its news service was, however, very defective, and readers who wanted to know all that was happening, either in India or in the world at large, had still to turn to the papers published primarily for Englishmen, which in this respect were much better equipped. Literate opinion had ceased to be purely local, and was interested in what happened outside India. The menace on the frontier was to some extent realised, and exercised a restraining influence in political discussion ; on the other hand the early defeats in the Boer War (1899–1902), and the delay in bringing it to an end, led some Indians to doubt whether England was as strong as they had supposed ; while the success of Japan against Russia (1904–1905), popularly represented as the victory of Asia over Europe, stimulated nationalist sentiment in a remarkable way. The main features of Indian response to these stimuli, and to others which will be indicated further on, were the growth of a feeling of national self-respect, a tendency to self-assertion, a claim that India should not be regarded as inferior to any other nation, and indignant protests against anything like discrimination against Indians living abroad.

The reaction of opinion to events in India itself followed similar lines, but from the nature of the case it tended to take an anti-English tinge, and to coalesce with the racial feeling which, as we shall shortly see, was growing up. If an official act was to be criticised, it was usually the act of English officials, and Englishmen had to bear the blame ; any instance of high-handed conduct, or misconduct, by an Englishman—a planter, a subordinate on the railway, or a soldier out shooting—was ' good copy ' for a section of the press, which would not have been interested in similar acts done by Indians ; and, speaking generally, the tendency was to attribute all India's evils to English rule. The prevailing ignorance of Indian history counted for much in this development. The text-books in use a generation ago were very inadequate, for historical research had made but little progress, while the Victorian complacency of their tone made their Indian readers all the more inclined, by a not unnatural reaction, to accept at face value the alternative accounts put forward from time to time of a great and glorious past blighted by the devastating rule of the English, or by the plague of western civilisation which the English had introduced. It is true that voices of eminent Indians were raised on the other side, men who realised the benefits which had come from the West as well as their attendant drawbacks; but in such matters attack is easier than defence, and incidents like the imposition of countervailing excise duties mentioned in the last chapter contributed very materially to the supply of ammunition.

It would be a mistake, however, to infer that all Englishmen were becoming unpopular, for individuals who responded to the new Indian feelings could become heroes in Indian eyes. The point may be illustrated by contrasting the first and last Viceroys of this period. Ripon was a good party man, who held office in successive Liberal administrations over nearly half a century with credit, though without particular distinction; but the nature of the measures introduced in his time, particularly the repeal of the Press Act and the Ilbert Bill (mentioned below), combined with his personal attitude to win for him unexampled popularity among the literate classes. Curzon, an administrator of the highest distinction, who did more for the material advancement of India than any Viceroy since Dalhousie, won a corresponding unpopularity, partly by some of the measures which he introduced, but mainly by some tactless utterances, which expressed all too clearly his scornful attitude towards Indian aspirations.

During this period, then, an important section of Indian literate opinion became organised for expression, and found its collective voice; the Left was vocal, but the Right remained almost silent, and practically unorganised. Operating on the Left flank, and directing their attention largely to the illiterate masses, were people who were often

AGITATION

described by the general name of agitators. These did not constitute a homogeneous body. Some of them were honest fanatics, careless of anything but their immediate object; some were men with grievances, real or imaginary; some were journalists in search of circulation; and a few were mere criminals, eager for troubled waters in which to fish; but, while their motives varied, the result of their activities was either to set class against class, or to set one class, or all classes, against the government. Examples of the former will be given later on; here we will instance the agitations directed against the government which were aroused by the Age of Consent Bill and by the measures taken to prevent the spread of plague.

The framers of the Indian Penal Code, having regard to the prevalence of early marriage, had fixed ten years as the 'age of consent,' that is to say, the age below which a wife's consent is not a valid defence against a charge of rape. Attention was directed to this provision of the law by the tragic death of a child-wife as the result of her husband's violence, and by the Act passed in 1891 the age was raised to twelve, still very low when judged by western standards. The Bill had the approval of many progressive Hindus, but a violent agitation against it appeared among some sections of the community in two centres, Calcutta and Poona; the cry of 'religion in danger' was raised in both places; and in the latter the attack developed into abuse of non-Hindus in general, whether Moslems or Europeans. In these centres the agitation was largely open, but in some places remote from them it was carried on below the surface; the word was passed round that Hinduism itself was threatened, and a feeling of vague alarm was produced in the minds of many who had no knowledge of the facts, but were led to think in a general way that the government was hostile to their cherished institutions.

The protagonist at Poona was a Brāhman named Bal Gangādhar Tilak, an able educationist and journalist, who soon after became the leader of the Extreme Left in the Congress. It was he, too, who took the most prominent part in the plague agitation which began in 1897. Indian memories of this disease had become blurred; outbreaks of cholera and smallpox were familiar incidents, but plague was a new terror, for which ordinary people were ready to grasp at any explanation that might be offered. At this period there was no way of fighting the epidemic beyond the time-honoured segregation of infected persons; house-to-house visits for this purpose were offensive to Indian ideas of privacy; and, since Indian voluntary workers could not be obtained, British soldiers were sometimes employed to search for suspected cases. The conduct of the soldiers detailed for this duty at Poona was violently attacked in Tilak's journal, and the attack developed into an indictment of the British government as a whole, in terms which led to Tilak's conviction for sedition, after two English officers had been assassinated. In this case, too, the agitation in Poona was largely open, but, as plague spread through the country, its advance was preceded by vague terror, which agitators, working below the surface, tried, and sometimes with success, to mould into concrete hostility to the government and its officers; 'plague riots' became a familiar heading in the newspapers; and endeavours to control the epidemic were rendered ineffective by the tacit resistance or open opposition of the people.

We now turn from the national to the sectional side of Indian politics, and must begin with a word of caution. For descriptive purposes it is necessary to write separately of national and regional, of racial and communal, movements, but it must not be supposed that these proceeded independently of each other; they were sometimes closely interlocked, and always they reacted on each other in such a way as to produce what looked to the casual observer like purposeless chaos. The clue to the labyrinth is the spirit of self-assertion, and the aspiration towards collective self-respect, manifested sometimes by sections and sometimes by those who had grasped the idea of India as a whole; sections claimed their due place in the emergent nation, the nation claimed its due place in the world, and since sentiment rather than reason was at work, it was inevitable that the claims should sometimes overlap.

Among regional movements we may glance at the claims put forward in the Marātha country, and in Bengal. In the former the cult of Sivājī, the great Marātha leader, was initiated in the 'nineties, largely through the efforts of Tilak. Sivājī was depicted as a national hero, almost as a demigod, and the celebrations organised in his honour created extraordinary popular enthusiasm in the home-country of the Marāthas. The movement had, however, also communal and racial implications, for Sivājī was glorified at the expense of the Moslems whom he successfully resisted, while the alleged prosperity of his subjects was contrasted with the ruin of India under British rule.

Geographical conditions tended, as we have said in an earlier chapter, to cut Bengal off from the rest of India, and in Moslem times it was regarded as a region with a life of its own ; it was the first part of India to experience, and respond to, the new influences introduced by the Company's rule ; and throughout the nineteenth century it retained a distinctive position. For administrative purposes, however, it was grouped with Bihār, Orissa and Chota Nāgpur in a single province, which eventually proved to be unworkable, and in Curzon's time the decision was taken to split it into two ; Eastern Bengal was jooined to Assam to form one province, Western Bengal with Bihār and Chota Nāgpur constituted the other. The announcement of this partition made in 1905 provoked a storm of protest from the Hindus of Bengal, a storm which took the government entirely by surprise ; they received the sympathy of politicians in other parts of India, but the feeling was essentially regional, and the ' motherland ' which had been ruthlessly ' torn in two ' was Bengal, not India. The revolutionary movement in this region, which we shall have to describe in the next chapter, had some of its roots in this agitation, the significance of which for our present purpose lies in the evidence it furnishes of the reality and depth of the regional patriotism which existed—unnoticed until its expression was provoked.

The main racial development of the period was the growth of hostility to Europeans in general, and Englishmen in particular. A most important factor in this development was the agitation directed against the Ilbert Bill, introduced in 1883. The Bill, which took its popular name from the Legal Member of Council who was in charge of it, though not its author, was a modest measure designed to remove an administrative anomaly. We have seen that Indians were first employed as magistrates merely to relieve overworked Englishmen of the less important cases, and at first there was neither need nor demand for giving them power to try Englishmen, whose cases were heard only by English magistrates specially empowered for the purpose. By about 1880, however, Indians who had entered the Civil Service were becoming senior enough to be appointed District Magistrates, and it was an obvious anomaly that under the existing law the chief authority in a district could not dispose of cases which might be within the competence of one of his subordinates. The Bill designed to remove this anomaly met with furious opposition from the unofficial English element in Bengal and Bihār, mainly the growers of tea and indigo, who, living in districts remote from the capital, objected to be placed in the power of an Indian magistrate; and their attitude had the support of many local officials, headed by the Lieutenant-Governor of Bengal. Their hostility was based directly on racial grounds, and, by some of the leaders and their supporters in the press, was expressed in terms which far exceeded the usual limits of political controversy; a section of the Indian press naturally replied in kind; and the racial issue was fairly joined. A compromise was eventually arranged, but much mischief had been done, and throughout a large part of India a definite tendency towards estrangement had come into existence—a tendency which, as we have seen, was manifested increasingly in a large section of the Indian press.

The compromise included one provision which had unfortunate results in practice. Under it Europeans were entitled to claim that they should be tried by a jury on which at least half the jurors should be of their own race ; and, except in a few places, the material for competent juries was scanty. Most Europeans of position were exempted from serving, on one ground or another, while the comparatively large and growing classes of men, whether European or of mixed race, employed in subordinate posts on the railways, or in shops and factories, were sometimes inclined to regard themselves when serving on a jury as champions of racial superiority rather than impartial judges of fact. Some failures of justice undoubtedly occurred, more were asserted or imagined, and every case in which a European was accused by an Indian offered an opportunity for racial recrimination in the press and elsewhere.

As the century drew towards its end, racial estrangement became manifest in the sphere of social relations. Indians of position had ceased to be content with the conditions we have described in an earlier chapter, under which 'society' was represented mainly by the Englishmen living in each administrative centre; and some of them began to seek admittance on a footing of equality to this local society, usually typified by a club, to which English officers of a certain rank were in practice admitted as a matter of course, while other candidates were subjected to the ordeal of the ballot. Some unfortunate incidents resulted ; here and there Indians were blackballed, or their names were withdrawn to avoid that result ; and petty local squabbles were magnified by gossip in such a way as to take on the appearance of a general movement. Very few Indians, however, were personally affected by such incidents as these. The self-respect of a much larger number was wounded from time to time by the discourteous behaviour of individual Europeans, usually though not invariably holding quite subordinate positions, but asserting claims to superiority on the strength of their blood ; and every wound of the kind contributed its quota towards the general feeling which was growing up. The result over a large part of India was that, while most English officers had many Indian friends, and some were popular with Indians as a body, the English came to be regarded as an exclusive society, hostile to Indian social aspirations, and determined to keep Indians in the subordinate position from which they were trying to escape.

The word 'communal' has come into use in India to describe the claims put forward by adherents of particular creeds, or sections of them, to what they regard as their due share in the general life of the country. The Parsees and Christians have made no such communal claims; those of the Sikhs affect only the Punjab; those of domiciled Europeans and the mixed race [1] concern a wider area but are numerically unimportant; and the present survey may be confined to two communities, the Moslems and the depressed Hindu castes.

In the towns, and still more in the villages, Hindus and Moslems ordinarily live in amity side by side, on the basis of respecting each other's feelings; but this amity is liable to be disturbed at any time by disputes which may lead to terrible scenes of violence and bloodshed. The two principal sources of such disputes are cow-killing and processions. Some Moslems like beef, and are not inclined to abstain from it in deference to Hindu reverence for the cow and her progeny, while the ritual of their creed recognises the sacrifice of a cow [2] on one of their great festivals, that which commemorates the deliverance of Isaac, or, as Moslems say,

[1] The nomenclature is treacherous here. In early days men of the mixed race were called 'East Indians,' or more contemptuously 'half-castes'; and the term Eurasian was coined in order to avoid hurting their feelings. In time, however, this name also acquired a contemptuous flavour, and the Indian government acceded to the request of the community to be called Anglo-Indians. The latter term is consequently ambiguous. Throughout English literature it bears the precise sense of a person of British birth who has lived long in India, but in recent official documents and in the contemporary press it means a person of mixed race.

[2] In technical language the sacrifice of some animal at this festival is *sunna*, or obligatory in the second degree, on every free Moslem who has the means to provide one. According to the treatise most widely accepted by Indian Moslems as authoritative, 'The sacrifice established for one person is a goat, and that for seven a cow or a camel. If a cow be sacrificed for any number of people fewer than seven it is lawful, but it is otherwise if sacrificed on account of eight' (*The Hidaya*, tr. C. Hamilton (London, 1870), p. 592).

Ishmael ; both Hindus and Moslems have periodical religious processions with loud music, and disturbance of worship by the noise of a procession not infrequently provokes retaliation. We have very little knowledge regarding the frequency of disputes arising from these causes, or others of less importance, during the Moslem period ; we know only that they occurred from time to time. Under British rule such disputes have been frequent, but the great majority of them have been adjusted in a friendly way through the mediation of local officials or residents of position, and in nearly every case where the peace has been broken the mischief has been caused by agitators, who have stirred the religious sentiments of the people to a point where conciliation has become hopeless.

In the 'eighties a movement for the abolition of cow-killing was started by Dayānand, the founder of the Ārya Samāj ; it was taken up vigorously in many places, and the result was a deplorable embitterment of religious feeling, with many riots and other crimes of violence, which made the early 'nineties a landmark in the history of the relations between Hindus and Moslems. The activity of this particular movement eventually declined, after much mischief had been done, but by this time the new spirit of self-assertion was at work in both communities. Some earnest Moslems initiated a movement to purify Islam in India from various Hindu practices by which it was in their eyes contaminated : some equally earnest Hindus exerted themselves to bring Moslem, and also Christian, converts back to what they regarded as the true fold ; and these conflicting propaganda, which are still active, helped to maintain the tension between the two communities. It would be quite unjust to say that Hindus and Moslems had become mutually hostile in the mass, but there was in fact some increase of mutual suspicion, a greater tendency to look for causes of offence, an inclination to settle disputes by violence, and a correspondingly enlarged scope for the efforts of agitators ; while at the same time the activities of the press gave a new importance to each local dispute, exaggerated accounts of which might provoke a reaction in distant parts of India.

The new spirit of self-assertion was manifested among Hindus of both the traditional and the eclectic schools of which we have spoken. The most thorough-going adherents of the former school now maintained that traditional Hinduism was wholly good, that western civilisation was wholly bad, and that it was the duty of every Hindu to do everything he could to save India from the poison offered by the West : such teaching inevitably tended to reinforce both the nationalist movement and the racial bitterness which we have described. The eclectics, represented by the Ārya Samāj, preached very much the same gospel, if ' Hinduism ' is taken in the sense in which they understood it, as those parts of traditional Hinduism which should be retained ; but their advocacy of cow-protection brought them into conflict with Moslems as well as Europeans.

Among Moslems the earlier doctrine of the obligation to rebel had practically disappeared, and it was now generally agreed that they might lawfully live as subjects of the British government in India, while the full acceptance of western education, the fruit of Sir Sayyid Ahmad's teaching, had brought with it a new tendency to take an active part in politics. But a conflict of loyalties had come into existence. Moslems were Indians, and the ideals of Indian nationalism appealed to many of them in the same way as they appealed to Hindus; but many of them clung to their older, and wider, ideal of a universal brotherhood, and a theocracy independent of racial or geographical limitations. The question which they had to ask themselves, Are we Moslem Indians, or Indian Moslems ? lies at the root of the activities of the community during the last half-century. In the period with which we are now dealing, the most noticeable activity was organisation for defence against the attacks of Christian missionaries and of the Ārya Samāj ; Islam, like other communities, became self-assertive, and the tendency of the time was towards increased insistence on the orthodox creed, and determination to maintain the distinctive position of its adherents. The Caliph, the vicegerent of God on earth, was still a living reality, and Indian

THE DEPRESSED CLASSES

Moslems watched with anxious eyes the vicissitudes of Turkey, the Sultan of which then occupied that position;[1] up to the year 1905, and later, large sections of the vocal community were Moslems first, and Indians next.

Inside Hinduism, a movement towards self-assertion arose among the lowest castes, described variously as 'depressed,' or 'untouchable,' who under the existing Hindu system suffered from many social and economic disabilities, but had hitherto accepted their position as natural. This movement owed much to missionary activities. The older Protestant missions were for the most part evangelist rather than proselytising; they welcomed sincere converts, but their main occupations were preaching and teaching. From about 1880 onwards, however, American missions spread over large parts of India, and devoted themselves particularly to the depressed classes; some of them were definitely proselytising agencies, and all of them brought a distinctive atmosphere of freedom and progress into their work. They gained many converts, but their influence extended much more widely, so that the depressed classes, here and there, began to ask why they remained depressed, and to assert a claim to a better position. The same result followed from the work of the Salvation Army, which started a little later among the lowest classes of all; and by the end of our period the condition of the 'untouchables' had become a living question.

Among the higher castes the reaction to this movement was twofold. Some people stood firm by tradition, and would hear of no change; but others recognised frankly that the tradition was a bad one, and that the claims of the depressed classes were in substance justified, while they felt it as a slur that it had been left to foreigners to do what Hindus should have done. The latter view gave an impetus to the idea of organised social service, which hitherto had made little headway among Indians; some Hindus now set out to do as the missionaries had done, and improve the lot of the lowest classes within the pale of Hinduism;

---

[1] This statement represents the view popularly held in India; its technical accuracy has been questioned.

and philanthropical societies of different types came into existence.

The new spirit of self-assertion inevitably manifested itself in the field of culture as well as politics ; it found expression in the literature produced during the period, in music and the drama, in the renascence of Indian art, in the study of science, and in the pursuit of organised amusements ; in all these activities Indians set out to do what Englishmen did, and, if possible, do it better. Literary journals began to appear, theatrical companies went on tour, amateurs of music organised concerts, all on English models, but increasingly with Indian inspiration. The new Indian art arose in the schools of Calcutta and Bombay ; the guidance in the earliest stages came from a few English teachers, but they based their lessons on what had survived in India, rather than on contemporary European practice, and, while external influences could not be entirely excluded, they were in fact transmuted, so that the new art, which has now become so familiar in the West, is in the true Indian tradition of grace and beauty.

The advanced study of science had still to be pursued abroad, for up to the end of our period the facilities in India remained scanty, though the new policy inaugurated by Curzon was shortly to bear fruit in institutions for higher scientific and technical education. Indian names now appeared in increasing numbers in the Tripos lists at Cambridge, where there was an Indian Senior Wrangler in 1899, and papers by Indians began to find a place in the transactions of English learned societies ; scientific research was becoming a part of the life of India.

It was not, however, for science only that students came from India to England, and their numbers increased largely during this period ; there were 160 in 1887, but twenty years later there were more than 700 ; and this rise in numbers was inevitably accompanied by a decline in the average of quality. The proportion of failures rose ; the increased numbers made it easier for Indian students to form little societies of their own and more difficult to mix with British students; a few Indians in England got into trouble; the failures helped to lower the high opinion that Indian students of an earlier generation had won in England and contributed something to the social estrangement of which we have already written.

The most important factor working in the contrary direction was the spread of organised amusements. Polo, the great game of the nomads of Central Asia, was played in India in Mogul times, but it seems to have died out except in parts of the Himalayas; English officers reintroduced it in the plains, where it was taken up with ardour, particularly in the Rājput States, and East and West met on the polo ground in an atmosphere of sportsmanship and cordiality. The distinctively English games, cricket and football, hockey and lawn tennis, came to the schools and colleges in the wake of English education; and during this period of social estrangement the general experience was that the playing-field was the place where Englishmen and Indians could meet on the most satisfactory terms. Nor is it irrelevant to recall that in the same period the genius and sportsmanship of Ranjītsinhjī, subsequently the Jām of Nawānagar, brought a revelation of hitherto unsuspected Indian qualities to the masses of the people wherever cricket was seriously played.

CHAPTER XLIX

UNREST AND REFORMS, 1906–1914

Viceroys : LORD MINTO, 1905–1910 ;
LORD HARDINGE, 1910–1916.

THE years which intervened between the departure of Lord Curzon and the outbreak of the War were characterised on the one hand by important constitutional changes, and on the other by dangerous revolutionary conspiracies : before dealing with these topics, we will review very briefly the general course of events. In 1911 King George V visited India in state, and was welcomed, by peasants as by Princes, in a way that left no doubt of the devotion of the people to the person of their Emperor. The occasion was taken to announce certain measures on which the Government had decided, among them the transfer of the capital of India to a new city to be built at Delhi, and the reconstitution of Bengal as a single province, separate from Assam on the east, and from Bihār with Orissa and Chota Nāgpur on the west.

The sentiment of devotion to the Emperor of India must be distinguished from acceptance of a position within the British Empire. The great bulk of Indian literate opinion regarded the British connection as desirable, or at least inevitable, but there was a small, though vocal, minority which sought its termination, and their position was strengthened by a general feeling of resentment against the treatment of Indians in some of the Dominions. The trouble came to a head in South Africa, particularly in Natal, where there was a large Indian population, partly under indenture, and partly 'free,' to use the term which was applied to those whose indentures had expired; but the word was not strictly appropriate, for free Indians were subjected to differential taxes and other disabilities, which stamped them as inferior beings. In the Transvaal also the position was difficult : in the days of its independence the British government had protested with justice against the way in which Indians were treated, but the position accorded to them after annexation was worse than before. A period of agitation in South Africa, and indignant protest in India, led to the decision, taken in 1911, to prohibit further emigration to Natal. At the same time Indian opinion became by degrees more and more hostile to the indenture system as a whole, which was regarded as inconsistent with the sentiment of national self-respect, and in 1915 the Indian government decided that it must come to an end.

On the frontier correct, though not altogether friendly, relations were maintained with the Amīr Habībullah, who continued to seek direct contact with the government in London, while the recurring trouble with the independent tribes was kept within moderate dimensions. A new and dangerous situation had, however, developed in this region. In the nineteenth century the tribesmen had been unable to obtain arms of precision, but just at its close a trade in these, which was known as ' gun-running,' came into existence in the Persian Gulf, and modern rifles and ammunition began to reach the tribesmen, first through Baluchistan and then through Eastern Persia. This trade assumed large proportions about 1906 ; four years later it was checked by a rigorous blockade of the Gulf, but by that time the mischief had been done, and the tribes had become effectively armed, so that the potential danger in this region was greater than it had ever been.

In India itself, the population increased substantially ; the first violence of the epidemic of plague began to show signs of weakening, and in the towns, though not yet in the country, other diseases such as cholera were slowly coming under control. The mileage of railways and canals increased steadily, trade prospered, and in some parts of the country the new departments of agriculture and co-operative credit began to make their mark. The chief feature in the economic life of the period was, however, the movement in favour of industrial development. In its origin this movement was largely sentimental, and, at first, it was not very practical: the literate classes felt it to be discreditable that India should import goods which might be made in the country, national self-sufficiency was accepted as a political ideal, and in some regions it found expression in a boycott of imported commodities. The sentimental argument was reinforced strongly by the practical need for finding employment for educated men. The public services could absorb only a small proportion of the increasing annual output of the colleges, the existing professions were overcrowded, and Indians looked with jealous eyes on the factories owned and staffed almost entirely by foreigners. The main result of the discussions which took place was to emphasise the need for more science in general education, and for additional facilities for technical instruction and research; these needs had already been recognised by the authorities, but it was only when academic opinion was reinforced by a popular demand that the various governments began to act on a scale commensurate with the demand.

The outstanding concrete achievement of the period was the establishment of a modern iron and steel industry in Chota Nāgpur, at a centre where the three main requirements, ore, coal and limestone, could be assembled. The enterprise is interesting as the first example in India of large-scale industrial planning. The earlier pioneers of factory industry had started on modest lines, and expanded their operations by degrees; but the group of Indian financiers who projected this enterprise began by employing European and American experts, who, after elaborate investigations, produced plans for works on a scale unknown in India and designed throughout in accordance with the most recent science and practice of the West. The main difficulty in realising their designs lay in the fact that, while the projectors considered protective duties for a limited period to be an indispensable condition of success, free trade was still

INDUSTRIAL DEVELOPMENT

the accepted doctrine in England, and no help could be expected from John (later, Lord) Morley, who became Secretary of State in 1905. This difficulty was overcome by a scheme of assistance devised by the government in India, comprising guaranteed orders for rails and various concessions of other kinds; a company, then the largest financial concern in India, was successfully floated; and the new towns of Jamshedpur and Tatanagar, named after the original promoter, Mr. Jamsetji Tata,[1] arose in the jungle, planned, like the rest of the enterprise, on modern scientific lines.

As time went on, the aspiration for industrial development broadened, and literate opinion concentrated on economic questions, next only to politics. The poverty of the masses, the scope for agricultural improvement, the possibility of restoring the old handicrafts, the merits or demerits of free trade, the conditions of life of the factory workers, these and other connected topics came into prominence. Their discussion was characterised by much ignorant and impatient idealism, but it served to bring home the need for greater and more precise knowledge; and economic science began to assume a new importance in the universities, which at the end of our period were constituting separate faculties and appointing whole-time professors in a subject which, at its beginning, was regarded as a mere makeweight to be 'crammed' in the hope of securing a few extra marks in an examination.

This, however, was only one among many developments in the field of education. A forward movement had been started by Curzon, and the Universities Act, passed in 1904, had made it possible for these bodies to become something more than examiners, to exercise some control over the affiliated colleges, and to organise post-graduate study; but certain provisions of the Act, and notably its tendency to increase the amount of official control, were so unpopular that the realisation of its objects was delayed. Technical and vocational instruction received some though not

[1] Jamshed is the classical form of the name; Mr. Tata himself used the popular spelling Jamset-ji.

adequate attention and increased grants were made for the education of boys in primary and secondary schools. The action taken by the government was in harmony with the development of literate opinion, which was now beginning to realise the need for educating the people as a whole. During this period the most prominent figure on the Left Centre was Gopal Krishna Gokhale, himself an educationist of distinction; and it was he who, by a Bill which he introduced in 1911 but which was not accepted by the government, first brought the idea of universal primary instruction into Indian practical politics; he and his associates had a clear vision of India as a whole, and felt the necessity for bridging the gulf between the small highly-educated class and the masses of the people.

The same vision was prominent among the causes which led to increased discussion of the problems of social reform. The largest of these problems, the reconstruction of village life, had not as yet come prominently before the public, and at this time the discussions were concerned with the classes rather than the masses; but attention continued to be given to the position of the 'untouchables,' Gokhale and others insisting that Indians, who were claiming equality with other civilised nations, should aim at equality among themselves. So far as the upper and middle classes were concerned, social reform meant partly a relaxation of the rules of caste, but chiefly a change in the position of women —better education, later marriage, abandonment of the practice of seclusion, opportunities for taking as active a share in the open life of the community as they already took in the life of the family behind the veil. On these topics very much was said, and something was accomplished; the majority held firmly to the old ways, but here and there pioneers of the new showed the courage of their opinions; and a gradual change set in, cumulative in its operation, which was destined eventually to transform the whole position.

We now pass to the constitutional changes which were made in this period. Curzon, who left his mark on almost

THE LEGISLATURES

every other branch of Indian administration, had omitted to reform the legislatures which were out of date; but the Congress was insistent in its demands, and eventually put forward the objective of responsible government such as existed in the Dominions. This objective did not commend itself either to Minto in India or to Morley in Whitehall, who between them elaborated a scheme, known popularly by their joint names, for enlarging the existing legislatures and extending their powers, but formally disavowed any intention of introducing responsible government. The ' Morley-Minto ' scheme came into force in 1909.

With the increase in the number of legislators it was possible to extend the arrangements for the representation of special interests, and the hybrid composition of the councils now became more marked. In the local constituencies, which consisted of delegates chosen by the members of municipal and rural boards, the practice of election was formally recognised, and organised interests also returned their own members without the formality of recommending for nomination. The most important change in this direction was the recognition of the Moslem community as a special interest. At the outset of the discussions, Moslems, who as we have said in the last chapter were now taking an active part in politics, showed that they were unwilling to take their chance of election by constituencies in which the voters would be predominantly Hindu, and put forward a claim to separate Moslem electorates, with the number of members fixed on the basis of the importance rather than the size of the community; this claim was accepted by the government in the face of Hindu protests, and the principle of communal representation was formally incorporated in the constitution.

The legislatures consisted of three elements, officials, elected members, and non-officials nominated mainly to represent unorganised interests. In the provinces officials were in a minority, and the government could be out-voted if elected and nominated members held together; but in the central council there was still an official majority. Various new powers of criticising and initiating policy were given to the councils, but the chief practical result was that the unofficial members rapidly acquired very great influence over the conduct of the administration ; in point of form they could not do very much, but they could press their own views, put the government on its defence, and give a lead to public opinion throughout the country. Minto and Morley might disclaim any intention of introducing parliamentary institutions in India, but the effect of their work was to establish a number of legislatures working on definitely parliamentary lines, and lacking only the one institution—ministerial responsibility—which is the essence of the parliamentary system. The administrations in India remained responsible, in the last resort, to Parliament, not to the legislatures where they had to defend their policy ; and they might still have to defend a policy which they did not approve, but which was imposed on them from London. There was thus an element of unreality in the proceedings ; Indians could put forward large schemes of dubious practicability, confident that they could never be called on to bring them into operation ; and both in construction and in criticism encouragement was given to loose, irresponsible talk at a time when the interests of India required that her politicians should be brought more directly into contact with reality. Concurrently with the change in the legislatures, steps were taken to introduce an Indian element in the higher administration. In 1909 an eminent Indian lawyer was appointed a member of the Viceroy's Executive Council, and about the same time two Indians were included in the Secretary of State's Council in England.

The other outstanding feature of the period was the emergence of revolutionary conspirators, drawn mainly from the student class; their activities constituted a serious menace to the public peace, but their numbers were trifling, and included only a minute proportion of the large student population, the great bulk of which had no sympathy with their methods. The enrolment of students for this purpose had been originated by Tilak at Poona in the course

STUDENT CONSPIRATORS

of the agitation described in the preceding chapter; associations were formed ostensibly for physical culture, but in fact for the furtherance of the promoters' designs; and the murders of 1897, which open the long list of political assassinations, were committed by members of one of these societies. Tilak refrained from active agitation for some time after his first conviction, but his views were unchanged, and in 1907 his propaganda was affecting not only students, but also factory workers in the cities, and peasants in the villages, of western India. In 1908 a series of articles in which he preached violence, approved of murder, and welcomed, if he did not advocate, the use of bombs in 'political warfare,' led to his conviction, and during the six years which he spent in confinement there was a respite from conspiracy on the western side of India.

Bengal was the main centre of conspiracy during this period. Resentment of the partition of the province, combined with the pressure of middle-class unemployment, led to the adoption of the methods which Tilak had originated; and their spread was facilitated by the peculiar organisation of the schools. In other parts of India most of these institutions received grants in aid, and were accordingly subject to a certain amount of supervision; but in Bengal there were also private schools, receiving no grants, independent of control, and many of them organised to provide the largest possible quantity of 'cramming,' rather than education, at the lowest possible price. It was from these institutions that the bulk of the conspirators were recruited, badly taught lads, despondent of their future, burning with patriotism, and accepting uncritically whatever they heard from their leaders, or read in the extreme section of the press. Their activities included assassination, gang robbery, and enforcement by violence of the boycott of foreign goods.

Assassination was obviously employed in the hope of paralysing the executive by terrorism, and various attempts were made, sometimes with success, on the lives of high officers, from the Lieutenant-Governor down, on Indian police officers who had done their duty, and on Indians who had helped the police with information or in other ways;

with this object bombs were used as well as pistols, and attempts were made to wreck trains. Gang robbery was practised as an expedient to raise funds for the purpose of the conspiracy; pickets of students tried to enforce by violence the boycott which had been declared against imported goods; there was a definite attempt to revert from the new Rule of Law to the older régime of force. Efforts were also made to extend the conspiracy to other parts of India; as a rule they were unsuccessful, but there was an outbreak of crime in the Punjab, where some sections of the population had grievances of their own. Simultaneously a centre of conspiracy was established in London, where the murder of an English officer and an Indian gentleman at a social gathering brought the public into contact with this aspect of the situation; and in the United States also a conspiracy was formed to organise rebellion in India.

For the most part the administration met the outbreak of crime with the resources provided by the existing law, but it was considered necessary to take new powers to control the press, a section of which had adopted the practice, initiated by Tilak at Poona, of openly urging its readers to break the law; an Act passed in 1908 made it possible to suppress newspapers of this kind, and two years later the Press Act instituted, not a censorship, but a system of control, under which direct incitement to crime disappeared. In Bengal, however, the taste for violence had been acquired and the conspiracies continued to function, nor were they greatly affected by the announcement of the reconstruction of the Province, because the movement was, as we have said above, rooted in the economic distress of the middle classes; in some other parts of the country also there were occasional manifestations of similar activities below the surface, and an attempt on the Viceroy's life in 1912 showed that the new capital of Delhi was within their scope.

The use of violence for political ends was opposed openly by three sections of Indian opinion, while it was condemned in private by nearly everybody of importance. The Princes, who had hitherto held aloof from affairs in the provinces, were alarmed by the influence of the extremist press, and

VIOLENCE IN POLITICS

in reply to a communication from the Viceroy most of them urged that it should be brought under effective control; Gokhale and other Hindu leaders of the Left Centre took a strong line against the methods of the extremists; and the Moslem League, which contained elements of Right, Centre, and Left, affirmed its loyalty to the British government. This League came into existence in 1908. Moslem opinion had been almost leaderless since the death of Sir Sayyid Ahmad ten years before; but the prospect of constitutional changes brought home to the community the need for effective organisation, new leaders now emerged, and henceforward the League was to play an important part in Indian politics.

Regarded as a whole, the period was characterised on the surface by sectionalism rather than nationalism; Hindus were sharply divided among themselves, while they were separated from Moslems by the latter's claim to a distinctive position in the constitution; and some other communities were beginning to feel the influence of the Moslem example. Below the surface, however, the current of nationalism was gaining in strength, and in particular was beginning to affect the silent Right as well as the vocal Left; some young landholders and merchants were falling into line with the professional men whom their fathers had distrusted, some of the States were becoming increasingly conscious that their interests were bound up with those of India as a whole; the leaven was spreading gradually through the lump.

It was during this period that changes which had occurred in the internal life of the States began to show their results, and while some were still behind the provinces, a few were drawing level with them, or even tending to take the lead. Financial reform had made much headway; regular systems of budget and accounts had been introduced; the land-revenue was frequently assessed by officers borrowed for the purpose from a neighbouring province, who brought their own methods with them; surplus funds were being invested in securities or in remunerative public works; the old ideal of a full treasury, on which the ruler could draw at his pleasure, was giving place to modern conceptions of public finance. In education, sanitation and other branches of administrative activity the example set by British India was being followed, or occasionally bettered. Mysore in the south and Gwalior in the north had started on the road of deliberate economic development. In Hyderabad special interest was being taken in Urdu literature and culture. Baroda had made much progress in spreading primary education, and was prominent in social reform. In the far south, Travancore and Cochin had a literate population relatively much larger than any other part of India. These were the leaders, but in other States also the Ministers, who were in many cases borrowed from the provinces, were working towards the standards which were familiar to them. Diversity was still prominent, and some of the Rājput rulers held to the old traditions, but taken as a whole the life of the States was being assimilated to that of British India.

CHAPTER L

THE RESULTS OF THE FIRST WORLD WAR

Viceroys: LORD HARDINGE, to 1916;
LORD CHELMSFORD, 1916-1921.

THE War brought to India a distinctive position in the British Empire, and a first instalment of responsible government, accompanied by a definite hope of the ultimate attainment of what is now called ' Dominion status,' that is to say, a status within the Empire equal to that enjoyed by dominions such as Canada or Australia. These changes were not to any appreciable extent due to pressure from outside ; they resulted rather from the reaction of opinion to the facts of the time, and primarily to the great fact that India had proved to be a source of strength in the crisis which the Empire had to face.

When the War began in 1914, the external situation was comparatively favourable so far as India was concerned. In the opening weeks a German cruiser made a demonstration on the east coast, but thereafter the supremacy of the Royal Navy of England ensured the tranquillity of the Indian seas. On land, Nepal and Tibet supported the Allies, and the Amīr of Afghanistan remained loyal to his engagements, though his country was seriously disturbed through the activities of numerous German agents. The collapse of Russia in 1917 involved new danger in this direction, since, owing to the weakness of Persia, the road through Turkey to Kābul lay open to Germany, and the enemy became active on the west of Afghanistan ; but the course of the War in other directions prevented this danger from materialising, and Afghanistan itself was not invaded.

India passed through three stages, initial excitement, reaction towards apathy, and then a new and vigorous effort to meet the danger caused by Russia's collapse. On the first news of war, the Princes offered the resources of their States, as well as their personal services, and the classes whose trade was fighting were naturally enthusiastic at the chance of practising it; these results were expected, but what surprised many observers was the manifestation of a similar spirit among other classes, literate and illiterate, whose ordinary interests lay elsewhere. The decision to despatch Indian forces to France received an extraordinary popular welcome, for it gratified the sentiment of national self-assertion which was present in the consciousness of the few, and unconsciously influenced far greater numbers; for the moment political controversy was in abeyance.

As the War proceeded, the excitement waned and politics revived. The Congress held at the end of 1915 was presided over by Sir S. P. Sinha, who had been the first Indian member of the Viceroy's Council, and shortly after, as Lord Sinha, was to be the first Indian member of a British government, and the first Indian Governor of an Indian province. In his presidential address he brought out clearly the position as it presented itself to the Indians for whom he spoke; the Morley-Minto constitution led nowhere, and he asked for a clear declaration of the British objective in India, and a definite ideal towards which Indians could work. The same need had impressed itself on Lord Chelmsford, who had been serving with his territorial regiment in India for some time before his appointment as Viceroy; shortly after taking up his post he formulated the objective as self-government within the British Empire, and he submitted tentative proposals for the first steps to be taken in that direction.

While these proposals were under discussion by the authorities, an attempt was made to restore unity among Indian politicians. The Extreme Left reappeared in the Congress of 1916; and at the same time an agreement, known as the 'Lucknow pact,' was reached between the Congress, predominantly Hindu, and the Moslem League, which ended for the time the dispute over the position to be assigned to the latter community, and recognised its claims to separate electorates and to a specified proportion of seats in the legislatures. Thereafter Indian politicians were busily engaged in drafting paper constitutions until August, 1917, when Mr. E. S. Montagu, the Secretary of State for India, announced the decision of the British government on the main question which Lord Chelmsford's proposals had raised. The announcement was in the following terms :

> 'The policy of His Majesty's Government, with which the Government of India are in complete accord, is that of the increasing association of Indians in every branch of the administration and the gradual development of self-governing institutions with a view to the progressive realisation of responsible government in India as an integral part of the British Empire.'

The announcement went on to emphasise that progress must be gradual, that the stages must be determined by the British government, and that the pace must depend on the co-operation of Indians and their development of a sense of responsibility.

This announcement, while it excited some surprise, aroused little opposition in England. It is probably correct to say that up to 1914 very few Englishmen had given serious thought to the future of India. Ordinary people knew it as a distant dependency, plagued by a few irresponsible politicians and agitators, but progressing under British rule, and they were content to leave the matter there. The events of the War brought the dependency nearer to their minds, and to their hearts. Indian troops in France, and in half a dozen other theatres of war, represented a material contribution to the forces of the Empire; and feelings were stirred by various picturesque incidents of the time, which operated to make it appear natural and reasonable that the dependency should develop into a dominion. The inclusion of Indian representatives in the Imperial Conference held in 1917 and 1918 was in accordance with the new spirit, as was the agreement reached in the former year that India should have precisely the same power as the Dominions to regulate the admission of subjects of other portions of the Empire. This agreement paved the way for a settlement of some of the disputes regarding the status of Indians which had arisen with Canada and Australia; and it was supplemented by a resolution passed by the Conference of 1921, which recognised that Indians lawfully settled in one of the Dominions were entitled to the ordinary rights of citizenship. South Africa, however, dissented from this resolution, and six years had still to elapse before its relations with India were placed on a more satisfactory footing.

The objective having been decided, the Secretary of State visited India and conferred with the Viceroy regarding the first steps to be taken on the road leading to it. The questions at issue were discussed with the provincial governments and leading Indian politicians, and the result of their labours was the Report on Indian Constitutional Reforms (known popularly as the Montagu-Chelmsford Report), which was published in the summer of 1918. A Bill based on it was examined, and substantially altered, by a Select Committee of Parliament, and eventually became law as the Government of India Act, 1919. Before summarising its provisions we must return to India, where the announcement of the objective had wrought a change in the political situation.

The immediate reaction was gratification, coupled with some surprise, at a declaration which went a long way towards meeting nationalist claims, and the unofficial constitution-makers pressed eagerly forward. Closer study soon brought men into contact with the realities of the situation, and opinions began to diverge. The Right became nervous about the future; the Extreme Left saw a chance for further agitation; and sectionalism again made head, for communities and interests became concerned to strengthen their own position in the new constitution. The Left Centre, which had been weakened by the death of its leader, Gokhale, in 1915, withdrew from the Congress, which thus came to represent the Extreme Left, and it also lost the support of the Moslem League. The times, too, were unfavourable to calm discussion of political questions. The early part of 1918 saw a vigorous organisation of India's resources against the danger of enemy action in Asia; the season was bad, and famine conditions appeared in some parts of the country, though the need for relief proved much less than had been anticipated; towards the end of the year the world-outbreak of influenza wrought with terrible effect, doubling the normal death-rate of the entire country; it was a time of deep distress, anxiety and unsettlement.

It would be a mistake, however, to infer that the internal situation had been free from anxiety up to this calamitous year. In Bengal the revolutionary conspiracies had been actively pursued, with a long tale of murders and other crimes; and the conspirators were in touch with German agents who were attempting to smuggle arms into the country, and to organise an attack on Burma by way of Siam. In the Punjab there was for a time a revolutionary movement among the Sikhs, originated by the American conspiracy mentioned in the last chapter, which operated through Sikh immigrants in British Columbia, and an outbreak of violent crime occurred which required special measures for its suppression. In northern India generally, a section of Moslem opinion was gravely perturbed by the fact that Turkey, which was regarded as the seat of the Caliphate, was allied with Germany, and consequently at war with India; and a number of young Moslems crossed the frontier and joined the fanatical element among the border tribes, where a fantastic plot was hatched for establishing Moslem rule in India with German help. India as a whole stood by the Government, but there were elements in the population, numerically small but active and dangerous, which sought to overthrow it. The extent of the danger was clearly brought out in the report of a committee which was appointed in 1917, and which is known from the name of its chairman as the Rowlatt Committee.

Economic stresses were not without effect in this direction. India as a whole profited for the time by war conditions; her primary products were in increasing demand at higher and higher prices; the systematic organisation of the supply of munitions resulted in a rapid development of industrial production, part of which has proved to be permanent; there was a general rise in wages, and an increased volume of profitable trade. The dangerous elements of the population did not benefit by these movements, but they were materially affected by the rise in internal prices which necessarily followed on the demand for export; times were very hard for those whose income was fixed in money; and the strain on the middle classes, from whom practically all the conspirators were drawn, was sufficient to drive young men to lawless courses.

Public finance was necessarily affected injuriously, for the increased revenue derived from industrial and commercial activity, together with various new or enhanced taxes, was not sufficient to cover the cost of war, and the unproductive debt, which by 1914 had practically disappeared, again became important. The most striking result, however, was the break-down of the currency system under which the country had prospered since the beginning of the century. To explain how this occurred would require a review of war finance throughout the world, and we can only record the outcome; the conditions of supply and demand made the token rupee worth more than the established fraction of one-fifteenth of a sterling pound, a unit which was no longer equivalent to the old English standard of a fixed amount of gold; the depreciated pound could be bought for fewer rupees, and the rate of exchange began to rise. To dispose of a complex and technical subject, we may add that the rise continued after the war was over, and on the advice of a strong committee of financial experts the rupee was fixed at one-tenth of a gold pound. This measure ended in a spectacular fiasco, and for some years the rupee was left to find its own level, but in 1926 it was stabilised at the value of 1s. 6d. which had emerged in the open market.

In social life, it may fairly be said that the racial estrangement of which we have written was lessened by the experiences of the years of war. Comradeship in the field, a sense of common danger, the heart-searchings and revision of standards which characterised the time, all contributed

THE NEW CONSTITUTION

to initiate the change which has since occurred. The Montagu-Chelmsford Report closed with an eloquent appeal to both races, which, though it did not use the term, was couched in the spirit of the old Indian principle of *maitri*, or friendliness, on which Asoka had laid stress more than twenty centuries before; and friendliness has gained much ground in the years which have since elapsed.

We must now summarise the steps which were taken in pursuance of the announcement of policy made in 1917. That announcement dealt with two different things, the service question and the constitution. As regards the former, it was decided that the superior services, formerly called imperial, but now known as 'all-India,' should be opened to recruitment in India; for some of them recruitment in England was closed, and these were destined to become purely Indian when the existing English element retired; for others, in particular the Civil Service, recruitment went on in both countries, so arranged as to ensure a progressive increase in the Indian element. These measures operated for a time to reduce the political importance of the service question as a whole; but the government was still obliged to consider the conflicting claims of various communities to a share in appointments, so that recruitment could not become a purely automatic process; and a strong Indian demand continued for further reduction of the European element and of the powers of the Secretary of State.

As regards the constitution, the position of the Secretary of State remained formally unchanged, but a convention was recognised to the effect that he would not ordinarily interfere in purely fiscal matters where the Government of India and the Legislative Assembly were agreed, and it was admitted that the new responsibilities which were entrusted to Ministers in the provinces must be respected in Parliament. At the same time an old anomaly disappeared. The Secretary of State had hitherto been both master and agent of the Indian government; he had given them orders, and he had acted for them in the purchase of stores and various other matters of a business character. In 1920 a High Commissioner was appointed in London, to take over some of the agency business, for which he was responsible to Delhi, not to Whitehall, while the Secretary of State retained his statutory functions of superintendence and control over the government.

In India the position of the central government, which now comprised three Indian members out of seven, was weakened in two ways: it lost the power of interfering in those provincial activities which were transferred to Ministers, as explained below, while the clear-cut distinction which was drawn between central and provincial finance operated to restrict its intervention in the latter domain. The central legislature was entirely remodelled, and two chambers were formed, the Assembly and the Council of State, both of them hybrid in composition. In the larger body, the Assembly, two-thirds of the members were elected, half of them by local constituencies, the rest by constituencies representing communities or special interests; the remaining one-third were nominated, some being officials and others representative of unorganised interests. The government was thus placed in a minority on any question on which the bulk of the non-official members were opposed to it; but on all matters of importance it could override a decision of the Assembly, and legislate with the concurrence of the Council of State, which contained a substantial minority nominated by it, while the majority were elected by constituencies with a very narrow franchise, and tended to represent the Right or the Centre rather than the Left. The practical effect of these provisions was that the unofficial members of the larger body could exert very great influence in debate, and still more in committee; but they were not in any way responsible, for they knew that in any matter of importance the government would have its way.

Parallel with this central legislature, but not organically connected with it, was the Chamber of Princes. In the practice of the nineteenth century the government had dealt with each State separately, and the Princes had not maintained direct relations with each other; but, as the unification of the country proceeded, the need began to be felt for some arrangement by which their common views could be ascertained and expressed, and informal conferences had taken place during the War. This practice was now formally established, but from the nature of the case the new Chamber was purely consultative, and had no executive authority, while several of the larger States and some smaller ones decided to stand aloof.

It was in the provinces that the main constitutional changes were made. The view taken at the time was that the principle of ministerial responsibility to the legislature must be introduced, but that it was not yet possible to apply it to the whole range of provincial administration; and this view led to the arrangement which came to be known as dyarchy. Each of the larger provinces was placed in charge of a Governor, who had an Executive Council, partly English and partly Indian, and also a body of Indian Ministers. The departments of the administration were grouped as 'reserved' and 'transferred.' The reserved departments were administered by the Governor-in-Council, responsible ultimately to Parliament; the transferred departments were administered, in the official phrase, by the 'Governor acting with his Ministers.' These Ministers were chosen by him from the legislature of the province, and could hold office only with its approval, that is to say, they were responsible to it for the departments transferred to their charge, but not for those which were reserved to the Governor-in-Council.

There were some minor differences between provinces in regard to the allocation of departments, but, broadly speaking, law and order, revenue and finance, were reserved, along with the power to initiate taxation, while local government, education, sanitation and economic development were transferred to Ministers, so that the scope of their responsibility, while it was limited, was wide. It was obvious that such an arrangement would be difficult to work, and the Governor, in his individual capacity, was invested with various powers to be used in case of need; but the practicability of the scheme depended in the last resort on the attitude of those who had to work it, on co-operation between the two sides of the provincial government, and still more on legislators prepared to give it a fair chance of success.

The single-chamber provincial legislatures were, like the central Assembly, hybrid in their composition, which varied from province to province. Neglecting minor variations, they consisted of a relatively small group of officials and non-official nominees, and a preponderating majority of elected members, chosen by three classes of constituencies, local, communal and special, the general object being to secure the representation of all the important classes and interests of a heterogeneous population—the towns and the villages, Moslems, Sikhs and Europeans, universities and landholders, merchants and planters, and so on. Elections were direct, and the franchise, though still very narrow by comparison with England, was much wider than anything which India had previously known. The introduction of dyarchy was thus an act of faith. An electorate, mainly illiterate and almost wholly inexperienced, was to choose representatives who should have power to control the Ministers charged with the economic and social development of the province: the capacities of the electors, and the qualities of their representatives, could not be estimated in advance; there were grounds for anxiety as well as hope; the one thing certain was that the new constitution was an irrevocable breach with the past.

CHAPTER LI

INDIA AFTER THE FIRST WAR, 1919–1943: EXTERNAL RELATIONS

Viceroys : Lord Chelmsford, to 1921 ;
Lord Reading, 1921–1926 ;
Lord Irwin, 1926–1931 ;
Lord Willingdon, 1931–1936 ;
Lord Linlithgow, 1936–1943 ;
Lord Wavell, 1943–1947.

With the introduction of the constitution of 1919, the history of India merged in current politics ; a federal constitution for the whole of India including the States was devised and enacted by the British Parliament in 1935, partial effect being given to it in the spring of 1937. Before, however, the new constitution could be fully brought into force the second world war broke out in September 1939. It then became clear that India would need another political constitution in the post-war period, and a change took place in the attitude of the British Government in regard to the responsibility for framing it.

It is at present too early to form a proper estimate of the events that have taken place in India in the past thirty years ; all that can be attempted here is to give a brief narrative of the progress of the country between 1919 and 1937, together with an even briefer and more incomplete account of the period between 1937 and 1947.

Before describing the social and political developments that have occurred in this period it may be well to sketch briefly the country's external relations. We shall begin with Afghanistan where Amir Habibullah had been on the throne since 1901, and had held firm during the first world war to his pledged neutrality, despite internal and external pressure. He was assassinated in 1919 and his third son Amanullah succeeded him. India was then passing through a critical time, owing to serious political disturbances in the Punjab, which will be described in the next chapter. Amanullah, an impetuous and inexperienced young man, seized the opportunity to invade the North-West frontier of India. He was repulsed, and after protracted negotiations a treaty was concluded in November 1921. Following upon this treaty Afghanistan entered into direct diplomatic relations with the British Government in London and with other countries. In 1926 the Amir assumed the title of King of Afghanistan. He initiated a number of social and administrative reforms in his State; these proved premature, and as the result of more than one internal revolution there were changes of rulers. Nādir Shah ascended the throne in 1929 and resumed friendly relations with the British and Indian Governments. During the disturbances, British representatives at Kabul and many Indian residents had been in great peril, but they were rescued in time by the Royal Air Force—a remarkable feat for those early days of aviation. Nādir Shah was himself assassinated in 1933 and was succeeded by his son Zahir Shah, who had the advantage of the services of his two uncles: Hashim Khan as Prime Minister and Shah Mahmed Khan as War Minister. Hashim Khan resigned at the end of 1946 and was succeeded by Shah Mahmed Khan.

We have briefly described in Chapter XXVII the difficulties that have been encountered by the Indian Government at various times in formulating a definite policy for its sphere of interest in the tribal territory bordering on Afghanistan. It has been pointed out that a solution for these difficulties does not lie either in a 'forward policy' or in a 'closed border policy' but rather in measures which would provide adequate means of livelihood to the tribes, thereby weaning them from their raiding proclivities. This is the policy which was pursued with a great measure of success. Shortly after the close of the first world war, Waziristan, the central section of this borderland, was the scene of serious disturbances. In 1923 and following years, permanent garrisons were established in this tract, communications were improved, the country was opened up, and a satisfactory understanding was effected with the tribes. Except for occasional trouble, this policy has on the whole proved successful in Waziristan though constant vigilance remains necessary. Elsewhere on the border there has been comparative peace since the last Afghan war.

Indian Moslems have always been interested in the fortunes of the countries in the Middle East where Islam is the religion of the people, while constitutional changes in these countries have been watched by all politically-minded Indians. Thus the rise to power of Ibn Saud in Arabia, the fall of the Kajar dynasty in Persia and the election by a Constituent Assembly of Reza Shah Pahlevi as a ' constitutional monarch ' were noted by many sections of the Indian public. Some feeling was caused in India by developments in Iraq when the opportunities for trade and employment secured by Indians during the first great war were restricted in subsequent years. Anglo-Egyptian controversies in the 'twenties and 'thirties have aroused much interest among Indian politicians. The difficulties in Palestine derived from the divergent claims of Jews and Moslems have certain similarities to Indian problems of the day, and the policy of the mandatory government has been closely observed in India.

For a time the chief interest of Indians, and particularly of Moslems, was centred in events in Turkey. The rise of Mustapha Kemal in 1920, the rejection of the Treaty of Sevres and the struggle with Greece were followed with much sympathy by educated Moslems in India, who organised Red Crescent Missions for the relief of wounded and destitute Turks. The attitude of the British Government at the time towards Turkish aspirations was deeply resented by Indian Moslems and also by many Hindus. Militant Moslems organised a Khilafat (Caliphate) party, the avowed object of which was agitation for the restoration of the Sultan of Turkey as Khalifa (Caliph) of Islam to his pre-war status. The religious turn thus given to the movement attracted many adherents, and for a time the Khilafat party acted in concert with the Congress, a development which will be more fully described in a later chapter. When, however, the Sultan left Turkey and the Treaty of Lausanne was signed in 1923, it was realised that the new Turkish republic had nationalist rather than religious or Pan-Islamic aims. The Khilafat agitation died down, but Indian interest continued unabated in the social and diplomatic activities of the Turkish republic.

On the northern border of India, relations with Tibet remained friendly. The cordiality of the understanding with Nepal was strengthened by the Treaty of 1923, and subsequently it established direct diplomatic relations with Great Britain. In the last quarter of a century cultural and commercial intercourse between the two countries was considerably developed.

Beyond Nepal lies China, a great country with which India had many contacts in the early centuries of the Christian era. In more recent times, a direct connection between the two countries arose from the export of opium to China, to which reference was made in Chapter XLVI and XLVII. The trade was open to serious misunderstanding in international circles, and in the early years of this century the Indian Government took progressive steps for its termination. No opium has been exported to China since before the first world war, and all export of this drug from India was prohibited. During the last fifty years a substantial trade was developed in the supply of Indian textiles to China, and many Indian merchants settled along the coastal belt of the country. The political changes that took place in China were followed with interest in nationalist circles in India, and when the conflict with Japan began in 1931, the sympathies of the Indian public were strongly on the Chinese side. Since the commencement of the second world war, military as well as cultural contacts received a powerful impetus, and missions have been exchanged.

India's cultural relations with Japan were always more slender than with China, though the military triumph of Japan over Russia in the early years of this century and her rapid progress in commerce and industries created a deep impression in India. Before the first world war and while it lasted Japan was able to establish an extensive trade with India, buying her raw cotton and exporting to her textile and other consumption goods. This trade was further developed after the first world war, and a commercial treaty was concluded between the two countries in 1934. Some Indians went to Japan for technical training, but they have played little or no part in the industrial progress of India. Since Japan's aggression in China all sections of Indians have condemned her policy and her diplomatic methods, while more recent events along the coast of China and in Malaya and Burma caused much injury and suffering to Indian nationals in those countries.

After the conquest of Burma by the British Indian Government, that country had been constituted a province of the Indian Empire and the system of justice and administration had been assimilated to the Indian model. Availing themselves of the opportunities in a comparatively undeveloped country, a large number of Indians, traders and merchants, agriculturists and professional men, migrated to Burma and made it their permanent home, while manual labour in her ports and industrial centres was mainly performed by workers who went there for short or long periods from the east coast of India. With the rise of a nationalistic feeling in Burma the immigration of Indians came to be resented; the economic interests of Burma, where secondary industries are few, were often in conflict with those of India, and a feeling originated that Burma did not receive proper financial consideration from the Indian Government. The answer of the Indian public was that the cost of the conquest, pacification and administration of Burma had been for many years met from Indian revenues and no adequate recompense had been received. These sentiments hardened during the discussions preceding the constitutional settlement of 1935, and it was then decided to separate Burma from India, thus placing her in direct contact with the Government of England. This measure was followed by trade and financial agreements between India and Burma. Unhappily they did not lessen the tension between the Burmese and the Indians in Burma. There were anti-Indian riots and outbreaks which gave rise in their turn to considerable feeling in India. The Japanese invasion and occupation of Burma in 1942 brought about a completely new situation which will be touched upon in a later chapter.

Ever since the beginning of this century the condition of Indian settlers in countries overseas has agitated the minds of the Indian intelligentsia. We have seen in Chapters XLIV and XLIX that in the nineteenth century the needs of newer countries for cheap labour were met by the recruitment of indentured emigrants from the congested areas of India, and that in 1915 the Indian Government finally abolished the system. In 1922 legislation was enacted in India regulating the emigration of unskilled labour and enabling the government to adopt measures for the prohibition of such emigration to any country where conditions were not satisfactory. Excluding Burma, the largest numbers of Indian emigrant labourers are to be found in Ceylon and Malaya; Indian agents have been posted in these countries to watch over questions concerning wages, welfare and citizen rights of Indians. Difficulties have usually been settled by negotiation between the respective governments.

Apart from the indentured labour which went to South Africa in early days, there has been in recent decades an influx from India, both to South Africa and to the countries in East Africa, of comparatively smaller numbers of traders, artisans and professional men. It will be recalled that the position of Indians in the Dominion of South Africa was the subject of serious complaint for a long time; after the first world war the situation became acute in Kenya also. In addition, small parties of Indian traders and artisans who had emigrated to Australia, New Zealand and Canada found that they were not accorded the same citizenship rights as other subjects of the British Crown.

As we have briefly mentioned in the previous chapter, the topic was discussed at meetings of the Imperial Conference. In 1918, a resolution of the Conference affirmed the right of each self-governing community of the British Commonwealth to control by immigration restrictions the composition of its own population, and in 1921 another resolution, South Africa dissenting, admitted in principle the claim of Indians settled in other parts of the Empire to equality of citizenship. Since then, as the result of a mission undertaken by the Rt. Hon. Mr. Srinivasa Sastri, and subsequent negotiations, most of the disabilities of the small body of Indian settlers in Australia, New Zealand and the greater part of Canada have been removed, though Indians have not the right of fresh immigration to these Dominions. India's relations with these Dominions are now of a very friendly character, and the help offered and given to India during the famine of 1943 by Canada and Australia has been warmly appreciated. Trade contacts were developed by the exchange of High Commissioners with Australia and New Zealand in 1941 and Canada in 1942.

In Kenya some improvement in the position of Indians was effected in 1924, but the prohibition of Indian settlement in the highlands has continued, and the disabilities of Indian settlers are still frequently the subject of complaint.

It is with the Dominion of South Africa that Indian relations have been most strained. There are roughly two hundred thousand Indians in that country and it is estimated that more than 80 per cent. of them are now South African born. The disabilities of Indians are of long standing, and from time to time new legislation has further threatened their existing status. After the 1921 Imperial Conference, prolonged negotiation with exchange of missions took place directly between the two countries. Ultimately the Cape Town Agreement of 1927 recognised that Indians domiciled in South Africa and wishing to conform to western standards of life should be enabled to do so. Assistance was to be given to Indians who wished to leave South Africa. A number of outstanding questions were disposed of and an Indian Agent (now a High Commissioner) was stationed in South Africa. The Agreement was renewed in 1932 and, although there were many minor difficulties and differences of opinion, relations continued to be friendly until 1943, when an acute controversy arose over legislation restricting the right of Indian settlers to acquire land in certain areas in Durban and Natal. The South African Government found itself unable to accede to Indian representations, and the

Indian legislature in 1943 passed a Reciprocity Act with a retaliatory intent.[1]

Since the first world war there has been a steady improvement in the status and position of India in the councils of the British Commonwealth. Indian members were summoned to the War Conferences in 1917 and 1918 and were able to represent Indian views. The Conference of 1917 resolved that India should be represented at all future Imperial Conferences, and Indians have taken an active part in later meetings. It will be recalled that an Indian (Lord Sinha) was for a time a Minister of the Crown in England. Indians shared on an equal footing with representatives of the Dominions in the deliberations of many Imperial committees appointed to deal with questions of economic policy.

In the Naval Treaty which followed the Naval Conference of 1930, India was definitely recognised as a component unit in the Commonwealth. Representatives from India played a prominent and independent part in the Imperial Economic Conference at Ottawa in 1932 and in subsequent conferences in London. Finally, Indian representatives attended during the second world war the War Cabinet in London on the same footing as representatives from the Dominions.

In the international sphere, too, the first world war effected a momentous transformation in the position of India. The part India had played in the conduct of the war was recognised when her representatives shared in the peace negotiations and became signatories of the Treaty of Versailles and of the Covenant of the League of Nations. From the outset of its formation, India took an active part in the work of the League, though there was some complaint in nationalist circles that India was never elected to a seat in the Council of the League. Indian delegates made their mark in the Assembly and in the standing or temporary commissions of the League as well as in ancillary bodies such as those concerned with the control of narcotic drugs. The

---

[1] Negotiations were in progress in the spring of 1944 for an amicable settlement of the differences between the two countries, which proved abortive.

delegates to the Assembly have been led by an Indian since 1929 and an Indian representative (H.H. the Aga Khan) presided over the session of the Assembly in 1937.

In the International Labour Organisation India has achieved an even more prominent position. Labour questions are now of great significance in India, and it has been realised at Geneva that it is necessary to accord to India an important share in the work of the Organisation. Delegates representing the Government, employers and workers under Indian leaders have actively participated in Conferences and Committees and made valuable contributions, while an Indian was elected President of the annual Conference in 1927. India has been recognised among the chief industrial countries of the world and has a permanent seat on the governing body of the Organisation. On the other hand, the proceedings and resolutions of the Organisation have largely influenced the public and legislatures in India in concerting measures for the welfare of labour.

Similarly, India has been welcomed at all recent international conferences on questions relating to economics, communications and transport, and has also been represented at international gatherings deliberating on military and naval matters. An Indian representative sat with Dominion representatives on the British Empire delegation at the Washington Naval Armaments Conference in 1921, and India had her own delegate at the London Naval Conference in 1930. She was also fully represented at the Geneva Disarmament Conference at Geneva in 1932–1933 and in 1945 at the San Francisco Conference when the Charter of the United Nations was agreed by fifty Allied Nations, India was represented by an entirely Indian delegation which secured a notable position in the great assembly and was one of the original Members of the United Nations as she had been of the League of Nations.

Indians now participate on equal terms in unofficial international gatherings such as those of the Parliamentary Union, the World Employers' Organisations and the Pacific Conferences. In the cultural sphere, too, notable developments have occurred in this period. Exhibitions of modern

Indian art have been held in London and at Continental capitals. World interest in Indian antiquities was stimulated by the discoveries of the prehistoric civilisation of the Indus basin. At Oriental Congresses, Indian scholars have made important contributions. An authoritative deputation from the British Association for the Advancement of Science took part in a sister gathering in Calcutta, and in 1943 there was a symbolic meeting in India of the Royal Society of London. Poets like Rabindra Nath Tagore and Muhammad Iqbal have been enthusiastically received in other parts of the world.

These developments have provided knowledge and experience of international affairs not only to the growing number of Indians who have taken part in them, but also to the Indian public generally. Ignorance and misconception regarding the outside world are being dissipated. Indian culture and Indian problems have acquired fresh interest for many countries in Europe and America. India has been brought increasingly into the main stream of the life of the world.

MAP IX

INDIA
Provinces and States
English Miles
0 100 200 300 400 500

▨ Indian States

MAP X

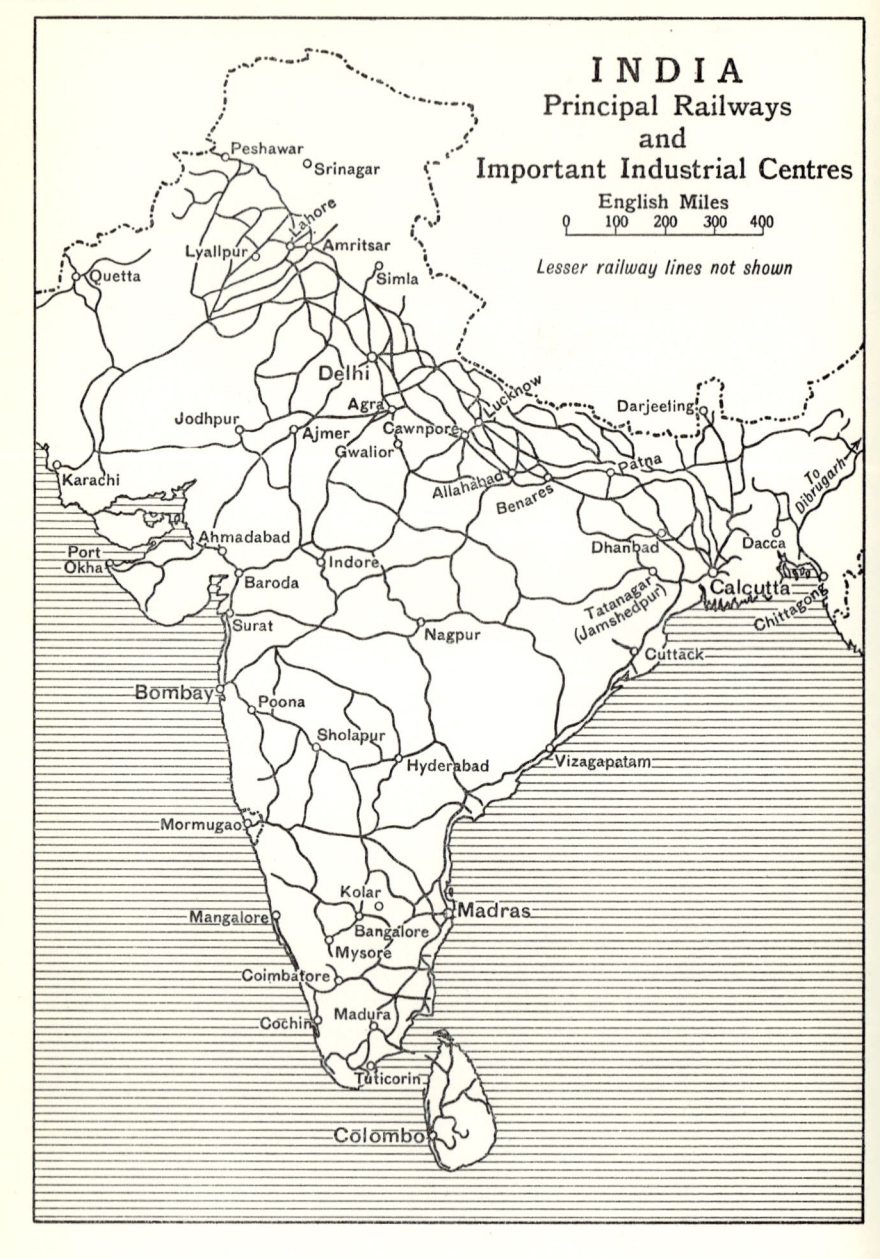

CHAPTER LII

CONSTITUTIONAL QUESTIONS: FIRST PHASE

WE have traced in the previous chapter the striking developments that took place in the period between the two world wars in the international relations of India. It will be well to bear in mind that the Reform Act of 1919 did not in itself effect any formal change in the powers of the Indian Government in this respect. The Governor-General in Council did not become responsible to the Indian legislature but continued to be responsible through the Secretary of State to the British Parliament, both in the sphere of policy and in that of legislation and administration. In actual practice, however, the Indian Government was allowed an increasing freedom in the internal as well as in the external sphere, so long as its action was not in conflict with major interests of British policy. An understanding was established that the appointment of Indian delegates to Empire and international gatherings and the instructions issued to them should be the joint concern of Delhi and Whitehall. In certain matters the relaxation of control was more definite. As a concrete example may be cited the permission to conduct direct negotiations with the Dominions and particularly with South Africa. An instance of more general and of far-reaching importance was the ' Fiscal Convention ' whereby it was conceded that, if the Indian Government and the legislature were agreed in matters relating to tariff policy, the Secretary of State or the British Parliament would not interfere. It was this ' Convention ' which enabled the Indian Government to abolish finally the ' countervailing excise duties,' to initiate the policy of ' discriminating protection ' and to conclude the Ottawa Agreement of 1932 and the Indo-Japanese Commercial Treaty of 1934. These various measures will be described in later pages.

In the present chapter we shall examine the working of the constitutional machinery provided by the Act of 1919 until it was superseded by the Act of 1935. The constitution of 1919 was introduced in India in most unfavourable circumstances. The year 1918 closed, as already stated, in widespread distress and anxiety. The monsoon had been unsatisfactory and a severe famine was apprehended in many parts of the country, but fortunately measures based on the experience of previous occasions were adopted in good time and conditions did not prove as grave as had been feared. Prices were high and there was considerable distress among people with fixed incomes and among urban and factory workers, wages not having kept pace with prices. Altogether a general post-war *malaise* affected all classes of the population.

Many sections of political Indians were not willing to admit that the proposals for the new constitution embodied an adequate measure of reform, and the Congress rapidly passed under the domination of the Extreme Left. A new leader for the Congress emerged in the person of Mr. Mohandas Karamchand Gandhi. A lawyer and a resident of Gujarat, he had lived for many years in South Africa, and had been foremost in ventilating Indian grievances there; since then he had actively supported Indian participation in the first world war. On his return home towards the end of the war, his earnestness of purpose combined with the simplicity and austerity of his personal life won for him great influence amongst all classes of the Hindu population and a commanding position in the ranks of the Congress.

It was in this unsettled atmosphere that Bills were introduced early in 1919 in the unreformed Legislative Council to give effect to the recommendations of the Rowlatt Committee. They were opposed by all sections of Indian politicians on the plea that the provisions would seriously interfere with individual liberty and were not suitable for enforcement at a time when far-reaching reforms were in contemplation.

Mr. Gandhi, who became the apostle of 'non-violent non-co-operation,' now advocated the adoption in India of the practice known as 'passive resistance'; he and his supporters announced that if the Bills were passed they would be disobeyed, and a furious agitation was conducted on these lines. The Bills were enacted in March, but before they were put in force there was an outbreak of violence, first in Delhi itself and then in the Punjab and a few other parts of India. At the same time came the troubles on the North-West Frontier caused by the Afghan invasion mentioned in the last chapter. In some districts of the Punjab the civil administration broke down and was replaced by martial law. The measures taken by the military administration, especially the firing with fatal effects on a large crowd assembled at Jalianwala near Amritsar, caused an outburst of feeling all over India. Gradually the civil administration was re-established in the Punjab and order was restored. A commission of enquiry condemned some aspects of the military administration, but the memory of the incidents remained long in the mind of the people.

The cleavage of opinion in India regarding the proposed constitution widened during the consideration of the Reform Bill in Parliament in the autumn of 1919; by the time it was passed in December of that year, the Left Centre in Indian politics now known as the 'Moderates' or 'Liberals' had formed themselves into a new party, composed mainly of men who had acquired experience in the political life of the country and in the legislative organs in the previous three decades.

The objective of this party, no less than that of the Extreme Left, was the attainment of Swaraj or self government in India, but it did not envisage separation from the British Commonwealth. The 'Moderates' were willing and ready to utilise the Act of 1919 with a view to securing as rapidly as possible a position for India similar to that of the Dominions. The Congress, which now represented the Extreme Left, resolved that 'Swaraj,' literally, self-government, must be attained 'within one year' by means of 'non-violent non-co-operation' with the Government.

It boycotted the elections for the new legislatures so that the 'Moderate' party, among whom there were Hindus as well as Moslems, constituted the bulk of the legislatures when they were inaugurated in the beginning of 1921.

At this critical period Moslem opinion in India was seriously perturbed over the events in Turkey and the terms of peace that were proposed for her after the first world war, and among militant Moslems opinion soon passed into action. In the north a movement was organised to desert India for Afghanistan, and large numbers underwent great hardships before the survivors ultimately returned to India. The more ardent spirits among Moslems now began to act in concert with Mr. Gandhi and the Congress party, while there was trouble among the Sikhs also in the Punjab and the country generally was unsettled. The Congress and the Khilafat party jointly proclaimed the policy of 'Civil Disobedience,' urging that objectionable laws should be disobeyed, though without violence. The result was serious and widespread violence among the masses who listened to such teaching, but had neither the training nor the discipline necessary for the practice of non-violence. On the Malabar Coast in the south-west of India the mixed Arab race known as Moplahs, who are zealous Moslems, broke into open rebellion in the summer of 1921 and for a short time established a reign of terror over their Hindu neighbours. Ultimately, a large section of Hindus came to disbelieve in the concordat between the extreme followers of the two religions, while the nationalistic developments in Turkey deprived the Moslem zealots of their inspiration. During these events, the Government and the new legislature were in accord in their determination to maintain the rule of law. Gradually the alliance between the Congress and the Moslem extremists was disrupted and the non-co-operation movement of 1921 collapsed. The conviction and imprisonment of Mr. Gandhi in the spring of 1922 did not provoke any renewal of disorder, and he was released a year later on grounds of health.

Meanwhile the legislatures were settling down to their new powers and functions, and their proceedings, both at the Centre and in the provinces, were conducted in an orderly and dignified fashion. At the Centre the officials and non-officials cordially co-operated in various important measures of reform. The Press Acts of 1908 and 1910 were substantially modified and a satisfactory compromise was reached about the racial discrimination in criminal procedure which had given rise to the storm over the Ilbert Bill in the 'eighties of the previous century. A new and liberal labour code was enacted and attention was given to the position of Indians overseas. A beginning was made in the appointment of Indians to commissioned ranks in the Army. The Government accepted the policy of ' discriminating protection ' recommended by a ' Fiscal Commission.' The financial and budget proposals of the Government were subjected by the Assembly to careful scrutiny.

On two points a conflict emerged between the Government and the legislature, particularly in the last session of the new Assembly. The non-official members had been watching constitutional developments in Ireland and the Middle East and, desiring to strengthen their hold over the leftist elements in the country, urged on the Government a quickening of the pace of constitutional reform, but met with no sufficient response. A more serious disagreement occurred on a taxation proposal. For reasons that will be explained in a later chapter deficits had occurred for several years in the finances of the country. Among the measures put forward by the Government to balance the budget was the doubling of the salt tax. This tax had a long history, and in the viceroyalty of Lord Curzon the Government had substantially reduced the duty in recognition of the fact that salt was a prime necessity for the agriculturists and their cattle. In the spring of 1922 the Government withdrew a proposal for enhancing the duty in deference to the views of the Assembly, but in the following year, when the proposal was renewed and rejected by a large majority in the Assembly, the Viceroy ' certified ' the enhancement of the duty under his special powers.

In the provinces, Ministers were appointed by the Governors from among the elected members to take charge of the ' transferred ' subjects, while some of the ' members of council' entrusted with the reserved subjects were non-official Indians, landholders, lawyers or industrialists belonging to the right wing of Indian politics. A number of useful legislative measures were carried through in the different provinces such as the Calcutta Municipal Act in Bengal, the Bombay Local Boards Act, the Madras State Aid to Industries Act, the Oudh Tenancy Act and certain Village Administration and Primary Education Acts.

There was financial stringency in all the provinces since the existing resources left little margin, after defraying the ordinary expenses of administration, for the development of the 'nation building' departments which were in the charge of Ministers. Though finance was a 'reserved' subject, Ministers who mostly belonged to the Moderate party feared that proposals emanating from them for enhanced taxation would give a handle to the Extreme Left who were outside the legislatures. In Madras the non-Brahmins who formed a compact party secured a majority among the non-officials in the legislature, and the Governor (Lord Willingdon) selected his Ministers from among them, thus bringing into effect a two-party system. Elsewhere the elected members followed sectional interests and the Ministers had often to lean on the official members for the support of their measures.

At this time a change took place in the attitude of some of the important leaders of the Congress party towards the new constitution. They felt that complete abstention from the constructive work that was being performed by the new legislatures tended to alienate the sympathy with Congress views among the intelligentsia. At the general elections in the autumn of 1923 they decided to stand as candidates with the avowed intention of 'destroying the constitution from within.' They were able to make much play with the defeat and discomfiture suffered by the members of the Assembly in their attempts to resist the doubling of the salt tax and to quicken the pace of constitutional advance. The Congress leaders were also able to point out how limited in actual practice was the power enjoyed by the Ministers in the provinces to advance popular education, improve public health or raise the standard of living. Some of the

THE NEW LEGISLATURES

Congress candidates had suffered detention or made other sacrifices during the movements in the immediately preceding years, and this counted in their favour with the electors. Many Congress men now entered the legislatures, and their proportion increased still further after the elections of 1926.

These new entrants to the legislatures, although vowed to destroy the constitution by obstruction from within, conformed to the traditions already established and, except in two provinces, the administration proceeded on the lines initiated in 1921. In Bengal and the Central Provinces it was made impossible at times for Ministers to hold office, and the Governor had occasionally to take over the administration. Progressive legislation continued to be enacted both at the Centre and in the Provinces, and in many cases received the support of Congress members. But there existed no longer the harmony and goodwill that prevailed in the first Legislative Assembly. With the advent of the new element among its members the Assembly devoted much of its time to arguments for further and immediate reforms in the Constitution, which the Government resisted on the ground that the Declaration of 1917 did not necessarily imply Dominion status for India and that no major changes were possible before the Royal Commission provided for in the Act of 1919 after an interval of ten years made its investigation and report.

During these years the unrest in the country became more or less localised : conspiracy was active in Bengal, the Sikh trouble continued in the Punjab and the factory workers in Bombay and elsewhere, now partially organised in trade unions, were additional sources of disturbance ; but the main cause for anxiety was a growing bitterness between Hindus and Moslems, which resulted in murderous outbreaks in widely scattered places. It cannot be asserted that at that time these recurring communal riots had general support on either side. In essence they were of the type described in an earlier chapter—local grievances, magnified by fanatics or agitators until passions became inflamed, and they were deplored by good men of both communities. Hindus and Moslems still acted together on many occasions in the legislatures and were equally insistent on further constitutional advancement. But both communities began to realise that full self-government for India could not be very distant and it was necessary to be vigilant in regard to their respective rights. The Government decided at this time on improving the emoluments of the superior civil services coupled with a large and progressive increase in the Indian element. In some of the services, such as Education and Public Works, only Indians were to be recruited ordinarily. Moslems and some of the minor communities now claimed a proportionate share in all grades of governmental services, and the fixation of this share became another element of discord.

The Moslem League was revived in 1924. While expressing its adhesion to the demand for Dominion status for India and a parliamentary system of government, the League re-affirmed the necessity for separate electorates and claimed full and complete autonomy for the Provinces, the sphere of the Central Government being confined only to matters of general and common concern. This last proviso was meant to give the Moslems a freer hand in the Provinces of Bengal and the Punjab where there was a Moslem majority in the population. At the same time a section of Hindu politicians became dissatisfied with the Congress profession of neutrality between the two religious communities and were apprehensive that Hindu interests would be sacrified in order to placate the Moslems. These militant Hindus organised themselves as the Hindu Mahāsabhā (Association).

These developments, combined with the apparent reluctance of the British Government to hasten the date for further constitutional advance, led some of the leaders of the different parties to confer together early in 1928 and to appoint a Committee to draft an agreed constitution. The draft report with some modifications was adopted by an ' All Parties Conference ' in the autumn of 1928 and was to be placed before an ' All Parties ' Convention. But finally neither the Congress nor the Moslems accepted the recommendations of the draft report, and no Convention was called together. The proposals, which need not detain us, were forgotten in the course of other important developments that took place in Indian politics at this moment.

The reader will recall the provision in the Act of 1919 for a Royal Commission to be appointed after ten years to review the working of the constitution. The Conservative Government in power in England decided to shorten the period, and in the late autumn of 1927 appointed a small commission consisting entirely of members of the British Parliament with Sir John (later Lord) Simon as Chairman. The non-inclusion of a single Indian in the Commission offended the strong sentiment of national self-respect that now prevailed in the country. The Commission visited India early in 1928 and again in the following cold weather. It was at first boycotted in India but eventually the difficulty was partially overcome and assistance was obtained from certain sections of Indian opinion. The Commission issued its report in May 1930. But before that date two striking events marked the course of Indian politics.

A Labour Government came to office in Great Britain in the summer of 1929 and the Viceroy (Lord Irwin, later Earl Halifax) visited England. On his return to India in October he made two announcements. The first was: 'In view of the doubts which have been expressed both in Great Britain and India regarding the interpretation to be placed on the intentions of the British Government in enacting the statute of 1919, I am authorised on behalf of His Majesty's Government to state clearly that, in their judgment, it is implicit in the Declaration of 1917 that the natural issue of India's constitutional progress as there contemplated is the attainment of Dominion status.'

The second announcement indicated that on receipt of the Report of the Simon Commission and before the British Government framed its own policy they would assemble a conference in London representing all sections of Indian opinion, including the Princes, to discuss with them all aspects of the problem.

The proposed inclusion in this conference of representative Indian princes needs a word of explanation. It will be recalled that in 1921 a Chamber of Princes had been established at Delhi with consultative functions and a number of states, large and small, now belonged to it. The Viceroy presided over its formal deliberations, and Indian Government officials attended meetings to assist in the discussion of matters of common interest to British India and the states. But there was no organic connection between the Chamber and the Indian legislature. Nevertheless, the economic and cultural interests of British India and the states were so intermingled that changes in the former were bound to have reactions in the latter. It was recognised on all sides that no long-term settlement of the constitutional problem of British India could ignore the question of its relations with the states.

The final recommendations of the Simon Commission may be briefly summarised. It agreed that dyarchy in the provinces should be developed into full responsible government, the Governor retaining special powers for the safety of the Province and the protection of minorities. The franchise was to be extended and the legislatures enlarged. In the Centre, in order that a federation of the provinces might ultimately be possible, the members of both houses were to be elected by the Provincial Councils. There was to be no change in the Central Executive. An All-India federation was deemed to be the ultimate aim, but was not considered immediately practicable. 'Dominion status' was not mentioned and doubts were expressed about the feasibility of a parliamentary system of government in India.

The Report of the Commission lost all importance in the eyes of Indian politicians in view of the pronouncements made several months earlier by the Viceroy about Dominion status for India and the summoning of a Round Table Conference in London. The 'Moderates,' both Hindu and Moslem, welcomed the announcements and as a rider expressed the hope that the Conference would be called together to frame a scheme of Dominion constitution for India. The Congress, under the influence of the extreme left sections of the party, refused to accept Dominion status as a substitute for complete independence which now became its aim; it also declined to send any representatives to the London

Conference. A fresh movement of 'civil disobedience' was launched in the spring of 1930, one of the principal features being a march under Mr. Gandhi's command to the sea coast of Gujarat to extract salt in violation of the laws on the subject. As in 1921, the movement, purporting to be non-violent, soon culminated in violence in practically all parts of the country. On this occasion, however, the Moslem community as a whole kept aloof. The Government took the usual measures to cope with the trouble and many of the leaders, including Mr. Gandhi, were detained in jail. The disturbances continued to the end of the year. Meanwhile the first session of the Round Table Conference was held in London in November and December.

Among those who attended were several rulers and some prominent state Ministers. The Congress refused co-operation but representative men were invited from all the other parties in India, Moderates and Moslems, the Hindu Mahasabha and the Indian Christians, the European and Anglo-Indian communities, the Sikhs and the depressed classes. There were also spokesmen of all three British parliamentary parties. At the very outset of the proceedings, in response to a suggestion from a Moderate leader, the Maharaja of Bikaner, speaking on behalf of the Princes, supported the claim for Dominion status and endorsed the proposal that India should be united on a federal basis, which the Princes would join of their own free will, provided their rights were guaranteed. The rulers further stipulated that the federal government must be largely responsible to the federal legislature. A Committee then made detailed proposals regarding the Legislature and the Executive. Other committees dealt with provincial autonomy, franchise, defence and the services, and submitted agreed recommendations. On the question of minorities, there was general concurrence that 'separate electorates' should be retained, but no agreement was secured on the questions whether this privilege should be accorded to minorities other than Moslems and whether this privilege should disappear after a certain time. Mr. MacDonald, the British Prime Minister, wound up the proceedings of the first session with the statement that the British Government 'accepted the proposals for full responsible government in the Provinces and for responsible government with some features of dualism at a federalised centre.' He added that any safeguards that might be imposed would be so framed and exercised as not to prejudice the advance to full responsibility. In order to give the Congress leaders an opportunity to consider this statement the Indian Government unconditionally released Mr. Gandhi and his associates. This was followed by conversations between the Viceroy and Mr. Gandhi, resulting in the so-called 'Gandhi-Irwin' pact of March 1931. Civil disobedience was to be effectively discontinued and reciprocal action was to be taken by the Government. The situation now rapidly improved and normal conditions were restored.

The second session of the Conference was held in the autumn of 1931. Mr. Gandhi attended it as the sole spokesman of Congress. Otherwise the composition of the Conference was much the same as at the first session except that representatives of the National Government in Great Britain replaced those of the Labour Government. The discussions centred mainly on two points, the dyarchy in the federal government and the minority representation. Mr. Gandhi refused to accept dyarchy at the Centre and he failed in his endeavour to secure agreement on the communal question. The representatives of all the minority communities joined together in the demand for separate electorates for themselves. At the end of the proceedings the National Government, which now included members of all British parties, re-affirmed the policy set forth at the close of the first session.

In India there was meanwhile a recurrence of civil disorder. The Congress complained that the Gandhi-Irwin pact was not being observed and reiterated its determination to accept no settlement short of complete independence for India.

The agricultural population were suffering from the severe fall in the prices of primary products as the result of the world economic crisis, and Congress partisans encouraged a no-rent campaign in many provinces. There was trouble in the North-West Frontier Province and there was a revival of terrorism in Bengal. The Government, with Lord Willingdon at its head, took steps to suppress the outbreak. Several Congress leaders, including Mr. Gandhi who on his return from London had associated himself with the activities of his party, were detained in jail. Congress co-operation in the work of the Round Table Conference came to an end.

Prior to the meeting of the third session of the Conference, committees appointed by the British Government toured India to make detailed enquiries on the subjects of franchise, finance and the participation of the States in the proposed federation. Since there was no prospect of an agreement on the communal question, Mr. MacDonald, the Prime Minister, announced the government scheme known as the 'Communal Award.' Separate electorates were to be provided for all the minority communities as well as for the Moslems in Bengal and the Punjab where they constituted a majority. The 'depressed classes' were recognised as a minority community entitled to separate electorates. Moslems where they were minorities and also Sikhs and Hindus in the Punjab received weightage. The 'Communal Award' was particularly obnoxious to Mr. Gandhi, then in jail in Poona, since it purported to divorce the depressed classes from the Hindus. He started a 'fast' to avert what was in his opinion a calamity and in deference to his views the caste Hindus as well as the depressed classes accepted a scheme known as the 'Poona Pact' by which the depressed classes were granted much larger representation; in return they would 'first elect a panel of candidates and from this the members of the legislatures would be elected by the general body of Hindu voters including those of the depressed classes.' This 'Pact' has ever since been resented both by caste Hindus as having substantially reduced their representation and by the 'scheduled castes' (as the depressed classes came to be called) on account of the interference of caste Hindus in their representation.

The third and last session of the Round Table Conference was held in the autumn of 1932. The main discussions concerned the methods of election to the federal chambers and the financial and other safeguards proposed by the government. After the dispersal of the Conference the British Government elaborated their draft proposals, which were carefully scrutinised by a Joint Committee of Parliament with the assistance of a number of Indians invited for the purpose. The Government of India Bill which emerged from these discussions was passed in 1935. In the ensuing chapter we shall briefly summarise the provisions of the new law and examine to what extent it has been possible to work it in practice.

CHAPTER LIII

CONSTITUTIONAL QUESTIONS: SECOND PHASE, 1935-1942

THE Constitution Act of 1935 had three features: provincial autonomy, dyarchy at the Centre, which was to include the States, and the exclusion from this Centre of relations between the States and the Paramount Power. In all cases reservations and safeguards were provided. The Federal Government at the Centre was not to be set up until a number of States sufficient to constitute half the total States population of India agreed to join the federation. On the outbreak of war negotiations for the accession of the States to the federation were suspended and have not since been renewed.

The relations between the States and British India have come into great prominence in recent years. The earlier history of these relations has been described in previous pages. In the time of Dalhousie two principles emerged in the treatment accorded by the British Government to the rulers of Indian States. We have explained how the principle of Lapse was subsequently abandoned but the principle of Paramountcy was retained. Canning restated in 1860 the doctrine of Paramountcy and laid down ' two great principles which the British Government followed in dealing with the States: (1) that the integrity of the States should be preserved by perpetuating the rule of the Princes . . ., and (2) that flagrant misgovernment must be prevented or arrested by timely exercise of intervention.'[1] These principles guided the action of the Government on subsequent occasions, and in the last quarter of a century

[1] Butler Committee's Report, para. 22, Cmd. 3302.

the Paramount Power had to intervene in several instances of gross misrule by Indian Princes. In 1926 Lord Reading held, with the approval of the British Government, that the supremacy of the Crown ' is not based only upon treaties and engagements but exists independently of them and quite apart from the prerogative in matters relating to foreign powers and policies, it is the right and duty of the British Government, while scrupulously respecting all treaties and engagements with the Indian States, to preserve peace and good order throughout India.'

The States occupied two-fifths of the area and included nearly one-quarter of the total population of India. Although there were more than five hundred States, some one hundred and twenty whose rulers were members of the Chamber of Princes in their own right made up by far the greater part of State territory and population. There was great diversity among the States in size as well as in their political, economic and cultural condition. The largest State in size was Kashmir with an area of 86,000 square miles, and the largest State in population was Hyderabad numbering sixteen million. At the other end of the scale were more than three hundred petty States covering in the aggregate an area of a little over six thousand square miles and with a total population of about a million. A noteworthy fact is that the great majority of the rulers of the States and also the greater part of their population belonged to the Hindu faith.

Over the States and the rulers the authority of the Crown, until the passing of the Act of 1935, was exercised through the Indian Government, which legally consisted of the Governor-General and his Executive Council. After the constitutional changes and pronouncements of 1919, some rulers began to be concerned respecting their future position should British India attain responsible government in course of time. Controversies had also arisen over the claims of some States to a share in British Indian maritime customs receipts and on other economic questions. A committee, under the chairmanship of Sir Harcourt Butler, was appointed in 1927 to report upon the relationship between the Paramount Power and the Indian States and to enquire

STATES AND FEDERATION 489

into the financial and economic relations between British India and the States. The view of the Committee on the first point was in accord with the opinion expressed by Lord Reading and has been summarised in Chapter XLII. On the second point the Committee indicated certain methods of adjusting relations but made no detailed recommendations. The Committee added a significant remark : ' We hold that the relationship between the Paramount Power and the Princes should not be transferred without the agreement of the latter to a new government in British India responsible to an Indian legislature.' It was not therefore without good reason that representative rulers and some of their ministers were invited to the Round Table Conference. We have described the attitude adopted by them at its sessions and the origin of the Federal scheme adopted in the Act of 1935.

Under this Act the Federal Legislature was to be bicameral. Two-fifths of the members of the Upper House and one-third of the Lower House were to be nominated by the rulers of all but the petty States we have mentioned above. Six members of the Upper Chamber were to be nominees of the Viceroy, the rest of its members being elected directly by ' separate electorates ' in territorial constituencies in the Provinces. The British Indian members of the Lower Chamber were to be elected by the Provincial legislatures.

Lists of subjects were prescribed on which the federal and provincial legislatures were respectively competent to legislate ; there was also a concurrent list of subjects in which both had jurisdiction. It was left to the Governor-General to decide, when occasion arose, whether a residuary subject was to be in the competence of the federation or of a Province.

The Executive was to consist of Ministers appointed by the Governor-General from among the members of the Legislature and was to be responsible to it. Two important subjects, defence and external affairs, were to be reserved and administered by ' counsellors ' responsible to the Governor-General. Supplies for these subjects were open to discussion in the Legislature but not open to vote. Legislation relating to coinage, currency and the constitution could not be introduced without the previous sanction of the Governor-General, who had also a 'special responsibility' for the financial credit and stability of the federation. He had certain other 'special responsibilities,' similar to those of provincial governors, which will be enumerated later.

Each ruler, before he joined the federation, was at liberty to limit the subjects in which federal jurisdiction was to apply in his State. In other internal matters the ruler was to be left free. The authority of the Paramount Power was to be exercised through a Crown Representative and not through the Government of India. The same person could be both Crown Representative and Governor-General, though their functions were different. This last change was effected in April 1937 when the Indian Government ceased to exercise the functions of the Crown in its relations with the States.

The federal system did not come into operation, and the constitution of the Central government in British India remained the same as it was under the Act of 1919, being under the control of the Secretary of State and responsible through him to the British Parliament. The Central Legislature was still governed by the rules that were in force under the old Act. The Legislative Assembly was last elected in 1934 and the Council of State in 1937. The life of both bodies was extended from time to time.

Turning to the provincial field, Burma was separated from India and now has direct relations with England. In India two new provinces were created : Sind was separated from Bombay and Orissa was carved out of the older provinces of Bihar and Madras. Of the eleven provinces thus constituted, Sind and the North-West Frontier had a preponderantly Moslem population. In the Punjab Moslems formed 57 per cent. of the population, the rest being Hindus and Sikhs. In Bengal 55 per cent. were Moslems, the rest were practically all Hindus. In each of the remaining seven provinces there was a very large Hindu majority.

Taking British India as a whole, Hindus, including scheduled castes who used to be described as the depressed classes, constituted 65 per cent. of the population and the Moslems nearly 27 per cent. Other communities made up the remaining 8 per cent.

By the Act of 1935, bicameral legislatures were established in six provinces. The franchise qualification, mostly on a property basis, was substantially lowered for the Assembly (the Lower House) and the number of its members was considerably increased. Separate electorates were provided for Moslems, Sikhs, Indian Christians, Anglo-Indians and Europeans. Representatives of the Scheduled Castes were elected in the manner described in the previous chapter. There were also seats for special interests, such as landholders, labour, commerce and industry. Room was found for a limited number of women elected according to religion. No seats were reserved for officials and the governor had no nominees.

In the Upper Chambers (Councils) a few seats were filled by nominees of the Governors. In Bengal and Bihar a considerable proportion were elected by the Lower House. The remaining seats were distributed between the different communities in territorial constituencies. For both Houses weightage was allowed for the minority communities except for Hindus in Bengal.

The executive was vested in a Council of Ministers appointed by the governor from among the elected members of the legislature and the executive was responsible to it. The financial resources of the provinces were sharply demarcated from those of the Centre. The authority of the legislature and the executive extended to all subjects which were within the competence of the provincial government as a whole in the constitution of 1919. Ordinarily, the Central government and the Central legislature had no longer any control over these subjects. The officers of the Indian Civil Service, Indian Police and Indian Medical Service employed in the provinces were recruited on an All-India basis by the Secretary of State and were subject to rules prescribed by him. The governor, who was appointed by the Crown and was responsible to the British Government through the Governor-General, had certain 'special responsibilities.' Among them were the prevention of grave menace to the peace or tranquillity of the province or any part of it, the protection of the civil servants just mentioned, the safeguarding of the legitimate interests of minorities and the prevention of discrimination against British commercial interests. The Governor-General was invested with similar responsibilities for the federation, but these were not in operation as a federation had not been established.

A chapter of the Act was devoted to provisions intended to safeguard British subjects belonging to the United Kingdom and companies incorporated there from any form of discrimination either in the provinces or by the federation.

An important section of the Act laid down that if the constitutional machinery broke down in a province, the governor should undertake all the legislative and administrative powers of the province, subject to the authority of the Governor-General (and not the Indian Government). In anticipation of the second world war, emergency powers were given by special legislation to the Governor-General and the Centre to be exercised in case of necessity.

We have given only a condensed summary of a very lengthy and complicated piece of legislation. Dyarchy was to prevail in the federal government, defence and external affairs being under the sole control of the Viceroy. Both he and the governors were endowed with many special powers. The Act prescribed a number of safeguards not only for minority communities but also in the interests of United Kingdom subjects residing in India. Superior civil servants were placed outside the control of the Indian governments. Obviously this was not a Dominion constitution. But an official spokesman stated[1] in the course of the debates on the Government of India Bill that 'special arrangements, ... freely negotiated and agreed' (between the United Kingdom and India) 'are not inconsistent with the ultimate attainment of the position of a Dominion within the Empire.'

[1] Hansard ccxcvii (1934–5), 1611–13, quoted by Coupland: 'Report on the Constitutional Problem in India,' Part I, *The Indian Problem*, p. 146 (O.U.P., 1942).

REACTIONS TO 1935 ACT

The new constitution met with a very mixed reception in India. The Liberals disliked the safeguards but were prepared to work the constitution both in the Provinces and in the Centre. The Moslems, while objecting to the federal constitution, were willing to utilise the provincial constitutions 'for what they were worth.' According to the Moslem view expressed at the time, it was preferable to have full responsible government in British India alone rather than a federal government including a preponderance of Hindu representatives from the States. The Congress condemned the new Act outright. Dyarchy combined with the representation of the States through nominees of the rulers made federation entirely unacceptable to it, while the provincial constitutions were in its eyes vitiated by the safeguards. The government commenced negotiations with the States in order to secure the accession of a sufficient number to the federation. Meanwhile it put in force the portion of the Act relating to provincial constitutions.

Provincial elections on the new basis were held early in 1937. Both the Congress and the Moslem League took an active part in the elections. The Congress stated again that its members would enter the legislatures in order to destroy the constitution from within. It published a manifesto advocating radical measures for the benefit of the rural and urban population. The 'communal award' was a special object of attack in this manifesto. The Muslim League demanded the safeguarding of the minority position of the community. It also had an advanced social programme. In the result the Congress secured large majorities in the six Hindu provinces and in the North-West Frontier. In Bengal and the Punjab, Moslems had an assured majority. In Sind and Assam there were several small parties and the situation was confused.

Coalition ministries began to function in April 1937 in the two provinces last mentioned, while in Bengal and the Punjab also proper ministries were constituted. The Congress Working Committee (popularly known as the Congress High Command) which directed the activities of all its provincial organisations, now decided that Congress members must not accept office in any province unless the governor gave an assurance that he would not use his special powers of interference. The governors, in view of the terms of the constitution, could give no such undertaking, and in order to carry on the administration appointed non-Congress ministers from the legislature. At this juncture the Viceroy (Lord Linlithgow) issued an appeal setting forth that within the narrow field of their responsibilities the governors were anxious 'not merely not to provoke conflicts with their ministers . . . but to leave nothing undone to avoid and to resolve such conflicts.' He added, however, that the interests for which the safeguards were intended must not be sacrificed. In conclusion he declared that he was himself determined 'to strive towards the full and final establishment in India of the principles of parliamentary government.' Thereupon the Congress removed its bans and Congress ministries were installed in seven provinces.

The provincial ministries had varying fortunes. In the Punjab, the Premier, Sir Sikander Hayat Khan, a statesman of ability and experience, formed a composite Ministry of Moslems, Hindus and Sikhs, and kept it together until his death in 1942, and his policy was continued by his successor. In Bengal the first Premier held office till March 1943, but the shifting politics of the different parties in the province, particularly the rise of the Moslem League, led to many changes in the composition of the ministry, and in the governments between 1943 and 1947 the majority of the ministers belonged to the Moslem League. In Assam and Sind no party enjoyed a clear majority and the governments proved unstable. In the six Hindu provinces where the Congress was predominant, the ministries were composed of Hindus and such Moslems as accepted the Congress policy. In these provinces and in the North-West Frontier the ministries held together until the outbreak of the second world war, when they resigned for reasons which will appear later. The constitutional machinery thus broke down and the governors took over the administration. Later, in Orissa, a non-Congress coalition ministry was formed in 1941, and in the North-West Frontier a Muslim League ministry took office in 1943.

PROVINCIAL MINISTRIES

In all the provinces the ministries were in the pre-war period confronted with the usual difficulties in the maintenance of law and order, but there was no serious failure anywhere. In October 1939 the Viceroy (Lord Linlithgow) acknowledged that they had conducted their affairs 'with great success' and had achieved a distinguished record. In most provinces much social legislation was passed. But there were vigorous complaints in Bengal, and to a less extent in the Punjab, of strong communal bias in the measures of these two governments. On the other hand, Moslems in the United Provinces and in Bihar declared that their interests were sacrificed and that they suffered oppression in various forms. The introduction of compulsory Hindi in the schools in Madras was resisted and the educational measures of the Central Provinces Government received special condemnation from Moslems both inside and outside the province.

The governors did not find it necessary to take any action in these matters in the exercise of their special responsibility. Nevertheless these and similar complaints widened the breach between Hindus and Moslems all over India. Congress propaganda in the countryside was met by an equally active and extensive propaganda by the Moslem League. The Hindu Mahasabha continued to object to the non-communal professions of the Congress and to urge a more militant attitude on the part of the Hindus. The Moslem League now claimed, not without dispute, that it was the only representative Moslem organisation in the country. A gradual change also took place in its views on a constitution for India. At first the League had condemned the federal proposal because it feared that the States nominees would perpetuate a Hindu majority in the legislature. Later, the view was propounded that in the circumstances of India parliamentary government might be possible provided it was not government by the majority party alone. Finally, in the spring of 1940, it was resolved [1] that no constitutional plans would be acceptable unless 'geographically

[1] Moslem League resolution—Lahore Session, 1940; Coupland II, pp. 196, 206.

contiguous units are demarcated into regions which should be so constituted with such territorial adjustments as may be necessary that the areas in which the Moslems are numerically in the majority, as in the north-western and eastern zones of India, should be grouped to constitute " independent states " in which the constituent units shall be autonomous and sovereign.' This is the scheme which is now known as ' Pakistan ' (a newly coined word meaning ' the land of the pure ').

Meanwhile there was a reaction in the States too against a scheme of federation with the provinces. The rulers could not fail to note the objections of the Congress and the Moslem League to the accession of the States. The Congress displayed an increasing interest in constitutional reform in the States, an agitation for which among their subjects had begun before the Round Table Conference and was a natural concomitant of constitutional ferment in British India. The position of the British government was that it would not obstruct proposals for constitutional advance initiated by the rulers but could not press them to initiate such changes.[1] The Congress at first declared that it would not itself operate in the States and ' the burden of carrying on the struggle must fall on the people of the States.'[2] Later, however, the Congress expressed its readiness to take a more active share in the agitation, and Congress leaders took a prominent part in meetings of the All-India States Peoples' Conference.[3] Several of the leading States and some small States became the scene of conflicts. These localised disturbances were checked but the reluctance of the States to join an all-India federation became more pronounced. The negotiations regarding Federation between the Crown Representative and the States, suspended since the outbreak of the war, did not therefore make rapid progress.

The States, however, did not stand still in the matter of constitutional reform. Among the larger States, Mysore was the most progressive in this respect. It had a bicameral

[1] R. Coupland : Report, Part II, *Indian Politics*, p. 169 (O.U.P., 1943).
[2] *Ibid.*, p. 172.   [3] *Ibid.*, p. 174.

REFORM IN THE STATES

legislature with substantial powers to discuss all legislative and financial proposals; two out of the five ministers were non-official members of the legislature. In Cochin a system of dyarchy was in operation. In Hyderabad, under a scheme promulgated some years ago but not in full operation, the electors were grouped not by religious communities but on a system of functional representation. About half the Assembly was to be elected, and with certain reservations it was to be empowered to discuss legislation and the budget. Similar constitutions functioned in Kashmir and Rampur. In Gwalior, Indore and Baroda, the legislatures were fashioned after the Mysore model but with more restricted powers. A beginning was made in Rajputana, where a constitution on a comparatively advanced model was adopted in the State of Jaipur. Some of the smaller States also established legislatures or Advisory Councils with varying powers.

Another reform of considerable importance had made progress in the States in recent years. The judiciary in most of the larger States was completely overhauled and only qualified men were recruited. In many instances the judiciary was separated from the executive, and all the larger States now possessed competent high courts. The smaller States had naturally some difficulty in this matter, but there was a movement among them, as in Orissa and the Punjab, to establish joint high courts exercising jurisdiction over several contiguous States. Similarly the small States combined to organise adequate police forces for their territories. The Crown Representative had in recent years repeatedly urged on small States generally to combine or federate among themselves for administrative purposes.

Reference has been made to the existence of several hundred small 'States' which were difficult to differentiate from 'estates,' large or small, in the British provinces. Most of these minute territories were situate in western India and their slender resources made it impossible for them to perform the duties of a modern government. For the past century their administration for all practical purposes was in the hands of British officials. They had no representation in the Chamber of Princes. It was decided to attach these fragmentary areas to larger contiguous States which would be responsible for their administration and the improvement of their social conditions. In promulgating this decision Lord Linlithgow made the important declaration that ' the ultimate test of fitness for the survival of any State is, in his opinion, capacity to secure the welfare of its subjects.'

We shall now narrate briefly the events that followed the Viceroy's proclamation in September 1939 that war had broken out between the King-Emperor and Germany. The Congress party met and expressed its condemnation of Nazism and Fascism but declared that, since war had been proclaimed without seeking or obtaining the consent of the Indian people, it could not associate itself with the war effort unless India was ' declared an independent nation and present application given to the status to the largest possible extent.' The Moslem League promised support to the war effort only on condition that no constitutional changes were made without its consent and approval. Other parties expressed wholehearted support but asked for some constitutional advance. The Viceroy replied that Dominion status was already envisaged by the British government as the goal of its policy, and that at the end of the war it would be prepared to modify the 1935 scheme to meet Indian views. This was not deemed sufficient by the Congress. Ministers of all the Congress provinces resigned and the governors undertook their administration.

A change of government took place in Great Britain in May 1940; Mr. Winston Churchill became Prime Minister and Mr. Amery was appointed Secretary of State for India. Early in August the Viceroy made an announcement on behalf of the British government which gave a completely new turn to the constitutional problem of India. Hitherto the declared policy had been that the stages and details of constitutional progress in India were to be finally determined by the British Parliament. Indians were now told that the framing of a new constitution would be primarily their own responsibility, and that after the war a representative Indian body would be set up for this task. The British government, before transferring their responsibilities, would require to be satisfied that the new government in India would not be one whose authority was denied by large or powerful elements in Indian national life to whose coercion they could not be parties. Meanwhile all parties and communities were invited to co-operate in the prosecution of the war.

The 'August offer' pleased the Liberals and the Hindu Mahasabha. The Moslem League did not reject it but demanded equal representatation with the Hindus. The Congress was not content to wait until after the war. It adopted a policy of 'individual civil disobedience' as a moral protest, and many Congress leaders and followers were imprisoned during the following months.

A year later the Executive Council of the Viceroy was considerably enlarged and had a substantial majority of Indian members. About the same time, a National Defence Council, projected with the Viceroy's announcement of August 1940, was established consisting of thirty members selected from all parts of India including the States. At its periodical meetings, under the presidency of the Viceroy, war measures were discussed.

The attitude of the two major political parties did not prevent the gradual intensification of India's war preparations during the first two years after 1939. Japan came into the war in December 1941, and in the early months of the following year had striking and rapid successes in the seas and countries to the east of India. Singapore, Malaya and the islands of the Indian Archipelago were occupied by the enemy, Burma was invaded and India was threatened.

In March the British Prime Minister described the situation as a crisis in the affairs of India and announced that Sir Stafford Cripps, a member of the War Cabinet, would fly to India with a 'Draft Declaration' on behalf of the British government 'to rally all the forces of Indian life to guard their land from the menace of the invader.' Sir Stafford Cripps spent three weeks in Delhi and discussed the proposals with the leaders of all parties as well as with the spokesman of the Princes.

The declared object of the Draft Declaration was the creation of a new Indian Union which should 'constitute a Dominion associated with the United Kingdom and the other Dominions by common allegiance to the Crown but equal to them in every respect, in no way subordinate in any aspect of its domestic or external affairs.' To this end it was proposed that :

(1) Upon the cessation of hostilities, a constitution-making body was to be set up consisting of nominees of the States and elected representatives of the provincial legislatures.

(2) Any province or provinces were to be free not to join the Indian Union and, in that case, these would be entitled, if they so wished, to form a Union or Unions of their own.

(3) The obligations of the British Government, including its undertakings for the protection of racial and religious minorities, were to be safeguarded by a treaty between it and the constitution-making body.

(4) Until a new constitution was framed, the British Government was to remain responsible for the defence of India with the help of an Indian Government composed of members of all parties and with the full co-operation of the Indian peoples.

The long-term proposals were not acceptable to the Congress leaders for two main reasons. First, in the constitution-making body the States were to be represented by the nominees of the rulers and not by persons elected by their subjects. Secondly, the unity of India might be jeopardised by the non-accession of a province or of the states. The Congress spokesman, however, stated that the Congress was prepared to accept the short-term proposal dealing with the period of the war, putting aside all questions about the future, if a 'truly national government' 'with real responsibility and power' were immediately formed.

The Moslem League rejected the scheme because in its view the primary object of the proposals was to create *one*

Indian Union, and the creation of more than one Union (that is, the Pakistan scheme) had been 'relegated only to the realm of remote possibility.' The League also disapproved of the method proposed for the election of the constitution-making body. The Sikhs protested vigorously against the possible severance of the Punjab from an All-India Union. The States wished their treaty rights to be guaranteed as a condition of their taking part in the framing of the constitution.

Sir Stafford Cripps had hoped that the principle of the Draft Declaration would be accepted apart from the scheme for the constitution-making body, and then a national government could be formed for the duration of the war. The Congress demanded a definite agreement that when a national government was appointed the Viceroy would abstain from exercising his constitutional power to overrule it in case of grave necessity. This demand could not have been met without an amendment of the existing constitution by legislation which the government was not prepared to undertake during the war. Owing to all these circumstances the negotiations broke down and Sir Stafford Cripps returned to England. The Secretary of State then stated in Parliament that though the Draft Declaration was withdrawn, its broad principles continued to be the policy of the government.

The failure of the Cripps Mission ushered in a period of acute political anxiety and disturbance in the country. In July the Working Committee of the Congress passed a resolution declaring that British rule in India must end immediately, and that if the appeal for the withdrawal of Britain failed, the Congress would be compelled, under the leadership of Mr. Gandhi, 'to utilise all the non-violent strength it had gathered since 1920.' This resolution created serious apprehension in the minds of all other parties in the country and was unequivocally condemned by them. But with a few dissentient votes the resolution was confirmed on August 8th at a largely attended meeting of the All-India Congress Committee at Bombay. The following day the Congress was declared by the Government to be an unlawful association. Mr. Gandhi and many members of the Congress were arrested and placed under detention. The serious disorders that broke out in various parts of India in the autumn of 1942 were gradually suppressed by the end of that year and Mr. Gandhi was unconditionally released in May 1944 on grounds of health.

The position of the constitutional questions dealt with in these two chapters can best be summarised in the words of Mr. Churchill, the British Prime Minister, in the House of Commons in September 1942 :

' The broad principles of the declaration made by His Majesty's Government, which formed the basis of the mission of the Lord Privy Seal (Sir Stafford Cripps) to India, must be taken as representing the settled policy of the British Crown and Parliament. These principles stand in their full scope and integrity. No one can add anything to them and no one can take anything away.'

CHAPTER LIV

DEFENCE AND FINANCE

IN the second world war India was confronted with very different problems from those with which she had to contend in the first. The primary need was for mechanised equipment and for men capable of handling it, while in the first war, though equipment of a simple character was required, the need of man-power was paramount. In the second world war India was first threatened in the West. Later, not only had she to be prepared for invasion from the East, but she had to mobilise her forces to attack in the East. While in the first world war her maritime defence was left almost entirely to the British Navy, in the second she herself made an increasing contribution to the naval operations of the war. The gradual development of India's defence measures between the two wars will be outlined in the following paragraphs.

We have described in Chapters XLIII and XLVII [1] the changes wrought in army organisation in India after the Mutiny and again early in this century. After the first world war approximately one-third of the army in India consisted of British forces with European personnel. The Indian Army proper, about a hundred and fifty thousand strong, was composed of infantry and cavalry with British officers. There was no Indian artillery or Air Force and there were very few Indians among the commissioned officers in the Indian Army. Recruitment for the army was practically confined to the northern areas of the country. The duties of the Royal Indian Marine were restricted to troop transport, port supervision and marine survey. A

[1] Pp. 371 and 421–2.

small contribution of £100,000 a year was made to the British Navy. India also made a free grant of a hundred million sterling to the British exchequer towards the cost of the first world war. The defence budget rose to 68 crores [1] in 1922; as a result of retrenchment it was reduced to 62 crores in the following year.

At this time there were insistent complaints among the Indian public and in the legislature regarding the defence organisation. It was contended that the cost, which amounted to nearly 30 per cent. of the combined Central and Provincial revenues, was too high and led to the starving of agencies for improving the standard of life of the people. The commissioned ranks of the army had been formally opened to Indians, but the number admitted was insignificant and no arrangements existed for their systematic recruitment and training. It was also urged that a national army should be built up and enlistment in the ranks should be open to all classes of the people in every part of the country.

Measures were adopted by the Government in the years that followed to meet this criticism. The strength of the army was reduced and by the exercise of economy the defence budget was brought down by 1935 to 44 crores. Welcome relief, amounting to a million and a half sterling annually, was received from the British exchequer towards the cost of British troops in India. Arrangements were made for the training of selected young Indians at Sandhurst, and when an Indian Artillery and an Indian Air Force were brought into existence, Indian trainees were sent to Woolwich and Cranwell. Schools were started to provide pre-cadet training. 'Indianisation' of the officers' cadres proceeded slowly. It was first restricted to eight selected units and then to one division of the army. After the inception of the second world war it was applied to the entire Indian Army, and candidates for commissions in the Army and the Air Force were recruited from all parts of India. The proportion of Indian to British officers was estimated to exceed 35 per cent.[2]

---

[1] For the sterling value of a crore, please see footnote at p. 407, *ante*.

[2] General Molesworth's lecture at the East India Association. *Asiatic Review*, January 1944, p. 3.

DEFENCE REORGANISATION

In the Indian Air Force, except for some attached R.A.F. personnel, all men and officers were Indians. Recruitment for the ranks of the army was thrown open to all communities and provinces. Moslems constituted a little over a third of the Indian Army when enlistment was mainly restricted to the north-western areas of the country. This proportion decreased when caste Hindus and scheduled castes from other provinces were permitted to volunteer.

The character and strength of the Indian Army was completely transformed within a short period. The need for modernising it was realised even when the defence budget was being curtailed. Detailed schemes were framed which were later accepted with modifications by an expert committee under Lord Chatfield, to which the British Government gave its conditional assent. The second world war began before the necessary changes could be completed. To meet the demand for adequate and increasing quantities of equipment and munitions urgent questions of industrial development were tackled. New factories were established, labour was trained, transport and storage were improved. In the engineering and other war industries the numbers employed rose from 400,000 in 1939 to more than a million in 1945, while in the ordnance factories the numbers rose from 17,000 to 116,000.

Meanwhile changes had taken place in regard to maritime defence. The Royal Indian Marine whose history went back to 1612 was converted into the Royal Indian Navy and Indian officers were admitted to the executive as well as the engineering side. Beginning in 1934 with half a dozen small ships, the Indian Navy developed into a force of substantial size, recruited from all parts of India numbering more than 30,000 in 1945 as against 1,673 in 1939. During the war new vessels were built in India and outside. The young Indian Navy saw service as far west as the Atlantic and as far east as Australia. The new Indian Air Force also won laurels in association with the Royal Air Force in the East, the personnel rising rapidly from 300 in 1939 to 23,000 in 1945, when it was given the title of Royal Indian Air Force. By 1946 the Force had eight fighter and two transport squadrons.

Before the second world war broke out the Indian

Government realised that in order to ward off a possible attack precautionary measures should be taken beyond the borders of India. The customary watch was maintained on the North-West Frontier and army contingents were despatched to Malaya, Aden and Somaliland. In official circles, however, the idea prevailed that no expansion of India's land forces was necessary to enable them to fulfil the role for which they were likely to be required. This belief was rudely shaken by the fall of France and the entry of Italy into the war in the summer of 1940, which made the sea route to the west through the Mediterranean almost impracticable. A recruitment campaign was started and large numbers of volunteers immediately came forward. The shortage of shipping, the hazards of the sea, the long sea route, and the requirements of other fronts made it, however, increasingly difficult to obtain sufficient supplies of modern equipment, as India was not, in spite of the measures mentioned above, in a position to supply all her own needs. It was also difficult to train officers sufficiently fast to cope with the large numbers of volunteers. The position gradually improved, and the rate of enlistment was augmented until, at the end of 1945, the Indian defence forces numbered close on two million. But for this additional strength it would have been a hopeless task to attempt to meet the severe strain on Empire man-power that developed during the crucial period of the war. The casualties numbered 180,000—of whom one in six was killed ; 6,500 merchant seamen were among the killed and missing.[1] With these troops, numerous contingents of the armed Forces of the leading Indian States were embodied for service against the enemy in India and overseas. These contingents were equipped according to modern standards and the conditions of their employment were improved. Nor should we omit to mention the military assistance given by the Nepalese Government and its gallant troops.

At the same time as the number under arms in India was increasing the organisation of supply was strengthened in

[1] *Statistics relating to India's War Effort* (Government of India Publication, 1947), p. 2.

all directions. Except for certain special articles India became largely self-sufficient for her military needs and was even in a position to export enormous quantities of war material to western theatres of war. An Eastern Group Supply Council was set up at Delhi to co-ordinate the needs and the available supplies of the Empire countries east of Suez. India in fact became an important arsenal for Middle East operations : she produced vast quantities of small arms, artillery, ammunition, grenades, etc. : and though her output of scientific and optical instruments was negligible in 1940, she had produced by 1945 more than 70,000.[1]

The Indian contingents originally sent to the Middle East received substantial reinforcements. Their exploits in Iran, Syria and Iraq, in the African continent from Somaliland to Tunisia and also in Italy are the subject of pride and glory to all Indians. They also won fresh renown in Italy, and General Mark Clark, the American Commander-in-Chief of the Allied Armies in Italy, paid tribute to their 'splendid fighting record.' Lord Wavell, who commanded Indian troops in different theatres of war, acknowledged that 'it was due to the soldiers that India sent and the material she supplied that we held the Middle East and that debt must not be forgotten.'[2] It is noteworthy that out of 154 Victoria Crosses, 30 were awarded to the Indian Army of which 27 were won by Indian Officers of the Indian Army.

Unfortunately the Indian troops sent east met a different and entirely undeserved fate. After the treacherous aggression of Japan the defence forces available proved inadequate in Hong Kong, Malaya and Singapore. Indian soldiers there shared the evil fortune of their British, Canadian and Australian comrades and were either killed or taken prisoner. More prolonged fighting occurred in Burma, but eventually the Indian and British troops there also proved too few and too poorly supported by air power. They had to conduct a most arduous retreat to Assam through roadless and unhealthy jungle country. The enemy penetrated into the interior of Assam, but it was finally hurled back. Indian troops also took a very active part in the re-conquest of

[1] *Ibid.*, p. 11.   [2] *Asiatic Review* (January 1944), p. 14.

Burma, and in the words of General Leese fought magnificently. At the same time large numbers of civilian Indians were also evacuated to India from Burma. They suffered much hardship and many died on the way. The arrangements for the reception in India of the survivors severely taxed the energies and resources of official and non-official agencies who undertook the task.

At the beginning of this chapter we indicated how the defence forces of India had been suddenly compelled to swing over from the west to the east owing to the threat of invasion by the Japanese based on Burma, and Allied forces, Indian, British, American, Nepalese and Chinese were massed for the re-occupation of Burma. These events had important repercussions and new contacts were brought about between India and the United States and between India and China. Some American forces were based on India and large quantities of war material arrived from America. An Indian Mission was posted in the United States; India secured diplomatic representation both in Washington and in China, Sir Girja Shankar Bajpai being appointed to Washington as Agent in 1943 and as Ambassador in 1947, and Sir Zaffrullah Khan as Agent in Chungking in 1942. Chinese soldiers were trained within Indian borders; road and air communications were developed between the two countries.

All these war commitments could naturally not be met within the budgetary limits for the defence forces we have discussed above. This brings us to a review of Indian governmental finance since the days of the first world war.

The constitutional reforms of 1921 and 1935 involved fundamental changes in the financial relations between the Centre and the provinces. The periodical allocation of certain sources of revenue to the provinces, supplemented occasionally by money grants, inaugurated in the 'seventies of the last century, had been made permanent in 1912. This system, known as 'Provincial Settlements,' had to be more closely defined when the Montagu-Chelmsford reforms conferred a measure of autonomy on the provinces. They were then granted full control over certain heads of revenue with the power of enhancing or reducing taxation within those limits. Of the various sources of governmental income, the receipts from customs duties, income tax and railways were naturally assigned to the Centre, while land revenue, excise and a number of smaller items were allotted to the provinces. This division, however, would have left a large financial deficit in the Centre, and after prolonged discussion it was decided by the British Government that the provinces should contribute varying but gradually decreasing sums to the Central exchequer. The provinces complained that this arrangement left them little scope for expanding their income though they were burdened with the increasing charges of the 'nation-building' departments. Bengal, in particular, with its permanently fixed land revenue, found itself faced with serious difficulties. Fortunately the position at the Centre gradually improved and the provincial contributions were at first reduced and finally abolished in 1928. In spite of this relief the financial resources available to the provinces remained narrow, and in the years following the world economic depression the Centre had to grant subventions to some needy provinces. After the Constitution Act of 1935 came into force, the situation again altered, and the changes then introduced will be dealt with later.

We may now turn to the financial fortunes of the Central Government. For some years these were at a low ebb. We have seen that the Government sustained heavy losses as a result of the currency policy adopted in 1919. The effort to support a two-shillings exchange rate was ultimately abandoned and the rupee gradually found its level at 1*s*. 6*d*., where it has remained ever since. Other causes still further aggravated the financial situation. As a result of the expenditure in the first world war there was an increase in interest charges and the unproductive debt had risen, though this still remained small in comparison with that of other important countries. The Afghan war of 1919 also left an appreciable financial legacy. A severe depression followed the short-lived trade boom which had marked the cessation of hostilities in 1918. Recovery in the countries which consumed the bulk of India's exports was slow and the external trade of India suffered accordingly; customs receipts fell sharply; prices in India were high; labour troubles affected production and transport and substantial wage increases had to be granted to all grades of private and governmental employees. Heavy deficits occurred in the budgets of 1921 and 1922 and were only partially met by increased taxation. These facts account both for the salt tax controversy to which we have referred in an earlier chapter and for the desire expressed by the legislature for a reduction in military expenditure.

Happily the tide turned by the middle of the 'twenties. Industries prospered, there was a large expansion in the external and internal trade, and receipts from customs, income tax and railways showed substantial increases. The Government was able to devote its attention to a programme for the improvement of communications and other civil requirements.

The economic slump which overtook the world in 1929 caused a fresh crisis, and its effects were felt in India for nearly three years. This disastrous period again coincided with a time of political and industrial unrest in the country. The prices of primary commodities which constituted the bulk of India's exports suffered a catastrophic fall; the prices of manufactured goods imported by India also fell but not to the same extent. Internal trade was affected by political disturbances. There was acute distress among the agricultural population. In some provinces, notably in the United Provinces, rents as well as land revenue were reduced. In 1931 the pound sterling went off the gold standard and the rupee, which was linked to the pound sterling, followed the same course. The Government was able to weather the storm by rigid economy, fresh borrowing and enhanced taxation, particularly increases in the customs duties and income tax.

Another important factor which helped the financial position of India at this time was the outflow of gold from the country which began in 1931. As we have said in earlier chapters, the main feature of India's trade through the centuries was the absorption of the precious metals; India

MOBILITY OF CAPITAL

sold more goods than she bought, and the balance was adjusted by imports of gold and silver, which were largely absorbed in hoards. This feature, in a reduced form, outlasted the great changes in commerce which marked the nineteenth century, and it culminated in 1924–25 when the net import of gold surpassed all records. Owing to the fall in prices during the depression, agriculture ceased to offer a livelihood to the peasants of large areas, and many of them met the position by selling their hoarded gold. The persistent export of gold was helped by the fall in the relative value of the rupee and much, though not all of it, was drawn from the peasants' stores of coin and jewellery. Economists, who had been accustomed to consider the accumulated hoards as a store of potential capital, regretted that a substantial proportion of them had been spent on current needs, but the phenomenon also indicated a change in the popular attitude in regard to the mobilisation of capital.

Though temporarily checked during the earlier crises of the second world war, the habit of saving had spread among the people at large and was fostered by the Government during the two wars by the issue of savings certificates and defence loans in different forms. The general result of these changes was a marked increase in the mobility of capital funds throughout the country. The co-operative movement played a part in this change; in spite of some failures and disappointments, it established itself in many parts of the country as a living force. The small working capital of 24 crores of rupees in 1921 had risen by 1943 to over 120 crores of rupees. The number of societies, the number of members, and even the loan transactions had quadrupled within that period.[1]

The changes in the financial machinery of India that have taken place in the last quarter of a century may now be considered. We have seen in an earlier chapter that after the crisis of the 'sixties, banking remained almost entirely in European hands. Thirty years later the collapse of

[1] *Recent Social and Economic Trends in India* (Government of India publication, 1946), p. 24, plate 34.

several small English banks through fraud or mismanagement served further to deter Indians from entering the field ; but the rise of the nationalist spirit after 1905 brought into existence a large number of Indian banks, mostly of a modest size. A few of these survived the first world war, and since then new Indian banks have been organised, several of which are conducted on sound lines and have made considerable progress. Signs are not wanting that the old and indigenous banking methods of the country may soon be transfused into a system of national banking on wide modern lines. Another important development of the period was the amalgamation of three presidency banks into the Imperial Bank of India. For a time this institution was entrusted with some of the functions appropriate to a central bank, and it also opened a large number of new branches in commercial centres which were till then destitute of modern banking facilities. A central bank in the strict sense was constituted in 1934 under the name of the Reserve Bank of India, and furnished very useful assistance to the currency and financial operations of the Government.

Insurance and accounting, like banking, used to be almost entirely in European hands, but after the first world war Indians entered these and other fields of financial activity. For a time there was danger that the movement would suffer from an unhealthy growth of unsound and incompetently managed institutions, but this was checked by legislation imposing safeguards and supervision. Most of the life insurance business in India is at present in the hands of Indian companies, but the major part of other forms of insurance is still managed by non-Indian companies.[1]

The Constitution Act of 1935 introduced further changes in the financial relations between the Centre and the provinces. The finances of the latter were then made completely independent of Central control. Half the income tax collected by the Centre was allotted to the provinces, subject to certain reservations for a temporary period and during the war. This provided the provinces with an

[1] *Recent Social and Economic Trends in India* (Government of India publication, 1946), pp. 60–61, plates 31–32.

WAR EXPENDITURE AND INFLATION

expanding source of revenue. In addition, the existing debt owed by five provinces to the Centre was completely extinguished, while in the case of the remaining provinces it was consolidated on favourable terms. Moreover, grants-in-aid were to be continued for an indefinite period to four needy provinces—namely, Assam, Orissa, Sind and the North-West Frontier; the United Provinces were promised a grant-in-aid for five years.

The provinces utilised their independence and comparative prosperity by substantial reductions of land revenue and in some cases by a policy of prohibition which has naturally affected the income from excise duties. They imposed, however, certain new taxes within their competence and were able to allocate larger funds to schemes of social advancement such as education, agriculture and public health.

In the Centre, war expenditure naturally dominated all other issues. India entered into a financial settlement with England regarding Indian defence expenditure during the war. In principle she agreed to pay, outside her pre-war normal defence expenditure adjusted in accordance with the subsequent rise of prices, the cost of such war measures as could be regarded as a purely Indian liability by reason of their having been undertaken by India in her own interests. She also agreed to pay a lump sum of one crore towards the cost of Indian defence forces employed outside India. In actual practice many of the war measures referred to served the joint interests of India and Great Britain and the costs were allocated in a manner agreed between the two governments.

During the five years 1939-40 to 1943-44 the total expenditure of the Indian Government at the Centre slightly exceeded 1,000 crores. Of this, defence expenditure amounted to 795 crores, an excess of 570 crores over the sum India would have ordinarily spent on defence but for the war.

India's war expenditure during those years naturally increased progressively. It is clear from what has been said above that the British Government also spent large sums in India for the purchase of supplies for various theatres of war and for the maintenance of a base in India for operations in the east. All this was paid for by placing sterling into the account of the Reserve Bank of India. Against this the Reserve Bank issued rupees for actual disbursement. Expenditure by the United States government in India led to similar consequences. A large sterling balance in this way accumulated in England, thereby enabling the Indian government not only to repay or repatriate the whole of its sterling debt, but also to acquire the remaining interests of the British shareholders of a number of Indian railway companies. Nevertheless a substantial credit balance in sterling was still owing to India.

These operations increased the amount of currency available which, among other evils, had aggravated the famine that occurred in Bengal in 1943. The government was slow in enforcing the necessary measures. The inflation of 1942 could have been met by the adoption of the usual methods. Their early adoption might have proved unpopular, but shipping difficulties and the political situation made it impossible to implement them.

In 1943, however, steps were taken to control the inflation. Taxation was considerably increased and an extensive propaganda for saving resulted in adding 279 crores to defence loans. Imports were increased, and the Governments of Great Britain and the United States provided gold to defray their rupee expenditure. Supplies were controlled, rationing introduced and prices stabilised.

The great financial and other resources put at the disposal of the Allies during the war received generous acknowledgment at the Bretton Woods Conference in 1944 when Lord Keynes, referring to the help given to the Allies, particularly by India, said that 'our effort would have been gravely, perhaps critically, embarrassed if they had held back from helping us so whole-heartedly and on so great a scale,' and added that ' when the end is reached and we can see our way into the daylight we shall endeavour, without any delay, to settle honourably what was so honourably and generously given.'[1]

[1] Rowland Owen, *India: Economic and Commercial Conditions* (H.M.S.O., London, 1949), p. 35.

CHAPTER LV

ECONOMIC DEVELOPMENTS

A REMARKABLE quickening of the national life of India has taken place since the first world war. This has been specially noticeable in the economic field. Many developments in the means of communication greatly facilitated this ' speeding up.' Under this head we may record first the creation of new seaports. The numerous creeks and open roadsteads, which in earlier days had sufficed for Indian seaborne trade, were practically useless in modern conditions, and thirty years ago there were only five really serviceable ports on the entire seaboard : Bombay, Madras and Calcutta with Chittagong at one extremity and Karachi at the other. The gaps between these were reduced by the construction of several new harbours, such as Vizagapatam, Tuticorin and Cochin, with substantial benefit to seaborne commerce. The States furthered this movement by the building of some smaller ports on the coasts of Kathiawar and Gujerat. Indian shipping and shipbuilding were developed at the same time. Down to the eighteenth century Indian vessels had been active in Asiatic waters and, later still, many of the wooden ships of the East India Company were built in Indian yards. India lost this industry when steamships came into vogue. Practically all the shipping in the Indian trade at the beginning of this century was non-Indian, although more than fifty thousand Indian seamen from Assam, Bengal and Bombay were employed in them. These men won commendation for their courage, industry and discipline in active service in all the oceans both in peace and in war. The Legislature was anxious in the early 'twenties to encourage and develop an Indian mercantile marine, but the only concrete step adopted by the Government at the time was the establishment of a school for nautical cadets. The second world war, however, gave a powerful impetus to the movement. Ships registered in India increased in number and tonnage, but the war took a heavy toll ; the total losses amounted to more than 24,000, including country craft.[1] Indian yards were kept busy building and repairing warships and merchant vessels.

On land the railways, which had inevitably suffered during the first world war, were overhauled with increase of efficiency. Local supplies of material and equipment were developed, and during the second world war Indian railways lent substantial aid to the operations in the Middle East. Despite the shortage of rolling stock which arose out of the export of much needed engines and wagons to the theatres of war the Indian railways carried a much heavier burden than before, chiefly as a result of military movements : the number of passengers increased by 75 per cent. ; the number of passenger miles more than doubled.[2] The total tonnage increased by more than 12 million tons, mainly attributable to military traffic.[3] One of the striking results of India's sterling accumulations has been that, with one exception, all Indian trunk lines have now been completely nationalised. There was no longer much scope for new trunk railways in India, but the coming of the motor produced great and rapid changes in the mobility of the rural population. The motorbus or the more primitive lorry penetrated into the villages and became the most popular means of travel. The road system of the country did not prove equal to this new strain. The Centre made large grants to the Provinces for road improvements,[4] but progress was slow. In Bengal particularly, owing to the nature of the country, good roads were few, and little was done to develop transport along the

---

[1] *Statistics relating to India's War Effort* (Government of India Publication, 1947), pp. 33 *et seq.*
[2] *Ibid.*, pp. 33 *et seq.*
[3] *Ibid.*, pp. 33 *et seq.*
[4] See R. N. Poduval's *Finance of the Government of India* (Delhi, 1951), p. 14. ' The increase in the excise duty on motor spirits was from time to time allotted to the Road Development Fund set up with the object of making disbursements to Provincial Governments and to Indian States for expenditure on road development schemes.'

rivers, many of which were silting up. An urgent need existed throughout India for new and improved roads and for a proper co-ordination of rail, road and river traffic.

From the middle of the nineteenth century India has enjoyed a cheap, reliable and progressive system of posts and telegraphs. The number of telephones increased from 37,000 in 1923 to 116,000 in 1944,[1] and many trunk telephone lines were erected, greatly facilitating internal trade. External commerce was assisted by the establishment in 1926 of the beam system of wireless in addition to the existing cables. India, moreover, lies on the main route of air transport between the west and the east. Air liners began to arrive in India in 1927, and a regular air mail service between India and England came into operation two years later. Thanks to the Empire Air Mail scheme which was inaugurated in the early 'thirties, air transport in India was developed at great speed and private enterprise could justifiably claim a large share of the credit for the progress made.[2] Indian companies organised services linking up all the large cities in the country, and even before the second world war travellers could journey from India to Europe in less than three days. Aviation has a great future in the country in view of its distances and the settled weather which prevails for long periods during the year.

This progress in communications has not only helped in the development of agricultural and industrial production, but has also facilitated the marketing of the products. The agricultural policy initiated by Lord Curzon at the beginning of the century is now bearing fruit, and through his influence the Imperial Agricultural Research Institute at Pusa received a donation of £30,000 from Mr. Henry Phipps of Chicago.[3] The scientific staff then organised were quick to realise that their immediate task was to improve the quality and yield of the crops already grown. An Imperial Sugar Breeding Station was established at Coimbatore and Institutes of Animal Husbandry and Dairying, and the rapid rise

[1] *Recent Social and Economic Trends in India* (1946), p. 17.
[2] *Ibid.*, p. 17.
[3] Wadia & Merchant, *Our Economic Problem* (Bombay, 1954), pp. 378 *et seq.*

of the new science of genetics to which India has made important contributions all helped in the improvement of stock. The whole field of Indian agriculture was carefully surveyed in 1927 by a Royal Commission under the Marquess of Linlithgow, and on its recommendation an Imperial Council of Agricultural Research was established with the primary function of promoting and co-ordinating agricultural, veterinary and marketing research in the country. Its work was to be periodically reviewed by a disinterested expert. The first to be appointed was Sir John Russell who in 1934 made comprehensive recommendations relating to scientific research to be carried out in the universities, the extension of the work of the departments and the commercial exploitation of useful discoveries.[1] The Indian Agricultural Research Institute at Delhi, through its research into basic problems of all India importance, has contributed much to the improvement of soil fertility and improved varieties of seeds capable of resisting drought, disease and insect pests.[2]

The Provinces and the States co-operated in the work of the Imperial Council of Agricultural Research, and ample funds were made available. Important results have been achieved. New and more profitable strains of wheat were introduced in extensive areas; much of the best cotton country, which produced only coarse fibre, began to be cultivated with medium staple, and after the beginning of the second world war was sown with long staple cotton. Sugarcane production was revolutionised, on the basis of varieties of cane which were deliberately created to replace the less productive type formerly grown. India has now a modern sugar industry capable of supplying all her own requirements. Valuable work has been accomplished in combating plant diseases and in popularising the use of fertilisers. Attention has been devoted to the improvement of livestock, and new marketing methods, including standard marks, have been introduced.

[1] Wadia & Merchant, *Our Economic Problem* (Bombay, 1954), pp. 378 *et seq*.
[2] *India 1953* (a Reference Annual published by Ministry of Information & Broadcasting, Government of India), p. 254.

POSITION OF PEASANTS

The agricultural resources of India were further enhanced during the period by the construction of several new and important irrigation canals. The waters of the Indus were harnessed by the Lloyd Barrage, then the largest work of its kind in the world, and the agricultural potentialities of extensive tracts in Sind, formerly nothing but desert, have been thereby completely altered. New canals were constructed in the Punjab, considerably adding to the prosperity of that Province and adjacent States. The Cauvery canals in Madras and the important Sarda canal in the United Provinces were completed. The Central Waterways, Irrigation and Navigation Commission was constituted in 1945 to act as a co-ordinating organisation with the authority to undertake construction work.[1] Before 1947 over Rs. 1,500 crores (£1,125 million) had been invested in major irrigation works in undivided India, which had an irrigated area of 72 million acres out of a total cultivated area of 298 million acres: i.e., 24 per cent.[2]

The lot of the peasant was also ameliorated in other ways. Originally, in Provinces where the land revenue was temporarily settled, the principles and methods of assessment could be changed by administrative regulation. Since the 1919 reforms, however, these regulations were incorporated in statutes which the legislature alone could amend. In many cases, the standard of assessment has been substantially lowered and the interval between revisions of assessment has been lengthened, thus leaving a larger margin in the hands of the landholders and tenants. In all the northern Provinces new legislation materially improved tenancy rights, notable instances being the comprehensive measures passed by the Congress ministries in the United Provinces and Bihar. In Bengal, the financial incidence of the permanent settlement caused much controversy, and a commission was appointed to investigate the question. Its recommendations for the amendment of the system, however, proved too expensive for the resources of the Province.

[1] *Ibid.*, p. 217.
[2] Rowland Owen, *India: Economic and Commercial Conditions* (H.M.S.O., London, 1949), p. 162.

Other measures were also adopted in several Provinces to help the cultivators. Peasant finance has always been a serious problem in India, and the lack of education among the rural classes made the progress of the co-operative credit movement slow and fitful. Statutory prohibition of the alienation of land to non-cultivating classes was tried in certain areas. Another palliative was applied in some Provinces in the shape of Acts providing for the compulsory reduction of a peasant's indebtedness to his moneylender. It remains to be seen whether, in the absence of alternative means of borrowing, this procedure will not deprive the peasant of the finance he needs to carry on his business.

Though much had been done for the improvement of agricultural production, there was no ground for complacency. It is true that the concrete measures we have described had helped large numbers of peasants to realise that profitable changes might be introduced in the methods they learned from their fathers. Flexibility, which is so essential to the success of modern agriculture, was taking the place of the old rigidity. Many other improvements were however overdue. The peasants' holdings continued to be too small and scattered for the use of modern mechanical appliances. Much remained to be done in the way of the substitution of grains of higher nutritional value for those being sown. The population, as we shall see in the next chapter, was growing at a rate which rendered the whole situation extremely precarious, and any sudden or unforeseen circumstance was liable to bring about a severe calamity. The truth of this observation has been strikingly illustrated by the serious food shortage that occurred in several parts of the country in 1943, culminating in an acute famine followed by epidemic diseases in the Province of Bengal. On his appointment as Viceroy, Lord Wavell immediately flew to Bengal to see to the measures urgently needed to cope with the Bengal famine. In July 1944 the Indian Government appointed a mixed commission of Englishmen and Indians under the chairmanship of Sir John Woodhead, formerly Governor of Bengal. They made an elaborate investigation and estimated that about 1·5 million deaths occurred as a direct result of the famine and epidemics which followed in its wake.[1] They assigned blame to both the Central and the Provincial Governments for delay in the adoption of the necessary measures, for inadequate control and for mistakes in policy; certain sections of the public were not free from blame. Several causes undoubtedly contributed to this result, but in the view of the Commission, much could and should have been done at least to mitigate, if not to avert, so great a tragedy.[2]

The belief was at one time held that the increasing pressure on the land could be alleviated by the diversion of the population to other avenues of employment and more particularly to industry. The great expansion of industry that has taken place in India in the last few decades has, however, been accompanied by a large and rapid increase in the total population of the country, and the proportion of industrial workers to agriculturists has actually diminished. An increase in the production of food, and more particularly of food with higher nutritive and protective value, is as urgently necessary to-day as it was fifty years ago.

The demand for industrial products among the rural classes was limited and was mainly supplied by village artisans. The cottage industries of India thus continued to display great vitality and tenacity. The hand-loom industry, in particular, was fostered by provincial governments and ardent nationalists. At the same time there was a remarkable development in the factory production of various classes of consumption goods such as sugar, matches, cigarettes, glass, cement and chemical products, articles which are mostly in use by the urban classes. The success that attended the entry of Indians into the cotton textile industry in Bombay was followed in the early years of this century by a wider movement of industrial enterprise prompted by the new nationalist spirit. We have recorded the establishment of the steel industry which proved of immense value to the country during the first world war. There was at the time a marked shortage of many articles

[1] Famine Inquiry Commission: *Report on Bengal* (Government Press 1945), p. 110. [2] *Ibid.*, pp. 104-7.

for which India had learnt to rely on seaborne imports, and this affected not only the life of the people but also the requirements for war and defence. A commission appointed by the Government under Sir Thomas Holland examined the question of industrial development and made important and far-reaching recommendations. The Indian Munitions Board, organised for the purposes of the first world war, also helped to develop local industrial resources. All the established industries of the country, textiles, steel and engineering, flourished during the first war, but they had lean times in the immediate post-war years.

Hope had been entertained that after the first world war was over the Government would follow an active industrial policy. The new constitution, however, stood in the way. Industries became a provincial subject and the Provinces did not possess the necessary resources in money or staff to pursue a policy of development. The Central Government also suffered from financial stringency in the early years after the first war. The result was that the recommendations of the Holland Commission for research, technical education and other measures remained in abeyance. Two avenues, however, remained open to the Centre, and these were followed. The State itself in India was a large purchaser of stores required for civil and military purposes and for the national railways, and a vigorous policy of utilising and encouraging indigenous sources of supply for these purposes was adopted with very satisfactory results. The other line of policy took advantage of the fiscal independence secured under the new constitution by introducing a system of ' discriminating protection ' devised to encourage industries for which raw material was available in the country and for which labour could be trained. To obtain the benefit of the privilege it was also necessary for the industry to show that protection would eventually not be needed. Protection was in this way granted to a large variety of industries such as iron and steel, woodpulp and paper, sugar and cotton and silk manufactures. Although in some of these cases it was no longer needed the duties were maintained during the second world war

CHANGES IN COMMERCE

The necessity of transporting coal over long distances to areas where raw materials are available has often hampered industrial progress in India. The development of hydro-electric schemes has helped to overcome this serious drawback, and notable advances in this respect were made in several Provinces and States.

The vast changes in India's industrial development brought about by the second world war cannot yet be chronicled, but some reference has been made to them in the chapter on defence. Meanwhile the need for planning and research became urgent and at a meeting of the post-war reconstruction committee in 1943 the position in respect of the replacement of capital goods after the war was examined.

Industrial and commercial developments are naturally linked closely together. Turning to the changes in the landmarks of Indian commerce, it may be noted that the progress of the Indian textile industry resulted in a decrease of the imports of cotton textiles from Great Britain. The 'fiscal convention' enabled the Indian Government to abolish the countervailing excise duties which had been a long-standing political grievance among all classes of Indians. Fresh controversy arose over the system of imperial preference which the United Kingdom proposed to adopt. When this question was first mooted in the early years of the century, the Indian Government under Lord Curzon had firmly held that India's tariff policy must be framed in her sole interests.

The matter came up anew in 1932 when the United Kingdom expressed its intention to adopt a system of mutual preference among Empire countries. It was understood that, unless India fell into line, her export trade to Great Britain would be prejudiced in competition with other Empire countries. This would have been a serious blow, inasmuch as the United Kingdom was the best customer for India's goods. At the Ottawa conference the Indian delegation proposed certain preferences for goods from the United Kingdom in return for preferences for Indian exports to that country of at least equal value, and these recommendations were accepted by the Indian Legislature. This was followed by a commercial treaty with Japan in 1934. That country was in those days the principal consumer of India's surplus raw cotton, mostly of low grade, and it was advantageous to India to secure a firm trade in the commodity. The war naturally made this agreement inoperative and after the defeat of the Axis powers the question of new commercial relations with Japan had to be considered as soon as the formal resumption of diplomatic contacts became possible. In 1947 a trade mission was sent to Japan from India to ascertain the basis for a new treaty between the two countries.

Many changes have taken place in the nature of the goods exported and imported by India. Jute and tea are still prominent among exports, but India sends abroad much larger quantities of textiles than formerly, and her exports of raw cotton have correspondingly declined. Manufactured articles now constitute a larger proportion of India's exports than in former years, and this feature is likely to be more marked in the future. Industrial development is naturally reducing the quantity and varieties of consumption goods imported into the country, but the need of capital goods such as machinery and vehicles has increased and is likely to continue to do so, judging by the figures of the immediate post-war orders. In the years preceding the second world war an active policy in furtherance of the external commerce of the country was adopted by the Government through the institution of a service of trade commissioners charged with the important duty of promoting Indian business and posted at different commercial centres of the world beginning with the United Kingdom (1918), Germany (1931), Italy (1935), East Africa (1938) and U.S.A. (1939).

Labour questions have necessarily come to the front in the new conditions. The factory brought with it many problems which at first did not receive attention either from the Government or from the intelligentsia, and a sordid life in squalid surroundings came into existence for the workers. A distinctive feature of the Indian problem is still that the majority of the workers do not yet regard the city as their permanent home ; they came largely from the villages which

LABOUR LEGISLATION

they revisit from time to time and to which they hope eventually to retire. Often the men do not bring their families, and town life, in crowded unhealthy tenements deprived of all amenities, is a disagreeable episode which is endured only for the relatively high wages it offers. The workers come from distant Provinces, belong to different communities, and sometimes speak different languages. There is consequently less impetus towards combination and improvement than would be found in a permanent urban population.

Up to the end of the first world war the factory workers were almost wholly unorganised, and the rise in wages lagged far behind the sudden rise of prices. Periods of unrest followed, marked by many strikes; gradually there was adjustment of wages, partly as the result of the activity of trade unions which now multiplied with rapidity. The history of the unions has been chequered; some of the leaders were men with personal or political axes to grind, while the idea of discipline was still foreign to many of the members. There was also much internal dissension in the movement. On the whole, however, the trade union has become a fact of Indian life and the movement has begun to throw up reliable and disinterested leaders. It has helped to secure many benefits for the workers, and it has had some share in influencing labour legislation since the first world war.

Labour laws in India were below modern standards when as a member of the International Labour Organisation she found herself confronted with world opinion on these questions. The constitutional reforms of 1919 came into operation at the same time, and the Central Legislature was empowered to legislate on all labour questions except housing. Legislation on housing was a matter for the Provinces, which in addition were given authority to legislate on all labour questions with the exception of mining, subject to the over-riding authority of the Centre. The administration of all labour laws, with the exception of mining, was entrusted to the Provinces, under Central control. As the Provinces had very limited financial resources they were unfortunately often unable to provide adequate machinery for the enforcement of the laws.

The Central Government undertook with considerable vigour the task of modernising labour legislation.[1] It received full co-operation from the Legislature and on the whole adequate support from the employers. An entirely new labour code came into being. Acts were passed for the regulation of factories and mines, a system of workmen's compensation was introduced, trade unions were legalised and protected, and a tentative trade disputes law was enacted. But owing to financial stringency the Government abandoned various measures that had been initiated for enquiries and research. The appointment of a Royal Commission under Mr. Whitley (formerly speaker of the British House of Commons), however, partially met this need, and the report of the Commission in 1931 formed the basis of further legislation. The laws already passed were liberalised, their scope was widened, and the regulations governing labour in tea plantations in Assam were remodelled.

With the introduction of the 1935 constitution, further changes took place in the powers of the Centre. While it still retained full control over mines, it could no longer compel Provinces to enforce new laws on labour subjects unless it granted financial aid to them. The Centre therefore adopted the practice of passing model laws which the Provinces were free to enforce or not as they chose. It is doubtful whether a diversity of labour laws among the Provinces will be of advantage to the country.

Since the change in the constitution, new ground was broken in some Provinces by the regulation of labour in shops and commercial establishments. In Bombay a comprehensive Industrial Disputes Act was passed.

India may congratulate herself on the progress already achieved in labour legislation, but important gaps remained to be filled. With few exceptions, little was done to improve the miserable conditions in which industrial workers were

---

[1] For a full account see A. C. Chatterjee: *Federalism and Labour Legislation in India* (I.L.O., Montreal, 1944). Reprinted from the *International Labour Review*, Vol. XLIX, Nos. 4–5, April-May, 1944.

LABOUR LEGISLATION

housed all over the country. They had no security against sickness, old age or unemployment. In 1943, however, a scheme of sickness insurance which had been drawn up was reported to be in an advanced stage of preparation, and a committee appointed by the Government of India in 1943 under the Chairmanship of Sir Joseph Bhore drew attention to 'the appalling conditions of overcrowding in industrial areas, particularly in Calcutta, Bombay, Madras and Cawnpore, where a large influx of workers to war industries brought about indescribable and intolerable conditions,' and made far-reaching recommendations.[1] The urgency and importance of these subjects admits of no doubt. 'India's industrial prosperity would be bought at too great a price if it involved the sacrifice of the well-being of her working classes.'[2]

[1] Report of the Health Survey and Development Committee (Delhi, 1946), Vol. IV, paras. 192 and 194.
[2] See footnote, p. 526.

CHAPTER LVI

SOCIAL PROGRESS

A LARGE increase in the population of India in the last twenty years has focused attention on the problem of its effect on the social progress of the country. The first accurate census of the whole of India was taken in 1891, when the total population was reckoned to be 280 millions. In the last census, in 1941, this figure had risen to 389 millions, a difference of no less than 109 millions in fifty years. There had been only a moderate rise in the first three decades of this period, the normal rate of growth being checked by the famines and the epidemics of bubonic plague and influenza described in previous chapters. From 1921 onwards however there were no serious positive checks of this kind, and the census figures indicate a 10 per cent. increase between 1921 and 1931 and a 15 per cent. increase in the following ten years. These rates of increase would not adversely affect countries where the standard of living was already comparatively high. But in India a very large proportion of the inhabitants are under-nourished, insufficiently clad and miserably housed, and this rapid increase of population inevitably brings in its train problems which may perhaps seem almost insoluble. Industrial and commercial development will not prove an adequate remedy since, as we have seen, it can at the best provide a livelihood for only a small fraction of the additional population. A great increase in agricultural production will be required even to maintain the existing standard of life if the growth of population continues at the present rate, and at first sight the outlook does not appear to be very favourable. The available land in India which has not

INCREASE IN POPULATION

already been brought under cultivation is very limited as large tracts are needed for pastures and forests. The reclamation by irrigation works of the Punjab and Sind deserts was completed, and a high priority has been assigned to irrigation projects in the reconstruction programme of the Government. A research irrigation station was established in 1943 in Bengal where this difficulty was particularly acute as in the short space of ten years the population has increased from fifty to sixty millions. Undoubtedly much can be done and is being done to increase the productivity of the soil, but progress can only be gradual in view of the obstacles already mentioned in an earlier chapter. On the other hand the expansion of medical relief and hygienic measures are bringing under control epidemic diseases which have hitherto acted as checks to the growth of the population of the country. In these circumstances it is clear that in order to raise the standard of living of the masses in India above its present low level not only is it necessary to promote industrial and agricultural development, but changes in social habits and customs are also needed to reduce the present high birth-rate. Such changes were in fact recommended by the report of the National Planning Committee who advocated the establishment by the State of birth control clinics and the raising of the marriage age.[1]

The improvement of public health has received attention, and the report of the Bhore committee is not only a mine of information on health matters but is also an authoritative guide for all concerned in improving the national health.[2]

The death-rate has varied between twenty-two and twenty-five per thousand, while the birth-rate is approximately thirty-five per thousand, and largely owing to the poor expectation of life of those who survive, nearly half of the entire population of India is under twenty years old. Much has been done to check the ravages of smallpox and cholera, but malaria continues to be endemic in most parts of the country and hyperendemic in certain particularly

---

[1] *Report of National Planning Committee* (Bombay, 1949), p. 148.
[2] *Report of the Health Survey and Development Committee* (Delhi, 1946), Vol. IV Summary, pp. 34–36.

unhealthy localities. It was estimated in 1946 that at least 100 million persons in the sub-continent suffer from malaria every year and that the annual mortality for which that disease is responsible either directly or indirectly is about two millions.[1] Fairs and pilgrimages, bringing as they do large numbers of people together, are a potent cause of the spread of infection. Towns and cities are developing without planning or the provision of open spaces and there is a consequent increase in tuberculosis. It was estimated in 1946 that about 2·5 million infective patients of tuberculosis existed in the country and about 500,000 deaths took place each year from this cause alone.[1] With the development of communications there is closer contact between urban and rural localities and both suffer equally from any serious epidemics. Habits of hygiene based on religious injunctions no longer afford sufficient protection; there is need for more extensive sanitary measures and for the inculcation of the principles of hygiene and health not only for the cure but also for the prevention of disease.

The governments at the Centre and in the Provinces realised the dangers of the situation. Health had been a ' provincial subject ' since 1919 and the Ministers everywhere displayed much interest in combating the existing evils, but action on any large scale had been possible only since the improvement in the financial resources of the Provinces. The health organisations were progressively strengthened and measures for propaganda and demonstration were adopted. The Central Government maintained a few research institutions on restricted lines and appointed a committee to survey the position and formulate proposals for the future.

Simultaneously with the spread of sanitary knowledge, schemes were being developed for the provision of extended medical relief. The indigenous medical systems continued to be favoured by large sections of the people and were being modernised by the application of new methods. Western systems of medicine and surgery had grown increasingly

[1] *Report of the Health Survey and Development Committee* (Delhi, 1946), Vol. IV Summary, pp. 34-36.

in popularity through the last hundred years and were practised in the towns by a considerable number of well-trained doctors, but the villages were too poor to be able to utilise their services to the necessary extent. The Provinces and States experimented with travelling doctors and dispensaries, and also established a large number of stationary hospitals. All these developments will undoubtedly bring about a rapid improvement in the health of the country, and the benefit will be apparent in the physique, efficiency and longevity of the workers.

Reference has been made to the increasing contact between the towns and villages brought about by the development of communications. The drift forwards and backwards from the villages to the factory towns has had the same result. There are indications of a great change in the mentality of the rural population, to which many causes have contributed. Among these is the co-operative movement, which is in many villages a living force. Another factor in the early years of this period was the determination of the Indian soldiers, particularly in the Punjab, to raise their standard of life towards that of the French peasants among whom they had lived in the first world war. No doubt soldiers and sailors in all parts of the country were activated by the same motives when they returned home from service overseas. The Government of India recognised that the demobilised Indian soldier would be one of the most powerful agents in the readjustment and development of society after the war, and their tentative plans included the creation of a fund to be used for the permanent benefit of former service-men. The Government had also under consideration the creation of a network of employment offices for discharged members of the armed forces and also educational and technical training schemes to enable them to qualify for technical and professional employment.'[1] The political movements of the last twenty-five years also had their influence on the rural population. The spread of education in the villages had an important effect on the

[1] *International Labour Review* (June 1943), Vol. XLVII, No. 6, pp. 755 and 756.

s

mind of the villager and on his capacity to adopt new ideas and new methods. The Kasturba Gandhi Trust, founded in 1945 in memory of Mr. Gandhi's wife is devoted solely to the improvement of the lot of village women. A generation ago the widening gap between the literate classes and the rural population constituted a threat to the future of India; later the gap narrowed and there were signs of the development of more reasonable relations between country and town than those which had come down from the eighteenth century.

The towns grew rapidly in number and size. By the end of the second world war more than one-eighth of the entire population of the country now lived in towns, while in the Province of Bombay over a quarter of the people were town-dwellers. Industrial and commercial development naturally brought about this increase in the urban population, and some of the principal towns displayed an abnormal growth. In over a dozen cities the population increased more than fifty per cent. in ten years, and the Census Commissioner observed that urbanisation was proceeding ' with all the drawbacks of lack of control, squatters' freedom and general squalor.' [1] His predecessor had stated that in 1931 [2] over a third of the population of Bombay suffered from gross over-crowding. Improvement trusts are operating in some of these cities, but clearly there is need everywhere for long-term planning and stricter control. Reasonable sanitary conditions should not be permanently sacrificed, specially as unhygienic conditions in the cities now soon affect the villages. The urgent need of establishing new industrial centres instead of expanding the already overgrown cities is also apparent.

Educational activities provided an important additional link between urban and rural localities. Formerly literacy was largely confined to the upper and lower middle classes in the towns, but it now extended downwards in the towns and outwards into the villages. After the 1919 reforms the Provinces had been very active, and notable progress was achieved in Bombay, Bengal, Madras and the Punjab,

---

[1] Census of India 1941, Vol. I, p. 26.
[2] Census Report 1931, Vol. I, p. 52.

EDUCATIONAL CHANGES

though other provinces like Bihar and the United Provinces had much leeway to make up. Some of the States, such as Travancore, Cochin and Baroda, were the most advanced parts of India in elementary education. Literacy was now progressing much more rapidly among women than among men, though the percentage of literate women was still much lower than that of literate men. According to the Census Report of 1941, taking India as a whole more than one-fifth of the male population could read and write, but only one in every twenty women could do so. This disparity, though still excessive, was rapidly becoming less marked, and this is the most hopeful feature of Indian social progress. In the past the two main obstacles in the way of elementary education in India were finance and the paucity of qualified and suitable teachers. The governments in India were now ready and willing to provide adequate finance, while the gradual spread of literacy in the villages, specially among the women, helped to create a reservoir from which teachers could be drawn and trained. No doubt is entertained by competent observers that the reluctance of the villager to send his child to school has completely disappeared from most parts of the country. The efforts made in the past to extend elementary education in rural localities did not provide a curriculum to meet the needs of the village lad but only made him desirous of becoming a townsman. Much study accompanied by many experiments was devoted to the solution of that problem, but no definite educational policy was put forward by the Indian national leaders till 1937 when a conference, presided over by Mr. Gandhi, drew up a plan for basic education which became known as the Wardha Scheme. Free and compulsory education for seven years in the mother tongue, coupled with training in a basic craft taught as a medium of education rather than as a vocational craft appears to be the main purpose of the scheme.

Indian educationists desirous of reforming the present methods of secondary education were confronted by the same problems. These were considered by a Central Advisory Board of Education which was reconstituted in 1935 so as to include all schools of opinion, official and unofficial.

Provision was also made later for the appointment of women and Indian statesmen to the Board. Reporting in 1944,[1] the Board drew attention to the failure to provide a national system of education, but mentioned with approval the progress that had been made in the years between the two world wars, stating that the number of children attending primary schools had risen from six to twelve million, and the number attending secondary schools had increased from one to nearly three million. They also recommended the adoption of a compulsory and free education for all children between the ages of 6 and 14, and they did not overlook the importance of adult education.

In the past all secondary school students aimed at entering a University and securing a degree. The majority failed to do either, and the lack of technical or vocational qualifications together with the very narrow range of openings available to persons with a purely literary training caused in ordinary times serious unemployment. The growing industries of the country need an increasing number of skilled craftsmen imbued with the desire of rising to the higher grades of employment, while modern agriculture requires men properly qualified to organise and improve the resources of the land. A distinct trend is now noticeable towards an adequate development of vocational and technical education, and a number of properly equipped institutions have been established. A powerful stimulus has been imparted to this movement, both by the recent world war when many youths were trained in war factories and by the adoption of the recommendations of the Central Advisory Board of Education. The appointment of an all India Board of Technical Education with Mr. N. R. Sarker as Chairman laid down the foundations of all future advance in this direction.[2] An appreciable number of promising young workers also had the advantage of training for a period in the industries of the British Isles. These men will provide a nucleus in India for the dissemination of new ideas and new

[1] 'Progress of Education in India,' *Decennial Review 1937–1947* (1948), Vol. I, Part III. The Report of the Central Advisory Board of Education under the Chairmanship of Sir John Sargent, pp. 231–319.
[2] *Ibid.*, pp. 271 and 272.

methods in craftsmanship. Improved facilities are now available in the country for higher education in engineering and other branches of technology. To achieve immediate results, however, a scheme for Overseas Scholarships for advanced technical training was inaugurated at the end of 1944, and a project for sending 500 students abroad annually was, in spite of almost insuperable difficulties, successfully launched. The provincial governments and the states selected students for this training in Europe and America.[1] Most of these young men secured theoretical and practical knowledge of the right kind and found employment in Indian industries, thus serving as a useful link between the industries of the east and of the west.

The universities of India have undergone many changes in outlook and organisation since 1920. An expert commission under Sir Michael Sadler, appointed during the first world war to enquire into the constitution of the Calcutta University, made a wise and elaborate survey of the whole field of secondary and university education. Their recommendations bore fruit in the reorientation of the work of the older universities and in the establishment of several new universities of a modern type, in the Provinces as well as in the States. Indian universities no longer confined themselves to mere examinations of college students but, with a very few exceptions, became teaching institutions, with or without some constituent colleges, and their aim was to foster research and scholarship while providing a corporate life for the students and the staff. Much valuable work was accomplished, specially in subjects such as the sciences, economics, history and philology. Links were established with learned bodies in Europe and America, and the work of Indian scholars received recognition in all parts of the world. One aspect of the new developments deserves particular notice in an account of Indian social progress. The universities have thrown themselves into the study of Indian economics, and thus coming into closer touch with the facts of life they have grasped that the problem of national poverty must be solved in the villages. Realising that better

[1] *Ibid.*, p. 288.

farming and better living must go hand in hand, many of the younger university students, both men and women, have turned their attention to social questions and rural problems and are actively co-operating in the movement popularly known as ' village uplift.'

Indian universities, like similar institutions in other countries, developed professional education. Law has always been a popular study in India, and the law colleges attracted most of the students after they graduated, but there are now many young men taking up engineering and technological subjects. India already possesses several well-equipped schools of medicine, several of them having been raised to college standard, and existing medical colleges have increased in number,[1] but their number needs to be still further increased and the facilities for clinical research enhanced if a sufficient supply of qualified physicians is to become available for the rural population. To promote the development of post-graduate education in all branches of medical science, the Government of India initiated an Overseas Scholarship scheme in 1946, and in 1947 enlarged its scope to embrace dentistry and nutrition.[2]

An educational problem which has been engaging attention in India is the medium of instruction in the secondary schools and colleges. Until a generation ago the text-books were all in English, which was also the language in which the students were taught in the colleges and many secondary schools. This resulted in providing a medium of communication common to educated persons all over the country, but naturally the creative and critical faculties of the learners suffered. In most provinces, instruction in secondary schools was given in the language of the locality, while English was taught as a compulsory second language. The main object of Macaulay and Bentinck in deciding that, except in the primary stage, education should be imparted in English has now been fully achieved. The contact with the west secured by the spread of English education has

[1] 'Progress of Education in India,' *Decennial Review 1937–1947* (1948), Vol. I, Part III. The Report of the Central Advisory Board of Education under the Chairmanship of Sir John Sargent, p. 176.
[2] *Ibid.*, p. 178.

THE WOMEN'S MOVEMENT

wonderfully vitalised the chief Indian languages. They have become the vehicles of flourishing literatures in prose and verse and are now used for the composition of historical, technical and scientific works of value and originality.

A similar development took place in the newspaper and periodical press. Those written and printed in English enjoy a circulation among readers in all parts of India, but the needs of the Provinces and more particularly of the villages are supplied by excellent periodicals and by many newspapers published in the provincial languages.

Many of the contributors to these periodicals are women. A promising feature of secondary and university education in India is the rapidly increasing number of girls who now attend the schools and colleges, many of them distinguishing themselves in competition with men students. The Central Education Department has also taken steps to promote the raising of standards in all branches of University studies and in 1946 a University Grants Committee was appointed. In accordance with their recommendations, large grants were made to the Delhi University and to the Muslim University in Aligarh, and to the Hindu University in Benares, more particularly to further women's university education. It was the Board's considered opinion that educational facilities should be available for both sexes and that the contribution to India's prosperity which would result from the early and thorough exploitation through education of the vast potential resources of brain power now latent in India's womanhood can scarcely be over-estimated.[1] Women now form no inconsiderable proportion of those who are taking to literary or scientific research on the one hand, and to professional education on the other, and they are also prominent in other branches of cultural progress in the country. In the period under review there was a renaissance of Indian arts, in painting and music, drama and dancing, and among the exponents of these arts were many gifted and well-trained women.

This remarkable movement among women and girls naturally exercised a deep influence on social habits and

[1] *Ibid.*, p. 284.

customs. The most striking difference which a casual observer would notice between the India of thirty years ago and the India of to-day is the breakdown of *purdah* or the seclusion of women. This custom, which obtained among the higher and middle classes of the north, will probably disappear completely in another generation. Along with this change much-needed reforms in marriage customs are taking place. The age of marriage among men and girls is gradually rising, and the minimum age has been fixed by a law,[1] passed in 1930, at eighteen for men and fourteen for girls. The re-marriage of Hindu widows, which was formally legalised nearly a hundred years ago, is now more frequent than was the case at the beginning of this century and is not unknown in the most orthodox families. Polygamy, though legally permissible for Hindus and Muslims, was practised only by a very small minority in both communities. Social opinion is now definitely arrayed against the custom, and women of both communities are leading the crusade for its abolition.

These changes in the status of women in India have been largely brought about by women themselves, and although at present confined mainly to the middle classes, they cannot fail to produce corresponding changes among the poorer classes in towns and villages. Women have always exercised a great though unobtrusive influence on social life in India, and the new ideas will gradually affect the outlook of the entire people.[2] There is reason to believe that as a result a solution of the population problems discussed above will be reached. The child-bearing age is already being narrowed and there is a growing desire for a high standard of life; it may be hoped that while the birth-rate will decline, the children of the future will be healthier and will grow up to be more robust citizens.

Important changes are also to be noted in other aspects of Indian social life. Caste restrictions are being relaxed in all parts of the country: a Hindu is now free to choose

---

[1] Child Marriage Restraint Act, 1930.
[2] For a full account of this development, see Atul C. Chatterjee's book *The New India*, 1948 (George Allen & Unwin, London).

almost any occupation he likes, and the limitations concerning food, drink and social contacts with people of other castes are far less strict than they were formerly. All the indications point to their gradually becoming obsolete. A greater rigidity has persisted in the rules prohibiting marriage between persons of different Hindu castes, but the reformed Indian legislature legalised such marriages [1] and they are now fairly common.

The social changes we have described began before the first world war and have since gathered momentum, bringing the sexes together in the open life of India. The principles of freedom and progress have won the day and are likely to bring about even more fundamental changes in Indian society.

[1] Hindu Marriage Disabilities Removal Act 28, of 1946.

CHAPTER LVII[1]

CONSTITUTIONAL QUESTIONS : THIRD PHASE 1942–1947

ONE result of the Cripps Mission was to show how wide and fundamental the divergence of aim between the Congress and the Moslem League had now become. Throughout the following five years this continued to thwart all endeavours, both by the British authorities and by the party leaders themselves, to find a basis of agreement, and eventually rendered the partition of India inevitable. It is therefore convenient at this point, for a better understanding of subsequent events, to summarise briefly the attitudes of the two parties towards each other and towards the British Government as they had developed by 1942.

The first aim of the founders of the Indian National Congress had been the fusion of the different elements of India's population into one national whole ; and though the bulk of its membership was Hindu it consistently claimed to be a non-communal body, and did in fact always include some influential Moslems such as Maulana Abul Kalam Azad who was its President in 1942 and again in 1945–46 ; in its rejection of the Cripps proposals it emphasised (while disclaiming any thought of compulsion to prevent secessions) that it was wedded to the unity, as well as the freedom, of India. As regards freedom Congress policy had passed through three stages ; in 1907 the moderate section had pronounced self-government within the British Empire to be its objective ; in 1927 under Gandhi's influence and after

[1] In the new Chapters LVII and LVIII, the honorific prefixes of Mahatma and Quaid-Ul-Azam before the names of Gandhi and Jinnah respectively have been omitted. They are now historic characters and such prefixes have consequently become unnecessary.

shedding its Liberal members it became finally committed to the goal of complete independence, and ultimately in the ' Quit India ' resolution of August 1942 (p. 501) to a demand for immediate independence. Its attitude to the problem of Moslem-Hindu antagonism, when the growth of this feeling could no longer be ignored, was that it was a by-product, and even a deliberate creation, of British rule, and that if only the British would relinquish power and responsibility, the Indian parties would then succeed in settling their domestic differences.

The Indian Moslem League, founded in 1906 to promote Moslem interests, extended its objectives in 1913 to include some form of self-government for India. In that year it was joined by Mahomed Ali Jinnah, a congressman, who became its President in 1916 and made the Lucknow Pact with the Congress (pp. 454–55). This common platform did not survive the non-co-operation campaign of 1919–22, which caused a rift in both parties (p. 476), and the outbreaks of communal violence which followed. Communal tension further increased in view of the prospect of further constitutional reforms, and in 1929 all the Moslem parties agreed upon a programme drafted by Jinnah for preserving Moslem minority safeguards and also for complete provincial autonomy and for increasing the number of Moslem provinces and the strength of the Moslem position therein. In 1934 Jinnah again became President of the League. He hoped for co-operation with Congress, as in 1916, and for the formation of Congress-League ministries in the provinces. But the Congress as the National Party, after its sweeping victory in seven provinces in the 1937 elections, entertained hopes of absorbing the League. It formed single-party governments, and required that any Moslem members of them should be, or become, congressmen. The League deeply resented this rebuff and was completely and permanently antagonised. Jinnah re-organised it to win the support of the Moslem masses, and it became an active political force in opposition to Congress, and in particular to Congress Moslems, winning an impressive number of by-elections in the Moslem constituencies. At the same time it passed wholly under the direction of Jinnah who was re-elected to its presidency in each successive year. As regards its attitude to the British Government, it drew level with Congress in 1937 by declaring for the establishment of full independence in India ; and in the following years entrenched itself in the position that it was the only body qualified to represent Moslems, and that as such and on the basis of the proviso to the British offer of 1940 (p. 499), it had the right to a full voice in any plan for a future constitution. After 1937 the League's own policy swung rapidly away from an Indian federation of autonomous units towards the thesis that the Moslems were a separate nation entitled to form an independent State. In 1939 it declared that Moslem India was 'irrevocably opposed to any federal objective which must necessarily result in a majority community rule under the guise of democracy,' and that India was composed of various nationalities and did not constitute a national State. The Lahore resolution of 1940 (pp. 495–96) clearly contemplated partition. It was vague as to the extent of the areas claimed, but at the time of the Cripps Mission Jinnah indicated that the Pakistan claim included the whole of Bengal and the Punjab.

After the failure of the Cripps Mission some moves were made within the Congress towards reconciling the League. In April 1942 Mr. C. Rajagopalachari of Madras proposed consultation with a view to agreement on the basis of acknowledging the claim to separation if the League persisted in it when the time came to frame a constitution. The All-India Congress Committee rejected these suggestions and resolved that it could not agree to any proposal to disintegrate India by giving liberty to any component part of it to secede. But Mr. Rajagopalachari persevered, and in March 1943 during Gandhi's detention obtained his personal approval of a draft formula for a Congress-League settlement. This proposed that the League should co-operate in forming an interim government, and that, if and when the British relinquished power, contiguous Moslem-majority districts in the north-west and east should be demarcated by a commission, that in these the issue of separation should be decided by plebiscite, and that in the event of separation an agreement should be made for safeguarding defence, commerce, communications and other essential subjects. In July 1944 Jinnah criticised these terms as being dependent on too many uncertainties, but accepted an invitation from Gandhi himself to meet him. Long discussions ensued in September between the two leaders, Jinnah clothed with authority from the League Council, Gandhi acting as a private individual prepared to use his influence with Congress. These aroused considerable hopes, but the results were disappointing; the talks began at cross purposes and ended in agreement to differ. They helped, however, to clear the ground of misunderstandings and define more precisely the basic differences between the parties, which were three-fold: the territorial extent of a separate State and the method of deciding this; the measure of its sovereignty, and last and most important the timing of its establishment. Jinnah claimed for Pakistan the Punjab, Sind, North-West Frontier Province, Baluchistan, Bengal, and now also Assam, within their existing boundaries (though subject to adjustments subsequently agreed to be necessary). He argued in effect that the hundred million Moslems of India, with their distinctive ways of life and thought already felt themselves to be, and were, a separate nation, and that this conception should be embodied in separate statehood with an adequate territory, which, since it could not include all of them, should comprise each of the two large zones where they constituted an over-all majority of the population. Gandhi rejected the two-nation theory and insisted that, if Moslem Indians in some provinces and in parts of others wished to live in separation from the rest of the Indian family, the wishes of all the inhabitants of the areas in question must first be ascertained. Secondly, Jinnah desired total separation without any limitations on Pakistan's sovereignty save such as she might afterwards accept by international agreements for security and neighbourly behaviour, whereas Gandhi proposed that provision should be made in the treaty of separation itself for the administration of subjects which must necessarily continue to be matters of common interest, a proposal which seemed to imply some federal or joint authority for these subjects. The third source of disagreement was the question whether Pakistan should be established after the withdrawal of the British or, at latest, simultaneously therewith. Gandhi in accord with accepted Congress doctrine held that the freedom of India from foreign domination was a pre-requisite for practical steps to settle the Hindu-Moslem problem, and that Congress and League should first take common action to achieve that single objective. Jinnah described this as putting the cart before the horse; he insisted that agreement for a Hindu-Moslem settlement should precede independence, and that the establishment of Pakistan must itself form part of any joint demand for the independence of the peoples of India.

Meanwhile there had been no break in the general political deadlock resulting from the ' Quit India ' resolution and the detention of the Congress leaders. Lord Wavell became Viceroy in the autumn of 1943, and had first to devote his attention to the measures urgently needed to cope with the Bengal famine before beginning to consider the possibilities of easing the political situation. But Gandhi was given an opportunity of making representations against his detention, and some correspondence followed between him and the Viceroy, who urged that Congress should abandon non-co-operation and join in helping India's economic and political progress. In some further correspondence after his release Gandhi revived the proposal made by Congress in April 1942 (p. 501), that a national government responsible to the Central Assembly should be formed. This proposal had to be rejected for the same reasons as before, but in doing so Lord Wavell suggested that good progress might be made if the Indian leaders would co-operate in a transitional government within the existing constitution, first reaching agreement in principle on the method of framing a new constitution; and that preliminary work on the latter might then begin at once, thus shortening the period of transitional government after the war. The Gandhi-Jinnah talks which followed soon after this shewed the difficulty of such an agreement in principle between the two major parties. But the limited objective of a satisfactory interim government was seriously studied in the winter of 1944-45 in non-official circles. Thus the Congress leader in the Assembly, Bhulabhai J. Desai, made some tentative suggestions for a Congress-League agreement to the League deputy leader, Liaquat Ali Khan, who personally thought them a possible basis for discussion if an approach to Jinnah were authorised by Gandhi. These suggestions were that each party should nominate an equal number of members of a Cabinet which would function within the existing constitution but on the understanding that it would not seek to use the Viceroy's reserve powers in order to enforce measures refused by the Assembly. About the same time a committee under the Liberal leader, Sir Tej Bahadur Sapru, recommended to Lord Wavell amendments of the constitution to provide for an interim government of Indians commanding the confidence of the parties in the legislature, and to extend the powers of the latter and eliminate the official element from its composition. This committee also made suggestions in regard to the future constitution-making body and indeed the future constitution itself; it was opposed to Pakistan, and favoured the principle of Hindu-Moslem parity of representation but only if the Moslems agreed to give up their separate electorates.

At the end of March 1945 Lord Wavell visited London and had lengthy consultations with the British Government, which on June 14th issued a statement of their policy. This re-affirmed the Cripps offer of 1942 and expressed the hope that Indian leaders might be able to agree on a procedure for determining India's permanent future form of Government; meanwhile the British Government realised that the war with Japan and the planning of post-war economic development required a relaxation of political tension and the co-operation of all sections of the population, and to this end suggested the following provisional changes within the framework of the existing constitution. All members of the Viceroy's Executive Council except the Commander-in-Chief should be selected from among leaders of Indian political life and should include equal proportions of Moslems and of Hindus (other than those belonging to the Scheduled Castes).[1] Lord Wavell was to call a conference of political leaders from the centre and the provinces and invite from them a list of names from which to make his selection. The conduct of the ordinary external affairs of British India was to be in the hands of an Indian member (instead of the Viceroy being in direct charge of them as had been the practice) and the Indian Government could send fully accredited representatives to countries abroad. It was hoped that as a consequence of co-operation at the centre there would be a resumption of responsible government in the provinces where the Congress ministries had resigned, and that in all provinces governments would be based on the participation of the main parties.

Lord Wavell in a parallel announcement in India described the proposals as a stride forward, and while making it clear that they in no way prejudiced the final constitutional settlement, stated that one important task for the new Council would be in due course to consider the means by which agreement on a future constitution could be achieved. He forthwith invited to a conference at Simla the Presidents of the Congress and of the Moslem League and other political leaders from the central legislature and the provinces. Those members of the Congress Working Committee who were still in detention were released, and the Congress Party decided to take part in the Conference. Gandhi had also been invited and went to Simla though he decided not to participate formally in the proceedings. The Conference opened on June 25th and accepted the proposals in principle, but ended in failure because it was unable to agree about the composition of the Council ; the Moslem League, in accordance with its claim to be the only representative Moslem organisation, sought an assurance which Lord Wavell was unable to give that all the Moslem members would be members of the League.

Shortly after this a Labour Government took office in the United Kingdom. It adhered, like its predecessor, to the principles of the Declaration of 1942, and was able in

[1] See p. 485.

SIMLA CONFERENCE

view of the end of the war to initiate an effort to solve the whole constitutional problem on that basis. The Cripps offer had contemplated that a constitution-making body should be set up immediately after the war and the provincial elections which would then be necessary, and that, unless some other form were agreed upon, it should be composed of persons elected on a system of proportional representation by the new provincial assemblies together with representatives of the Indian States. With the end of the war the time was ripe for an endeavour to carry out this intention and as a preparatory step to hold general elections; during the war there had been none to the central assembly, nor to the provincial assemblies and it was in any case desirable to renew these bodies and obtain an up-to-date representation of political opinion. On September 19th, 1945 Lord Wavell announced the British Government's proposals; immediately after the elections he was to hold discussions with representatives of the new provincial assemblies and of the Indian States to decide the method by which a Constituent Assembly might be formed (whether as proposed in the Cripps offer or otherwise) and its powers and procedure, and was also to take steps to form an interim Executive Council which would have the support of the main Indian parties.

The ban imposed upon Congress as an unlawful association (p. 501) had been lifted after the Simla conference, and in September its All-India committee met and passed a number of resolutions. These criticised the new British proposals as a mere repetition of the Cripps offer designed to cause delay, re-affirmed the 'Quit-India' resolution of August 1942, declared Congress policy to be negotiation when possible and non-violent direct action if necessary, and decided to contest the elections on the issue of immediate transfer of power. As regards any right of separation from an Indian union, in order to clear up a discrepancy between the earlier pronouncements the Working Committee adopted a new resolution which laid its emphasis on the unity of India but contained a proviso that no territorial unit inhabited by a homogeneous people would be forced to stay in against its will. The Moslem League also entered the elections on a platform of opposition to the British proposals, concentrating on the Pakistan issue and claiming that this should be settled before constitution-making began.

Thus the first reactions in India to the new British initiative were to sharpen the opposition between the principal parties, and seemed to offer little prospect of co-operation either in planning a new constitution or in the tasks of government during the transitional period. The British Cabinet was anxious to dispel suspicions of its purpose and make its full significance clearer. It accordingly arranged in December that a Parliamentary inter-party Delegation should visit India to make personal contacts with leading Indians and convey to them the general desire of the British people that India should speedily attain independence as a partner in the British Commonwealth.

The results of the elections, which were held in the cold weather of 1945–46, confirmed beyond question that the policies of the two parties had the support of the masses of their respective constituents. In the 'general' constituencies the Congress had an overwhelming success against such opposition as was offered by Moderates, the Hindu Mahāsabhā or other groups. In the separate Moslem constituencies the League substantiated its claim to be the mouthpiece of Moslem opinion by winning all these seats in the central and in four of the provincial assemblies, all but two in Bengal and a large majority of them in each of the other provinces except the North-West Frontier Province where it improved its position but where Congress held the majority of the seats; the anomalous strength of the Congress in this Moslem-majority province was due to the support of a widespread Pathan nationalist movement which since 1931 had made common cause with it against the British. After the elections ministerial governments were formed in all the provinces for the first time since 1940; during the intervening period they had existed sometimes in only four, and at no time in more than six of them. Congress governments now again took office in most of the provinces. The League was able to form a government in

Bengal and a precarious one in Sind ; in the Punjab there was still a coalition government of Hindus, Sikhs and non-League Moslems.

For the British Government events since September 1945 emphasised the difficulties of finding some basis on which Indians could work together in building their future constitution, and at the same time the necessity of making every effort to do so ; the cleavage between the two great parties was more pronounced than ever ; each had defined its policy and received an emphatic endorsement from its electorate ; cross currents and moderating influences were weaker. On February 19th, 1946 (when the results of the elections to the centre and to some of the provincial assemblies were known) Mr. Attlee, the British Prime Minister, announced that in view of the critical importance of forthcoming discussions the Cabinet had decided with the full concurrence of the Viceroy to send out three of its own members, Lord Pethick-Lawrence (Secretary of State for India), Sir Stafford Cripps and Mr. A. V. Alexander, to seek, in association with the Viceroy, an agreement with leaders of Indian opinion on the principles and procedure relating to the constitutional issue. In a speech in the House of Commons on March 15th he emphasised that the purpose was to help India to set up the machinery for making her own decision on her future ; he added that he hoped she might choose to remain within the British Commonwealth with the advantages which this offered her, but that she was free to choose otherwise if she wished.

The Cabinet mission arrived in India on March 24th and after long separate discussions with leaders of the Congress and Moslem League succeeded in bringing them together in conference under their respective Presidents, Maulana Azad and Jinnah. No progress could be made on machinery without considering also the broad basis of the future constitutional structure ; independence in union implied a single constituent body ; independence subject to partition presupposed two separate ones. Though in the Conference each party was prepared to make some concessions, it proved impossible to close the whole of the gap between them. Eventually therefore on May 16th the mission and the Viceroy with the approval of the British Government published a statement giving their own conclusions on the fundamental issue of partition and outlining a plan both for policy and machinery which they recommended as coming nearest to reconciling the views of the parties. Impressed by the Moslems' genuine fear of becoming subject to a permanent Hindu majority at the centre, the mission first carefully examined the possibility of a separate and fully sovereign state of Pakistan, either consisting of the six whole provinces claimed or alternatively confined to Moslem-majority areas; for the full claim it had been argued that this territorial extent was necessary for viability, but it would mean that nearly 45 per cent. of Pakistan's population would be non-Moslem including large minorities in Bengal and the Punjab and a majority in Assam, and the mission considered that the basic argument in favour of Pakistan was equally valid for excluding non-Moslem areas from it. On the other hand a compromise on the latter basis was at that time quite unacceptable to the League; and the mission also were averse from the partition of Bengal and of the Punjab, each possessing its own language and tradition, and the bisection of the Sikh community which it would entail. Moreover against either alternative the mission had to weigh the administrative and economic reasons for preserving the unity of India, especially in respect of defence and communications, and the difficulties that Pakistan itself would be divided into two widely separated zones, and would inherit one or both of the two most vulnerable external frontiers and be insufficient in area for a defence in depth.

The mission therefore turned to other methods of securing Moslems in control of their own vital interests, and recommended a constitution on the following lines. There was to be a Union of India, but its functions would primarily be restricted to Foreign Affairs, Defence, Communications and the finance required for these subjects; all others would belong to the provinces, but provinces should be free to form 'groups,' with group executives and legislatures, and

POSITION OF THE STATES

each group could determine which provincial subjects should be taken in common; there would thus be a three-tier constitution (so far as the group system was adopted)—first a centre with minimum powers, next group governments to administer subjects excluded from the centre but transcending provincial boundaries, such as economic planning, and last the individual provinces; the provision for grouping would enable contiguous Moslem provinces to consolidate, and also in general help to counter the danger of fragmentation which would result from provincial autonomy coupled with so narrowly restricted a centre. As a further safeguard for Moslems, any motion in the Union legislature which raised an important communal issue would require the consent of a majority of the representatives voting from each of the two major communities. Moreover the constitutions of the Union and of the groups were to be subject at ten-yearly intervals to reconsideration if demanded by any province (a provision which was taken by the League at any rate to imply liberty to secede from the Union).

On the problem of the Indian States the mission recorded a separate memorandum. They pointed out that when British India became independent (whether inside or outside the British Commonwealth) the old relationship between the Crown as paramount power and the rulers could not continue. The void caused by its disappearance would have to be filled either by a federal relationship between the new government and the States or by particular political arrangements. Looking to the future the mission hoped that the States would strengthen their position both by levelling up their standards of administration and by introducing representative institutions where these did not already exist, and that the smaller ones would form or join administrative units large enough to be fitted into the new constitutional structure. During the interim period it would be necessary for the States, with the help of the Crown representative if desired, to start negotiations with British India for the future regulation of matters of common concern especially in the economic and financial fields, and to arrive at an understanding with the probable successor authorities that the existing arrangements on these matters should continue until new ones were completed. Meanwhile the mission assumed for the purpose of its own plan that the States as well as the provinces would be embraced in the Indian Union, and that they would retain all powers other than those which they ceded to it. The precise form which the States' co-operation with the new government would take was to be a matter for negotiation during the process of constitution-making. The Standing Committee of the Chamber of Princes welcomed all these proposals. They endorsed the recommendations for internal reforms in the States, decided to appoint representatives to a joint consultative committee with the central government to reach agreement on matters of common concern, and appointed a negotiating committee to represent the States in the making of the Union constitution.

The mission devised an appropriate machinery for making a constitution on the broad basis which they had described. There would be a constituent assembly composed of representatives of the provinces, and at a later stage of the States also, in the proportion roughly of one to a million of their populations. Initially the States would be represented by their negotiating committee. The allotment of seats to each of the eleven major provinces would be divided between the ' general' (*i.e.* mainly Hindu [1]) and the Moslem communities (and in the Punjab the Sikhs also) in proportion to their populations in the province ; the representatives of each community [1] in the provincial legislative assembly, voting separately, would elect its allotted number of members of the constituent assembly. This assembly would at once hold a preliminary meeting to settle formal business and would then divide itself into three sections consisting of the representatives of three groups of provinces ; the first representing the solid block of six Hindu-majority provinces, Madras, Bombay, the United Provinces, Bihar,

[1] For these purposes all persons who were not Moslems or Sikhs were reckoned in the ' general ' community ; for example it included the eleven European members of the Bengal Legislative Assembly, but the latter decided to take no part in the election.

the Central Provinces and Orissa, would be overwhelmingly Hindu ; the second would represent the Punjab, North-West Frontier Province and Sind and would have a Moslem majority over Hindus and Sikhs (though some of the Moslems might be pro-Congress) and the third section would represent Bengal and Assam together and would have a small Moslem majority, though Assam by itself was mainly non-Moslem ; there were to be added to the first section one representative of each of three minor (Chief Commissioners') provinces and to the second section one from British Baluchistan. Each of the sections thus formed was to proceed (by a simple majority unless otherwise agreed) to settle constitutions for the provinces in its group, and to decide whether there should be a group constitution, and, if so, with what provincial subjects it should deal. This procedure, which for the initial purpose of constitution-planning definitely arranged the representatives of provinces in a Hindustan-Pakistan pattern, was an essential feature of the plan for an over-all compromise between the parties, on the basis of which the mission could carry out its first duty of setting a constitution-making machinery in motion. But an important safeguard was provided which preserved the essence of the optional grouping implied in the mission's sketch of the eventual constitution ; any province after the first election under its new constitution was to have power through its newly elected legislature to opt out of any group in which it had been placed.

The Constituent Assembly was to re-assemble as a whole to settle the Union constitution and was to be free to make its own decisions, but any proposal to vary the basic provisions of the plan, or raising an important communal issue, would require a majority of the representatives of each of the two major communities who were present and voted. In dealing with the problems of fundamental rights, the protection of minorities and the administration of backward areas, it would be assisted by an Advisory Committee appointed at its preliminary meeting to report on these matters and advise whether they should find their place in the provincial, group or Union constitutions. For the period of constitution-making, the mission and the Viceroy desired that the central administration of India should be carried on by an interim government resting on the support of the major parties with Indian leaders in charge of all portfolios [1] including Defence as well as External Affairs, and that this transitional government should have the greatest possible freedom in its direction of affairs though independence was to wait till the new constitution came into operation.

The sincerity of the British desire and purpose to ensure the early independence of India was clearly proved by the patience and sympathy with which the mission had laboured to promote agreement between the two parties, and, when this failed, to work out a most satisfactory compromise. In commending their plan to the Indian leaders and people, they pleaded that even though it did not completely satisfy all parties it should be accepted and operated in the spirit of mutual accommodation and good will which statesmanship demanded, and asked that the danger of violence and disturbance which lay in the alternative to doing so should be seriously considered. The first response of the major parties to this appeal was remarkably favourable when compared with the extreme positions which they had originally taken up. The Moslem League had entered the conference fortified by the proceedings of a convention of League members of provincial legislatures held in April, at which the demand for Pakistan and a demand for a separate constitution-making body had been unanimously urged in most uncompromising language, and the participants had individually pledged themselves to their cause and to obedience to the League in any movement launched by it for the attainment of their goal. But though so deeply committed, the League was now willing to co-operate in the proposed machinery; it regarded the compulsory grouping of provinces in sections as an adequate substitute for entirely separate bodies, and in a resolution of June 6th accepted this scheme, in the hope that it would ultimately result in the establishment

[1] In March 1946 the British Parliament had removed the previous statutory limitation under which three members of the Viceroy's Council had to be persons with official experience.

INTERIM GOVERNMENT

of a complete sovereign Pakistan, while reserving the right to revise its attitude at any time during the progress of constitution-making. The Congress had been anxious for a stronger centre with powers extending to currency, customs and planning as well as a general power to take action in grave emergencies. It had proposed that the constituent assembly should first draw up such a constitution and that only after this the provinces might of their own accord form groups to consider other matters. It strongly objected to the initial automatic grouping into sections, especially on behalf of the North-West Frontier Province with its congress government and Assam with its Hindu majority, and held that in practice the representatives of a provincial assembly could not be compelled to enter a section against their will. Nevertheless after much discussion with the Viceroy and the mission, the Congress resolved on June 25th to join the constituent assembly, though adhering to its own interpretation on certain points, namely that there was scope for enlarging and strengthening the central authority and for ensuring the right of a province to act according to its choice in regard to grouping. Among the Sikhs on the other hand first reactions were entirely unfavourable to the mission's proposals which they regarded as a virtual acceptance of Pakistan. At first the Sikhs refused to follow the Congress lead, but later on they decided to agree to work the plan. Meanwhile the decisions of the two main parties encouraged hopes of getting the constitution-making machinery started, despite the serious differences between their objectives and their interpretations of some of the provisions.

The question of the composition of the interim government, however, again proved intractable, as it had done a year previously, and eventually led to a deadlock in the rest of the plan. The League were anxious for parity of representation with Congress. But in the new context of prospective independence the Congress objected in principle to a hard and fast rule of parity as being a dangerous precedent. It was also very anxious, as a national organisation, to maintain its right to include a Moslem among its own nominees, but this was precluded by the League's contention that all

Moslem representatives must be selected from the League. In view of the obstacles to an agreement, the Cabinet mission and the Viceroy in a further statement of June 16th again took the initiative. They proposed the names of six Hindu members of Congress, one of whom might be reckoned as representing the Scheduled Castes, five members of the League, a Sikh, an Indian Christian and a Parsee; an assurance was given to the League that no decision on a major communal issue could be taken by this government without the assent of each of the main parties in it. The statement also announced that if the major parties, or either of them, were unwilling to join in a coalition on these lines, the Viceroy intended to proceed with the formation of an interim government as representative as possible of those willing to accept the mission's statement of May 16th. The Congress, in their resolution of June 25th, which accepted the mission's long-term plan, rejected the proposals on the interim government. The mission (which had to leave India at the end of June) thereupon decided that in accordance with the announcement of June 16th a representative interim government should be formed as soon as possible, but that further negotiations to this end should be adjourned for a short interval while the elections to the constituent assembly, which had already been put in train, were taking place. Simultaneously, however, the League decided to join the government already proposed and Jinnah took strong exception to its postponement. He held that the long-term plan and the interim proposal hung together as a coherent whole, which had been accepted by the League but not by the Congress, and that the announcement of June 16th meant that in the circumstances which had arisen the Viceroy ought to proceed forthwith to form an interim government of those willing to join it; failing this, he urged that the elections to the constituent assembly should be postponed. It was not possible to give him satisfaction on either point, nor to dispel these misunderstandings and suspicion of the motives of the adjournment. The League was disturbed by this incident to an extent which seemed disproportionate to the occasion. The underlying cause, however, lay in the supreme importance which each side attached to the interim government and (especially in the case of the minority community) to safeguarding the security of its own position in it. If the League was barely satisfied with the proposal of June 16th, it was not prepared for additional concessions which it might be asked to make in further negotiations to satisfy Congress. Moreover as regards the longer-term proposals the League was seriously disturbed by the Congress reservation in regard to grouping and feared that this might wreck the plan at its inception—fears which were not unjustified as this matter became one of decisive importance at a later stage. The combined result of these fears and suspicions was to estrange the League, and it gradually withdrew from effective co-operation in the mission's plan.

Lord Wavell on July 22nd again made proposals for an interim government similar in composition to that proposed in June, but with the proviso that it would not be open to either party to object to names submitted by the other, and without any formal condition requiring the assent of both parties on communal issues since this was in any case implicit in the idea of a coalition. The League declined to join on these terms and at the end of the month the League Council resolved to withdraw its acceptance of the Cabinet mission's plan, and to resort to ' direct action,' when this might be deemed necessary, for the achievement of Pakistan. In August the President of the Congress, Pandit Nehru, was invited to make proposals for an interim government and, after he had sought the League's co-operation without success, a government was formed of prominent congressmen and some non-League Moslems as well as representatives of the smaller communities, with himself as Vice-Chairman. It was the Viceroy's hope in forming this government that the League might afterwards be persuaded to join it. The League declared August 15th as ' direct action ' day. This was followed by an outburst of grave communal disturbances in Calcutta. Further serious outbreaks of violence, though this was condemned by the leaders of both parties, followed in Bengal and soon afterwards in Bihar ; Bombay and the

United Provinces were also affected. The Viceroy renewed his efforts, eventually with success, to bring the League into the government, and on October 15th this was reconstituted with five League nominees under Liaquat Ali Khan taking the place of three Congress members. The League thus obtained its share in the control of the centre. But as an experiment in co-operation the government was a failure since it lacked any real unity or harmony of purpose. The first meeting of the constituent assembly, which had been elected with League participation in July and August, had been postponed but was now fixed for December 9th. This threatened to bring to a head the vexed question of grouping on which the Congress adhered to its reservations, holding that each province had the right to decide both as to its grouping and as to its own constitution. The League proposed that the meeting should be indefinitely postponed, and when this was negatived by Congress decided to boycott the assembly. In the hope of overcoming this impasse, conversations were held in London between the British Government, the Viceroy, Pandit Nehru and Sardar Baldev Singh (Sikh member of the Indian Government), Jinnah and Liaquat Ali Khan. These failed to bring the parties to an agreement. The British Government, however, reaffirmed that it was an essential part of the Cabinet mission's plan that, in the absence of an agreement to the contrary, the decisions of the assembly's sections on provincial constitutions and grouping should be taken by a simple majority vote of each section; and they urged the Congress to accept this view and so open the way for the League to participate in the assembly. They pointed out that if a constitution were framed by an assembly in which a large part of the population was not represented, the British Government could not contemplate forcing it on unwilling parts of the country, and that the Congress also had declared itself against such enforcement. But the deadlock continued. The Congress demanded that the League should either enter into the constituent assembly or resign from the interim government. The assembly met on the date fixed without its League representatives, and instead of dividing itself into sections proceeded to deal with the general basic principles of the Union constitution, while the League denounced its resolutions as illegal and invalid. In February the League proclaimed a non-violent campaign against the unionist government in the Punjab which led to serious communal rioting ; in March the ministry resigned and the governor had to take charge of the administration.

CHAPTER LVIII

PARTITION AND THE TRANSFER OF POWER

SINCE the continued dissensions between the parties made it impossible for the constituent assembly to function in the manner intended, and it was essential to bring a dangerous state of uncertainty to an end, the British Government on February 20th, 1947 issued a new statement of their policy in regard to the transfer of power. They announced that they intended in any case to take the steps necessary to transfer it into responsible Indian hands by June 1948 at the latest, and that preparatory measures would have to be taken in advance of that date; they still desired, if possible, to transfer it to authorities established by a constitution worked out by a fully representative assembly as proposed by the Cabinet mission; but if it should appear that such a constitution would not be ready within the time limit, they would have to consider to whom the powers of the central government of British India should be handed over, whether as a whole to some form of central government, or in some areas to the existing provincial governments, or in such other way as might seem most reasonable and in the best interests of the Indian people. At the same time the appointment of Lord Mountbatten as Viceroy was announced.

The definite determination to transfer power by a fixed date left no room for any lingering doubt of British sincerity or for excusing Indian dissensions on this ground; and it brought home to both parties the real necessity and urgency of finding some basis of agreement before the time limit expired. Lord Mountbatten's instructions were to endeavour first to obtain an agreement on the basis of the

MAP XI

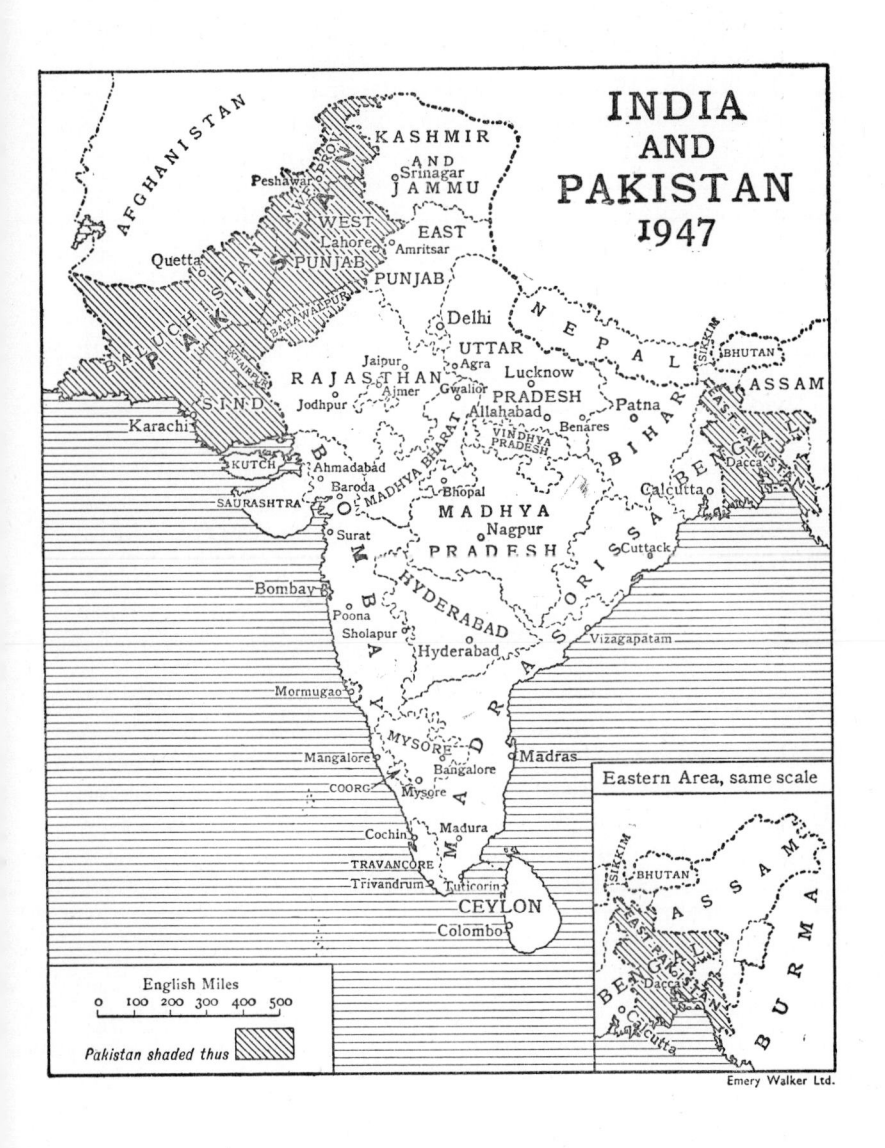

Cabinet mission's plan for a United India, and if by October he considered that there was no prospect of this, to report as to the steps which he advised for handing over power by June 1948. When he arrived on March 22nd, 1947, the communal situation was still threatening; the rioting in the Punjab had recently reached its height, and disturbances had started in the North-West Frontier Province also. In a short speech at his swearing-in ceremony he referred to the urgency of the tasks ahead and appealed to all to avoid any words or acts which might increase communal bitterness. Shortly afterwards a joint appeal was issued by Gandhi and Jinnah denouncing the use of force for political ends and calling on all communities to refrain from acts of violence and disorder and to avoid any incitement to such acts. The Viceroy was soon engaged in intensive discussions with political leaders and others, and found them unanimous on one point—that in order to stop communal strife and restore a peaceful atmosphere, it was essential to reach a decision, and announce it as early as possible, on the question how and to whom power was to be transferred, and thus put an end to the uncertainty which was itself an incentive to disorder. The Viceroy first endeavoured to obtain a decision of this question in the sense of the Cabinet mission's plan for an all-India union, as being ideally the best solution. But the essence of that plan was agreement between the parties; there could be no question of compulsion, and it at once became obvious that there was now no prospect of obtaining such an agreement. The Moslem League and the Congress had indeed at one time each agreed to work the machinery of the plan, but with different objects and different interpretations—the Congress in hopes of strengthening the central authority and avoiding the automatic grouping of provinces, the League provisionally, in reliance on the grouping system, and without ever abandoning its ultimate objective of a 'complete sovereign Pakistan.' It was now quite unyielding in its demand for complete partition, and it was clear that no other solution would be accepted peacefully. Partition therefore was the only alternative to coercion, and Lord Mountbatten next

MOUNTBATTEN AND PARTITION

turned to Congress to see whether it would be prepared to surrender the ideal of a united India. The policy of Congress, as embodied in its resolution of September 1945, was against coercion. For the sake of peace and the certainty of an early transfer of power, it was now prepared to agree to the unfortunate necessity of the division of India, provided that the peoples of large non-Moslem areas were not included in Pakistan against their will. This was the principle of self-determination which Gandhi had stressed in his talks with Jinnah in 1944. It was bound to involve partitioning Bengal and the Punjab, which was scarcely less disagreeable to the League than partitioning India was to others, but could be defended by the same logic. In the end, for the sake of peace and the early achievement of a sovereign Pakistan, Jinnah and the League acquiesced in a reduction of their full territorial claim. There were also other considerations favouring a compromise which may naturally have given cause for reflection on both sides. If the unity of all India could only be preserved as a loose confederation with a centre too weak to check centrifugal tendencies, there was a danger not merely of division but of fragmentation; and for the League the abatement of their territorial claim was made easier by the reflection that the inclusion of large irreconcilable elements in Pakistan might be more a source of weakness than of strength.

Meanwhile at an early stage in his discussions Lord Mountbatten himself reached the conclusion that partition on the basis of popular consent was the only fair and practicable solution of the problem and the one which offered the best chance of acceptance. Accordingly, while still consulting the political leaders on points as they arose, he provisionally prepared for eventual consideration by all the parties concerned a plan of partition and machinery for ascertaining the popular will. At the beginning of May this was submitted to the British Government and in the latter part of the month he went to London for consultations on it. In the form which it finally took as part of the Plan of June 3rd it contained the following provisions. There was to be no interruption in the work of the existing constituent assembly which contained the majority of the representatives of all the provinces except Bengal, the Punjab, Sind and British Baluchistan; but contingent provision was made for a new and separate constituent assembly to represent the peoples of Moslem-majority provinces and areas, who might opt to join it by decisions taken through the provincial assemblies elected in 1946 or in two cases by referendum. In Bengal and the Punjab the issue of partition was to be decided by their assemblies sitting separately in two parts, one part representing the Moslem-majority districts (as indicated by the 1941 census) and the other the rest of the province; a simple majority vote by either part for partition was to be decisive, after which each part would decide whether to join the existing constituent assembly or the new one. The Sind legislative assembly and British Baluchistan would also take their decisions as between these two alternatives. As regards the North-West Frontier Province, two of its three representatives were already taking part in the existing constituent assembly, but in view of geographical and other factors it was to have an opportunity, if the Punjab was partitioned, of reconsidering its position through a referendum to the electors of its legislative assembly. Similarly, if Bengal was partitioned, a referendum would be held in the contiguous Moslem-majority district of Sylhet in Assam to decide whether it should be amalgamated with eastern Bengal. The detailed boundaries of new provinces resulting from partition were to be investigated and demarcated by Boundary Commissions on the basis of ascertaining the contiguous majority areas of Moslems and non-Moslems within the districts, and taking other factors into account. The membership and terms of reference of these commissions were to be settled in consultation with those concerned.

The essence of the plan was to provide machinery by which Indians themselves would decide on their future constitutional arrangements. Unfortunately a decision to partition the Punjab was bound to cut across the important Sikh community owing to the pattern of its distribution in the province. The Viceroy anxiously considered whether any solution was possible which would keep the Sikh community more together. But in March before his arrival a resolution by the Congress on behalf of the Sikhs had been received expressing their wish that the Punjab should be divided according to predominantly Moslem and non-Moslem areas, which in fact meant on a line nearly bisecting their own community. That was at a time when the Cabinet mission's plan for an all-India government (which the Congress hoped to strengthen) was still in the field. Now that division of the Punjab would probably involve its partition between two separate states the case was somewhat altered. But in any case under the partition plan it was not possible to preserve the unity of the Sikh community without departing from the basic principle of division by areas to meet the wishes of the two major communities. It could only be hoped that as a key community in Punjabi politics the Sikhs might be able to improve their position by negotiation with the other parties. It was arranged that the terms of reference to the Punjab Boundary Commission should be drawn up by a committee nominated by the party leaders including those of the Sikhs.

The part of the plan so far described satisfied the need for an early answer to the question to whom the British should transfer power. A further question, to which different considerations might apply, was the timing of the transfer. Was this to wait until the constituent assemblies had completed their work and duly constituted governments were ready to receive it, or until the preparatory work of setting up separate administrations had proceeded far enough to ensure a smooth transfer to provisional governments? Was the date announced to stand or to be anticipated? At the time of the Cabinet mission's plan the British Government had contemplated retaining their responsibilities under the existing constitution until a new one was made by a constituent assembly in which Congress and League co-operated and the dispute between them was thus settled. But there was no longer the same reason for delaying the British withdrawal when once the dispute between the parties was settled by an agreement to separate.

Moreover there was now a time limit for withdrawal, and there was in any case hardly time enough for the constituent assemblies, especially the new one, to work out satisfactory constitutions before June 1948. The view has been strongly held, however, in some well informed quarters, that in order to ensure a smooth and peaceful transfer, the British withdrawal should have been deferred until the important administrative changes involved in partition were well on their way to completion. The main administrative services had been built up on the basis of a united India, and it was certain that the task of dividing them, while at the same time maintaining the efficiency of the civil administration, would be difficult and complicated. On the other hand there were the considerations that the acceptability of the partition plan rested largely on its promise of early independence; that it was becoming increasingly difficult to keep the interim coalition government together; and that the settlement itself might be jeopardised by a delay in the transfer of power. In any case the decisive factor in the problem was that the major political parties had repeatedly emphasised their desire for the earliest possible transfer of power, the British Government were in full sympathy with this desire and there was no constitutional obstacle to meeting it. Lord Mountbatten suggested, and the British Government agreed, that pending new constitutional arrangements, power could be transferred on a Dominion status basis by the simple expedient of continuing the Government of India Act of 1935 with the amendments necessary for this purpose. It was therefore proposed to transfer power during 1947 on this basis either to one or to two successor authorities according to the results of the measures prescribed for ascertaining the popular will.

This plan for the transfer of power was approved by the British Government after their consultations with Lord Mountbatten, and was supported by all parties in Great Britain. On his return from London he invited the Indian party leaders to a joint meeting, and asked them to accept the plan as one which, though it could not wholly satisfy the principles of any of them, was a fair solution and the

TWO INDEPENDENT DOMINIONS

best that was possible in the interests of the country. In this spirit it was accepted by the Congress leaders, the Sikh representative, Baldev Singh, and also by Jinnah with assurances that he would recommend it to the Moslem League Council for their confirmation. The plan was accordingly announced in the statement on Indian policy of June 3rd, 1947.[1] The Viceroy had a separate interview with Gandhi, who as the champion of Hindu-Moslem unity was specially distressed at the prospect of partition, and he too acquiesced in the plan as being the only basis on which Hindus and Moslems had been able to reach agreement, and at the meeting of the All-India Congress Committee on June 14th he spoke in favour of the resolution confirming its acceptance.

After the announcement of June 3rd preparations were at once commenced for the administrative changes which partition would involve. A committee of the interim government was set up, and towards the end of June was replaced by a Partition Council with an enlarged authority and membership, to deal with civil issues, including the transfer of public assets and liabilities. Agreement was reached on the principles and procedure to be adopted for the division of the Indian armed forces and their reconstitution as separate Dominion forces. As a precaution against outbreaks a joint Indo-Pakistan military force was formed for despatch to areas of potential trouble. On July 19th the interim government was reconstituted on the lines of separate provisional administrations for India and Pakistan. A Joint Defence Council was inaugurated under Lord Mountbatten's chairmanship to provide for future consultation on major defence problems between the two Dominions.

The results of the steps prescribed for ascertaining the popular will were in favour of the incorporation in Pakistan of the Moslem-majority districts of Bengal and the Punjab, the provinces of Sind and British Baluchistan, the North-West Frontier Province and Sylhet. These steps were completed in time to enable the British Parliament to enact on

[1] Cmd. 7136.

July 18th an Indian Independence Act setting up two independent Dominions of India and Pakistan as from August 15th, 1947. This Act gave full sovereign powers to the Legislature of each Dominion, to be exercised in the first instance by their constituent assemblies, both for making new constitutional provisions and in other matters; pending new provisions the Government of India Act, 1935, was to provide an initial constitutional basis subject to the express provisions of the Independence Act and to other necessary alterations; up to the end of March 1948 at the latest the Governors-General were given wide powers to issue orders both for making such alterations and for dividing the administrative machinery, authorising the temporary continuance of existing services and activities and other transitional purposes. When the Independence Bill was drafted it had been hoped that for the initial period of transition an effective co-ordinating link between the governments of the two Dominions might be established by the appointment of Lord Mountbatten as Governor-General of each of them, and the Act included an enabling provision to cover this possibility. But this was not used, as on the Pakistani side it was eventually considered desirable that Jinnah should become Governor-General of the new State from its inception, though the decision that nevertheless Lord Mountbatten should still remain as Governor-General of the Indian Dominion was welcomed by the Pakistani as well as by the Indian leaders.

The Independence Act also brought to an end the King's suzerainty over the Indian States and the existing agreements with them and also those with the frontier tribes, thus leaving the new Dominions free to negotiate fresh ones. The plan of June 3rd, 1947 had related only to British India. As regards the Indian States the policy announced in the Cabinet mission's memorandum of May 1946 (p. 551) remained unchanged. Some of the Princes, following the lead of the Maharaja of Bikaner, had sent representatives to the constituent assembly; others following the Nawab of Bhopal, Chancellor of the Chamber of Princes, had hesitated to do so pending a settlement of the dispute between the parties. With the approaching transfer of power and consequent lapse of the old relationship between the States and the Crown, urgent consideration had to be given to the position of the States ; and it was desirable, if possible, in the interests of all concerned that some form of federal relationship should be established between the individual States and either India or Pakistan as might be appropriate in view of geographical and other factors. In order to facilitate this on a uniform basis, the Viceroy circulated a draft instrument of accession for discussion ; this in the form it received at the end of July provided for accession in respect of Defence, External Affairs and Communications. There were in all about 565 States, the great majority of which were geographically linked with India. By August 15th all the States, with the exceptions of Kashmir, Hyderabad and Junagadh, had signified their accessions either to India or to Pakistan. The transfer of power also entailed the lapse of agreements on matters of common concern to the States and British India, by virtue of which a system of co-ordinated administration of such matters had grown up. The accessions in respect of communications ensured continuity of administration in one important field, but there were many other technical subjects, such as customs and transit, in the financial and economic fields, on which new agreements would have to be made between the States and the successor authorities. The Independence Act provided for continuance of the old agreements until denounced by either side ; but the States were also advised to enter into ' standstill agreements ' with the new authorities for the continuance of existing arrangements till new ones could be made. Two States Departments were set up in readiness for partition to conduct the relations of India and Pakistan respectively with the States.

The end of British rule and the creation of two new and sovereign States, freely associated with others within the Commonwealth, is a natural point at which to bring the present work on the history of India to a close. The transfer of power, dimly foreseen by Elphinstone as a desirable consummation, was the outcome of a policy consciously pursued for thirty years since the Montagu announcement of August 20th, 1917; but the roots of that policy stretch back to an earlier epoch in the history of British India. The first foundations, on which it afterwards became possible to build a political structure culminating in self-government, are to be found in the solid administrative work and material progress, and above all in the growth and fostering of liberal ideas, which were characteristics of British rule since the first part of the nineteenth century. The former provided the requisite basis of political and economic security; the latter made a more direct contribution, by attracting the natural genius of the Indian people towards the development of that type of political self-consciousness which could only be satisfied by national freedom in the form of parliamentary democracy. Throughout the later process of political evolution, till towards its end, the unity of India was implicit in the objective of Indian freedom. But one great obstacle to the attainment of this objective was the difficulty of reconciling the legitimate claims of the majority with those of the large Moslem minority. As independence drew nearer, the natural fears and stresses between them grew more acute, until Indian nationalism ultimately engendered a separate Moslem national self-consciousness. In the Cabinet mission plan a supreme effort was made to produce a synthesis. But when this failed, independence in separation became, by the consent of both parties, the only practicable conclusion.

APPENDIX

INDIAN NOMENCLATURE AND CHRONOLOGY

THE facts brought together in this Appendix will, it is hoped, be of some service to those readers who may wish to pursue the study of Indian history in more elaborate works or in the original sources.

I. NOMENCLATURE

1. *Representation in English.*

The first obstacle confronting the student is the number and variety of unfamiliar and uncouth names, many of them spelt differently in different books. Apart from minor sources, the names are drawn from three principal linguistic systems, Sanskritic, Dravidian and (through Persian) Arabic, each of them with various sounds unknown in English; to attempt precise representation of all these sounds in one set of characters means doubling or trebling the alphabet by the introduction of new letters or the use of diacritical marks, which are at once meaningless and repulsive to ordinary readers; and in the text of this book we have preferred to adopt the simplified method of transliteration used in the *Imperial Gazetteer of India*, which is more generally known than any alternative. This method may be summarised as follows.

(1) Forms which have won admission to the English language are retained, in spite of the fact that they may diverge widely from the correct Indian orthography. Calcutta, Bombay and Madras, Cawnpore, Lucknow and Delhi, are all good English, though bad transliteration.

(2) Where there is no accepted English form, the letters used have precise values, intended to give, not the actual pronunciation, but as near an approach to it as the English alphabet permits.

Vowels.—Three short vowels, *a*, *i* and *u*, are employed, pronounced as in the series, *putty*, *pity*, *put*; the sound of *a* in *patty* is not represented in Indian written languages. The five

572 INDIAN NOMENCLATURE AND CHRONOLOGY

long vowels, $\bar{a}$, $\bar{e}$, $\bar{\imath}$, o, and $\bar{u}$, are sounded as in *mart, mate, meet, mote, moot*; the long Indian $\bar{a}$ is almost exactly represented by the English *-ar*, when the *r* is not sounded separately. At one period Persian speakers introduced in India an $\bar{a}$ sounded as *aw*, which accounts for such words as nabob (properly transliterated *nawwāb*); this sound is not distinguished in the written languages though it is heard occasionally in some parts of the country, especially Bengal.

Consonants are meant to be pronounced as in English, but *g* is always guttural (*get*), and *j* palatal (*jet*); the distinction between *s* (*hiss*) and *z* (*his*) is always observed; on the other hand the Persian sounds represented by *v* and *w* are so nearly identical that precision in the use of these letters is scarcely possible, and they are also interchangeable in reproducing the languages of Western India.

Aspirated Consonants.—Where *h* follows another consonant, it is necessary to distinguish. *sh* has the English sound (*she*), and *ch* is palatal (*church*, never *choir*), but *bh, chh, dh, th*, etc. represent a range of aspirated sounds which are very important in Sanskritic languages, but are absent from Persian, and are practically never heard in England; some idea of the nature of the sound can be got by saying 'uphill' rapidly as a single word. *gh* and *kh* are ambiguous. In Sanskritic names they are aspirated sounds; in Arabic and Persian they are sounded in a way unknown in ordinary English, but to be heard in Scotland and Ireland, as in *loch, lough.*

It may be added that the pronunciation of Arabic was materially altered in Persia, and Arabic names used in India are pronounced Persian fashion; thus the name familiar in Europe as Ottoman appears in Persia and India as Usmān.

The system of precise transliteration most commonly used in England is that which is recommended by the Royal Asiatic Society, and is published periodically in the Society's *Journal* (e.g., January, 1935, p. 267). Modern books usually contain an explanation of the system used in them, but the older sources are unsystematic, and contain many distorted forms; some clues to these are given in the next section.

As regards pronunciation in general, it may be said that the chief difficulty arises from the English habit of accenting one syllable strongly and slurring the others: Indians give every syllable approximately the same value, saying (e.g.) Hi-mā-la-ya, where Englishmen say Himaláya.

2. *Distortion.*

Classical Sanskrit is characterised by complex groups of consonants, and the speech of ordinary people tended to break down and simplify these : thus the Sanskrit *sutra* was written in the old vernacular as *sutta*, Krishna became Kishan, and the Rāshtrakūta clan became known as Rāthor. At the present day this tendency is reversed, and classical forms are becoming more popular among educated Indians ; and in the earlier period it is sometimes doubtful whether a Sanskrit form has been broken down or a popular form has been Sanskritised. Distortion is, however, found mainly in foreign sources.

Greek.—Much knowledge of the early history of India is drawn from Greek sources, which, it will be understood, are based not on Sanskrit but on the simpler language which the Greeks heard spoken in the country. They usually provided terminations to conform to the precise rules of their own language, and, having no palatal characters in their alphabet, they made shift with their sibilants : thus, hearing of the great ruler Chandragupta, probably in the simplified form Chandragutta, they transformed him into Sandrokottos. Having no *h* of their own, except at the beginning of a word, they were naturally puzzled by the Indian *h*, which is always sounded, and sometimes represented it by the letter which is known in English as *chi*, but was really the aspirated guttural *kh* ; thus Brāhmans became Brachmanoi.

Chinese.—For some periods Chinese sources are important. The phonology of China was, however, so different from that of contemporary India that Indian names took on forms unrecognisable to ordinary readers, and their identification is a task for specialists ; Mālava, for instance, became in Chinese Mo-la-p'o.

Portuguese.—The practice of the Portuguese is important, partly for understanding their own literature, and partly because both Dutch and English at first depended on Portuguese interpreters, whose peculiar forms thus acquired a wider currency. Like the Greeks, the Portuguese provided their own terminations, the masculine *-o* and feminine *-im*, strongly nasalised. They had the usual difficulty with the palatal sounds ; *j* was represented by *z*, but, curiously, they regularly wrote *ch* as such, though in their language that combination is pronounced *sh*. They had difficulty, too, with the sound of *h* which they met in India, sometimes writing (e.g.) Mafamed for Muhammad ; and, having no *w*, they commonly represented its sound by *b*. Groups of consonants were obstacles to them, and they often inserted additional vowels ; while the transposition of letters (metathesis) sometimes occurred. That considerable distortion might result may be seen in their word *zaburro*, which represents *juwār*, the Indian name of the sorghum millet.

Dutch and English.—As has just been said, Dutchmen and Englishmen at first depended largely on Portuguese interpreters, and some very curious forms reached Western Europe, to undergo further distortion there by copyists and printers. As time went on, Dutch and English discarded interpreters, and some of the seventeenth-century writers of both nations reproduced Indian sounds with remarkable exactitude, though the Dutch, like the Greeks and the Portuguese, had to represent the palatals by sibilants. In the next century, however, the arrival in the country of European troops, usually uneducated, resulted in some extraordinary distortions, examples of which can be found in the classical glossary known as *Hobson-Jobson* (London, 1903), which is an indispensable companion to the student; and the nineteenth century was well advanced before any serious attempt was made to secure precision or uniformity in the English representation of Indian names.

3. *Place Names.*

Scientific study of Indian place names has scarcely begun, and the popular etymologies, which the inhabitants are ready to furnish on demand, are no more trustworthy in India than elsewhere. The largest single group, however, which comprises about one-third of the total, can be described in precise terms. These consist of a personal name or designation, with a suffix (or in a few cases a prefix) of the same general nature as the English -ton or -ham. The formation of such names can be traced back in the literature for several centuries, and it is quite certain that they refer either to the founder of the place, or to the individual, whether human or divine, in whose honour it was founded, or under whose protection it was placed.

The most usual suffixes drawn from Sanskritic languages are: -*nagar* (city); -*pur*, -*pura* (town); -*grām* or -*gāon*, corruptly -*gong* (village); -*ganj*, -*hāt* (market); -*garh*, -*kot* (fort); -*ghāt* (river-crossing or mountain-pass). The languages of South India furnish -*pet* (town); -*pattanam*, corruptly -patam (town or village); -*palle* (hamlet); -*konda* (hill); -*drug* (fort); while Persian-speaking conquerors contributed -*shahr* (city), and -*ābād* (founded by). Linguistic form is not, however, a certain clue to the history of a place, for the suffixes have been used freely, and to take one example, the names in the series Rāmpur, Shāhjahānpur, Lyallpur, commemorate respectively a deified Hindu hero, a Mogul Emperor, and a British Lieutenant-Governor. The Persian suffixes, indeed, denote that the name cannot be older than the thirteenth century, but the place may be far older, for the conquerors on occasion renamed an ancient site on their own lines; the name Allahabad, for instance, dates from the reign of Akbar, but the history of the place goes back to a much earlier period.

INDIAN NOMENCLATURE AND CHRONOLOGY

Of the other place names, all that can be said at present is that local tradition may sometimes be true, and that etymology may sometimes furnish a probable explanation; but the presumption is that they are old, because extant documents disclose no recent methods of formation other than the personal name with prefix or suffix.

4. *Personal Names.*

India has not yet developed a complete system of surnames in the strict sense, though their use has of late spread rapidly among the upper and middle classes. The need for something of the kind, to distinguish between individuals bearing the same personal name, has, however, long been felt in India as elsewhere, and we meet occasionally in history most of the elements from which English surnames have been derived—the patronymic, the tribe name, the place name, and the rest—used in the case of individuals, and sometimes, but not always, transmitted to their descendants.

Hindu personal names were usually, though not invariably, derived from some deity or hero, or from a shrine, or sacred river, and frequently in the form of expressions written in two words, as Gaṅgā Prasād ('Boon of the Ganges'). Names denoting attributes of a deity are also common, especially for women, as well as others drawn from flowers, gems or other beautiful objects, as Padmā (lotus), Motī (pearl), or Ushā (dawn). In addition, there are titles appropriate to particular families, occupations, or castes, such as Singh (lion), which is now affixed to the personal name by nearly all Rājputs, and by some men of other castes.

The early invaders from Central Asia brought to India names which were as strange there as they are now in England, and even in the Moslem period we meet such outlandish forms as Sabuktigīn or Iltutmish. These, however, soon gave way to the regular Moslem system of personal names, which may be derived from the Hebrew patriarchs, as Ibrāhīm or Yūsuf (Abraham, Joseph), or from prophets and champions of Islam, as Muhammad or Husain, or may be expressions with a religious significance, as Abdullāh ('Slave of Allah'), or Alāuddīn ('Standard of the Faith'). The number of such names is limited, and there was often room for confusion between individuals; in such cases a second name was commonly added, which might be drawn from the tribe, or birth-place, or occupation, of the person concerned, or might be a mere soubriquet. Thus Alāuddīn, the great king of Delhi, was called Khaljī, from the name of the tribe to which he belonged, to distinguish him from an earlier ruler of the same name, whose military activities had earned for him the soubriquet of Jahānsoz, or 'World-burner'; but even with such aids as these it must be admitted that the frequent recurrence of names is a serious obstacle to western students of the Moslem period.

There is also some risk of confusion in the case of Parsees. Their personal names were commonly drawn from the select band of heroes of old Persia, such as Suhrāb and Rustam, or Bahrām and Khurshed, with the honorific suffic -*jī*; and the father's name was added to that of the son, giving, for instance, Suhrābjī Rustamjī as the name of an individual. The community was, however, quick to imitate the English practice of using surnames, which were commonly drawn from occupations, as Modi (steward), and the risk of confusion between individuals has thus been reduced.

5. *Titles, Designations, etc.*

Hindu rulers were apt to employ high-sounding titles for themselves, but it does not appear from the extant literature that any of them established a regular system of titles to be conferred on their subjects in general. It may be noted that the series of titles, Rāja, Rāo, Rānā and Rāi, with their compounds, properly imply sovereignty, and, strictly speaking, would not be available for the subjects of a Hindu ruler.

The Turkish conquerors introduced a regular system with three ranks of nobility, Khān, Amīr, and Malik, which, except for the fact that they were not hereditary, may be thought of as the equivalent of Duke, Earl, and Baron. In Central Asia the title of Khān was strictly confined to the chief of the horde, whose principal commanders were designated Amīr. When the Turkish rulers in India adopted the title of King (Bādshāh), Khān inevitably depreciated in value, and was conferred on the principal nobles, occasionally with an honorific addition, such as Khān Jahān ('Duke of the World'); Amīr then became the second rank, while for the third use was made of Malik, which is derived from an Arabic root originally denoting sovereignty.

Under the Afghan rulers of the fifteenth century further depreciation occurred, for every gentleman called himself Khān, a practice which has survived among that race. Akbar restricted the use of this title, and in the Mogul empire Khān was again employed as part of the titles conferred on courtiers of merit. Amīr was employed more widely to denote a courtier in general, and its plural form, Umarā, was currently used for the courtiers as a body; but European visitors took this form as singular, and in the seventeenth century one constantly reads of the 'Oomrahs,' where the reference is to the nobility. With the

INDIAN NOMENCLATURE AND CHRONOLOGY

decay of the Mogul empire, titles steadily became longer and more sonorous, till the mere words Khān and Amīr lost most of their honorific value; and so it has come to pass that at the present day Khān, which sufficed for the world-conqueror Chingīz, and was beyond the reach of Tīmūr, may appear as the surname of a gentleman of Afghan race, or as part of the title conferred on a subordinate official, while it has been assumed very widely by some classes of converts from Hinduism.

The Moguls introduced the practice of conferring titles on their Hindu subjects, employing for this purpose the designations originally appropriate to sovereignty, and from the sixteenth century onwards the connotation of these becomes increasingly indefinite; Rāja may still denote a sovereign ruler, but it is often a title enjoyed by a subject of position, such as a large landholder; while Rāi, apart from its use in titles, has been assumed by many men of position.

More perplexing to foreigners than the official system of titles is the mass of honorific designations created by popular usage, drawn originally from occupation or from religious, social or literary position, sometimes assumed without adequate justification, and now frequently developing into surnames. Thus the specialisation of functions among Brāhmans gave rise to such terms as Pandit (Sanskrit scholar), Chaube (learned in the four Vedas), or Upādhyāy (literally, teacher); the familiar Bābū originally denoted social distinction, but has been degraded in popular usage; Thākur ('lord' in the sense of 'deity') is appropriated usually by Rājputs, though in some places it is applied to Brāhmans, and in the form Tagore it has become the surname of one of the most eminent Brāhman families of Bengal; and various other honorific designations have been used by Hindus. Among Moslems they are perhaps even more prevalent, the commonest being Munshī (writer, claimed also by some Hindus), Maulavī (Islamic lawyer), Hāfiz (one who has memorised the Koran), Hājī (one who has made pilgrimage to Mecca), Mirza (prince, gentleman), Mīr or Saiyid (a descendant of Muhammad), and Sardār (a high military title, used also by Sikhs).

II. Chronology

In the Sanskrit classics the past is reckoned by 'aeons' and 'ages,' running back for thousands of millions of years, but this reckoning has no significance for the historical period. As time went on, a practice grew up under which conquerors established new eras, dating usually from their accession to the throne, and a large number of such forgotten eras have been recovered by modern scholars; knowledge of them is indispensable for the study of coins and inscriptions, but the general reader is only concerned with two, the Vikrama and the Saka.

The *Vikrama era* begins in 58, or possibly 57, B.C. According to tradition it was established by Vikramāditya, a king of Ujjain, who defeated the Sakas; but there is reason to believe that the founder was in fact the Saka king Azes I, who ruled in northern India (*Camb. Hist.*, i. 571, 581), and that it was carried south with the extension of Saka rule. Whatever its origin, its use became widespread, and under the name Samvat it is still employed by many Hindus.

The *Saka era* begins in A.D. 78. Most authorities hold that it was established by the Kushān king Kanishka, and gives the year of his accession, but some scholars put that event about half a century later, and find another origin for the era. It obtained a wide currency in India.

The *Hijra era*, denoted by A.H., was introduced into India by the Moslem conquerors; it runs from July, 622 A.D., the date of the flight (*hijrat*) of Muhammad from Mecca to Medina. Whatever era was used by Hindus, their year was kept fairly close to the seasons by periodical intercalation; but the Moslem year follows the moon, not the sun, and contains only 354, or occasionally 355 days. The resulting divergence from the seasons as determined by the course of the sun is a serious administrative inconvenience in an agricultural country, and Akbar established for revenue purposes a solar year, which is known as *faslī*, and is still familiar in many parts of India. It started from 963 A.H., but necessarily fell gradually behind, so that, e.g., 1304 *faslī* corresponded to 1314 A.H. (1896–7). Akbar also introduced the *Divine era* (*Ilāhī*), which ran from his accession in 1556, and was intended to supersede the Hijra, but it did not last for long; his successors usually reckoned dates by 'regnal' years, that is to say, a new era began at the accession of each Emperor and ended with his death, but they also maintained the Hijra era as the permanent basis of their chronology. Precise conversion of Islamic dates to Christian is a treacherous task; the most convenient materials for the purpose will be found in Sir Wolseley Haig's *Comparative Tables of Muhammadan and Christian Dates* (London, 1932); but a rough approximation can be obtained by deducting three per cent. and adding 622.

Finally it may be recalled that there are two pitfalls in dates of the *Christian era*, which was used increasingly in India from the sixteenth century onwards. (1) At one time the year began on 25th March; this was changed to 1st January in Portugal in 1556, in Holland in 1583, and in England in 1752. Dates given in the records of these countries therefore need adjustment between New Year's Day and Lady Day up to the years stated, and it is now usual to indicate the pitfall by writing, e.g.,

5th January, 1601/2. (2) The old, or Julian, calendar had too many leap years, and in the sixteenth century its year had fallen ten days behind the correct solar year. The error was adjusted in the new, or Gregorian, calendar, which was adopted by Portugal in 1582, by Holland in 1583, and by England in 1752. Dates given in records of those countries, up to the year stated, have consequently to be increased by ten days up to 1700, and by eleven days thereafter.

INDEX

ABDURRAHMĀN, 406, 414
Abul Fazl, 210, 212
Accountants, village and pargana, 225
Accounting business, 51
Achin, 234, 235
Aden, 72, 73, 200
Administration : Hindu, 17, 23, 27, 50-2, 54, 88-90, 106, 107, 121 ; Turkish, 153-7, 168, 169 ; Sayyid and Afghan, 179, 180, 208 ; Akbars', 221-30 ; later Mogul, 232, 250, 251, 280-2 ; Golconda, 244 ; British, 295-304, 314-16, 333-8, 392, 459-61, 473, 489-92
Adoption, 28, 352
Advisory Committee, 553
Afghan wars : first, 345-9 ; second, 405-6 ; third, 464, 475, 509
Afghanistan ; position in tenth century, 133, 134 ; in Aurangzeb's reign, 252-3 ; independent state, 268, 322, 326, 327, 345-9, 366, 404-6, 413-15, 443, 451, 463-5.
Africans, 181, 182, 260
Aga Khan, H.H., the, 471
Age of Consent Bill, the, 431
Agitators, 430-2, 437
Agra, 179, 205, 219, 220, 242
Agrarian questions (modern), 377, 383-5, 518-19
Agricultural improvement, 157, 169, 227, 283, 418, 419, 517-19, 529
Ahalya Bāī, 320
Ahichhatra, 61
Ahimsā, moral principle, 54
Ahmad Shāh Durānī, 268
Ahmadābād, 184, 379, 380
Ahmadnagar, 183, 217, 232, 240, 243, 248
Āīn-i Akbarī, text, 221, 303
Air Force, 504, 505
Air transport, 517
Ajanta, site, 95
Ajmere, 158, 159, 207, 329, 353
Ajodhya, 89, 289 ; *and see* Kosala
Akbar, Mogul Emperor, 210-29

Akbar, Prince, 210, 253, 254
Akbarnāma, text, 212
Alāuddīn Bahman Shāh, 174
Alāuddīn Khaljī, 88, 162-6
Albuquerque, Afonso de, 199, 200
Alexander, A. V., 549
Alexander the Great, 45-7, 73
Alexandria, 67, 73, 96
Aligarh, 397 ; University, 537
All-India Board of Technical Education, 534
All-India Congress Committee, 542, 547, 567
All-India States Peoples' Conference, 496
All Parties Conference, 1928...480
Allahabad, 16, 108, 219, 278
Amānullah, 464
Amarāvatī site, 79, 80
Ambar, Malik, 243
Ambhi, 47
Amery, Rt. Hon. L. S., 498
Amherst, Lord, 330
Amīr Khusrū, 189
Amīrs of Sind, the, 347
Andhra kingdom, 63, 69, 75, 80-2
Angkor, 138
'Anglo-Indians,' 5, 436, 491
Animists, 32, 33, 121
Annam, 138, 139
Antialcidas, 65
Arabs, 5, 112, 116, 134, 135, 198-200
Arakan, 2, 216, 245, 252, 349
Aravalli mountains, 158
Archaeological Survey, the, 396
Architecture : origins, 9, 56 ; Gupta period, 93, 94 ; later Hindu, 126, 177, 188 ; Turkish, 177, 184, 189, 190 ; Mogul, 219, 220, 242 ; modern, 396
Arcot, 265 ; *and see* Carnatic
Armagon, 237, 246
Armenians, 5, 288
Armies, standing, 52, 106, 120, 153, 165
Army organisation (British), 333, 372, 421, 422, 477, 503, 504-5, 506
Arthasāstra, text, 27, 49

INDEX

Artillery, 201, 205
Arts and Crafts: early, 9, 13, 17, 130, 140, 184; Akbar, 228; Shāh Jahān, 242; Aurangzeb, 251; decay, 286, 289, 290, 279; renaissance, 472, 533
Ārya Samāj, the, 398, 438
Aryan people and language, 4–6, 10–15
Asceticism, 31, 41, 42, 46, 52
Asiatic Society of Bengal, the, 303
Asoka, 53–7, 87
Assam, 106, 251, 252, 330, 353, 433, 494, 507, 526, 543, 550, 553, 555, 564
Assassination (modern), 432, 449, 450
Assaye, battlefield, 323
Assembly: the Legislative, 460, 477, 478, 479, 490, 491, 547; Bengal, 552 *n.*; Constituent, 547, 553, 555–6, 558, 559, 563–4, 568
Assignment of revenue, 26, 153, 222, 225, 232, 281
Astrology, Astronomy, 67
Attlee, Rt. Hon, C. R. (later Earl Attlee), 549
Auckland, Lord, 331, 345, 346
Augustus, Roman Emperor, 73
Aurangzeb, Mogul emperor, 244, 249–63, 276
Australia, 456, 468, 469
Austrian Succession, War of the, 270
Ayūb, Khān, 406
Azad, Maulana Abul Kalam, 540
Azes I, 69

BĀBUR, 179, 204–6
Babylon, 72
Bactria, 44, 46, 64, 65, 68, 76, 241
Bādshāhnāma, text, 242, 247
Bāgh, site, 95
Baghdad, 112, 134
Bahlol, 179, 180
Bahmanī kingdom, 174–7, 182, 183
Bājī Rao, 323
Bajpai, Sir Girja Shankar, 508
Bālāditya, 98, 99
Balban, 160–2
Balharā kingdom 116
Bali, 137
Balkh, 241; *and see* Bactria
Baluchistan, 112, 217, 403, 404, 543, 553, 564, 567
Bāna, 104
Banerji, Surendra Nath, 427
Banjāras, itinerant merchants, 165, 166, 286
Banks, 378, 511

Bantam, 234
Barbaricon, 74
Barley, 10, 17
Barlow, Sir George, 324
Barnett, Dr. L. D., quoted, 125
Baroda, 452, 497, 533; *and see* Gaekwar family
Barros, João de, 203
Bassein, Treaty of, 323
Batavia, 233, 326
Beas, river, 45
Benares, 16, 17, 37, 61, 148, 187, 250, 340; University, 537
Bengal: early, 3, 38, 61, 87; Pāla dynasty, 113, 114, 149, 150; Sena dynasty, 150, 191; Turkish rule, 152, 161; independent, 168, 180, 181, 187, 209, 266; Mogul, 207, 209, 216; British, 278, 297–300, 352, 433, 449, 457, 479, 485, 490, 495, 509, 514, 516–17, 520, 543, 548–50, 553, 557, 563, 564, 567; Islam in, 191; partition, 433; reunion, 442; Legislative Assembly, 552–3
Bengali language, 187, 194, 342; *and see* Vernacular languages
Bentinck, Lord William, 330, 337, 536
Berār, (Moslem) 183, 217; (British) 353
Berlin, Treaty of, 405
Besnagar; *see* Vidisā
Bhagavadgītā, text, 37, 124
Bhakti, doctrine, 124, 125, 193–5, 290, 342
Bhārhut, site, 62, 66
Bhoj, Rāja, 151
Bhonsle family, the, 267, 310, 323, 329; *and see* Nāgpur
Bhopal, Nawab of, 568
Bhore, Sir Joseph, 527
Bīdar, 177, 183
Bihār: early history *see* Magadha; Gupta period, 86, 89; Harsha, 111; Pāla dynasty, 114, 149, 150; Gaharwārs, 150; Turkish, 152; Afghan, 207; Mogul province, 216; joined to Bengal, 266; British, 278, 297–300, 353, 433, 490, 495, 519, 533, 552, 557
Bījāpur, 183, 184, 241, 243, 244, 254
Bikaner, Maharaja of, 483, 568
Bindusāra, 53
Birth control, 529, 538
'Black hole,' the, 273
Board of Control, the, 313
Board of Revenue, 315
Board of Trade, 314, 315
Boer War, the, 429

INDEX

Bombay : city and island, 246, 261, 307–10, 378–80 ; presidency, 329, 335, 353, 478, 479, 490, 532, 552, 557
Borneo, 136
Borobudur, shrine, 137
Boundary Commissions, 564
Brahmā, 31
Brahman, 21
Brāhmans, 18–21, 30, 31, 42, 43, 123 ; abroad, 136–8
Brahmaputra, river, 2, 3
Brāhmī script, 38, 39
Brahmo Samāj, the, 342, 343, 397
Brazil, 201
Bretton Woods Conference, 514
'Brinjarrees' ; *see* Banjāras
British Association for the Advancement of Science, 472
British Commonwealth : India's status in, 470–2, 548, 549, 551, 569
British Government, 542, 545, 558, 560, 563, 565 ; attitude of parties towards, 1942...540
British India, end of, 568–70
British sincerity, 560
British withdrawal, 565–6
Broach, 74
Broeke, Pieter van den, 235
Buddh Gaya, site, 66
Buddha, Buddhism, 40–3, 54, 55, 65, 76–8, 89–91, 98, 108, 109 ; decline, 122–4, 150 ; outside India, 136–40
Bughrā Khān, 161
Bundelkhand, 150, 354
Burhānpur, 184
Burma, 1, 138, 139, 330, 349, 353, 381, 403, 467 ; separation, 467, 490 ; Japanese invasion, 467, 499, 507 ; *and see* Arakan
Bussy, Charles de, 271
Butler Committee, 488–9
Buxar, battlefield, 277

CABINET MISSION, 549, 551–3, 555–8, 561, 562, 565, 568, 570
Calcutta, 261, 262, 269, 273–5, 301, 303, 341–3, 478, 557 ; capital of India, 374, 379, 431, 442 ; University, 535
Calico ; *see* Cotton goods
Calicut, 199
Caliph, caliphate, the, 112, 438, 457, 465–6
Cambodia, 138, 139
Camoens, Luiz de, 203
Campbell, Sir Colin, 371
Canada, 456, 468, 469

Canals, 356, 357, 408, 519 ; *and see* Irrigation
Canning, Lord, 366–73, 376, 426, 487
Canton, 287, 288
Cape Town Agreement, 1927...469
Capitulations, 234, 236, 237
Carnatic, the, 265, 271, 272, 279, 309, 311, 319 ; annexed, 321
Caste : defined, 17–19 ; among Aryans, 14 ; development, 24, 51, 52, 127 ; in Islam, 192 ; accretion of foreigners, 100 ; modern, 343, 356, 394, 446, 538–9
Cattle, 13, 90 ; venerated by Hindus, 30
Cauvery, river and canals, 357, 519
'Cave'-temples, 95
Cawnpore, 369, 370, 379
Ceded and Conquered Provinces, 324, 333, 334 ; *and see* North-Western Provinces
Celebes, 136
Central Advisory Board of Education, 533–4, 537
Central India Agency, the, 353
Central Provinces, the, 353, 479, 553
Central Waterways Irrigation and Navigation Commission, 519
'Cesses,' 129, 299
Ceylon, 55, 117, 149, 326, 381, 468
Chaitanya, 194, 342, 397
Chalukya dynasties, 102, 103, 115, 116, 149
Champa, 138, 139
Chandel dynasty, 127, 150, 151
Chandernagore, 274
Chandragupta I, 86
Chandragupta II (Vikramāditya), 88
Chandragupta Maurya, 35, 46, 48–52
Chariots, war, 13, 119
Charter Acts, the : 1813...315, 343 ; 1833...315, 336, 337, 400 ; 1853...352, 372, 400
Chatfield, Lord, 505
Chauhān dynasty, 151
Chauth, 258
Chelmsford, Lord, 453–6, 463
Chiefs, *passim* ; term explained, 157 ; under Turks, 163, 164 ; under Akbar, 217, 218 ; in eighteenth century, 284
Child, Sir Josia, 262
Child marriage, 28, 128, 446, 538
China, intercourse with, 134, 135, 139, 140, 287, 408, 466, 508 ; paramount over Kashmir, 113
Chingiz Khān, 158, 221
Chitor, 206, 218

INDEX

Chittagong, 245, 252, 261, 515
Chola kingdom, 63, 102, 116, 149, 172, 174
Cholera, 380, 420, 529
Chota Nāgpur, 353, 433
Christianity in India, 83, 121, 202; *and see* Missionary enterprise
Chronicles, 34, 144, 188, 251
Chronology, 35, 577-9
Churchill, Rt. Hon. Sir Winston S., 498, 499, 502
Cis-Sutlej States, 327
City governors (Mogul), 224
'Civil disobedience,' 475, 476, 483, 484
Civil Service, the Indian, 295-7, 314-16, 400, 423, 427, 459, 480, 491, 492
Clark, General Mark, 507
Clive, Robert, 272-9
Coal, 339, 379, 523
Coasting trade, 72-4, 202
Cochin, 175, 199, 246, 452, 497, 515, 533
Coffee, 386
Coimbatore, 517
Coinage : early, 59, 60, 65, 77, 129; Turkish, 168; Afghan, 228; Mogul, 228, 229; British, 338; *and see* Rupee
Collectors (revenue), Mogul, 225; British, 315
Colombo, 246
Commandants, Mogul, 223, 224
Commander-in-Chief, the, 373, 421, 545
Commerce, inland : (early) 130, 156, 208, 228, 251, 286-8; (British), 277, 297, 377-9, 523-7, 543
Communal Award, 485, 493
Communal claims and disputes, 436-9, 447, 451, 454, 459, 462, 479-80, 495, 559, 562
Communications, 515-17, 531, 543, 550, 569
Concubinage, 292, 364
Congress, the Indian National, 427, 428, 447, 454, 456, 465, 474-6, 478-9, 482-5, 493-6, 498-502, 540-9, 555-8, 562-3, 565; and the war, 498 ; and individual civil disobedience, 409 ; Working Committee, 493-4, 501, 546-7; Governments in provinces, 548 ; Hindu membership of, 540 ; President of, 540, 549, 557
Congress League : ministries in provinces, 541 ; settlement, 542 ; agreement, 545
Conjeeveram, 85, 102, 103, 127

Conspiracies, 448-50, 457, 479
Constituent Assembly, 547, 553, 555-6, 558, 560, 563-6, 568
Constitution, the Indian : under Pitt's Act, 1784...313 ; 1858... 371-3 ; Morley-Minto scheme, 447, 448 ; Montagu-Chelmsford scheme, 455, 456, 459-62, 481, 508; Reform Act of 1919...463, 473-9, 481, 488, 490, 508, 524; Act of 1935...463, 486, 487-96, 498, 508, 512-13, 525, 566; August offer, 498-9 ; Draft Declaration, 499-502, 545-6
Constitution of the Union, 551-3, 559
Consumption goods, 521, 524
Co-operative credit, 419, 511, 520, 531
Copper, 10, 285
Cornwallis, Lord, 313-20, 324, 381
Coromandel Coast, 201, 235, 237, 248, 270-2
Cottage industries, 521
Cotton, 10, 13, 17, 45, 518, 524 ; *and see* next entry
Cotton goods : production and trade in, 74, 130, 140, 201, 235, 238, 248, 286, 287, 338 ; modern industry, 379, 380, 523, 524
Council, Secretary of State's, 374, 448
Council of State, the, 460, 490
Councils : Aryan, 13 ; Hindu, 17, 23 ; Tamil, 84, 121 ; British, *see* Executive, Legislative Councils
Countervailing duties, 416, 417, 430, 473, 523
Court of Wards, the, 384
Courtesans, 85, 107, 128
Courts of law (British), 295, 300, 301, 315, 372, 392
Cow-killing, 30, 146, 176, 218, 250, 436, 437
Cranwell : training of Indians at, 504
Criminal law : early, 90, 107, 121 ; Turkish, 161-3, 166, 169 ; Afghan 208, 209; Mogul, 224, 232; British, 336-8, 392
Cripps, Sir Stafford, 444 ; mission, 499-502, 540, 542, 545, 547
Crown Representative, 490
Currency, 555
Curzon, Lord, 413-15, 418, 420, 421, 430, 445, 446, 477, 517, 523
Customs duties, 249, 297, 408, 416, 555, 569 ; *and see* Protection
Cyrus, 44

INDEX

Dacca, 246, 252
Dacoity, 336, 450
Dāhir, 120
Daibal, 74
Dalhousie, Marquess of, 348–62, 487
Danes, the, in India, 235, 322
Darius I, 44, 72
Dasyus, 12–15
Daulat Rao Sindhia, 320
Dayānand, 398, 437
Death rate, 529
Debt, Agricultural, 383–5, 419
Debts, Public, 289, 406–11, 417, 458, 509, 513, 514
Deccan, the, 174
Defence expenditure, 513–14
Defence measures development, 503–8, 543, 550, 554, 567, 569
Delhi, 152, 159, 168, 169, 242, 268, 306, 319, 324; the mutiny, 369; imperial capital, 442, 450, 475; University, 537
Demetrius, 64
Deogīr, 162, 168, 172–4
Depressed castes or classes, 90, 107, 439, 446, 485, 491, 546, 556
Desai, Bhulabhai J., 545
Devapāla, 114
Dhār, 151
Dharma; *see* Sacred Law
Dharmapāla, 114
Dharmaśāstras, texts, 22
Diamond-fields, 285
Diet: Aryan, 13; Hindu, 90, 128
Dīn Ilāhī (Divine Faith), 214
Diplomacy, art and practice, 119, 276
'Direct Action,' 557
Disraeli, Benjamin, 405
Diū, fortress, 200
Diūl, 74
Dīwānī of Bengal, the, 278, 297
Dominion: of India, 568–9; of Pakistan, 568–9
'Dominion status,' 453–5, 479, 480, 481, 482, 483, 492, 498, 566, 568
Dost Muhammad, 345–9, 404
Draft Declaration, 499–502
Drama, 67, 92, 93, 440, 537
Dravidian peoples and languages, 4, 5, 12–16; religion, 83–5
Drugs, intoxicating or narcotic, 128, 408; *and see* Opium
Dufferin, Lord, 374, 413, 424
Dupleix, Joseph, 271, 272
'Dustucks,' 277, 296, 297
Dutch East India Company, 233–9, 274, 322
Dutch East Indies, 136, 137
Dyarchy, 461, 462, 482, 484, 492, 493

East India Company; *see* Dutch, English, French
Eastern Group Supply Council, 507
Economic developments, 515 *et seq.*
Economic slump, 1929...484; 509–510
Economics, study of, 445, 532
Education, 340–4, 358, 359, 365 *n.*, 393–5, 445, 446, 449, 531, 532–7; military, 504; secondary schools, 533–4; vocational and technical, 534
Edward VII, 402
Elections: general, 547–9; provincial, 547
Elephants in war, 119, 153
Elgin, eighth Earl of, 376
Elgin, ninth Earl of, 413
Ellenborough, Lord, 345–7
Ellora, site, 95, 127
Elphinstone, Mountstuart, 569
Emergency powers, 479, 492
Emigration, 381, 443, 468–9
Empire: idea of, 24, 106, 119, 146; Indian, proclaimed, 402
English East India Company, 233–9, 261–3, 269–72, 294–6, 313–15, 515; in Indian eyes, 359–62; abolished, 371
Espionage, 52, 163, 166
Eucratides, 64, 65
Eurasians: *see* Anglo-Indians
Exchange: *see* Rupee
Excise duties, 408, 513; *and see* Countervailing duties
Executive Councils, 294, 373, 448, 460, 461, 491, 499, 545, 547
External Affairs, 554, 569

Factories (ordinary sense), 339, 379, 380 419, 444, 521, 524–5
'Factory (historical sense), 234, 235
Fa-hien, Fa-hsien, 89–91
Family, the Hindu, 28
Famine (old sense), 4, 39, 51, 128, 169, 247, 248, 300, 357, 358; (new sense) 358, 365 *n.*, 377, 409, 410, 417, 418, 457, 469, 474, 514, 520–1, 544
Farming of revenue, 154, 167, 168, 244, 283–5, 298–300
Farrukhābād, 266, 307
Fatehpur, Sīkrī, 219, 220
Federation, 463, 482–90 *passim*, 492, 493
Female infanticide, 337, 344 *n.*
'Feringees,' 245, 252
Financial history, 508–14; *and see* Public Finance
Fīrūz, 170, 171

INDEX

Fiscal Convention, 473, 521
Foreign Affairs, 550
Forests, 408
'Fort,' term explained, 234
Fort St. David, 270
Fort St. George ; *see* Madras
Fort William ; *see* Calcutta
Franchise, 460, 462, 482, 485, 491
Francis, Philip, 294
French East India Company, 261, 269-72, 278, 322
Frontier policy : Hindu traditional, 23, 38 ; Asoka's, 54 ; Turkish, 158 ; Mogul, 252, 253 ; British, 345-7, 413-16, 443, 464

GAEKWAR family, the, 267, 310, 329
Gaharwār dynasty, 150, 152
Gama, Vasco da, 198
Gandamak, Treaty of, 404, 405
Gandhāra, 64, 69 ; sculpture of, 78, 79
Gandhi, Mohandas Karamchand, 474, 475, 476, 483, 484, 485, 501, 502, 533, 542-3, 562, 563, 567
Gandhi-Irwin pact, 484
Ganesh, Rāja, 180
Ganges Canal, 357
Ganges, river, 2, 3, 16
Gangetic plain, the, 3, 12, 16, 17
Gaur, 106, 161, 207
Geneva Disarmament Conference, 471
George V, 442
Ghaznī, 143, 152
Ghūr dynasty, 149, 152, 153
Gingee, 258
Gladstone, William Ewart, 405
Goa, 200-2, 246
Godāvarī, river, 53 ; canals, 357
Goddard, Colonel William, 309, 310
Gokhale, Gopal Krishna, 446, 451, 456
Golconda, 183, 184, 241, 243, 244, 254 ; diamonds, 285
Gold, 10, 74, 285, 411, 510-11
Good Hope, Cape of, 198, 326
Gopāla, 114
Governors : Turkish, 153-7 ; Mogul, 224, 225 ; Governors-general, 294, 305, 313, 473, 488, 490, 492, 568 ; Governors, provincial, 490, 491-2, 494
Greeks in India, 64-7 ; *and see* Alexander the Great
Gūjar, : caste, 100 ; dynasty, 113-15
Gujarāt : early, 49, 68, 69, 100 ; Turkish, 166 ; independent, 181 ; Mogul province, 216, 248 ; British, 329, 515

Gujrāt, battlefield, 348
Gulbarga, 174, 177
'Gun-running,' 443
Gupta empire, 86-96
Gurjaras, 100 ; *and see* Gūjar
Gurkhas, 329 ; *and see* Nepal
Gwalior, 152, 159, 207, 215, 310, 452, 497

HABĪBULLAH, 414, 443, 463
Hafiz, 189
Haidar Alī, 265, 279, 311
Haileybury College, 303, 332, 400
Hanumant Rao Moré, 276
Harappā, site, 9
Hardinge, Lord, 442, 450
Hardinge, Sir Henry, 347, 348, 352
Hardwār, 16
Harsha, Harsha-vardhana, 104-11
Harshacharita, text, 104
Hārūn, Caliph, 134
Harvest glut, the, 129, 130, 226, 377-9
Hashim Khan, 464
Hastings, Marquess of ; *see* Moira, Lord
Hastings, Warren, 294-312
Havelock, Sir Henry, 370
Hawkins, William, 236
Headmen of villages, 121, 225, 283
Hector, the, 236
Heliodorus, 65
Hellenic culture, 45, 66, 67
Hemū, 215
Herat, 345, 349
High Commissioner, the, 460
High Courts, 371
Himalayas, 1, 2
Hīnayāna, 78, 108
Hindi, language, 6 ; *and see* Vernacular languages
Hindu Kush mountains, 2, 139
Hindu, Mahāsabhā, 480, 495, 499, 548
Hindu Membership of Congress, 540
Hindu Sāhi dynasty, 143, 147
Hinduism : emergence of, 16-21 ; described, 22-33 ; extension, 46 82-5, 103 ; Gupta, 90-2, ; Kanauj, 108 ; tenth century, 118-31 ; fifteenth century, 193-5 ; modern, 361, 397-9, 431, 437-9, 479-80 ; outside India, 136-8
Hindustani, language, 6, 187, 290 ; *and see* Vernacular languages
Hiuen Tsang ; *see* Yuan Chwang
Holkar family, the, 267, 310, 319, 323, 329
Holland, Sir Thomas : Commission, 522

INDEX

Homosexual practices, 155
Hong Kong, 507
Hooghly, river and port, 245, 261, 262
Horses, 13, 175, 201
Housing, 525, 526–7,
Hoysala dynasty, 149, 172–4
Humāyūn, Mogul emperor, 206, 207, 209
Humāyūn the Oppressor, 182
Huns, 5, 65, 97
Huvishka, 80
Hyderabad, 265, 271, 279, 309, 310, 319–21, 353, 452, 488, 497, 569
Hydro-electric schemes, 523

IBN BATŪTAH, 169
Ibn Saud, 465
Ibrāhīm Lodī, 179, 205
Iconoclasm, 94, 146, 156, 176, 250, 253
Ilbert Bill, the, 430, 434, 477
Iltutmish, 160
Imperial Agricultural Research Institute, 517
Imperial Bank of India, 512
Imperial Conferences, 455, 468, 469, 470
Imperial Council of Agricultural Research, 518
Imperial Preference, 523
Imperial Service troops, 422
Imperial Sugar Breeding Station, 517
Impey, Sir Elijah, 301
Incarnations, 31, 122, 125, 194, 195
Income tax, 408, 416
Indenture system; see Emigration
Independence, 554–5, 568
India, *passim*: defined, 1; described, 1–6; Dominion of, 568–9
Indian Agricultural Research Institute, 518
Indian Christians, 556
Indian Independence Act, 568–9
Indian Munitions Board, 522
Indians in England, 343, 394, 400, 440, 441
Indigo, 238, 248, 386, 387
Indo-China, 137–40
Indo-European language, 11
Indore, 354, 497; *and see* Holkar family
Indus plain: 3, and *passim*; early civilisation, 9, 19, 472; Aryan, 12; foreign territory, 44–7; *and see* Punjab, Sind
Indus river, 2, 45, 519; ports, 74
Industrial development (modern), 339, 379, 419, 444, 445, 505, 521–7, 529

Inflation, 514
Influenza, 457
Inheritance, 28, 211, 212
Inscriptions, 39, 53–5, 75, 81, 117; abroad, 136–8
Insurance business, 511
Interim Government, 555–8, 566–7
Intermarriage: among Hindus, 18, 127; Moslems and Hindus, 170, 185, 186, 218; Portuguese and Indians, 202
International Labour Organisation, 471, 525
International relations development, 470–2
Interpreters, 50
Intoxicants, intoxication, 128, 163, 182, 211; prohibition, 513
Iqbal, Muhammad, 472
Iraq, 465
Iron and steel, 17, 285, 444, 521
Irrigation, 51, 81, 128, 150; Moslem period, 171; modern, 356, 357, 418, 519, 529
Irwin, Lord (afterwards Viscount Halifax), 463, 481, 484
Islam: described, 144–6; reaches India, 112, 144–8; spreads, 190–2; declines, 291; revives, 397, 437; in politics, 438, 447, 454, 457, 465, 476, 480; modified by Hinduism, 192; eastward of India, 137–9
I-tsing, 136

JAHĀNGĪR, Mogul emperor, 217, 218, 231–3
Jai Singh, Rāja, 256
Jainism, 40–3, 122; persecuted, 109
Jaipāl, 143, 144
Jaipur, 497
Jalālābād, 346, 347
Jalāluddīn Khaljī, 162
Jalianwala incident, 475
Jamshedpur, 445
Janjīra, 260
Japan, 140, 429, 466–7, 474, 499, 507, 524; war with, 545
Jauhar, rite, 148, 218
Jaunpur, 178, 179, 215
Java, 136, 137, 233
Jesuits in India, 202, 212, 214, 231, 232, 236, 240
Jews, 5, 122, 288
Jhānsī, 158, 352
Jhelum, river, 47, 64
Jinnah, Mahomed Ali, 541–4
Jizya, tax, 145, 146, 156, 218, 250, 291
Jodhpur; *see* Mārwār
Jones, Sir William, 11, 35, 302, 317

INDEX

Journalism, 341, 342, 361, 392, 426, 429, 432, 434, 450, 477, 537
Judges: Mogul, 224; British, *see* Courts of law
Jumna river, 17, 62, 327; canals, 357
Junagadh, 569
Jūnāgarh, 81
Jungle tribes, 4, 17, 32, 33, 118, 121
Jury, trial by, 434, 435
Jute, 339, 379, 524

KABĪR, 193–5
Kābul, 204, 209, 216, 268, 345–7, 405, 406, 464
Kāfūr, Malik Nāib, 166, 167, 172, 173
Kaikubād, 161
Kailas temple, 127
Kajar dynasty, 465
Kākatīya dynasty, 149, 172, 173
Kālidāsa, 92
Kalikātā; *see* Calcutta
Kalinga, 53, 54, 61, 63, 87, 102, 116
Kālinjar, 151, 152, 208
Kampil, Kāmpīla, 17, 61
Kāmrūp, 106
Kanauj, 89, 91, 104–8, 113–15, 147, 150
Kānchipuram; *see* Conjeeveram
Kandahār, 217, 232, 241, 268, 347, 404, 406
Kanishka, 76–80
Karachi, 74, 515
Karma, 20, 21, 31, 125, 398
Karnāl, 268
Kāshī; *see* Benares
Kashmīr, 98, 113, 181, 190, 216, 326, 348, 488, 497
Kasturba Gandhi Trust, 532
Kathāsaritsāgara, text, 127, 128
Kathiāwar, 65, 69, 515
Kausāmbi, 61, 62
Kautilya, 27, 49
Kemal, Mustapha, 465
Kenya, 468, 469
Kerala kingdom, 63, 116, 174
Keshab Chandra Sen, 397
Keynes, Lord, 514
Khajurāho, 127, 150
Khalīfa; *see* Caliph
Khan, Liaquat Ali, 545, 558
Khan, Sir Zaffrullah, 508
Khāndesh, 181, 217
Khānua, battlefield, 206
Kharoshthī script, 38
Khilafat party, 465–6, 476
Khizr Khān, 178
Khmer empire, 138

Khusrū, Prince, 211
Kingdoms, subordinate, 24, 50, 54, 61, 106
Kingship: Aryan, 12, 13; Hindu, 17, 23, 38, 110, 118, 123; Islamic, 145; Turkish, 153; rule of succession, 118, 156, 210
Kistna, river, 54, 174; canals, 357
Kitchener, Lord, 421
Konkan, the, 1, 257, 260
Koran, the, 144
Korea, 140
Kosala, 36, 37, 41, 61
Krishna, 31, 37, 194, 195
Krishnadeva, 183
Kshatriyas, 18, 42, 43, 101; *and see* Rājputs
Kurus, 36, 38
Kushāns, 75–80
Kutbuddīn Aibak, 153, 154, 160
Kutbuddīn Mubārak Shāh, 167

LABOUR conditions: early, 107, 130; modern, 387, 419, 458, 471, 477, 524–7
Labour Government, 481, 546–7
Lāharī-bandar, 74
Lahore, 147, 152, 179, 205, 327, 399
Lake, Lord, 323
Lakhnautī; *see* Gaur
Land revenue and tenure: early, 25, 26, 50, 51, 107, 128, 129; under Turks, 156, 157, 164, 165, 167–70; Sayyids and Afghans, 179, 180, 208; Akbar, 223–7; Shāh Jahān, 241; later Mogul, 282–4; British, 297–300, 317, 318, 333–5, 348, 359, 382–5, 408, 513, 519
Landholders, 157, 267, 284, 298–300, 334, 335, 382–5, 388, 519, 520
Languages of India, 5, 6, 536–7
Lansdowne, Marquess of, 413
Lapse, Principle of, 351, 352, 487
Laswārī, battlefield, 323
Lawrence, Sir Henry, 348, 370
Lawrence, Sir John (later, Lord), 348, 368, 369, 376
League of Nations, the, 470–1
Leese, General Sir Oliver, 508
Legal practitioners, 302, 389, 390
Legislation, 120, 314, 316, 337, 372, 478, 479, 489, 490, 519, 526; *and see* next entry
Legislative Councils, 372, 424, 425, 447, 448, 460–2, 474, 476–7, 489, 491, 497
Linlithgow, Lord, 463, 494, 495, 498, 499, 518
Lloyd Barrage, the, 519

INDEX

Local government (British period), 262, 402, 423, 424
Lodī dynasty, 179, 180
London Naval Conference 1930...471
Lucknow, 289, 370, 371
'Lucknow Pact,' the, 454, 541
Lytton, Lord, 376, 405, 406, 426

MACAO, 287
Macaulay, Thomas Babington, Lord, 301, 336, 343, 392, 536
MacDonald, J. Ramsay, 483, 485
Madagascar, 135
Madras : factory, city and port, 246, 262, 270–2, 278, 279, 309–11 ; presidency, 322, 335, 353, 478, 490, 532, 542, 552
Madura, 85, 172–4
Magadha, 37, 48, 53 ; for later history, see Bihār
Magistrates (British), 315, 316, 434
Mahābhārata, text, 36, 37, 159, 219
Mahābīr, Mahāvira, 40–3
Mahādjī Sindhia, 282, 310, 319, 320
Mahānadī river, 53
Mahārāshtra, 80, 254
Mahāyāna, 78, 108
Mahendrapāla I, 114
Mahmūd of Ghaznī, 147, 148
Maitri, moral principle, 54, 459
Maiwand, battlefield, 406
Makbūl, 170, 171
Malabar, 74, 198, 199, 476
Malacca, 198, 200, 246
Malaria, 380, 420, 529–30
Mālava, 104, 105
Malay Peninsula, 134, 137–9, 149, 468, 499, 507
Mālwa : early, 49, 61–3, 69, 151 ; under Turks, 166 ; independent, 181 ; Mogul province, 215 ; Marāṭha, 267, 329 ; modern, 353
Māndū, 184
Mansūr, Caliph, 134
Manu, Laws of, 22, 26 ; translated, 317
Marāthas, 101, 254–61, 266–9, 279, 281, 282, 285, 433 ; *and see* next entry
Marāṭha wars : first, 306–10 ; second, 323, 324 ; last, 328, 329
Marine, Royal Indian, 503–4, 505, mercantile, 516
Markets, 377–9
Marriage law and customs, 28, 538
Marshall, Sir John, quoted, 19, 66, 126
Martand, 126
Mārwār, 253, 254
Masulipatam, 235, 237

Maues, 69
Maukhari dynasty, 99, 105
Mauritius, 320, 326, 381
Maurya empire, 48–62
Māyā, doctrine of, 125
Mayo, Lord, 376, 418
Medicine, : art of, 67 ; profession, 388, 401, 491, 529–30, 536
Meerut, 369
Megasthenes, 49–52
Menander, 66
Mercenary troops, 120 ; *and see* Sepoys
Mesopotamia, 9, 10, 39, 60, 71
Metcalfe, Sir Charles, 331, 344
Methwold, William, quoted, 29
Mewār, 206, 218, 232, 253, 254, 257
Miānī, battlefield, 347
Middle classes, the, 388–90, 444, 449, 458
Mihira Bhoja, 114
Mihiragula, (or -kula) 97–9
Milinda ; *see* Menander
Mining, labour laws, 525
Minority communities, 483, 484, 485, 492
Minto, first Earl of, 326–8, 343, 396
Minto, fourth Earl of, 442, 447, 448
Mīr Jafar, 274, 276, 277
Mīr Jumla, 252
Mīr Kāsim, 276, 277
Mīrā Bāī, 193
Missionary enterprise : under Asoka, 55 ; Hindu, 437 ; Moslem, 192, 437 ; Portuguese, 197, 202 ; modern times, 341, 342, 360, 365, 439
Mithridates (I and II), 68
Mocha, 72, 73
Mogul empire : foundation, 204–9 ; character, 210–12 ; history, 212–263 ; disintegration, 259, 265–72 ; end, 369
Mohenjo-daro, site, 9, 10, 19, 38, 39, 71
Moira, Lord, 328–30, 342
Molucca Islands, 140
Monasteries, 91, 94, 109, 123
Money ; *see* Coinage, Rupee
Moneylenders, legislation, 519
Mongols, 158, 160, 161, 163–5, 170, 171
Monson, Colonel William, 323
Monsoon, the, 3, 4 ; *and see* Famine
Montagu, E. S., 455, 456, 570
Moplahs, 5, 135, 476
Morley, John, Lord, 420, 445, 447, 448
Mornington, Lord *see* Wellesley, Marquess of

INDEX

Moslem institutions, etc.; see Islam
Moslem League, the, 451, 454, 456, 480, 493–6, 498–501, 540, 541–2, 544–50, 554–9, 562–3, 565; and war effort, 498; Pakistan, 496, 500–1, 542–5, 548, 550, 553–5, 557, 562–3, 567–8; Council, 543, 557, 567; Governments, 548–9; President, 541, 549
Motor traffic, 516
Mountbatten, Earl, 560, 562–3, 566–8
Muhammad, Bahmanī king, 176
Muhammad, prophet of Islam, 112, 144
Muhammad, son of Balban, 161
Muhammad, son of Tughluk, 167–170
Muhammad Ghūrī, 152, 153
Muhammad Hakīm, 209, 216
Muhammad Shāh, 267, 268
Multān: Arab, 112; Turkish, 147, 161; independent, 181; Sikh, 327; British, 348
Music, 85, 107, 128, 188, 219, 251, 440, 537
Musketry, 201, 205, 223
Muslin,; see Cotton goods
Mutiny, the, 366–71
Muttra, 61, 63, 69, 147, 220, 250
Mysore, 54, 265, 279, 309–11, 318, 320, 321; State, 321, 352, 452, 496–7

NĀDIR SHĀH (1733), 268
Nādir Shāh (1929), 464
Nāgpur, 329, 352, 379; and see Bhonsle family
Nālandā, 109, 137
Nānā Phadnavīs, 308, 323
'Nana Sahib,' the, 370
Nānak, 193–5, 326
Nanda dynasty, 48, 49
Napoleon I, 320, 326
Narasimha, (Narsinga) 182, 183
Narbada, river, 2, 62
Nāsiruddīn Mahmūd, 160
Natal, 381, 442, 443
National Defence Council, 499
National Party, 541
National Planning Committee, 529
Nationalism, 391–7, 399, 426–32, 451
Naval Conference and Treaty, 1930, 470
Naval power, 199, 237, 260
Navy, Royal Indian, 505
Navigation, inland, 3, 286, 356
Nawāb, term explained, 265
Nāyaks, 244
Negapatam, 246

Nehru, Pandit, 557–8
Nepal, 329, 330, 366, 421, 453, 466, 506
New Zealand, 468, 469
Nirvāna, 41
Nomad migrations, 65, 82; their fate in India, 100, 101
Nomenclature: representation in English, 571–2; distortion, 572–4; place names, 574–5; personal names, 575–6, titles, 576–7
Non-co-operation movement, 475, 476
No-rent campaign, 484
North-West Frontier Province, 415, 484, 490, 494, 543, 548, 553, 555, 562, 564, 567
North-Western Provinces, 324, 353; and see United Provinces
Northbrook, Lord, 376, 405
Northern Circars, the, 271, 279, 322
Novelties, demand for, 231, 238, 239
Nuddea, 187, 340
Nūr Jahān, 231, 232

'OCEAN OF STORY'; see Kathāsaritsāgara
Oligarchies, 38
Omichund, 275
Ophir, 72
Opium, 128, 288, 408, 417, 466
Orissa, 38, 217, 267, 353, 490, 494, 497, 553
Ormuz, 200, 246
Ottawa Agreement 1932...470, 474, 523
Oudh: early, see Kosala; independent, 266, 277, 278, 306, 307, 319, 322; British, 352, 353, 359, 360, 370, 371, 478
Outram, Sir James, 370
Overland route, the, 354
Overseas Scholarship schemes, 535, 536
Oxus, river, 139

PACIFIC CONFERENCES, 471
Pahlavas, 68, 69
Painting, art of, 95, 126, 188, 219, 251, 290, 395, 440, 537
Pakistan. see Moslem League
Pāla dynasty, 113, 114, 123, 149, 150
Pallavas, 82, 87, 102, 115, 116
Panchāla, 38, 61, 63
Pāndus, 36
Pāndya kingdom, 63, 116, 172, 174
Pānīpat, battlefield, 205, 215, 268
Paramountcy (British), 324, 352, 487, 490

INDEX

Parliament and India, 263, 294, 295, 311, 313, 332, 358, 371, 373, 400, 423, 456, 473, 481, 486, 490, 498, 502
Parliamentary Union, 471
Parmeshar, Supreme Being, 194
Parsees, 5, 122, 134, 214, 288, 339, 378, 380, 556
Partāb Singh, Rāna, 218
Parthians, 65, 68, 69
Partition, 542, 560, 562-7 ; Council, 567
'Passive resistance,' 475, 476
Pathan, 548
Patna, 48, 86, 89, 91, 277
Pattala, 74
Pawār dynasty, 151
Peacock Throne, the, 242
Pearls, 74, 285
Peasants, help for, 519-20
Penal Code, the, 392, 431
Pepper trade, 74, 135, 197-201
Permanent Settlement, the, 300, 317, 318, 333, 335, 388, 519
Persecution, 91, 109, 122, 240, 250, 327
Persia, 44, 45, 68, 80, 217, 232, 241, 267, 268, 327, 345, 349, 465
Persian Gulf, 72, 73, 443
Persian language and literature, 189, 219, 303, 360
Peshāwar, 76, 139, 327
Peshwās, the, 266, 307, 329, 370
Pessimism, 21, 40, 42
Pestilence, 380
Pethick-Lawrence, Lord, 549
Philosophy : in the Rigveda, 13, 14; Hindu, 20, 21, 32, 67, 123, 187 ; Islamic, 189
Phipps, Mr. Henry, 517
Phoenicians, 72
Pilgrimage, 130, 131, 527
Pindāris, the, 328
Piracy, 201, 202, 245, 252, 260, 261
Plague, 380, 420, 431, 432, 443
Plan of June 3, 1947...563-4, 567
Planting system, the, 385-7, 434
Plassey, battlefield, 274
Police, 208, 228, 232, 241, 286, 316, 491, 497
'Political,' special Indian sense, 352, 354
Politics, 426-40, 451, 454, 456, 475-9, 480, 493
Polo, 160, 441
Polygamy, 12, 28, 127, 343, 538
Pondichery, 270, 279, 322
Poona, 256, 266, 319, 320, 431, 432
Poona Pact, 485

Population, 380-2, 420, 443, 490-1, 496, 520, 528-9
Portuguese, the, 5, 197-203, 233, 245, 246, 261
Porus, 47, 49
Post Office, the, 354, 355, 517
Prabhākara-vardhana, 105
Prākrit languages, 40, 93
Prayāg ; see Allahabad
Precious stones, 74, 285
Presidency towns, the, 300, 402, 423
Press, the ; see Journalism
Price control, 165, 166
Primogeniture, 118, 385
Princes, the Chamber of, 460, 481-2, 483, 488, 498 ; Standing Committee, 552 ; Chancellor, 568
Printing, 290, 303, 304
Prithvīrāj, 151
'Private trade,' 277, 296
Professions, 302, 388-90, 536
Prohibition, 513
Proportional representation, 547
Prose, development of, 304, 395
Protection (fiscal), 287, 379, 408, 416, 444, 473, 477, 522, 523
Provincial constitutions, 491-3, 558
Provincial ministries, 477-9, 493-5
Provincial services, 423
Provincial Settlements, 508
Public finance : Mogul, 229, 233, 251 ; British, 305, 406-12, 416, 417, 458, 460, 461, 477, 478, 504, 508-14
Public health, 529-31
Public instruction ; see Education
Public services : under Akbar, 221, 222 ; British, 295, 296, 315, 316, 399-401, 422, 423, 459, 480, 491
Public works, 333, 355-8, 409
Pulakesin II, 103, 106
Pulicat, 235, 236, 246, 262
Punjab : early, 44-7, 64-9 ; Turkish, 147, 181 ; Mogul, 215, 216 ; Persian and Afghan, 268 ; Sikh, 326, 327, 345-8 ; British, 348, 353, 421, 422, 450, 457, 464, 475, 479, 490, 495, 497, 519, 529, 531
Purānas ; coins, 60 ; texts, 37, 92
Purandhar, Treaty of, 308
Purchas his Pilgrimes, 239
Purdah, 29, 127, 185, 446, 538
Pūrus, 38
Pusa, 517
Pushyamitra, 62

QUETTA, 404
'Quit India' resolution, 541, 544, 547

INDEX

RACIAL feeling, 387, 429, 430, 434–6, 459
Raghunāth Rao, 308
Railways, 355, 356, 358, 361, 408–11, 516
Rajagopalachari, C., 542
Rājarāja, 116
Rājārām, 258, 259
Rājataringinī, text, 34
Rājputāna, 3, 158, 215, 216, 253, 254, 282, 329, 497 ; Agency, 353
Rājputs, *passim* : origins, 101 ; found new kingdoms, 157 ; their chronicles, 188 ; oppose Moguls, 206 ; loyal to Akbar, 217, 218 ; alienated by Aurangzeb, 254 ; oppressed by Marāthas, 324 ; adhere to British, 329 ; *and see* Kshatriyas
Rājyasrī, 105
Rājya-vardhana, 105
Ram Mohan Roy, 337, 342, 343
Rāma, 31, 35, 194, 195
Rāmakrishna, 398
Rāmānand, 193
Rāmānuja, 124, 125, 193
Rāmāyana, text, 35, 36, 194
Rampur, 497
Ranjīt Singh, 326, 327, 345, 346
Ranjītsinhjī, Jām of Nawānagar, 441
Ranthambhor, 159, 207, 216
Rāshtrakūta tribe, 102, 113 ; *and see* next entry
Rāthors (= Rāshtrakūtas), 115, 116, 253, 254
Ratī, unit of weight, 59
Raziya, 160
Reading, Lord, 463, 488, 489
Rebirth, doctrine of, 14, 20, 21, 31
Reciprocity Act, 1943...470
Record of Rights, 334, 343
Recreations, 13, 441
Red Sea (trade route), 72–4
Reform Act, 1919...473, 475
Regulating Act, 1773 ... 294, 301 305
Regulations, 314, 336
Religion : Aryan, 13, 14 ; *and see* Christianity, Hinduism, Islam
' Reprisals,' 237
Reserve Bank of India, 512, 514
' Residents,' term explained, 314
Reza Shah Pahlevi, 465
Rigveda, text, 10–15, 19
Ripon, Marquess of, 413, 423, 430
River traffic, 516–17
Roads, 286, 355, 516
Roberts, Sir Frederick (later, Lord), 406

Rock-temples, 95
Roe, Sir Thomas, 236
Rohilkhand, 266, 307
Rohilla war, 306
Roman trade, 73, 74
Round Table Conferences, 482–6, 489, 496
Rowlatt Committee, the, 457, 474–5
Royal Society, 472
Rudra : *see* Siva
Rudradāman, 80, 81
Rule of Law, the, 316, 334, 336, 348, 362, 392, 476 ; resisted, 450, 476, 483
Rupee, the, 228, 338 ; exchange-value, 411, 412, 416, 458, 509, 510
Russell, Sir John, 518
Russia, 345–9, 404–6, 413, 414
Rutlām, 158
Ryotwārī tenure, 285, 335

SABUKTIGĪN, 143, 144, 154
Sacred Law, the, 22–31
Sacrifice, 19, 20, 31, 125
Sadler, Sir Michael, 535
Safeguards, in 1935 Act, 492, 493
Sailendra empire, 136, 138
St. Thomé, 235
Sākala, 64 ; *and see* Sialkot
Sakas, 65, 68–70, 80, 88
Sākiyas, 41
Sakyamuni ; *see* Buddha
Sālbai, Treaty of, 310
Salsette, 307, 308
Salt, 224, 285, 407, 416, 477, 478, 483, 510
Saltpetre, 238, 246, 286
Salvation Army, the, 439
Sambhar, 151
Sambhujī, 257, 258
Samudragupta, 86–8, 96
Sānchī, site, 66
Sandeman, Sir Robert, 404, 415
Sandhurst : training of Indians at, 504
Sandrokottos ; *see* Chandragupta Maurya
San Francisco Conference, 1945...471
Sangrāma, 206
Sankara Āchārya, 124
Sanskrit : language, 6, 11, 93, 302 ; literature, 34, 92, 93, 126, 188 ; studies, 187, 290, 340, 343
Santāl Parganas, 3
Sapru, Sir Tej Bahadur, 545
Sarda canal, 519
Sardesai, Mr. G. S., quoted, 282
Sarkar, Sir Jadunath, 251, 269, 276
Sarker, Mr. N. R. 534

INDEX

Sasānka, 106, 109
Sastri, Mr. Srinivasa, 469
Sātāra, 329, 352
Satraps; see Sakas
Savings campaign, 511, 514
Sayyid Ahmad Khān, Sir, 397, 427, 438
Sayyid dynasty, 178, 179
Scheduled castes; see Depressed classes
Science, study of, 67, 393, 440, 444, 532
Sculpture: origins, 10, 56; development, 66, 77-80, 95, 96, 126, 177, 188; Islamic, 189; modern 396
Scythians, 5; and see Sakas
Seaports, 515
Sea traffic, 71-4, 134-41, 198-202, 271, 286, 287, 353, 376, 515
Secretary of State for India, the, 371, 374, 459, 473, 490, 549
Seleucus I, 46, 49
'Self-determination,' 563
Sena dynasty, 150, 152, 191
Sennacherib, 72
Sepoys, 270, 280; and see Mutiny
Serampore, 341, 342
Serfdom, 25, 30, 387
Seringapatam, 319, 321
'Settlement'; see Land revenue
Seven Years War, the, 273, 278, 279
Shāh Alam, 268, 277, 278, 306
Shāh Jahān, Mogul emperor, 240-9
Shah Mahmed Khan, 464
Shāh Shuja, 345-7
Shāhjī Bhonsle, 255
Shāhu, 258, 259, 266
Shaikh Sadi, 189
Sher Ali, 404, 405
Sher Khān (later, Sher Shāh), 206-9, 221
Ships and shipping, 71-4, 287, 515-16
Shore, Sir John, 320
Sialkot, 64, 69, 98
Siam, 138, 139
Siddhārtha Gautama; see Buddha
Sīdīs, 260
Sikander the Iconoclast, 190
Sikander Shāh, Lodī, 179, 190
Sikander Hayat Khan, Sir, 494
Sikhs, 326, 327, 345-9, 457, 476, 479, 490, 501, 550, 552 and n., 555-6, 564-5
Silk, 246, 287
Silver, 10, 17, 74, 201, 238, 271, 285, 411
Simla, 374
Simla Conference, 546-7, 549
Simon Commission, the, 481, 482

'Simultaneous examinations,' 423, 427, 459
Sind: early, 64, 68; under Arabs, 112; independent, 181, 326; Mogul, 217; Persian and Afghan, 268; British, 347, 353, 490, 494, 518, 527, 543, 549, 553, 564, 567
Sindhia family, the, 267, 310, 323, 329
Singapore, 499, 507
Singh, Sardar Balder, 558, 567
Sinha, Sir S. P. (afterwards Lord), 454, 470
Sirāj-ud-daula, 273, 274
Sīta, 35
Siva, Sivaism, 19, 31, 46, 125, 194
Sivājī, 255-7, 276, 433
Skandagupta, 97
Slavery: Aryan, 13, 14; Hindu, 30, 51, 130; Moslem, 145; Turkish, 154-6, 176, 180, 181; abolished, 337, 338; the slave trade, 381
Smallpox, 380, 420, 529
Sobraon, battlefield, 348
Social life and relations: Tamil, 84, 85; Hindu, 90, 107, 127, 128, 363; Moslem, 292, 340, 363; European, 291-3, 362-4, 435, 441, 458, 470-2
Social reform, 317, 343, 397, 398, 428, 446, 519, 527, 528-39
Social service, 439, 535-6, 538-9
Solomon, King, 71
Somnāth, 148
Son, river, 207
South Africa, 135, 456, 468, 469-70, 473; and see Natal, Transvaal
Sovereignty, European, 262, 263, 271, 295
Spice trade, 74, 140, 197-200, 236
Sreni, 19
Srivastava, Mr. A. L., quoted, 276
Srīvijaya, 136
States, Indian; origins, 267, 284, 324, 329, 330; history, 351, 352, 376, 412, 422, 451, 454, 460, 487-490; and federation, 483, 490, 496; constitutional reform in, 496-7, 547, 551-5, 568-9; judiciary, 497; the small states, 489, 497-8
'Statutory civilians,' 401
Steel industry; see Iron and Steel
Stone Age, 9
Subletting, 383
Sūdras, 18
Suez Canal, 376
Sugar, sugar-cane, 17, 238, 416, 417, 518
Sulaiman, merchant and writer, 116

INDEX

Sumatra, 134, 136, 137, 149, 233
Sunga dynasty, 61–3, 66, 69
Supreme Court, the, 295, 301, 372
Surat, 235, 236, 248, 257, 261, 428 ; Treaty of, 308
Sutlej, river, 327
Suttee, 29, 46, 105, 128, 218, 250, 337, 343
Swarāj, 428, 475

TAGORE, Rabindra Nath, 472
Taj Mahal, the, 242
Tālikot, battlefield, 177, 183
Taluk, Talukdar, terms explained, 283
Tamil kingdoms, 63, 75, 102, 116, 174 : language, literature and culture, 84, 85
Tamluk, 89
Tanjore, 127, 321
'Tanks,' special Indian sense, 356
Tāntrism, 291
Taptī, river, 1, 2
Tārā Bāī, 259
Tarāorī, battlefield, 152
Tariff policy ; *see* Protection
Tata, Jamsetji, 445
Tatanagar, 445
Tavernier, Jean-Baptiste, 242
Taxation, 27, 107, 130, 224, 228, 249, 297 ; British, 407, 416, 458, 477, 478, 483, 512, 514
Taxila, Taxiles, 47, 54, 61, 64
Tea, 339, 386, 524
Telegraphs, 354, 355, 403, 517
Telephones, 517
Temples, 94, 95, 126, 127
Thānesar, 99, 104–6
Thībaw, 403
Thomas, Apostle, 83
Thuggee, 336
Tibet, 111, 140, 413, 414, 453, 466
Tilak, Bal Gangādhar, 431–3, 448, 449
Tīmūr, 171 ; his *Institutes*, 303
Tipu, 311, 318, 320, 321
Tobacco, 128, 283
Todar Mal, 227
Tons, river, 62
Toramāna, 97
Torture, 244, 281, 282
Trade commissioners, 524
Trade unions, 479, 524, 525, 526
Tranquebar, 235, 322
Transfer of power, 560, 562–3, 566, 569
Transhipment trade, 135, 198–200
Transitional government, 554
Transmigration ; *see* Rebirth
Transvaal, 443

Travancore, 175, 312, 319, 452, 533
Tripartite Treaty, the, 346
Tuberculosis, 530
Tughluk, 154, 165, 167
Tukārām, 256
Tulsī Dās, 194
Tunga-bhadra, river, 174
Turkey, modern, 465–6, 476
Turkish kingdom, the : establishment, 152 ; character, 153–9 ; history, 160–71 ; end, 178
Turkistan, 133, 139, 345, 404, 413
Turks, the : early movements, 98, 143 ; character, 144, 155 ; in India, 147–77 ; results of their rule, 185–95
Tuticorin, 515
Twist, Johan van, quoted, 247

UDAIPUR ; *see* Mewār
Ujjain, 54, 62, 63, 69, 310
Unification, of India, 354, 391–6, 499–501
Uniformity administrative, 392
United Nations, 471
United Provinces, 421, 495, 510, 519 533, 552, 558 ; *and see* North-Western Provinces, Oudh
United States, the, 450, 457, 508
Unity of India, 550, 562–3, 565–6, 570
Universities, 359, 393, 445, 535–6, 537
'Untouchables' ; *see* Depressed castes
Upanishads, texts, 20
Urbanisation, 532
Urdu language and literature, 290 ; *and see* Vernacular languages

VAISHYAS, 18
Vākātaka dynasty, 96
Vakīls ; *see* Legal practitioners
Vālmīki, 35
Vandalism, 79, 94, 190, 396
Vardhamāna ; *see* Mahābīr
Vardhana dynasty, 99
Vazīr, the, 153
Vernacular languages and literature, 126, 188, 193, 194, 290, 304, 394, 395, 495, 536–7
Versailles, Treaty of, 470
Viceroys : Hindu, 54 ; Mogul, 223 ; British, 371, 374, 544, 546, 549–50, 554 *and n.*, 555–8, 560, 562, 564–5, 567, 569
Victoria, Queen, 402
Videha, 37, 38, 40, 61
Vidisā, 62, 63, 65
Vijayanagar, 174–7, 182, 183, 243, 244

Vikrama, era, 70
Vikramāditya, 69, 70
Village uplift, 536
Villages, 12, 24–6, 121, 131 *n.*, 387; term defined, 24
Vindhya mountains, 1–3
Vījī Vora, 288
Vishnu, Vishnuism, 19, 31, 125, 194, 195
Vizagapatam, 515
'Voyage,' term explained, 234

WAGES; *see* Labour conditions
Wahābīs, 360
Wanidwash, battlefield, 279
War of 1793–1815...320, 326
War of 1914–18...453–8, 470, 503, 504, 520
War of 1939–45...463, 470, 492, 498, 499, 503, 506–7, 516, 547; the political parties and, 498
Warangal, 172–4
Wardha scheme, 533
Warfare: Aryan, 12, 13; Hindu, 119, 120, 175; Turkish, 175; Portuguese, 201; Mogul, 205, 223; European, 270, 280, 312
Washington Conference, 1921...471
Wavell, Lord, 463, 507, 520, 544–7, 557
Waziristan, 415, 464–5
Weaving, 10, 13, 140, 248, 338, 379, 521; *and see* Factories
Wellesley, Colonel Arthur (later, Duke of Wellington), 321, 323
Wellesley, Marquess of, 320–4, 341

West Africa, 201
Western Ghats, 1, 198, 254, 355
Wheat, 10, 17, 518
Wheeler, Sir Mortimer, 9 *n.*
White Huns, 97–9
Whitley Commission, 526
Wilberforce, William, 343
Willingdon, Lord, 463, 478, 485
Wireless, 517
Women, position of: Aryan, 12; Hindu, 17, 28, 29, 127, 128, 537, 538; Moslem, 185, 211; modern, 398, 446, 491, 537–8
Wood, Sir Charles, 358
Woodhead, Sir John, 520
Wool, 10, 13
Woolwich: training of Indians at, 504
World Employers' Organisations, 471
Writing, art of, 10, 38, 39; materials, 39, 144

XERXES, 45

YĀDAVA dynasty, 149, 172, 173
Yakūb Khān, 405, 406
Yasodharman, 98, 99
Yuan Chwang, 98, 104–9
Yueh-Chi, 65, 68, 75, 76

ZAHIR SHAH, 464
Zamīndār, term explained, 157; *zamīndārī* tenure, 285
Zoroastrianism, 134